Battles of the Civil War

A Captivating Guide to the Battle of Fort Sumter, First and Second Manassas, Pea Ridge, Shiloh, Antietam, Chancellorsville, Vicksburg, Gettysburg, Chickamauga, and Atlanta

Free Bonus from Captivating History (Available for a Limited time)

Hi History Lovers!

Now you have a chance to join our exclusive history list so you can get your first history ebook for free as well as discounts and a potential to get more history books for free! Simply visit the link below to join.

Captivatinghistory.com/ebook

Also, make sure to follow us on Facebook, Twitter and Youtube by searching for Captivating History.

Table of Contents

Part 1: The Battle of Fort Sumter

A Captivating Guide to the First Battle of the American Civil War

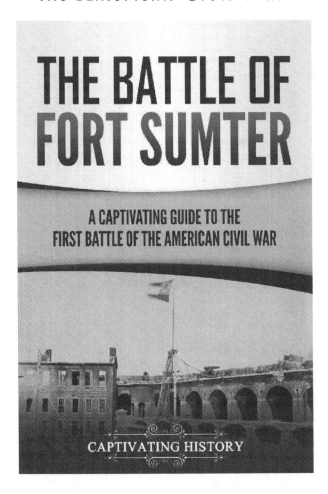

Introduction

By 1861, the United States of America was not united on the issue of slavery. The country was in a no man's land of confusion, as both modern and outdated ideologies coexisted. The more industrialized North followed the new path paved by other countries in which slavery was a thing of the past, with the future depending on factories, services, and hard-earned professions to form the bedrock of the economy. The "Old South" extended across the Southern states from the Atlantic Ocean in the east to a little west of the Mississippi River, including Texas. The Southern economy was based primarily on farming and the trade of agricultural goods, particularly cotton, with the rest of America and also with Europe. The lifeblood of the South was its plantations, most of which had become wealthy over several generations by using enslaved Africans for labor.

By the time of President Abraham Lincoln's election in late 1860, it was evident that the South could no longer hold on to its disappearing past. As the US frontier began to develop toward the west, Lincoln was adamant that the new territories of the country would not include slavery. When referring to existing slave states in the South, the newly elected president remained diplomatic but was clear. He said that "I believe this government cannot endure permanently half slave and half free." When Lincoln took office in March of 1861, he promulgated that he would not abolish slavery immediately or without negotiations with the South. However, after experiencing decades of short-lived, failed compromises with the federal government on the issue, the slave-owning states decided to permanently break away from the Union and form their own independent government.

President Lincoln was being pulled into a war he did not want, but he refused to recognize the legitimacy of the Confederacy. Friends became foes overnight, as military personnel and civilians alike needed to choose a side. Many would have preferred compromise and could identify with the validity of the arguments of both the North and the South. But in the four-year-long American Civil War to follow, there could be no quasi allegiances. From the start of the Southern secession in December 1860 until President Lincoln's inauguration three months later, the country existed in a high state of tension. Neither side would capitulate on its ideologies, but neither side wanted to be seen as the aggressor. With the eyes of the world upon them, this mighty nation, which had fought so hard for independence from Britain less than a hundred years before, turned against itself and against the very foundations of its Declaration of Independence, which promoted collectivity.

As the Confederacy began to assert itself by claiming ownership of previously held federal property, the Union government was forced to retaliate. Like children snatching toys, the first painful argument occurred in the Charleston Harbor of South Carolina over an island stronghold known as Fort Sumter, as neither side would relinquish the prize. Occupied by a tiny, underequipped garrison of Union soldiers who refused to evacuate, the Confederates started the first battle of the Civil War by opening fire upon the vulnerable island in April of 1861. Within two and a half days, the fort came under Confederate control, as the Federals, who had put up the best fight possible, were forced to surrender and be redeployed north out of enemy territory.

Two years into the Civil War, by the summer of 1863, the Union had established a naval blockade through the ocean surrounding southeastern America, as well as up the mighty Mississippi River. However, until the last moments of the war in February 1865, Fort Sumter remained under Southern control—the only break in the chain of Union supremacy along the coast and perhaps a symbol of the South's determination to see the fight through to its bitter end, come what may.

Chapter 1 – Prelude to the American Civil War

The American Civil War lasted from April 12th, 1861, to May 9th, 1865, during which time the Southern slave-owning states of America fought for their independence against the Northern federal United States government, also known as the Union. Since the Southern insurrection was never officially recognized by the American president of the time, Abraham Lincoln, the newly formed Confederate States of America (CSA), or the Confederacy, was a Southern breakaway government; this was why they were referred to as the "Rebels."

The Northerners, also known as the "Yankees," were pulled into a fight that President Lincoln did not desire. Lincoln (1809-1865) was a representative of the Republican Party, and he was voted in as the sixteenth American president in November of 1860. His open views against slavery posed a direct threat to the Southern states that depended heavily on slaves for their plantations and, therefore, their economic prosperity and quality of life. By the 1860s, the Northern US states were heavily dependent on the more modernized industries of manufacturing rather than farming or the production of cotton.

Slavery had been abolished in other developed countries decades before the Civil War broke out. When Lincoln took office in March of 1861, he was cautious in his announcements regarding slavery in his inauguration speech. Lincoln's election four months beforehand had heralded panic in the South, and in December of 1860, the state of

South Carolina was the first to announce its secession from the Union in order to govern independently. By February of 1861, six more states had seceded—Mississippi, Florida, Alabama, Georgia, Louisiana, and Texas—to form the CSA. Several more slave-owning states had the potential to secede, and President Lincoln was clear on what he thought about this in his first speech as president.

In this speech, President Lincoln placed the onus on the insurgents not to start a civil war and called for peace. The president went on to allay the fears of the Southerners and confirm that their peace, personal security, and property were not in danger. He reiterated that he would not abolish slavery in the states where it already existed but was intent on ensuring it not be established in the more unsettled western territories of the US. It was perhaps Lincoln's intention to slowly dismantle slavery as it existed in the South, but unfortunately, the Confederacy's open declaration of war with the bombardment of Fort Sumter a month later forced the president to rescind these initial olive branches and eventually enforce the harsh Emancipation Proclamation. The proclamation banned slavery in the rebelling states by September of 1862 (to take full effect on January 1st, 1863) in the midst of the bloody battles.

The president's initial words had not reassured the South, and by April of the year he took office (and after the Battle of Fort Sumter), four more states—Virginia, Arkansas, Tennessee, and North Carolina—had seceded. Eleven of the existing thirty-four American states had officially joined the Confederacy. (Missouri, Kentucky, Maryland, and Delaware remained "hung" states throughout the Civil War; they were slave-owning territories to which the Confederacy lay claim but remained mostly loyal to or were controlled by the Union. West Virginia split from Virginia in June 1863 to rejoin the Union.) President Lincoln's four-year term in office, which ended with his assassination on April 14th, 1865, was defined entirely by the American Civil War—a fight he had never wanted to engage in. With a Union victory occurring less than a month after his death, slavery was eventually abolished in the US.

The root causes of the Civil War were deep and complex and are still debated by historians to this day. The soldiers of the North became known as the "Blues" or the "Bluecoats." The soldiers of the South were known as the "Grays." This is because of the uniforms that they wore. An estimated 600,000 to 750,000 soldiers were lost in over 10,500 engagements in the four-year-long bloody struggle for sovereignty (not counting the approximate 50,000 and 80,000 deceased civilians and slaves, respectively).

The South was brought to its knees, as plantations, property, and infrastructure were destroyed. These had once formed the foundation of a booming agricultural economy and supplied both America as well as international markets, particularly Europe. Four million slaves (13 percent of the US population) were emancipated, creating a sudden dichotomy of altered social structures and an immediate and urgent need for job creation, which was not especially forthcoming.

The Battle of Fort Sumter near Charleston, South Carolina, which lasted from April 12th to April 14th, 1861, was the official start of the American Civil War. When the Confederates began an unprovoked attack on the federal stronghold, which they believed to be their newly acquired property, President Lincoln pronounced war. However, the US president refused to recognize the shadowy form of the self-proclaimed CSA, so he would not correspond through their elected president, Jefferson Davis (1808-1889, a Democratic Party politician who had previously served as the secretary of war for the US). Instead, he continued to communicate with the legally elected US governor of South Carolina, Francis Pickens. Francis Wilkinson Pickens (1805/07-1869) was a politician and firm supporter of the concept of the Southern plantation autocracy, also known as "plantocracy." Although a stalwart secessionist, he had been legally elected as state governor of South Carolina as part of the US democratic system. Pickens would go on to sanction the attack on both the federal USS *Star of the West* as well as Fort Sumter.

The South would not capitulate to the evolving federal stance on slavery and stood firm behind an outdated and morally reprehensible (especially from today's viewpoint) set of ideologies. The Rebels chose war above reason, believing that foreign powers such as France or England would support their efforts in the long term, which they did not. (Europe was the main international market for Southern cotton.) The result was four years of bloodshed and mayhem and economic ruin for the South from which they would never entirely recover. Many influential people in the military and politics on both sides of the divide believed that war could be avoided, but many did not. April 12th, 1861, was the tipping point that started the determined and sustained aggression that became the American Civil War.

Chapter 2 – Fort Sumter Becomes a Target of War

One of the first tasks of the Confederacy was to seize Union land and property in the South and remove the federal presence from US military bases, forts, and strongholds throughout their territories. These bases were particularly situated along the southern coastal extremities of North America and along the major waterways and inlets, such as the Mississippi River and Charleston Harbor. Since the federal government considered the CSA to be an illegal entity, this was an open act of sedition toward the Union. Lincoln had stipulated in his inaugural speech that the state of the Union was in perpetuity, and therefore, all Southern states were under US laws with administrative and military infrastructure belonging to the federal government. Charleston had been the epicenter of the slave trade since colonial times, and as the primary symbol of a disintegrating establishment where plantation owners and slave owners ruled the world, it was fated to be the location of the start of hostilities.

Like most of the US forts, Fort Sumter had been built in the 1800s. After the War of 1812, which lasted from 1812 to 1815, a series of forts were planted along the US coastline. Fort Sumter began to be built in 1829 upon an artificial island that was constructed using an existing sandbar exposed at low tide. Named after the revolutionary war hero of the South Carolina militia, General Thomas Sumter (1734-1832), the fort was built in the middle of the water channel that naturally protected Charleston. Three land forts—Fort Moultrie, Fort Wagner, and Fort

Gregg—were simultaneously built to provide full frontal protection against enemy naval approaches. Seventy thousand tons of granite were imported from New England to build up the land under Fort Sumter, upon which a timber structure was laid as a foundation. An elaborate plan for an impenetrable brick fort was designed—a pentagon standing 50 feet (15 meters) above the low-water mark with walls 5 feet (1.5 meters) thick.

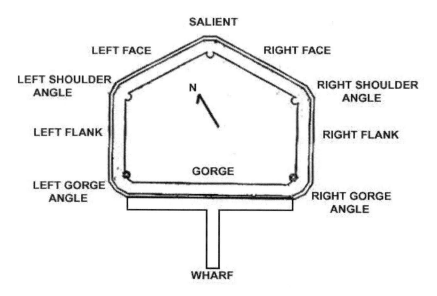

A drawing of Fort Sumter showing a five-sided structure. The non-exposed wall, or gorge, is attached to the wharf.
https://commons.wikimedia.org/wiki/File:FtSumterDrawing.jpg

However, by the start of the Civil War in 1861, the fort as initially conceived was still not complete or ready for action. Technical engineering and legal issues, as well as a lack of funds, plagued the project so that only a shell of the original structure, approximately 180 feet (55 meters) long on an island one hectare (2.4 acres) in size, was constructed. Essentially, only the exterior of the fort stood, which was in stark contrast to its original design that would have created one of the most impressive strongholds in the world. The three-story battery for 135 heavy guns housing up to 650 men never materialized. If it had, the result of the Battle of Fort Sumter could have been starkly different. When the Federals moved into the structure under cover of darkness at the end of December 1860, only fifteen cannons were mounted, and the central parade ground was a mess of rubble, abandoned ordnance, and empty gun carriages. Local tradesmen, presumably loyal to the Confederacy, who lived in the fort were corralled into a room and guarded for the duration of the Union occupation.

Only two forts in Southern territory remained in the Union's hands by April of 1861—Fort Sumter and Fort Pickens, which was off the Florida coast. All other federal property and buildings (including government offices, railways, and post offices) in the South—from Texas to Florida—were now under Rebel control. Fort Sumter occupied a central position, as it stood where the river surrounding Charleston met the open Atlantic Ocean. Fort Sumter stood approximately 6 kilometers (3.7 miles) southeast of Charleston across the bay. Charleston was an important town in Charleston County, South Carolina, and was situated toward the end of a promontory of land. This peninsula extended southeast into Charleston Harbor and was formed by the confluence of the Ashley, Cooper, and Wando Rivers. Surrounding Fort Sumter was a series of islands separated from the mainland by rivers. James Island lay just half a kilometer (a third of a mile) to the southwest, while Morris Island was not much farther away to the south. Sullivan's Island was approximately 2 kilometers (1.24 miles) northeast.

Fort Sumter stood as a sentinel amongst these landmasses, guarding Charleston Harbor against any unwanted visitors who approached by sea. The island was approximately 853 kilometers (530 miles) southwest of the Union capital of Washington, DC, via land and slightly farther if approached via ocean along the eastern coast of the US. In December of 1860, the Union commander in charge of Fort Moultrie, US Army Major Robert Anderson (1805-1871), took it upon himself to abandon the fort in the wake of South Carolina's secession from the Union. He had been appointed as the lead commander at Moultrie in mid-November when the secessionist rumble had grown louder; the war office thought it prudent to tighten its grip on the Southern fortifications. Major Anderson was appointed, as he was a long-standing military officer who could whip the rather lethargic and desultory group of approximately eighty Federals into reasonable shape.

The indefensible Fort Moultrie lay about 1.75 kilometers (one mile) northeast of Fort Sumter across the bay on the tip of a peninsula of Sullivan's Island. Moultrie was vulnerable to Confederate militia, who were just itching to oust the Federals from their shores. Major Robert

Anderson had the foresight to know that the Union forts in Charleston Bay would inevitably be attacked. He wrote to the US War Department, requesting further companies of soldiers to man the forts. He also asked for masons, craftsmen, and engineers to enhance the fortifications, as well as other provisions and weapons, including heavy field guns. His requests were ignored, as the sitting government before Lincoln believed that to honor his requests would mean an open act of war toward the Southerners. It must be remembered that many who sat in government at this time had Southern sympathies and were all too eager to put the Federals in a compromising position.

Fort Moultrie received only one new addition, an engineer named Lieutenant Richard Kidder Meade (1829-1862), a Virginian who switched to the Confederacy after the Battle of Fort Sumter in May 1861 but died of typhoid fever the following year. Anderson and his men's position at Fort Moultrie was too vulnerable to be tenable. The fort was mostly open to the land, where large sand dunes made the approach easy. Flammable homes surrounded the fort, which only confirms that it was an impossible position to defend. Furthermore, it was Anderson's assessment that if the Rebels commandeered Fort Sumter first, they could turn the guns on Moultrie. Before waiting for orders, Major Anderson disabled (spiked) the heavy guns he could not move from the land fort and transported the smaller cannons and his eighty-five personnel to Fort Sumter.

Major Anderson was a lifelong military man for the US Army. He hailed from Kentucky—a divided state—but had always been loyal to the Union, as had his father before him, who had also been a major. After four decades of serving the army, Anderson was close to retirement when the Civil War began. After the Battle of Fort Sumter, Anderson was promoted to brigadier general and put in command of Union armies in Kentucky and Rhode Island until his retirement in 1863. On December 26th, 1860, less than a week after South Carolina had seceded, Anderson secretly began transporting the men of companies E, F, G, H, and I of the 1st US Artillery (sometimes combined as companies E-G and H-I) to the incomplete but more defensible island of Fort Sumter. At this stage, the fort had less than half the required cannons due to budget cuts by President James Buchanan (1791-1868, in office as the fifteenth president of the United States from March 1857 until March 1861).

President Buchanan was a "lame-duck" president, as he had stood idly by while the Confederacy stole federal property in the South since his term was coming to an end. Although he was known to have Southern allegiances, he purported that he could not take any action against the CSA, thereby putting the Federals already posted in the South in significant jeopardy. Anderson's men consisted of a mix of native-born Americans as well as European immigrants—specifically Irish, German, English, Danish, and Swedish. The conditions within the fort were desolate, and it would be three and a half long months before the men received fresh supplies after they had surrendered after the Battle of Fort Sumter.

Unfortunately, Major Anderson's timely and astute move to Fort Sumter was seen as a hostile tactic by the Confederate government of South Carolina. The Southerners did not want Yankees in their forts at all and would accept nothing less than a full withdrawal from the area. By the end of December, the Confederacy had retaliated by using its militia troops (no official Confederate armies existed yet) to occupy the abandoned Fort Moultrie. They captured its fifty-six guns and began repair works, using mostly slave labor. The militia proceeded to take over all other federal positions in the Charleston area, including Fort Johnson on James Island, a battery on Morris Island, and Castle Pinckney (manned by a single occupant), a fortification in Charleston Harbor. By December 30th, the Confederates had captured the federal arsenal in Charleston, acquiring twenty-two thousand weapons, and they then proceeded to build and arm numerous forts in the Charleston area, which included an unusual floating battery (heavy artillery unit).

On January 9th, 1861, the steamer USS *Star of the West* was repulsed by South Carolina militia cadets from Morris Island and then later from the captured battery at Fort Moultrie. The *Star of the West* was bringing extra troops and supplies to Fort Sumter. These shots, which diverted the ship from reaching the fort, can be considered as the first official shots of the American Civil War. South Carolina Governor Pickens, as well as other senior Confederate officials, continued to insist upon a Union evacuation from Fort Sumter, which the federal government ignored. The following day on January 10th, Florida declared its secession from the Union, causing a small fort off its far western shores, Fort Pickens, to become a target of war. Fort Pickens would become one of the few forts in the South that remained in Union hands throughout the war. Some historians argue that the first official shots of the Civil War occurred on January 8th as the Union fought off Rebel civilians in order to occupy Fort Pickens.

Shortly after, the other five of the first seven Confederate states announced their official secession. War was imminent. Major Anderson sent away all unnecessary civilians from his fort, including inessential workmen and the families of some of his soldiers and officers. (Women and children had been present with the battalion at Fort Moultrie and then followed the men to Fort Sumter, where they spent over a month before being required to evacuate. Those who did not go to New York remained in lodgings in the Charleston area and visited their men in the fort.) Anderson sent all vulnerable persons north to New York by the end of February, and besides his limited battalion, he retained forty-three workmen. Major Anderson proceeded to make Fort Sumter ready for an attack, most importantly by erecting the loose cannons. Installing forty-five cannons, especially up at the top tier of the fort, was no easy feat, as the gun barrels could weigh up to eight tons. Ultimately, most of these installed guns were never used for the Battle of Fort Sumter.

By April of 1861, Fort Sumter was low on supplies, particularly food and fuel, which was estimated to run out by April 15th, making resupply urgent. The men were living on tiny rations of food; luxuries such as coffee and tobacco were unavailable, and there was virtually no wood to burn during the cold, damp winter and spring months. President Lincoln sent word to Governor Pickens on April 4th that he was dispatching vital supplies to Fort Sumter, which excluded ammunition, weapons, and soldiers. He stipulated that the supply ship would be unarmed and that if the vessel was fired upon, he would engage in land combat to enforce the supremacy of the US government. The Confederates felt betrayed by the new US president, and Confederate Secretary of War Leroy Pope Walker (1817–1884, who also served as a brigadier general in the field as well as a military judge for the Confederacy) telegraphed General Beauregard, who was in charge of the South Carolina militia, on April 10th. He instructed the general to demand an evacuation of Fort Sumter immediately. In the event that the Union was genuine in its desire to remain in the fort or had the audacity to accept a resupply, Beauregard had been instructed to "reduce" the stronghold (i.e., destroy it).

In the meantime, Lincoln was sending a fleet of ships toward the Charleston Bar—a series of submerged shoals about thirteen kilometers (eight miles) from Charleston. The first vessel to arrive was the USS

Harriet Lane on the evening of April 11th. The remainder of the fleet under Gustavus V. Fox (1821–1883, a US naval officer) included the sloops-of-war USS *Pawnee* and USS *Powhatan*, which carried motorized launches and about three hundred sailors. Three tugboats were also sent along with the armed screw steamer (motorized steamer) USS *Pocahontas* and the steamer *Baltic*, which included two hundred troops of the C and D companies of the 2nd US Artillery. In keeping with President Lincoln's promise not to send forces toward Fort Sumter, Captain Fox's instructions had been to use the smaller supply-only vessels to restock Fort Sumter. If he received retaliation from the Confederacy, he was supposed to bring in the naval ships and soldiers who waited farther out toward the open ocean away from enemy guns.

Of the eighty-five men stationed in the Fort Sumter garrison, besides Major Anderson, eight commanding officers oversaw sixty-eight noncommissioned officers and privates, eight musicians (part of the regimental band who would play through the surrender ceremony), and noncombatant workmen. Most of the men had spent several happy years at Fort Moultrie near the summer resorts and bustling city life of Charleston. Their escape from the mainland under cover of darkness with their few supplies and rations was in stark contrast to the service they had recently been used to.

In addition to the fifteen guns that were already in position at Fort Sumter, Major Anderson oversaw the placement of a further forty-five guns between their arrival at the fort and the start of hostilities. These sixty guns had been positioned around the fort, although there were insufficient men to operate them. The guns were arranged in three enclosed levels within the fort walls, or casemates, as well as on the central parade field. Ultimately, the middle level of the casemates went unmanned due to a shortage of men. The top tier, which was exposed, became too dangerous to operate in the heat of battle. Unfortunately, all the forts in the Charleston area had been designed to protect an onslaught from the sea, with their guns and gun positions designed to defend incoming ships from the Atlantic Ocean. Fort Sumter had not been engineered to protect itself from its own shores, artillery fire from the land, or close-encounter amphibious attacks.

Chapter 3 – The Battle of Fort Sumter Begins

In March of 1861, Brigadier General Pierre Gustave Toutant (P. G. T.) Beauregard (1818-1893) was placed in charge of the Rebel forces in South Carolina by Confederate President Davis. Beauregard was the first general officer for the South, and he had previously served the US Army as a civil engineer and distinguished military man. (He was instrumental in convincing President Davis to surrender in 1865 and went on to work for African American civil rights in his home state of Louisiana postbellum, becoming a wealthy businessman.) General Beauregard took the South Carolina militia under his wing and trained them to use heavy artillery (cannons and field guns) in anticipation of a siege against Fort Sumter. In a strange twist of irony, Union Major Robert Anderson had trained General P. G. T. Beauregard in artillery at the US military academy West Point several decades earlier. The pair had become close, and Beauregard served as Anderson's assistant for a time after his graduation. In the spring of 1861, these two former comrades worked hard to prepare their men for an overwater artillery battle against one another that would not only officially begin the American Civil War but would also serve as a tragic example of how friends became foes overnight.

The Confederates had the advantage of both position and resources, and the men under General Beauregard built up an impressive array of armaments (ordnance) during March and April of 1861 that all pointed toward Fort Sumter. By the start of the Battle of Fort Sumter, the Rebels had established nineteen coastal batteries (collective units of heavy guns) around the bay. In and around Fort Moultrie, there was a formidable battery: twenty-four heavy guns including columbiads (large caliber smoothbore cannons for long distances and perfect for shore defense), howitzers (mid-range weapons between artillery guns and heavy mortars), thirty-two- and twenty-four-pound smoothbore single-shot cannons, heavy mortars (short-barreled artillery with a high arcing range), and other cannons. The floating battery was shielded and positioned near Moultrie, and it contained four cannons. Fort Johnson on James Island had five heavy field weapons, including four mortars. Finally, Cummings Point (the "Iron Battery") on Morris Island boasted an impressive thirteen artillery weapons, including mortars, cannons (as well as one rifled cannon), and columbiads. The Confederate batteries were protected by shields and iron bars. Beauregard also had six thousand troops at his disposal, as well as an abundance of extra militia and civilian volunteers from South Carolina and surrounding Southern states hankering to take a shot or two at the Yankees. In the end, he used about five hundred men to engage in the battle with Fort Sumter—one Yankee to every six Rebels.

With the odds overwhelmingly against them, Major Anderson and his men were increasingly becoming trapped like rats in a cage. As their resources dwindled, they were informed that the Union fleet with supplies was on its way, but they were not given the exact date of arrival. Meanwhile, by April 9th, the Confederate cabinet had voted in favor of attacking Fort Sumter before the resupply vessels could arrive. (The Confederate capital was then located in Montgomery, Alabama, but later changed to Richmond, Virginia.) Until that point, both the leaders in the North and the South had been reluctant to act as the aggressors. Both sides knew that after the first move, there was no going back. The Confederate Secretary of State Robert Toombs (1810–1885) was the only individual to oppose the attack, stating with truth and wisdom, "[the attack] will lose us every friend at the North. You will only strike a hornet's nest...Legions now quiet will swarm out and sting us to death. It is unnecessary. It puts us in the wrong. It is fatal." Toombs had always been opposed to the war and resigned from Davis's cabinet as a result of the Battle of Fort Sumter. He joined the field once the war had begun in earnest, but he no longer played a role in the politics of the Confederacy.

During Thursday, April 11th, and the early hours of April 12th, General Beauregard used three of his subordinate commanders—Colonel James Chestnut, Colonel James A. Chisholm, and Captain Stephen Dill Lee—to correspond with Major Anderson in Fort Sumter. Captain S. D. Lee (1833-1908) was an American politician, Confederate officer, and educator. He began the war as an aide to General Beauregard before becoming a general in the main theaters of the war (Western and Eastern Theaters). Colonel James Chestnut Jr. (1815-1885) was a US lawyer and politician who served as both a Confederate congressman and officer in the Civil War. His wife, Mary Chestnut (1823-1886), was the famous wartime diarist whose memoirs went on to be published as a key source of information about the war.

These three men had been given sovereign power by General Beauregard to decide whether the fort should be attacked, but some historical sources suggest that the Confederacy had already decided to use Fort Sumter as an example. The secessionists would fire upon the fort as a message to President Lincoln and the Union that their Confederate government was to be taken seriously. In retrospect, the negotiations during Thursday night of the 11th seemed little more than a professional courtesy.

As the small boats moved backward and forward through the night delivering messages between the fort and the mainland, it became clear that the South wanted a fight. Major Anderson had capitulated under the pressure of a potential attack by stating he would evacuate by April 15th if no supply vessels had reached them. This was too conditional a withdrawal for Beauregard, and at 3:20 a.m. on Friday, April 12th, Major Anderson was informed that the Rebels would attack Fort Sumter in one hour. Anderson escorted the senior officers back to their small boat, and after shaking hands with each one, he announced, "If we never meet in this world again, God grant that we may meet in the next."

True to his word, General Beauregard ordered the first shot to be fired from Fort Johnson at 4:30 a.m. Acting under the orders of Captain George S. James, Lieutenant Henry S. Farley was the first American officer to officially open the Civil War when he fired from his battery of two 10-inch siege mortars on James Island. Beauregard knew that his ammunition rounds would last only forty-eight hours, so he had signaled the batteries surrounding Fort Sumter to unload their ammunition in a counterclockwise direction around the bay, waiting for two-minute intervals between each discharge. Soon the sky above the fort was alight with fire, and the booming of guns brought Charleston residents out of their beds to watch the pre-dawn display. But the arcing and exploding balls and shells were only sent toward Fort Sumter for the first two and a half hours. Major Anderson withheld any counterfire until after dawn at 7 a.m.

On April 12th, more Union naval vessels as part of Fox's relief effort arrived on the scene. Captain Fox himself arrived on the *Baltic* at 3 a.m., but the remainder of the ships were only on site by 6 p.m. on the first day of battle. Considering the Union had not coordinated the arrival of the flotilla with the beginning of an unanticipated bombardment, the rescue mission's appearance on that day was a miracle. (The *Powhatan* never arrived, having been redirected to relieve Fort Pickens in Florida, which was receiving similar treatment as Fort Sumter.)

Captain Fox was unable to resupply Fort Sumter on Friday, April 12th, as his small ferrying boats were repulsed by the constant maelstrom of ballistic firing. He wisely waited for all his warships to be present, but on Saturday, April 13th, the seas were too rough for his boats to approach the fort safely and achieve the desired moorings. Fox would need to wait until darkness on Saturday night to relieve the Union; by that time, the battle was already over.

Chapter 4 – In the Heat of the Battle of Fort Sumter

Within Fort Sumter on the morning of Friday, April 12th, once the sun was up, Union Captain Abner Doubleday fired the first shot at the Iron Battery upon Cummings Point and missed. Not only did Anderson not have enough men to discharge the sixty cannons at his disposal, but he was also particularly reluctant about using the best-situated cannons upon the top tier of the fort (the parapet or barbette tier). The barbette guns were ideally placed to fire the most accurate, damaging shots, but Major Anderson was concerned that the men assigned to employ these guns would be the most vulnerable of all; after all, they would have been raised up and exposed to incoming Rebel shots. Only twenty-one guns on the lowest tier could be employed. It was unlikely that the cannons would find their mark due to their limited range. The guns could not achieve the correct angle when pointed through the narrow embrasures (slits) of the battlement walls. The Federals also had limited ammunition, which was unlikely to last more than thirty-six hours. The Union guns included three Howitzers, as well as columbiads and other cannons, but no mortars. In lieu of mortars (high-arcing trajectory ballistics), the men installed ten-inch columbiads. Their bases were dug into the parade ground and pointed sky-high to improve their ballistics.

However, some of the most problems facing Anderson's men were a lack of cloth, gunpowder, cartridges, and fuses for the cannonballs. Anderson's only choice was to send unexploding solid iron balls or heated shots toward the enemy, which, even if they found their target, could do little damage to the abundant shoreline of batteries. Also, there were only seven hundred ammunition bags, which were used to send ignited gunpowder projectiles at the enemy at the start of the battle. Men inside the fort worked furiously to sew more, using every bit of blanket and piece of cloth or clothing available. They eventually turned to Major Anderson's personal sock supply in desperation.

The major was reduced to employing just six of his guns in the heat of the battle—two aimed at Cummings Point, two at Fort Moultrie, and the final two pointed toward James Island. These were fired slowly to conserve ammunition. Anderson split his men into three groups, working them in shifts to conserve their energy. The remaining men stayed in the bombproof sections of the fort for their protection, with the shifts changing every two hours. Eventually, the resting men would be occupied putting out fires in the wooden barracks and shifting explosives away from the flames.

Fort Sumter was pounded over thirty-four hours from April 12th to April 13th, although there were no direct fatalities on either side of the battle lines until an ammunition accident occurred at the very end, which claimed the lives of two Union soldiers. (A similar accident claimed the life of one Confederate soldier during the battle.) Upon inspection during the cessations in firing (such as at dusk), there was evidence of mortar damage to the fort, indicating that few of the three thousand shells and cannonballs had found their mark. This was mostly due to the vast distances required to fire accurately at the fort over the water. The real damage to the fort had been from fires caused by the hot shots, also known as heated shots. Hot shots were cannonballs heated in smoldering furnaces to extraordinarily hot temperatures before being fired upon the enemy. These balls did not explode when they found their target but caused the objects around them to ignite and spread fires.

Although Fort Sumter was a mostly masonry structure, its internal ramparts, including much of the living quarters for the men, were primarily made of wood. Heated shots were originally designed for bombarding wooden ships at sea, and they proved an ideal weapon during the Battle of Fort Sumter, as they smoked out the Federals from their island stronghold. A welcome storm sent rain showers to extinguish the flames caused by the hot shots on the evening of April 12th, but this was the same weather that prevented the resupply boats from bringing aid the next day. The Union held their fire through the night, but the Confederates continued firing about four shots an hour. However, it was the fear of an amphibious infantry attack during the night that concerned the Federals the most. They stayed awake to be aware of any potential landings, which thankfully never occurred.

On Saturday, April 13th, the Rebels resumed a full artillery bombardment on Fort Sumter, and by noon, every wooden structure in the fort, including the main gate, was on fire. Three hundred unused barrels of gunpowder were stored in a magazine (ammunition storage building), and as the fire approached, the soldiers attempted to move the barrels to prevent them from exploding on site. When this became too dangerous, as the flames licked closer to the magazine, Major Anderson called off the effort and sealed in the remaining barrels with earth and rubble. Only approximately fifty of the barrels were stored safely in various casemates away from the fire, and there are records that state that two-thirds of the unmoved barrels were thrown into the sea as a precaution. (Apparently, these barrels formed themselves into pockets upon the water, with the currents bringing them ever closer to Fort Sumter instead of away from it. When ignited by the cannonade, the barrels formed moving islands of flames with tall, smoking plumes.)

Fort Sumter itself had become a furnace, as the federal soldiers who were not at work laid facedown in their bombproof sections with wet handkerchiefs covering their faces. The impossibility of the Yankees' situation was not lost on the Southerners, who whooped with support every time the fort managed a counter shot. Eventually, it was the fear of his men being burned alive that forced Major Anderson's surrender. The Union men were surrounded by the enemy, who cheered and jeered from the shorelines at those in the fort as well as those floating hopelessly on the resupply vessels. In Anderson's mind, the North had no choice but to capitulate.

Although the Rebels won the day, it was not without admiration and respect for the Northerners, who had put up the best fight under difficult conditions; after all, they were hopelessly underprepared and outnumbered. In retrospect, though, the American Civil War was inevitable, as the unstoppable force that was the North met the immovable object that was the South. The dramatic and deadly pantomime that unfolded across America would have found its source and outlet at some point; it just happened to be at Fort Sumter in April of 1861.

Chapter 5 – The Surrender of Fort Sumter to the Rebels

By lunchtime on Saturday, April 13th, 1861, the Union flag had been shot from its pole in the center of the parade ground. By this time, Fort Sumter had suffered through thirty-four hours of near unceasing artillery barrages. The Confederates had unleashed three thousand rounds of high-arcing ballistic trajectories toward the Yankees, who had defended their fort and their flag as best they could. At 1:30 p.m., Confederate Colonel Louis Wigfall took it upon himself to commandeer a small boat and head for the fort to begin peace negotiations. Unfortunately, these peace talks were not coordinated with General Beauregard, who was headquartered in Charleston, nor were they discussed with his senior subordinates, including Captain Stephen D. Lee.

Colonel Louis Trezevant Wigfall (1816–1874, a former US senator from Texas and later a leading secessionist) set out from Morris Island amidst the bombardment that continued from the other islands surrounding the fort. Wigfall held his sword aloft with a white handkerchief trembling in the wind upon its end. He was offering the Union an opportunity to withdraw, knowing they could not raise a white flag themselves since their standard had fallen and were too occupied scurrying back and forth within the fort simply trying to stay alive. Wigfall traveled of his own accord with a fellow officer, and the boat was rowed by a pair of slaves across the open sea, with all of them risking their lives to present Major Anderson with an armistice.

Upon meeting with Major Anderson, Colonel Wigfall negotiated the terms of a withdrawal. An evacuation was the Federals' last resort, as their ammunition was nearly out, and the men were tired, hungry, and in need of medical assistance. The Union vessels had never managed to reach them and remained immobile, anchored beyond the Charleston Bar and out of the reach of Southern ordinance. As fires continued to burn within the fort, Anderson verbally agreed upon a truce at 2 p.m., with his consolation prize being that no lives had been lost under his command until that point. The major's reluctance to send his men onto the ramparts had considerably added to the preservation of his men; however, it also potentially contributed to the loss of the battle. Needless to say, a Northern win at Fort Sumter was virtually an impossibility, and the battle had really been more of a heroic attempt to defend themselves against the ring of enemy shore batteries—an enemy that strongly desired their exit from secessionist territory.

The Union managed to hoist the flimsy white handkerchief on a temporary flagpole that could be seen by the Confederates upon each promontory of surrounding land. (Some reports state that the white flag was also jiggled from some of the embrasures so it could be seen at all enemy points.) In Charleston, a delegation of officers who were not aware of Wigfall's negotiations thought that the Union had made the first move toward peace and hastily paddled their way toward the fort. This delegation included Captain Lee, as well as the former mayor of Charleston, Porcher Miles, and Roger Pryor. Apparently, Wigfall and Beauregard had not spoken for two days, and Wigfall had not had the authority to broker a deal. Major Anderson was outraged, and to add further insult to the debacle, General Beauregard had simultaneously seen the Union's white flag and sent a second group of senior officers toward the fort.

Luckily, General Beauregard's final terms were similar to Wigfall's, and after the terms were put into writing, the surrender proceeded. The terms of the final surrender were virtually identical to the initial terms negotiated during the night of April 11th —a quiet withdrawal by the Federals, who could take their personal possessions and firearms, including uniforms, that would then be transported by Confederate vessels to the safest and closest Northern port or naval transport available. A withdrawal ceremony honoring the Union, including a salute to the flag, was also permitted.

The Union's formal surrender occurred at 2:30 p.m. on April 13th. The guns finally fell silent, but the Federals actually evacuated the following day on Sunday afternoon, April 14th. The agreed Union evacuation ceremony was held at 2 p.m. on Sunday, and the Union soldiers safely lined the upper-level casements for the first time in several days. As per the proud Major Robert Anderson's terms of withdrawal, the truce included a one-hundred-gun salute—a discharge of ammunition that had ironically been impossible during the battle. Unfortunately, during this display, more specifically on the forty-seventh shot, a pile of cartridges was accidentally ignited by a spark. The explosion badly wounded Privates Daniel Hough, Edward Galloway, and George Fielding, as well as several other members of the gun crew of Company E. The salute was stopped short at fifty shots.

The less severely wounded men were treated by the onsite surgeon, Samuel W. Crawford. Private Hough was mortally wounded and buried within two hours in the parade ground—this was the first fatality of the Civil War (his arm was blown clean from his body). Privates Galloway and Fielding were later transferred to Chisholm's Hospital in Charleston, where Galloway died within a few days. Fielding was released after six weeks but had lost an eye. Hough and Fielding were two of the three fatalities of Fort Sumter as a result of a tragic accident. The Confederate soldiers escaped unscathed to fight another day, except for one unfortunate Rebel soldier who had been mortally wounded by a misfiring cannon.

A photograph of Fort Sumter taken on April 15th, 1861, with the victorious Confederate flag flying in the central parade ground. The casemate levels can be seen along the right.
https://commons.wikimedia.org/wiki/File:Fort_Sumter,_April_15,_1861.jpg

The remaining federal troops were placed aboard the Confederate vessel *Isabel,* and after a night's rest, they were disembarked onto Union Captain Fox's *Baltic,* which at last could be of some use. The Federals of the Fort Sumter garrison were eventually unloaded in New York City and welcomed as heroes with a parade on Broadway. Major Anderson, who was also deemed a hero, had salvaged the tattered Union flag from the fort, and it became an item of deep patriotism for the war. The flag is displayed in the fort's museum today.

Major Anderson's correspondence to Union Secretary of War Simon Cameron en route to New York shows his pride in the Union's efforts to hold the fort at all costs, as well as perhaps a considerable degree of folly and arrogance in the Union's actions to hold the stronghold against all odds. Anderson does not show much remorse in defending a virtually indefensible fort, especially considering that the families of the deceased and badly wounded soldiers were also affected by his arguably unnecessary withdrawal parade. (He also disgracefully turned away shipments of food donated in goodwill from the South Carolina government before the battle.) Nevertheless, the returning Federals were saluted as heroes by passing vessels all throughout their voyage north and into New York Harbor.

Major Anderson's letter to Cameron (1799–1889, in office from March 1861 until January 1862) stated:

"Having defended Fort Sumter for thirty-four hours, until the quarters were entirely burned, the main gates destroyed by fire, the gorge walls seriously injured, the magazine surrounded by flames, and its door closed from the effects of heat, four barrels and three cartridges of powder only being available, and no provisions remaining but pork, I accepted terms of evacuation offered by General Beauregard, being the same offered by him on the 11th instant, prior to the commencement of hostilities, and marched out of the fort Sunday afternoon, the 14th instant, with colors flying and drums beating, bringing away company and private property, and saluting my flag with fifty guns."

By 4:30 p.m. on April 14th, Fort Sumter was filled with Confederate soldiers of the recently formed Company B of the First South Carolina Artillery Battalion, as well as a volunteer company of the Palmetto Guard, which was a local militia group. (The Confederate States Army, most of whom were volunteers, had come into full force by March.) The Southerners' first job was to douse the flames that still burned around the buildings. After their first night in the fort, three soldiers of the Palmetto Guard, who had manned the Iron Battery, fashioned a headboard for Hough's grave. As the Federals were transported by steamboat to their awaiting flotilla, hordes of Charlestonians lined the shores and occupied boats in the bay to witness the withdrawal. In silent respect to their enemy soldiers, the Rebel military bared their heads as the *Isabel* passed.

General P. G. T. Beauregard was likewise hailed as a hero in the South, and he went on to serve as the lead commander in the first land engagement of the Civil War—First Manassas, also known as the First Battle of Bull Run, in northern Virginia in July of that same year. The Battle of First Manassas, which played out in the decidedly active Eastern Theater of the Civil War, was another resounding Confederate victory, as thirty-five thousand unseasoned Yankee soldiers high-tailed it back to Washington, DC, in a rout. Beauregard continued to play a significant role in the Civil War in both the Western and Eastern Theaters before returning to his native Louisiana after the war.

Chapter 6 – The Outcome of the Battle of Fort Sumter

Fort Sumter was the first action of the American Civil War, which served to bring hundreds of thousands of volunteer soldiers to the capital of Washington, DC, over the next few years. In response to President Lincoln's call for support, Northern loyalists and men keen for employment brought their families and possessions and camped around the capital wherever they could. Similarly, Southern volunteers rallied behind the Confederacy, emboldened by the first win of the war. Lincoln assumed the war would be short and decisive, and at first, he requested only seventy-five thousand men be conscripted for ninety days. After the North's staggering and embarrassing loss at the first full land engagement of the war—the First Battle of Manassas or Bull Run in July of 1861—the president realized that the war would be neither short nor easily won. More soldiers were then called for conscription for far longer periods of time.

President Lincoln's call for support to raise an army to subdue the South was the act of aggression he had wanted to avoid. In response, the four final slave-owning states of what would become the Confederacy seceded shortly after Fort Sumter—Virginia, Arkansas, Tennessee, and North Carolina. Politicians and senior military men employed throughout the federal government of Washington, DC, resigned their posts and moved southward to support the Rebel movement. Even some of the federal soldiers from the Battle of Fort Sumter abandoned their blue uniforms for the gray of the Confederacy, as the battle lines had now clearly been drawn. The Union began the war with a naval blockade around the eastern and southern American coastline and up the Mississippi River that divided the country in two. This blockade was designed to stop the South from trading, as well as inhibit the movement of goods, men, and supplies during the war. However, it only came into full effect after the Siege of Vicksburg in the summer of 1863 when the Mississippi finally came under the control of the Union. However, Charleston Harbor and its forts remained in Confederate hands for the duration of the war, leaving an annoying and obvious gap in the Union blockade.

Several attempts during 1862 and 1863 were made to retake Charleston Harbor from land and from sea, but all were a failure. First, the Battle of Secessionville in June of 1862 was an overland approach along James Island to take Charleston. The First Battle of Charleston Harbor in April of 1863 was the first naval assault to recapture Fort Sumter. Union Rear Admiral Samuel Francis Du Pont (1803–1865), who was the commander of the South Atlantic Blockading Squadron, arrived in Charleston Harbor with nine ironclad warships or monitors, the largest dispatch of monitors at that time. The poorly coordinated attack was further marred by unfavorable weather conditions. The valuable vessels also needed to be cautious of underwater mines planted by the Rebels. The flotilla took 500 hits from about 2,200 rounds that were fired from shore artillery under the command of General Beauregard. Shots were also fired from Fort Sumter itself. Eventually, the flotilla maneuvered through the heavy currents out into the safety of the open ocean; despite the retreat, they had managed to unleash about 140 rounds on the fort and its surroundings.

One of the ships used in the First Battle of Charleston Harbor, the USS *Keokuk*, sank the day after the battle 1,300 meters (1,400 yards) offshore of Morris Island. The Confederates worked to salvage the vessel's guns and place them within Fort Sumter, which they were attempting to rebuild using five hundred enslaved Africans. (The Rebels used slaves in abundance to build and repair many important strongholds and other wartime infrastructure; sometimes, they even forced them to fire upon the enemy against their will.)

The next bombardment of Fort Sumter was during the Second Battle of Fort Wagner in July of 1863, which continued until September. This was an attempt to seize Confederate artillery positions on Morris Island. The final amphibious effort to take the fort was on September 8th and 9th, 1863—the Second Battle of Fort Sumter. This was the last Union attempt to retake the stronghold, and it failed, apparently due to ongoing disagreements between the military and naval commanders. This second attempt by the South Atlantic Blockading Squadron ended in a debacle, as the operation was undermined by poor communication, reconnaissance, and planning. When a small party of Federals managed to land at the fort, a warning was sent out by the Rebels within the fort, alerting the artillery at Fort Johnson as well as the CSS *Chicora* to begin counterattacking. The US naval squadron departed, and over a hundred Union soldiers were captured upon the shores of Sumter.

For the next eighteen months after the Second Battle of Fort Sumter, the Union Navy didn't make further attempts to retake the fort but instead continued to pound it with heavy fire (using fifty thousand projectiles, which resulted in three hundred Confederate casualties). The fort—by then little more than a pile of rubble—remained in Confederate hands until shortly before the close of the Civil War, until February 1865. The fort had ceased to become a valuable defensive stronghold for the Rebels, who had by then turned to other methods to protect the harbor. They mainly used defense mechanisms, including land batteries and sharpshooters, underwater exploding mines, and small naval armadas. The naval fleet included the first working small submarine, which unfortunately killed more Confederates than Federals because of its rudimentary engineering. (In 1864, the submarine exploded and sank only to be rediscovered in 1995 in the waters off Charleston.)

The Rebels evacuated Fort Sumter as well as Charleston when Union Major General William T. Sherman (1820-1891, a military man, businessman, educator, author, and one of the most prominent leaders of the Civil War) successfully outflanked the city during the Carolinas campaign. The Carolinas campaign, which took place from January to April 1865, was the final campaign of the Western Theater. The Union officially reoccupied Fort Sumter on February 22nd, 1865. Union companies E to I (including the band) were reassigned and went on to fight for their country, seeing considerable action at times in some of the war's major battles. In 1866, they returned to the peaceful manning of forts in New York Harbor.

The de facto end of the American Civil War is often considered to be April 9th, 1865, when Confederate General in Chief Robert E. Lee (1807–1870) surrendered his Army of Northern Virginia to Commanding General of the US Army General Ulysses S. Grant (1822–1885) at Appomattox Court House, Virginia. General Lee's surrender was roughly in tandem with General Sherman's final victory of the Carolinas campaign at the Battle of Bentonville, North Carolina, in March. By April 18th, Sherman had defined the terms of surrender with the opposing Confederate general, Joseph E. Johnston (1807–1891, a distinguished career US Army officer and civil engineer who fought for the Confederacy). General Johnston convinced Confederate President Davis that the South needed to surrender in toto, and the terms of capitulation with Sherman were debated until the end of April.

The Union, knowing that the remaining Southern surrenders were inevitable, took the opportunity to hold a victory celebration at Fort Sumter five days after the Appomattox surrender on April 14th, which was exactly four years after Major Robert Anderson was forced to remove the US flag from the ramparts of the fort. This was a symbolic celebration that served to close off the Civil War where it had begun. Major General Anderson had been promoted and had also retired in the interim, but he came away from his sickbed to raise the Union flag once again at this key fort in the South. However, in retaliation, a Confederate sympathizer assassinated Union President Lincoln on the same evening at the capital in Washington, DC.

After the war, Fort Sumter was somewhat rebuilt, although only to the level of two tiers. Eleven gun-rooms were also created that incorporated 100-pound Parrott rifles. However, until the end of the 19th century, the fort was mostly used as a lighthouse, with fresh preparations for war appearing at the turn of the century for the Spanish-American War (1898) and the Second World War (1938–1945). But Fort Sumter did not see action after the American Civil War; instead, it became a preeminent national monument in 1948 under the control and care of the National Park Service and American Battlefield Trust.

A telegraph message was discovered 147 years after it was first sent by Governor Pickens to a cotton and shipping merchant in New York; it was dated April 14th, 1861. The message included, in part, "Fort Sumter surrendered yesterday after we had set all on fire...F. W. Pickens." During the Battle of Fort Sumter, Confederate supporters from South

Carolina had lined the shores near the fort, cheering as the Union men were overcome and surrendered. Had they known of the four years of death and horror that would follow, of the loss of their sons, lands, and livelihood, they may not have cheered but rather wept. Only a month before, the American president had stressed that their country need not be divided over slavery but rather work together to find a common solution. But the fundamental difference in ideologies between the North and the South drove events onward to a final and disastrous outcome for the South.

Conclusion

The Battle of Fort Sumter was very evidently just a small part of the Civil War. The US president, whose election had apparently instigated state secession to form the Confederacy, was unwilling to capitulate on his desire to prevent new states from adopting slavery. However, he was also equally unwilling to be the aggressor in the events leading to the Civil War. The federal government fought against the Rebels in defense of what they had spent almost a century building since gaining independence in 1776.

President Lincoln was called into a national fight that he remained in for the duration of his time in office, as well as for the rest of his life, which ended tragically and prematurely with the close of the Civil War. The American South, which had been so determined to adhere to a vanishing colonial past reliant upon enslaved human beings, was fatefully drawn to clash with the advancing North, which was intent upon following global trends and advancing industrialization. Ironically, the American Civil War, like all wars, provided a decisive and unforeseen boost to advancements in manufacturing, engineering, and transportation. The North, with its superior resources, raced to develop ironclad naval ships, armaments, roads, railways, medical provisions, and other necessities to ensure their victory over the South.

The South's fatal thinking that international trading markets of the US, such as England and France, would come to their aid was the fundamental error in the formation of the Confederacy. Slavery had been abolished from these countries and their colonies decades beforehand,

and no matter the foreign appetite for Southern cotton, the federal government of America was too large an ally with whom to pick a fight. During the Civil War, the international stage remained deathly quiet, and no matter how vigorously and honorably the Rebels fought, they were pinioned in their Southern fortress and surrounded from land and sea by the Union. As the Southern soldiers began falling in their thousands, the Confederate resources also became curtailed and shriveled by the ravages of war. It would only be a matter of time before the South needed to bend a knee to the North.

Ironically, it was the very act of war by the South that forced President Lincoln's hand to resolutely abolish slavery in their territories sooner than he had intended; this was done through the Emancipation Proclamation, which took effect in January of 1863. Until the start of the war, Lincoln had teetered on the fringes of ensuring his loyalty to the North while maintaining open communications with the South. After Fort Sumter and as the war advanced, the president became less conciliatory, as it was apparent that only a hard line with the Rebels would work.

If the South had been willing to negotiate years earlier, they could have avoided the deaths of hundreds of thousands of Americans, as well as the humiliation and near devastation of their agricultural economy and way of life that was the outcome of the American Civil War (this would have more than likely been affected regardless since slavery was uprooted). But the Rebels would not reason and refused to imagine a life without slavery. They, as well as many in the North, which became more and more obvious as time passed, had difficulty seeing previously enslaved people as their equals, as American citizens with a right to vote, own land, and work for wages. The Southerners' dangerously outdated principles led them into a hasty and ill-calculated fight, and as the first guns sounded around Charleston Harbor in the early hours of April 12th, 1861, few Confederates understood that their seminal victory at the Battle of Fort Sumter would simply not be worth it in the long run.

Part 2: The First Battle of Manassas

A Captivating Guide to the First Battle of Bull Run That Took Place at the Start of the American Civil War

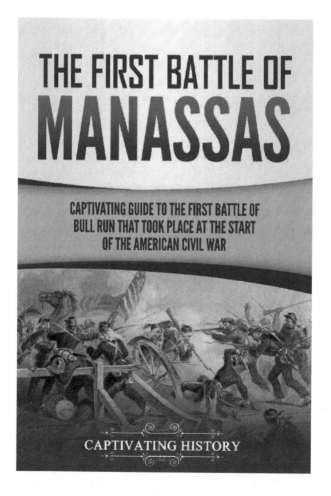

Introduction

When the Republican candidate Abraham Lincoln was elected to office as the president of the United States at the end of 1860, his open intention to end the expansion of slavery sent a wave of panic through the Southern states of America, as they relied heavily on slave labor for their plantations. Between December 1860 and May 1861, eleven US states seceded from the federal government to form an unrecognized, independent Confederate government. Not willing to negotiate on the issue of slavery, which had been abolished in the rest of the Western world decades before (for instance, the abolition of slavery in most British colonies had occurred in August of 1834, including the Caribbean), Southern militias began open warfare with their previous government by attacking Fort Sumter in Charleston, which was located within the Confederate state of South Carolina, in April of 1861. This attack was the official start of the American Civil War—only later named as such since both the Northerners and Southerners intended the fighting to be short and decisive, with both sides expecting to be the victors.

After Fort Sumter, the Northerners reached a fervor of desiring a confrontation with the Southern Rebels as the pre-war statement "On to Richmond!" echoed through the North, a sentiment that was driven strongly by the press, the general public, and by certain political elites. Many seasoned military generals advised against the war or at least suggested a significant delay in order to gather and train troops. These veterans' warnings were ignored, as military field seniors and their troops, as well as President Lincoln and his cabinet, were swept up in the tide of teaching the states that had seceded a lesson they would never forget. The Yankees (a pejorative term Southerners used for Northerners) believed that by capturing the Southern capital of Richmond, located deep in Virginia, in one quick, efficient militaristic move, they would quell the South's voice forever. The Northerners were neither correct nor prepared for the next four years of bloody fighting that defined the American Civil War, which lasted from 1861 to 1865. The Northern Union had underestimated the South's degree of determination, as they wanted to protect their sovereign rights and, more specifically, to own slaves.

The First Battle of Manassas, which took place on July 21st, 1861, was the first official land engagement of the American Civil War, even though the war officially started with the bombing of Fort Sumter in Charleston. At the Battle of First Manassas, approximately seventy thousand Union and Confederate troops met near the strategic Manassas Railroad Junction, which linked the vital food-producing farmlands of the Shenandoah Valley to the west with the slave market of Alexandria on the Potomac River to the east and, more importantly, sent rail links south into Virginia and the other Southern states. The Union Army, having approached from the capital of Washington, DC, was required to cross the Bull Run River (or Bull Run Creek) to face the enemy. Thus, the battle became known to the Northerners as the First Battle of Bull Run.

The troops on both sides were "green" and underprepared. The terrain was difficult to navigate, and the approach to the battlefield was long and arduous, especially for the Northerners. The approximate final numbers that came close to the battlefield were 28,450 on the Union side and 32,230 on the Confederate side of the total 35,000 and 34,000 combatants, respectively. Only approximately half of the engaged troops saw direct combat, which resulted in the relatively low causalities for such a heated battle (4,878 wounded, dead, and missing combined).

Confederate General Pierre Gustave Toutant-Beauregard (better known as P. G. T. Beauregard; 1818–1893), who led the Southerners, had tactical control and could engage more of his field since they fought on home ground. Civilians, including close relatives of the soldiers, the press, and politicians, joined in that day and lined the battlefields to take notes, observe, sketch, sell food, or simply enjoy a day out with a picnic and brandy!

The horrifying death and destruction that ensued sent stunned civilians and beleaguered soldiers hurrying back to the capital with the realization that the war to come would be long, bloody, and hard-won. Although the Southerners were the victors of the First Battle of Manassas, they retreated to regroup and strategize. Both the Union and the insurgent Confederacy had learned significant and humbling lessons on that fateful day in July 1861. Both sides withdrew to deal with their injured pride, make difficult decisions that would take the war forward, garner resources for the long fight, and build up more substantial fighting armies than the fledglings they had let loose.

In an ideal world, the carnage at the First Battle of Manassas would have sent the leaders of the North and South to the negotiation table rather than the war office, but sadly, it did not, and both sides became more resolved than ever to destroy their enemies who had, until so recently, been their allies.

Chapter 1 – A Short Background on Manassas

The Battle of First Manassas (also written as the First Battle of Manassas) is known as the First Battle of Bull Run in the North, and it was fought on July 21st, 1861, in northeastern Virginia within the counties of Fairfax and Prince William. The battle occurred by the Bull Run River, which runs in a southeasterly direction and separates the counties of Prince William on the west and Fairfax on the east. Both armies were over-confident and underprepared, but ultimately, the Confederates won the day by overrunning the Union Army with fresh reinforcements. The First Battle of Bull Run was a staggering and embarrassing defeat for the Northerners, but an anonymous correspondent for the *Atlantic Monthly* (a Boston-based literary and cultural magazine) cast light on this early defeat by stating, "Bull Run was in no sense a disaster...we not only deserved it, but needed it...Far from being disheartened by it, it should give us new confidence in our cause."

His words would prove prophetic, as the Federal Army (the Northern, US, or Union Army) began preparing for a real war in which they would ultimately be the victors. The North's previous attitudes to the newly formed Confederacy had largely been that the rebellious South would quickly and easily be quelled. Those who knew differently and who had been engaged in the War of 1812, which was part of the Napoleonic Wars, were unfortunately too old, for the most part, to be included tactically within the American Civil War.

The sixteenth American president, Abraham Lincoln (in off. March 1861–April 1865), had been snuck into office under cover of darkness to protect his identity and prevent any potential assassination attempts. This was in stark contrast to the future Confederate President Jefferson Davis (1808–1889), who served for the duration of the Civil War and was greeted in Richmond, Virginia, a few months later in 1861 with a brass band and crowds of civilians throwing flowers his way. Davis had been a United States senator from Mississippi for four years before the war, and he also served as the US secretary of war from 1853 to 1857.

Lincoln's election to office is considered as one of the causes of the American Civil War, although the origins of the war were many and were not only deeply entrenched within American society but had also been long in the making. The true causes of the Civil War are still debated and cannot, in truth, be attributed to a single person or event. At the time of Lincoln's election, there were thirty-four American states, with the Northern and Pacific states being largely supportive of his policies. The Southern states required slave labor (specifically the descendants of African slaves) for their large plantations and to support their heavy reliance on an agricultural economy, mostly in cotton.

President Lincoln was intent upon preventing the spread of slavery into newly acquired American lands and territories that extended toward the west and southwest of the country. The Southerners, in opposition to Lincoln's views, began seceding from the Union to form the Confederate States of America. This secession was not recognized by the federal government nor by the international community and led to the American Civil War, as Lincoln sought to reincorporate the South into the Union and find a solution to the issue of slavery.

The Confederate States of America (CSA) lasted for the duration of the Civil War. The eleven states that eventually broke away from the Union—South Carolina, Mississippi, Florida, Alabama, Georgia, Louisiana, Texas, Virginia, Arkansas, Tennessee, and North Carolina—were all within the "Deep South" of the United States, particularly toward the southeastern extremities of North America. The Confederacy was originally created with only seven states, with Virginia, Arkansas, Tennessee, and North Carolina joining after the official start of the Civil War in April 1861 (and the attack on Fort Sumter in South Carolina). The Confederate capital was moved on May 29th, 1861, from Montgomery, Alabama, to the far more strategic location of Richmond,

Virginia, six days after Virginia seceded. Although Missouri and Kentucky technically remained part of the Union, the Confederacy claimed them as their own due to the high number of Confederate sympathizers in those areas, and it ran an illegitimate shadow government in these states.

The nation's capital, Washington, DC (the District of Columbia), on the east of the Potomac River, which essentially formed a dividing line between the North and the South, remained the Union capital during the Civil War. It also became the home of many slaves who fled the South. Washington, DC, was extremely close to Rebel territory, so it was well defended and well fortified during the war.

The city of Manassas in northeastern Virginia was nothing more than a railroad crossing during the American Civil War, although it was the most strategic rail node for the Confederate Army (also known as the Rebel Army). Manassas Junction, as it was known, linked Washington, DC, eastern Virginia, and the Potomac River with the Shenandoah Valley west of Manassas across the Blue Ridge Mountains. Most importantly, the railroad connected to the Confederate capital of Richmond, which lay 153 kilometers (95 miles) south of the Manassas Junction. The settlement of Manassas grew around the rail junction after the Civil War and was incorporated in 1873—eight years after the end of the Civil War. The Shenandoah Valley was considered the breadbasket for the Confederacy during the Civil War, and while the Confederates occupied it until the autumn of 1864, the valley was used as a strategic juncture from which to launch raids on the Union states of Maryland and Pennsylvania (north of Maryland), as well as haranguing Washington, DC. Despite the fact that the Confederacy was victorious in both the First and Second Battles of Manassas (with the second battle occurring in August 1862), the Manassas Junction and surrounding railroads were controlled by the Union forces for most of the Civil War.

Chapter 2 – Prelude to the First Battle of Bull Run

The American Civil War officially began on April 12th, 1861, when the Confederates attacked the Union stronghold of Fort Sumter near Charleston in South Carolina. South Carolina, which is below Virginia and separated by North Carolina, was entrenched within the "Deep South" but was still vulnerable to attack. Fort Sumter was in reality attacked by the South Carolina militia, not the Confederate Army, as the Confederate Army had not yet been conscripted.

The attack was instigated by the Southerners' insistence that their Ordinance of Secession, which had been ratified by the individual states between the end of 1860 and the beginning of 1861, be recognized and upheld by the Union government. According to the Union government, these resolutions were illegal and unenforceable, as the rebellious states were still technically a part of the United States. As mentioned above, President Abraham Lincoln's election in November 1860 prompted the Southern states to draft resolutions to secede. Lincoln's open opposition to slavery posed a direct and serious threat to the Southern way of life, including their economy and social fabric.

Since Fort Sumter was the start of the Civil War, it is important to look into the battle in a bit more detail. Charleston Harbor, where Fort Sumter was and still is located, is an inlet at the junction of two rivers leading to the Atlantic Ocean and sheltered at the entrance by Morris Island and Sullivan's Island. After the signing of the Ordinance of

Secession, the South stipulated that the US Army abandon their position near Charleston, which they did not. The Federal Army was moved, however, by Major Robert Anderson (1805-1871) from the vulnerable position it held at Fort Moultrie on Sullivan's Island to Fort Sumter, which was located on an island that dominated the entrance to Charleston Harbor. The US president at the time, James Buchanan (1791-1868, in off. March 1857-March 1861), sent reinforcements on an unarmed ship, but it was attacked and forced to withdraw. All Union property, except for the fort, was seized by the South Carolina militia. Between January and April 1861, the army within Fort Sumter was technically under siege.

In March, Brigadier General P. G. T. Beauregard, the first general officer of the Confederate States Army, became the commander of the Charleston forces. (P. G. T. Beauregard, who served the US military from 1838 as a brevet major before joining the Confederacy, was also known as "Little Napoleon" or "Little Frenchman" due to French being his first language. He later played a pivotal role in the First Battle of Bull Run.)

Once Lincoln took office, the president decided to send reinforcements to Major Anderson's men during the siege. This, along with the US Army's refusal to evacuate Fort Sumter, led to the bombardment of the fort. Cannons began firing on the fort in the early hours of April 12th, and it lasted for thirty-four hours. The Federal Army was significantly outgunned, and it eventually surrendered, agreeing to evacuate. (No fatalities were incurred on either side during the Battle of Fort Sumter, but unfortunately, there was an accident during the surrender in which a gun explosion killed two Federal soldiers.) The incidents surrounding Fort Sumter were the official start of the American Civil War, although the initial bloodshed of the war was attributed to the Baltimore riot a week later in Maryland, in which sixteen soldiers and civilians lost their lives and hundreds were wounded.

After the start of the American Civil War, newly elected President Abraham Lincoln, who was inaugurated on March 4th, 1861, called on his loyalists for support and requested seventy-five thousand volunteers to aid his efforts to quell the rebellious South (the US Army at that time stood at about fifteen thousand). Lincoln officially issued a proclamation on April 15th, 1861, a few days after the bombardment of Fort Sumter, declaring the South's actions as an insurrection against the United States.

Virginia was one of the states that seceded, and it was a key state by virtue of its strategic proximity to the US capital of Washington, DC. Since the capital was surrounded by the state of Maryland—a slave-owning region that could potentially have become part of the Confederacy—Lincoln worked hard to prevent losing Maryland to the South. He ultimately achieved this by imprisoning secessionist ringleaders, and he narrowly prevented Washington, DC, from being surrounded by enemy territory during the war. The federal capital remained close to the front lines of the fighting during the Civil War and saw constant influxes of wounded soldiers and escaped or emancipated slaves. DC lay only 175 kilometers (109 miles) northeast of the Confederate capital of Richmond in Virginia.

Federal General George B. McClellan (1826–1885, who served two terms of service for the US military from 1846 to 1857 and again from 1861 to 1864), was given command of the principal Union Army of the Potomac, and he built 53 kilometers (33 miles) of fortifications to protect the nation's capital. The Confederate Army never had any intention of directly attacking the supremely protected capital, but it made a few feints for Washington, DC, mostly to confuse and distract the Northerners. The Confederates mostly fought on the south of the Mason-Dixon Line— the line that separated the northern states of Pennsylvania and Maryland from Virginia to the south. This demarcation was put in place in the mid-18th century and became the de facto division between the Northern free states and the Southern slave states during the Civil War. (West Virginia, which is south of the Mason-Dixon Line, only separated from Virginia in 1863 to become part of the Union.)

Most of the military leaders of both the North and the South had been prominent members of the Mexican-American War, which lasted from 1846 to 1848. Although the war, like many other conflicts, had multiple reasons for starting, it was kicked off by the US annexation of Texas in 1845, in which America ultimately gained the territory from Mexico. Many of the Southern leaders had gained their experience as members of the United States military, so the Civil War's call to arms was painfully personal on both sides, but it was seemingly inevitable. To reinforce how connected soldiers from both the South and the North were, most senior military men on both sides had trained together at West Point, a military academy in New York, and had served in many wars on the same side.

The First Battle of Manassas arose due to the Confederate Congress's plan to hold its meeting at Richmond on July 20th, 1861. The Northern press and general population wanted their government to take action and tame the insurgent South once and for all before the advent of the congress. War fever had spread across the country, and decisive action was becoming imminent. Thousands of Federal troops were gathering at Washington, DC, although these were mostly unseasoned volunteers who set up rudimentary camps around the capital. Many in the North believed that the capture of the Confederate headquarters of Richmond would end the war once and for all.

There had been little time for preparation or training for both the Northern and Southern troops. The voices of reason that spoke against the war in Congress were largely ignored, such as the veteran military commander Winfield Scott (1786-1866), who had fought in the Mexican-American War and every other significant American war since 1812. As the commanding general of the US Army at the start of the Civil War, Scott's opposing ideas to Lincoln's, as well as his advancing age, meant that he stepped back as the head of the US Army in favor of Brigadier General Irvin McDowell (1818-1885). Scott had misgivings about the appointment of McDowell, as well as about attacking the Confederacy head on. His wise counsel as an experienced veteran was largely ignored since he was too old to join the field. Most importantly, Scott recommended a delay on the advance on Richmond, which ultimately led to the First Battle of Bull Run, since the volunteers who had been called up needed more time to train. Scott had been in favor of relying entirely on the experienced and trained US military core personnel.

On July 4th, 1861, President Lincoln asked Congress for 400,000 troops and $400 million "for making this contest a short, and a decisive one." The North's confidence was so great that soldiers were conscripted for an initial period of only three months. Thirty-five thousand Union troops marched from the capital of Washington, DC, to strike at twenty-two thousand Confederate men on July 16th, 1861, who had converged near the river of Bull Run in northeastern Virginia, doing so to specifically defend the Manassas Railroad Junction that brought supplies and food from the west and north to the Confederacy.

As mentioned, Lincoln employed Brigadier General McDowell to lead the Federal troops south, break the backbone of the rebellion accumulating at Manassas, and clear the way to Richmond. The US president was advised by McDowell to avoid the onslaught since the American troops were not sufficiently trained or prepared for battle. However, Lincoln knew that the same would be true of the Southern forces, so he continued with the engagement regardless. McDowell had been headquartered at the abandoned mansion of the Confederate defector Robert E. Lee in Arlington County at the far northeastern corner of Virginia before he led his troops toward the small settlement of Centreville. (General Robert E. Lee served for the duration of the Civil War under the South's banner, but like many of his contemporaries, he had previously served the US Army, acting as a colonel from 1829 to 1861.)

Centreville, which was forty-two kilometers (twenty-six miles) west of DC, would serve as the intermediary point and temporary headquarters for the Union on their approach to Manassas. Centreville lay eleven kilometers (seven miles) northeast of Manassas, with the Bull Run River lying approximately equidistant between the two points. Their movement was unobstructed by Confederate troops, who had started moving back toward the junction once they'd received intelligence of the Union march.

McDowell reluctantly drove his troops southwest toward Manassas Junction. His Army of Northeastern Virginia formed the corps of what would later become the Union Army of the Potomac. The Union Army of Northeastern Virginia contained five infantry (foot soldier) divisions (the 1st to the 5th Division), which were arranged into three to five brigades each. Most of the brigades had artillery batteries. Artillery batteries could be fixed or mobile (naturally, the approaching army had exclusively mobile artillery), containing heavy gunnery and other long-distance field weapons such as cannons (heavy field guns), howitzers (a variation of the cannon for more indirect bombardment via shelling), rifled artillery (heavy field rifle guns), mortars (portable explosive launchers with short, thick barrels and short-range, high-arc detonation trajectories), and the multi-barreled Gatling gun (similar to modern-day machine guns, firing up to six hundred rounds a minute). The average battery would have six to twelve ordnance pieces (mounted mobile heavy guns).

The generals in charge of the five divisions were, respectively, Brigadier General Daniel Tyler, who commanded the largest 1st Division, with four brigades led by Brigadier General Robert C. Schenck, Colonel

Erasmus D. Keyes, Colonel William T. Sherman, and Colonel Israel B. Richardson; Colonel David Hunter led the 2nd Division, containing two brigades headed by Colonels Andrew Porter and Ambrose Burnside; Colonel Samuel P. Heintzelman led the 3rd Division, with three brigades headed by Colonels William B. Franklin, Orlando B. Willcox, and Oliver O. Howard; General Theodore Runyon led the 4th Division, and he did not have brigades nor divisions for engagement but commanded seven regiments from New Jersey and one regiment of New York volunteer fighters and militia; and finally, Colonel Dixon S. Miles led the 5th Division, with two brigades led by Colonels Louis Blenker and Thomas A. Davies.

This original Army of Northeastern Virginia also had a cavalry of about four hundred men and their horses. Typical weapons of the war included edged, personal combat weapons, such as short swords, bayonets (generally attached to the end of rifles), knives, swords, and sabers. There was a general shortage of sidearms, rifles, and muskets, but these typically included both the single-shot and the newly developed repeating muskets, revolvers, pistols, and carbines. Crude rocket launchers, hand grenades, and landmines were also used.

McDowell's troops moved slowly, which gave the appointed commanding officer of the Confederacy, General P. G. T. Beauregard, time to send for additional troops and supplies from the Shenandoah Valley. Aided by a prodigious spy network that had been operating in the Union capital, the Confederate Army was waiting, and it was as prepared as possible for the arrival of the Northern troops. Confederate Brigadier General Joseph E. Johnston (1807–1891) was stationed in the valley, and by outmaneuvering the Federal forces, he was able to march approximately twelve thousand men toward Manassas. Johnston had served as a brigadier general in the US Army from 1829 to 1861, after which time he joined the Confederacy as a general until the end of the Civil War.

Despite the fact that these additional Confederate troops (adding to a total of approximately thirty-four thousand overall) joined the battle in its later stages, it is estimated that both the Northern and Southern armies could only put approximately eighteen thousand of their men to good use during the Battle of Bull Run owing to the awkwardness of the battle scene (in topographical and tactical terms) and the general confusion that accompanied the battle.

In June of 1861, in anticipation of a Northern onslaught toward Richmond, Confederate forces used slave labor to reinforce the exposed eastern approach to Manassas (the Bull Run River protected the northern approach), building an extensive series of fortifications and placing strategically located cannons at high points. Signal Hill, eleven kilometers (seven miles) directly south of Centreville across the Bull Run River, would prove to be a key strategic node of the battles to come. Local plantations and their beautiful homes were used as headquarters, redoubts, forts, and field hospitals, and they protected the east-west orientated Orange and Alexandria Railroad leading to the port of Alexandria on the Potomac River. (Alexandria was the site of an important slave market.)

Chapter 3 – Skirmish at Blackburn's Ford

The site of the forthcoming battle was a mere forty kilometers (twenty-five miles) west-southwest of the enemy capital of Washington, DC. Although Bull Run flows mostly in a northwesterly to southeasterly direction, the section around which the First Battle of Bull Run occurred was where the river makes a mostly northerly to southerly transit through the landscape, which means that the attack strategies of the two armies included crossing Bull Run from approximately west to east and vice versa. A turnpike road (a toll road), Warrenton Road, from Centreville crossed the Bull Run River at Stone Bridge and eventually formed a crossroad on the western side of the river with Sudley Road before reaching the town of Gainesville. Almost five kilometers (three miles) north upstream of Stone Bridge on Bull Run River was Sudley Springs (Sudley Ford), an unmanned ford that permitted crossing in shallow waters.

The Confederacy was prepared for the arrival of the Union troops. They had received a dispatch via their spy network, which was run mostly by society women and young girls from Washington, DC, that a battle in mid-July was imminent. The Confederacy was aware that by July 16th, 1861, the Federal Army was on the march, and the slow progress of the Northerners gave the Southerners time to send for reinforcements.

General Beauregard—the dashing Louisianan who had heralded a heroic standing through the bombardment of Fort Sumter—was the man assigned to move twenty-two thousand Southern troops—the Confederate Army of the Potomac—to an encampment near the little-known river of Bull Run in order to defend the Manassas Rail Junction. Beauregard's initial plan had been a bold and overconfident one of sending for reinforcements and extra troops to pincer the Federal Army in a dual west and east attack at the enemy's flanks. He intended to encircle and disarm the Northern Army and then march northeast to capture both Washington, DC, and the state of Maryland. However, upon consideration, the protection of the Manassas Railroad Junction became Beauregard's primary concern, and he decided to keep his troops in their original place, but he still called for reinforcements since he knew that his twenty-two thousand troops faced thirty-five thousand Union men. (McDowell's army was the largest ever assembled in North America.)

Beauregard's Confederate Army of the Potomac consisted of seven infantry brigades, containing most of the fighting men (19,500), one cavalry unit (about 1,500 men), several additional legions and regional battalions, and almost 40 pieces of field artillery organized under five batteries (about 800 men). The leaders of the brigades were, respectively, Brigadier General Milledge L. Bonham, Brigadier General Richard S. Ewell, Brigadier General David R. Jones, Brigadier General James Longstreet, Colonel Philip St. George Cocke, Colonel Jubal Early, Colonel Nathan G. Evans, and Brigadier General Theophilus H. Holmes (leading the reserves).

In the Shenandoah Valley to the northwest, Confederate General Johnston was holding his position to defend the crucial agricultural land necessary to feed the South. He was threatened by eighteen thousand Northern troops to his approximate twelve thousand men, which were under the command of Major General Robert Patterson (1792-1881), who served three periods of service for the US Army, with his career ending in 1861. Patterson's men of the Department of Pennsylvania were stationed to prevent access to the capital and, more crucially, to block any attempts by Johnston to send his troops southeast to join Beauregard at Manassas.

In this second and most critical concession for the North, Patterson failed. Both Johnston and Beauregard had been poised to move to the aid of the other upon the start of the engagements. When Union forces officially began moving on Manassas, Johnston responded and craftily maneuvered his troops south to support Beauregard. Patterson's inability to prevent military reinforcements from reaching Bull Run was considered the principal cause of the Union's defeat of this first major land engagement of the war, and it brought Patterson's military career to an end, as he was pressured to leave the army.

Johnston had been headquartered in Winchester, Virginia, 89 kilometers (55 miles) northwest of Manassas and 121 kilometers (75 miles) west-northwest of Washington, DC. When General Beauregard informed Confederate President Jefferson Davis that he needed aid since skirmishes and gunfire were already present along his front lines, the Winchester troops safely decamped the valley to move swiftly toward Bull Run. This was done without any major issues since Patterson had inexplicably moved his troops along the Shenandoah Valley, which meant they were out of the path of the Confederate troops. (Some reasons for Patterson's early withdrawal include his men having reached their ninety-day conscriptions, not having received sufficient supplies from Pennsylvania, and General Winfield Scott, who was then the commanding general of the US Army, requiring him to join up with McDowell's army.)

Under Johnston's orders, Brigadier General Thomas J. Jackson (1824–1863) led his brigade from Winchester on July 18th, 1861, protected by the three-hundred-strong 1st Virginia Cavalry of Colonel J. E. B. ("Jeb") Stuart (James Ewell Brown, 1833–1864). Thomas J. Jackson is a notable name in Civil War history books, although he might be more familiar to readers by his nickname of Stonewall Jackson, which was given to him due to his role in the First Battle of Bull Run. He served the US Army from 1846 to 1861 as a brevet major and then the Confederacy until 1863. Jeb Stuart is another notable name of the war, and he served as the captain of the US Army from 1854 to 1861, ending his career as a Confederate major general. Both men died in the Civil War.

Overall, the Confederate Army of the Shenandoah consisted of four brigades of three to five infantry regiments, each totaling approximately twelve thousand men, including the cavalry. Each brigade commanded one artillery battery with a further twenty pieces for the general field. The addition of the Shenandoah Army would bring the Confederate total to about thirty-four thousand men—just one thousand short of the Northerners. The battle would be equally pitched, but ultimately, it was possibly the unknown arrival of waves of the Shenandoah men during the critical dates of July 19th to July 21st, just before and during the First Battle of Bull Run, that caught the Union unawares. (In fact, McDowell had been assured via Patterson that the Shenandoah Army had not left the valley!) The Shenandoah troops gave the Confederates fresh reinforcements and renewed strength that the unseasoned Federal troops could not match. Toward the main pitch of the battle on the afternoon of July 21st, when it became apparent that the Confederates would win, most Federal troops chose to flee the battlefield upon their own consideration to the astonishment of the Union generals. The overwhelmed and exhausted Yankees then scampered back to Washington, traumatized by their first real experience of war.

The four Shenandoah brigades were commanded by Brigadier General Thomas J. Jackson, Colonel Francis. S. Bartow, Brigadier General Barnard E. Bee, and Brigadier General Edmund K. Smith (replaced during the battle by Colonel Arnold Elzey, 1816–1871, who served the US Army from 1837 as a captain before joining the Confederacy), respectively. Colonel A. C. Cummings of the Virginia Volunteers was also present on the battlefield.

While Johnston was bringing his men down from Shenandoah and McDowell was organizing his attack plan for the Union, Beauregard moved his troops behind the natural line of defense of the Bull Run River. Confederate President Davis had already ordered all troops to move north from Richmond (153 kilometers or 95 miles directly south of Manassas) and Fredericksburg (97 kilometers or 60 miles north of Richmond). The Confederate troops were spread along the western edge of the Bull Run River for approximately eight kilometers (five miles), from Stone Bridge on the Warrenton Turnpike to Union Mills (a stagecoach point) in the south. Aware that both sides of the military corps were novices, Beauregard spread his troops along the stretch of river that would most likely be the scene of the ensuing battle. He concentrated his troops at the fords (shallow points) of the Bull Run River, which averaged twelve meters (forty feet) wide in most places.

Bull Run had steep banks and deep sections that would have been difficult for even experienced troops to cross. Beauregard had, however, left the northern stretch of Bull Run, from Stone Bridge to Sudley Springs, unmanned. When the fighting began at 10 a.m. on Sunday morning, July 21st, toward the Sudley Road Turnpike, Beauregard,

Johnston, and most of their men had already spent hours waiting before the continual sound of gunfire to the north made them realize their mistake in focusing on the lower reaches of Bull Run.

McDowell intended to proceed cautiously and planned to move from east to west and attack Beauregard's right flank, as close to the Manassas intersection as possible. However, after arriving at Centreville on Thursday, July 18th, the same day Johnston and twelve thousand Rebels were sneaking out of Shenandoah, the Union general conducted a reconnoiter of the intended approach and decided against this initial maneuver. In McDowell's absence, Brigadier General Daniel Tyler (1799-1882, who completed two terms of service for the US Army, the second during the Civil War) was ordered to take the lead division and probe the roads toward Bull Run—giving the impression that they would take Manassas head on. Tyler was joined by Colonel Israel B. Richardson (1815-1862, who served two terms with the army but lost his life the following year at the Battle of Antietam). Unfortunately, Tyler exceeded his orders, and in an act of insubordination that would later be attributed to the loss of the battle, he allowed his troops to exchange fire with the Rebels across Bull Run.

Furthermore, the overexuberant brigadier general tested the Rebels' defenses at Blackburn's Ford (marked on the 1861 map as "Blackfords Ford"), just south of Mitchell's Ford (located west of Centreville). Blackburn's Ford was 5.5 kilometers (3.5 miles) downstream of Bull Run, south of the pivotal Stone Bridge—a bridge of stone that marked the main thoroughfare to Centreville along the Warrenton Turnpike. The Confederate troops, led by Brigadier General James Longstreet (1821-1904, who served the US Army as a major from 1842 to 1861 before joining the Confederacy), remained hidden in the woods on the western bank. Tyler, wanting to ascertain the extent of the entrenched enemy across the river, moved his force forward toward the river. He was arrogant enough to discharge artillery power and send out troops to encourage front-line skirmishes since he saw evidence of the enemy about.

After this initial onslaught by the opposition, the Confederates leaped into action, using musket firepower to send Tyler's men retreating in confusion after half an hour of fighting. Later that afternoon, both sides unloaded hundreds of rounds of artillery fire on one another across the river to no effect for an hour. Essentially, each party seemed to be testing the others' readiness, capabilities, and resources.

The Confederate infantry at Blackburn's Ford was later joined by more troops and artillery, thinking that the main battle had begun. Confederate Colonel Jubal A. Early (1816-1894, who served two terms in the US Army before switching allegiance to the Confederacy during the Civil War, ending his career as a major general) had marched his brigade for three kilometers (two miles) from the headquarters at the McLean House (owned by William McLean, a retired general from the Virginia militia). On the other side, Union Major General William Tecumseh Sherman (1820-1891, who served two periods in the US Army, including postbellum, and would go on to be a key figure for the Federals) arrived late, and his men did not experience heavy fighting.

Unfortunately, the gross inexperience and under-preparedness of all parties were apparent when soldiers allied to the Confederacy sent as reinforcements began firing on their own men at this initial skirmish at Blackburn's Ford. The confusion was connected to the uniforms, as the Southerners were required to wear gray and the Northerners dark-blue, although this coding was not entirely enforced at this point in the Civil War (it remained an issue for the entire duration of the war because the material for uniforms was in short supply). Many volunteers had arrived for battle in their home uniform colors, which sometimes meant Northerners were wearing gray and the Southerners blue! This appalling oversight was listed as one of the contributing factors to the overall confusion of the day since, even under the best conditions, it was difficult to tell foe from friend due to the fighting, yelling, and constant gun smoke.

Eventually, the Union troops retreated under the constant fire of the Confederates. About 150 lives were lost that day on both sides.

Tyler was satisfied that the enemy was in full force and was ready to be engaged at a later point. Although he had completely overreached and even breached his orders, he had ascertained the general positions of the Confederate troops around Blackburn's Ford and had specifically located the extent of their left flank.

Due to the engagement at Blackburn's Ford, McDowell decided not to attack the enemy directly in the direction of Manassas Junction but rather to make a sneak attack from the northwest, far above Stone Bridge. McDowell dispatched his chief engineer, Major John Barnard, to scout a suitable crossing, and he returned with two propositions, including the easily navigable Sudley Ford.

Tyler's foolishness could have potentially undermined the entire Battle of Bull Run three days later since both Confederate leaders, Jubal Early and James Longstreet, later agreed that the Yankees' "licking" at Blackburn's Ford provided a considerable boost to the Confederate Army's confidence, particularly of the soldiers who were young and inexperienced in war. (McDowell's lack of confidence in Tyler also became apparent, and it would play out to the Union's detriment three days later.) Although technically neither side had really "won" at Blackburn's Ford, the disorderly manner in which the Federal troops retreated and the fact that they retreated when they should have never engaged in the first place contributed to the illusion that they had lost.

Chapter 4 – The Battle of First Manassas Begins

McDowell's decision not to execute a frontal assault on the enemy meant sending his troops far upstream of the Bull Run River in order to close in on the Confederate left flank. This new plan was executed three days later on Sunday, July 21ˢᵗ, since the Federal forces needed to regroup and strategize their main attack plan. This three-day delay was later seen as one of the main causes of the Union loss at Bull Run since the Rebels had time to call for more troops and reinforcements from farther north—specifically Johnston's Shenandoah Valley brigades and cavalry. In the interim, many of the Union volunteer soldiers' ninety days of service had been completed, and they were found by civilians wandering back to Washington, DC, on the eve of the first real battle of the Civil War!

The civilians, excited by the contradictory news that the North had won the skirmish at Blackburn's Ford, were setting out in their private carriages with picnics and champagne to enjoy the final showdown of the war, as, according to their neighbors and the press, it was a battle in which the Yankees were sure to win! Congressmen and press officials joined the civilian crowds to observe and record the ensuing events, which they would later either prematurely report as a Union win, grossly exaggerate, or deeply regret participating in as the battle turned into a rout, with Federal troops sent scampering without permission back to Washington, DC, at the conclusion of the fateful battle.

General Johnston and his commanding units had made haste out of Winchester under Johnston's claim that "Beauregard was being attacked by overwhelming forces...Every moment is precious...for this march is a forced march to save the country." This communique was not true, but it was effective in rallying his troops, who hustled across the Shenandoah River, up Blue Mountain Ridge, and through the Ashby Gap of the Blue Mountains. Jackson's brigade was the first to arrive at the Manassas Gap Railroad Station at Piedmont (now Delaplane), and he loaded as many of his troops as possible into railroad freight cars. The overloaded locomotives took eight hours to cross the last fifty-five kilometers (thirty-four miles) to reach the Manassas Rail Junction in the late afternoon of Friday, July 19th. The rest of Johnston's army straggled into the Confederate camps over the next twenty-four hours, with Johnston arriving at midday on Saturday, July 20th. The last remaining Confederate troops to arrive on the day of battle (Sunday, July 21st) were Brigadier General Edmund Kirby Smith's 4th Brigade of the Army of the Shenandoah.

Johnston, being senior in rank to Beauregard, at first wanted to take command of the Confederate forces, but he later realized this was best left to General Beauregard, as he was more familiar with the terrain. Beauregard's original plan was to cross the lower Bull Run near Blackburn's Ford and, moving from west to east, attack the enemy's left flank.

Ironically, Union Brigadier General McDowell's adjusted plan of moving upriver and crossing Bull Run from east to west to attack the enemy's left flank would have sent both armies chasing each other's tails in a pinwheel movement. McDowell's poor intelligence network had led him to commission the first American aviation unit to aid in his decision of initial attack—this was none other than the United States Balloon Corps! McDowell employed the services of the *Enterprise*, the first civilian-operated hot air balloon, complete with a telegraph system that provided aerial surveillance of Confederate troops by the Union. (The Balloon Corps was officially in operation for use during the Civil War from 1861 to 1863, but it was never considered to be especially successful.) McDowell is rumored to have joined the civilian aeronaut Professor Thaddeus Lowe in an aerial reconnoiter over the anticipated battleground of Bull Run to make preliminary observations of the field.

The facts of Lowe's participation in the First Battle of Bull Run are contradictory and unsubstantiated, except that he was commissioned in June of that year to survey the surrounding area. Apparently, McDowell, and then later Tyler, were impressed by Lowe and sent those sentiments to Washington. Another account speaks of Lowe being accosted by his allies, the Federal troops, while hovering within firing distance above them during the First Battle of Bull Run. He had not thought to take evidence of his military allegiance when he followed the troops to Centreville. The account—possibly a commission to check on the enemy's movements after the battle on July 24th—tells of Lowe being too afraid to descend in friendly territory because he could not prove his allegiance. He ended up being swept behind enemy lines but made a lucky escape back into Union territory, where he reported that the enemy had retreated and were not making an approach on Washington. Whatever the true account of Lowe's adventures, he was successful enough during this period in the war for Lincoln to approve the Balloon Corps and for more military-grade balloons to be manufactured.

Regardless of the true basis for McDowell's decision to attack via Sudley Springs, it was the correct one. The enemy was located from Stone Bridge southward, particularly around Blackburn's Ford, where they anticipated another full onslaught. At 2:30 a.m. on Sunday morning, McDowell sent about fifteen thousand men under the divisions of Hunter and Heintzelman about five kilometers (three miles) along the Warrenton Turnpike (approximately halfway toward Stone Bridge) to then turn northwest on a road that ran parallel to Bull Run leading to Sudley Springs. (Sudley was located about five kilometers or three miles north of Stone Bridge by a direct route along the river.)

The Northern Army heading for Sudley marched in three columns. David Hunter (1802-1886) was serving his second term of service for the US Army as a major general and marched that day on his fifty-ninth birthday. Samuel P. Heintzelman (1805-1880) had served the US Army for his entire adult life, and he had also finally achieved the rank of major general. Both generals were leading volunteer armies who were not used to marching and had never experienced open warfare. Tyler's division of eight thousand men had been dispatched by McDowell directly toward Stone Bridge to create a diversion away from the bulk of the army marching north, and Richardson's retinue was sent to Blackburn's Ford.

Confusion immediately ensued during both advances from the Warrenton Turnpike. Tyler's 1st Division blocked the forward movement of Hunter's and Heintzelman's 2nd and 3rd Divisions. The 1st Division arrived at Stone Bridge at 6 a.m., but once the 2nd and 3rd Divisions had eventually turned right off the turnpike, they found the route to be little more than a cart lane and stumbled forward in the dark along un-scouted roads. By the time the approximately fifteen thousand northward-moving troops had reached Bull Run at Sudley, it was 9:30 a.m. (two to three hours later than planned). The sixteen-kilometer (ten-mile) approach had included several necessary rest and refreshment stops for the unconditioned troops, which eventually worked considerably in their disfavor as they were spied upon when passing near Sudley.

McDowell's overall plan was to draw the enemy up from the lower fords by sending in Hunter's and Heintzelman's men from the north, allowing the remainder of the Northerners to cross the southern fords and surround the Confederates or at least block the Southerners' movement across Bull Run. The two divisions that McDowell had sent to guard Stone Bridge and Blackburn's Ford were required to execute feints and mock charges to distract and confuse the enemy.

In the early hours of Sunday morning, a Union 20-pounder shell came whizzing into the detached kitchen of the McLean homestead, where General Beauregard was then stationed, near Blackburn's Ford. Nobody was hurt, but Beauregard's breakfast had been ruined. (There are contrary reports that this incident actually occurred on July 18th at the skirmish of Blackburn's Ford at dinnertime.) This was the signal that the battle had begun. A 30-pounder Parrott rifle, a cannon weighing three tons, was also discharged by the Union near Stone Bridge at about 6 a.m., plus more artillery fire from Stone Bridge extending south toward McLean's Ford from the Federal side. (These massive field rifles would later be confiscated by the winning Confederate side.)

Beauregard sent orders to all the commanders stationed along the Bull Run fords, but for some reason, the orders either did not reach the recipients, or they were drastically incorrect. Brigadier General Richard S. Ewell (1817–1872, who served the US Army as a captain from 1840 before joining the Confederacy and went on to play a significant part in the Civil War) was ordered to lead an attack at Union Mills but instead received a message to stand his ground and hold fire. Two other

Confederate regiments, including the reserve brigade under Brigadier General Theophilus H. Holmes, were expected to move forward in support of Ewell, but only one received correct orders, which resulted in a single unit moving forward alone. Beauregard's impression was that the battle had begun since it seemed as if a full-frontal attack was occurring along the southern reaches of Bull Run from Stone Bridge downstream to Union Mills. Not knowing that he had, in fact, been fooled by the Union's tactics, he stuck by his original plan of crossing the river to attack the enemy's left flank for several more hours, although it was never executed.

In the interim, Confederate Captain Edward P. Alexander, from his hilltop station on Signal Hill, spotted the Union soldiers near Sudley and sent a timely signal flag warning to Colonel Nathan Evans (1824-1868, who served as a US captain from 1848 until joining the Confederacy as a brigadier general for the Civil War), who was positioned at Stone Bridge with a small retinue of men. (Evans had sent a number of his men to intercept a potential direct threat from Tyler at Stone Bridge, although he soon realized that these were Union feints because of the minimal firing.) Alexander had used the flag signaling method of aerial telegraphy (flag semaphore or wigwag) by using a single flag to transmit, "Look out for your left! You are turned!" A courier scout also arrived from Sudley to get Evans's attention. The Union plan had been to cross the river in the dark and to descend upon the enemy in a surprise attack, but the lateness of their arrival at the ford enabled the signalman to see the sun reflecting off metal as the army moved.

The signaler's message reached Evans nearly thirteen kilometers (eight miles) to the northwest. Evans, taking nine hundred of his men, or eleven of his fifteen companies (as well as his aide, who never left his side and carried a small barrel of his favorite whiskey), rushed north at about 9 a.m. to meet the Union, leaving Stone Bridge pitifully manned with four companies of the 4th South Carolina and two guns.

Tyler's demonstrations, which had been acting as a pinning maneuver to hold the enemy, could have become an outright assault, in which he would have likely overrun the men at Stone Bridge. By 10:15 a.m., the first column of the Federal troops, led by the 2nd Rhode Island Regiment (part of Hunter's men under Colonel Ambrose Burnside), had confronted Evans's 1st Louisiana Battalion on a hilltop behind which Evans had positioned his men with two guns. Matthews Hill, where

Evans' men lay in wait, was located in the crook of the northern extremities of the battlefield just south of where Sudley Road met Bull Run.

Thus, the first official frontal engagement of the Battle of Bull Run began. Evans was attributed with considerable courage, as he and his men were vastly outnumbered for several hours while they held off the Union troops and awaited the remainder of the Confederacy. Evans was described as "being everywhere" during the thick of the battle. His leadership was credited as a significant contributor to the South's victory that day. The Confederate forces under Evans spread out on Matthews Hill (above the Warrenton Turnpike and a small tributary leading to Bull Creek) in a thin line, and they effectively blocked the enemy's approach for a time.

At first, the battle on Matthews Hill (a low rise in the landscape) was relatively evenly matched, with soldiers and leaders being wounded, sometimes fatally, on both sides. Major Chatham R. Wheat's (1826-1862, who had served three years in the US Army before joining the South) 1st Louisiana Special Battalion, the "Wheat's Louisiana Tigers," charged at one point, causing confusion in a delaying spoiling attack (an attack meant to disrupt the opposition's plans). The "Tigers" were a semi-mercenary unit organized by Wheat and known for their exceptional bravery and fierceness but also their wild ill-discipline. These approximately five hundred men heralded from New Orleans, Germany, and Ireland, and they were considered socially inferior street fighters. Wheat received a Union bullet straight through his lungs during the First Battle of Bull Run that he ultimately survived—the first recorded in US battle history.

Within an hour or so, reinforcements began arriving on both sides of the battlefield to surge the fighting forward. Union Colonel Ambrose E. Burnside (1824-1881, who finished his military career as a major general at the end of the Civil War before going into politics), leading a brigade under Hunter's Federal 2nd Division, arrived from Sudley Springs from the north. Burnside's men included those under Major George Sykes (1822-1880), who commanded the Regular Infantry Battalion consisting of eight regular army companies from various regiments—the only regulars (official soldiers) in the Union field at that time. Next to arrive at the field was Colonel Andrew Porter of Hunter's 2nd Division and Colonel William B. Franklin of Heintzelman's 3rd Division.

Like Burnside before them, the colonels erroneously sent their men in piecemeal to be defeated in quick succession. Approaching each engagement piecemeal and not engaging the full force of the Union at any point would spell the day's defeat for the Federal forces. However, there was general confusion and poor coordination on both sides.

Brigadier General Barnard Elliott Bee Jr. (1824-1861, who served the US Army as a lieutenant colonel from 1845 to 1861 before joining the Confederacy) and Colonel Francis S. Bartow (1816-1861, fresh to military service) arrived from the south, having been sent by Johnston in aid of the Confederates. These additions brought the Confederates' total numbers to almost three thousand within the eye of the battle on Matthews Hill, but they were still vastly outnumbered. Neither Bee nor Bartow would survive the day, but both were attributed with courage and their considerable efforts in holding back the Yankees. (They were two of the first most senior officers to lose their lives during the Civil War.)

Bee ignored Evans's orders to stay back, and coupled with Evans's refusal to withdraw, Bee swooped forward to defend the line. Bartow followed to protect Bee. At about 10 a.m., Tyler sent Sherman north from Stone Bridge to join the action on the hill and to attack the Confederate's right flank. The battle of Matthews Hill had turned in favor of the Union, as the Confederates were practically encircled and outflanked, fighting three to one.

Between 11:30 a.m. and noon, the Confederacy began disassembling and moving back beyond the Youngs Creek tributary and the Warrenton Turnpike, and they were covered as they withdrew by Captain John D. Imboden (1823-1895, new to service), who commanded a light artillery unit of 107 men. Southern troops began coalescing around the safety of Henry Hill—a high point near Henry House (home of the Henry family) below the southern intersection of Warrenton and Dumfries (Dumfries, or Sudley, Road led north to Sudley Springs).

When Bartow retreated back over the turnpike south of Stone Bridge toward Henry Hill, he did so with only four hundred remaining soldiers (he had lost at least half of his men). Although the Confederate troops ultimately retreated in sporadic confusion, they had prevented the Union Army from crossing Youngs Creek of Bull Run and then Warrenton Turnpike. The Confederates still retained the critically important objective of the Manassas Railroad Junction. The battle on Matthews Hill had lasted for about two hours, but it was simply the forerunner to the main battle.

Overly enthusiastic observers from the North sent early and incorrect correspondence back to Washington that they had won the day. Without waiting for official military confirmation at the close of the engagement, the Northern press immediately began running stories of success, sending further ignorant observers and civilians toward the battlefield.

Chapter 5 – In the Heat of the First Battle of Bull Run

The area around Henry Hill was the battle site for both the First and the Second Battles of Manassas, the second being fought almost one year later in late August of 1862. The battle on July 21ˢᵗ, 1861, would rage during the afternoon on the northern grassy open slopes of the 730-meter (800-yard) gradual rise of the hill. (The southern slopes were mostly forested.) The house that topped the hill was home to the eighty-five-year-old widow of Dr. Isaac Henry and her grown children. The bedridden widow, who was unable to leave the house, was mortally wounded on the day of the battle when a Union artillery projectile crashed through her bedroom wall, causing many injuries (and supposedly blowing off her foot). She died later that day from the trauma and was the only civilian casualty of the First Battle of Bull Run.

Union Brigadier General Irvin McDowell had urged his troops south, following the retreating Confederates to regroup just north of the Warrenton Turnpike. Instead of taking the opportunity to hound the enemy south, McDowell took up a position on Dogan's Ridge across the valley, sending volleys of heavy fire to the enemy on Henry Hill. McDowell hesitated for several hours, continuing to build his reinforcements as his troops still crossed Bull Run.

This delay allowed time for the Southerners to prepare for a battle on Henry Hill, where they formed an army of about 6,500 men (and about 13 cannons), including fresh units from Brigadier General Johnston who had not fought in the morning. At this point, the Confederates were still outnumbered by the approaching Union Army, which was approaching from the north by at least two to one. General Beauregard was also still naturally concerned about the Union forces that remained along the southern sections of Bull Run, as they could cross at any moment to encircle the Southerners from behind. He dispatched Bartow toward Stone Bridge. It would be Bartow's final engagement.

Colonel Bartow rejoined the battle near Henry Hill under the orders of Beauregard to deal with the insurgents over Stone Bridge. His horse was shot from beneath him, and he received a bullet wound, but Bartow simply changed horses and continued the fight. His demise occurred when he rode forward, swinging his cap, yelling to his boys to follow him. He was mortally wounded in the chest and died shortly after on the battlefield. His last words were apparently of encouragement for his troops to continue the fight. The remainder of Bartow's 7th Georgia Regiment obeyed and eventually beat back the fatigued Federal troops, who had been fighting all day. Although the Georgia regiment suffered greatly and had been significantly reduced in numbers, they managed to destroy the enemy battery at Stone Bridge, much to the relief of General Beauregard, who considered it a vulnerable point that made the enemy approach very accessible. (Bartow was posthumously elevated to the rank of brigadier general due to his role in the battle, and his final words of "They have killed me, boys, but never give up" have been immortalized on his gravestone.)

The core nucleus of the Southern army on Henry Hill included "Stonewall" Jackson and his 1st Brigade of the Shenandoah of more than two thousand men. Stonewall positioned his men along the leeward eastern crest of the hill out of the direct line of fire. His thirteen cannons were positioned slightly farther up on the crest of the hill to fire upon the approaching enemy. Behind him was Bee, who would later issue the words that immortalized Jackson's nickname of "Stonewall" in history.

At 1:30 p.m., the overconfident McDowell ordered two Union batteries (under Captains James B. Ricketts and Charles Griffin) up the western side of Henry Hill, which were met at short range by Confederate artillery and musket fire. McDowell had unfortunately sent his batteries of longer-range weapons ahead, whose firepower extended over the heads of the Confederate troops, and the distance was too close for the guns to take effect. The 33rd Virginia Regiment leaped from the brush to dispatch with the Union cannoneers and let loose such a volley that an observer described the Union battery divisions' situation as a tragic scene, "It seemed as though every man and horse of that battery just laid right down and died right off."

The surviving Northerners of the batteries drew back to the safety of Sudley Road to rejoin their colleagues but were set upon by a surprise attack by Colonel Jeb Stuart's cavalry on their right flank. The Union guns abandoned on the hill were commandeered by Jackson's men and turned against the Northerners. Under Jackson's command, who told his men to "yell like Furies!" his Confederate troops rushed down the hill, yelling at the enemy as they took ownership of the heavy artillery. It would be the first of the notorious "Rebel yell" that the Southerners used for the remainder of the Civil War.

The Northerners fought back, and at this point, they were still the aggressors and outnumbered their opponents. The Union artillery changed hands again back to their rightful owners. And again, the Southerners swooped down the slope to retake the guns. The Northerners fought back. As the battle rose and fell, each side risked exposing their flanks as they charged. The Union artillery changed ownership several times that afternoon during charge after countercharge, with neither side able to retain their position. The Federals repeatedly fought within meters of Jackson's line, but the general would not budge. He held the line and earned his stalwart nickname.

Farther afield, McDowell's troops had mostly taken command of battlefields surrounding Henry Hill, although, by 4 p.m., his troops were tiring. New troops arriving from Sudley Ford extended the line west across Sudley Road and were showing signs of surrounding the enemy and cutting off their direct line to Manassas.

With the arrival of new Confederate troops in the late afternoon, which joined the focus of the main battle west of Sudley Road, the tide began to turn in favor of the Southerners. The Union Army's insistence on attacking the Confederacy "in bits and pieces" reduced their initial advantage, and by late afternoon, they were no longer in a position to surround the Southerners and forge their way to Manassas Junction.

Union Colonel Sherman had sent two charges up Henry Hill to attack Jackson's right flank (one being the "Highlanders" in their tartan pants), but both had been a failure due to the continual confusion over uniforms and flags. The soldiers' inconsistent attire, as well as the similarity between the Northern and Southern flags that were held aloft of fighting troops, had caused significant hesitation in attacking companies— particularly to the detriment of the Union men, who often found themselves virtually upon their enemy before realizing who they were.

To further add to the confusion over allegiances, the Union Zouaves, the 11th New York Volunteer Infantry (modeled on the French mercenary light infantry companies of the same name), an elite unit organized by Officer Elmer E. Ellsworth (1837–1861, who died before the battle but was a close personal friend of President Lincoln), wore red-striped trousers and fez caps in the likeness of their North African brothers! The Zouaves proved to be fierce, unconventional fighting men who were well-coordinated and trained and remained in the thick of the battle for most of the day. ("Remember Ellsworth!" became a rallying Union battle cry, as the men felt loyalty to Ellsworth's commitment to his men.)

Earlier that day, Sherman was fired upon by Confederate Colonel Wade Hampton III's legion, which had moved in to support the right flank and support Jackson. Hampton's men and horses were fresh but panting from their recent exertion of making their way from the railroad station. His unit contained artillery, infantry, and cavalry (about 650 men).

The final Union brigade to reach the battle scene at about 3 p.m. was under the command of Colonel Oliver O. Howard of Heintzelman's division. Howard (1830–1909, a career army officer) had been instructed to turn the enemy's left flank away from the main battle. (Until then, he had been stationed to protect Sudley Ford.) Holding his position on Chinn Ridge, west of Henry Hill over Sudley Road, Colonel Howard was met with overwhelming numbers of Confederate forces that had been sent to swing around the west. The Southern units under Colonel Early and Brigadier General Bonham had been pulled away from the southern fords to join the left flank of the Confederates. The last of the Confederates to join the heat of the battle toward the west was Brigadier General Smith (and, subsequently, Colonel Elzey of the Shenandoah 4th Brigade soon after Smith was wounded), freshly arrived from Shenandoah. The additional Southern units made a crushing full-frontal attack on Howard, who sent his men into battle in small, vulnerable units in waves of unsuccessful counterattacks. (Smith's troops had just completed a ten-kilometer, or six-mile, journey from the train.)

The Confederates had crippled the Union's right flank, and the Federals were in danger of being surrounded, as their exit route north was blocked. Tyler, who had by this point retaken Stone Bridge, for some reason did not bring aid to the Union's left flank, even though he had three infantry brigades and heavy artillery available. (It has been suggested that he never received orders to do so, as McDowell, who was in the heart of the battle, was distracted.)

Similar to the western extremity of the battle, the Federals in the east were also weakening, as Colonel Keyes of Tyler's 1st Division, including 150 men, had been repulsed by the Rebels. On top of that, Confederate Jeb Stuart's cavalry had ridden east to add to the squeeze. When the Confederates saw the Northerners begin to fall back in exhaustion and confusion, the entire Southern line was ordered forward by Beauregard, including the Confederates now in control of Henry Hill. Jackson progressed down Henry Hill, capturing artillery as he moved. Jeb Stuart's artillery swept through sections of the Union, sending them hurrying backward in disarray.

By 5 p.m., McDowell's army was certifiably in chaos and disintegrating. His final orders to Tyler to bring fresh troops across Bull Run to attack the far left, as the Confederacy had done to them in the west, could not be executed because Tyler's pinning forces were already in full retreat—without orders to do so. (Later, some of these units would at least hold the road to Centreville, allowing for the disgraceful Federal withdrawal.)

Panic and disorder had set in on the Northern side, and unfledged soldiers abandoned the scene in an unspecified retreat. It was mid-summer and stiflingly hot in the heat of battle, and the volunteer fighters had lost their romantic notions of the glory of war, no matter how patriotic their original intentions had been. (Essentially, McDowell had led a ragtag crew who were underdisciplined, poorly armed, and poorly outfitted for the job at hand.) As mentioned above, the lack of correct uniforms on both sides had meant troops unleashing firepower on friendlies and sometimes allowing the enemy to approach and overwhelm them, thinking they were allies. The inconsistent uniform debacle occurred many times on both sides throughout the day. To add to the allegiance confusion, the Confederate flag of blue, white, and red with a circle of stars and thick stripes was almost impossible to tell apart from the United States Star-Spangled Banner in the midst of fighting. (The Confederates later changed their flag to a large starred cross, which is still seen in the South today.)

McDowell's and other senior officers' attempts to halt the deserting troops proved futile. He posted rear guards at the various crossroads and fords that marked the retreat of the demoralized troops, who were being harried home in fear. These guards consisted mostly of Porter's men, Sykes's Regulars, and Ellsworth's "Fire" Zouaves of the 11th New York, who experienced heavy casualties as a result. Hordes of Northern soldiers clogged the retreat to Centreville and collided with civilians and their carriages along the way. There were reports of soldiers throwing down their weapons and belongings, stealing horses, and fleeing the scene of battle any way they could. In some instances, the Union retreat became a frenzy, as the petrified soldiers' way out was blocked by exploded and abandoned gun carriages and ambulances. For example, a carriage blocked the bridge over the Cub Run tributary of Bull Run toward Centreville, which created mass panic. Kind citizens in Washington, DC, who received and aided the troops when they eventually arrived in the capital over the next few days, spoke of traumatized, famished, dehydrated men, shaken and half-mad by their first experiences of war.

Dead and dying men and horses, as well human body parts, scattered the battlefields. Dying men had embraced their foes in their last moments. Some of the wounded had simply died of dehydration in the ten-hour-long battle. The local private buildings—churches, houses, and barns—were used as field hospitals and became the sites for horror stories. One Southerner who approached a manor house field hospital described "piles of legs, feet, hands and arms, all thrown together, and at a distance resembled piles of corn at a corn-shucking." The rudimentary facilities and lack of medical help at the time required excessive amputations, often in any space and on any table available, including in grand dining halls or church benches. For those left wounded, slow deaths and gangrene often became their fate, and rampant diseases such as dysentery and scarlet fever swept through sickbays and healthy camps alike.

The Southerners made a preliminary and vague attempt to chase their enemies north and cut off their route to the capital, but they eventually allowed them to flee—but not without sending heavy firepower at their retreating backs. Toward the end of the day, Confederate President Jefferson Davis joined the victorious Beauregard and Johnston on Henry Hill to discuss whether the pursuit of the enemy was advantageous, but in all honesty, the Confederate forces were in similar disarray as their enemy and were just as depleted. So, the Southerners stayed put, regrouping and withdrawing their men over the following days. (A day-long rainstorm on Monday, July 22nd, contributed to the Confederacy's decision not to pursue the enemy and also added to the heavy and horrifying atmosphere as Union troops limped into Washington in desperate need of aid.)

Most of the Union artillery abandoned on the battlefields was captured by the Confederates. Beauregard's paranoia about the Confederacy's now exposed right flank toward Union Mills, as well as a rumor that the enemy had turned and was approaching from the southeast, sent the victors hurrying to ensure the Federal forces had not returned. By this time, it was nightfall, and with the hastily retreating and completely shattered Union Army heading home in a rout, which would later be referred to by the Southern press as "the Great Skedaddle," the Confederates had won the day and the first real land battle of the American Civil War.

Chapter 6 – Retreat and Reprisals

President Abraham Lincoln had remained awake all of Sunday night for news of the battle. Word finally reached him. "General McDowell's Army in full retreat through Centreville. The day is lost. Save Washington and the remnants of this army." Upon hearing this, an emergency cabinet meeting was immediately called, in which Lincoln's secretary of war, Simon Cameron (whose brother had died the previous day at Bull Run) put the nearest town to Washington, DC, Baltimore, which is sixty-four kilometers (forty miles) northeast of DC on high alert in case of an attack, and they also ordered all organized militia to defend the capital. Due to media fallacies, most of the North awoke on Monday morning believing that the North had won, not realizing that the day would be marked as "Black Monday" from thereon.

The federal government was devastated by the news of the loss, more so because it meant a protracted and expensive affair going forward. The Union's original idea to enlist men for a mere ninety days was altered to up to three-year conscriptions, and Lincoln signed a bill for a further 500,000 men to enlist. It was the end of innocence and idealism in the North and signaled the premature end of many career army officers' terms of service—both for the North, where blame needed to be apportioned for the dismal failings at Bull Run, and for the South, for at the end of the Civil War, previous US Army officers were not allowed to serve the Union.

Although Union General Patterson's career was brought to an end due to his failure to prevent Confederate reinforcements from reaching

Bull Run from the Shenandoah Valley, General Johnston later admitted that after the enemy's defeat at Bull Run, it was the presence of Patterson's men to the north that prevented him from chasing the limping Federal Army back to Washington, DC, and the incumbent complete annihilation of part of the Union (and perhaps even a frontal assault on the capital).

The First Battle of Bull Run saw the first fatality of a senior officer on either side—Brigadier General Barnard E. Bee. Bee was dispatched under Johnston and was attributed with the nicknaming of "Stonewall Jackson" when he was purported to have declared during the battle, "There is Jackson standing like a stone wall. Let us determine to die here, and we will conquer. Rally behind the Virginians!" It was never ascertained whether this likeness was meant as an insult or a compliment to Jackson, and since Bee died within twenty-four hours after the end of the battle from a shot through the stomach, it was never confirmed whether he spoke these words or what he meant by them. (Whether Bee was, in fact, annoyed with Jackson for not moving forward is not important since both leaders experienced the largest share of the day's fighting. Jackson's brigade fought alone for almost four hours in the eye of the main battle, and they experienced 50 percent of the casualties suffered that day—his actions were later considered particularly heroic.)

McDowell's misgivings about the battle had proved correct, but the federal government felt obliged to remove McDowell from his position at the head of the leading military division due to the failure of the First Battle of Bull Run. McDowell was frank in admitting that he had struggled to coordinate and control his troops on and off the field, enabling the final scramble to DC, during which time he had failed to gather and calm the soldiers in the aftermath of the battle. McDowell's plan had been ambitious and complicated, and it was further exacerbated by his never having led such a large body of troops before. But then again, nobody in the country ever had! McDowell was also later criticized for having engaged too personally in the battle rather than acting as a general and coordinating the troops. Beauregard and Johnston on the Southern side had been commended for leading from behind and funneling fresh troops forward, strategically placing them where their impact would be best. The Southerners' bird's-eye view approach to the First Battle of Manassas had ultimately given them the tactical upper hand.

What remained of the Northern Army of Northeastern Virginia was then combined with the troops from Washington under Brigadier General Joseph K. Mansfield (1803-1862, who died during the war), as well as the Shenandoah men under Major General Nathaniel P. Banks (1816-1894). Major General George B. McClellan ("Young Napoleon") was put in charge of these combined troops, which were known as the main US Army of the Potomac from thereon. McClellan was attributed with training and organizing the Army of the Potomac before being appointed as the commanding general of the US Army in November of that same year. However, McClellan's leadership did not last long, and he was removed from his position in March of the following year, 1862. McClellan did not share the same views on politics or war strategy with President Lincoln; in fact, he even ran against Lincoln as the opposing Democratic nominee in the 1864 presidential elections. After being removed, McClellan would not serve as a military leader in the field again. Despite McClellan's fall from grace, he is attributed with rallying the crucial Army of the Potomac, whose numbers swelled from 50,000 to 168,000 during the four months of his involvement—the largest military force the US had raised until that point. He is also attributed with significantly fortifying the capital with forts, artillery, and cannons to the extent that the city was considered "impregnable."

The battle had been the largest and bloodiest in US history until that point. The First Battle of Bull Run cost the Confederacy 387 fatalities, 1,582 wounded, and 13 missing men. The Union Army had lost 460 men, 1,124 wounded, and a significant 1,312 were missing—assumed captured. (During the entire Civil War, an estimated 620,000 to 850,000 military deaths were recorded, and almost 60 percent of these were Union deaths.)

At the site of Sudley Church, just north of Sudley Springs, the congregation had had the foresight to cancel their morning services as thousands of Union troops and artillery crossed the ford on July 21st, 1861. Later that day, the church would be the scene of a makeshift Union hospital and graveyard for wounded and dead men. Three hundred injured Federal troops were abandoned at the church due to a lack of sufficient transportation. When the Confederates eventually caught up with the retreating enemy near Sudley, they apparently found too many Yankees to capture and hold successfully, so they eventually gave up on taking prisoners. The wounded who were not captured by the Confederates near Sudley Church and who did not die were aided by the church members and their neighbors. Private John Rice, whose life was saved, returned in 1886 to pay for the rebuilding of the church, which was completely destroyed in the Second Battle of Manassas.

After the Battle of First Manassas, the Confederates retained their defensive position within the safety of the Southern states and made no move to attack the capital, although it was feared by many Northerners. The Southern military was in disarray, too, even though the field and the victory had been theirs. The South had won this first significant encounter, but leaders and soldiers of both sides were considerably humiliated, learning what arrogance and inexperience could get them. The Southern celebrations were subdued as the Confederate President Jefferson Davis announced from Richmond, "We have won a glorious though dear-bought victory. Night closed on the enemy in full flight and closely pursued." Johnston was employed to build the main Southern Army of Northern Virginia, which continued as the South's bastion for the duration of the war.

The collateral damages of the four-year-long war to come, which would include rampant disease, homelessness, economic ruin, the loss of civilian life, destruction of historical buildings and essential farmlands, and, most critically, the loss of able-bodied men (whether they be sons, fathers, etc.), were not considered. After the First Battle of Manassas ended, both Northerners and Southerners withdrew to lick their wounds and rebuild their armies for further onslaughts.

Conclusion

Ultimately, the Northerners' defeat at Bull Run in the summer of 1861 filled the Southerners with false confidence that they could "lick the Yankees" at every turn. The inexperience and under-preparedness of the Federal forces became starkly apparent. The Southerners, fighting mostly for loyalty and honor, which were connected to deep family ties and old social principles, were, at first, perhaps stronger opponents and more brazen, and they were seemingly more disciplined in this first confrontation. Since it was the North's intention to remove the Southerners' right to own slaves, the Civil War was more personal for the Southerners as their way of life was being threatened.

On both sides of the Mason-Dixon Line, war veterans had predicted the spate of unsteady and cavalier battles that marked the first few years of the Civil War and knew from experience that the war would be neither short nor certain. Civilians alike, who had brought their private carriages and picnics to oversee the battle as a form of entertainment, were shocked and traumatized by the brutality of what unfolded and what this meant going forward. Americans realized they might be living through a real war with gruesome consequences on both sides.

The rapid and glorious victory expected by both assailants at the start of the Civil War never materialized; instead, the First Battle of Manassas was a prelude to the four-year-long bloody outcome of the American Civil War. In an age before rapid media responses or definitive intelligence networks, rumors steeped upon rumors, and ignorance mounted amongst soldiers and civilians alike, creating an atmosphere of confusion and belligerence that laid the foundations for the war to come. On both sides, inaccurate and premature news of victory ran like wildfire through the affected states and was even used as untrue propaganda by the Northern and Southern presses.

This first major land engagement of the Civil War was typical of the chaotic and premature battles during the first year or two of the Civil War, demonstrating that the fighting units were undertrained and uncoordinated. Men were assigned piecemeal, without an awareness of allied units or how to protect one another. Attacks were frontal and unnecessarily brutal with higher than necessary fatalities. Tactical intelligence, most specifically a lack of adequate maps, was slow, inconsistent, and sometimes entirely absent. Finally, battlegrounds were poorly chosen and difficult to navigate. The First Battle of Bull Run initiated military operations in what became known as the Eastern Theater—the battles east of the Appalachian Mountains, including West Virginia, Virginia, the District of Columbia (DC), Maryland, the northern seaports of North Carolina, and Pennsylvania. (The Western Theater included the southern states of Dixieland, between the Mississippi River to the west and the Appalachian Mountains to the east. A further three theaters were named in which key battles of the war occurred.)

The Battle of First Manassas was the first of seven major Civil War battles of the Western Theater, and the state of Virginia would prove to be the site of some of the bloodiest fighting of the American Civil War. Ironically, the old stalwart state of Virginia had at first resisted secession from the Union because of loyalties that linked back to the founding of America in 1776. It was one of the last regions to join the Confederacy, and divisions in opinion eventually led to the creation of West Virginia in 1863, which split from its home state to join the Union.

The refusal of the South to negotiate the abolition of slavery or some sort of reasonable intercession of its gradual dismantling had prompted the American Civil War, although there were other factors behind the war. The natural loyalties of the Southerners to one another and to their home states—regardless of their opinions about slavery—drew them indiscriminately toward the battle lines. Thus, many American military men who had fought side by side for decades ended their careers as they faced old comrades and colleagues.

Ultimately, the North won, and slavery was abolished, but in the process, the country lost one of its finest presidents, and the South lost its dignity and faced economic and social collapse. The whole of America became responsible for filling the void left by the devastation of the war. If the First Battle of Manassas had taught the two sides anything, it would have been to negotiate and not to fight, but unfortunately, this first real engagement of the war instead stoked the fires of both sides.

Part 3: The Battle of Pea Ridge

A Captivating Guide to the Battle of Elkhorn Tavern, which was an American Civil War Clash in Arkansas That Took Place in March of 1862

Introduction

Toward the end of the harsh and lingering winter of 1861/62, the Federal Army of the Southwest embarked on a near-impossible campaign into the enemy territory of northern Arkansas. Their mission had first been to flush Confederate forces from southern Missouri, a state that technically remained part of the Union for the Civil War. However, Union General Samuel Curtis was not content until he had infiltrated the Confederate state of Arkansas and put pressure on the Southern army lurking near their strongholds of Fort Smith and the state capital of Little Rock.

Abutting the Indian Territory to the west and the Mississippi River to the east, Arkansas was a western outpost for the American Civil War. The terrain was rocky and wooded, full of treacherous ravines and steep escarpments with only a few bad roads traversing the landscape. Railroads to the area were limited or nonexistent, and the waterways were low and unnavigable. The twenty-six thousand Northern and Southern soldiers who engaged in the Battle of Pea Ridge marched for days on low rations through near-impenetrable territory to surprise their foes. Notwithstanding the frozen ground, snowstorms, and vastly limited supplies, the troops were required to travel light and with speed.

The final full-throttle clashes between the armies unfolded in the first week of March upon an area of high ground known as Pea Ridge in northwestern Arkansas. The ridge was the flattest and most open of the surrounding terrain; it could be easily defended by the Union and not easily approached by the Confederates (also referred to as the Rebels,

Southerners, or the Grays—they largely fought in gray coats when they could muster uniforms). The Confederates fought with a mixture of volunteer soldiers and unlisted guerilla fighters of the Missouri State Guard. The Southerners, under General Earl Van Dorn, were driven into an impossible situation, devoid of true military planning and grossly infringing on their basic human rights. Although it was one of the few occasions in the Civil War in which the Rebels vastly outnumbered the Yankees, Van Dorn's inexperience, impatience, rampant hedonism, and feverish state led to a series of bad decisions that imperiled his entire Army of the West and resulted in the death of three of his senior commanders and the capture of three more.

When the Southerners limped from the battlefield after their defeat at Pea Ridge, the starving, exhausted army all but disbanded. Van Dorn scuttled the remnants of his men east into Mississippi, leaving Arkansas vulnerable to the Federals (another name for the Union men; they are also referred to as Northerners, Yankees, or Bluecoats—they typically fought in uniforms that were dark blue). By 1863, the Union would be in full control of northern and central Arkansas, including the strategic nodes of Little Rock, central Arkansas, and Fort Smith adjunct the Indian Territory.

After the Battle of Pea Ridge, the victorious Union under Curtis marched south and took the town of Helena on the Mississippi River by July of 1862. Exactly a year later, Helena would prove vital to the Union's success at the Siege of Vicksburg, Mississippi, heralding the pivotal turning point in the Civil War from which the South could not recover.

Chapter 1 – Prelude to the Pea Ridge Campaign

On Christmas Day of 1861, the Union commander of the Department of the Missouri, Major General Henry Wager Halleck, placed Brigadier General Samuel Ryan Curtis in command of the Army of the Southwest, which was headquartered in Saint Louis, Missouri. Curtis was to replace Brigadier General Nathaniel Lyon (1818-1861), who had been instrumental in taking a stand for the Union in Missouri in the early stages of the war. Lyon was a lifelong military man for the US government, but he was killed at the Battle of Wilson's Creek (also known as the Battle of Oak Hills)—the first major engagement of the Trans-Mississippi Theater fought on October 10th, 1861, near Springfield, Missouri. Lyon had made considerable strides in ensuring most of Missouri, including the pivotal riverside town of St. Louis, remained in Union hands. His efforts prevented Missouri from officially joining the Confederacy. General Lyon was the first Union senior commander to be killed in the Civil War.

General Halleck (1815-1872) or "Old Brains" was a US Army officer, scholar, and lawyer, and he went on to serve as the commanding general of the US Army from July of 1862 until March of 1864. He has been criticized throughout history as being a tactically inferior military man, but there can be no doubt of his considerable administrative skills as the head of the armies. The American Civil War had been raging for less than nine months—it began in April of 1861—so it was not at the point where it was, in fact, considered a civil war. The Southern states of the newly formed Confederate States of America (the CSA, the Confederacy, or the South) began ceding from the Union government (the North) in December of 1860, a month after the election of President Abraham Lincoln (1809–1865, in off. March 1861–April 1865).

The Confederate states eventually included eleven of the thirty-four existing states and were in open opposition to Lincoln's clear intent to stop the expansion of slavery across the United States of America. The states that seceded were South Carolina, Mississippi, Florida, Alabama, Georgia, Louisiana, Texas, Virginia, Arkansas, Tennessee, and North Carolina. West Virginia split from Virginia halfway through the war in June of 1863 to rejoin the Union. Kentucky and Missouri, abutting the east and west of the mighty north-south running Mississippi River, were divided states and straddled the border of the North and the South. These two states technically had official Confederate Congress representation throughout the war, as well as declarations of secession. However, they also harbored many citizens who were loyal to the Union and endured a heavy Union force presence throughout the war. Neither Missouri nor Kentucky ever officially joined the Confederacy in toto.

The full spectrum of the causes of the American Civil War is complex and debated to this day, but suffice to say that the South wanted a degree of autonomy it could not achieve as part of the Union. The Southern wealth in natural minerals, abundant agricultural lands, and strategic arterial waterways leading to national and international markets provided the Southerners with the impetus to retain their hold on slave labor. They were willing to fight the Federals to the death in defense of their colonial way of life and its associated economic benefits. The four-year-long Civil War that ensued was longer, bloodier, and more expensive than anybody, including the American president, could have anticipated. And the South's loss of this war undermined its economic and moral stability for generations to come.

General Samuel Curtis (1805–1866, a US Army officer, engineer, lawyer, and Republican politician who helped to found the party) had been actively appointed to the US military as a commander since June of 1861, whereupon he had resigned his political position and his congressional seat. The Army of the Southwest was created with Curtis's appointment on December 25th, 1861, and it was primarily composed of troops from the Department of Missouri. Originally, the Army of the

Southwest contained three divisions commanded by Brigadier General Franz Sigel, Brigadier General Alexander Asboth, and Colonel Jefferson Columbus Davis. General Sigel (1824-1902)—a native German by birth and immigrant to the United States—was not a popular commander with his direct superiors, but he had received recognition from President Abraham Lincoln for conscripting German-speaking immigrants to fight for the Union. Upon Curtis's appointment to head the Army of the Southwest, Sigel had threatened to resign since more than half of Curtis's army at that time were of German or other European origins. Sigel felt that the appointment should have been his.

General Curtis's solution was to further divide his army into four divisions and place General Sigel at the head of the two divisions with the largest number of immigrants—the 1st and 2nd Divisions. The Battle of Pea Ridge was destined to be the highlight of General Sigel's military career, as he was considered an inept general even though he was an excellent recruiter. The immigrants, who spoke virtually no English, were known to repeat in chorus, "I'm going to fight mit Sigel," and this statement became a song of the Civil War. Major General Peter Joseph Osterhaus (1823-1917), also a German immigrant, was placed in charge of the 1st Division, and Brigadier General Alexander "Sandor" Asboth (1811-1868), a Hungarian immigrant, was in charge of the 2nd Division.

Colonel Jefferson Davis (1828-1879, a military man with a controversial career who was promoted to brigadier general after the Battle of Pea Ridge and has no relation to Confederate President Jefferson Davis) was placed in charge of the only division of the Army of the Southwest that was constituted entirely of English-speaking Americans. This was the 3rd Division. General Curtis's 4th Division was created to bring an ethnic balance to his army, and he placed Colonel Eugene Asa Carr (1830-1910, a lifelong military man who would go on to receive the Medal of Honor for his actions at the Battle of Pea Ridge) at its helm. The Pea Ridge campaign, which lasted from February to July of 1862, would mark the pinnacle of the Army of the Southwest's operations.

The Pea Ridge campaign transpired in the wartime geographical region known as the Trans-Mississippi Theater. This arena was one of six official theaters used to zone the armies and battles of the Civil War. This particular theater included operations within the states west of the Mississippi River but not as far as the Pacific coastline. Although the exact parameters of the Trans-Mississippi Theater changed over the Civil War, it mostly included the states of Louisiana, Arkansas, Missouri, Kansas, the Indian Territory (now Oklahoma), Texas, New Mexico, and Arizona. (Some historians refer to the Trans-Mississippi Theater as part of the Western Theater, which was technically the collection of states along the eastern embankment of the Mississippi River but still "west" of the Eastern Theater.)

In the early stages of the war (1861 and 1862), Missouri, on the western embankment of the Mississippi River with Arkansas to its south, was dominated primarily by ongoing disputes between its allegiance to the North or the South. Missouri became a nominal Confederate state in November of 1861 as part of a dubiously inconsistent political maneuver. But the Union still dominated most of the state, and ultimately, the permanent military presence indicated under which banner the state would fall. By December of 1861, Missouri was distinctly divided in terms of occupation by both the Union and the Confederacy. This deadlock included the presence of secessionist militia under the unofficial Missouri State Guard across the western and southern extents of Missouri. The Federal Army held a large arsenal of armaments at St. Louis at the northeastern extremity of Missouri, approximately at the midpoint along the border with Illinois. (St. Louis is very strategically placed at the confluence of the Mississippi and Missouri Rivers.) The Federal presence extended through the northern and eastern extremities of Missouri, and they controlled the majority of railroads and waterways.

At the beginning of the Pea Ridge campaign, Arkansas was definitively a Southern state, but a fortuitous and strategic move by the Yankees after their success at Pea Ridge in early March of 1862 saw them overrun and occupy the northern half of Arkansas by mid-July of that same year. The Battle of Pea Ridge was critical in that it decided the fate of Missouri for the remainder of the Civil War. Missouri would be a Union stronghold— a coup for the Federals who could use the territory as a headquarters in the trans-Mississippi. Missouri was a significant foothold for the Union to have, as it ensured a supply line into the Trans-Mississippi Theater until the end of the war. Northern Arkansas also remained under Union control until the end of the war, with its state capital of Little Rock being captured by the Federals in 1863.

The Confederate Missouri State Guard (MSG) was not officially a Southern army and did not have to report to the CSA headquarters in

Richmond, Virginia, to Confederate President Jefferson Finis Davis (1808-1889, an American Democratic politician and previous US secretary of war) nor to the Missouri capital of Jefferson City (officially in Union hands), 209 kilometers, or 130 miles, west of St. Louis. Major General Sterling Price (1809-1867, also known as "Old Pap," a legislator, congressman, and governor of Missouri) was a CSA commander of the regular army for the duration of the war, although he assumed command of the MSG in its unofficial capacity as a "guerilla leader" during 1861 and 1862 until the Battle of Pea Ridge.

The MSG had their own coat of arms based on the Missouri state flag—golden bears on a blue background. Their leader, General Price, was prone to obstinacy and insubordination. Price had approximately six thousand to eight thousand men under his command at any one time, and they were considerably deficient in organization, training, and logistical leadership. The MSG volunteers came and went under their own auspices and provided their own supplies, clothing, and weaponry. Despite the voluntary and guerilla-style tactics employed by the Missouri State Guard, they had won a series of important battles in the run-up to Pea Ridge. The Battles of Carthage (July 1861, southwestern Missouri), Wilson's Creek (August 1861 near Springfield, Missouri), and Lexington (September 1861, western Missouri), pitched on the Ozark Plateau, had all been MSG victories, but the Southerners still failed to dominate Missouri or force the state to officially secede to the Confederacy.

This failure was in part due to a distinct split in the Confederate forces within the Missouri Department of the Trans-Mississippi Theater. Brigadier General Benjamin McCulloch (1811-1862, a lifelong military, militia, and law enforcement man who served much of his career in Texas and was a longtime friend of David "Davy" Crockett) had been conscripted since the start of the war to build the Army of the West. He did this mostly by recruiting from Texas, Arkansas, Louisiana, and the Indian Territory. The army eventually included members of the Cherokee, Choctaw, and Creek nations. General McCulloch split his headquarters between Fort Smith, Fayetteville, and Little Rock, and he performed miracles arming, equipping, and supporting his troops at the far western extremities of the Civil War theaters. (Fort Smith was 146 kilometers, or 91 miles, south of the Arkansas-Missouri border on the western boundary of Arkansas with the Indian Territory and an important strategic node leading west.)

Although Generals McCulloch and Price had been involved in the Confederate victories in Missouri until that point, the two commanders had little regard for one another and strongly criticized each other's leadership styles, armies, and long-term military plans to take and hold Missouri. The Missouri State Guard under General Price dominated southwestern Missouri, while General McCulloch's army shored up northwestern Arkansas. Thus, it was imperative that these two disparate groups cooperated in their efforts to drive the Union from Missouri and prevent the Northern movement into Arkansas. Unfortunately, this was not to be.

As a result of the Confederate Arkansas and Missouri regiments' inability to agree, Major General Earl Van Dorn (1820–1863, a notorious ladies' man who was shot dead by a jealous husband in May 1863) was placed in overall command of the Trans-Mississippi District as part of the Confederacy's Department Number Two. General Van Dorn had been a distinguished US Army officer before joining the Confederacy, but he went on to make staggeringly poor military decisions that led to the Southern loss at Pea Ridge. He was a close personal friend of President Davis, and he was unusually offensive-minded. (Two other senior Confederate commanders had refused the appointment before Van Dorn was selected by the president.) After taking command on January 29th, 1862, Van Dorn combined the feuding Southern armies of the trans-Mississippi into the Army of the West, setting up his headquarters at Pocahontas, northeastern Arkansas, a cheeky thirty-two kilometers (twenty miles) from the border with Missouri. Van Dorn was intent upon striking at the Yankees in the spring of 1862 when conditions made the Ozark Plateau of southwestern Missouri more navigable.

Subsequently, General Sterling Price was commissioned into the official Confederate States Army on March 6th, 1862, as a major general, just in time for the start of the Battle of Pea Ridge. During the winter of 1861/1862, Price had been slowly and painfully enrolling his men into the official volunteer Confederate service; just two out of the original nine brigades of the former MSG participated in the confrontation at Pea Ridge as volunteer soldiers. Price was destined to lead a hybrid army of militia and CSA soldiers during Pea Ridge—a situation not to be repeated for the remainder of the war. On March 17th, after the Battle of Pea Ridge, General Sterling Price merged the remainder of his Missouri State Guard into the Confederate Army of the West.

Both Northerners and Southerners knew that gaining the state of Missouri was the key to ultimately winning the territories west of the Mississippi River. From Missouri, states to both the North and the South could easily be accessed, as well as the strategic lifeblood of the Confederacy—the Mississippi River and its major tributaries such as the Missouri and Ohio Rivers (draining into the Mississippi River from the northwest and the northeast, respectively). The Federal win at Pea Ridge went relatively unnoticed at the time by contemporary media but also by historians afterward, although it is now recognized as a critical turning point in the war that laid the foundations for a succession of Federal wins thereafter. The leading General Curtis is now acknowledged as having executed revolutionary military maneuvers not before seen in North American military history.

Chapter 2 – Events Leading to the Battle of Pea Ridge

Once Van Dorn arrived in Arkansas, he began organizing the Confederate troops under their various commands and recruiting new troops. Brigadier General Benjamin McCulloch brought about eight thousand Texans with, and General Sterling Price had approximately seven thousand Missourians. Fresh additions included two regiments of almost two thousand men from the Indian Territory—the 1st and 2nd Cherokee Mounted Rifles under General Albert Pike. General Pike (1809-1891), a Freemason, author, orator, lawyer, and military man, commanded the Indian Territory for the Confederacy in the Trans-Mississippi Theater for most of the war. Pike was instrumental in assisting Native American tribes reclaim land from the federal government; he also acted as an envoy to establish peace treaties with the Native Americans.

Along with General McCulloch, General Pike had trained three Confederate regiments of Native American cavalry before the Battle of Pea Ridge. Pike's Native Americans would at first experience success during the battle before falling back in disarray when the Federals counterattacked. Later in the Pea Ridge campaign, in May of 1862, Pike was ordered to send troops from the Indian Territory to Arkansas. He refused to do so and proceeded to resign from his post. After considerably dramatic events hereafter, including a warrant for his arrest and his disappearance into the Arkansas mountains, his resignation was eventually accepted in November of 1862, and he took the role of court justice in Arkansas in September 1863. Pike was considered a determined and dangerous white supremacist against blacks in his day, but he appeared to consider the Native Americans as his allies and treated them with care.

Confederate Brigadier General Benjamin McCulloch had two principal commanders: Brigadier General James McQueen McIntosh (1828-1862, a career soldier and cavalryman) and Colonel Louis Hébert (1820-1901, a soldier, educator, engineer, and writer). McIntosh was renowned for fighting on the frontier and would lead the Confederate cavalry (horse-mounted troops) at Pea Ridge. Unfortunately, the battle would be his demise, as his brazen courage finally got the better of him. Hébert was a popular infantry leader who would be wounded and captured at the Battle of Pea Ridge, but he lived to complete the war as a brigadier general. (He was released a few weeks after Pea Ridge in a prisoner-of-war exchange only to be recaptured at the Siege of Vicksburg in July of 1863. He was released again in another exchange in October of that year.)

Union General Samuel Curtis's Pea Ridge campaign began in mid-January 1862 in Lebanon, Missouri—halfway between St. Louis and Pea Ridge. Telegraph Road ran southwest from St. Louis into Arkansas through Lebanon, linking many points of engagement between the Northerners and Southerners. One of these points included the hamlet of Bentonville, located in the far northwest of Arkansas, approximately fifteen kilometers (nine miles) south of the Missouri border. There was also Fayetteville, which was south of Bentonville, about forty kilometers (twenty-five miles) from the Missouri border. Bentonville was part of Benton County—the most northwestern county of Arkansas—and would be the site of the Battle of Pea Ridge.

The Union campaign would finally end at Helena on the Mississippi River, approximately equidistant along Arkansas's eastern border. The campaign ended on July 12th, five months after it started, and it covered a distance of 1,126 kilometers (700 miles). In retrospect, the Pea Ridge campaign has been considered the most successful set of military maneuvers after General Ulysses S. Grant's capture of Vicksburg within the first two years of the war.

Federal General Henry Halleck was rightly concerned that the continued presence of the Missouri State Guard would eventually force the state to secede to the Confederacy. So, he began gathering his forces under Curtis deep in the winter of 1861/62. Curtis eventually commanded twelve thousand men, and his instructions were to permanently flush the Southerners from Missouri or destroy them in the process. This command meant removing the enemy from their winter headquarters at Springfield, Missouri, 89 kilometers (55 miles) southwest of Lebanon—about 161 kilometers (100 miles) northeast of Bentonville.

Curtis's and Sigel's men made quick work of this preliminary order, and by February 17th, Confederate General Price and his Missouri State Guard had been routed from Missouri. They fled into Arkansas, following Telegraph Road. The Federal advance over the frozen winter grounds along poor roadways had taken the Southerners by surprise, and they abandoned Springfield by February 13th. Since McCulloch had taken the opportunity to visit the Confederate headquarters in Richmond over the winter, he was absent when Price called for assistance in the south. General Price realized he needed to escape the unfortified Springfield and head south to join McCulloch's troops if no one could come to his aid.

Both Confederate Generals McIntosh and Hébert had been hesitant to join Price at Springfield in the absence of McCulloch. However, once they were made aware of the Federal move south, pushing at the backs of Price's men, the Southerners leaped into action to prepare for a Union invasion into Arkansas. The Rebels in Arkansas had overwintered between Bentonville and Fort Smith, and they began marching toward the state border to block Union progress.

Curtis exercised a sustained pursuit of the Rebels over the state line: an event that was not repeated for the duration of the Civil War, whose battles generally ended in routs, retreats, or stalemates. After a series of skirmishes and as the Yankees pushed the Rebels out of Missouri, Curtis telegraphed Halleck, saying, "The flag of our Union again floats over Arkansas." The Federal troops were triumphant and celebrated their accomplishment with pomp and song.

Later that day, however, Curtis's troops met with a considerable skirmish with McCulloch's fresh troops under General Hébert at Dunagin's Farm just south of Little Sugar Creek along Telegraph Road. Little Sugar Creek was a stream in northwestern Benton County that flowed west along the south of Pea Ridge. It joined the Big Sugar Creek, which flowed along the north of the ridge to form the Elk River on the west of the ridge. This skirmish was to be the first real engagement on Arkansas soil, but it ended with nightfall.

However, the Union situation was not without its risks. The farther the Union moved south, the farther they moved away from their supply bases in northeastern Missouri, particularly the railhead supply station at Rolla, which was equidistant between St. Louis and Lebanon. Also, the greater the distance the Federals put between themselves and their strongholds north, the more easily the Rebels could encircle their army from the rear and block their routes home.

This unlikely incursion at Springfield by the Federals during the harrowing winter months had been exactly the surprise attack that General Halleck anticipated. That winter was a brutal and freezing affair, replete with snowstorms and frozen ground. The soldiers marched through sleet and freezing rain on low rations, their limited clothing frozen to their bodies. As Generals Curtis and Sigel marched their men south, they came upon the bodies of the dead and dying mules and horses, as well as discarded supplies, broken wagons, and exhausted Rebels. The Federals scooped up the stragglers as captives, but they were not quite sure what to do with the extra men who they could ill-afford to maintain.

The rout had taken place upon the Ozark Plateau—a vast limestone intrusion spreading across the southern half of Missouri and the northern half of Arkansas. The plateau was the most rugged and sparsely populated region in the United States, and it was difficult to penetrate in the best conditions, let alone in a hurry in the depths of winter. The complete lack of waterway access (the rivers were low in winter) and railroads on the Ozark Plateau required Curtis's army to travel light along the primitive, rural roads. Supply wagons were reduced to the bare minimum in terms of food, overnighting, medical equipment and supplies, armaments, and ammunition. Food supplies were rationed according to expected days on the road, so foraging and hunting proved vital in sustaining the men, particularly as winter turned to spring. This paring back of unnecessary baggage would be a signature move for both the Northerners and Southerners during the Pea Ridge campaign. But when taken too far, it became a dangerous and tenuous manner in which to move troops.

The well-planned and thoughtful General Curtis had requested a quartermaster from the Union regulars to aid in his campaign. Captain

Phillip Henry Sheridan (1831–1888) had subsequently been employed as supply master to Curtis's troops. (Phillip "Fightin' Phil" Sheridan was a lifelong military man, and he was extremely popular with his commanders. He rose quickly through the ranks during the Civil War, finally serving as general of the army upon his death. Sheridan was also instrumental in the demarcation and preservation of Yellowstone National Park in Wyoming). This appointment would prove to be one of Curtis's secret weapons of war, as Sheridan worked wonders maintaining the supply lines north and issuing only what was necessary to troops in combat. Captain Sheridan's frugality ensured that the Federals could move as quickly and easily as possible toward and eventually through enemy territory.

After the skirmish at Dunagin's Farm on February 17th, the Confederates slunk back to Cross Hollows—a cantonment (temporary military quarters) nineteen kilometers (twelve miles) south of Bentonville. McCulloch arrived back from Virginia a few hours later to the delight of his troops. The Federals did not pursue further at this point and camped for two days in Little Sugar Creek valley to recuperate. During this time, Curtis identified the limestone bluffs running along the southern extremity of Pea Ridge and north of Little Sugar Creek as an ideal line for fortifications in the event that the Confederates pushed back toward Missouri again.

But General Curtis was not satisfied with merely pushing his foes over the state line; he wanted to infiltrate Arkansas and possibly overcome the region with a Federal presence so strong that it was forced to capitulate to the Union. By February 18th, Curtis had already sent General Alexander Asboth to reconnoiter the areas around Bentonville, as well as the way to Cross Hollows. Asboth was greatly assisted by pro-Unionist civilians who provided information about roads and Rebel movements.

Just after the Confederacy had been formed in 1861 and before Arkansas officially joined in May of that year, the Federals had removed their arsenal inventories from the two depots at the capital of Little Rock and Fort Smith—about 257 kilometers (160 miles) northwest of Little Rock. General McCulloch, with his tiny force of fewer than nine thousand men, had been the only Rebel army positioned in Arkansas until the arrival of General Van Dorn. At that time, Arkansas had the smallest population and the least infrastructure of any Confederate state. It was considered a rugged wilderness permeated by a few crude roads and virtually impenetrable topography. McCulloch had decades of frontier experience in Texas (including with the famous Texas Rangers), and although he had limited military experience, he was the best candidate for maneuvering through rough, unchartered terrain.

By February 19th, 1862, the Southerners had retreated farther into Arkansas territory rather than being trapped in Cross Hollows and against the White River that ran to the southeast. (The White River was a 1,162-kilometer or 722-mile river originating in the Boston Mountains of northeastern Arkansas, running northeast into southern Missouri before turning southeast back into Arkansas and ending its journey at the Mississippi River.) After destroying the cantonment, the Rebels arrived at Fayetteville and made a clumsy and incendiary attempt to capture their stores and lay waste to the town so the Federals could not benefit in any way. (The Confederate supply transports, such as horses and wagons, remained farther south, and individual soldiers were instructed to grab what they could carry.) Eventually, 10 days and 193 kilometers (120 miles) after leaving Springfield, McCulloch's and Price's armies settled in the Boston Mountains on the southern extremities of the Ozark Plateau. The Boston Mountains lay just north of Fort Smith, separated by the Arkansas River. The Union sent cavalry raids all around Fayetteville and other areas north of the Confederate encampments to confuse the enemy. The full Yankee army moved as far as Cross Hollows, about nineteen kilometers (twelve miles) south of Little Sugar Creek.

The Pea Ridge campaign was one of the few occasions in the Civil War in which the Union men were outnumbered. Curtis's Army of the Southwest was strung out all the way from Rolla to Pea Ridge (about 322 kilometers or 200 miles), and the men fortified strategic nodes along the way and also provided a safe route in case of a retreat. Curtis had approximately ten thousand men under his command, while the Confederacy had around sixteen thousand at the time of the engagement in March.

The rate of attrition of troops on both sides was very high owing to the tough winter conditions and lack of supplies. The Northern supply line was stretched and vulnerable, so Curtis decided to hold his position. However, he split his army into two to encourage foraging and living off the land. He remained with the 3rd and 4th Divisions at Cross Hollows and sent General Sigel's 1st and 2nd Divisions about twenty-four kilometers (fifteen miles) just west of Bentonville to McKissick's Creek. Sigel was already showing deeply concerning signs of erratic and insubordinate behavior, but Curtis didn't know how to alter the circumstances—he needed all the men and commanders at his disposal.

All of the Union divisions were a distance of about nineteen kilometers (twelve miles) south of Little Sugar Creek, and the plan if the Confederates attacked was to concentrate their scattered detachments and retreat onto the southern bluffs of Pea Ridge.

Chapter 3 – Approach to Pea Ridge, March 6th, 1862

Pea Ridge was a high, flat, partially open area of land that straddled the border of southwest Missouri and northwest Arkansas. Rising between two east-west running creeks—Big Sugar Creek to the north in Missouri and Little Sugar Creek to the south in Arkansas—Pea Ridge was an unusually convenient ground for a pitched battle in the Trans-Mississippi Theater, whose terrain was generally riverine, wooded, rocky with steep ravines, closed off, and difficult to navigate (unlike the more expansive battlegrounds of the Eastern and Western Theaters). Equidistant between the creeks on the eastern end of the ridge was Elkhorn Tavern. The Telegraph (or Wire) Road had gained its name from an overland mail service along the route that became disestablished at the start of the war. Elkhorn Tavern was an important stopping point for the mail coaches, although it was actually a private residence of the Cox family and situated at a major crossroads.

A reconstruction of Elkhorn Tavern photographed in 1907, Benton County. It was originally built in 1840 as a private residence and became a critical juncture on the roads leading southwest through Arkansas. (The tavern faces Telegraph Road.) Mrs. Polly Cox, alone without her husband, hid in the cellar with her family during the battle, and they were unharmed, although the tavern and outbuildings were severely damaged.

During the Confederate scupper from Springfield, General Van Dorn had been at Pocahontas, preparing for a northeastern Arkansas attack on Missouri. Upon receiving news of the events of mid-February, he hurried as fast as he could, taking an arduous nine days to reach the Boston Mountains. Along the way, Van Dorn fell into an icy river and became dangerously ill. He spent the rest of the campaign giving orders from a field ambulance. Having abandoned his previous plans, Van Dorn was to take charge of both armies (the Missouri State Guard and McCulloch's and Pike's men). Knowing they outnumbered the enemy, Van Dorn marched north on the offensive. Delirious with fever, General Van Dorn proceeded to issue premature and ill-conceived orders that would seal the fate of his Army of the West. He would force them to march eighty kilometers (fifty miles) north with virtually no food or shelter. After the Rebel whipping at Pea Ridge, his poor army was forced to repeat the journey south in even worse conditions.

Within less than two days of his arrival in the Boston Mountains, Van Dorn had unilaterally decided upon a plan of attack, having discovered that the Union Army was divided. He would rush his army north past Fayetteville and do a western about-turn onto General Sigel's troops at McKissick's Creek. Knowing that he had superior numbers, Van Dorn anticipated victory and then planned to march east to dispatch with the remaining 3rd and 4th Divisions of the Federal Army at Cross Hollows. The Southern general anticipated the way to St. Louis would be open and available for the taking.

The Confederate plan required considerable speed, and Van Dorn's solution to this was for his troops to travel so light that they would be victorious against the enemy within three days of setting out. Food rations would only be provided for three days, and the men were restricted to the bare minimum in ammunition, clothing, camping, and cooking supplies. The bulk of these necessary supplies were abandoned in the Boston Mountains. The shortsighted, impulsive, overconfident, and arguably inhumane Van Dorn expected his men and their animals to subsist on captured Yankee rations as well as foraging! Van Dorn was not familiar with his subordinates—a strangely combined ragtag army—nor the geography to be traversed. To complete this lunatic expedition, only two days of rations were sent out with the men instead of three. (Also, trailing ammunition wagons followed the Confederates north but spent a large part of the Battle of Pea Ridge far west of the action at Camp Stephens, near the intersection of Little Sugar Creek and the detour road north, awaiting instructions that never came!)

On March 4th, 1862, the largest Confederate army ever to be raised west of the Mississippi River departed on a counter-offensive mission from the Boston Mountains. Accompanied by sixteen thousand men and sixty-five cannons, General Van Dorn continued to issue orders from his ambulance. The Confederate Army of the West had a three-to-two advantage in manpower and a four-to-three advantage in firepower and artillery over the Union Army of the Southwest.

But the Confederate march north was a disaster, as a late winter snowstorm slowed progress (the Confederates had been allowed no tents and only one blanket per man), and their food rations were used up by midday on March 6th before they arrived in Bentonville. Union General Curtis had received word via a small spy network by March 5th that the Rebel Army was on the move toward them. Curtis immediately informed Sigel, and both wings of the army concentrated their troops and prepared to move. The Union columns skidded hurriedly through the freezing conditions of the day and night of March 5th, and by the morning of March 6th, they were filing into place along the southern high ground of Pea Ridge. The Union spent the day fortifying the ridge against a southern approach across Little Sugar Creek (just south of the ridge), digging trenches, establishing makeshift redoubts (defensive works), and other hurried fortifications with the timber, earth, and materials that were available. Also, fortunately for the Northerners, they had the foresight to block a subsidiary road, the Bentonville Detour, which led around their right flank to the west and toward their rear, with a tangle of timber.

Just two Northern divisions under General Sigel's rearguard unit experienced action on their route to the Pea Ridge ramparts on March 6th. Sigel had tarried in Bentonville to enjoy a hot breakfast at the local hotel and was almost cut off from the remainder of the Union Army. (General McIntosh had planned to surround Sigel's errant mob, and the Union's 36th Illinois was temporarily captured but later escaped when McIntosh fumbled the expedition. Sigel was able to speed through with the remainder of his troops.) After a six-kilometer (four-mile) running fight through the snow east of Bentonville, the dilatory Sigel and his six hundred men of the rearguard safely reached Pea Ridge. Sigel had also unfortunately removed a cavalry unit from the Confederate path north and also sent an almost four-hundred-man taskforce west, which would not see the battle at Pea Ridge. Although there are no formal records of General Curtis's displeasure with General Sigel's lackadaisical approach to war, his failure to put Sigel in a significant position of command until the final day of the Battle of Pea Ridge, March 8th, spoke of his mistrust of Sigel and his inability to rely on his supporting commander. (Curtis was also present on that final day to keep a close eye on Sigel, who performed brilliantly.)

But Van Dorn's plan had failed. The Yankee Army were reunited and safely protected on the rugged bluffs behind Little Sugar Creek and straddling Telegraph Road, while his own men were freezing, exhausted, and starving. The Confederate drop-out rate along the way had been considerable, and historians have no definite way of concluding exactly how many Southerners eventually engaged in battle in the days to come. (The eventual number is estimated at twelve thousand to thirteen thousand.) The desertion rate is estimated to be up to a third of the army, with large groups of exhausted, frozen, and famished soldiers collecting along the wayside.

The ever-hasty Van Dorn then forced his men to continue the march on the night of the 6th along the Bentonville Detour in an attempt to cut off the enemy at their rear and prevent a retreat into Missouri. Both subordinate Generals Price and McCulloch were appalled and suggested that their men rest and make a move the next morning. However, Van Dorn refused, and a thirteen-kilometer (eight-mile) march began for the beleaguered men.

Although the Confederates got through the Union's felled timber blocking the route, it delayed the already glacial pace of the moving columns by a further four hours. By dawn on March 7th, the Confederate Army was stretched out along the full thirteen-kilometer front, from the leading divisions of the Army of the West at Telegraph Road to the tailing divisions (General Pike's Indian Brigade) still in the Little Sugar Creek valley.

Chapter 4 – The Battle of Leetown, March 7th, 1862

General Van Dorn was both deliriously feverish and happy that he had achieved his ends and encircled the enemy. But Van Dorn's long line of straggling troops was still trailing far behind in their decrepit state. The intrepid general chose to take them on a shortcut along Ford Road that joined the Bentonville Detour to Elkhorn Tavern running west-east along Pea Ridge. Ford Road turned off the Bentonville Detour at Twelve Corner Church (which remains standing) and then passed between Big Mountain to the north and Little Mountain to the south. In reality, Ford Road was little more than a lane. Leading south off Ford Road was the Leetown Road that joined with a hamlet of the same name.

The village lay just 2.5 kilometers (1.5 miles) north of Little Sugar Creek, and the first engagements of the Battle of Pea Ridge were set to unfold from 1 p.m. to 4 p.m. in the fields just north of Leetown. (Leetown had been named after a farmer from the area and was established in 1840.) General Van Dorn chose to split his army on the morning of Friday, March 7th, to hasten their approach to their destination of Elkhorn Tavern. The leading troops under General Price, including a mixture of Missouri State Guard and volunteers, were to circumnavigate around the north of Big Mountain (a rugged, wooded rise in the landscape) and eventually join with Telegraph Road leading south to Elkhorn Tavern. The tired men under Generals McCulloch and Pike were to follow Ford Road east to hasten their journey. Both sections of the Confederate Army needed to rejoin at Elkhorn Tavern—three kilometers, or two miles, east of Leetown—by the afternoon. General Van Dorn still believed the Union to be concentrated along the southern escarpment of Pea Ridge facing Little Sugar Creek. He intended on making a pounce for their rear and prevent a retreat after demolishing them since his army lay between the Federals and the route north to Missouri.

Although Union General Curtis's scouts had informed him early on Friday morning that there was evidence of approaching Rebels along both Ford Road and north of Elkhorn Tavern, he believed these to be decoys. He was convinced that only some men had been sent to detract from an expected full-frontal attack by the entire Army of the West from the south across Little Sugar Creek. Curtis was incorrect, and it was one of the few occasions that he was taken off-guard during the Pea Ridge campaign. The Union general sent just 15 percent of his army north toward Leetown under General Peter Osterhaus, principally to protect his supply wagons in the open fields below Elkhorn Tavern. Curtis would later send another 15 percent of his men under Colonel Davis after Osterhaus, as well as half of Colonel Carr's 4th Division, directly toward the tavern. The remainder of the Army of the Southwest under Generals Sigel and Asboth remained in situ behind the Pea Ridge fortifications.

During midmorning, Osterhaus's troops moved north, unknowingly heading toward the full force of Confederate General McCulloch's army. Osterhaus and his approximately thousand men were accompanied by Colonel Cyrus Bussey's small cavalry force of about six hundred men (from the 1st, 4th, and 5th Missouri Cavalry and the 3rd Iowa Cavalry) with just three heavy field guns and two supporting batteries (heavy field gun units—the 4th Ohio and the Independent Missouri Battery) to support the infantry (men on foot). By 1 p.m., the Union had moved through Leetown and past farmer Samuel Oberson's cornfield that led to a line of woods in front of Wiley Foster's farm to the south of Ford Road.

General Osterhaus, who rode ahead, caught sight of McCulloch's six-column-wide advancing army and their weapons glinting in the midday sun. At this stage, his men were outnumbered five to one. He realized the enemy grouping was far more than a diversion and sent word south for backup from the main Federal Army. He also knew that he needed to act quickly to prevent the Rebels from reaching Elkhorn Tavern, as they would then be able to recombine their force and jeopardize the

Northern supply wagons. Osterhaus wasted no time in instructing Colonel Bussey to fire the heavy guns into the Confederate Army at once in an attempt to engage a battle and prevent the forward march. His tactic was successful and drew three thousand cavalrymen under General McIntosh in a colorful charge across Foster's wheatfield toward the Union's advanced cavalry unit.

With the Comanches' war cry ringing in the air, the Confederate 6th, 9th, and 11th Texas Cavalry, the 1st Texas Cavalry Battalion, and the 1st Arkansas Cavalry Battalion careened forward in a chaotic and effective charge. Overwhelming the advanced Federal guard with vastly superior numbers, they scattered the Union cavalry and captured the three guns in a rout that sent men and riderless horses in all directions. On the Union cavalry's left flank, General Pike's 1st and 2nd Cherokee Mounted Rifles had picked their way through the woods and dispatched with any stragglers in the rout. (There were unsubstantiated rumors of scalping.)

Federal survivors of the skedaddle hurried south through the woods and over Oberson's Field, meeting with the approaching infantrymen who were just entering the field. The Union cavalry called to their comrades to turn back against the Rebel onslaught, but Commander Greusel shouted, "Officers and men, you have it in your power to make or prevent another Bull Run affair. I want every man to stand to his post." The 2nd Brigade commander of the 1st Division Infantry Regiment, Nicholas Greusel (1817-1896), who commanded his 36th Illinois unit, the 12th Missouri Volunteer Infantry, and two Illinois cavalry companies, had been referring to the First Battle of Bull Run of July 1861—the first official battle of the Civil War fought in the Eastern Theater. In this battle, the Federals had been routed from the field despite having all the advantages of numbers and tactical approach.

Greusel's warning hit home, and by the time Osterhaus galloped through in retreat, he was thankfully met by a calm and orderly defensive bastion of Bluecoats holding the line on the southern side of Oberson's Field. But Federal reinforcements had not yet arrived from Little Sugar Creek, and McCulloch's army of approximately seven thousand men and four artillery batteries were likely to make quick and gruesome work of the Blues. Luckily for the Yankees, the Confederates were in considerable disorder on Foster's farm on the other side of the woods. Greusel took the opportunity to fire heavy shell power toward the Grays to both confuse and distract the enemy while he waited for reinforcements. His ploy worked, as the Native Americans, who had never experienced artillery shelling before, fled the field and didn't play much more of a role in the battle. The remainder of the milling Confederates (who did not have an open view of the Federals through the woods and weren't sure of their numbers) realized they were unable to march farther east toward Elkhorn Tavern, leaving their rear exposed to oncoming Federals.

General McCulloch had no choice but to turnabout and engage with the force upon Oberson's Field. Unfortunately, he failed to communicate his decision to the overall commanding General Van Dorn, who was on the northern detour approaching the tavern. Thus ensued the full Battle of Leetown, which lasted until late afternoon on March 7th—this was the western denouement of the Battle of Pea Ridge.

The Leetown Road ran north-south through Morgan's Woods—to the east of Foster's and Oberson's fields and joining Ford Road to Leetown. General McCulloch, an experienced Texas Ranger, fatefully took it upon himself to reconnoiter the western extremities of the battle lines and do an advanced scout of the enemy on his own. Unfortunately, Greusel had sent forward a vanguard unit of pickets to hold the northern line of Oberson's Field. When they saw a shadowy figure moving on horseback through the woods, the jittery Federals fired without question, killing General McCulloch immediately with a shot through the heart. It was hours before Confederates found his body and realized what had happened.

General McIntosh was finally given command of the Confederate Army in the late afternoon but met a similar end to McCulloch when he brazenly rode ahead of the dismounted infantry divisions, which were picking their way through the woods toward the Union lines. In the interim, the Northerners and Southerners had been skirmishing between the two fields. When McIntosh emerged from the woods into enemy territory, followed by his army, Greusel's 36th Illinois was ready and unloaded a maelstrom of firepower. General McIntosh fell from a bullet through the heart not 200 meters (220 yards) from where McCulloch had died.

After losing two of their most vital commanders, the Rebel infantry assault on the west of Leetown (the Southern right flank and the Northern left flank) dissipated in the leadership vacuum. Meanwhile, Confederate Colonel Hébert arranged his infantry divisions east of

Leetown in Morgan's Woods—the 4th, 14th, and 15th Arkansas and 3rd Louisiana. Not knowing that his superiors were dead, Hébert hesitated to make the combined attack that had been agreed with McCulloch. Eventually, in the late afternoon, he began moving his troops forward to the nonexistent right flank of the Union Army that did not extend beyond Leetown.

But Union Colonel Davis had been dispatched north by General Curtis from Little Sugar Creek and arrived just in time to repulse the Rebels. Davis's 1,400 men in three Illinois and Indiana regiments also included the 2nd Illinois Light Artillery Battery. Colonel Julius White's brigade of the 37th and 59th Illinois formed the advance guard that would fortuitously but unknowingly directly block Hébert's advance through the woods. When Hébert's men inadvertently crashed into White's men in the woods, a close and intense firefight erupted. Amidst the smoke and confusion, many of the soldiers were required to lie flat on their bellies to engage in combat.

But the Federals on this eastern flank were outnumbered and began to be pushed back. A posse of Rebels even escaped west to Oberson's Field and temporarily took command of two artillery guns before being chased back. Colonel Davis sent a brigade of two units—the 18th and 22nd Indiana—under Colonel Thomas Pattison to the east to outflank the oncoming Rebels. Colonel Hébert's 14th and 15th Arkansas veered left, changing the front lines toward the east.

In the fierce tangle of fighting that ensued, the Union commander of the 22nd Indiana was killed (Colonel John A. Hendricks), and Colonel Hébert and Colonel William C. Mitchell of the 14th Arkansas were separated from their men in the smoke and confusion. A third Confederate commander, Colonel William F. Tunnard of the 3rd Louisiana, became vulnerable when he collapsed from exhaustion. Although the fighting in Morgan's Woods reached a stalemate, Confederate commanders Hébert, Mitchell, and Tunnard were ultimately captured by the Northerners, leaving the Southerners with only one senior commander, General Pike, who could not have known of this fact at the time.

Hébert's men fell back to Foster's farm, appalled to discover over two-thirds of McCulloch's army aimlessly milling about on the back lines west of Leetown. They had done nothing to assist with the breakthrough on their left flank and could easily have overrun the enemy. By 4 p.m., the battle near Leetown was over, with staggering losses to Confederate lead commanders but very few fatalities to their army, which had not engaged much. The vastly outnumbered Union had been both lucky and tactically effective, using good leadership and pivotal decisions to fend off the enemy. The Bluecoats had most importantly prevented the two Southern armies from uniting at Elkhorn Tavern to deal the intended blow to the Army of the Southwest.

Hereafter, General Pike only managed to take charge of half of McCulloch's confused and dispirited army. He marched them north around Big Mountain to join General Price's rearguard by midnight. Some of the remaining units, including one Native American unit, removed themselves from the battle altogether and drifted west away from Elkhorn Tavern. Colonel Elkanah B. Greer of the 3rd Texas Cavalry corralled the remaining men and followed Pike's route toward Elkhorn, bringing a bedraggled, exhausted, and starving group of troops to join the Southern army at dawn on Saturday, March 8th. (Colonel Greer, 1825-1877, was the de facto commander after McCulloch and McIntosh, but many hours had elapsed before he knew of his superiors' deaths and Pike's withdrawal.)

The newly arrived Confederates from Leetown had been without food or rest for two days and could not realistically be committed to the battle ahead—the second defining day of the Battle of Elkhorn Tavern. General Van Dorn's high-risk, high-reward approach to Pea Ridge had failed to include correct staffing arrangements before their departure from the Boston Mountains. After the Leetown debacle, the Confederates' ammunition wagons remained at Camp Stephens, nineteen kilometers, or twelve miles, west across Pea Ridge. By the morning of March 8th, when Van Dorn was finally headquartered at Elkhorn Tavern, the general's haste and lack of attention to planning and detail would have a fateful impact.

Chapter 5 – The Battle of Elkhorn Tavern, March 7th - 8th, 1862

When General Curtis had been informed early on the morning of March 7th that two Confederate approaches were coming for his army's rear, he dispatched General Osterhaus and then Colonel Davis toward Leetown and also Colonel Carr toward Elkhorn Tavern. Carr took half of his 4th Division (about 1,400 men) with him since General Curtis still believed the northern encroachment of the Rebels to be a diversionary tactic. Apparently, General Curtis was known for his rather traditional and stiff approach to battle, which would serve him well in the days to come; in the meantime, though, he had been outfoxed by Van Dorn, who had stealthily lit campfires in front of Little Sugar Creek to keep the enemy guessing. The vulnerable Union supply wagons stretched out in farmer Benjamin Ruddick's cornfield south of the tavern and adjacent a small store on Telegraph Road—Pratt's Store—about 2.4 kilometers (1.5 miles) from Elkhorn Tavern.

The part of Telegraph Road that came from the north, circumnavigating east around Big Mountain, passed through an extensive, rugged, and wooded gulley, the Cross Timber Hollow, before ascending onto the high ground of Pea Ridge just north of Elkhorn Tavern. At the tavern intersection, Huntsville Road led in from the east from the village of Huntsville. A short distance south of the tavern, Ford Road led in from the west to join Telegraph Road. Finally, not far east from the Elkhorn Tavern intersection was Clemon's Lane, which ran south off

Huntsville Road, parallel to Telegraph Road. Ruddick's Field lay between Telegraph Road and Clemon's Lane, and Clemon's Field lay to the east of the lane. Big Mountain lay to the northeast of the intersection, and the Battle of Elkhorn Tavern (Battle of Pea Ridge) would play out at the southeastern extremity of the mountain's base. (Big Mountain stretched from Twelve Corner Church in the west to Elkhorn Tavern in the east.)

Colonel Carr had a decade's worth of experience fighting Comanches in Texas and was known to be a vigorous and sometimes insubordinate military man. Although General Price's men who had circumnavigated Big Mountain had dwindled to approximately five thousand (with ten artillery batteries but limited ammunition caissons or containers), they would still outnumber the Union by about one to three in the initial stages of the Battle of Pea Ridge. Carr arrived at Elkhorn Tavern at noon with Colonel Grenville M. Dodge's brigade of the 4th Iowa, 35th Illinois, 3rd Illinois Cavalry, and the 1st Iowa Battery, which he quickly dispatched to guard the right (east) of Telegraph Road at the top of the ridge. (Colonel Grenville Mellen Dodge, 1831–1916, a soldier, politician, businessman, and railroad executive, played a considerable role in the Civil War as an intelligence officer and went on to have a glittering postbellum career.) Carr also employed the small group of the 24th Missouri, which had been guarding the supply wagons. Colonel Carr waited for his quarry to come to him—he had the high ground and the element of surprise, although the Union would remain considerably outmanned and temporarily outgunned for the remainder of the Battle of Pea Ridge, which lasted until midday on March 8th.

The Rebels reached Cross Timber Hollow gorge at about the same time as the Federals, and a series of skirmishes ensued between the advanced guards from both sides in the lowlands near a tanning yard. When the Confederates realized the enemy was upon them, they spread out in a west-east line, straddling Telegraph Road. They navigated across the awkward terrain below the steep incline leading up onto Pea Ridge with men of the MSG to the left flank and Confederate soldiers to the right. Three hundred feet above them (ninety-one meters or a hundred yards), a thin blue line of enemy forces held the ridge blocking Telegraph Road south. The Southerners advanced on the Northerners, albeit at a snail's pace. Even though the soldiers were tired and hungry, they were required to attack uphill through a rough and wooded landscape.

Similar to the scene that was unfolding near Leetown at that exact moment, Colonel Carr realized that he was vastly outnumbered and sent word to General Curtis for reinforcements. In the meantime, he prepared for an offensive against the foe and bought the Union two hours in delay tactics by firing battery artillery from the Union's four guns into the oncoming soldiers. The Confederates' twenty-one heavy guns answered back, and a "perfect storm" of artillery firepower ensued. Colonel Carr is noted for saying, "Give them hell boys," and his enthusiastic and reckless engagement would eventually earn him several bad wounds, a promotion to brigadier general, and the Medal of Honor. He had profound loyalty and respect from his men, as he cavorted along the front lines, encouraging, directing, and inspiring them.

By 2 p.m., General Curtis had sent a brigade of a further thousand men to Carr's aid. The Federals were now outnumbered by two to one. Colonel William Vandever hurried north from Little Sugar Creek with the 9th Iowa, 25th Missouri, and the 3rd Iowa Battery. Soon, a Missouri cavalry with two more guns, captained by Frederick W. Benteen, and then the 8th Indiana battalion and the 1st Indiana Battery arrived. The Union repeatedly sent infantry and cavalry charges down the slope, but the Rebels held firm, probably in the belief that McCulloch's men would soon be joining them along Ford Road and cutting off their attackers at the rear. But this was not to be, and Van Dorn only learned of the battle at Leetown in the late afternoon.

When the Confederate general realized he would need to retreat or attack, he instructed his men to form a wide arcing front to envelop the enemy at its flanks. By 4 p.m., the Missouri State Guard was successfully upon the high ground and threatening the Union's right flank. Stretching for 1.5 kilometers (a mile) to the east of Elkhorn Tavern, the Southerners now extended well beyond the Yankees' limited line. As the Union's left flank also began to be encroached upon, Colonel Carr condensed his troops, making a frontal assault by General Van Dorn possible. (Van Dorn had taken command of the Southern right flank, while Price had control of the left flank.) The Rebel breakthrough eventually came near Elkhorn Tavern, and as the Southerners burst forth upon the Federals around Telegraph Road, clearing the woods and the dense smoke of gunfire, they were less than ninety meters (a hundred yards) from their enemy. A maelstrom of firing ensued for thirty minutes, with men falling on both sides.

But the Union men were overwhelmed and could not sustain the onslaught. Eventually, their line began to collapse on the left, and then the center around the tavern gave way. The Yankees began to retreat, salvaging most of their heavy guns except for two and unleashing a final round of artillery power at the enemy before withdrawing down Telegraph Road. As the Union reformed in Ruddick's Field south of Elkhorn Tavern, Lieutenant Colonel Francis Jay Herron's 9th Iowa held the rearguard. Herron (1837-1902) was wounded and taken prisoner by the Rebels; he would be exchanged not long after Pea Ridge. He also received both a promotion to brigadier general and the Medal of Honor for his actions at Pea Ridge.

But the Confederates finally had the prize—the coveted Elkhorn Tavern—and General Van Dorn would eventually roll up in his ambulance to make it his headquarters for one brief night before the final denouement of the Battle of Pea Ridge on March 8th.

The Battle of Elkhorn Tavern with the Confederate troops rushing at the Union artillery and the Union infantry pulling hurriedly back behind their guns in a retreat on the evening of March 8th, 1862.

It was now dusk, and the quickening darkness and smoke from gunfire created a gloomy affair. As the Rebels pushed through at Elkhorn

Tavern, half a mile (eight hundred meters) to the east, General Price managed to advance two thousand of his men as well as eleven guns by the late afternoon to encroach upon the Yankee right flank, crossing east of the tavern through Williams Hollow. (Price had been wounded but continued with his arm in a sling. Carr was triply wounded but also continued to lead.) As the enemy moved west down Huntsville Road, Union Colonel Dodge swung his men to face east across Clemon's Field. The Federals were ensconced behind timber obstructions and had a clear view across the field and the approaching army. (Colonel Dodge had been responsible for creating the obstructions across the Bentonville Detour at his own suggestion.)

Price had no choice but to send his troops in a full-frontal attack in the diminishing daylight. The Confederates sustained heavy losses as their troops moved against the foe piecemeal and in a state of considerable exhaustion. But eventually, the sheer overwhelming numbers of Southerners pincered the Union at Clemon's Field, and Dodge withdrew his men toward Elkhorn and then farther back to join the Union contingent at Ruddick's. Colonel Carr was frustrated at the retreat, but sufficient reinforcements had not been forthcoming in time, and the day was ending—there was nothing further he could do except regroup south of Elkhorn.

In the interim, General Curtis had been graced with time to move the full, unwieldy bulk of their supply wagons from Ruddick's Field. The accumulated Army of the Southwest had done an about-turn during the afternoon when Curtis finally understood that the threat from the north was not a decoy but the full Confederate Army of the West. The Union men were now established along the southern line of the flattened Ruddick's cornfield as day turned to night. Behind the thin blue line at the front, the remainder of the army moving north from Little Sugar Creek (including General Asboth's 2nd Division and Sigel's remaining men) would eventually coalesce with the supply wagons farther south and be safely away from the enemy. When the remaining Federals under General Osterhaus and Colonel Davis moved in from the west after the battle at Leetown, the united Union Army faced north. General Curtis had maneuvered his battalions and their equipment 180 degrees from their originally entrenched position facing south over Little Sugar Creek— an orderly and intelligent move that would not be repeated in the Civil War. Curtis's headquarters were now at Pratt's Store.

As the Bluecoats condensed across Telegraph Road behind Ruddick's Field, at about 6:30 p.m., General Van Dorn made a last stab at the enemy before nightfall. He had lost half of his original army, so just three thousand Confederates made this final rush against the Blues. The Confederates met with devastating results, as they were relentlessly pushed back across the clear, open fields. Both armies retreated to reorganize as March 7th-one of the longest days of many of the men's lives—ended.

By the dawn of March 8th, Curtis's army had reunited and was ready for another day's battle. General Sigel had marched his divisions in circles all night only to arrive just before dawn. Also, the wounded General Asboth pleaded with General Curtis to retreat rather than fight, an attitude likely shared by many of the troops who felt trapped between the Rebels and Little Sugar Creek, but Curtis was confident.

Unbeknownst to the Union, the Confederate troops around Elkhorn Tavern were not ready for battle. Besides the deserters who'd wandered west after the engagement at Leetown, the Southerners had neither food, nor water, nor ammunition. They sustained themselves by scavenging through the fallen haversacks of Union troops and abandoned sutlers' (civilian provisioners) wagons. The ammunition caissons would never arrive from Camp Stephens. The straggling Southern troops arriving from Leetown via the north of Big Mountain were in a bad way. General Van Dorn was not in a position to start a battle on Saturday morning, and yet the pugnacious commander would not retreat.

General Curtis needed to remove the Army of the West from their position around the tavern on Pea Ridge since they were blocking his route north. He was temporarily cut off, and although Van Dorn did not start a fight on the morning of the 8th, Curtis methodically moved his troops into battle position across Telegraph Road and was ready to begin an engagement at 8 a.m. Although the Confederates were in no realistic state to do so, they fought back, and the first action of the day consisted of Southern and Northern artillery probing the landscape, coming forward to fire and then retreating back into the woods. Curtis had directed General Sigel into a primary position overseeing the six batteries (heavy gun units) of the Union on the left wing. This proved to be a strategic move, as Sigel's superior experience with artillery outweighed his erratic and itinerant behavior leading to the Battle of Pea Ridge. The 1st and 2nd Divisions under Sigel found the high ground on the western approach and settled in. Colonel Davis held the center with his 3rd Division, and Colonel Carr's 4th Division oversaw the right wing.

The Union's left flank extended far to the northwest, with General Asboth at the extreme end of the line, followed by General Osterhaus. By midmorning, Sigel calmly moved his batteries farther up the western side of Telegraph Road to face northeast and came much closer to the Rebel lines. The Union now fought along a dogleg, threatening to overcome the enemy's right flank. It was one of the few occasions of linear engagement in the Civil War in which a full army was deployed in an impressive and visible arcing line. Sigel pounded the enemy with twenty-one guns for two hours, firing approximately 3,600 rounds at a rate of more than thirty shots a minute. The Confederates returned fire from twelve cannons amidst exploding shells, and the inferno was heard over eighty kilometers (fifty miles) away in Fayetteville.

Eventually, the sustained cannonade was too much for the Southerners; their guns began to fall silent, and they started retreating piecemeal from the battlefield, disappearing through the woods north back into Cross Timber Hollow or slinking east down Huntsville Road. (Both routes eventually led south after circumnavigating the battlefield.) The Union would experience a near textbook military engagement that morning. After a calm pelting of the enemy by artillery fire, they extended their lines, simultaneously closing in to pinion the left and right flanks. Under the continual volley of fire, the Confederate line was disintegrating, their morale degenerating, and their ammunition almost spent. It was the Union's cue to send in an infantry charge.

At 10:30 a.m., the Union guns ceased their barrage as all able soldiers of General Curtis's ten thousand-strong army rushed forward in a pitched assault, which included cavalry charges. On the far western flank, Asboth's men routed the last remaining Cherokee Mounted Rifles from their position. Osterhaus pushed against the Confederate 1st Missouri Brigade under Adjutant General Lewis Henry Little. (Little, 1817-1862, had assumed increasing responsibilities in regards to command since the previous day's battle of Elkhorn Tavern, which earned him a promotion to brigadier general the following month. By the end of the fighting on March 8th, Little became the de facto commander of Price's troops, but he was killed later that year in September at the Battle of Iuka.)

As Union Colonel Davis held the center, Colonel Carr's division on the right flank received most of the onslaught as the Rebels retreated eastward along Huntsville Road. Federal records of these final engagements of the Battle of Pea Ridge describe a classic and momentous military display in which artillery, cavalry, and infantry worked harmoniously and effectively together to rout their adversaries from the field.

Yelling, playing their drums, and flashing the deadly bayonets of their guns, the Federals made quick work of flushing the Southerners from the field, rushing at them from the south and west. Van Dorn and Price made a hasty exit east along Huntsville Road at about 11 a.m., shamefully leaving many of their troops behind. At this point, most of the Confederate soldiers escaped in all directions in a humiliating rout, with just a few fighting bravely until the end, such as Colonel Benjamin Rives of the 3rd Missouri, who was killed while enforcing a rearguard unit for retreating troops. General Pike and the Confederate artillery escaped north up Telegraph Road and back into Cross Timber Hollow, and some hurried west along Ford Road. Eventually, most of the Southern army followed their leaders along Huntsville to the east. The split and disintegrating retreat of the Rebel Army did not prompt General Curtis to pursue, and by noon, the field was theirs. (General Sigel did mistakenly take many of his men on a northeastern excursion in pursuit of Van Dorn in defiance of Curtis's orders, although he had to turn back the next day when Curtis refused to send reinforcements. Sigel had been under the mistaken belief that the Rebel Army had fled into Missouri, whereas they had all eventually turned south.)

Chapter 6 – Outcome of the Battle of Pea Ridge

Elkhorn Tavern served as a temporary field hospital during the Battle of Pea Ridge for both the Yankees and the Rebels, and it remained as a hospital for weeks after the battle as soldiers recovered. Similarly, every possible building in Leetown was used as a field hospital. The armies in the remote Trans-Mississippi Theater often went without sufficient medics and doctors, and once the smoke had cleared atop Pea Ridge, General Curtis was tasked with collecting and caring for both Northern and Southern wounded men. The Battle of Pea Ridge claimed approximately 13 percent of the Union field and an estimated 15 percent of the Confederate field in deaths, severe injuries, and persons missing.

The Federal Army suffered 1,384 casualties, including 203 deaths, 980 wounded, and 201 missing. (Carr's and Davis's divisions had suffered the most, with 682 and 344 casualties, respectively.) Although true records of the Southern losses from Pea Ridge were not forthcoming, the estimates are conservatively two thousand casualties of the estimated twelve thousand to thirteen thousand men who eventually engaged. Of these casualties, two generals had been killed (McCulloch and McIntosh), one mortally wounded (General William Y. Slack of the Missouri State Guard's 2nd Brigade), and one wounded (Price). (Slack was heralded by General Price as being one of the bravest men of the battle, as he took responsibility on many occasions for missing or inept superiors. He died from a bullet wound several weeks after the battle and was posthumously promoted to brigadier general.) Four Confederate colonels had been captured, wounded, or mortally wounded. The loss of so many senior officers greatly affected the Confederacy.

When General Curtis learned that most of the Army of the West were retreating back toward the Boston Mountains, he knew that Missouri would remain safely in Union hands. Many of the Southerners deserted the army at this point, as the extent of their starvation became more dangerous than the enemy they had so recently faced. After two weeks, a ragtag and vastly diminished mob of Rebel soldiers coalesced near Van Buren on the Arkansas River just north of Fort Smith. By April, the remnants of the Army of the West had been moved east over the Mississippi River into the Western Theater to contribute to apparently more important causes. This left Arkansas vulnerable to the Federal presence. Without clear Southern leadership or a functioning army, General Curtis took the opportunity to infiltrate deeper into Arkansas by the end of April 1862.

General Halleck had instructed Curtis to rendezvous with General Frederick Steele (1819–1868, a lifelong military man prevalent in the Trans-Mississippi and Western Theaters) in Batesville, Arkansas, on May 2nd. (Batesville, Arkansas, was about 161 kilometers, or 100 miles, northeast of Little Rock.) Halleck had instructed Curtis to send half of his Army of the Southwest under Generals Davis and Asboth east across the Mississippi River. General Curtis reorganized his army into three divisions. Steele took command of the Army of the Southwest's 1st Division, while General Carr commanded the 2nd Division and General Osterhaus the 3rd Division. (Davis and Carr had been promoted after Pea Ridge, and Osterhaus's promotion to brigadier general would follow in June 1862.) The recombined army remained at approximately ten thousand men strong, with six thousand infantry, three thousand cavalry, and one thousand artillerymen.

Curtis came within eighty kilometers (fifty miles) of the state capital of Little Rock before realizing his supply line north was in jeopardy. The Army of the Southwest turned east and followed the White River toward the safety of the Mississippi River from which provisions from the north could be sent. Along the way, the Federals needed to deal with difficult terrain as well as Rebel outlaws (bushwhackers), which considerably complicated and slowed their journey. In June of 1862, the Union's supply situation became so serious that the US Navy attempted to send provisions up the White River, only to be halted at St. Charles (about sixty-four kilometers, or forty miles, west-southwest of Helena) on June 17th by a Confederate bombardment of artillery from the shore. This skirmish at St. Charles saw the sinking of US ships as well as the disablement of the USS *Mound City*. There were many Federal deaths. Union forces disembarked to counterattack the Rebel emplacements, while the remaining supply envoy (with food and supplies for men and their horses and mules) continued upriver to a low water point at Clarendon from where it could go no farther. (St. Charles and Clarendon were about sixty-four kilometers, or forty miles, apart.)

In order to reach Clarendon as quickly as possible, General Curtis made a bold decision to cut his tenuous supply lines north to Rolla and force his men to live off the land. This would allow them to move as quickly as possible through challenging enemy territory. (It was the only real occasion in which Union troops were forced to live entirely off the land. Although General Grant would claim his men had done the same during the Vicksburg campaign, it was later proved that it was not true and that they had, in fact, been well supplied throughout.) The Union march through the eastern river counties of Arkansas proved to have an economically devastating effect on the state, as General Curtis proceeded to emancipate slaves as he moved, thus permanently undermining the plantations en route. His men also plundered and pillaged as they traveled, destroying property to the value of $1.5 million. At least three thousand emancipated slaves and their families joined the army's march, and others fled north into Missouri.

Along their journey, the Federals dealt with irregular skirmishes from Southern military forces attempting to block and disrupt their passage through Arkansas. As a result, they suffered some fatalities, captures, and destruction of supplies. (The Union detachments were scattered due to their need to forage, which made it difficult to keep the men concentrated and protected.) The Rebels made one last attempt to cut off the Army of the Southwest's progress by sending a newly formed Rebel force under Southern Major General Thomas C. Hindman (1828-1868, a lawyer, politician, and Confederate officer who had been fighting in the Western Theater) toward James Ferry at the Cache River— about ten kilometers (six miles) from the hamlet of Cotton Plant, Woodruff County. Cotton Plant was approximately halfway between Little Rock and the Mississippi River and en route to the supply boats at Clarendon, to which the Yankees were heading.

On July 7th, the Federal Illinois and Wisconsin infantry vanguard under Colonel Charles Hovey (1827–1897, an educator, college president, and military man) as part of Steele's 1st Division met with a force of about five thousand Rebels led by Brigadier General Albert Rust near James Ferry. (Rust, 1818–1870, was an Arkansas politician, businessman, and Confederate commander who led in the Eastern, Western, and Trans-Mississippi Theaters.) The Battle of Cotton Plant (or the Battle of Cache River) that ensued included five Rebel regiments of Texas cavalry, three regiments of Arkansas infantry, one artillery battery, and several smaller units. The Confederates were inexperienced, poorly coordinated, irregularly trained and equipped, and armed only with what they had brought from home. But they had taken the Federals by surprise as the Bluecoats crossed the Cache, and they had not experienced a full engagement since Pea Ridge in March.

By mid-morning, it seemed as if the Grays would finally halt Curtis's columns, as they were repeatedly pushed back toward the river. However, slowly but surely, newly arrived Federal reinforcements crossed the Cache River (which was low and passable), allowing the Federals to begin outnumbering the Rebels by two to one. But General Curtis chose to send forward just the necessary reinforcements to meet the unknown Confederate force. This type of military engagement, known as a "meeting engagement," prevented Curtis from applying the full force of his army, which was strung out for miles along the Cache River.

The first Federal reinforcements upon the field were the 1st Indiana Cavalry, as well as their artillery. They caused plenty of damage to the enemy by creating confusion and then mass panic. The Confederates fled, and the Union forces who had engaged pursued them for a few miles before ending the fight. The Southern ambush around Cotton Plant had become a rout, and they fled from the field in a humiliating fashion. The profoundly demoralized Rebels who were still alive or not captured melted back into the Arkansas countryside, leaving the Federals with an unobstructed march onward.

The Battle of Cotton Plant resulted in 63 Federal casualties, including 6 deaths, and there were approximately 120 Confederate deaths and many wounded, most of whom were reported to have died after hurrying from the scene. White and black men died side by side, as well as umpteen horses and mules. The battle was reported as horrifying and bloody, with bodies strewn everywhere and the river water running pink with blood. Many Southerners involved in this minor battle deserted the army after the appalling mismanagement by their commanders.

The Army of the Southwest arrived at Clarendon on July 9th, one day after the Federal flotilla had left after abandoning hope of reconnecting with the Army of the Southwest. Curtis pushed his army onward from the White River to the Mississippi River. Curtis's army arrived at Helena, Arkansas, on the banks of the mighty Mississippi on July 12th. Helena remained in Union hands for the remainder of the war, and it proved to be a vitally strategic jumping-off point for General Grant's Vicksburg campaign in 1863.

Helena also became one of the first critical places for the recruitment of black troops, which proved vital to the defense of Helena and other Union strongholds along the arterial lifeblood of the Mississippi River over the next few years. The Battle of Helena on July 4th, 1863, was a Union victory, which ensured that Helena would remain in Federal hands. (This battle took place at the end of the Vicksburg campaign, which is considered to be the turning point of the Civil War that broke the back of the South.) In August 1862, the Union soldiers, as well as emancipated slaves, built Fort Curtis, which became the primary Federal bastion in the small town. Over time, the Army of the Southwest was eventually incorporated into the Army of the Tennessee and the Army of the Mississippi once the region had stabilized in favor of the Yankees.

After the Union success at Pea Ridge and the Army of the Southwest's subsequent foray through Arkansas, the Trans-Mississippi Theater was quite firmly within their grasp. The geographical and tactical distance from the Southern headquarters in Richmond, Virginia, and the Confederates' lack of a permanent and official base west of the Mississippi River saw an unusual development in Southern leadership and fighting in the trans-Mississippi. Random acts of guerilla warfare led by Southern sympathizers dominated the states of Missouri, Kansas, and the Indian Territory for the remainder of the war. After the Union victory at the Siege of Vicksburg in July of 1863, the Yankees controlled the extent of the Mississippi River, dividing the Southern states in two and further isolating the regions west of this mighty waterway. The Southern commander in charge of the Trans-Mississippi Department at the time was General Edmund Kirby Smith (1824–1893). His regions of Arkansas, Missouri, Texas, Louisiana, and Arizona Territory, and the

Indian Territory became known as "Kirby Smithdom" after the fall of Vicksburg in accordance with his greater government's lack of control west of the Mississippi River thereafter.

In Missouri, although the Union retained overall control of the state for the remainder of the war, frequent guerilla raids occurred, particularly along the western extremities of its border with Kansas. The secessionist sympathizers responsible for these incursions were known as bushwhackers. In Arkansas, the Union retained its hold on the north, finally taking back control of the coveted Fort Smith and Little Rock in 1863.

The remaining elements of the Missouri State Guard were invigorated to fight once more in 1864 under General Sterling Price when he unsuccessfully attempted to retake Missouri. Certain units of the MSG continued to operate west of the Mississippi River until the end of the war. They still acted as renegades and were set apart from official Confederate control, but nonetheless, they were still under the command of appointed and recognized Southern leadership.

The Trans-Mississippi Theater still remains an obscure and often overlooked arena of the American Civil War. The Battle of Pea Ridge is considered the most important official conflict of the war in this theater. This theater was vast in geographical extent but extremely limited in terms of authority figures, organized armies, settlement infrastructure, and continuous supply lines, making it perhaps one of the more dangerous theaters in which to fight. Minor battles and skirmishes continued in the trans-Mississippi but without permanent or far-reaching repercussions. Both official and guerilla engagements included activities within the Indian Territory, and almost eight thousand Native Americans were eventually conscripted to aid the Confederacy, including a commanding general.

Although Native Americans also fought for the Union, they were never officially conscripted into the regular army. A strange dichotomy existed in 19th-century North America wherein Southerners refused to live or fight alongside emancipated slaves (they forced enslaved blacks to fight for them), but they fought against the Northerners for the rights of Native Americans. This included fighting together with Native Americans, and some of them even commanded their own brigades. To add to the confusion, the Native Americans were also known to swap allegiances between the North and the South depending on a variety of factors, so they could not be relied upon.

The Union's success in Arkansas against overwhelming odds meant a permanent reversal in the balance of power in the Trans-Mississippi. Union troops from Missouri and Arkansas could now be filtered to other Civil War theaters as Missouri remained securely a Federal state. The soldiers in the Trans-Mississippi Theater had seen some of the most brutal actions of the Civil War due to the hazardous terrain of the western wilderness and limited infrastructure, supplies, engineer corps, and medical assistance (those fighting in the Eastern Theater, for instance, could head back to Washington, DC, after a battle or south to Richmond). Not to mention, the men in the Trans Mississippi had to deal with inclement and sometimes deadly cold weather.

In retrospect, knowing what we do about General Van Dorn's atrocious leadership and his subordinates' inability to make good decisions, it was always obvious that the Union would be victorious at Pea Ridge. But to the Federal soldiers huddled in their tents during a snowstorm along Little Sugar Creek in the days before the battle, success was not an obvious result. They were outnumbered in enemy territory in impossible terrain and appalling weather. They were taken by surprise by Van Dorn's rear sneak approach, and they were alarmingly separated from their route home. From March 6th to March 8th, 1862, the soldiers of the Army of the Southwest were not sure of their fate. When victory came calmly and quickly on the final day of battle, they were overwhelmingly relieved and heartened—the Union had never taken a win for granted.

Conclusion

At the time of the American Civil War, Missouri was considered the gateway to the west. On the western side of the north-south running Mississippi River, it was the southernmost state that technically remained part of the Union for most of the Civil War. Abutting Confederate Arkansas to the south, Missouri was a pivotal departure point for the Federals' fight in the Trans-Mississippi Theater.

But as much as the Yankees wanted to retain control of Missouri, the Rebels wanted to snatch it away, and sympathies remained mixed in both Missouri and Arkansas for the entirety of the war. After the Union's success at Pea Ridge, Missouri was theirs, although they did have to deal with guerilla skirmishes and one or two failed attempts by the Southerners to recapture the state. Pea Ridge and the Confederates' subsequent scuttle into Mississippi left northern Arkansas open for Federal occupation. By 1863, the year after the Battle of Pea Ridge, the Federals controlled central Arkansas as well the state capital of Little Rock. The Union victory of Pea Ridge left Missouri and, most importantly, St. Louis secure in Northern hands. The Federals were able to concentrate on other war theaters, specifically on the application of essential reinforcements in capturing the Mississippi River.

The Battle of Pea Ridge is heralded as one of the key turning points in the Civil War. It enabled a cascade of Union victories to follow, leading to the North ultimately being victorious over the South. Although it may be obvious that the federal government, with its abundant resources and international connections, was always going to win the Civil

War, the real grit of the Northern and Southern disagreement was fought along the frontier, where opposing loyalties ran high and where blood was the only price to pay to defend a disappearing way of life or, conversely, the introduction of a new set of ideologies.

With the controversial "Indian Territory" immediately to the west of Arkansas, the men of the Pea Ridge campaign fought within a vortex of mixed and changing realities. Old, new, enslaved, and quasi-American citizens, Native Americans, and freshly arrived European immigrants melted into a kaleidoscope of confusion, self-interests, shifting loyalties, undisciplined military maneuvers, and sometimes cowardice and mayhem. The result was resoundingly a Union victory but against all odds. The Yankees could not take their win for granted, as the continued fickleness and obscurity of the Trans-Mississippi kept them continually looking over their shoulders as they navigated and eventually held enemy territory.

The strongly Unionist Mississippi River town of St. Louis in northeastern Missouri was a prize that the Rebels sorely wanted. If the Southerners captured St. Louis, they would have Missouri and thus the entire territory west of the Mississippi River. St. Louis, as the most commercial and industrialized center of the western frontier, was too juicy a fruit for Confederate General Van Dorn and his Army of the West to ignore. All that stood in his way was the Northern Army of the Southwest under General Curtis and the radically hostile landscape of the Ozark Plateau.

Blind to all reasoning and logic, Van Dorn continued a winter campaign that the Federals had begun. In the haze of feverish delirium, he commanded troops from his sickbed and subjected a vastly superior army of sixteen thousand men to inhumane conditions as he attempted to achieve the impossible. Van Dorn's political ambitions, coupled with his militaristic weaknesses, allowed an army of ten thousand men to lick them. To add to this considerable humiliation, his troops admitted to being more afraid of starving or freezing to death than being killed by an enemy bullet.

The spectacular Southern failure at Pea Ridge was only made worse by a near-perfect military execution of artillery, infantry, and cavalry across the field of battle by the Union in the final denouement on March 8th. The Rebels were scuttled from the field, disappearing in every direction to find food and succor for their demolished pride. But the headstrong Van Dorn still didn't take responsibility for the loss. Instead of digging in with his troops to defend Arkansas, he took the ragtag mob that remained and hustled east over the Mississippi River and into the Western Theater, leaving Arkansas vulnerable.

The Battle of Pea Ridge, and in fact the entire Trans-Mississippi Theater of the Civil War, is an oft-overlooked aspect of underlying events that led to the Union's ultimate success. Without the stalwart and tactical Curtis and his fine posse of leaders, the whole western region could have fallen to the South. All the states directly east of the Mississippi River would have been exposed to Confederate pressure, and so on and so forth all the way to the Atlantic Ocean. But General Curtis and his men held firm. They neither panicked nor retreated, and glory became theirs in a few intense and memorable days.

Part 4: The Battle of Shiloh

A Captivating Guide to the One of the Bloodiest Battles of the American Civil War

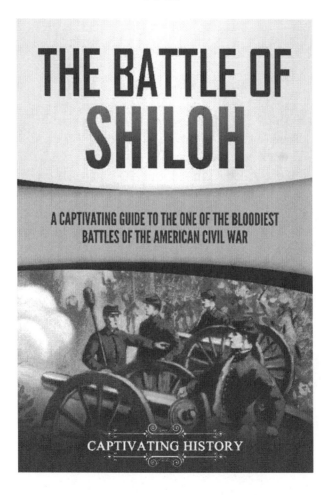

Introduction

On April 6th and 7th, 1862, the armies of the Union and the Confederacy clashed near the small Methodist church called Shiloh in southeastern Tennessee along the Tennessee River. The word "Shiloh" means "place of peace" in Hebrew, but for many Americans at the time and since, the word took on a new meaning, for the Battle of Shiloh was the bloodiest battle fought on the North American continent at that time, and it remained near the top of the list of deadliest battles when the war ended in 1865.

Re-creation of the original Shiloh church on the exact spot where it stood in 1862. The battle raged in and around the church at one point during the conflict. Courtesy Matthew Gaskill.
https://commons.wikimedia.org/wiki/File:Shiloh_Church.jpg

After 1865 and until relatively recently, the Battle of Shiloh was relegated to the back pages of history books, except among historians and Civil War buffs. The battles that took place in the eastern part of the country in the area around the capitals of the Union and the Confederacy (Washington, D.C, and Richmond, Virginia, respectively) were the focus of most of their attention. The stunning Federal (also referred to in the text as the Union, the Yankees, or the USA) defeat at the First Battle of Bull Run (also known in the South as the First Battle of Manassas), the drama between President Abraham Lincoln and General George McClellan, "Stonewall" Jackson's dashing Shenandoah Campaign, the talented general Robert E. Lee, the Battle of Gettysburg, and much else have always overshadowed the events in the Western theater of the Civil War.

However, it has been argued in more recent times that the battles in the Western theater and along the Mississippi River played a more decisive role in the defeat of the Confederacy (also referred to in the text as the CSA or the Rebels) than was previously believed, and it may have been the more important theater, as the Union cut key supply lines, drove deep into Confederate territory, seized or destroyed vital farming and industrial areas and ports, and eventually allowed General William Tecumseh Sherman to march to the Atlantic and threaten the rear of the bulk of the Confederate forces that were fighting in Virginia. For most of the war, the struggle in the East was mostly confined to Virginia, a small part of Maryland, and a town in Pennsylvania called Gettysburg. The Civil War in the West was fought over hundreds and eventually thousands of miles.

However, for the men that fought there and for the nation at large, the Battle of Shiloh was an absolute shock. It was the bloodiest battle of the war up to that time, and it saw more dead and wounded than the French and Indian War, the American Revolution, and the War of 1812 combined. It is no exaggeration to say that the news of Shiloh hit the people in both the North and the South in the same way as Pearl Harbor did decades later or even 9/11, which took place more than a century later.

Chapter 1 – Before the Battle

The Civil War began just shy of a year before the Battle of Shiloh. On April 13th, 1861, the Union fortress of Fort Sumter off the coast of Charleston, South Carolina, surrendered to the Confederate forces, which had been bombarding it for a day and a half. In command of the rebel guns pounding the fort was General Pierre Gustave Toutant Beauregard, a Louisianan and graduate of the West Point class of 1838, who excelled in the use of artillery. Beauregard (who is usually referred to by his initials, "P. G. T.," though he himself signed his letters as "G. T. Beauregard") would play a key role at Shiloh a year later.

General Beauregard in 1862, about the time of Shiloh. Courtesy National Archives.
https://commons.wikimedia.org/wiki/File:Gen._Pierre_Gustave_Toutant_de_Beauregard,_C.S.A - NARA - 528596.jpg

When reading histories of the Civil War and its battles, it's astounding how many times the word "shocked" is used to describe the reaction of both soldiers and civilians to an event, but in many ways, the American Civil War was the first "total war" in the modern sense. War was waged not only on the battlefield but also against civilians in cities, industries, agriculture, transportation, and, perhaps most of all, on the people's way of life and culture—that being slavery and the culture that supported it.

To us in the 21st century, the shock of the Southerners when their cities were bombarded and their slaves set free seems naive, but one must remember that, at the time, most wars were fought on isolated battlefields and that most of the casualties were the soldiers fighting on them. The carnage of the Civil War would largely remain on the battlefields, but many people, both within the country and overseas, were shocked by the amount of carnage they personally witnessed.

The Civil War was also the first war that was photographed to any large degree. While the camera technology of the day made it nearly impossible to capture battles as they happened, it was certainly able to take pictures of the dead, dying, and wounded. These photographs were also able to be seen almost immediately after the event, being displayed in newspapers, books, and exhibitions of the day, and the telegraph brought news of events on the battlefield almost as they happened. War was brought to people's front step during the Civil War, both figuratively and literally.

For about a decade before the war began, people all over the nation anticipated some sort of violent struggle between the North and South. While they did get a taste of the viciousness that could happen with the so-called "Border Wars" in Kansas and Missouri over the issue of slavery, virtually no one anticipated a nationwide conflict that would claim well over half a million lives.

It all started with Fort Sumter. The shock at the siege of Sumter was not at its casualty rate, as there were virtually none. No, the people of the country were shocked that the war, which had been brewing for some time, had actually begun. In the North, the shock was doubled by the fact that Sumter was a Confederate victory.

Three months after Fort Sumter, the armies of the North and the South clashed near the Bull Run creek near Manassas, Virginia, just some thirty miles south of Washington, D.C. The people, common soldiers, politicians, and many of the officers of both armies believed that once the "other side" got a taste of their "fighting spirit" and strength, the war would likely come to a rapid end.

Famously, people from Washington took trains and coaches out to the battlefield, where the armies, which were small at this point in the war, were massing, to watch the Rebels be defeated and then come to their senses and surrender. Instead, they saw the Federal troops defeated and had to join them in a panicked rout back to Washington.

Those in the South rejoiced over their victory, but they realized a number of things: they weren't strong enough to assault Washington, their soldiers and officers needed much more training, and that the war was not going to end any time soon.

A couple of smaller battles had been fought before Bull Run; their casualties numbered in the double digits. At Bull Run, just under five thousand men were killed or wounded. At Hatteras Inlet, after the First Battle of Bull Run, there were just over seven hundred casualties. At Ball's Bluff, Virginia, there were just over one thousand casualties. At Belmont, Missouri, there were nearly 1,500. At Mill Springs, Tennessee, there were 671. Forts Henry and Donelson in Tennessee saw a combined total of 17,517 casualties, the vast majority of which were Confederate prisoners. Wounded men accounted for most of the figures in the other casualties listed above. The total number for these battles was 26,195 men killed, wounded, missing, or taken prisoner.

By the time of Shiloh, many people had started to understand that the war was going to last much longer than they had initially believed but perhaps not *much* longer. And although the war had been bloodier than expected, people understood that, for the lack of a better phrase, "war is war."

The Strategic, Political, and Military Situation before Shiloh

The main Union Army in the East before Bull Run was commanded by Ohio General Irvin McDowell. His complete defeat at the hands of General P. G. T Beauregard led to his dismissal and the appointment of General George B. McClellan, who, like many of the higher-ranked officers of the Civil War, had fought in the Mexican-American War (and, in McClellan's case, with distinction). McClellan's skill in organizing the Department of the Ohio and his leadership of a small contingent of troops at the victory at Philippi (in what was to become West Virginia in 1863) on June 3rd, 1861, led to both rapid fame, as Philippi was the first land battle of the war, and rapid advancement.

McClellan was appointed the commander of the Military Division of the Potomac, meaning he was in charge of all Union troops in the Washington area. In August, this became the Army of the Potomac. McClellan was in command of the largest Union force, and he was second in military authority only to the famed hero of both the War of 1812 and the Mexican-American War, General Winfield Scott.

McClellan, even before the Civil War, had a reputation in the army as an excellent organizer and trainer of men. He also possessed a tremendous ego ("tremendous" might be an understatement), which only grew larger with the victory at Philippi, the adoration of the people of Washington, who greeted him as some sort of savior, and his appointment to command the largest section of the Federal army. His favorite nickname, which he encouraged but scarcely earned, was the "Young Napoleon." His troops also knew him fondly as "Little Mac," for he stood at about 5'8", which was actually just short of average at the time.

McClellan was indeed a great organizer and trainer of officers and men. Throughout his time in command, his troops seemingly adored him. He kept them well clothed, well fed, and, most glaringly, out of harm's way when Lincoln and others pressed him to lead his troops against the Rebels.

In the war's beginning stages, General Scott and his staff formulated a plan to subdue the Confederacy, which they dubbed the Anaconda Plan. Federal forces, which were greater in number on land and sea than the South, would pressure and attack the Rebels at all points: in the east near Richmond, down the vital Mississippi River, and all along the coast of the Confederacy, limiting transport and supply. They would squeeze the rebellion to death like an anaconda.

McClellan disagreed with this plan, but until Scott's resignation, which happened due to his ill health and being pushed aside by Lincoln in favor of younger officers (like McClellan), he was unable to do anything about it. However, when Scott retired, McClellan was put in overall command of the Union armies, so he was able to formulate the strategy he believed would win the war. This would be a grand plan in the style of Napoleon, which aimed at defeating the Confederacy in one overpowering campaign.

This campaign, known as the Peninsula Campaign, called for the landing of a massive Federal army behind the main lines of the

Confederate Army in Virginia, south of Richmond. This Federal army would swiftly move up the James River Peninsula, seize Richmond, defeat the Rebel army, and end the war.

In many ways, the plan was innovative, but it was also impractical. The movement of so many troops down the Virginia coast would surprise no one (especially with the many Rebel spies in Washington), and the James River Peninsula was a relatively narrow piece of land that would allow a smaller force to hold back a larger one since the larger one would be unable to maneuver.

On top of all that, McClellan, for all his skill in training and supplying his men, turned out to be *extremely* cautious. Historians have debated the reasons for this, but many have landed on the opinion that his caution was due to his fear of losing his reputation. Once he arrived on the peninsula, McClellan began making incessant demands for more men, falsely believing that the Confederate force opposing him was at least as big if not bigger than his own 105,000 men and his many guns. For most of the campaign, the Rebel force was outnumbered by McClellan's forces, and had he been more decisive, he may have actually drove "onto Richmond!" (as the Union battle cry went). However, his delays and slow movement allowed the Confederates under General Joseph E. Johnston to reinforce and dig in. In the end, the Peninsula Campaign saw a series of hard-fought battles, some of which were won by the Union, but the U.S. forces never came close to Richmond.

After the Peninsula Campaign, which lasted from March through July of 1862, McClellan was relieved of his command of all Union armies, but he was left in command of the Army of the Potomac. His hatred for Abraham Lincoln, whom he vilified as a military "amateur" pushing him into battle before he was ready, only grew. For his part, Lincoln began to look for a replacement for McClellan, which he found in 1863 after McClellan's failure to pursue Robert E. Lee after the bloody Battle of Antietam on September 17th, 1862.

McClellan's successors as commander of the Army of the Potomac were Generals Ambrose Burnside, Joseph Hooker, and George Meade, respectively. Each of them had their chance to lead the Union to victory. Meade came close, winning the Battle of Gettysburg in July 1863, but he did not pursue and destroy Lee as Lincoln urged. He was replaced in the spring of 1864 by Ulysses S. Grant—the victor of Shiloh.

Chapter 2 – The Men and Their Weapons

The average age of the Civil War soldier was just under twenty-six years old, which is older than the bulk of the soldiers today. Most of them, especially those from rural areas and those from the South, had never been more than fifty miles from their homes if that. For this and other reasons, even in the North, most soldiers referred to themselves as residents of their state rather than calling themselves an "American." It was only sometime after the war was over that people began referring to themselves as Americans.

Most of the men had been farmers before the war, even though the urban population was beginning to grow by the start of the conflict. Within the Union ranks, some three hundred different trades/careers are listed, such as carpenter, surveyor, teacher, locksmith, mason, machinist, blacksmith, shoemaker, and teamster (those who drove wagons or transported goods). A number of them were lawyers or dentists, and some common soldiers were even local politicians or ministers (state and county politicians often secured an officer's commission for themselves, whether they had experience on the battlefield or not). The vast majority of soldiers were used to leading hard lives and fending for themselves. Aside from drills, uniforms, following orders, and, of course, getting shot at, army life could be much easier than relying on oneself for an income, and the fact that most soldiers had experience working with their hands helped too.

By the end of the war, about 25 percent (about 500,000 of 2 million) of the men in the Union Army were immigrants. That figure was less in the Confederacy, which was perhaps around 10 to 15 percent. The immigrants in the Union Army came from all over Europe (Europe was from where most immigrants came until well into the 20ᵗʰ century). The same held true in the Confederate Army, though it had a higher proportion of Irish and English immigrants within its ranks.

Hundreds of thousands of black Americans flocked to the Union banner to fight for the freedom of their fellows and, many times, family members in the South. Until the latter part of the war, blacks were limited to non-combat roles as laborers, which included the awful task of recovering bodies from the battlefield and burying them. The contingent of black Americans in the Union Army in Tennessee at the time of Shiloh held such roles. Of course, the enslaved blacks of the South were forced to work as laborers for the Confederate Army and as servants for many of its officers.

The uniforms of both sides varied, though there was more "uniformity" in the ranks of the better-equipped Union Army than there was in the Confederacy. Men from the North wore Union blue uniforms and a variety of hat styles, while the Rebels wore a patchwork (sometimes literally) of clothing. By the mid-point of the war, most Southern troops were wearing either the famous gray or perhaps the equally numerous yellowish "butternut" uniforms, with their own style of hat, although both sides began to wear the famous "kepi" by the end of the conflict. In April of 1862, the weather in western Tennessee was mild, but it was made worse by the fact that virtually all the uniforms were made of hot, slow-drying, heavy wool.

The Rebels frequently wore their own shirts and shoes (if they even had them) on the battlefield, and tragically, a number of Southern units still wore their state militia uniforms, which, unfortunately, were blue. On the Shiloh battlefield, perhaps hundreds of Rebel soldiers were wounded and sometimes killed by their own side, as they mistook them for the enemy.

What the average soldier carried with them depended on which army they were in. Generally speaking, Union soldiers were better equipped than their Confederate counterparts.

The typical Union foot soldier wore a belt from which hung a bayonet scabbard, a cartridge box, and a cap box ("caps" were the eraser-sized percussion charges that set off the gunpowder within the rifle). The cartridge box would hold about forty cartridges, which, for most of the war for most men, were paper tubes surrounding a Minié ball and black powder. (A Minié ball was actually a bullet-shaped lead projectile about half an inch wide and an inch or so long; the name came from its French inventor.) The cartridge box was usually lined with tin to help keep the contents organized. Each cartridge box had a pocket or pouch for a cleaning kit. Union soldiers carried anywhere between sixty and eighty rounds of ammunition.

Cavalry and artillerymen had less equipment for both mobility and necessity. In the fight at Shiloh, the cavalry played a smaller role than in some of the larger battles to come.

Unlike the Rebel soldiers, who generally carried their belongings in a cloth bag or tied-up blanket (unless they could get their hands on Union equipment), the men in blue carried a cotton or canvas knapsack that was most often painted black in order to stiffen and waterproof it. A blanket or shelter-half (half of a pup tent—the other half was carried by a comrade) was strapped to the top of the knapsack. At times, overcoats were also carried on the top of the knapsack. Additionally, a canvas bag or haversack was worn over the shoulder in which a soldier would carry food, personal items, coffee, and extra ammunition, among other items. These were also often painted to help keep the contents dry, and they contained a removable liner, for, after a time, the sack would begin to smell from the bacon, coffee, and tobacco carried within. Rebel soldiers grabbed Union haversacks whenever they could.

Every soldier carried a canteen. Early canteens were made of two pieces of tin with a pewter spout and a cork stopper. Most canteens were carried or were encased in a cotton or wool cloth, which would keep water cool and helped to prevent noise. Union canteens were also prized by Rebel soldiers, but early in the war, the canteens on both sides were notoriously flimsy.

Soldiers carried a knife, spoon, and maybe a fork, as well as a tin cup and perhaps a small frying pan or canteen half for cooking. Issued rations were most often salt pork or bacon and hardtack, a hard, dry biscuit or cracker that could last ages and tasted like it.

A wide variety of weapons were used during the Civil War. Like almost everything else, the industrialized North produced more and better weapons, with the possible exception of larger cannons, than the

South. For a surprisingly long time, the men in gray used their own personal weapons brought from home. At Shiloh, most Rebel troops had never seen combat and were not able to be properly equipped. A great many carried shotguns or even old flintlocks from the Revolutionary War period. A handful even showed up with pikes or farming scythes.

However, most men at Shiloh, whether they were from the North or the South, carried the same or similar equipment as their comrades in other theaters of the war. Until close to the war's end, most men carried a muzzle-loading rifled musket. The advent of rifling (etching spiral grooves inside the barrel) meant both increased range and accuracy.

For those of you wondering why Civil War units lined up in rows and often fired at each other in standing positions, here are the answers. Firstly, until the advent of rifling, musket barrels were smoothbore, meaning it was just a simple tube. This meant limited range and limited accuracy, especially when you consider that many smoothbore weapons were made individually, not from prefabricated molds. To increase the effectiveness of these weapons, men were massed together. Within one hundred yards or so, this "wall of lead" was bound to hit something, at least most of the time.

However, with the advent of rifled barrels, which oftentimes came with sights, the effective range of these weapons increased manyfold. An average shot could hit a man-sized target with reliability at about three hundred yards away or even more. Sharpshooters might even hit something seven hundred to eight hundred yards away. This made the massing of the troops into the tight formations we see in Civil War books, movies, and re-creations a deadly error, and this tactic accounted for the high casualties at Shiloh.

An average soldier might load, fire, and reload his muzzle-loading weapon two or three times a minute. During the war, the self-contained bullet, with its own metal casing, powder charge, and projectile, was developed. Rifles now increasingly loaded at the breech, near the hammer. Even single-shot breech-loading weapons were faster than muzzle-loaders. Within a short time, rifles and carbines (a shorter barreled variant) began holding a number of rounds within them, making rapid fire possible. The famed Winchester rifle of the Old West was modeled on the Civil War-era Henry repeating rifle, which could hold sixteen rounds—fifteen in the tubular magazine that was under the barrel and one in the chamber, which was exceedingly dangerous since the weapon had no safety mechanism. To make things worse, dropping the weapon or jolting the hammer might cause a dangerous misfire.

Officers, cavalrymen, and some artillery soldiers carried pistols, which also came in a wide variety, some of which were actually variations of muzzle-loaders. Toward the end of the war, many of the pistols were quite similar to modern revolvers but oftentimes fired a larger caliber, making them quite deadly at close range.

The size and slow-velocity of Minié and round musket balls meant that, very often, wounds above the elbows or knees were fatal, and they usually blew a large hole open upon exiting the body.

Even deadlier was the artillery of the Civil War. At Shiloh, guns ranged from quite large 24-pound siege guns (named for the weight of the ammunition) to smaller 3- and 5-pounders. The armies of the Civil War also used mortars, which had a high trajectory, making them ideal for siege work (dropping shells over high walls), but very few if any mortars were used at Shiloh. These weapons bore little resemblance to modern mortars, as they were short, thick, and made of solid iron.

The cannons that were used at Shiloh and elsewhere during the Civil War fired a variety of ammunition. There was solid-shot, which is exactly what you think—a solid iron ball. There were explosive shells, hollow iron balls filled with black powder with a fuse that was cut to lengths depending on range. Spherical case-shot was similar to explosive shells, except they were filled with iron balls that would disperse upon explosion. Canister-shot was essentially a giant shotgun shell filled with iron balls, nails, scrap metal, or even rocks. Canister was used for close-range work, up to 250 yards. Double canister is just as you might imagine: two canister shells loaded at once. At Shiloh and other battles, canister was used to stop charges and break up formations.

If you've seen any movies about the Civil War, one of the most ubiquitous scenes is that of the army field hospital with its bone saws, screaming, bloody bandages, and piles of amputated arms and legs. Actually, it was at Shiloh that the first designated field hospital was located. It was a canvas tent with open sides and a couple of tables. It was not until after Shiloh and its horrible casualties that work began on developing a functional medical corps and hospital system. Until then, medical assistance took place wherever surgeons (or what passed for them) happened to be. Frequently, these were local homes. This occurred at Shiloh, and makeshift hospitals were set up on the Union steamboats that brought reinforcements down and across the Tennessee River.

Chapter 3 – Officers

Major General Ulysses S. Grant was the commander of the Army of the Tennessee at Shiloh, and he was also in overall command of the battle for the Union. At this stage of the war, Grant was a rising star, despite rumors of his heavy drinking. He had just won the Battles of Fort Henry and Fort Donelson on the Cumberland River northwest of Nashville, which allowed the Union to subdue those key Confederate strong points and protect the river traffic in northern Tennessee/southern Kentucky at a relatively low cost of Union lives. As a result of this and a Union drive into central Tennessee toward Nashville, the Confederates lost Kentucky to the Union and much of central and northeastern Tennessee.

Grant was born in Ohio in 1822, and he was raised in Illinois. He was the son of a tanner who believed his son would not amount to much. Grant's father couldn't be blamed, though, as his son showed virtually no interest or talent in anything except horses and riding, at which he absolutely excelled. To give his son direction, his father managed to secure Ulysses an appointment at West Point, where he graduated in the middle of his class in 1843.

In 1846, the United States went to war with Mexico. During the Mexican campaign, Grant, who did not agree with the US cause against Mexico, was assigned as regimental quartermaster of the 4th US Infantry, and he excelled at supply and logistics. He also saw combat at Palo Alto, Resaca, and Monterey, where he distinguished himself in a now-famous ride under fire to deliver a request for ammunition from surrounded troops. During the Mexican-American War, he became acquainted with a number of men he would both serve with and fight against in the Civil War, most famously the future Confederate commander Robert E. Lee.

When the war ended, Grant, who by this time was married with a growing family, held a variety of posts in the East and Midwest, but when he was sent west to California and the Oregon Territory to hold distant and boring posts, he fell into alcoholism. During the Civil War, rumors of Grant being drunk rose from time to time, but it's believed that the only case in which he truly drank to excess was during the long, slow siege of Vicksburg on the Mississippi River in the spring and summer of 1863, a year after Shiloh. At no time was Grant ever accused of being drunk during a battle or at a crucial moment.

Grant quit the army in 1854 and attempted to make it in a variety of businesses and farming; however, all of these attempts failed. The outbreak of the Civil War saw him working as a clerk in his father's saddlery in Illinois. He volunteered for the war effort, and due to his West Point and Mexican-American War experiences, he was shortly made colonel and, a month later, in August 1861, brigadier general. In the fall of 1861, Grant forced Confederate forces to retreat from Paducah, Kentucky. In November, he engaged the Rebels in Missouri and Kentucky, suffering a defeat and winning small victories while also making a name for himself in Washington, especially with President Lincoln, who was suffering from a plethora of generals who had no fight in them. Lincoln liked Grant's pugnacity.

In February 1862, Grant won the Union's first major victories at Forts Henry and Donelson while commanding the Army of the Tennessee. At Fort Donelson, the Confederates within the fort asked for surrender terms. Grant's reply? "Nothing less than unconditional surrender will be accepted." From that moment on, Ulysses S. Grant, or rather "U. S. Grant," was known as "Unconditional Surrender" Grant. Through February and March, Grant gathered men and supplies and, along with Union Western commanding general Henry Halleck, devised a plan to seize the key rail lines in Corinth, Mississippi, just south of the Tennessee border, about 120 miles east of Memphis.

Grant with an uncharacteristically long beard, which he trimmed just before Shiloh.
https://commons.wikimedia.org/wiki/File:Ulysses_S_Grant_as_Brigadier_General,_1861.jpg

Under Grant's command in his campaign to cut the key rail lines at Corinth were a number of other general officers: Lewis "Lew" Wallace (who would write the epic novel *Ben Hur* after the war), Don Carlos Buell (whose Army of the Ohio had just driven the Confederates out of southern Kentucky and the key cities of Clarksville and Nashville), Benjamin Prentiss (who had been a lawyer in Illinois before the war and was a Mexican-American War veteran), another Wallace (this one "W. H. L" for William Hervey Lamme, whose wife made her way to the battlefield to be with her husband), Charles Smith (whose division was probably the best-trained in Grant's army, many of whom had not seen combat), and Stephen Hurlbut (a native North Carolinian who had moved to Illinois before the war).

However, one general stands out from the others: William Tecumseh Sherman. Sherman had just rejoined the army after what was called "a severe bout of melancholia," which we know today as serious mental and emotional depression. Some in the army even called him insane, but Sherman had served with Grant before. He was actually his senior officer by date when they were both brigadiers. Grant and Sherman would be the Union's equivalent to Robert E. Lee and Thomas J. "Stonewall" Jackson, as both pairs of men seemed to know each other's thoughts seemingly before they were spoken and trusted one another implicitly.

In the case of Sherman and Grant, some have surmised the close bond between them stemmed from Sherman's defense of Grant when rumors of his drinking stalled his career just before and early in the war. Grant was one of the few men willing to take Sherman into his command after his serious bout with depression, which lasted about six weeks. Another of Sherman's supporters was the overall Union commander in the West, Henry Halleck, whom Sherman, a West Point graduate, had met during the Mexican-American War.

Sherman was tall, high-strung, and sometimes indecisive before battle, but during the battle, he, like Grant, seemed to develop a sort of preternatural calm, especially when others around him were panicking. When Sherman came to the battlefield at Shiloh, he was in command of some of the greenest troops in the Union Army, some of whom were more than a little leery about having a "crazy man" commanding them.

Sherman in the popular Napoleonic pose of the time, sometime after Shiloh.
https://commons.wikimedia.org/wiki/File:General_sherman.jpg

Southern Men

The men of the Confederate Army of the Mississippi were commanded by General Albert Sidney Johnston, another West Pointer who had graduated two years behind Confederate President Jefferson

Davis, with whom he was good friends. Johnston was a Kentuckian, but he had moved to Texas and took part in the Texas War of Independence. Although he joined as a private, he quickly moved up the ranks to become a senior brigadier general by the end of the war.

An event during this time may actually have cost Johnston his life almost thirty years later at Shiloh. He fought a duel with a fellow general and was shot through the hip, causing nerve damage that caused most of his right leg to go numb. At Shiloh, he was shot behind the right knee, but he paid it little mind until he nearly fell off his horse from the loss of blood—the bullet had severed a branch of his femoral artery, and he bled to death.

Before he met his fate at Shiloh, Johnston was known as the "Man of Three Republics"—he had fought for Texas, serving as its secretary of state during its short independence, the Federal army, and, finally, the Confederacy. Johnston was considered by many in the South to be its greatest general (that is before the rise of Robert E. Lee), but before Shiloh, he had been pushed ever southward by Ulysses S. Grant. At Shiloh, Johnston and his fellow general, P. G. T Beauregard, formulated a plan to push Grant's army against the Tennessee River and destroy it for good.

Painting of Johnston done at the start of the Civil War.

Beauregard, who had seen to the surrender of Fort Sumter and who had commanded Southern troops at Bull Run, thought himself the equal of Johnston, at least in rank, and superior to him in ability. During the Battle of Shiloh, Beauregard took over after Johnston's death, but a series of key mistakes by both generals may have cost the South the battle. Beauregard led troops throughout the war, in both the East and the West, and survived the conflict. He became a very rich man in New Orleans after the war, helping organize a scheme for the Louisiana lottery, successfully patenting a series of inventions for trolley cars, and becoming a novelist.

At Shiloh, Johnston and Beauregard commanded a force that included units under the command of Leonidas K. Polk (who had been an influential Episcopal bishop in Louisiana before the war), William J. Hardee (known as "Old Reliable"; he was born in 1815 and fought in the Second Seminole War in Florida and the Mexican-American War), John C. Breckinridge (a Kentucky politician and non-combat Mexican-American War veteran who was the youngest vice president in United States history, serving under James Buchanan, and who went on to become the last Confederate secretary of war), and finally Braxton Bragg (who also fought in the Second Seminole War and in Mexico with heroism, saving the unit under the command of one Jefferson Davis, with whom he became fast friends; in fact, Bragg's friendship with Davis may have saved his career during the Civil War, for he could be both competent and grossly incompetent and was known for arguing with just about everyone over everything. At one point later in the war, Confederate cavalry commander Nathan Bedford Forrest, who played a small role at Shiloh, threatened his life).

Chapter 4 – Prelude to the Battle

It was obvious to virtually all of the men in the Confederate Army of the Mississippi that the Union's next move would be to seize the railroad hubs and storage facilities at Corinth, Mississippi.

Corinth, Mississippi, is just south of the Tennessee/Mississippi border where the north-south Mobile and Ohio Railroad and Memphis and Charleston Railroad meet. Of the two, the Memphis and Charleston was the more important, for it was the only railway that led from the Gulf of Mexico to Richmond, the capital of the Confederacy. Cut that line, and the supplies and men going east to west (and vice versa) would have to go by wagon, which would both increase supply times and likely decrease their amount. The Union plan was to sever the western part of the Confederacy from the eastern part and to control the Mississippi, which would allow them to regulate the north-south passage of supplies and cut off the western Confederate states of Texas, Louisiana, and Arkansas from the rest.

Confederate spies and scouts had sent reports stating that the Union Army of the Ohio under Don Carlos Buell had been ordered to march west to rendezvous with the Army of the Tennessee under Grant. If that happened, the Union would outnumber the Confederates in the area by about two to one or more. As it was, Johnston was able to concentrate about fifty-five thousand men for the coming battle.

The Rebels took the idea of losing Corinth so seriously that they summoned virtually all of their troops stationed in Louisiana north to Corinth, leaving (unbeknownst to the Federals) New Orleans wide open.

Among these troops was Brigadier General Daniel Ruggles's artillery. He was born in 1810, graduated from West Point, and fought in the Second Seminole War and in Mexico, where he became acquainted with many of the men on the battlefield of Shiloh, including U. S. Grant. He had also fought with Albert Sidney Johnston during the Mormon Uprising in Utah. Ruggles would play a key role on the first day of Shiloh.

Similarly, General Leonidas Polk, who oversaw two divisions, was summoned from the fortified but poorly located Columbus, Kentucky, which he had seized in an attempt to prevent Union control of the Mississippi and which was now almost completely behind enemy lines.

Also joining the forces converging on Pittsburg Landing were Tennessean Benjamin Cheatham's some three thousand men. Benjamin Cheatham was a hard-fighting officer from Nashville who had also fought in the Mexican-American War and who, after the Civil War in his old age, would supervise much of the landscaping at Arlington National Cemetery, Robert E. Lee's former home.

In the middle of March, Grant began to move his forces southward. His headquarters were to be at Savannah, Tennessee, about nine miles north of the battlefield. When he arrived in Savannah, he set up his headquarters in William H. Cherry's mansion. Cherry was a pro-Union Tennessean, of which there were many, though most were located in the eastern part of the state.

When Grant arrived in Savannah, he found Union Brigadier General Charles Ferguson Smith's troops. Smith's forces were located on both sides of the Tennessee River, so Grant ordered them to be brought over by some of the 170 steamboats that he had taken upriver. The next day, Grant began deploying his troops southward. Five divisions would land at Pittsburg Landing (named after a whiskey maker named Pitt, who sold his product to the rivermen on the Tennessee before the war) about nine miles upriver from Savannah (the Tennessee River flows from south to north, so "upriver" is actually moving southward, against the current). One of Grant's divisions, under Lew Wallace, would be stationed to the west of Savannah on the western side of the river at Crump's Landing. In total, Grant had just under forty-three thousand men under his command.

Grant's superior, Henry Halleck, was concerned that Grant might do something rash before Buell's troops made their way to him, so he ordered Grant "to avoid a general engagement." Grant replied that he would not engage the enemy but that it would likely be impossible to avoid contact with the Rebels as he marched toward Corinth. Perhaps this made Halleck a bit nervous, for he reiterated sometime later that Grant and his generals were not to move until Buell arrived. "By all means keep your forces together until you connect with General Buell. Do not let the enemy draw you into an engagement now." Buell's forces numbered about thirty thousand men. When they did arrive, Grant would have the numerical advantage.

This fact was known to Johnston and Beauregard, who decided that rather than wait for Grant to besiege them in Corinth with twice as many men and more guns, food, and other supplies, they would attempt to surprise him at Pittsburg Landing, cut him off from the river and Buell, and destroy him. Once that was done, they could turn on the smaller forces of Buell and deal with him as well.

Speed was the key. But the Confederates were faced with a number of problems before they could get to Pittsburg Landing and fight Grant.

The Confederate forces near Corinth were made up of green troops, many of whom had had very little training at all. Although this problem plagued the Union as well, the Confederates suffered from it more. Even the basic commands of the complicated group maneuvers were new to them, and they were expected to march over twenty miles and enter a fight against a general who was on a winning streak.

Late on April 2nd, 1862, Johnston and Beauregard got word that Buell's army was approaching Savannah. Beauregard told Johnston, "Now is the time to go," for if Buell united with Grant, their plans were over. Johnston agreed, and the two set the ball in motion. They had hoped to be joined by General Earl van Dorn's army, which was somewhere on the other side of the Mississippi in Arkansas, but the generals in Corinth could not wait any longer. Either Van Dorn hadn't been found by the messengers they sent out, wasn't coming, or couldn't come or make it on time.

Johnston's plan was a good one. His orders for the men under his command were as follows: "In the approaching battle, every effort should be made to turn the left flank of the enemy, so as to cut off his line of retreat to the Tennessee River and throw him back on Owl Creek [a nearby wide and swollen body of water that would be impossible to cross in battle] where he will be obliged to surrender." Johnston hoped to get his army squared away (fed, supplied with ammunition, etc.), move out at dawn on the 3rd, march the twenty-plus miles, and attack Grant at Pittsburg Landing on April 4th.

His units were to march to a junction called Mickey's about eight miles south of Pittsburg Landing, overnight there, and attack the next morning, on April 4th. Even though Johnston was nominally in command, he and Beauregard seemed to have split duties, with Johnston making sure the plan was set and that the wheels were turning and with Beauregard planning the line of march and its coordination.

Johnston and Beauregard had about 28,000 men with them at Corinth, and these would be joined by about 12,000 more, which would all converge at Mickey's. General Bragg commanded 16,000 men, and General Hardee had just over 6,700. Breckinridge brought his corps that numbered 7,200 men, and Benjamin Cheatham brought 5,000 from the northwest.

The Confederate forces numbered just over forty thousand men (including some four thousand cavalry), which was about equal to Grant's force. Conventional military wisdom called for the attacking force to have at least a two-to-one advantage over the defenders, but in most situations during the Civil War, this was a luxury the men of the South simply did not have. The population of the Union states was twenty million. The population of the Confederacy was eight million, and while the Rebels were quite successful in raising an army much larger than should have been possible (after all, the bulk of their labor force consisted of millions of enslaved people), Confederate officers often relied on maneuvers, surprise, and unorthodox tactics to offset the Union's numerical superiority. It would have to be this way at Shiloh too.

With thousands of green troops at a time when orders were passed by written notes that were handed off personally or came by word of mouth, the CSA camp was slow and uncoordinated as it moved out on April 3rd. If you've watched movies about the Civil War or even the Napoleonic Wars, not much is said about the skill and timing needed to coordinate a march of twenty miles, much less an attack, especially at a time with very archaic communications systems. Of course, it would not be a very exciting movie. In order to reach the battlefield in a way in which troops can stay with their units, the order of battle deemed most effective by their generals had veteran troops arriving first, with their support, ammunition, and artillery right behind them, followed by less experienced troops, etc. Another question for the commanders would be which general did they want as the "point of the spear" of their attack? Perhaps there were veteran units commanded by a general who excelled at defense but who was hesitant on the attack, while another more inexperienced unit was led by more aggressive officers, etc.

Making things worse, it was spring in Tennessee, and while it had not gotten overly warm yet, the rain was a problem. It was not raining on April 2nd, but the roads were still sloppy from prior rainfall, which slowed things down before the men could even approach Mickey's. All of this combined to get the Confederates off to a very slow start, the first of many misfortunes that may have cost the Rebels the battle. By the close of the day on April 3rd, the lead Confederate forces set up camp some miles short of Mickey's. Making things worse, the road leading back to Corinth was clogged all the way back to the town with the rest of the army. Men had to fall out by the side of the road and rest as best they could.

The next day, Friday, April 4th, the day originally designated for the attack, brought rain—and lots of it. The ground was already wet, but now, it had become a quagmire. The roads in the rural area were all dirt roads and wagon tracks, and soon, they dissolved into nothing but mud. The route to Pittsburg Landing became a veritable swamp, which made walking difficult, not to mention horse-drawn wagons and cannons. The effort to move just a few miles did nothing but make the men tired.

Worse still, many of the men had already gone through the three days' rations they had been given the day before. Hunger from the exertion, the cold rain, boredom, and the weight of the rations all combined to cause many of the men to consume what they had on them, and they would go into battle on an empty stomach, which would have consequences during the fight.

It kept raining, delaying things another day, and on the night of April 5th, Johnston walked into a meeting of his commanders (Beauregard, Polk, Bragg, and soon to be joined by Breckinridge) and discussed the situation. Although they had been initially fired up for the attack, both Beauregard and Bragg were now against it. They suggested to Johnston that since Union cavalry and other scouts had engaged some of the Confederate pickets (small forces sent out to guard/watch the approaches to the main camp), Grant must know they were there and probably already prepared fortifications. Bragg and Beauregard argued that if that was the case, then an attack would be futile, and the Confederates needed to come up with another plan.

Johnston and Polk disagreed. Scouts, spies, and civilians in the area had reported that Grant's men were not entrenched anywhere and that the Union Army was still at Pittsburg Landing. What's more, Buell had not joined them yet. After some deliberation, Johnston gave the order. "We shall attack at daylight tomorrow!" Since the battle, many believe that Johnston was overly concerned with his reputation. His forces had been driven south by Grant, he had sustained two large and humiliating defeats, and the Northerners were driving into the heart of the Confederacy. After he gave the order, Johnston strode outside and met his brother-in-law, Brigadier General William Preston, and said, "I would fight them if they were a million." Perhaps Johnston was too carried away.

In actuality, the civilians, scouts, and spies reporting to Johnston were correct. Grant and his generals, particularly Sherman, had no idea that the Confederates were only a few miles away. Practically all of the Union commanders believed that the reports of a large Confederate concentration at and around Corinth meant that there would be a hard fight ahead when the Union men assaulted that important rail junction. They dismissed a number of reports coming in that told them the Confederates were much closer than that.

In Grant's mind, he would assault Corinth in overwhelming force, cut the Confederacy in half, and perhaps end the war. Also on his mind were Halleck's orders to not provoke a fight with the Rebels until Buell's army had united with Grant's. Therefore, the scouts and pickets sent out by Grant and his commanders did not venture very far from the main camp near the Tennessee River; they went just far enough to make sure the Rebels weren't too close but not far enough to perhaps accidentally run into a larger Confederate force and provoke a battle. Grant was so sure that no Confederates were "north of Corinth" (as his friend Sherman put it) that he hadn't even had his men dig in, thinking this might cause them to think defensively and worry that their commander had turned into a copy of one of those Union commanders in the East. Anyway, he planned to move out for Corinth soon.

Even so, some of the Union pickets reported hearing large groups of men in the distance and saw large groups of cavalry go by between wooded thickets not far to the south. In actuality, despite orders to the contrary from Johnston and most Confederate officers to keep quiet, many of the green troops, eager for their chance to "whup those Yankees," shouted, joked, and played the drums; some even blew trumpets or bugles. Little skirmishes between small groups of men in the area of Pittsburg Landing had been going on since the 3rd, and on the afternoon of the 4th, Union troops reported being fired on by a Confederate cannon. These reports were dismissed as local skirmishes with Confederate scouts sent to probe and see if Grant was moving toward Corinth. Even Sherman, known later in the war for his aggressiveness, dismissed the reports as the product of inexperienced officers' overactive imaginations, replying to one, "Oh, tut, tut! You militia officers get scared too easily."

On the morning of April 6th, 1862, with dawn appearing faintly on the horizon, the Confederates began to move into place for their attack on Grant's positions near Pittsburg Landing. On the Union's right and the Confederate's left stood a little log Methodist church, which had been built nine years before. It was called Shiloh, Hebrew for "place of peace."

Chapter 5 – The Battle

Sherman's troops were on the right flank of the Union line west of the Shiloh church. On that line was one of the nervous officers that Sherman was referring to in his quote above. This officer was Colonel Jesse Appler, who commanded the 53rd Ohio Regiment. Appler was too old to be on a battlefield, and he was the nervous type, but on Saturday afternoon, he had sent pickets farther afield than most of the other Union officers because of that nervousness. His troops were green and untrained, but they knew Confederates when they saw them, so they came back to Appler, saying that they had been fired on by a "line of men in butternut clothes," which they had. Those Confederate troops were the pickets of General Hardee's division. More reports were dismissed by other Union commanders as the fears of untried men. Still, Sherman did send Grant, who was rehabbing at Cherry Mansion in Savannah, having sprained an ankle the day before, a message, saying that he believed that two regiments, some cavalry, and a few cannons were about two miles away. He proposed capturing some Rebels and sending them back to Grant for questioning. Later on Saturday, Sherman wrote another dispatch to Grant, worded in the language typical of the time: "I have no doubt that nothing will occur today more than some picket firing...The enemy is saucy, but got the worst of it yesterday...I do not apprehend anything like an attack on our position." Interestingly enough, Sherman mentioned to a nearby reporter that he did think danger was near. The reporter asked Sherman why he did not report it, to which the tall, red-headed general replied, "Oh, they'd just say I was crazy again."

At 4:55 a.m. on Sunday, in the middle of the Union line, another officer was feeling the hairs on the back of his neck stand up. Colonel Everett Peabody, an engineer and railroad executive before the war and who was now in command of the 25th Missouri Volunteer Regiment, was alarmed by a report given by his cavalry commander, Major James E. Powell, which stated that an astounding number of Confederate campfires were seen not far from their position. Peabody ordered Powell to take about three hundred cavalry troopers and reconnoiter the area.

At the edge of a field about a half-mile from their lines, Prentiss's troopers ran headlong into the men of the Confederate 3rd Mississippi Infantry Battalion, commanded by Major Aaron Hardcastle. This was part of the brigade commanded by Brigadier Sterling M. Wood, which included men from Tennessee, Alabama, and Arkansas. The Rebels fired on Prentiss's dismounted men and fell back. The Federals moved forward, firing a volley, until they saw what no one had suspected—about nine thousand Rebels in gray and butternut, kneeling on a rise just ahead. Just then, one of the Mississippi men fired and killed Lieutenant Frederick Klinger. He would be the first casualty of what would become the bloodiest day of the war to that point.

The Confederates advanced on a narrow front as they approached the Union front lines. Hardee's corps marched in two ranks, one unit behind another, which was followed by the horses, wagons, and men of the artillery straining to pull heavy guns on the muddy dirt roads. Then came Bragg's large corps made up of five brigades, which were also in ranks of two. These were followed by the men of Polk's corps, who formed deeper ranks about a mile behind, and these were followed by Breckinridge's men, whose troops would serve as a reserve to go where and when they might be needed most. From the point where the Mississippi men met Powell back, the Confederate Army stretched almost two miles to the rear.

To the rear of Powell's fight with the Confederate vanguard was Colonel Peabody, who ordered reinforcements to be sent forward. But as they moved toward Powell, they were greeted by the sight of his retreating troopers, who were, in turn, followed by the mass of the Confederate Army of the Mississippi. At that, the officers in Peabody's camp ordered the alarm to be sounded, and drum rolls pealed through the Union camp. As they fell into some sort of order and prepared their weapons, their commanding general, Benjamin Prentiss, rode up to Peabody, yelling to be heard over the commotion. "Colonel Peabody, I will hold you personally responsible for bringing on this engagement!" To which Peabody replied that he was always responsible for his actions. It was lucky for the Union that Peabody had sent Powell forward, for if he had not, the first thing greeting the Union men in his camp would have been thousands of fired-up Rebels.

On the Confederate side, General Beauregard, who was getting the lay of the land and was familiar with the road conditions, still wanted to call off the attack, especially after knowing the Yankees had been alerted. At this point, it was too late. By the time orders went out and the men pulled back and sorted out, it's likely the Union would have been upon them. Instead of being on the attack against mostly unsuspecting troops or in Corinth in fortified positions, the Rebels would be on open and unfamiliar ground, with green troops attempting to fall back under fire. No, Johnston would have none of it, and he ordered Beauregard and the army to press on. "Tonight we will water our horses in the Tennessee!" he exclaimed.

Johnston told Beauregard to remain in the rear and organize the advance and direct supplies and reinforcements as they would be needed. He would advance with the troops and help coordinate the attack, which, as he had telegraphed Jefferson Davis earlier, would consist of "Polk in the left, Bragg the center, Hardee the right and Breckinridge in reserve." Johnston's plan was for Hardee to advance up the line of the river to cut off the Union from the escape route across it while the rest of his forces pressed the Union eastward in a large vise. For his part, it seems that Beauregard was on board with part of that idea, but he wanted to sweep the Union men eastward against the river and destroy them. As you can see, coordination of the Confederate command was lacking at Shiloh.

It was made worse when Albert Sidney Johnston rode forward with the attack. It was textbook, then and now, that an army commander should not put himself in harm's way, especially at the start of a battle. He should have remained in the rear, assigned aides to ride forward, and coordinate the Rebel attack from a safe position. No one is exactly sure why Johnston took the action he did on April 6th, and what's more, he followed the troops on the far Confederate right (the Union left) at the point farthest from the rest (and the majority) of his army. Perhaps he thought he should be at what he considered the lynchpin of his plan, cutting off the Union from the river. Maybe he thought that his presence would spur his men on; after all, he was a popular commander. Or perhaps he was eager to be in the field when he got his revenge against Grant for the defeats at Forts Henry and Donelson. Whatever the reason, he left Beauregard, who was hesitant about the attack and had different plans, in command and moved forward, at one point in the battle sending his own personal physician to the rear to aid wounded men and giving his own tourniquet to a wounded man on the field.

On the Union right, where Brigadier General William Tecumseh Sherman's 5th Division was positioned and where the nervous Colonel Appler of the 53rd Ohio had been raising the alarm for days, men started streaming northward from where Appler and his men had been hearing ever increasing and approaching fire. One man with his arm badly mangled ran past Appler and his aide, Lieutenant Ephraim Dawes, screaming, "Get into line! The Rebels are coming!" Appler ordered the men around him forward to form a skirmish line and sent another message to Sherman. Rearward, Sherman had had it with Appler's nervousness, and when the messenger returned to the older man, that was made clear. Sherman replied, "You must be badly scared over there." The timing of Sherman's message could not have been more ironically perfect, for as Appler and Dawes heard Sherman's reply, they saw hundreds of men advancing on their right, polished gun barrels glinting in the glare of the rising sun.

At that, Appler exclaimed, "This is no place for us!" and sounded the retreat, which, despite the colonel's semi-panic, was exactly the right call to make. After retreating back some distance from their camp, Appler's men took up a good position on the top of a bush-covered rise and waited for the Rebels to come closer.

Sherman knew that Confederates were in the area, but he was convinced that what Appler saw was simply a reconnaissance in force. Nonetheless, he rode forward to see for himself. When he arrived at Appler's position, he looked through his binoculars and realized that Appler was right, but before he had time to react, a lieutenant named Eustace Ball yelled out to him, "General, look to your right!" Just then, some Rebel sharpshooters rose up about fifty yards from his position and opened fire. Sherman exclaimed, "My God! We are attacked!" and threw up a hand to protect his face as the Rebels fired. Sherman's orderly, Private Thomas Holliday of the 2nd Illinois Cavalry, took a fatal bullet and fell from his horse. Sherman was wounded in the hand, and as he rapidly backed away, he told his nervous colonel, "Appler, hold your position, I will support you," then galloped off. Sherman's behavior was unusual, but he would lead his men bravely and smartly for the rest of the battle.

Appler did hold his position for quite a while. The Confederates mounted a number of attacks across the rough ravine in front of his position. These men were led by an outstanding Southern general named Patrick Cleburne, who had immigrated from Ireland and had fought with the British Army before doing so. Cleburne would go on to fight in some of the major battles to follow in the West, but that morning, he and his troops found themselves struggling against muddy, swampy terrain covered in tree stumps and roots on that ravine in front of the 53rd Ohio. This caused his formation to split into two sections, with Cleburne in command of the one thousand men (the 23rd Tennessee and 6th Mississippi) in front of Appler, with the rest of his brigade getting scattered through the thick woods, something that was beginning to happen throughout the Confederate line.

Appler's men opened up on the Southerners as they entered the former Union camp. Behind his riflemen, the 1st Illinois Light Artillery opened fire on the Rebels. Cleburne later reported, "Musketry and artillery at short range swept the open spaces between the tents, with an iron storm that threatened certain destruction for every living thing that dared to cross." The 23rd Tennessee broke under the fire. Cleburne rallied about half of the men from the Tennessee brigade and half from the Mississippi brigade and moved forward, screaming the notorious "Rebel yell." Another blast reduced his ranks even further, but the Rebels kept coming, even though they were being destroyed in the process. After the second push by the Rebels, Appler called a retreat, and many of his men ran away in panic, though two companies of men remained in position under the command of Lieutenant Dawes.

All across the Confederate left (Union right), the Rebels came on and on, but the Union men under Sherman on the far right and Prentiss to his left fought desperately to hold their ground. The Rebels had hoped that Hardee's men would break through the Union lines, but that was not happening. Bragg's corps, with nearly sixteen thousand men, moved to the left to press the attack.

If you ever visit the Shiloh National Battlefield, perhaps the first thing that will strike you is its size—it's very small, only 5.8 square miles. Within this space, eighty thousand men were crammed together in fields, woods, and ravines, fighting to the death. No wonder the death toll was so high. When walking the grounds, it is hard to imagine eighty thousand men fitting into the area, much less fighting, but they did.

As the battle grew in intensity between 6 and 7 a.m., Ulysses S. Grant was taking breakfast at the Cherry Mansion in Savannah just a few miles away. He heard the rumble of guns and walked out onto the porch of the house to listen. He turned to his men, limping past them on his sprained ankle, saying, "Gentlemen, the ball is in motion. Let's be off." Before he went aboard his personal steamboat, the *Tigress*, he sent two notes for reinforcements: one to Buell, urging him to hurry, and the other to Brigadier General William Nelson, whose 4th Division of the Army of the Ohio was already filing onto the eastern bank of the Tennessee. Grant ordered Nelson to move south along the east bank opposite Pittsburg Landing, where some of the many steamboats with his forces would meet Nelson and bring them across the river to join the fight. This may have been an error on Grant's part because he could have ordered Nelson's troops to be brought on board the ferries at Savannah so they could be steamed upriver (remember, the Tennessee flows south to north) to Pittsburg Landing rather than have them march south for nine miles first, but that is what happened.

Pittsburg Landing today looking north toward Savannah. Courtesy Matthew Gaskill.
Chris Light, CC BY-SA 4.0 <https://creativecommons.org/licenses/by-sa/4.0>, via Wikimedia Commons https://commons.wikimedia.org/wiki/File:Tennessee_River_(Pittsburg_Landing).jpg

Grant's personal riverboat, the Tigress (center), at Pittsburg Landing shortly after the battle.

Before Grant got to Pittsburg Landing, he stopped just a short ride away at Crump's Landing, where he had stationed Lew Wallace and his 3rd Division and told them to prepare to move. Wallace told Grant that he had heard cannon fire and that he had made his men ready, but Grant did not give him orders to move at this time. He likely should have, for later in the day, a series of confusing events involving Wallace, his reception of spoken over written orders, and his unfamiliarity with the terrain would lead to his delay in getting to the battlefield.

Farther south, General Prentiss and Colonel Peabody were taking the brunt of the Confederate attack. General Johnston had arrived and ordered the Rebels to mount a massive bayonet charge across about three hundred yards of relatively open field. Though they sustained high casualties and the Union men fought hard, the Rebels' charge, which was accompanied by thousands of men giving the notorious "Rebel yell," broke the men in Prentiss's position, causing many of them to panic. These men, soon to be joined by others in Federal units nearby, fled all the way back to Pittsburg Landing. Nothing could stop them, and nothing, from threats to calm reassurance, could get most of them to return to the front lines. Worse still, the men from Prentiss's division, many of them bloody with their own blood or the blood of others, ran through units coming up from the rear, sowing panic among a good many of them, especially among the green troops. "We're cut to pieces! The Rebels are coming! We're whipped!" were only some of the cries that went up. (As a side note, in the bibliography, you can find a link to an old newsreel of very old Confederate veterans giving the crowd a much appreciated "Rebel yell.")

While the Southerners victoriously pushed Prentiss's back in the center and sent hundreds panicking to the rear, they may have also cost the Confederacy the battle. On the march to Shiloh, many of the untrained and ill-disciplined men had gone through their rations and had not had anything to eat for over twenty-four hours. The shock and quickness of their attack had been such a surprise that the men in Prentiss's camp (almost two brigades of them) had just woken up, which means hundreds of cook fires were still burning with pots full of soup, bacon, biscuits, and hot coffee. At that point, hordes of hungry Rebels stopped in their tracks and began to loot the Union camp. Not only did they help themselves to the Yankees' food, but they also began looting personal belongings that had been left behind and even engaged in debates over whether Southern or Northern women were more attractive.

Even General Johnston, the highest-ranking Confederate soldier in the West and the second-highest in the whole army (Adjutant and Inspector General Samuel Cooper was the highest), could not get the Rebels moving again. When he saw one of his officers emerge from a Union tent with an armful of loot, he scolded him, saying, "None of that, sir! We are not here for plunder!" The officer gave Johnston a chastened look, and the general then picked up a Union tin cup and said, "Let this be my share of the spoils for the day." Johnston held the cup and used it as a pointer for the rest of his life, which was soon to be coming to an end.

Though many of Prentiss's men had panicked, he and his officers were able to gather together about one thousand men along an old wagon track dividing a dense thicket to the rear and slightly east of his original position. At about that time, Union general Stephen Hurlbut sent two of his brigades to aid Prentiss along what became (and is now) known as the "Sunken Road." His third brigade was sent to reinforce Sherman's forces on the right.

If you refer to the map a few pages back, you'll see that Prentiss's original position was in the center of the Union line. When his position was lost, Sherman was forced to order his brigade commanders to pull back, lest the Rebels drive past the Union left and catch the Yankees in a vise. This was at about 9 a.m., and the battle had been going on for a good four hours already. Sherman gave an aide this message: "Tell Grant if he has any men to spare I can use them. If not, I will do the best I can. We are holding them pretty well just now. Pretty well; but it's hot as hell."

At this time, Grant was sending messages to Lew Wallace to "hurry up your command as fast as possible," but a series of misunderstandings delayed Wallace's movement, and when he did move, he took the wrong road. A march that should have taken him two hours at most ended up taking nearly seven. However, though Wallace's men did not take part in the battle on Sunday, they and Nelson's troops, who were also being hurried by Grant but did not arrive until sunset, would be fresh for the fight on Monday. They had twenty thousand fresh men, plus what Grant already had against the Confederates, who were fully committed with no reinforcements available.

Throughout the morning, on the Rebel left and center, the back-and-forth fighting and repeated charges, combined with the thick undergrowth and woods, smoke from the guns, and the confusion that comes in every battle, caused the Confederate forces to become intermingled. Commanders lost their men and vice versa. Men from Mississippi were fighting in units made up of Tennesseans, with different combinations like this happening all along the line. The Rebel generals conferred in person or through messengers and decided, after some time, that commanders would no longer be responsible for their units but for those men who fell within certain areas. Even this was ineffective to a large degree, and the chain of command broke down. This happened to a lesser degree in the Union ranks, but by noon, the fighting at Shiloh had become a "soldier's fight," with lieutenants, sergeants, corporals, and veteran privates leading the men nearby.

Despite Johnston's plan, most of the fighting took place in the center and left of their line. The original plan called for the main Rebel thrust to move near the river to cut off the Union line of retreat and force their surrender or annihilate them. However, as the battle evolved and as the confusion grew, more and more units from both sides followed the most basic of orders: go where the firing was. In the morning and early afternoon, most of the fighting was done at the center and left. What's more, the units that were assigned to push along the river were unfamiliar with the area, and between the thick growth and the deep ravines, which were oftentimes filled partly with water, the Rebels' field of view was limited. They could not see the river, but they believed they were pushing toward it, but this was because their maps were aligned incorrectly. Had they been able to continue their push forward later in the day, they would have ended up a few hundred yards inland, far from their objective.

In the center of the line, the 1,000 men under General Prentiss, which had combined with the roughly 1,500 reinforcements under the command of General W. H. L Wallace, took up positions in the woods in front of the Sunken Road. After a short lull, in which both sides attempted to reorganize their men and come up with a strategy going forward, the fighting in the center picked up again around 12:30, and it soon became absolutely ferocious.

At 12:30, Confederate colonel Randall Gibson moved his 13th Louisiana Infantry brigade (of Bragg's corps), along with what men he gathered, and launched the first of what would be about a dozen Confederate attacks on Prentiss's position. The first attack, which was met with thousands of rifles supported by cannons, was bloodily repulsed, as were the next and the next and the next. Soon, the Rebels in the area were calling this position the "Hornet's Nest" for the sound of thousands of rounds buzzing through the air.

One of the men in the Hornet's Nest was Colonel Peabody, who had ordered Major Powell forward earlier in the morning. Peabody sustained three wounds when a Minié ball hit him in the face, killing him instantly. Major Powell had also fallen by that time.

General Prentiss.
https://commons.wikimedia.org/wiki/File:General_Benjamin_Prentiss.jpg

Colonel Gibson.
https://commons.wikimedia.org/wiki/File:Randall_Lee_Gibson_(circa_1860).jpg

Colonel Peabody.
https://commons.wikimedia.org/wiki/File:Col-Everett_Peabody.jpg

Throughout the day, more and more Confederate troops were ordered to or gravitated toward the Hornet's Nest. Gibson's men moved into the Hornet's Nest three times, only to be cut to pieces. More and more Confederates then took their place. Along the Union right, General Stephen Hurlbut moved into position to prevent the Rebels from driving through a gap in the Federal lines, but by late afternoon, he was pushed back. On both sides of the Hornet's Nest, Rebel troops moved in, yet Wallace's and Prentiss's men held on.

This began to change at about 4:30 when Brigadier General Daniel Ruggles moved almost sixty cannons about three hundred yards from the Hornet's Nest. This was the largest concentration of artillery on the North American continent to that point. They opened at this relatively close range, sending explosive balls and canister into the Hornet's Nest.

Ruggle's position today with the Hornet's Nest in the distance. Some fifty-five cannons sit at the Shiloh Battlefield today. Courtesy Matthew Gaskill.

By 5 p.m., elements of fourteen of the sixteen Confederate brigades on the battlefield that day began to surround the Hornet's Nest. By this time, the Union men inside the Hornet's Nest had begun to retreat from the area before the Confederate trap could close on them.

As they moved to the rear, Union General W. H. L Wallace was hit in the back of the head with a Minié ball, which exited from his left eye socket. The men surrounding him, including his brother-in-law, attempted to bring him to the rear, but the fighting was so severe and his wound so horrible that they had to leave him on the field for dead. Amazingly, the next day, he was alive found by advancing Union troops. His wife, Ann, had traveled to Savannah from Illinois before the battle, unbeknownst to her husband, and had arrived at Pittsburg Landing the night before, the beneficiary of a special pass signed by Ulysses S. Grant. Her husband's brigade chaplain brought her the news of Wallace's death as she attempted to aid wounded men on the many steamboats that acted as makeshift hospitals. The next day, she was told that her husband had been found and was still alive, but barely. For the next three days, she sat with him as he flowed in and out of consciousness. On the third day, he squeezed her hand tightly, looked at her with his good eye, and passed away.

As the Confederate ring tightened, Prentiss realized that escape was impossible and that a relief force was not coming. He and his officers ordered the men remaining in the Hornet's Nest to surrender. Over two thousand Union troops gave themselves up. Later that evening, Prentiss was afforded the treatment his rank was due and dined with Beauregard and other Rebel generals. Beauregard, who famously sent a telegraph back to Jefferson Davis that the Confederacy had won a "complete victory," chuckled when Prentiss told him and the others, "You gentlemen have had your way today but it will be very different tomorrow. You'll see! Buell will effect a junction with Grant tonight and turn the tables on you tomorrow." Prentiss was later exchanged for Confederate officers, and he fought on until he retired in 1863, feeling that, despite being lauded as a hero by Grant and the press, the desk-bound higher-ups had it in for him, as they kept posting him to camps away from the action.

At about the same time that evening, Confederate cavalry Colonel Nathan Bedford Forrest dressed some of his troopers in captured Union clothing and told them to scout the Union lines. He reported what they told him to his brigade commander, General Ronald Chalmers, that the Union was "receiving reinforcements by the thousands, and if this army does not move between this and daylight, it will be whipped like hell before 10 o'clock tomorrow." His report went up the line, but he heard nothing. At 2 a.m., he scouted the Union position himself and returned to camp, excitedly reporting what he had seen to General Hardee, who had been asleep. Hardee merely told Forrest to "keep a bright lookout" and rolled over. By all accounts, Forrest was mad enough to murder.

At 2 p.m., though, that was all in the future. On the Confederate left, General Cheatham's troops, along with elements of Bragg's corps, had begun pushing Sherman's and General John A. McClernand's forces back toward Pittsburg Landing. It was at this point that elements of the Confederates' left began to head toward the firing in the Hornet's Nest, but enough of them continued pressing the Union men on the left, back closer to the Tennessee River. As you can see from the last map,

Sherman's and McClernand's forces retreated toward Tilghman's Branch, a wide creek that was even fuller due to the heavy rains from the last days. The position was an excellent one for defense; in addition to the swollen creek, the Federals sat upon a steep rise leading up from the water on the other side.

After attempting to reorganize their troops, the Confederates began to assault Sherman's position across Tilghman's. Each time they were torn to pieces. It was there that the Confederate advance would halt later that afternoon.

On the Confederate right, which was supposed to have been the focus of the battle, fighting was taking place within a peach orchard (now known to history simply as the "Peach Orchard") to the left of Prentiss's position in the Hornet's Nest. These ten acres of blooming peach trees would have been the ideal spot for a picnic. The wind was blowing slightly, and peach blossoms were floating down to the ground. By the end of the day, the trees had been torn apart, the blossoms soaked with blood and trampled into the mud.

General Johnston had moved along the center of his line earlier in the day, attempting to organize attacks, instructing officers, and trying to make sure ammunition went where it was needed. By about 2 p.m., he was at the left of his line, pushing his men forward in an attempt to drive them between the Union men and the river, about half a mile to the east.

The men of General Breckinridge had attempted to push the Yankees out of the Peach Orchard quite a few times, but by the time Johnston arrived, the dead, wounded, and pieces of men from both sides littered the ground. Confederate officers were running about, trying to get their men in order for yet another attack when Johnston came riding up. He called out, "Men! They are stubborn! We must use the bayonet!" And as the men formed ranks, he rode in front of them, tapping each bayonet with his tin cup souvenir as he rode by. Then he moved in front of them, yelling, "I will lead you!"

Seemingly, Johnston's presence and his ability to organize and calm the officers lit a fire under the units in front of the Peach Orchard. He spurred his horse onward, and he and his men charged at almost full-speed into the guns of the Union men defending the area. The Rebels, whooping and howling the Rebel yell, were unstoppable this time. They tore through the orchard and began pushing the surviving Yankees backward, as the map below illustrates.

Just north of the Peach Orchard was a small pond. The men from both sides quickly gave it a name—"Bloody Pond." As the battle flowed around them, wounded men from both sides, some missing limbs, others with their entrails dragging behind them, pulled themselves to slake their thirst brought on by the loss of blood. Many died at its banks, and soon, the entire pond was red from the hundreds of men lying around it.

After leading the charge into the Peach Orchard, Johnston came riding back to the Confederate rear, his shirt torn in many places from bullets that had whizzed closely by without striking him. One of his thigh-length riding boots had been struck in the sole so that its heel was flapping under Johnston's stirrup. At first, Johnston appeared to be fired up, then suddenly he reeled in his saddle. His aide, former Tennessee Governor Isham Harris, who had volunteered to be Johnston's aide, jumped onto Johnston's horse behind him, holding the general up with one arm. He asked, "General, are you hurt"? Johnston replied, "Yes, and I fear seriously." Harris took the general into a shallow ravine nearby and helped him off his horse. As was mentioned earlier, Johnston had left his personal doctor with the wounded at another spot on the battlefield and had also given his tourniquet to another soldier to aid a wounded comrade. Harris searched Johnston's body and couldn't find anything until he saw that the general's right boot was leaking blood. Johnston had been wounded behind the right knee. The numbness in his leg had caused him to either not feel it or dismiss it as a light wound, but the bullet had nicked a branch of the key femoral artery. Within minutes, he was dead. Albert Sidney Johnston was the highest-ranking officer of either side to fall on the battlefield in the entire Civil War.

The men of the Union fell back on the Owl Creek Ravine, north of the Peach Orchard. The ravine was over one hundred feet deep with a steep slope. There, they received reinforcements from Grant, including cannons that were loaded with canister and double-canister. In the assaults that followed, the few Confederates that managed to make it out of the ravine were blown off its slopes by short-range cannon and musket fire. Most of the men trying to dislodge the men in blue at Owl Creek were stopped cold in the ravine, many of them caught in a crossfire from hell where the ravine took a turn. Making things worse for the Confederates near the river were two Union gunboats, which began shelling them throughout the rest of the day and into the night.

All through the day, Grant wondered with increasing anger as to where Lew Wallace and his brigade were. He sent a messenger back to Crump's Landing in the late morning. It took him some time to find Wallace in the first place, and when he did, he was given the inexplicable reply that Wallace would only respond to orders in writing. Riding back to Grant, his messenger explained the situation to the general, who fumed and authorized his aide to write out orders to Wallace in his name. Two more messengers were sent back to Wallace to no avail—the general, whose troops fought well and were well led the next day, had taken the wrong road and would not arrive until after nightfall.

As night fell, the lead troops of Buell's army began pouring into Pittsburg Landing. General William "Bull" Nelson, who was broad and well over six feet tall, got off his ferry and became furious at the sight of over a thousand men at the landing, standing about, crying, laying down, or wandering about senseless—these were the men who had begun running from the field earlier in the day and who were joined by others throughout the battle. Nelson was absolutely mad with anger and waded into the crowd of men, striking some of them with the flat of his sword and threatening to begin shooting them. He even ordered his personal escort to draw sabers and "trample these bastards into the mud!" As this was happening, another Union unit was brought across the river, and as they attempted to disembark, they were stormed by the panicked men on the shore, whom they had to fight off with rifle butts. These men (units from Ohio and Illinois) actually made it to the front lines at Owl Creek, and their cannons helped to fight off the Confederate assaults there.

For his part, General Nelson sent a messenger to Grant, asking him for permission to begin shooting deserters. A call from General Grant to see him at his headquarters and the pleas of his aides calmed General Nelson down.

U. S. Grant had had a close call earlier in the day. As he was riding behind the lines to get an idea of the situation, a nearby aide had his head blown off by a shell. A splinter from that shell hit and cracked Grant's sword scabbard. Now, at about 6 p.m., Grant wondered whether or not General Buell meant to send more than just Nelson's troops across the river. He stood above Pittsburg Landing near his headquarters and pondered the situation. An aide approached him and waited for orders from Grant, who was talking to himself. The aide overheard him say, "Not beaten yet by a damn sight."

Grant didn't need to worry. All through the night, Buell's men came over the Tennessee River and set up camp near Grant's headquarters. At one point, however, some of his officers began wondering whether or not they would be better moving east across the river themselves and fighting another day. One of these was Sherman, who voiced doubts about the situation to other officers, but when he approached Grant at about 9 p.m., finding him quite a few yards from his headquarters, standing under a tree in the rain, he said nothing except to state the obvious. "Well, Grant, we've had the devil's own day, haven't we?" Grant barely looked up and said, "Yes. Whip them tomorrow though." Sherman dismissed all ideas about moving to the far side of the river after that.

Grant had taken his place under the oak because his headquarters and the area around it were full of wounded men, their limbs being sawed off by surgeons. The screaming and cries were more than Grant could take, and he had wandered off to be alone with his thoughts. Before Sherman came up, he had tried to get out of the rain and went back to his headquarters, but the screams of the wounded were just too much for him, so he returned to his place under the tree, lantern in one hand, cigar in his mouth.

That night, a thunderstorm struck the Shiloh area. Under the glare of lightning, troops saw and heard horrific things. One of those men was Confederate soldier Henry Morton Stanley, who was a Welsh immigrant in the 6th Arkansas Brigade. He had been captured toward the end of the day. As he sat with his fellow prisoners, he, like many others that night, listened to the moans and screams of the wounded in the field, and worse, he saw wild hogs feeding on the dead and nearly dead. Stanley would free himself from captivity by volunteering to join the Union Army, but he was discharged after suffering a serious illness. He then joined the Union Navy and served on board the USS *Minnesota* as a clerk. If his name sounds familiar, it's because he went on to become a world-famous explorer and found the lost Dr. Henry Livingstone, who had disappeared in his search for the Nile. Stanley's (supposed) famous line was "Dr. Livingstone, I presume?"

On the Confederate side, a sequence of serious mistakes were made. First was Beauregard's ill-timed telegraph to Jefferson Davis claiming "total victory." Next, many of the tired officers and men of the Confederacy simply dropped where they were or were ordered to move back to the rear, with some, namely Polk's men, going back near their starting point that morning. Worse, no real effort was made to organize the scattered men and units to prepare for a possible Union attack the next day, and no additional ammunition was brought forward, at least not to most of the units.

Conclusion

By the next day, April 7th, Ulysses S. Grant had forty thousand men at his disposal. Half of these men were fresh. Most of them were from Buell, the bulk of whose forces had made it across the river during the night. Just shortly after sundown, Lew Wallace's troops arrived after their unintended detour and were put into the line.

Against the Union's forty thousand men were about twenty-eight thousand Rebel troops, virtually all of whom were exhausted and ill-prepared for the Union counterattack, which began at about 6 a.m. For about two hours, the Rebels held the Yankees and even mounted two surprisingly savage counterattacks in the mid-morning, but the Union forces were too much for them. By about two in the afternoon, they had been pushed back past their original starting point, and Beauregard ordered them to fall back to Corinth. Grant's men did not pursue them until the next day, allowing the Southerners to escape to Corinth, which was besieged from April 29th to the 30th, finally falling into Union hands.

Over twenty-four thousand men were killed, wounded, or went missing at Shiloh, the worst toll of the Civil War up to that time. And despite the bloodshed at Gettysburg, Petersburg, and the other places fought in the South, the Battle of Shiloh still remained in the top ten of the war's bloodiest battles.

Shiloh showed the nation that the war was going to take much, much longer and be much bloodier than had ever been imagined. Immediately after the battle, many people in the North criticized Grant for the slaughter at Shiloh. Many in Washington pressured Lincoln to dismiss him, but the president replied, "I can't spare this man; he fights!" Of course, Grant went on to command all the Union forces from the beginning of 1864 to the war's end, and he also became the eighteenth president of the United States.

Both sides made glaring errors at Shiloh. The men of the South underestimated Grant's willingness to fight, they lacked discipline in their march toward the battle, Johnston should never have gone to the front as he did, and, most of all, the officers of the Confederacy let their men down by not reorganizing and resupplying their men at the end of the first day.

On the Union side, the overconfidence of Grant, Sherman, and others caused them to be surprised by the Rebel attack on April 6th. Had they dug in, perhaps more men would have lived, and the battle might have ended much sooner. The lack of Grant's, Wallace's, and Nelson's urgency in reinforcing Pittsburg Landing also cost lives. Still, the Battle of Shiloh was another Union victory, and it was especially important to them since the men in blue were being defeated time after time in Virginia and Maryland.

Part 5: The Battle of Second Manassas

A Captivating Guide to the Second Battle of Bull Run, A Significant Event in the American Civil War

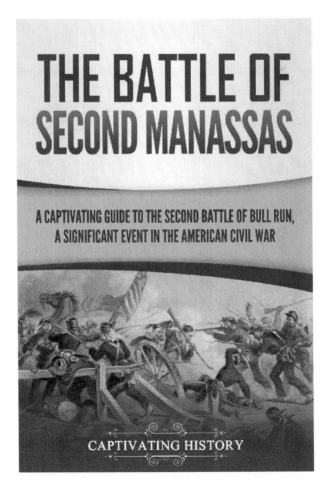

Introduction

Just a little over a year after the First Battle of Manassas, which occurred on July 21ˢᵗ, 1861, the Second Battle of Manassas unfolded, lasting from August 28ᵗʰ to August 30ᵗʰ, 1862. Second Manassas was fought upon the original battle site in northeastern Virginia near the Bull Run River and the strategic Manassas Railroad Junction. Unlike the first occasion, the troops on both sides were more seasoned and had battle experience. Generals and soldiers alike knew more about the horrors and outcomes of war, and their arrogance had been significantly reduced from the start of the Civil War in April 1861. In the Battle of Second Manassas, also known as the Second Battle of Bull Run in the North, the number of troops was doubled, but sadly, the ensuing casualties more than quadrupled. The Battle of First Manassas was the bloodiest and most intense conflict up to that point. The Battle of Second Manassas brought the Civil War to a new record of combative destruction.

Besides fighting on the same turf, other eerie similarities linked the Battle of First Manassas to the second one. The Confederates were triumphant in both, owing mostly to poor leadership on the Union side, which resulted in poor tactical decisions. The Federal forces (another name for the Northerners or Union Army) were technically fighting on familiar ground with a far larger force, and the odds had been overwhelmingly with them at the start of the fighting on both occasions. Also, similar to the year before, the losing Federal troops, fighting in swelteringly hot summer conditions, were routed back to Washington, DC, heavily hounded by the Confederate troops. A dramatic thunderstorm ensued in the days after Second Bull Run, something which had also occurred on what was dubbed "Black Monday," which followed the Federals' failure at First Bull Run.

Both the First and Second Battles of Manassas brought Union military careers to an end, as scapegoats for the North's failure were unjustly sought out and then penalized. The Confederates watched with glee as some of the Union's best leaders were axed in retaliation for essentially making good decisions, at least in comparison to the poor ones that came from their superiors, during the Battle of Second Manassas.

Also, both battles reinforced the North's and South's resolve to obliterate the enemy. What had started as a series of skirmishes in the spring of 1861 was now evidently a serious civil war, and the ideological and economic differences at the root cause of the war turned into a permanent bloody divide that would continue until the spring of 1865.

The Battle of Second Manassas opened a gateway for the Southerners to enter previously unchartered Northern territory, bringing the war to the doorstep of the Union's capital of Washington, DC. Defeat, as well as the approaching winter of 1862, turned the Confederates home, but the Civil War would rage for a further two and a half years.

Chapter 1 – Context of the Second Battle of Manassas

The American Civil War, which lasted from April of 1861 to May of 1865, mainly began over the issue of slavery. The American states south of the Mason-Dixon line (an imaginary line devised in the 18th-century and which divided the "North" from the "South"), which relied heavily on slave labor for their plantations, conspired to break from the Union and form their own government.

Eventually, eleven Southern states ceded from the existing thirty-four states of the Union between December of 1860 and April of 1861 to form the Confederate States of America. These states were North and South Carolina, Mississippi, Virginia, Florida, Alabama, Georgia, Louisiana, Texas, Arkansas, and Tennessee. (In 1863, West Virginia split from Virginia to join the Union.) The Confederate capital was created in Richmond, Virginia. The North remained part of the Union government, and their people became known as the "Yankees" to the Southerners (a term that formerly referred to Americans in general). The Southern slave states formed an illegal government led by President Jefferson Davis (1808–1889, an American politician who had served two terms in the US military before acting as the president of the Confederacy from 1861 to 1865).

Although the bombing of the Federal stronghold of Fort Sumter in Charleston, South Carolina, in April of 1861 by the Southerners had been the real start of the Civil War, the Battle of First Manassas (also known as the First Battle of Manassas or the First Battle of Bull Run) was the first official land engagement of the war. The First Battle of Manassas was fought on July 21st, 1861, in which approximately seventy thousand Union and Confederate troops faced a day-long confrontation around the Bull Run River in northeastern Virginia. (The river separates Prince William County to the west and Fairfax County to the east.) The Battle of First Manassas, which was ultimately a Confederate victory, was the biggest and bloodiest battle in the United States until that point, in which approximately 4,800 men lost their lives or were wounded. The Federal troops hightailed it back to Washington in shame, and President Lincoln's war office finally realized the enormity of the task ahead and that the war with the South was going to be long, bloody, and expensive.

The area near the First Battle of Manassas remained a crucial strategic node of fighting during the Civil War because of the Manassas Railroad Junction. This junction connected the Orange and Alexandria Railroad that ran west-east toward Alexandria on the Potomac River, which had a slave market, with Washington, DC. It also linked with the Manassas Gap Railroad, which ran northwesterly over the Blue Ridge Mountains into the Shenandoah Valley. The Shenandoah Valley was the agricultural heart for the Southerners since these fertile farmlands provided the food that was sent via the Manassas Railroad Junction to the South.

The Battle of Second Manassas is also referred to as the Battle of Groveton since there was much fighting near this hamlet, which was located about ten kilometers (six miles) northwest of Manassas Junction. Second Manassas unfolded on the west of the Bull Run River in Prince William County, extending from the Sudley Ford north along the Bull Run River to include Stony Ridge and the wooded area around Groveton to the west and then south to the crossroads around which the First Battle of Bull Run had unfolded. This crossroads was the intersection of the west-east Warrenton Turnpike that led to Centreville and crossed the Bull Run at Stone Bridge and the north-south Manassas-Sudley Springs Road. The fighting reached as far south as the Union Mills railroad crossing, ten kilometers (six miles) south downstream of Stone Bridge.

The location of the Battle of Second Manassas was within what was known as the Eastern Theater of the Civil War. This region included Washington, DC, Maryland, Virginia, Pennsylvania, and the coastal ports of North Carolina. (The Eastern Theater was one of five theaters during the Civil War. The main engagements of the war took place in the states south of the Mason-Dixon line, although fighting took place on the other side of the country as well in states like California, New Mexico, and Arizona.)

From April until July of 1862, the Federal Army, led by Major General George B. McClellan, the "Young Napoleon" (1826-1885, served two terms of service for the Union, the second during the Civil War, resigning in 1864 to run as a political opponent to Lincoln), was engaged in the Peninsula campaign as head of the main Union Army of the Potomac. This campaign was intended to be an amphibious pincer-like attack on the Confederate capital by using the two rivers that flank the Virginia Peninsula—the York and the James—to lay siege to Richmond. (The Virginia Peninsula extends from Richmond southeast toward the Atlantic Ocean.) In March of 1862, McClellan left a strong force to cover the capital but shifted a large amount of his army south to Fort Monroe on the tip of the peninsula, where the York and James Rivers met, which was about 161 kilometers (100 miles) southeast of Richmond.

In naval terms, the Peninsula campaign was a failure, but McClellan nevertheless managed to battle his way up the peninsula in a series of land engagements, eventually arriving near Richmond in late May. The Rebel troops (another name for the Southern or Confederate forces) had moved down from northern Virginia to defend the capital against McClellan, and from May 31st to June 1st, the Battle of Seven Pines (also known as the Battle of Fair Oaks or the Fair Oaks Station Battle) took place on the outskirts of Richmond. The Confederates stopped the Union from penetrating their capital, although technically, the battle was a stalemate.

During the Confederates' repulsion of the Union forces, leading Confederate General Joseph E. Johnston (1807-1891, a career soldier who served the United States from 1829 until changing allegiance to the South) was wounded and subsequently replaced by the more aggressive and tactical General in Chief Robert E. Lee (1807-1870, a career military man who served the US Army from 1829 before becoming part of the Confederate Army) in June of 1862. (Lee was one of the very patriotic US officials who agonized over joining the South and made his decision at the last moment, not wanting the war to proceed. Ironically, his military prowess would make him a powerful opponent to the North in the coming years.)

Lee and his newly reformed and renamed Army of Northern Virginia made a final repulsive onslaught of the Union forces on the Virginia Peninsula during the Seven Days Battles. The Seven Days Battles were a series of seven battles fought over seven days, which eventually drove McClellan's army back down the peninsula. These battles ended with the Battle of Malvern Hill on July 1st, 1862, officially ending the Peninsula campaign. (Malvern Hill lies twenty-six kilometers, or sixteen miles, southeast of Richmond near the James River.) Although tactically the Union won at Malvern Hill, McClellan ended his campaign farther down the peninsula than where he had started. Essentially, the Northerners had been repulsed.

The Seven Days Battles saw stunning casualties on both sides. Of the ninety thousand Confederates, twenty thousand were wounded, killed, or missing. Sixteen thousand Union soldiers were reported wounded, killed, or missing out of the 105,000 men who had been engaged. However, once Confederate General Robert E. Lee felt certain he had the Yankees on the backfoot and that Richmond was safe, he turned his attention to northern Virginia, beginning the northern Virginia campaign of July to September 1862 and, subsequently, the Maryland campaign (or Antietam campaign) in September of that year.

After his performance on the peninsula, General Lee reformed his Army of Northern Virginia into two major corps, commanded by James Longstreet and Stonewall Jackson, who were both crucial, well-known, and larger-than-life figures of the war. James Longstreet (1821-1904) had served the United States Army from 1842 as a major before joining the Confederacy as a general during the Civil War. (Longstreet was one of the few Southerners who rejoined the US government after the war, becoming a US diplomat.) Jonathan "Stonewall" Jackson (1824-1863) had served in the US Army since 1846, ending as a brevet major, before joining the Confederacy as a lieutenant general. He died shortly after the Second Battle of Bull Run at the Battle of Antietam after being accidentally shot by his own men and subsequently contracting pneumonia. Both Longstreet and Jackson had proved their military might during the first land engagement of the Civil War—the Battle of First Manassas—where Jackson had acquired his legendary nickname of "Stonewall" after having stood his ground against the Union in a superhuman effort of resistance on Henry House Hill.

As the northern Virginia campaign continued, General Lee sent his troops north toward the Federal capital of Washington, DC. Jackson formed the left wing, and Longstreet (known as Lee's "Old War Horse" or "Old Pete") formed the right. The Confederate cavalry unit under Major General J. E. B. Stuart was a division under Jackson. James Ewell Brown ("Jeb") Stuart (1833–1864) was a debonair cavalier who had a reputation for bravado, as well as efficiency, and he became a trusted aide to General Robert E. Lee. (Jeb rode with a crimson-lined coat and an ostrich-plumed hat that were stolen by Northern soldiers just before the Battle of Second Manassas while they tried to capture Stuart himself. Apparently, the Yankees were just as delighted to capture the man's costume as they were the man!) He was killed in action in 1864 but played a significant role in the Civil War.

Stonewall led four divisions, as well as the cavalry, three of which were under the command of Brigadier General Charles S. Winder, Major General Richard Ewell, and Major General A. P. Hill. Longstreet led five divisions north, with the leaders including Brigadier Generals Cadmus Wilcox and James L. Kemper, Major General Richard H. Anderson, Brigadier General John B. Hood, Brigadier General David R. Jones, and Brigadier General Nathan G. "Shanks" Evans.

In the meantime, the "Young Napoleon" had been trying to convince Washington that he needed the full force of the Federal Army behind him if he was to recommence an attack on Richmond. (He had sent a telegram to Washington on July 2nd stating that he had faced an army two hundred thousand men strong, which was completely untrue!) McClellan held his position on the Virginia Peninsula at Harrison's Landing, where his campaign had begun. The landing was on the northern bank of the James River, forty kilometers (twenty-five miles) southeast of Richmond and about ninety-seven kilometers (sixty miles) upstream of the open ocean. (The York River forms the northern tributary of the Virginia Peninsula and the James River the southern boundary.)

At Harrison's Landing, the Confederate Army was protected by Union gunboats positioned on the James River, but McClellan was refused his request for reinforcements. The Union government was not prepared to recall their armies for one southern campaign that would leave the capital of Washington, DC, vulnerable. Also, in the heat of summer, the threat of malaria and yellow fever from mosquitos in the wetlands of the peninsula was not worth the risk. On August 4th, 1862, the fiery McClellan was ordered to return his troops to northeastern Virginia via the James and then the Potomac Rivers.

President Lincoln had been opposed to McClellan's plan to re-attack Richmond and was more intent upon defending the Union capital, sensing that the fighting would move north from southeastern to northeastern Virginia. He was correct, and he had the foresight to appoint a new commanding general of the US Army, which had been McClellan's role until March of 1862. Major General Henry Halleck (1815-1872) assumed command of the Federal forces in July of 1862 and remained in that position until March of 1864. Halleck, also known as "Old Brains," was not only a military man but also a scholar and a lawyer. He was unpopular as a military leader and was replaced by Ulysses S. Grant (1822-1885, a military man, public administrator, and politician) who went on to lead the Union to victory in 1865 and then served as the eighteenth president of the United States from 1869 to 1877.

Lincoln also appointed one of his relatives by marriage, John Pope (1822-1892), as the commander of the newly formed Army of Virginia, which was pulled together in late June. The Army of Virginia was assembled from the remnants of other Union armies scattered throughout northern Virginia, the Shenandoah Valley, and Washington. (Eventually, the army would consist of three corps of more than fifty thousand men, but it was disbanded after the stunning failure at the Second Battle of Bull Run. On September 12th, 1862, the Army of Virginia was merged into the Army of the Potomac, never to be reconstituted.) Pope had been active in the Western Theater (specifically in Missouri and Mississippi) and had experienced successes, which led to a haughty attitude of bravado based on ignorance. He was unpopular with leaders and soldiers alike to such an extent that there was evidence of broad-based hatred against him. And his promotion by the president to commanding general of the main Union army above his superiors did not help matters!

Pope was placed in charge of the Army of Virginia in July of 1862, making himself even more unpopular, specifically with the commanding general of the South, Robert E. Lee, when he began terrorizing the civilians of northern Virginia, which was technically Southern territory that the Northerners dominated during the war. Lee labeled Pope as a "miscreant" who ought to be "suppressed," as he took food and supplies from local homesteads and threatened to execute prisoners of war, suspected traitors, and civilians alike. Pope also had a broader, politically enforced objective from his president to begin influencing the Southern civilians by using the incentive of alleviating the hardships they were experiencing as a result of the war. General Orders 5, 7, and 11 aimed to compensate food-producing farmers who were loyal to the Union, annihilate Confederate guerilla operations, and prevent civilian hostilities toward the Federals. Unfortunately, in many cases, these orders were taken too far by the Yankees, who used them as an opportunity to plunder, pillage, and punish innocent people and their property.

The 1st Corps of the Army of Virginia was led by Major General Franz Sigel (1824-1902, a German American soldier and revolutionary who recruited many German-speaking immigrants to the Federal Army), who replaced Major General John C. Frémont (1813-1890, who served three terms of service for the US Army) and had resigned in disgust upon the appointment of Pope, who was technically his junior in rank. The 2nd Corps was led by Major General Nathaniel P. Banks (1816-1894, a politician and serviceman during the war), and the 3rd Corps was led by Major General Irvin McDowell (1818-1885, a career army officer who had been held responsible for the Northern defeat at the First Battle of Bull Run and demoted). Troops from Washington under Major General Samuel D. Sturgis formed the reserves for the Army of Virginia, and three separate cavalry brigades, under Colonel John Beardsley, Brigadier Generals John P. Hatch, and George D. Bayard, were attached to the three military corps.

McClellan was ordered to join forces in northern Virginia with Pope to form a substantial army that would be about seventy-seven thousand men strong. McClellan's addition to the Army of Virginia eventually included the Army of the Potomac's 3rd, 5th, 7th, and 9th Corps. (The 2nd and 6th Corps were promised for later since the Potomac Army would take time to move north from the peninsula.) The four Potomac corps were led by Major Generals Samuel P. Heintzelman, Fitz J. Porter, William B. Franklin, and Jesse L. Reno, respectively. One brigade of the Kanawha Division (a detachment originating from the start of the war named after a western Virginian valley) under Colonel Eliakim P. Scammon also joined with the Potomac additions, specifically at the start of Second Bull Run. Pope spread his body of men out in an arc across northern Virginia.

The right flank was positioned under Sigel on the Blue Ridge Mountains at Sperryville, Virginia, eighty kilometers (fifty miles) west of Manassas, protecting the Shenandoah Valley. The Union center was positioned a few kilometers northeast of Sperryville under Banks, and the left flank under McDowell was posted to Falmouth on the Rappahannock River, just north of Fredericksburg—halfway between Washington and Richmond. Lee, with a mere fifty-five thousand men, knew when the Army of the Potomac began withdrawing from the Virginia Peninsula and that they were on their way to join the northern forces. As the leading general of the Confederacy, he could not afford for the Union to combine forces, so he planned to intercept McClellan on his way north.

By mid-July, Jackson's men were on the move north, but Lee waited another month until mid-August, once he had received intelligence that McClellan was on the move, to send Longstreet to join Jackson. By August 15th, Lee had dispatched most of his men from Richmond to confront Pope. Lee's intention, which he repeated at the Battle of Chancellorsville of 1863, was to pin the enemy from the front using Longstreet and send Jackson to pinion their rear, thus attacking them from both ends.

Chapter 2 – Prelude to the Second Battle of Bull Run

General John Pope's main purpose was to protect the Shenandoah Valley, as well as Washington, DC, from the enemy. He also needed to protect Aquia Creek, an inlet near the mouth of the Potomac River from where he expected George McClellan's troops to arrive. Also, Pope needed to detract from McClellan's movement north of the Virginia Peninsula, so he planned to move his troops toward Gordonsville. Moving his troops was a decision counterintuitive to laying a wide defensive position across northern Virginia, but Pope was also in an impossible situation, not knowing whether to remain on the defensive or move to the offensive. Gordonsville lies approximately 160 kilometers (100 miles) southwest of Washington, DC, and 106 kilometers (66 miles) northwest of Richmond. The settlement of Culpeper, forty-five kilometers (twenty-eight miles) northeast of Gordonsville, was to become a crucial node during August of 1862. Unfortunately, Stonewall Jackson had beat Pope to Gordonsville and had occupied it with more than fourteen thousand men (possibly up to eighteen thousand men) since July 19th. (Jackson's men had arrived via railroad.)

Having decided Richmond was safe from McClellan, Confederate General Robert E. Lee dispatched most of his troops from the Southern capital. By the end of July, Jackson had been reinforced by a further ten thousand men under General A. P. Hill (1825–1865, who served the US Army from 1847 before switching allegiance to the Confederacy and who was shot dead by a Union soldier a week before surrendering to the Union). Lee's intention was to disable Pope's army before McClellan could reach him. McClellan, who did not agree with his orders from Washington to return north, delayed his removal from the peninsula until mid-August, eventually leaving a single corps behind. The Confederates had also received intelligence stating that it appeared Union Major General Ambrose Burnside (1824-1881, a soldier, politician, and industrialist who served the Federal Army from 1847 until the end of the Civil War) was moving his troops from North Carolina to join Pope. (Burnside had played an important role in the Battle of First Manassas. His 9th Corps eventually joined the action at Second Bull Run under Major General Jesse L. Reno, 1823-1862, a career officer who was tragically killed later that year in the Maryland campaign by a rookie Union soldier.)

At the end of July, Pope moved his headquarters into the field, but instead of waiting for McClellan's reinforcements, the general dispatched some of his forces to Cedar Mountain in Culpeper County, from where he could launch cavalry raids on Gordonsville. Pope sent out one brigade and one cavalry unit from Nathaniel Banks's corps to move south on August 6th. Pope intended to eventually charge on Gordonsville to capture the rail junction and to simultaneously detract from McClellan's movements north. (Cedar Mountain is thirty-two kilometers, or twenty miles, northeast of Gordonsville and sixteen kilometers, or ten miles, southwest of Culpeper.)

In response, Jackson advanced toward Culpeper on August 7th, where the central 2nd Corps of the Union Army was beginning to coalesce. Jackson's intent was to protect central Virginia by attacking the Federal vanguard and weakening Pope's army. He also intended to capture Culpeper (specifically the Union stronghold at Culpeper Court House) before the three Federal corps united. This divide and conquer tactic had proved successful in Stonewall's previous Shenandoah Valley campaign in the spring of that year, but the sweltering heatwave in early August 1862, as well as poor military instructions, ultimately did not allow Stonewall to repeat his earlier successes in northern Virginia in the same manner.

An advanced cavalry unit sent by Jackson alerted the Union to the advancing enemy. Pope immediately ordered Major General Franz Sigel's 1st Corps to march south to Culpeper, and Banks's men assumed a defensive line on a ridge above Cedar Run (Cedar Creek), eleven kilometers (seven miles) south of Culpeper Court House and just to the northwest of Cedar Mountain. The Confederates crossed the Rapidan River on the morning of August 9th and entered Culpeper County. Upon approaching the enemy on the ridge, the Battle of Cedar Mountain (also known as Slaughter's Mountain or Cedar Run) ensued, mostly as a series of intense artillery fighting until 5 p.m. that day. Confederate General Charles S. Winder (1829-1862, a career military officer) was leading the left flank division and met his end when he was badly mauled by a Union artillery shell. His replacement, as well as general confusion amongst the Confederate units, resulted in the lack of a cohesive attack plan by the Southerners. The Northerners, under Major General Nathaniel Banks, took the opportunity to attack Jackson's troops before they could advance.

A Confederate counterattack led by Major General A. P. Hill pushed Banks's troops back over Cedar Creek. Despite fighting back, by 8 p.m., the Union was in full retreat but hotly pursued and under heavy attack from the Confederates. However, Jackson's overall advance on the Northerners at Cedar Mountain was stopped by the arrival of Brigadier General James B. Ricketts (1817-1887, a career officer) of the 3rd Corps Army of Virginia, as he covered Banks's withdrawal. By 10 p.m., the determined Stonewall Jackson finally called off the chase for several reasons, most importantly because he was alerted that not only were the remainder of General Irvin McDowell's troops due to arrive but also that Sigel would soon be upon the scene.

The Confederates won the day, but Stonewall's intentions of dispatching with the Union Virginia Army piecemeal would not be realized. The Rebels fell back south of the Rapidan River to Orange Court House, thirty-one kilometers (nineteen miles) south of Culpeper. Jackson remained in position for a few more days, but realizing that the Army of Virginia was finally together, he withdrew his men to Gordonsville on August 12th. The Battle of Cedar Mountain had been the first official engagement of the northern Virginia campaign, and it effectively shifted the area of focused engagement of the Civil War from the peninsula to northern Virginia. The battle was considered a slaughter, and of the almost seventeen thousand Confederate and eight thousand Union troops that were engaged, there were approximately four thousand casualties—killed, injured, or missing. Commanding General Henry Halleck no longer felt confident in Pope's approach on Gordonsville with the wild and unpredictable Jackson still on the loose. He called off the Federal campaign, giving Robert E. Lee the upper hand to direct the following course of the war.

By mid-August, General Lee came upon the opportunity he had been looking for when he discovered Pope's Army of Virginia (sixty thousand strong) positioned in the confluence between the Rapidan and Rappahannock Rivers northwest of Fredericksburg. But on the morning of August 18th, a copy of his attack orders was stolen by a division of the Union cavalry—the same raid in which Jeb Stuart was almost captured. Pope withdrew his army out of harm's way the next day to the northern bank of the Rappahannock, but Lee continued to poke at the enemy. Four days of skirmishes, lasting from August 22nd to August 25th, ensued, but Pope held his ground. These included the Battles of Waterloo Bridge, Lee Springs, Freeman's Ford, and White Sulphur Springs, resulting in a few hundred casualties in total.

Heavy rains had swollen the river and made it impossible for Lee to breach. General Pope knew that he had less than a week to wait for McClellan's reinforcements to arrive, potentially bringing his numbers to over 100,000 men. On the rainy night of August 22nd, Jeb Stuart's cavalry reconnoitered the area around Manassas Railroad Junction and plundered the vulnerable Catlett's Station just south of Manassas. They were unable to burn the premises because of the wet conditions, but they made quick work of taking what they could. A captured dispatch book alerted the Confederates to McClellan's imminent arrival. The pressure on General Lee to devise an alternative plan increased, and he decided to infringe upon Pope's advantageous position by cutting off the Union railroad supply line to Washington, DC.

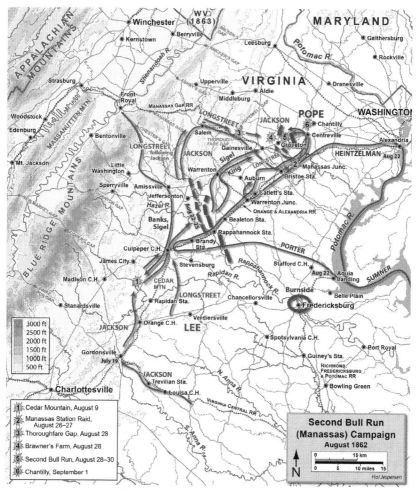

The northern Virginia campaign of Robert E. Lee's Confederate Army during August of 1862 that led to the Battle of Second Manassas (blue for Union forces, red for Confederate).

Hlj, CC BY-SA 4.0 <https://creativecommons.org/licenses/by-sa/4.0>, via Wikimedia Commons https://commons.wikimedia.org/wiki/File:Northern_Virginia_Campaign_August_1862.png

Lee conspired to send the intrepid Stonewall Jackson on an outlandish and daring feat north to circumnavigate the enemy in their protected position behind the river. Jackson was ordered to move beyond the enemy's front lines in a wide right flanking maneuver to the west, circling back down upon the Union's rear and effectively intercepting their clear route north, as well as cutting off crucial supply lines. Longstreet's wing was instructed to remain along the southern bank of the Rappahannock River to detract the enemy from Stonewall's movements. In the pre-dawn hours of August 25th, Stonewall Jackson's twenty-five thousand men embarked upon an eighty-seven-kilometer-long (fifty-four-mile) circling approach upon foot from the Rappahannock River, moving northwest and through the Thoroughfare Gap of the Bull Run Mountains. This loop essentially moved eastward to descend upon the Manassas Gap Railroad Junction, enclosing Pope's men within enemy territory.

It took Jackson less than forty hours to capture Bristoe Railroad Station of the Orange and Alexandria Railroad leading to Washington on August 26th. Bristoe was just five kilometers (three miles) south down the line of the most strategic rail node of the Civil War—the Manassas Gap Railroad Junction. The Confederates now held the rail link north, cutting off supplies and communication between the Yankees and their home turf. Not only was rapid communication via telegraph now stalled but so was the quick movement of all Union reinforcements south, including soldiers. Jackson's men were ordered to ransack the main Union supply depot at the Manassas Junction and burn what they couldn't steal to the ground. It was a daring and opportunistic attack, even by today's military standards. (Pope's men had previously led a raid to capture cavalry commander Jeb Stuart, who had managed to escape but left his famous cape and hat behind. These accouterments and other belongings, as well as his adjutant, were taken by the Yankees, which enraged Stuart. The cavalryman retaliated by plundering General Pope's headquarters at Catlett's Station—even farther south down the railroad—on August 22nd, making off with three hundred prisoners, $35,000 in Union payroll money, and other booty, including Pope's personal battle clothes and a copy of his attack plans!)

When General Pope received intelligence of Stonewall's infringement, he reacted immediately and chased the enemy to Manassas. Pope was emboldened by the idea of using the division in Confederate troops to first encroach upon Jackson and to then turn his attentions to Longstreet's thirty thousand men to the south. Technically, the odds of a Federal success in this maneuver were high—they outnumbered the Southerners by between one to two and one to four, depending on the military arrangements and the arrival of reinforcements.

But when Pope arrived at Manassas, the Southerners had already fled the scene, and Jackson was nowhere to be found. Reports reached Pope that the enemy planned to march upon the settlement and strategic

187

Union stronghold of Centreville, sixteen kilometers (ten miles) northeast of the junction across the Bull Run River. Jackson had, in fact, sent out several groups in mock feints to mislead the Union scouts. Without confirming the Confederate movements, Pope marched his full army toward Centreville to obliterate an enemy he knew was considerably less in number. But like a horse blinkered by a single goal, Pope had conveniently forgotten the remaining Confederate forces under Longstreet, who had moved north following Jackson. Pope also hadn't considered that Jackson was not on the march but rather lying in wait for the opportune moment.

As evening approached on August 28th, a column of Pope's men was west of the Bull Run River, across which the Warrenton Turnpike led over Stone Bridge to Centreville. The vanguard of Northerners was nearing the Confederate forces thought to be at Centreville. But Jackson's men were ready and waiting. The Southerners had set up their fireless camps along Stony Ridge near the village of Groveton, west of the Bull Run River. Stony Ridge lay north of the Warrenton Turnpike and northwest of the crucial intersection with Sudley Road, which eventually crossed the river farther north upstream at Sudley Springs Ford. The crossroads and surrounding lands had been the scene of the Battle of First Manassas a year before. When the Federal troops marched along the Warrenton Turnpike toward Centreville, they were completely unaware of the embankment of Confederates along their left flank, who were poised for action. The Union men were walking into a trap. Stonewall issued the orders, and the Battle of Second Manassas began.

Chapter 3 – The Battle of Second Manassas: August 28th–29th, 1862

General Robert E. Lee had anticipated the unimaginative John Pope's move north to Manassas, and once the Federals moved from the Rappahannock, he sent General James Longstreet in support of Stonewall Jackson—following the same circuitous route Jackson had taken from the enemy's grounds. The combination of Longstreet's and Jackson's troops would prove essential for a Confederate victory. Meanwhile, Jackson had cunningly secured his troops amongst the woods of Stony Ridge, and on Thursday, August 28th, Pope would spend an entire day unsuccessfully seeking out the enemy that he knew was somewhere near Manassas.

The unfinished railroad of the defunct Manassas Gap Railroad Company became strategically vital to the Confederates during the Battle of Second Manassas. The unfinished railroad ran south below and parallel to the wooded rise of Stony Ridge. The grading had been prepared in the late 1850s as an independent line to join Gainesville, just west of Manassas, to Alexandria on the East Coast. Work on the railroad had been suspended before the advent of the war for financial reasons, but the ground was laid for railroad construction, leaving a long trench line, which was ideal for warfare. The section where the ground was the most excavated became known as the "Deep Cut" as a result of Second Manassas.

Jackson's shenanigans around the Bristoe and Manassas stations on Wednesday, August 27th, had not been conducted entirely without conflict. Stonewall's rearguard unit under Major General Richard S. Ewell (1817-1872, "Old Bald Head" or "Baldy," a career US army officer who joined the Confederacy and was a key figure under Lee and Jackson) was attacked by Union forces near Bristoe Station during the afternoon, in what became known as the Battle of Kettle Run. The Union unit led by Major General Joseph Hooker (1814-1879, "Fighting Joe," a career US Army officer who served three military terms for the US, including in California) had advanced from Catlett's Station along the Orange and Alexandria Railroad, searching for the Confederate miscreants. Ewell put up a strong resistance before retreating to join the bulk of Jackson's troops at Manassas Junction. There were up to six hundred casualties in the Battle of Kettle Run—killed, wounded, and missing.

Also, on the 27th, Union General George W. Taylor (1808-1862, a career military man who served one term in the US Navy and two in the US Army) of the Northern 1st New Jersey Brigade was called west from Alexandria to deal with the skirmishes that were apparently ensuing around Manassas. Upon reaching Jackson's forces near the junction and realizing the full might of the enemy, the brigade made a hasty retreat back over the railway bridge at Union Mills, south of the Warrenton Turnpike. The Confederate forces chased Taylor's men back over the bridge in a rout during what is known as the Battle of Manassas Station. Union General Taylor died four days later from a leg injury sustained that day, but he was immortalized in the poem "The General's Death" by the modern Irish poet Joseph O'Connor.

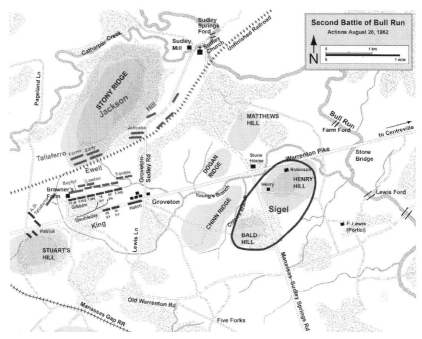

Arrangement of troops at the start of the Battle of Second Manassas on the evening of Thursday, August 28th, 1862, showing the unfinished railroad below Stony Ridge (red for the Confederates and blue for the Union).

Hal Jespersen, https://www.cwmaps.com/, CC BY 3.0 <https://creativecommons.org/licenses/by/3.0>, via Wikimedia Commons https://commons.wikimedia.org/wiki/File:Second_Bull_Run_Aug28.png

Stonewall's four divisions of men settled into the trees of Groveton Woods on Stony Ridge after they had plundered and burned all Yankee supply stations in and around Manassas Junction. Their encampments stretched from Sudley Church, where Sudley Road crossed the Bull Run River north at the Sudley Springs Ford to Groveton, three kilometers (almost two miles) to the southwest (very close to the old Manassas battlefield). Twenty-four hours later, in the early evening of Thursday the 28th, Jackson's quarry came to him when elements of Pope's army moved east toward Centreville, exposing themselves to Jackson's artillery.

The units of the Union column included those under Brevet Major General John P. Hatch (1822-1901, a career military man who led Brigadier General Rufus King's "Black Hat Brigade," who was absent due to epilepsy), such as General John Gibbon, Major General Abner Doubleday, and Brevet Major General Marsena R. Patrick. At about 6 p.m., General John Gibbon (1827-1896, a career US Army officer) was positioned around Brawner's Farm (home to the John Brawner family), south of the unfinished railroad and southwest of Stony Ridge. Gibbon was the chief of artillery for Major General McDowell, and he led the Black Hat Brigade of volunteers he had trained. (Gibbon was renowned for making them wear black hats and white leggings into battle, which his troops hated, and he awoke one morning to find his horse dressed in white leggings!)

The Black Hat Brigade was originally organized by Brigadier General Rufus King (1814–1876), who had served two terms of service with the US military, eventually resigning in 1863 because of his epileptic seizures. King had at first been responsible for the Black Hat Brigade, which was also known as the Black Hats, Iron Brigade of the West, and the King's Wisconsin Brigade. This brigade, made of the 2nd, 6th, and 7th Wisconsin Infantry Regiments, the 19th Indiana Infantry Regiment, and the 24th Michigan Infantry Regiment, was eventually incorporated into the broader division of the 1st Corps of the Army of the Potomac under King's command in March of 1862. (King had replaced McClellan in the role.) The Iron Brigade of the West fought entirely in the Eastern Theater of the Civil War, even though their members mostly heralded from states of other war theaters, particularly the Western Theater (the Midwest). This infantry brigade was renowned for its uniform dress, intense discipline, and tenacious fighting, but it also experienced the highest percentage of casualties in the war.

The Battle of Brawner's Farm began that evening as a prelude to the Second Battle of Bull Run when Jackson sent artillery fire whizzing over the heads of the Union around the turnpike. The ever-crafty and bellicose Jackson had ridden out earlier that day disguised as a farmer—much to the horror of his men—to assess the approaching enemy. Undetected, Stonewall returned to his men and announced an order to "Bring out your men, gentlemen!" The intrepid Stonewall knew he needed to draw the Union into a fight before they reached Centreville, where it was likely that the full might of the Union Army would rejoin once McClellan's men arrived on the scene.

Being an experienced artillerist, Union General Gibbon ordered a counter-fire from Battery B of the 4th US Artillery, and the crossfire had the desired effect of halting the forward movement of troops. Hatch's men were far to the front of the column, and Patrick's men at the back sought cover, leaving Gibbon and Doubleday (1819–1893, a career US

Army officer who had fired the first shot at the first engagement of the Civil War at Fort Sumter) to countercharge. Gibbon sent in 430 men of the 2nd Wisconsin Regiment, thinking he was attacking Confederate Jeb Stuart's cavalry, but in fact, the Northerners approached directly at Stonewall's main veteran infantry (the 800 remaining men of the previous 2,500 who had formed Jackson's "stone wall" at the First Battle of Bull Run). Pope had informed his men that Stonewall was already at Centreville, meaning the Yankees were less than prepared for Jackson's antics.

Gibbon sent his men back through the woods to sneak up the hill in an effort to capture the Rebel cannons. They met with the enemy in a series of indecisive skirmishes, as other units joined the fight on both sides. At first, Jackson's eight hundred under Colonel William S. Baylor (1831-1862, a lawyer and soldier who served the Confederacy) fired upon them in Brawner's orchard. Then, Jackson sent in three Georgia regiments under Brigadier General Alexander R. Lawton's brigade. (Jackson circumnavigated Major General Ewell's command.) As Gibbon added his 19th Indiana and the 6th and 7th Wisconsin Regiments (also part of the Black Hats), Jackson responded by sending Brigadier General Isaac R. Trimble's brigade to support Lawton.

The foes exchanged heavy volleys of musket fire as the men loaded and reloaded their weapons without pause for two hours. Jackson sent in horse artillery under Captain John Pelham (1838-1863, a skilled artilleryman who had never served in the US Army and was killed at the Battle of Kelly's Ford in March of 1863 in Culpeper County), which fired at the enemy from ninety-one meters (one hundred yards) away. Eventually, the Federals were overwhelmed three to one (6,200 men against 2,100) and separated from the enemy by a distance of a mere 46 meters (50 yards) in places. As one line fell back, another immediately took its place and unleashed a fury of firepower.

Doubleday sent in the 56th Pennsylvania and the 76th New York Regiments, which arrived after dark but were still repulsed by the Rebels. The battle ended at about 9 p.m., with Gibbon's men retracing their steps back through the woods below the farm. The Battle at Brawner's Farm was a stand-off, and the approaching darkness ended what Gibbon referred to as "a long and continuous roll."

Jackson had made his first move against the lagging Federal column near Groveton (also referred to as the Battle of Gainesville), but the resulting skirmish was inconclusive, as King's four thousand Union forces withdrew to Manassas Junction (although, as noted above, Hatch was the one who actually commanded them during this battle). In fact, the Confederates had sustained heavy losses in the savage fight, and two division commanders, Brigadier Generals Taliaferro and Ewell, were seriously wounded. (Ewell lost his left leg as a result of the battle and was out of action for the next ten months.)

William Booth Taliaferro (1822-1898) was a legislator and Confederate general during the war, and he was one of the few Southerners who served the US government both before and after the war. Brigadier General William E. Starke (1814-1862, a businessman who joined the Confederates for the war under Stonewall Jackson but was killed later that year in the Battle of Antietam) took over from General Taliaferro. During the Battle of Brawner's Farm, one in every three soldiers had been shot. Jackson's brigade had lost 40 percent of its men (1,250 men), and Gibbon's brigade lost between a third and half (1,150 killed, wounded, captured, or missing). However, the brief battle on the evening of the 28th revealed the Southern position, which drew the Union out for a battle over the next two days, exactly what Jackson had desired.

Meanwhile, Major General Longstreet, along with General Lee, were making their way toward Stony Ridge via the Thoroughfare Gap (Chapman Mill or Beverley Mill), arriving on the afternoon of August 28th, just one day's march away from joining the remainder of the Confederate Army. The Thoroughfare Gap ran through the Bull Run Mountains, about thirteen kilometers (eight miles) northwest of Gainesville. A few days earlier, Stonewall and his men had passed unencumbered through the gap—flanking their enemy on the right—but Longstreet was met by Union General Rickett's division, which blocked the eastern end of the pass.

James B. Ricketts had been sent to forestall Longstreet while Pope dispatched with Jackson at Manassas. Longstreet's leading Confederate division under Major General D. R. Jones (1825-1863, a career soldier who served in the US Army before joining the Confederacy) fought Ricketts near Chapman Mill, which changed hands three times in this intense set of skirmishes. The 1st Georgia Regulars fought the 11th Pennsylvania Regiment in a narrow quarry trench on the hillside above the mill. But Confederate Colonel Evander Law's brigade summited

Mother Leather Coat Mountain to the north of the gap, descending upon Rickett's right flank. A Confederate column also passed through Hopewell Gap several kilometers to the north, thus circumnavigating Thoroughfare and adding support to the Confederates with the high ground. By dusk, the Northerners were beaten and forced to withdraw via Gainesville toward Bristoe Station and Manassas Junction, leaving the way clear for Longstreet to join with Jackson. Longstreet's clearance of the Bull Run Mountains to join the action of Second Manassas ensured the South's victory.

At dawn on Friday, August 29th, the overconfident Pope began an assault on the Confederates, not realizing that Longstreet's men had cleared the Thoroughfare Gap and were on their way to join Jackson. Longstreet's twenty-five thousand men had begun their march that morning at 6 a.m. from the Bull Run Mountains. Pope was most concerned that the enemy would withdraw, as he erroneously believed after the Battle of Brawner's Farm, he had caught them on the backfoot in full retreat from Centreville, and he wanted to retain them in a pincer movement and force a fight, boasting that he would "bag the whole crowd." The Union spread out south of the unfinished railroad, with Ricketts on the far left, King near Groveton, and then McDowell's and Sigel's divisions spreading until Stone Bridge (technically, at that point, it was a wooden reconstruction) at the Bull Run River. Pope was positioned at Centreville, eleven kilometers (or seven miles) away, with three divisions and a fourth division northeast of Manassas Junction (south of the visual of the battle maps).

The Union general was overconfident in his belief that he commanded significantly more men than the Confederates and that the result of the battle would ultimately be a Northern victory. Pope was unaware not only of Longstreet, who would be on the scene within hours, but also of where his various units were. Pope believed McDowell and Sigel were blocking Jackson's route west over the Bull Run Mountains, whereas McDowell had been described by King's division as being "lost in the woods" somewhere near Groveton and south of the enemy. Sigel was even farther south near the turnpike intersection. In truth, all of Pope's troops were either south or east of Jackson, who was living up to his reputation as a "stonewall" and was settled and ready for battle on the 29th, free to make an escape back the way he had come through the Thoroughfare.

Jackson had sent General Jeb Stuart to round up elements of Longstreet's approaching army and position them strategically for the battle. Stonewall arranged twenty thousand of his own men along a 2.7-kilometer (1.7-mile) line to the south of Stony Ridge along the railroad grade. Two of Lawton's brigades, as well as Starke's division, were centered in the middle. Stonewall also ordered General A. P. Hill's "Light Division" to hold the Confederate left flank north toward Sudley Church near Sudley Ford of the Bull Run River, which would prove useful later that afternoon. Jackson also placed a cavalry unit, as well as a battery of horse artillery, to protect Sudley Ford from a Union crossing, which would have exposed the Confederate rear. Later that day, the Confederate artillery stopped Federal Brigadier General Orlando M. Poe's brigade after they had forded the Bull Run, although they were completely unaware that they were closing in on the enemy's rear. The Union was repulsed by heavy fire and forced to retreat, but Sudley Church was destroyed in the fighting. The Yankees made no further progress in crossing the Bull Run behind the Confederates for the remainder of Second Manassas.

On the morning of the 29th, Jackson was ready for Pope, although the Federals were in disarray. Union General Sigel's 1st Corps was used to make an initial assault on the enemy, and they formed a broad front at dawn, prepared to batter the enemy head on, reaching the front by 7 a.m. (Pope had concocted a far more complicated attack plan, but because of the arrangement of his scattered troops, the first assault ended as a frontal attack. In fact, Sigel had originally been ordered toward the enemy's left.) Sigel's men were instructed to advance and engage to ascertain the enemy's position, and by 10 a.m., the fighting was full-frontal, with the Confederates using the trench of the unfinished railroad as their protective dugout, particularly around the Deep Cut.

The Federals needed to approach the enemy up a gradual rise toward the trench until they were virtually upon the Southerners. For every Northern attack, there was a Southern counterattack. Major General Joseph Hooker's 3rd Corps and Major General Isaac Stevens's (9th Corps moved in to support Sigel (Stevens, 1818–1862, was a US Army career officer and politician who was killed shortly after in the Battle of Chantilly). To the east, men engaged in hand-to-hand combat in the woods near Sudley Road; some units became temporarily trapped behind enemy lines, and leaders of sub-divisions were killed or wounded, causing panic amongst their men. To add to the chaos, wounded men from the battle of the 28th from King's division were found after a night of suffering and needed to be removed from the battlefield. When sections of the Union fell back in disorder, the Confederates rushed forward, first with musket fire but also in personal combat, clubbing, bayoneting, and knifing their foe. The Union artillery in the south on Dogan Ridge (northwest of the Warrenton Turnpike intersection) pelted the enemy when they emerged from the woods, forcing a retreat.

However, by 12:30, the fighting had reached a stalemate. Pope arrived on the battlefield at about 1 p.m. to take command, and he deliberated whether to end the fighting altogether and retreat to Centreville since McDowell's and McClellan's troops were nowhere to be seen. When Pope received word that McDowell was close, he resumed the full-frontal attack on Jackson, sending two Union brigades toward the enemy in the afternoon to puncture the Southern line. These included Major General Samuel P. Heintzelman's 3rd Corps of the Army of the Potomac and Major General Jesse L. Reno's 9th Corps, as well as two of McDowell's divisions. (Heintzelman, 1805-1880, was a career army officer who was very prominent in the first years of the war—a World War II ship was named in his honor; Reno, 1823-1862, was a career army officer and "soldier's soldier" who fought alongside his men and was killed two weeks later at the Battle of South Mountain as part of the Maryland campaign.)

One brigade under Brigadier General Cuvier Grover (1828-1885, a US Army career officer), which was part of Hooker's division, attacked at 3 p.m., thinking they were backed by Major General Philip Kearny (1815-1862, a career army officer who died shortly after in early September at the Battle of Chantilly), although it was Stevens who held their retreat. Grover made straight for Confederate Brigadier General Edward Thomas's Georgia brigade. Like all other charges of the day, Grover's men attacked at point-blank range, followed by a bayonet charge and then hand-to-hand combat. Reinforced by two Carolina brigades, the Confederates fought back, but after clearing the woods, they were forced to retreat when exposed to Union artillery. Grover faced 350 casualties due to the charge. During the engagements of the day, the Union attacks were isolated, poorly supported or coordinated, and eventually repulsed with heavy casualties and no advancement or breakthroughs.

The two sides continued to fight across the unfinished railroad, with Pope dispatching three of his units toward the enemy, including Major General John F. Reynolds's Pennsylvania Reserves (Reynolds, 1820-1863, was a career US Army officer who played a key role in the American Civil War but was killed at the Battle of Gettysburg in 1863). The wooded battle scene made it difficult for either side to deploy artillery except toward the Union's left (the Confederate right), which included open fields between the woods and the rail grading. The right was the weakest part of the Confederate front line defense, which was held by Starke's division. Jackson added General Jubal A. Early (1816-1894, a Virginia lawyer and politician who served a prominent role as a Confederate general in the Civil War) and Colonel Henry Forno's "Louisiana Tigers" brigades to bolster Starke, as well as to form a right-flank link to Longstreet's men when they arrived. (The Louisiana Tigers started as a nickname for a small group of troops from Louisiana, but by the end of the war, the term applied to all Louisiana soldiers, as they had a reputation for fearless, hard fighting.)

While the Union attacks almost found success, it was an unsupported, piecemeal maneuver that did not have the desired result of breaking through the enemy line. The charges were repulsed as the Southerners fought back. The fighting continued all day, with it being General Pope's intention to hold Jackson in situ until the arrival of the Union 5ᵗʰ Corps of McClellan's army. The 5ᵗʰ Corps was led by General Fitz John Porter (1822-1901, a career US Army officer and highly respected by the enemy but who was constantly surrounded by controversy within his own army), whose military career would come to an end as a result of the events occurring during the Second Battle of Bull Run. Pope intended to use Porter's division to hammer at what he believed to be the right flank of Jackson's army near Groveton.

Ultimately, Pope wanted Porter to sever any possible joining of Longstreet's and Jackson's armies and to force a firm wedge between them by reaching Jackson's flank before Longstreet did. But Porter was too late. McDowell and some of his units, who had arrived on the scene, moved west with Porter from Bristoe Station. When Porter arrived with his ten thousand troops to cover the enemy's right flank, he was unexpectedly confronted with Longstreet's thirty thousand men, of which Pope was unaware, so Porter decided not to attack near Groveton. Longstreet had arrived on the morning of the 29ᵗʰ, just in time to join the Battle of Second Manassas, which would rage throughout that day and into the next, lasting until sundown of Saturday the 30th. (Some of Longstreet's units took longer to march from the Thoroughfare Gap, trailing in at 3 a.m. on August 30th.)

The Southern right flank was no longer at Groveton but extended far south and beyond where the Old Warrenton Road crossed the Manassas Gap Railroad. Porter and McDowell were not only outnumbered three to one but also widely separated from the remaining Federal Army, which fought mainly around Stony Ridge to the north. Jeb Stuart had also ridden out to halt the Union's right-flanking advance in a short, sharp shoot-out. Porter chose not to carry out Pope's discretionary orders to attack but held his position, subsequently defending the Union's left flank and preventing Longstreet from joining the main battle that day. McDowell moved to join Pope toward Manassas, who would only discover the arrival of Longstreet's men by 7 p.m. that evening. Unfortunately, Porter's decision not to attack later made him a convenient target for the North's loss at the Second Battle of Bull Run and led to him being unjustly court-martialed. (The specific and infamous order of Pope's on this day became known as the "Joint Order"—a contradictory set of instructions, which also included a potential overnight retreat to Centreville.)

Similarly, on the 29th, Confederate General Longstreet refused General Lee's orders to attack from his position on the right flank, stating, "The time was just not right." Longstreet was not sure of the enemy's strength and positioning. (Longstreet did, however, launch a few scouting parties that night, which resulted in brief skirmishes, to assess the enemy's positioning and strength.)

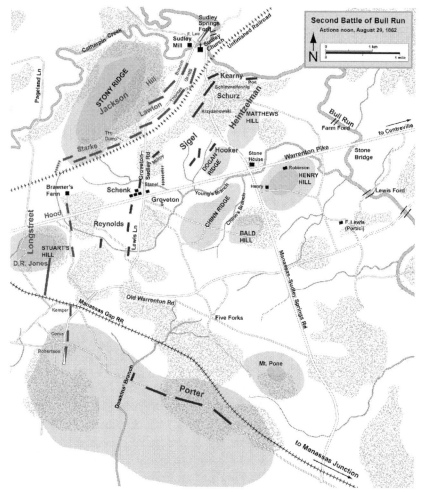

Arrangement of troops at noon on Friday, August 29th, 1862, during the first day of the two-day-long Battle of Second Manassas, showing Porter's troops advancing along the railroad toward the enemy's right flank only to find Longstreet's Confederate troops reaching far south of Groveton in excessive numbers (red for the Confederacy and blue for the Union).

Tired of waiting for Porter's attack to the west that never came, by 5 p.m., Pope had sent in the fiery, one-armed Philip Kearny to assault the Southern left flank. Kearny was facing off against General Hill across the incomplete railroad. A. P. Hill was the commander of the famous "Light Division" that had found fame (or notoriety, depending on which side one was) at the Seven Days Battles during the Peninsula campaign and went on to become a significant and integral part of the Confederate fighting force. The Light Division consisted of six brigades from six Confederate states (Virginia, South Carolina, Georgia, North Carolina, Alabama, and Tennessee.) Several batteries were attached to the Light Division. The brigade had originally been a unit under Longstreet, but a feud between Hill and Longstreet resulted in the transference of the Light Division to Stonewall Jackson's jurisdiction. The Light Division had played a crucial role in the Battle of Cedar Mountain and went on to ensure a significant defense of Southern lines at Second Manassas. (The naming of the "Light Division" was first referenced in June of 1862, but its origins are unclear.)

However, the Light Division had been fighting all day for at least nine hours, and Kearny's men began beating the fatigued soldiers back. Just when it seemed that the Federals would at last break the line, Jackson advanced a reserve force into the fray, led by General Early. Early's fresh reinforcements pummeled the Federals back to their starting positions.

Despite scrambled orders on both sides to attack as dusk approached, by nightfall, the Rebels still held their position in the woods above the incomplete railroad near Groveton. Both Northern and Southern sub-commanders had rejected Pope's and Lee's ideas for advancement, citing nightfall and chaotic and clogged attack routes as inauspicious for advancement. General Pope was disgruntled that Porter had not joined the battle to the south, but he felt sure he could obliterate the enemy on Saturday the 30th and chase the Southerners from Northern territory for good. He had noted several incidents during the day that erroneously indicated to him that the Confederates were in retreat. For the third day in a row, Pope would be unaware that the (now completely reunited) Confederate Army would be waiting and prepared for a battle on the ground of their own choosing.

Chapter 4 – The Second Battle of Bull Run: August 30th, 1862

The morning of the swelteringly hot Saturday passed quietly without fighting, and Pope took the time to devise a final assault on the Confederates, who he still erroneously believed were retreating. Pope had arrived at this conclusion because both Jackson and Longstreet had pulled back, but they were simply repositioning themselves. This was especially true of Longstreet's division under Lieutenant General Richard H. Anderson, "Fighting Dick" (1821-1879, a career army officer who joined the Confederacy for the war), which was the last to arrive at the scene from the Thoroughfare Gap in the early hours of the day. Anderson's men at first advanced too far, and realizing their mistake, they pulled back west toward the remainder of the Confederate troops. This brief withdrawal reinforced Pope's mistaken beliefs. The Southerners were still stubbornly in place, despite being technically outnumbered by the Union's approximate seventy-seven thousand men (an estimated sixty-two thousand that eventually engaged) to the Confederate's approximate fifty-five thousand. A series of fruitless but incorrect reconnoiters convinced Pope that the Confederates had not moved south toward their left flank, and peculiar orders sent several of Pope's units away from the battlefield—only a few of whom returned for battle later that day.

General Lee was hoping for a fight, and besides having his united army in place and ready for battle, he had established eighteen artillery pieces under Colonel Stephen D. Lee (1833-1908, who served in the US Army for seven years as a first lieutenant before joining the Confederacy as a lieutenant general—no relation to General Robert E. Lee) above the battle site northeast of Brawner's Farm, pointed at the open fields in front of Jackson.

After much deliberation, Union General Ricketts was sent toward the enemy at noon "in pursuit" of a withdrawing army. But he shockingly met the full onslaught of Jackson's men, and after his unit was thoroughly repulsed, he reported that the Confederates were still very much present and ready for battle. Unwilling to wait for further reinforcements from McClellan that had been late in coming (specifically the 2nd and 6th Corps), Pope decided to attack. There was wide controversy around McClellan's delay in sending further reinforcements from his position near Alexandria. A letter to McClellan's wife suggested he held back his units on purpose to teach Pope a lesson and to ensure he received a whipping, thus returning the full army to McClellan after Second Manassas, which was exactly what happened. It has also been suggested that Pope moved ahead without waiting for McClellan to claim any credit of victory. These entrenched, bitter, and ongoing brawls between leaders of the Union ensured many Northern failures in the first few years of the Civil War.

After noon, Pope decided to pincer an enemy he still believed was likely to retreat. He sent Porter, Hatch, and Reynolds west toward the enemy's right flank and Ricketts, Kearny, and Hooker east toward the left flank. Porter's division, along with reinforcements from McDowell, advanced in the afternoon at about 3 p.m., with five brigades of about ten thousand men ready to strike at Brigadier General Starke's division along the unfinished railroad's Deep Cut. (They were overseen by twenty-eight artillery pieces on Dogan Ridge to defend them.) Porter's 1st Division was led by Brigadier General Daniel Adams Butterfield (1831-1901, a New York businessman and general in the Civil War). This initial assault nearly broke through the Confederates' front right center, routing the Confederate 48th Virginia Infantry Regiment. (In haste, Pope prematurely reported a breakthrough to Washington.) When the South's ammunition ran out at certain places, they, specifically the Louisiana and Virginia regiments, began hurling rocks from the unfinished railroad toward the Union troops in desperation. The Federals took the opportunity to throw the rocks back! Meanwhile, McDowell, realizing the Southerners were not withdrawing, held his position on both Bald Hill (below Chinn

Ridge) and Henry House Hill.

Jackson needed to call on Longstreet for reinforcements—an unlikely move by the stalwart Stonewall. Longstreet, who was unable to move his troops toward the congested battle scene, sent forward his artillery instead under the command of Stephen D. Lee. The battery, as well as eighteen cannons, pounded the Union from the west.

Brevet Major General John P. Hatch had taken over the command of Brigadier General King, who'd fallen ill the previous evening with epileptic seizures. King's men included the Iron Brigade of the West (the Black Hats) that had been pummeled by Jackson on the evening of August 28th. The division, now officially under Hatch, joined Butterfield in the fight. (Hatch had been with McDowell and Porter the previous day as they moved up the Manassas-Gainesville Road toward Longstreet when they were set upon by Stuart.) The Union closed ranks and fought harder, but they could not withstand the Confederate firepower, and their attempts eventually stalled.

Porter, seeing the ensuing devastation, decided not to send further reinforcements to their death and called his men back to the protection of Groveton Woods. Butterfield's and Hatch's men fell back from the carnage at the Deep Cut, needing to cross open fields under a gauntlet of fire from Southern artillery before reaching the safety of Groveton Woods. They collided chaotically with reserve troops behind them, which were partially pursued by some of Starke's men, who were beaten back by the Union reserves. They had fought for an hour, and three thousand of Porter's men lay dead, dying, or missing in the field. Jackson's command, which was equally depleted, could not immediately counterattack, which allowed Porter to stabilize his men north of the turnpike.

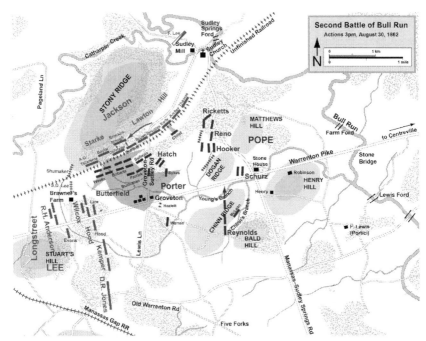

Arrangement of troops at 3 p.m. on Saturday, August 30ᵗʰ, 1862, during the second day of the two-day-long Battle of Second Manassas, showing Porter's troops attacking at the unfinished railroad. Stephen D. Lee's battery is seen in the west (red for the Confederacy and blue for the Union).

Map by Hal Jespersen, http://www.CWmaps.com, CC BY 3.0 <https://creativecommons.org/licenses/by/3.0>, via Wikimedia Commons https://commons.wikimedia.org/wiki/File:Second_Bull_Run_Aug30_1500.png

But a full onslaught by the Yankees was exactly the move General Robert E. Lee had anticipated, and he patiently waited for the fighting to subside before launching a counterattack on the exhausted Federal troops. By holding their position overnight along the ridge and maintaining the advantage of dominating the unfinished railroad, the Confederates had managed to lure the enemy into a fight and essentially maintained not only tactically the higher ground but also the upper hand. Stonewall had once again lived up to his name by not relenting, holding the ground that determined the battlefield and ultimately dominating the line.

The general of the Union 3ʳᵈ Corps, Irvin McDowell, seeing the line under Porter beginning to break down and withdraw, ordered General Reynolds north of the Warrenton Turnpike toward the enemy's left flank. (Reynolds had been positioned on Chinn Ridge, southwest of the

Warrenton Turnpike and Sudley Road intersection.) McDowell's intention was to bolster the weakening troops toward the Northerners' right flank. It would prove to be a disastrous decision since Reynolds's removal left a mere 2,200 men below the turnpike. The enemy, who were thick and strong to the north and west—with the Bull Run River to the east and the railroad to the south, blocking the Northerners' escape— could now easily rout the Northerners from the battlefield, which was exactly what they did.

General Lee used the opportune moment to unleash his army and ordered Longstreet to counterattack at 4 p.m., just when Porter's men were falling back. Pope had ignored warnings of a potential counterattack, and the Union's left flank below the Warrenton Turnpike was weak and largely undefended. Longstreet had quietly decamped more than three kilometers (two miles) past the Union's southern extremities. Lee simultaneously sent Jackson to approach the Union right. The Rebels had the Federals broadly pinned against the Bull Run River. The Rebels' five divisions spread out from Brawner's Farm in the north to Manassas Gap Railroad Junction in the south, forming a wall of attack west of the north-south aligned Manassas-Sudley Springs Road.

Longstreet used the weak point below the turnpike to overwhelm the entire Federal Army, sending thirty thousand fresh troops toward Henry House Hill to halt the enemy's retreat over Bull Run. The Confederate objective was to dominate the high ground of Henry House Hill—the key location of First Manassas—in order to rout and destroy the Federals by pushing them north, as they would be unable to ford the Bull Run at Stone Bridge.

At the front of this onslaught, the Confederates outnumbered the Yankees by ten to one. General John B. Hood's Texas Brigade led the charge for the Confederates, who focused on the strategic node of Henry House Hill. (Hood, 1831-1879, a career military man who served the US Army before changing to the Confederacy during the war, was a notorious buccaneer and aggressive leader, although Texas had not been his home state but where he was posted once completing the military academy.) Hood was supported by "Shanks" Evans's South Carolinians. (Nathan George "Shanks" Evans, 1824-1868, was a career military man who served the US Army before joining the Confederacy for the war. He had played a crucial role in the Battle of First Manassas, as he'd been the first to notice the enemy encroachment from the north over the Bull

Run. Dashing ahead with his barrel of whiskey, Shanks held off the enemy on Matthews Hill before the Southerners joined forces and retreated to join the full battle that ensued at Henry House Hill.)

Seeing the Rebels' plan, Porter sought out two Yankee regular brigades under Brevet Major General Robert C. Buchanan (1811-1878, a distinguished career military man who served forty years for the US Army) and Colonel Charles W. Roberts (1810-1875, a lawyer, civil engineer, and Union officer during the Civil War) to move south of the turnpike. But in the meantime, only two Federal brigades were in position to meet Hood's assault—Colonels Nathaniel C. McLean's Ohioans of Sigel's 1st Corps and Gouverneur K. Warren's of Porter's 5th Corps. McLean (1815-1905, a lawyer, farmer, and Union general during the war) held Chinn Ridge, while Warren (1830-1882, a civil engineer and Union officer) was slightly farther west (less than two kilometers or a mile).

The Confederates were at first met with Warren's two regiments of the 5th and 10th New York Zouaves. The Zouaves were an unusual unit modeled and trained in the North African Zouave mercenary style of combat, although its members were mostly firefighters from New York. The Zouaves had suffered severe casualties during the First Battle of Manassas when they acted as a rearguard for the retreating Union Army and also as they faced Stonewall on Henry House Hill during the stand-off that garnered him his reputation. Now, once again a target for direct and brutal combat, the troops received the full onslaught of the enemy, and half of the brave and charismatic thousand-strong Zouaves fell that day within a space of ten minutes. In terms of a single infantry regiment engagement, it was the biggest loss of life within a unit during the entire Civil War.

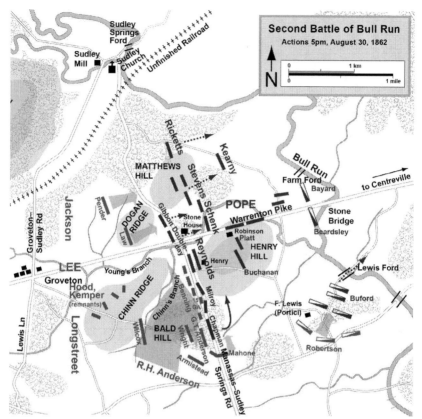

Arrangement of troops at 5 p.m. on Saturday, August 30th, 1862, during the second day of the
two-day-long Battle of Second Manassas, showing the approach of the Confederate forces
pushing the Union against the Bull Run River and forcing them to retreat.

Pope's reluctance to create a safety net for his withdrawing troops now
became a necessity. The enemy was upon them in vast numbers, and
they intended to block their escape route, not only from the battlefield
but also from Washington, DC. Pope, from his headquarters near
Dogan Ridge, had been preoccupied with intelligence that McClellan's
promised troops had finally arrived. Commanding General Halleck had
informed Pope that not only was the Army of the Potomac's 2nd and 6th
Corps at his disposal but also an additional corps, the 4th. (McClellan had,
however, been ordered to remain in Washington—the glory would all
belong to Pope!) But it was too late. Pope's men were being routed from
the field as he read the belated news.

A flimsy Union line of defense was used on Chinn Ridge (southwest of the intersection of Warrenton Turnpike and Sudley Road) to allow time for Pope, with the help of McDowell and Kearny, to build a real defense along Sudley Road and on Henry House Hill (southeast of the intersection and the site of the First Battle of Manassas). McLean was the first on Chinn Ridge to meet the enemy, and he had aligned his four regiments of 1,200 men and one small battery west toward the tide of Confederate troops. McLean was aided by another Federal artillery battery positioned north of the turnpike. Confederate Brigadier General Shanks, in support of Hood, rushed up the left flank of the ridge, but he was repelled by McLean. The Union line held, for the time being, giving Pope half an hour to get reinforcements to the heat of battle.

Pope sacrificed unit after unit while he bought time to establish his defense. All the while, the Federals were subjected to the "Rebel yell" (a loud roar adopted by the Southerners during the war) as they closed on the ridge. General Lee had withheld three divisions to take Henry House Hill, but night was falling, and Longstreet's troops were becoming tired and disorganized. Two of these three divisions were a distance from the battlefield, including General Richard Anderson's reserves. The third division under David R. Jones (1825–1863, a career army officer who joined the Confederacy in the Civil War and died of natural causes during the war) arrived fresh to join the mob on Chinn Ridge and push the Northerners back. At 5 p.m., Lee dispatched Fighting Dick Anderson's troops from Brawner's Farm to join the fighting. These three thousand new troops could have easily overrun the exhausted Northerners, and they almost did along the southern line of fighting where the Union was falling back. It was a crucial opportunity for the Southerners to take Henry House Hill, but they lacked coordination and discipline. In addition, Anderson curiously withheld their advance (the reasons for this reluctance never became clear).

The Union had by now managed to establish themselves in a defensive line along the upper eastern bank of Sudley Road. They unleashed musket fire on the Southerners, who stalwartly continued to advance under Colonel George T. Anderson's Georgia regiment. With Anderson's command to "Knock hell out of those blue shirts!" the Georgia regiment stumbled forward, but the Union line held. The enemy was within forty-six meters (fifty yards) of the Union line and continued to be pelted with musket and heavy artillery fire. But the Rebel Army pushed forward relentlessly. In places, the Confederates pushed through the Union line, and the Federal troops rushed forward to seal the breach.

By 6 p.m. that evening, Union forces under Colonel John Kolte made a final effort to push back the Southerners and recapture a battery that had been lost on Chinn Ridge. But Longstreet's men conquered and dominated Chinn Ridge and Bald Hill after almost two hours of the most intense fighting of Second Manassas. However, the Confederates' goal of Henry House Hill was unlikely to be realized since their numbers were heavily depleted, their troops exhausted, their ammunition low, and night almost upon them. Many of the Federals had moved or were moving to safety across Bull Run and into Fairfax County toward the Union stronghold of Centreville. They were greatly aided by the spirited defense on Henry House Hill by Reynolds's Pennsylvania Reserves and Brigadier General George Sykes's 2nd Division. Altogether, Pope had at least created a line of defense of four brigades along the western slope of Henry House Hill to both deter the enemy and protect his withdrawing troops. The Confederates had won the day's struggle, but their hopes of obliterating the Yankees were proving unlikely.

Darkness was falling when the Rebels managed to maneuver around the southern end of the enemy lines, and they were potentially in a position to begin a pincer-like flanking move upon the Union's left. General Jeb Stuart instructed the commander in charge, General Lewis Armistead (1817–1863, a career US Army officer who became a brigadier general in the Confederate Army but was killed the following year in the Battle of Gettysburg), to advance and envelop the exposed enemy line. But Armistead refused, citing darkness and heavy smoke as too confusing an environment in which to continue a fight—his men would not be able to tell friend from foe. Thus, the Confederate advance was temporarily halted.

Meanwhile, Jackson was pointing his artillery at the Yankees' direct line of withdrawal and began pelting the Union's right flank at 6 p.m., north of Henry House Hill. By 7 p.m., Pope had managed to establish a solid line of defense against Jackson. The Union held their defensive position until nightfall, but Pope understood the futility of continuing the fight and withdrew his remaining troops under cover of night, beginning about 8 p.m.

The final engagement of Second Manassas was a battle at about 7 p.m. between two cavalry units at Lewis Ford, south of Stone Bridge. Brigadier General Beverly Robertson (1827–1910, a career cavalry officer who changed allegiance for the Civil War) and Colonel Thomas Lafayette "Tex" Rosser (1836-1910, a cavalry officer and engineer who went back to serving the US after the war who was heralded by Jeb Stuart for his daring cavalry raids and tactical brilliance) of the Confederate cavalry under Jeb Stuart aimed to cut off the Union retreat by crossing Bull Run at Lewis Ford to encircle the enemy's rear. However, they were met by Union Brigadier General John Buford Jr's cavalry, which had superior numbers (Buford, 1826-1863, a career US Army cavalry officer, distinguished himself during the Battle of Gettysburg on July 1st, 1863). The fierce ten-minute encounter resulted in severe casualties on both sides, particularly amongst the leadership (with Buford being shot in the knee), but the Federal withdrawal was ultimately protected.

Leaving a line of decoy troops at the front, Pope hurriedly removed the remainder of his men, most of whom had crossed the Bull Run River by 11 p.m. The famous Stone Bridge over the Bull Run River along the Warrenton Turnpike had been destroyed by the Confederates in March of 1862, but a wooden one was rebuilt by the Union shortly after. Stone Bridge had proved a pivotal point during the First Battle of Bull Run, and when Pope withdrew his troops after the Second Battle of Bull Run, the Union destroyed the wooden bridge in their wake to prevent an easy Southern crossing. Pope's army retreated to the Federal stronghold of Centreville in failure and humiliation, just as General McDowell had done a year before. Admittedly, in 1862, the Union was in better shape than they had been in 1861, and they at least retreated in a calm and orderly manner, which was not the case in First Manassas.

The equally exhausted Confederates, who were low on ammunition, did not pursue the Yankees in the darkness. Lee telegrammed Confederate President Jefferson Davis after the battle, saying, "This army achieved today on the plains of Manassas a signal victory over the combined forces of Generals McClellan and Pope." For the Yankees, although technically the battle had unfolded behind enemy lines (in Southern territory), the area around Manassas in northeastern Virginia was largely under Union control for the Civil War, so the odds were significantly in favor of the Northerners. But the Rebels, using solid tactical maneuvers, exemplary timing, clear and steady commandeering, and unwavering resistance (so common of the Southerners), had once again won the day on the fateful grounds of Manassas.

Chapter 5 – Outcome of the Battle of Second Manassas

Amongst the multitude of General Pope's bad decisions before and during the Battle of Second Manassas, one question remains unanswered, and it's whether the tide could have turned in favor of the Union on Sunday, August 31ˢᵗ, had the Union remained in place to fight another day. Nightfall ended the events on Saturday 30ᵗʰ, and Pope had withdrawn his troops to save them from further suffering, but the Union had held the high ground at the end of the fighting on Saturday and also had three fresh corps from McClellan waiting near Centreville. There is a chance—given their higher numbers of fighting men and greater reinforcements of ammunition and artillery—that they could have regrouped and given the Confederates a beating.

On the Confederate side, Lee had given in to both Jackson and Longstreet at several points during the lead-up to and throughout Second Manassas, although he was technically the commanding general. Lee had reluctantly allowed Jackson's wild two-day flanking maneuver north to Bristoe Station and had relented to Longstreet's refusal to join the fight on August 29ᵗʰ. Although both instances of leeway were successful for the Confederates, this insubordination proved problematic later in the war when Lee struggled to control his headstrong generals to the detriment of his army.

The Union withdrawal from the battlefield at Second Bull Run did not officially end the fighting of the Confederate's northern Virginia campaign. Lee pressed his point and sent Jackson's exhausted troops to encircle Pope at Centreville and cut off their route back to Washington, DC. Thankfully, some of the Union cavalry detected the new enemy movement and alerted Pope to the approach, who was prepared. In the late afternoon of September 1ˢᵗ, some of Pope's forces intercepted the flanking wing of Jackson's, which had been sent to prevent the Union retreat to the Northern capital.

The enemy columns met at Ox Hill near Chantilly Plantation on the Little River Turnpike, eight kilometers (five miles) east of Centreville on the main road back to DC (thirty-four kilometers, or twenty-one miles, west of the capital). Jackson's divisions fought against two Union divisions under Major Generals Philip Kearny and Isaac Stevens, who were both sadly killed in the fighting. The Battle of Chantilly took place during a torrential thunderstorm—strangely reminiscent of the rainstorms of "Black Monday" after the Battle of First Manassas a year earlier. The battle was inconclusive and ended prematurely because of the weather, but it allowed Pope's army time to retreat back to Washington, DC, in comparative safety. Chantilly was officially the final battle of Lee's northern Virginia campaign.

The culmination of the Second Battle of Bull Run resulted in 14,462 Union casualties, including 1,747 killed, 8,452 wounded, and 4,263 captured or missing. It was a stunning defeat, with the casualties representing approximately 20 percent of those on the field. The Confederates listed 7,298 casualties, of which 1,096 were killed and 6,202 wounded—an equally shocking 15 percent of the field.

After the failure at Bull Run, Pope was relieved of his command on September 12ᵗʰ, 1862, along with the disbanding of the Army of Virginia, which had existed for a brief two and a half months. Three days after the end of Second Bull Run, Pope was posted to the Department of the Northwest, well out of the way of the "real" fight with the South. He was now responsible for Native American uprisings. However, he remained in service to the US government, returning as a key figure toward the end of the war. His Army of Virginia was merged into the Army of the Potomac, which included the three fighting divisions he had "borrowed" for Second Manassas.

McClellan was once again—albeit temporarily—in charge of the main Federal Army. McClellan was removed from the head of the main army in November in that year, 1862, due to ongoing disputes with President

Abraham Lincoln regarding tactical decisions and other political derision. He was replaced by the reluctant Major General Ambrose Burnside.

However, the humiliated Pope, who was responsible for the Northern loss, did not humbly accept responsibility for his actions but transferred the blame to other, more popular leaders. He mostly attributed the defeat of Second Bull Run to General Porter, accusing him of insubordination. Porter was subsequently arrested, court-martialed in November 1862, found guilty in January 1863, and dismissed from the military on January 21st in disgrace. Porter's open hostility toward Pope and the removal of his advocate, McClellan, from the military did not aid his cause. (McDowell is purported to have spoken against Porter in the hearing, potentially to save his own career.) Porter would spend many years defending himself against the official accusation of disobedience and misconduct. Fifteen years later, in 1878, a special commission exonerated Porter, confirming that his refusal to attack Longstreet resulted in a better, less damaging result for the Army of Virginia. His sentence was rescinded, as well as his dismissal from the army (although he officially resigned two days after being acquitted). Confederate commentator, Edward Porter Alexander (1835-1910), who served the Confederacy during the war as a brigadier general, wrote of Porter's dismissal, saying that the Confederates who knew Porter admired him greatly and considered his dismissal "one of the best fruits of their victory."

The Northern defeat at the Second Battle of Bull Run emboldened General Lee to continue with his campaign into enemy territory, and within the first week of September 1862, his troops splashed across the Potomac River into western Maryland. At this point, the Union was losing the war. The Maryland campaign continued through the first three weeks of September, with the campaign including the Battles of Harpers Ferry, South Mountain, and Antietam. Lee's real objective was the rail center of Harrisburg in Pennsylvania, approximately 193 kilometers (120 miles) north of Washington, DC. However, Lee and his army were repelled after the Battle of Antietam (also known as the Battle of Sharpsburg) on September 17th, 1862. After Antietam, Lee withdrew from Maryland back across the Potomac, and the Maryland (and effectively the summer) campaign ended. The Union forces did not pursue General Lee and the Confederates south. By the end of

September 1862, the area around Manassas Railroad Junction was firmly back under Union control.

Conclusion

The Yankees' staggering loss at Second Bull Run not only allowed General Lee to penetrate the Union states and threaten the capital but also brought the fight to the world stage. The Southerners were garnering international recognition for their cause, which could have led to both political support and funding from abroad and a far more virulent enemy for the Union. The Confederacy knew that with their smaller numbers and more vulnerable tactical position, they could never win the war alone, so they were essentially playing a delaying game, keeping the Union at bay until foreign intervention arrived. The formation of the Confederate States of America had been largely based upon their belief that their cotton, and therefore the preservation of their slave-driven plantations, was invaluable to Europe.

It was clear that the US government, while holding command politically and administratively in most of the country, was weak militarily—mostly due to poor choices in field leadership. The fiery temperaments and passionate, planned, and decisive actions of the Southern generals overwhelmed the weak bureaucratic decisions made in the North, which then leaked onto the battlefields of the Civil War. The Union was contributing to their own demise.

The events surrounding the Battle of Second Manassas and the infringement by General Lee into Maryland and Pennsylvania meant that the North was losing the war, but the South was making assumptions that did not hold true. The Confederate government had never been legally recognized by its parent federal government nor diplomatically acknowledged as independent by any foreign country. The Southerners assumed that the international demand for their cotton would bring a multitude of European countries to their aid, which never happened. (The main countries to import Southern cotton were England and France, and neither were prepared to go to war with the US over the Confederacy's demands.)

In the Western Theater, the Union had made greater gains, and, technically, the various failures in the Eastern Theater from 1861 to 1862 were "inconclusive" since no permanent invasion of enemy ground on either side unfolded. A month after the Battle of Second Manassas, on September 22nd, 1862, President Lincoln issued the Emancipation Proclamation, which declared that all slaves held in the Confederacy were now freed. Until this point, abolition had been a tacit cause for the Civil War; now, for the South at least, it was a reality.

Lee's brief soirée into Northern territory in the autumn of 1862 that completed the Maryland campaign ended in a stalemate at the bloodiest one-day battle of the war—the Battle of Antietam—on September 17th. The Rebels could go no farther north and were forced to retreat. The US president grabbed the opportunity to nail his Emancipation Proclamation to their retreating backs. The European countries that the Confederacy were so dependent upon for support had abolished slavery decades beforehand, and they relied heavily on the US for other imports, including a quarter of their food. Help from Europe would not come— the Confederacy were on their own. With this knowledge and in the certainty that they could muster more military might and resources than the divided and isolated South, the US government was now in control. They simply needed to patiently play the tactical waiting game so familiar to the South until their foes eventually ran out of resources.

Part 6: The Battle of Antietam

A Captivating Guide to an Important Battle of the American Civil War

Introduction

On September 17th, 1862, US President Abraham Lincoln got the great victory he had desired ever since the outbreak of the American Civil War over a year before. Declaring victory would give him the political breathing space he needed to do something that he had been pondering for some time—freeing the slaves.

The great victory Lincoln wanted took place near Antietam Creek in Maryland, near the town of Sharpsburg. The Union called it "The Battle of Antietam," and the Confederacy referred to it as "The Battle of Sharpsburg." It is known by both today, but "Antietam" is the more common usage.

The thing about the Battle of Antietam was that it wasn't really a victory for either side. It was more like a bloody stalemate, except for the fact that the troops of the North remained near the battlefield while the rebels moved to a position that was more suited for defense.

While the battle certainly was not the resounding victory Lincoln had hoped for, he was a very astute politician. If his troops were still on the field and the enemy was not, he won. Privately, though, Lincoln was both angered and horrified by the results of the battle, or rather the lack of them.

Though there were four battles to come (Gettysburg, Spotsylvania, Chickamauga, and the Wilderness) that were to be more costly in terms of men killed, Antietam, unlike the battles listed above, was fought during the course of one day and was, therefore, the single bloodiest day of the Civil War. And the losses were high—2,100 Union and 1,550

Confederate troops died that day.

Think of this: since 2001, approximately 2,440 American servicemen and women have been killed in the war in Afghanistan. On one single day in 1862, around 158 years ago, that number was exceeded by over one thousand soldiers. That does not take away any of the bravery of the soldiers fighting today; rather, it is simply meant to illustrate the intensity and costliness of the Battle of Antietam.

The Battle of Antietam is remembered today as being the bloodiest day in the Civil War, and as being the "victory" that Lincoln needed to issue the Emancipation Proclamation, but at the time, the reaction to the battle was far from unanimous. Lincoln, members of his Cabinet, Congress, the press, and the public hoped that General George McClellan would take advantage of the situation and pursue the retreating rebels back into Virginia and to their capital, Richmond. But as he had done so many times before, McClellan hesitated, coming up with reason after reason about why he could not chase the rebels down.

So, a short biography of George McClellan is a good place to begin this history of the Battle of Antietam.

Chapter 1 – "Young Napoleon"

In the mid-19th century, the idol of military men throughout the Western world was Napoleon Bonaparte. Even though he was ultimately defeated, he had taken on the world, almost won, and had done it in a way that hadn't been seen on the battlefield before. Audacity, speed, and surprise were the hallmarks of Napoleon's military career.

In the United States, which hadn't felt the brunt of Napoleon's invading armies, Napoleon was revered. Look at the pictures of the officers (and some of the enlisted men) of the Civil War—they pose like Bonaparte, with one hand tucked into his jacket, like the picture of Union General George McClellan below.

General George McClellan
https://commons.wikimedia.org/wiki/File:George_B_McClellan_-_retouched.jpg

The nickname "Young Napoleon" was given to him as he rose to take command of the Army of the Potomac, the main Union Army in the eastern theater of the Civil War, after a couple of small victories in western Virginia (in today's West Virginia, which was separated from Virginia in 1863).

At the time, the nickname, while bold, made more sense than it would later in the war. McClellan, who was born in Philadelphia in December 1826, had a stellar career before gaining control of the Army of the Potomac: he was second in the 1846 West Point class (which included future Confederate generals Stonewall Jackson, George Pickett, and A.P. Hill), distinguished himself in the Mexican-American War, returned to teach at West Point, led mapping expeditions on the frontier and explored routes for the transcontinental railroad, and went overseas as a military observer in the Crimean War.

In the years before the Civil War, McClellan had retired to private life and became an executive with the Illinois Central Railroad. There, he made important connections, including with the governor of Ohio, William Dennison Jr., who appointed McClellan as the major general of Ohio volunteers in 1861 shortly after the war began in April 1861. This promotion from private life to one of the highest ranks in the army brought McClellan to the attention of President Lincoln, who also received positive reviews about McClellan from the Ohio governor. Lincoln promoted McClellan to major general, a position that was right below Mexican-American War hero Winfield Scott, on whose staff McClellan had served in that war.

In the first truly planned action of the war (as opposed to incidental skirmishes) at Philippi in western Virginia in June 1861, McClellan's troops were victorious. Though small in scale compared to what was to come, the victory at Philippi (involving some four thousand men on both sides) reinforced the Northern notion that the war would be short. Naturally, the people in the South felt the same way at the beginning of the war.

The Battle of Philippi was also the first indicator to President Lincoln that McClellan was going to be a problem. Though McClellan wasn't announcing anything different than what was standing government policy in 1861, in western Virginia, he announced to the populace that his army would not interfere with slavery in the area. Answering rumors that the Union troops would encourage slave revolt, McClellan announced, "not only will we abstain from all such interference but we will, on the contrary with an iron hand, crush any attempted insurrection on their part." This was not within McClellan's authority to announce or enforce without orders, as those orders were supposed to come from the civilian authority—meaning Lincoln. McClellan quickly apologized to the president, but it was the first of many, and other apologies would come much slower with time, if at all.

Over a month after McClellan's fight in western Virginia, the Union lost the First Battle of Bull Run under General Irvin McDowell. With that shocking defeat, Lincoln began searching for a new commander of the Union armies in Virginia. Not only was McClellan appointed to head the Army of the Potomac, but he was also made the commander of all Union forces.

It became clear almost immediately that McClellan had a gift for organization, discipline, and instilling pride in his troops, all of which were lacking since the beginning of the war and especially after the First Battle of Bull Run. Though there were still problems in the quartermaster corps (the branch of the service responsible for the requisitioning and distribution of supplies), such as officers selling army goods for their own private gain, making sure their friends in the army got first choice, and bribery, McClellan and his staff went a long way to fixing the worst of the problems.

The general fired inefficient, lazy, and inept officers and had them sent into retirement or assigned to desk jobs or posts far from any action, and he also brought up new officers that were familiar with modern tactics, drills, and organization. McClellan made sure that discipline was enforced, which, deep down, most troops love—no one wants to go to battle with a mob of undisciplined men, especially when facing a skilled enemy. In time, the men loved McClellan, for while it was a fatal flaw in regard to his career, his cautiousness meant, at least to average soldiers, that "Little Mac" would not throw their lives away on a whim and without preparation.

McClellan was no stranger to what we today would call "spin." He courted the leading newspapermen of the day, was the toast of Washington society, and made political connections wherever he could. Soon, the newspapers, his men, and much of the Northern public was calling him the "Young Napoleon." McClellan did nothing to dissuade them.

And that right there was one of McClellan's biggest problems—his massive ego. He feigned modesty when he was called the "Young Napoleon," but deep down, many believe that he enjoyed it immensely and that it went to his head, which was already large from being second in his West Point class (he was bested by one point because of an athletic event) and having won some early, but small, victories in western Virginia.

As the war went on, Lincoln and others began to realize that McClellan was way too cautious for a general in command of a powerful army and perhaps was more concerned with not losing his army or reputation rather than winning victories. McClellan would not take this laying down, though; the general began describing Lincoln and his Cabinet in increasingly disparaging terms. He had to know reports of this would get back to Washington, DC, but he seemingly didn't care or incredibly did not know.

McClellan's first grand idea culminated in the Peninsula Campaign, an amphibious landing on the James Peninsula, which was south of Richmond and behind Confederate positions facing Washington. It was a great idea in many ways. It could possibly surprise the enemy. It also ensured that McClellan's Army of the Potomac, numbering in the neighborhood of 100,000 men during the summer of 1862, would be concentrated in a small area, which would allow them to bear down on the rebels with great force while having, at least for a time, the cover of the US Navy's guns. Conversely, however, the territory would also allow a smaller enemy led by skilled officers to keep the larger enemy bottled up. It all depended on leadership and boldness, the latter trait being something McClellan did not have.

At Yorktown, where the American Revolution ended, McClellan besieged a smaller CSA ("Confederate States of America") army under General John B. Magruder. Instead of maneuvering to defeat him or simply (in the parlance of WWII) "kick ass and bypass," McClellan left the much weaker force behind him to be "cleaned" up by US troops coming up from behind while McClellan pressed on toward Richmond.

Magruder shrewdly maneuvered his troops in sight of the Federal forces (another name used to refer to the Union) so they thought the rebels were much more numerous than they were. He also employed Quaker guns to make the Union general believe he had more artillery than he truly did. The phrase Quaker guns is a play on words, as the religious Quaker sect espouses to this day non-violence. These "guns" were actually logs painted black and leaned against rocks or set up on wheels in plain (but distant) sight of the enemy. Magruder had dozens of these "guns" deployed in the field.

Magruder also had spies and scouts, and the Confederates had double agents within the Federal camps and in Washington, spreading rumors about the immense strength of the Confederate forces. Of course, these were all gross exaggerations, as the Confederate forces in Virginia were outnumbered by the Union Army.

One of the most interesting things (and one of the most tragic in many ways) about the Civil War was that many of the officers knew each other, even if they were on the opposing side. Sometimes they were best friends, as in the case of Confederate General Lewis Armistead and Union General Winfield Scott Hancock. Whether they knew each other as friends, acquaintances, family, or just by reputation, many of the men who fought in the Civil War had served in the US Army before. That gave them a lot of insight into the tactical and strategic thinking of their enemy.

As mentioned above, McClellan had gone to West Point with some of the South's leading generals. He had also served in Mexico and was known to others, including Robert E. Lee. Most of them knew of McClellan's cautious nature before the war, and they played off of it during the conflict.

Urged to move by Lincoln during the Peninsula Campaign, McClellan began what was to become his ignominious trademark—asking for more troops. He had been supplied with the largest standing army in the history of the North American continent, and he still asked for more men, men that didn't exist. The draft wasn't instituted until 1863, and until that time, Washington was dependent on volunteers, and these men took time to train and outfit.

Lincoln complained about McClellan's lack of movement, which was made worse not only by the claims of Southern strength (which Lincoln, from his intelligence sources, likely knew to be an exaggeration) but also by McClellan's assurances that when he was ready, he would move with great speed. President Lincoln famously said, "If General McClellan is not using the army, perhaps he might let me borrow it." Just before the Peninsula Campaign, Lincoln removed McClellan from overall command of the Union armies, hoping that the general might be able to focus on the upcoming campaign near Richmond better. While McClellan seems to have known that he was out of his depth as the commander of all the Union forces, he still harbored resentment against someone who he believed knew nothing of military planning.

McClellan had written to his wife that he viewed Lincoln as "a well-meaning baboon." To McClellan, Secretary of State William Seward, who was 25 years older than the general, was an "incompetent little puppy. Before the Peninsula Campaign began, Lincoln, Seward, and Lincoln's private secretary John Hay paid a late-night visit to the McClellan residence to discuss the general's plans for the upcoming campaign. Informed that the general was out, Lincoln and his party decided to wait. A bit later, McClellan came in by another door and went upstairs to bed, despite being informed that the president of the United States and the secretary of state were waiting in his parlor. A half-hour went by before a servant came down and explained to the president that the general had "gone to bed." John Hay felt that the president should be incensed, but Lincoln only replied that is was "better at this time not to be making points of etiquette and personal dignity." He never visited McClellan's home again, though.

During the Seven Days' Battles at the end of the Peninsula Campaign, McClellan's armies, when they were engaged, fought well. Actually, they won more battles than they lost. However, they were outmaneuvered and fooled throughout the campaign into thinking the Confederate Army was much bigger than their own. By the end of the three-month campaign, which lasted from March to July 1862, the Union troops were dejected, and they were loaded on boats and sent home to Washington.

McClellan had been outmaneuvered and fooled by a new Confederate commander, as the old one, Joseph E. Johnston, had been wounded in the Battle of Seven Pines. The new commander of the Army of Northern Virginia, the main force of the CSA, was Robert E. Lee. At the end of the Peninsula Campaign, Lincoln relieved McClellan of his command, sending him into semi-retirement.

This enforced retirement would not last long, however. At the Second Battle of Bull Run (also known as the Second Battle of Manassas, which is what it was/is more commonly called in the South) in late August, McClellan's replacement, General John Pope, was routed by Robert E. Lee, and the Army of the Potomac was once again sent into disarray, as it had been after the First Battle of Bull Run.

In September, Lincoln reluctantly called McClellan back to duty, appointing him commander of "the fortifications of Washington, and all the troops for the defense of the capital." By this time, McClellan's caution, ego, and caustic pen and tongue had alienated the Cabinet as well, for all of them urged Lincoln not to reappoint "Little Mac." Lincoln admitted that reappointing McClellan was like curing a hangover with "the hair of the dog," but he told his secretary, "We must use what tools we have. There is no man in the Army who can man these fortifications and lick these troops of ours into shape half as well as he. If he can't fight himself, he excels in making others ready to fight."

So it was that George McClellan was in command of the Union armies in Virginia when Robert E. Lee devised his first plan for an incursion into the North to force "the Yankees" into a negotiated peace.

Chapter 2 – Southern Gentlemen

Where McClellan was cautious, Robert E. Lee was bold, as were most of his generals, most notably Thomas J. "Stonewall" Jackson. They were brought up in the Southern military tradition, hearkening back to the Revolutionary War days of Nathanael Greene, the American commander who, though a Northerner, fought a classic campaign against the more numerous British in the South.

Southern officers were also inculcated with the notion of honor and chivalry, and many sons of the Confederacy were brought up on tales of knights charging through enemy lines to save the day. And lastly, just like McClellan and many Northern officers, they idolized the military career of Napoleon Bonaparte and his audacious and revolutionary tactics. Unlike McClellan, though, they put them into action much more often.

Of course, the most famous man in the South was Robert E. Lee. Though he had lost a number of battles to McClellan in the Seven Days' Battles, he was so skillful in maneuvering his troops that he not only caused McClellan to retreat back to Washington, but he also convinced many in the North that his army was nigh to invincible—which, for a short time, it was.

But that reputation was to come after the Seven Days' Battles and after the subject of this book, the Battle of Antietam. Lee was to go on and win decisive victories at Fredericksburg and Chancellorsville in 1863 before moving on to his second incursion in the North at Gettysburg. There, he would sustain the defeat that many consider to be the turning point in the war, but even after that battle, and despite his seeming lack of judgment in ordering Pickett's suicidal charge, Lee caused US General Ulysses S. Grant much frustration in the defensive battles in Virginia until the war's end.

Lee had been offered the command of all Union armies after the Battle of Fort Sumter, the battle that started off the Civil War. He had already distinguished himself at West Point, both as a student and an instructor, in the Mexican-American War, and in the projects he had undertaken in the Corps of Engineers after that conflict. Lee was the man in charge of the Virginia militia that put down John Brown's anti-slavery rebellion at Harper's Ferry and was one of the most well-known and respected men in the US military, as well as the country in general.

But Lee's first loyalty was to the state of Virginia, which he (and many other Virginians) called their "home country." In those days, most people never traveled outside of their county unless they were in the army or navy, and they had very little contact with Washington, DC, or people from outside their state or even immediate area. Railroads were beginning to change that, albeit slowly, and it didn't really impact most of the people in the South, as railroad production there lagged far behind the North (which came to be a big factor in the Civil War), and the price to ride the rails was prohibitive for many. So, Lee, like many other Southerners, counted his loyalty to his state first and the Union second, especially when it came to the government telling them how to live.

Robert Edward Lee
https://commons.wikimedia.org/wiki/File:Robert_Edward_Lee.jpg

Of course, the main issue of the Civil War was slavery, though many at the time said that the issue was states' rights, an opinion that is still held today by some. Lee is hard to pin down on the issue of slavery in some ways. He was a slave owner and is recorded as having administered harsh punishments. He is also recorded to have set slaves free, and like some other leading Southerners, Lee believed that slavery would die a natural death. However, it wasn't up to the men in the North, who had no idea how much slavery was a part of both economic and social life (according to Southern thinking), to tell Southerners what to do with their "property."

Lee turned down Lincoln's offer, crossed the river to Virginia, then went to the Virginia Legislature and accepted their offer to lead the armies of Virginia, which were forming at that moment.

One of those units that were forming was the Virginia Military Institute Corps of Cadets, led by Major Thomas Jackson, soon to be known to all as "Stonewall." Jackson had been at West Point as well, graduating in 1846 with George McClellan, among others who would fight alongside and against him in the Civil War.

Many people familiar with the Civil War know that Jackson was what some might call an "odd duck." He burned with Christian religious fervor, yet when faced with the aftermath of the looting in Fredericksburg, Virginia, by Union forces, he wanted to "kill 'em all." Jackson often rode his horse or walked about with one hand in the air so as to "keep himself in balance." He sometimes would hold his leg out of the stirrup for the same reason. Most famously, he often sucked on lemons, which is a good idea when scurvy was a real danger, but he was often seen with a lemon in his mouth while riding or even during battle. Jackson wouldn't eat pepper because he thought it weakened his left leg, and he wouldn't send letters that would be in transit on the Sabbath but fought many of his greatest battles on Sunday. In his teaching tenure, he brooked no talking in class. One of his students, James Walker, who ironically would become a brigadier general under Jackson at Antietam, challenged Stonewall to a duel because Jackson singled him out for talking in class, an accusation that Walker believed to be false.

All was forgiven by the time of the Civil War, as Walker's testimony in Jackson's disciplinary hearing illustrates the view of most of the cadets that Jackson taught: "Major Jackson is a stranger [author's note: meaning "strange"] amongst us and brings from the field of his late brilliant achievements many singular and eccentric notions."

By the time of the Battle of Antietam, Jackson's eccentricities had partially endeared him to his men, and his victories, which included the First Battle of Bull Run, the Shenandoah Campaign, and the Second Battle of Bull Run, had made him famous throughout the South.

Thomas Jonathan "Stonewall" Jackson
https://commons.wikimedia.org/wiki/File:Stonewall_Jackson.jpg

As we discuss the Battle of Antietam and the events leading up to it, we will introduce you to other leading figures, both from the South and the North.

Chapter 3 – The Men Who Fought, Their Equipment and Uniforms

Most of the time when we read of the Civil War, we read about the men we've mentioned above or other leaders, like Ulysses S. Grant or William Tecumseh Sherman. Though there are books and movies that do talk about the lives of the average soldier, they seem to be few and far between. So, let's take a little time to talk about the men who did the bulk of the fighting and most of the dying in the American Civil War.

If you look at the old hurried films of the beginning of World War I in nations throughout Europe, crowds seem to be going crazy at the prospect of war. Today, when a nation is attacked, as in the case of 9/11, a grim determination sets in, and perhaps there is talk about how quickly the enemy will be beaten, but there is seldom joy. At the start of WWI, as you can see in those films, the people in the crowds when war was announced or when the soldiers began to march off actually seemed happy. Of course, we know that they learned very quickly that WWI was going to be very different than anything anyone had experienced in history before, and that joy turned into grief and anger very quickly.

The Civil War was the same way. There are famous tales of crowds riding out to Manassas Junction, Virginia, from Washington, DC, to see what they expected to be a "grand sight," to use the parlance of the time. Many believed the Federal Army would rout the Southerners in one quick go. As the men in (mostly) blue came running back from the front lines, some of them with arms, hands, and eyes hanging off, those same crowds panicked, and at least some of them began to realize their ideas about a glorious war might be incorrect.

The men who initially fought felt the same way, at least those who had not done any fighting, which was most of them. Most of the men in the army who had fought in the Mexican-American War were either officers or retired, and there was a limited number of non-commissioned officers who had done some fighting on the frontier. However, most of the men who filled the ranks of the "Blue and the Gray" had no idea what they were getting into.

By the time the war began in 1861, people on both sides had known it was coming for some time. A civil war had almost happened during the "nullification crisis" of 1832-33, and tensions flared up again during the years before the war in a low-level guerrilla war in Kansas over the spread of slavery. The "nullification crisis" involved radicals from the South, who were led by Southern firebrand John C. Calhoun. Calhoun and others believed that President Andrew Jackson and the federal government were taking too much power for themselves, and they asserted that states had the right to "nullify" any federal law they found ran contrary to the laws of their states or wishes of their legislature. Jackson threatened an invasion of Calhoun's home state of South Carolina, and so, the "nullifiers" backed down, but the tensions between the Southern states and the federal government would remain.

One of the many sad things about the Southern cause was that many of the men in the rank and file had more in common with their Northern brethren working in factories and, to an extent, slaves than they did to their officers. The poor whites of the South were largely illiterate and barely educated. They fell to sickness with great regularity, considering the climate and the state of hygiene and health in the 19th century. The upper classes in the South held most of the power, and a relatively small number of families in each state or county held most of that power.

Though there was some upward social mobility in the South, the agricultural nature of the Southern economy did not allow the same social climbing that happened in the North. There were, of course, exceptions, such as in the case of Nathan Bedford Forrest, who built a fortune trading slaves.

Still, the men of the South who filled the ranks of the Confederate armies could hold themselves above somebody—the slaves. And the Southerners were full of resentment toward the Northerners, who believed they could tell Southerners how to run their lives.

For the men of the North, the issue was unity. A sizable minority did care about the slavery issue, and more began to care as they moved into the South and saw the conditions that the vast majority of slaves lived in, but maintaining the unity of the fairly new nation, which wasn't even one hundred years old yet, was their main cause. To them, the Southerners were betraying what the American Revolution had been fought for, what many of their forefathers had died for. Additionally, many Northern officers, after having been stationed in the South, realized the very class-conscious and increasingly outdated Southern society, seeing in it shades of the very aristocracy the men of the Revolution had fought against.

Of course, there were men on both sides who simply fought because that's what their countrymen were doing; they didn't want to be accused of cowardice or of not being a patriot. Some joined for the adventure. Many new immigrants in both parts of the country joined to prove themselves Americans. And some simply joined for a paycheck.

Weapons and Equipment

What did the men of North and South go to war with? As opposed to today's American soldier, who many times goes into the field with eighty or more pounds, carrying everything from ammunition to basic medical equipment, technology, and MREs, the Civil War soldier, for the most part, carried the bare minimum into battle. As a rule, the soldiers were never far from their supply trains, and if they were, they were notorious scroungers—especially the Northern soldiers in the final campaigns of the war.

Generally speaking, the Union soldier was better outfitted than his Southern cousin. As you can see in the following picture, the Northern foot soldier went into battle or on the march carrying a wool blanket atop his knapsack. In that knapsack was his half of a two-man tent, a groundsheet, an overcoat, and personal effects, such as a Bible, razor, sewing kit, etc. He carried his rifle, a forty round cartridge box, a sheathed bayonet, a box for the caps used for firing his weapon (in the early stages of the war), a leather haversack, a cloth-covered canteen, and a tin cup. Of course, this was the average load for the Union soldier—each man made it his own according to his preference and the forbearance of his officers.

Unfortunately for the men of both sides, their uniforms were made of wool. Not only was this hot in the summer, but it was also itchy. Linen blouses helped somewhat. The Union soldier wore boots or shoes with a square toe, sometimes referred to as "gunboats." The standard issue by the end of the war was a blue uniform, though throughout the war and especially at the beginning, many units (coming as they did from state militias of different traditions and histories) wore various different uniforms, and the colors, hats, and pants varied greatly, as you can see below.

Though the Confederates had a great deal of variety in their uniforms to start the war, much as the Union men did, by the end of the war, the standard Confederate uniform was either grayish or butternut. In the 1930s, President Franklin Delano Roosevelt honored the survivors of the Civil War by beginning his speech, "Veterans of the Blue and the Gray," but it's more likely that most men in the Confederate armies wore butternut or a mix of both.

As you can see from the following picture, the Confederate soldier was generally not as well equipped as his Northern counterpart. This only got worse as the war went on, as the Union would blockade the main Southern ports and take more Southern territory.

Though many Southern soldiers wore the same style of forage hat, or "kepi" as the Northerners, it was gray. Many rebel soldiers wore variations of the slouch hat you see above. Like the Yankees, the rebels wore a jacket covering a linen shirt and occasionally an overcoat. In the winter campaign of 1862, which culminated in the bloody Union defeat at Fredericksburg, many of the Southern soldiers did not even have shoes, let alone overcoats. Southern soldiers often took better clothing off dead Union soldiers or prisoners of war.

"Johnny Reb," as the common Southern soldier was referred to in both the North and the South, carried a blanket slung over his shoulder and maybe a groundsheet or shelter-half, a partial tent, if he was lucky. Oftentimes these were wrapped around extra articles of clothing, such as socks or gloves. Naturally, he carried his weapon, cartridges, cap box, and usually a wooden canteen. Additionally, the Southern soldier often carried a knife in addition to his bayonet.

When the war began, both sides were armed with virtually the same weapons, which meant that capturing the enemy's stores was exceedingly important, especially for the rebels, as most of the weapons production was in the Northern states. As the war went on, blockading the Southern coastline and cutting their supply lines was important to the North in order to prevent what weapons the South could buy overseas or make themselves from getting to their men on the front.

In a book of this length, we are limited to talking about the basics and what most men were equipped with. Let's start with the most common infantry weapon of the war, the Springfield Model 1861. The first long gun to equip iron sights as a standard feature, the Model 1861 was a .58 caliber gun firing a Minié Ball— think about that for a moment. The American heavy machine gun of World War II and today is the Browning .50 caliber. It will tear or blow a man apart. Anti-aircraft carriers of WWII mounted four of these guns on a single mount, and though it was technically "illegal" to use against men, it was done all the time. Its nickname was the "Meatgrinder." Now, think of hundreds of .58 caliber guns all aiming at much the same point, which is what happened during the Civil War. It is no wonder that Antietam remains one of the bloodiest days in US history.

The ammunition of the Springfield 1861 was the Minié ball, pictured above. As you can see from the spelling, the name has nothing to do with the size of the projectile (and it's clearly not a ball). It was named after its inventor, Claude-Étienne Minié, who designed the French Minié rifle used in the Crimean War.

To fire the 1861 Springfield, as well as other muzzle loading weapons, with the Minié ball, the soldier poured gunpowder down the barrel of the gun (this was a proscribed amount, though more or less could be added for range), then sent the ball down the barrel until it rested on the gunpowder at the bottom. In the case of the Minié ball, the hollowed end allowed the powder to be packed into the bullet rather than around it, as with a musket ball. This also meant that the bottom of the ball flared out and lodged itself in the rifled grooves of the barrel, which, when fired, would send the projectile spinning.

For those of you unfamiliar with firearms, "rifling" means that the inside of the barrel was etched with spiral grooves. In the case of the Minié ball, when the thinner bottom of the cartridge flared out, it provided a block of the gases that propelled the ball. This was different than the older musket ball, which lost power with gases escaping around the sides of the ball as it traveled down the barrel. The rifling of the barrel and the spin put on the projectile meant that rifles (as opposed to the smoothbore musket used previously) had greater range and were much more accurate.

This is one reason why the formation fighting that took place during the Civil War was so deadly. Previously, men grouped together because smoothbore muskets were notoriously inaccurate. Grouping together allowed them to multiply the effect of their weapons and perhaps hit *something*. What the men of the Civil War (especially the officers) did not realize was that with rifling, those formations were essentially a slow-moving target that could hardly be missed. Add the Minié ball and the size of the caliber, and the battlefields of the Civil War were butcher's yards.

A well-trained soldier could fire the Springfield three times a minute. Its effective range was just under three hundred yards, give or take. The rifle was just under 56 inches long and weighed a bit over 9.5 pounds.

Before the mass production of the Springfield, both sides of the war used the British-made Enfield 1853, which was, in most respects, just like the Springfield, except it was manufactured overseas. This would become problematic during the war, especially for the South, not to mention they were fairly expensive.

In the war's last year, breech-loading rifles, carbines (shorter-barreled and lighter rifles, mostly for cavalry use), and repeating rifles were used by some units of the Union Army. Breech-loading meant the projectile, now with powder contained in the cartridge, was inserted at the base of the barrel, meaning no powder pouring or ramming was needed. The advent of the repeating rifle meant that multiple cartridges could be loaded into the weapon and fired one after the other, only stopping to reload a clip of bullets. Obviously, this gave the Union Army a great advantage over the Confederate soldiers, whose own experiments with breech-loading rifles were abortive.

As was mentioned, the men carried a variety of arms, especially at the beginning of the war. This held true for officers and their sidearms as well. Most officers, at least for dress or formal situations, still wore a sword, and some (especially in the cavalry) wore it in battle.

Most Union officers (and some Confederates) carried the Colt M1861 Navy .36 caliber six-shot pistol. The effective range of this gun was between 75 to 100 yards, though most times when the pistol was employed, action was at much closer range. About 40,000 Model 1861s were produced during the war. Many Confederate officers carried a similar weapon, the Colt Model 1860, which was larger in caliber—.44, just like the character Dirty Harry in the movie *Magnum Force* (1973).

The large caliber and relatively slow velocity of Civil War firearms combined with the use of the Minié ball meant that a great deal of damage was done when a soldier was hit. Usually, the ball flattened out when entering the body, and if it didn't hit bone, it continued its way out, usually creating a large exit wound.

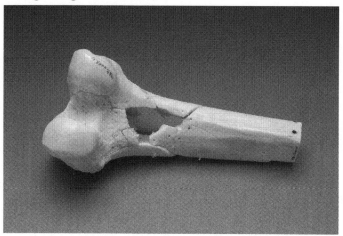

Upper thigh (femur) hit by Minié ball
https://commons.wikimedia.org/wiki/File:Gunshot_femur.jpg

Obviously, there were a great many ways to die on the Civil War battlefields. Aside from the weapons described above, artillery in its various forms caused many deaths. However, most of the deaths of the Civil War came not from battlefield injuries but from diseases and post-operative infections.

One of the most famous images of the Civil War is that of the battlefield hospital and the amazing number of amputations done there. Personal accounts of the war and some extant photographs describe and show mountains of arms, legs, hands, and feet cut off in order to save a life. Unfortunately, through most of the war, cleanliness wasn't only next to impossible; its importance wasn't yet realized.

Dirty instruments, hands, bandages, floors, and bedding all meant that many of the men who had survived the battlefield, even with relatively minor wounds, were all in danger of dying from infection. It was not until the US Sanitary Commission, which was formed in 1861 and included many influential and powerful women, lobbied Congress and the military that conditions in the battlefield hospitals began to change, leading to a drop in infection rates, at least in the North. This was also at a time when the idea of germs was just taking hold, and only those at the cutting edge of medical knowledge began to accept the idea.

Those were some of the ways a man could die during the war. But what kept him alive? Well, their field rations—those carried by the men or by units nearby on the march—were hardtack and salt pork. Hardtack is essentially a biscuit or a cracker made from water and flour. Sometimes salt is added. The resultant "hard" cracker has an exceedingly long shelf life, but it is relatively flavorless and could almost break teeth unless softened with more water.

Salt pork is just that—pork salted to preserve it for long periods of time to prevent spoilage. Both of these items increased thirst, which was never a good thing in a situation where water was limited, the weather sometimes hot, and the uniforms made of wool. In camp, the menu varied, but bacon was a staple and a favorite. This was not the healthiest diet, but it wasn't all that different from what they ate at home. Salt and sugar were the prime ways people added flavor and preserved food back then.

Of course, as there have been in all armies throughout history and the world, there were the men skilled at "scrounging"—finding things to add to meals, whether this was done by hunting, wheeling and dealing, or stealing. A good scrounger helped keep men's spirits up, and many Civil War era diaries are filled with tales of men getting their fill of chicken, turkey, deer, and, of course, some kind of alcohol while sitting by the campfire, playing cards, and singing songs.

Toward the end of the war, with much of the South's agricultural land taken over, its ports blockaded, and its railways cut or occupied, starvation set in for both the armies of the Confederate and civilians. Though many Southern armies had a good reputation for not "foraging" (a polite word for "stealing"), whether in its campaigns in the North or at home, in the last year of the war, desperate times called for desperate measures. Many Southern civilians also began to hide what little they had from their own armies.

Obviously, as we know from the tales of "Sherman's March to the Sea" and other episodes, Union troops in the South were notorious for pillaging and raiding Southern farms and homes, especially if they were plantations, as they were the very symbol of the Southern aristocracy.

Chapter 4 – Battle of South Mountain and Harper's Ferry

Throughout the Civil War, General McClellan's reputation went from bad to worse. Much of this had to do with his caution, which may have cost the country tens of thousands of more lives. At times, McClellan had the means and opportunity to win the war, but his fear of losing rather than risking everything to win prolonged the conflict by years.

Adding to McClellan's bad reputation was the discovery of his private letters and writings, as well as contemporary accounts of his comments on Lincoln, the Cabinet, the conduct of the war, and his boasting about his military acumen. Adding to that was his running for president in 1864 on the Democratic ticket and calling for a negotiated peace with the South.

However, as was stated, McClellan may have been a braggart and overly cautious, but he did know something about battles. He did win, though he could have won bigger, and he did rebuild the army twice. Historians have stated that the best use of McClellan's talents would have been as a staff officer or at the head of the Quartermaster Corps, where he likely would have excelled.

Still, in the prelude to the Battle of Antietam, McClellan won a battle that is much overlooked by history—the Battle of South Mountain. But the Union also lost an important battle in the time just before Antietam at Harper's Ferry.

The Battle of South Mountain took place in the hills of western Maryland, near the area where Camp David lies today. In early September 1862, Robert E. Lee, fresh off the Confederate victories at the Second Battle of Bull Run and Jackson's Shenandoah Campaign, launched an invasion of Maryland with the ultimate goals of taking pressure off Richmond, cutting Union supply lines to Washington from the "breadbasket" of Pennsylvania, and perhaps forcing Lincoln to a negotiated peace. Lee's broader goal was the seizure of the capital of Pennsylvania at Harrisburg, an important river port at the time, but to do that, he would have to make his way through Maryland first and reduce the Federal garrison at Harper's Ferry, located in western Virginia.

The Union garrison at Harper's Ferry contained some 14,000 men and significant amounts of artillery. It was meant to be a check on any rebel moves northward and to keep the confluence of the Shenandoah and Potomac Rivers clear of rebel interference. It was a very strong force, and in the right hands, it could have stalled or perhaps stopped any Confederate drive north into Pennsylvania.

However, in command of the Harper's Ferry garrison was Colonel Dixon Miles, who, among other things, was likely an alcoholic. He was also eccentric and aging, though the two might not have been mutually exclusive. He had developed the odd habit of wearing two hats at a time—the reason is lost to history, but perhaps he simply didn't remember the first one was there.

Harper's Ferry was familiar to Lee and Jackson. They were both native Virginians, and Jackson had grown up in the western part of the state. He was present when John Brown and his comrades were hanged after Lee put down the rebellion at Harper's Ferry, commanding a contingent of Virginia Military Institute cadets sent there to help keep order.

One good thing about the town of Harper's Ferry itself is that it commands the local river traffic. Unfortunately, it is also surrounded by steep hills and cliffs, giving any commander determined enough to get cannons on them a decided advantage. Miles was determined, but he only placed a few guns and two thousand men on the most tactically important heights, known as Maryland Heights, and left nearby Loudoun Heights undefended. He chose to place most of his men to the west, convinced that the rebels were going to attack across the flat plains to the west of the town.

Lee knew that he would have to eliminate or bottle up the forces at Harper's Ferry if he wanted to advance farther north. What he did was to become his trademark in later battles: he divided his weaker forces to engage the enemy where he was least expected, with both audacity and speed. Lee sent Stonewall Jackson, who commanded about 30,000 men, to take care of Harper's Ferry, while he moved with the rest of his army, about 20,000 men, in the direction of Hagerstown, Maryland.

Over the course of the next three days (September 12th-15th), Jackson moved his artillery and most of his men into the hills surrounding Harper's Ferry, the same hills that Miles thought the Confederates would believe to be insurmountable. Skirmishes occurred over those days, but Miles believed he could hold out—that is until Jackson's guns began to bombard the town from the heights above, followed shortly after by an infantry attack by his most aggressive commander, fellow West Pointer A.P. Hill.

Though the fighting was heavy for a short time, Miles realized that the positioning of Jackson's guns and his advantage in numbers would eventually defeat the garrison. Still, critics say that Miles, aware that Lee was moving troops nearby, should have held out as long as possible in order to delay any possible rebel moves northward. As it was, McClellan, realizing that Harper's Ferry was likely to fall, had begun to move the bulk of his army in the direction of Harper's Ferry, either to relieve the town or to engage "Bobby" Lee (as McClellan called him) and defeat him once and for all. Should this happen, Lee was going to need Jackson's men, and Jackson was under orders to eliminate the threat of Harper's Ferry, leave a small garrison there, and then move with speed to rejoin the bulk of the Army of Northern Virginia.

Any extended period of time that Miles could hold out would have been useful, but after three days of Jackson maneuvering and placing his guns, the battle was essentially over in one day. Miles surrendered after his forces took minimal casualties; sadly, he was one of them, dying from complications from a terrible leg wound. The Confederate dead numbered less than 40, and the Union dead was just over that number, at 44. The Union losses altogether, though, were rather high, with 12,419 missing and/or taken prisoner.

While the Battle of Harper's Ferry was going on, McClellan was engaging the Confederates at South Mountain, which was to the northeast of Harper's Ferry by some twenty miles. In actuality, South Mountain was not really a peak; it was more of a heavily wooded ridge, which included three main "gaps" through which roads for local commerce passed.

On September 8th, 1862, Lee summoned his commanders and issued "Special Order 191." Lee emphasized security and warned his commanders against telling too many of their men about the plans contained in his order. His adjutant signed a number of copies in Lee's name for Jackson, Hill, and a handful of other commanders and had them distributed. One of Lee's officers—no one is completely sure who—wrapped them around three cigars to help keep them dry and at some point dropped them unknowingly.

The man who found them, Corporal Barton W. Mitchell of the 27th Indiana Volunteers, who would die after the war from the recurring infection from a wound sustained at Antietam, found the orders and relayed them to his chain of command, one of whom authenticated Lee's adjutant's signature, having known him well before the war. Lee's plans went all the way to the top, and when George McClellan received them, he exclaimed, "Now I know what to do! Here is a paper with which, if I cannot whip Bobby Lee, I will be willing to go home."

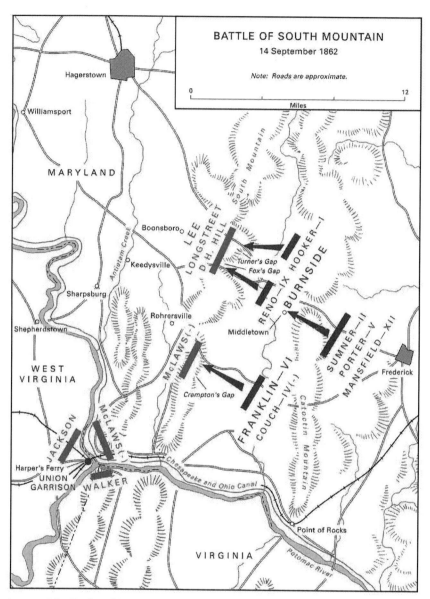

Basic map of the Battles of South Mountain and Harper's Ferry. Note the location of Sharpsburg and Antietam Creek to the east.

Lee's forces at South Mountain were sparse, and the Confederate general's hope was for Jackson to defeat the garrison at Harper's Ferry and come to the aid of Lafayette McLaws and D.H. Hill, wherever they were engaged, when Jackson freed himself from his assault. In the days before, Lee had sent McLaws and Hill eastward to reconnoiter both a route north and to find and assess Federal forces in the area of Frederick, some ten miles east of South Mountain.

Another Confederate force, under General James Longstreet, had been sent north toward Pennsylvania with the aim of reaching Hagerstown, Maryland, just a few miles south of the Pennsylvania border. Longstreet was one of Lee's most trusted generals, and he had a reputation for his skill with artillery. Even more so than other famous Southern generals, Longstreet had good friends that ended up in the Union Army. His West Point roommate, William Rosecrans, became a prominent Union general, as did John Pope and George Henry Thomas (one of the best Union generals and who became known as the "Rock of Chickamauga" for his unyielding stance there). Longstreet was a party-goer at West Point, resulting in many demerits and graduation near the bottom of his class. Football, slovenliness, tardiness, and drinking seemed to have a priority, which may be one reason Longstreet was good friends with Ulysses S. Grant, whose wedding he attended in 1848. He practically had to because Grant's wife, Julia Dent, was Longstreet's cousin. Longstreet was also good friends with future Confederate commanders Lafayette McLaws, George Pickett, and D.H. Hill.

Though he graduated near the bottom of his West Point class in 1842, Longstreet was an able commander. Like the other generals mentioned in this book, he took part in the Mexican-American War, serving on the staff of future president Zachary Taylor. He took part in many actions but was most notable for rescuing a group of outnumbered Americans from a charge by two hundred Mexican lancers, cavalrymen who fought with lances. In the fight to take Mexico City, Longstreet was involved in desperate hand-to-hand combat. He ended the war with a brevet (temporary battlefield) promotion after he had led a charge at Chapultepec, in which he was wounded while carrying the colors. The man he handed the colors to was George Pickett.

Longstreet's Civil War record was distinguished both before and after the Battle of Antietam, and though he was defeated more than once, he took part in some of the great Confederate victories of the early war and helped Lee in his brilliant defense of Richmond in the war's later stages. At Gettysburg, he played a controversial role that is still debated by historians today, as he begged Lee to give up the battlefield and redeploy his men before the disastrous Pickett's Charge ended the Gettysburg Campaign.

Longstreet during the war
https://commons.wikimedia.org/wiki/File:James_Longstreet.jpg

As the Confederate men took their defensive positions in the gaps at South Mountain, Lee sent word for Longstreet to return to the area to reinforce them, as the rebel troops in the gaps were vastly outnumbered. When Longstreet's troops did arrive at 3:30 p.m. on September 12th, after having marched over rough terrain for nineteen hours to get there, they came just in time to allow the Southerners to begin a strongly fought tactical retreat to better ground.

The fighting at South Mountain, as you can see from the map above, took place at three gaps. North to south, they are Turner's Gap, Fox's Gap, and Crampton's Gap.

McClellan, who had pursued Lee rather slowly at this point, changed his pace when he received the lost Special Order 191. Having previously believed, as he was wont to do, that the majority of Confederate troops faced him directly, he now knew that Lee had divided his troops into three branches, and McClellan meant to take advantage of it.

On the morning of September 14th, Union division commander General Jacob D. Cox launched an attack on the right flank of the Southern troops at Fox's Gap. There, his Ohio division overran the

North Carolinian troops of General Samuel Garland Jr., who was killed in action. After this, though, Cox stopped, waiting for further orders and allowing the Confederates to fortify their positions on the north flank of Fox's Gap.

To the north, General Ambrose Burnside, who openly admitted his lack of skill for greater command and who had turned down Lincoln's request to take command of the Army of the Potomac twice because of it, moved slowly and waited for orders from McClellan, who was slowly riding up the National Road (which led east-west from the coast through Virginia and Maryland) at the head of a large column of troops who cheered him on. Hearing that the battle was going on just a mile or two down the road, McClellan stopped his horse by the side of the road, tucked one hand in his jacket, and pointed toward the battle with the other hand. He remained that way for some time. It would have made a great statue, but many generals, including most Southern generals, would have been galloping toward the fighting and forcing their men into a trot. McClellan did neither of these things; instead, he gave general orders and presumed his subordinates would carry them out.

Burnside waited for one of his corps commanders, Joseph "Fightin' Joe" Hooker (who would replace Burnside as commander in chief when he accepted Lincoln's offer after Antietam), and at Fox's Gap, a usually aggressive Union general Jesse L. Reno moved slowly to reinforce the Union troops there.

At Crampton's Gap on the southern part of the mountain, 1,000 men of the CSA under General Howell Cobb faced 12,000 Union soldiers led by William B. Franklin, who, like his commander McClellan, believed he was facing more men than he actually was. Skirmishes took place most of the day until around 4 p.m. when Franklin's subordinate, Henry Slocum, got tired of waiting for his commander to give the order to advance with his whole force. Slocum led 12,000 Maine, New Jersey, Pennsylvania, and New York men right into the Southern position. At about that time, two regiments of Georgia troops showed up to reinforce Cobb, but it did no good. Wave after wave of Union troops came at them relentlessly, and by nightfall, the position was taken. One rebel soldier, George Neese, a gunner in the horse artillery, said, "the Federals were so numerous that it looked as if they were creeping up out of the ground."

At the gaps to the north, the battle had been going on with some severity all day. At about the same time that Slocum led his men at Crampton's Gap, Longstreet's troops arrived in position. At the base of the mountain, they had met Robert E. Lee, who received their cheers and urged them on. The Texas Brigade, which had been led by the aggressive General John Bell Hood (a Kentuckian who joined the South when his state remained in the Union) until he had been arrested, demanded Lee reinstate Hood to command. "Give us Hood!" they shouted. Hood had been arrested and removed from command after the Second Battle of Bull Run in August over a conflict with another Confederate general over some captured wagons, and he was with Lee's entourage when the men confronted Lee about it. Lee replied, "You shall have him!" and called Hood forward. Lee asked Hood to express "regret" over the wagon incident, but Hood refused. Lee, being in a no-win situation, then replied, "Well, I will suspend your arrest until the impending battle is decided."

Toward dark, the Union generals had begun to pressure the Confederates at Fox's and Turner's Gaps after hard fighting among rocks, trees, and underbrush. Although the Southerners held their positions when the fighting ceased at full dark, Lee, Longstreet, and D.H. Hill met to discuss their options and decided that it was only a matter of time before their positions were overrun. Rather than risk complete defeat and possibly a panic-fueled rout, Lee elected to orderly retreat back toward Sharpsburg, between the Potomac River to the west and Antietam Creek. During the fighting at South Mountain, Lee had received word from Jackson about the fall of the Union garrison at Harper's Ferry. That evening, Lee sent word to Jackson to head toward Sharpsburg.

On the other side, George McClellan sent word back to his wife, saying he had won a "glorious victory." A similar message went to Washington, DC. Lincoln responded, "God bless you and all with you. Destroy the rebel army if possible."

Chapter 5 – Antietam

Despite the setback at South Mountain, Lee was still determined to fight on Northern ground. He knew McClellan was cautious, but Lee also knew that he wasn't stupid and that if the Southern generals weren't careful, "Little Mac" might be able to wrangle the decisive victory he had been looking for.

Even with that knowledge, Lee decided to take up a dangerous position near Sharpsburg, a small town whose population today is only about 800. It was roughly the same in 1862. Behind Sharpsburg is the Potomac River, one of the widest on the North American continent. The river near Sharpsburg is not nearly as wide as it is near Washington, DC, but it is wide enough that Lee, if he and his forces were bottled up in the area, would probably only have one bridge with which to remove his army. If that were the case, and the Federal forces were on his heels, the Army of Northern Virginia would be shot to pieces.

But one thing that even the laziest of history students know is that Robert E. Lee was a gambler. Aside from that, the area did afford some defensive advantages. Sharpsburg itself was essentially in the middle of Lee's lines. The Potomac protected Lee's rear if McClellan attempted a wide flanking move; however, Lee and the entire country knew McClellan would not attempt such a move.

Antietam Creek ran from north to south in Lee's front. Many would actually call the creek a small river, and though there were places that were shallow enough for a man to cross in waist-deep water, three main bridges spanned the waterway.

A mile and a half or so above Sharpsburg was a series of woods, punctuated by farm fields on rolling hills. These were thick woods, which blocked one's vision and sound to some degree. As you can see from the map, they were named for where they lay—north, east, and west. The rebels positioned themselves around the West Woods, using the Dunker Church as a base of operations and an anchor point for their defense. The church was so named for a pacifist sect that baptized their congregants by "dunking" them, rather than using the more common method of pouring water on the head.

From north to south ran the Hagerstown Pike, the main roadway north that linked the larger town of Hagerstown to Sharpsburg, which was thirteen miles away. To the south of the woods and the Dunker Church, just to the east of the Hagerstown Pike, was the "Sunken Road," so-called because the wear and tear on the dirt surface had caused it to sink below the level of the ground around it. The Sunken Road was bordered on both sides in spots by a split-rail fence. After the battle, and to this day, the Sunken Road has been referred to as "Bloody Lane."

The Sunken Road
Chris Light at English Wikipedia, CC BY-SA 3.0 <https://creativecommons.org/licenses/by-sa/3.0>, via Wikimedia Commons
https://commons.wikimedia.org/wiki/File:Antietam_Sunken_Road.JPG

"Bloody Lane" immediately after the battle
https://commons.wikimedia.org/wiki/File:BloodyLaneAntietam.jpg

In the south, just outside Sharpsburg and near to Antietam Creek, was another Southern force, with Lafayette McLaws and R.H Anderson in reserve. Later in the day, the action in this area would be remembered for the slaughter that took place on the southernmost bridge over Antietam Creek. Then known as Rohrbach's Bridge, today it's known as Burnside's Bridge, for the Union general whose troops forced their way across it, taking immense casualties.

The battlefield of Antietam has been preserved and today resembles in many ways the field as it looked on that September day in 1862—rolling hills, cornfields, orchards, and fences, some of which gave cover and some which didn't

Chapter 6 – Dunker Church

One of the contributing factors in the large casualty count at Antietam was the confusion and lack of communication that took place, mostly on the Union side. There were also some unfortunate/fortunate (depending on whose side you were on) accidents, which made things even more confusing and bloody. To describe each unit action and maneuver that took place throughout the battle would require much more space than we have here. What follows is a general overview of the battle in the north around the Dunker Church and what had become known as simply the "Cornfield."

At 5:30 a.m., in the far north of the battlefield, Union General Joseph Hooker ordered three divisions to move out. General Abner Doubleday (the supposed inventor of baseball, although that claim, which Doubleday never made himself, has been discredited by modern-day historians) was on the right, General George Meade (who would lead the Union to victory the next summer at Gettysburg) was in the center, and on the left was General James Ricketts, another West Pointer and native New Yorker. The first two columns moved through the North Woods, and the last made their way to the East Woods.

As soon as Doubleday's men emerged from the North Woods, Confederate guns opened fire. The rebels were so accurate that they didn't have to fire many shots to find the right range, as their second shell tore into the 6th Wisconsin Brigade, killing two men and wounding eleven. Within a few seconds, Federal guns to the rear and on the flanks opened up, and a raging artillery duel began. Not only did the guns near the Hagerstown Pike and the advanced rebel lines open fire, but so did the guns on the rise near the Dunker Church. These were eight cannons from Jeb Stuart's forces, a dozen from Jackson, and another sixteen from batteries across the road from the church. Generally speaking, Confederate batteries consisted of four guns, while Federal units consisted of six.

The Union guns then joined the fray. Two miles away, across Antietam Creek, 24 heavy Federal guns opened fire. A journalist nearby attempted to count the blasts of these guns, which amounted to about sixty rounds per minute.

This was when five Pennsylvania regiments marched to the south of the East Woods and into the right side of the rebel line in front of the church. The Southern unit in this area was commanded by Colonel James Walker—the same man who had challenged Stonewall Jackson to a duel some years before. Walker was wounded and had to be taken from the field, but his men put up such a fight that the "Bluecoats" retreated.

General Joseph Hooker moved with his men toward the Dunker Church and the cornfield north and east of it. In that cornfield, Hooker and his men saw glinting Confederate bayonets among the stalks. So, he called up more guns, and six batteries opened fire on the cornfield, which was from now on known to men on both sides and history as *the* Cornfield. In his battlefield report, Hooker wrote, "every stalk of corn in the northern and greater part of the field was cut as closely as could have been done with a knife, and the slain lay in rows precisely as they had stood in their ranks a few minutes before."

Hooker called for reinforcements to press on, and on the Union left, General Rickett's 1ˢᵗ Brigade filed out of the East Woods and into the eastern part of the Cornfield, where stalks of corn still partially hid their advance, as well as what was waiting for them on the other side. Because the maneuvers and communications of the time required officers to be able to see and identify units personally, most flew the national flag and the flag of their unit(s). This was what the Union men did, and the Georgia unit waiting for them saw their flags coming at them through the corn. At about two hundred yards, the Georgians opened fire, which was then returned by the men in blue.

Two of the Union men in the Cornfield were brothers, German immigrants named Gleasman. One went down after being shot by a rebel sharpshooter some distance away. This was seen by his brother, who pointed and said, "There is the man who killed my brother, and he is taking aim now against that tree." At just that moment, he, too, was felled by the same man, falling next to his brother on the field.

From about 6 to 6:45 a.m., both sides poured in reinforcements to the area. At 6:45, Walker's unit, who had lost 40 percent of its men, began to retreat. The Georgians next to them remained, but they had taken even more punishment—a 50 percent casualty rate, and their commander had been killed, as had five Confederate unit commanders in the area.

As the gray line of Confederates was about to give, another rebel unit rushed into the fight, the Louisiana Brigade, which consisted of men mainly from New Orleans who were known as the "Tigers" (yes, the Louisiana Tigers—history is everywhere, LSU fans). These men charged into the Federal lines and drove them back toward the East Woods. One Union officer writing after the war called it, "the most deadly fire of the war...the dead and wounded go down in scores." To break up the Tigers' assault, Federal cannons were quickly brought to bear on the advancing Louisiana men, blowing the Tigers to pieces at point-blank range. Those who survived were then attacked by General Rickett's last reserve brigade. The fighting then shifted to hand-to-hand combat, at one point fighting over fallen Union colors. In trying to retrieve them, seven of ten men from the 90th Pennsylvania died. Private William Paul grabbed the colors and made it safely back to Union lines, and he won the newly established Medal of Honor for his actions. In the conflict near the East Woods, the units had lost nearly 50 percent of their strength.

At the same time as this was happening near the East Woods, the Union forces were pushing into the West Woods on the rebels' left. As they were coming down the western side of the Hagerstown Pike, they came under fire from still more men in the Cornfield. The Federal soldiers brought up cannons to deal with this, but as the guns were setting up, rebel sharpshooters began to pick their crews off. Within five minutes, more than half of the Union crews were dead or wounded.

Throughout the morning, in many different parts of the Cornfield on both sides of the Hagerstown Pike, unit after unit was thrown into the fighting. Wisconsin units and men were mixed in with New York units and men, and by about 6:45 a.m., they were about halfway to the Dunker Church.

As this happened, another Confederate counterattack occurred out of the West Woods. There, Brigadier General William Starke had the men from his two brigades line up along a wooden rail fence just thirty yards away from the Federal flank. In turn, some of the men from Wisconsin and New York wheeled right (think of a swinging door), and an artillery unit to the north opened up on the rebels. Within fifteen minutes, the rebels were reeling, and their commander was struck by three Minié balls and soon died. All along that fence line and into the Union position were dead and dying men, but the fighting raged on.

In the small "no man's land" between the two enemies, Confederate Captain R.P. Jennings lay wounded with another man. The two men argued about what the safest course would be—to try to run or remain where they were, as bullets were landing all around them. "I may as well be killed running as lying still," Jennings said, and he got up and amazingly made it back to the rebel lines.

All along the Pike, the men in gray were falling back toward the Dunker Church. These were Jackson's men, and many of the units had taken 50 percent casualties or more. Just when it looked like the Confederate left might break, 2,300 men in gray came tearing through a hole in the churchyard fence and toward the fighting, screaming their rebel yell, that unique battle cry of the South, which is explained generally by historian Shelby Foote in Ken Burns' miniseries *The Civil War* as a howl and a series of yips. These were the men of John Bell Hood's division, the Texas Brigade, and they were angry. The night before, Stonewall Jackson had promised them that they would be held in reserve and given time to eat a real meal, which they had not done in days. That morning, as they set up their fires and pots and got ready to sit down to eat, the call came for them to join the fighting.

No man likes having his breakfast interrupted, least of all when he hasn't really eaten in days and especially when he is being called on to perhaps go and die. So, they gathered their arms and ran into battle, surging through the churchyard and into the Cornfield, across the Pike and toward the East Woods. Hood himself followed, trying to maneuver his horse so that he didn't tread on some wounded man, for the field was almost invisible under the bodies.

The Texans pushed every Federal soldier in their path out of the way, sending them into a panic—at least those they didn't shoot down. Hood's Texans were soon joined by D.H. Hill's division, but the Texans took the brunt of the fighting in the Cornfield on the eastern side of the Hagerstown Pike. Barreling out of the field, Union men who had fought well all morning gave way to Hood. A Union private, no more than sixteen, stood on a knoll and tried to rally his comrades, yelling, "Rally, boys, rally! Die like men, don't run like dogs!"

Jackson sent a messenger to Hood, who replied back to Stonewall, saying that he would soon be pressed back unless he received reinforcements but that he would keep pressing until he no longer could. When the fighting did end, the 1ˢᵗ Texas Brigade was found to have sustained 186 men dead out of 226, an 82.3 percent casualty rate, the highest for any regiment throughout the costly war.

Back along the Pike to the west, the Federal units left in the area banded together and began to fire on the surging rebels on the other side of the road. Farther to the west, Confederate General Jubal Early's men were marching toward the Pike. Some Union guns fired westward, while others fired east. Forty out of one hundred of the battery's men were wounded or killed that morning. Other men jumped in to keep the guns firing, including General John Gibbon, the commander of the Federal center unit. One gun was positioned right in the middle of the road, and Gibbon noticed it was firing too high. He jumped down from his horse, lowered the elevation of the gun himself, and gave the order to fire through the wooden rails of the fence and into the rebels who were on the other side. At least a dozen enemy soldiers were blown to pieces by the canister shot. After the battle, a Union officer said he saw an arm fly thirty feet through the air.

The men in Gibbon's battery increased their firepower to double canister. Think of a shotgun switching from .20 gauge to .12 gauge or even .10 gauge. Three Confederate charges attempted to overtake the guns, and all three times they were beaten back. This took place between fifteen and twenty minutes. The Union men were soon going to be out of ammunition, and so, Gibbon called for a retreat. A total of 26 dead and mangled horses lay around the cannon, but the remaining Union men in blue found enough animals to limber (mount for traveling) their guns, and they made their way off the field while being under fire the whole time. They retreated, along with much of Joe Hooker's division, about three-quarters of a mile back toward Poffenberger's Farm, as you can see on the map above. Hood's men retreated themselves back to the West Woods. Seeing so few men with their general, a Southern officer asked

Hood, "Where is your division?" Foreshadowing the comments made after Pickett's Charge at Gettysburg, which would happen around a year later, Hood replied, "Dead on the field." Hood, a man noted for his aggression and who would become even more famous for it later in the war, said that Antietam was the fiercest fighting he had ever seen.

But it was only 7:30 in the morning, and the battle had been raging for about an hour. Hundreds were already dead and wounded, but only a small segment of both forces had been in action. There were still units to the south that had not been engaged at all.

After all of this fighting, the Union side still had reserves to throw into the battle, the troops led by General Joseph Mansfield. At 58, he was old for the time, and he had never led large groups of men in battle. Although he was a West Pointer and a veteran of the Mexican-American War, most of his career had been spent behind a desk or performing engineering duties. Worse still, his XII Corps was made up of many soldiers who had never seen battle and had little training. To try to keep some control of his rookie troops and to increase the force with which he hit the rebels, Mansfield ordered his men into very tightly bunched formations as they marched to battle at the center of the Union line. Other officers tried to dissuade him, arguing that this would increase casualties from Confederate artillery, but Mansfield would hear none of it.

As his men approached the East Woods, they came under fire. Mansfield then tried to maneuver his men into a firing formation. This took time, which made the situation even worse. At one point, Mansfield told one unit, the 10th Maine, to stop firing, as he believed their targets to be Union men. As his men protested, Mansfield took a fatal shot in the chest. His executive officer took command and finally got the men moving. And down toward the Cornfield they went.

That cornfield was only about 250 yards deep and about 400 yards wide, but in it were hundreds of bodies, both dead and wounded. That day, the Cornfield changed hands *fifteen times.* In an attempt to take over the Cornfield, the brigades of the XII Corps engaged with men of D.H. Hill's unit, men who had loaded their guns with "buck and ball" cartridges, which is a ball surround by pieces of buckshot. Most men that were hit by these shots did not die, but the wounded covered the battlefield.

Finally, at about 8:30 a.m., another Union force, led by General George Greene (a grandson of Revolutionary War hero Nathanael Greene), came marching from the northeast to flank the rebel position. Seeing a huge force of Federals marching their way, the battle-weary rebels in the Cornfield began to break. Another of Greene's brigades moved even farther south to attempt to turn the Confederate right flank. Soon, they were within sight of the Dunker Church, which had been the Union goal all morning. Greene's men were advancing toward the church so quickly, though, that he had to call a halt to their advance. His artillery was lagging behind, and unless they caught up, the advance would be pushed back. Greene called his men to a halt by calling out, "Halt, 102nd! You are bully boys but don't go any farther!"

As his artillery caught up, Greene ordered a charge and drove the last Confederate battery off of the plateau near where the Dunker Church stood. Some Union men cautiously peeked into the windows of the church, but they saw nothing but wounded rebels lying on the pews.

By this point, the Union held most of the area east of the Hagerstown Pike and had some troops in the West Woods, but there still were rebels in the woods as well. The lines in the north ended about two hundred yards east of the Dunker Church, and at about 9 a.m., the fighting on the northern part of the battlefield ended. It had been a slaughterhouse, but the day was still young.

Chapter 7: "Bloody Lane"

Antietam was chaotic. A thousand movements of units large and small were fighting over the same ground, as they had in the Cornfield. However, if one was to see the battle unfold from above, one would see that the struggle unfolded rather neatly, if that can be said about a battle in which thousands died. The fighting began in the north, near the Dunker Church and the Cornfield, then it flared up in the center, and the fighting ended in the southern end of the battlefield.

The next phase of the battle was no less bloody. In fact, as you can see from the title, this aspect of the battle was dominated by the struggle along what has become known to history as simply the "Bloody Lane."

The fighting in the center began almost by accident. A Union brigade under General William French had become separated from its division that was headed south, away from the fighting in the Cornfield area. The commanding general of the II Corps sent his son as a runner to find them, and when he did, he relayed his father's order that rather than moving back north to rejoin the rest of the corps, they should attack the Confederate center lines near a side road that headed straight east from the Hagerstown Pike.

French confronted men from D.H. Hill's division, which was a part of General James Longstreet's corps and who had seen three of five brigades torn to pieces in the fighting alongside the Pike. Now the rest of Hill's division would be involved in another bloody engagement of the Civil War.

Though Hill's 2,500 men were outnumbered by French's division, they possessed what in 19ᵗʰ-century parlance was "good ground." They sat atop a small gradual ridge in the road mentioned earlier—which had been sunken from years of traffic—with rail fences lining most of both sides of the road. For the rebels, this was a gift, as it was a trench they didn't have to dig, and the men from French's division were coming right at them. At this point in the battle, the men faced each other rifle to rifle, bayonet to bayonet, but no cannons were brought up until the fighting began to rage.

At 9:30 a.m., French attacked the Sunken Road, and men began to be cut down in rows, falling like cornstalks under the scythe. Most of the men in this attack were recruits that had never seen action. The second Union attack, just minutes later, was also made up of recruits, but they managed to beat back a counterattack by a brigade of Alabamians, who really should not have left the protection of the Sunken Road. Yet another attack, this time by three veteran divisions, was also stopped, the men mown down in action. Within about fifty minutes, French's division had suffered 30 percent losses.

Leaders on both sides soon realized that the battle had shifted south, and so, they sent more and more units to the area around the Sunken Road. Robert E. Lee sent over 3,000 men under Major General Richard H. Anderson to aid Hill and move his line farther to the right (eastward) in the hopes that they could envelop French's attacking division. Simultaneously, another 4,000 Union men moved in under Major General Israel B. Richardson to prevent French's division from being surrounded.

As soon as they arrived, the Union men launched their attack, the fourth on the Confederate position in an hour. In the vanguard was a brigade of Irish immigrants led by Thomas Meagher. Facing them on the other side were Irish immigrants in Hill's division. The Union Irish would suffer about 50 percent casualties before falling back.

At noon, the fifth Union attack began to push the rebels back. A number of Confederate officers had been killed or wounded in the fighting, and with their loss, the integrity of the rebel units began to break down. Finally, a unit of New Yorkers managed to flank the far right of the Southern line and fire down at them from a small knoll. Between the firing from their front and now from their left, the Southerners at the easternmost part of the road were slaughtered. As the rebels began to flee, artillery, personally led by General Longstreet, began to open fire on the pursuing Union men, breaking up their attack. A counterattack by the remnants of D.H. Hill's division almost succeeded in outflanking the Union left around the knoll, but the damage was done. Both sides were exhausted. In the fighting that took place there from about 9:30 a.m. to 1 p.m., a total of 5,600 casualties were sustained by both sides, with the Union suffering a bit more.

As the Confederates were moving away from the Sunken Road (already known as the "Bloody Lane" by this point), some of McClellan's officers urged him to throw in some men from his reserves, which numbered over twenty thousand infantry and cavalry. McClellan took the advice of Commander Edwin Sumner of the II Corps and remained in place. The advice of this corps commander likely reinforced McClellan's already cautious nature.

Still, the day was not over. Another part of the battlefield was about to erupt in the south, and it would be no less a slaughter than what had already occurred.

Chapter 8: Burnside's Bridge

When General Ambrose Burnside is remembered today, it is sadly during trivia contests about where the word "sideburns" comes from. However, Burnside and the men under his command should be remembered for the effort they gave in the Civil War, for it was a matter of life, death, and freedom.

As we have mentioned, General Burnside was a mediocre general, and he knew it. Burnside was better fitted for a lesser command than corps commander or commander of the army. That doesn't mean he did not give his all in the struggle because he did. It's just that, unfortunately, his all wasn't all that good.

Burnside's career was really a tragedy in many ways. He was a major player in the First Battle of Bull Run and took part in the ignominious retreat from that battlefield. He also played a major role at Antietam, which we will tell you about momentarily. After Antietam, Burnside was given command of the Army of the Potomac when Lincoln fired McClellan, and his first major battle with the Army of the Potomac was the Union slaughter at Fredericksburg in December 1862. After that, he, too, was fired and sent to the West, first to Kentucky, which was a quiet area, and then he took part (with some success) in the campaigns in Tennessee. This brought Burnside back to Virginia, where, again, he did not distinguish himself and was partially responsible for the disaster of the Battle of the Crater during the greater Siege of Petersburg in 1864. After the war, Burnside became a US senator, successful industrialist, and the first president of the National Rifle Association. But this was all in the future of the man who was supposed to take over a key bridge crossing Antietam Creek.

George McClellan's original plan was for the southern part of his armies to move against the men in gray in a diversionary attack to support the Union effort in the northern part of the battlefield, but a number of factors changed this plan.

Firstly, the orders for Burnside to launch his attack did not reach the bearded general until 10 a.m., by which time the battle in the north had been going on for some four bloody hours.

Second, the relationship between Burnside and McClellan had been strained for the past few days. They had been great friends since West Point when they were teenagers. McClellan had even helped Burnside out financially when they were in the private sector before the war. Now, McClellan had chastised his friend for moving too slowly, both in the lead-up to South Mountain and in the battle itself. A warning from McClellan that one was too cautious could be interpreted in a number of ways, but either way, a rebuke from the cautious "Little Mac" that one was being too careful was not a good sign.

Burnside also resented the changes in command structure that McClellan had recently instituted, which were in effect at Antietam. In essence, Burnside was formally acting as McClellan's second-in-command, in charge of both his own IX Corps and Joseph Hooker's I Corps. Before the battle, McClellan had changed this so that Burnside was only in command of his own corps, which, in truth, was an improvement and should have allowed his orders to be acted upon more swiftly. Whether this affected Burnside at Antietam or not, we cannot be sure, but the strain between the generals did affect those around Burnside, as they were not sure exactly what the chain of command was.

No matter what time Burnside's orders arrived or at what time he chose to move, one thing was clear: his task was not going to be easy. His front faced Antietam Creek, which in many places was too deep to ford. Three bridges crossed the creek in its run through the battlefield. Burnside's men were facing the southernmost bridge, known as Rohrbach's Bridge, which was named after a farmer in the area. However, there were fordable places in the area, and the plan was for the Union men to cross the bridge in a frontal assault on Confederate positions that could be easily seen, as well as across Snavely's Ford about a mile to the south. It was hoped that the ford would either have no defenders or would be lightly defended so that the Federal forces could swing around and trap the rebels in a pincer move. At least, that was the plan.

During the morning, while waiting for McClellan's orders to arrive, Burnside and his second-in-command, Brigadier General Jacob Cox, looked at the bridge and the land directly across from it. Neither man thought to check out the ground on either side of it or the depth of the water there. In places not so far away, the creek was waist-deep or a bit less. They knew it would not be easy to cross, but it would not be as difficult as marching directly across a bridge into the face of enemy cannons.

The bridge was an arched, stone structure (which has today been restored to its pre-war appearance) just wide enough for four men to cross in a line abreast. The sides of the bridge were about waist high. In other words, any man crossing that bridge was a sitting duck. If used in conjunction with one or two concurrent crossings of the shallow parts of the creek nearby, moving across the bridge might not go too horribly. However, that is not what happened that morning.

Burnside's Bridge today

Burnside had 12,500 men and 50 cannons on his side of the bridge. Had he acted sooner in the morning, he might have won the day for the

Union much earlier and saved countless lives. But he did not get his orders, was a cautious man by nature, and his reconnaissance was sorely lacking. If his scouts had been more on top of things, Burnside would have realized that Robert E. Lee had stripped the southern end of his front to reinforce the men fighting in the Cornfield and Bloody Lane.

Facing Burnside in the south were five weakened brigades, which consisted of about two to three thousand men in total, along with twelve cannons. Immediately in the area of the bridge were about four hundred men with six to eight guns. It is a military axiom that an attacker should have at least a two to one advantage. Burnside had a five or six to one advantage, but that was partially negated by the ground on the other side of the bridge. There was a high wooded bluff there that used to be the side of an old quarry, and therefore, in addition to the trees and large boulders, it provided excellent cover and vantage points.

The Southern general in command at the bridge was Brigadier General Robert Toombs of Georgia, a successful politician who was the first Confederate secretary of state. After Fort Sumter, he warned Jefferson Davis, the president of the Confederacy, that war should be averted, accurately perceiving the Union's reaction to conflict. "Mr. President, at this time it is suicide, murder, and will lose us every friend at the North. You will wantonly strike a hornet's nest which extends from mountain to ocean, and legions now quiet will swarm out and sting us to death. It is unnecessary; it puts us in the wrong; it is fatal."

Toombs had become disenchanted with some of his superiors, many of whom were West Point men, and he made no secret about it. Toombs felt them to be overly cautious. By the time of the Battle of Antietam, Toombs had determined that his military career would end once he distinguished himself in a great battle. In a letter to his wife, he said, "The day after such an event, I will retire if I live through it."

So, Toombs awaited what he could see was going to be an overwhelming number of Union troops. Leading south away from the bridge and toward Snavely's Ford was a dirt road, which was also in relatively plain view of the rebels on the western side of the river. If and when the Union men decided to flank the bridge, Southern sharpshooters would be able to line them up perfectly.

Behind the bridge and toward Sharpsburg, there were another twelve rebel cannons, and just east of the town were another small number of guns. The plateau where the guns were positioned would soon be called

"Cemetery Hill." These guns were firing at other locations on the battlefield just a little before 10 a.m. when an aide from McClellan galloped up to Burnside with orders to advance. The orders had been written at 9:10 a.m.–fifty minutes before. This was at the time of the rebel repulse of Hooker's troops in the north and while Federal troops were getting beaten back in the West Woods. McClellan had waited until he received word from his reserve VI Corps that they were marching up to the southern end of the battlefield to provide the added punch to break through the rebel lines once Burnside's men had crossed the bridge.

The honor (and it was an honor, at least to the officers in charge) of leading the first assault across the bridge was given to the Kanawha Division, which was made up of mostly Ohio men who had distinguished themselves at the Battle of South Mountain.

But before the Ohioans could try to storm across the bridge, the 11th Connecticut Regiment was going to try to take control of the bridge by moving out onto the span and laying down enough fire on the rebels for the Ohioans to advance. Having received their orders from behind the crest of a hill, the Ohioans began to climb. As soon as the 11th crested the hill, the Confederates opened fire.

Two companies moved to the right and two to the left. The men on the right were pinned down right away, but the men on the left, who were also under heavy fire, reached the road that ran parallel to the creek. Part of the regiment went down to the creek to see if they could cross on foot, but the water was four feet deep, and the current was strong and clearly in the view of the rebel riflemen, who opened fire on the men in the water. The 11th sustained 30 percent casualties in fifteen minutes.

The 11th's commander, Colonel Henry Kingsbury, attempted to lead his men on a charge across the bridge, but the Union men could not make any headway, and their highly regarded colonel was killed. Things only got worse from there.

The commander of the Kanawha Division, who was leading his men to the bridge, somehow got lost. Later it was discovered that neither he nor any of his officers had examined the ground they were supposed to take to the bridge, and so, instead of simply cresting the bridge as the 11th had done, they veered to the north for a quarter of a mile, under fire almost the whole time.

All this time, the men in the division commanded by Brigadier General Isaac Rodman were finding the going tough in their journey to reach Snavely's Ford to the south. Once again, the officers in charge had listened to their scouts but had not examined the ground, as the route to the ford was overgrown with brambles, rocks, and trees.

Next up at the bridge were two regiments, the 2nd Maryland and 6th New Hampshire. They, too, were stopped in their tracks with heavy casualties. All the while, McClellan, whose headquarters was some distance away, sent more orders to Burnside after already having sent several messages urging him to cross the bridge. The fourth said, "Tell him if it costs 10,000 men he must go now." When the fourth aide arrived, Burnside exploded on him, saying, "McClellan appears to think I am not trying my best to carry this bridge; you are the third or fourth one who has been to me this morning with similar orders."

Attempt number three began at 12:30 p.m. The brigade commander, Colonel Edward Ferrero, had been an etiquette and dance instructor at West Point and was a corrupt Tammany Hall politician from New York City before the war. He wasn't a soldier, but two of his regiments, the 51st New York and the 51st Pennsylvania, were good—as were their unit commanders. With his men assembled around him, Ferrero received a runner from Burnside, who told him, "It is General Burnside's special request that the two 51^{st}s take that bridge. Will you do it?" Ferrero's men were upset—they did not want to follow their commander across. Aside from being a bad soldier, Ferrero had recently suspended their whiskey ration. One of the soldiers yelled, "Will you give us our whiskey, Colonel, if we take it?" He answered, "Yes, by God, as much as you want!" That did the trick.

However, promise of whiskey or not, the 51sts had a hard time taking the bridge. They hunkered down behind sections of stone wall near the bridge and tore apart sections of rail fence, piling them up for cover, all while under heavy fire. After half an hour of intense fire, the men of the 51sts noticed the shots were slowing down. The weight of Union numbers, as well as their own casualties and slowly disappearing ammunition, forced the Confederates to begin an orderly withdrawal. A Union captain, who was joined by two color-bearers and their guard, moved onto the bridge. As they were halfway across, the Union men saw the last remaining Confederates running to the rear.

The Union had the bridge, but it came at a high cost. They suffered 500 casualties to the Georgians' 150. Additionally, three hours had gone by, which Robert E. Lee used to summon reinforcements from other sections of the battlefield. And General A.P. Hill's division had just arrived after a seventeen-mile march from Harper's Ferry.

Making matters worse, after the bridge was taken and a foothold had been secured on the other side, Burnside's officers made another blunder. They hadn't brought ammunition across the bridge with them, at least not enough to sustain an assault on the rebel positions just outside Sharpsburg. Over the next two hours, a traffic jam ensued. Wagons, cannons, horses, and men were all moving this way and that on the narrow bridge. All the while, Robert E. Lee was preparing another welcome for the Union men.

At 2:30, A.P. Hill's 3,000 men arrived on the field. Lee positioned them on his right flank, which extended northeastward to the Boonsboro Pike. On the Pike itself, Union troops under General Robert C. Buchanan held a position to block any rebel movement in the center but didn't dare advance close to Sharpsburg, as the area around the road was open to fire from both sides. Worse still for the Federals, the ground moving toward the town and away from the creek was sloped, and the rebels had the high ground.

At 3 p.m., Burnside gave the order. For the next two and a half hours, the Union assaulted the rebel positions. Fighting was particularly intense (not that it was not intense all along the line) in the area near the Otto House and the Sherrick House, along a small creek that ran to the Antietam Creek.

By 5:30, the rebels had had enough. In the time since the end of the war, much has been said about the bravery and passion of the Southern troops, and they surely had it. However, it should be remembered that the men in blue had it as well, as they walked essentially into the mouth of Hell, directly into the rebel guns, and despite taking thirty, forty, and fifty percent casualties, they continued to attack until the battle was theirs.

Unfortunately, at the time, the Union armies were led by men who were not ready for the decisive action that was needed to claim total victory. In Sharpsburg that evening, civilians hunkered down in basements or fled the town in panic. Many rebel soldiers expected the Federals to arrive at any minute. Once the sun went down, however, Lee and the other rebel commanders were relatively sure that no more Union attacks would take place, though they made themselves ready in case it happened.

McClellan had over 12,000 men yet to see battle. He could have moved them past his exhausted soldiers and likely taken the town. McClellan might have ended the war by trapping Lee and his army on the eastern side of the Potomac. But he was convinced, once again, that Lee had more men than he really did and that the "wily silver fox" (as many referred to Lee) was planning a counterattack at any moment.

Lee had no such attack planned. The next day, there was a short truce arranged to remove the injured men from the field and exchange the wounded that had been taken as prisoner. That evening, Lee began his withdrawal back into Virginia, and the war would go on for two and a half more years.

Conclusion

The Battle of Antietam remains the bloodiest single-day battle in American military history. Lincoln, his Cabinet, and virtually everyone in the Union were sickened at the cost. Though he and his men spun the battle as a Union victory, which it technically was, everyone knew that a huge opportunity had been lost and that likely thousands of men had died for nothing.

That was all except for George McClellan, who was sure he had won a great victory and prevented Lee from launching another assault into the North. Once again, he was wrong. Lincoln waited until the midterm elections to fire McClellan, as the general had powerful allies and was well-liked by his troops. Besides that, the president could use McClellan's recognized organizational powers to help the army recover after the battle. But in November, McClellan was done, never to return.

The casualties in the battle were as follows: 12,410 Union, including 2,108 dead, with the Confederate casualties at 10,316 with 1,546 dead. People were still finding bleached bones of unburied bodies years later.

There was one positive that came out of the Battle of Antietam. On New Year's Day 1863, Lincoln issued the Emancipation Proclamation.

That on the first day of January, in the year of our Lord one thousand eight hundred and sixty-three, all persons held as slaves within any State or designated part of a State, the people whereof shall then be in rebellion against the United States, shall be then, thenceforward, and forever free.

However, historians will tell you that, in effect, the Emancipation Proclamation really did not do anything at all. The slaves mentioned were not in the Union's border states (slave states that had declared their support for the Union), and nothing Lincoln could say would free the states "then in rebellion." Still, the Civil War was about freedom, and the Emancipation Proclamation let the South know that the war would continue until they were defeated. The Emancipation Proclamation was a necessary step in the eventual passing of the Thirteenth Amendment to the Constitution, which was passed shortly before Lincoln's assassination and abolished the practice of slavery.

Part 7: The Battle of Chancellorsville

A Captivating Guide to an Important Battle of the American Civil War

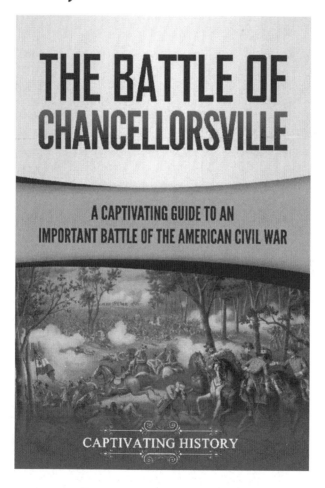

Introduction

Through the centuries, there have been battles that have transcended time. While many battles (some of them quite decisive in their own quiet way) have been assigned a place as a historical footnote, others live with us, sometimes centuries or even millennia after they took place.

The Stand of the 300 at Thermopylae, Alexander's defeat of the Persians at Gaugamela, Caesar's victory over the Gauls at Alesia, the revolutionary victories of Napoleon before his defeat at Waterloo (itself a symbol of utter defeat), the American victory at Yorktown to end the Revolutionary War, Gettysburg, the Battle of the Somme in World War I, Pearl Harbor, Stalingrad, the Bulge, the Tet Offensive...and so many more.

For military scholars, armchair historians, and "buffs" of the American Civil War, there is one other battle that should be included on that list, for it was a masterpiece of military planning and execution, though, in the end, its impact was less decisive at the time than it might have been on the officers and men who studied it afterward.

The Battle of Chancellorsville took place in 1863. One hundred fifty-seven years later, what Robert E. Lee and Thomas J. "Stonewall" Jackson did on that battlefield in Virginia is still being taught at the United States Military Academy, also known as West Point, and other military schools around the world. This battle, more than any other in the Civil War, cemented these two Southern military leaders as legends, as bold and innovative battlefield commanders. In fact, the battle has come to be called "Lee's Perfect Battle." Jackson, however, would not live to enjoy the laurels of their victory, but that we will discuss in great detail toward the end of this volume.

With their victories at Chancellorsville and at Fredericksburg, which took place immediately afterward, the Confederate Army was able to mount its invasion of the North, which ultimately took them to a small town in Pennsylvania named Gettysburg—but that is a battle for another time.

Chapter 1 – Background

Let's be clear—the American Civil War was fought over slavery. Some may argue that the conflict was fought over "states' rights," and there can be a logical point made for that. However, the one "right" the South was fighting to keep the most was slavery.

Since its inception, the United States had been wrestling with itself over the issue of slavery. How could a nation founded on the principle that states "All men are created equal" allow the enslavement of others? People today still wrestle with that. They needn't do so. For most white people in the South and a good many in the North, "Africans" (the polite name that many in the community were referred to as) were not people.

By the beginning of the Civil War, Africans had been in bondage in North America for about two and a half centuries. They were captured or bought (from other Africans or Arab slave traders) in Africa and then brought to the Western Hemisphere. They were also bred into slavery. Children and their parents were torn from each other, just like chattel animals. With the ratification of the US Constitution in 1787, slaves were labeled as "three-fifths" of a person for tax, census, and political reasons.

In the years between the establishment of the United States and the start of the Civil War in 1861, the government and the people of America wrestled with the question of slavery. By 1852, with the publication of Uncle Tom's Cabin by Harriet Beecher Stowe, many in the North were pushing for the abolition of slavery in the entire country or, at the very least, the prevention of new "slave states" being established.

In the South, where the economy was based on agriculture, the sentiments to limit or eliminate their virtually cost-free source of labor didn't fall on deaf ears—in fact, it enraged the people. The North, which was much more populous than the South, was also far richer and was seen by many (especially by the ruling classes in the southern part of the country) as pushy and power-hungry. To them, it seemed as if the men in the North were trying to gain more power by eventually freeing the slaves. The liberated black Americans would naturally side with the Northerners politically, and the Southern way of life, which was seen, at least by those on top, as "genteel and aristocratic," would be made extinct.

A war was fought in the 1850s in Kansas and Missouri, two territories vying for statehood, and this war became a literal battleground for the question over the expansion of slavery. By the end of 1860, virtually everyone in the United States believed that a civil war was inevitable, and on December 20th of that year, South Carolina became the first state to secede from the Union.

It's also interesting to note (and some Southern apologists use this for their "states' rights" argument) that a number of states in which slavery was legal remained in the Union. These were Maryland, Delaware, Kentucky, and Missouri (though the latter two had a significant number of men fighting for the South).

Chapter 2 – North and South: Comparisons

Within a short period, the eleven states that eventually made up the Confederacy seceded from the Union. Too many in South, this had been a long time coming, but when it came, the South was woefully unprepared for what was to come.

In the South, there was a popular misconception that the Northerners would not fight to keep the South in the Union, or at the very least, they would not fight for long, especially once they had their noses bloodied. For reasons that could form their own book, many of the men of the South, whether they were from the upper classes with aristocratic bearing and ideas of martial "honor" or from the tough farmers and backwoodsmen, felt that the men of the North were soft, that they were either city boys that had no experience fighting or farmers whose rich soil almost grew crops on its own with little hard work involved.

This preconceived notion also meant that the South's material unsteadiness was either overlooked or downplayed by many. The South was overwhelmingly agricultural, with its few industries located mainly in the cities on or near the coast, such as Richmond, Charleston, and Atlanta. This also included their limited war-making capacity. The Confederates did not have the arms that they needed when the war broke out, and that's why some of the South's initial moves were to seize federal arsenals and army bases in the South.

However, as it would become increasingly clear, the South was unable to move troops as effectively as the North due to the lack of railroads. By the second half of the war, the North was able to shift troops rapidly from one part of the country to the other as their strategies demanded.

Lastly, the South's greatest weakness was its lack of manpower. Twenty-two million people lived in the North, while nine million lived in the South. Of these nine million people, over three million were slaves. This large number of the slave population also meant that a sizable portion of the white Southern male population had to remain out of uniform, as slave uprisings were a constant worry during the war. Amazingly, however, in the first year of the war, before the North became very serious about the conflict, the Confederate forces in the field almost equaled that of the Union.

Despite all of these problems, the South did have some advantages during the war. First and foremost, they did not have to attack the North. The defenders almost always have an advantage in modern wars (and some historians believe the US Civil War to be the first "modern" war)— the South could fortify and defend. They did not have to waste their manpower in an invasion of the North, which is why some still question Robert E. Lee's decision to do so in the summer of 1863, but that's a story for another time.

The Confederacy also had a distinct advantage in leadership. While there certainly were bad Southern generals, at the beginning of the conflict, the scales of leadership were decidedly tipped in the Southerners' favor. While the following is a generalization, many of the leading Southern families expected their sons to serve at least some time in the military, as it was the "manly" thing to do. A disproportionately large segment of the United States Army's officer corps was from the South, and many of those, such as Lee and Jackson, had combat and leadership experience in the Mexican-American War in the 1840s.

At the beginning of the war, many, but not all, of the Northern generals were political appointees or had been desk-bound for a long time. It was not until about the mid-point of the war that the lower and mid-level officers of the North, who were young and capable with combat experience under their belts, moved into top leadership positions.

But those leaders were not present at the Battle of Chancellorsville in the spring of 1863.

Chapter 3 – Summary of the Battles before Chancellorsville

The Battle of Chancellorsville came at almost the mid-point of the Civil War, and though they certainly had setbacks, the Confederate Army did unexpectedly well–unexpectedly well to the men in Washington, DC, in 1861, that is. As with most wars, both sides believed their armies would sweep forward and end the war quickly. If you ever hear a general or politician saying, "The war will be over by Christmas," you can almost be assured that it will *not*. History bears that out.

Very generally speaking, the men of the Union looked at their foes as outnumbered and outdated, at least in regards to their aristocratic thinking and ideas of "honor." They also thought of the average Southern soldier as a barefoot backwoodsman who was not all that smart. They were right about the first one, though–the South was certainly outnumbered. However, the Southern ideas of honor and their so-called aristocratic thinking were overblown, and these ideas actually sometimes played to the South's benefit, as the men in the South followed natural leaders and oftentimes appointed them on their own. All too often in the North, officers were often political appointees, desk-bound officers who hadn't seen a battlefield in years or ever, or men who simply bought their way into a general's uniform.

One of the more stereotypical views the North of the South was the aforementioned backward "backwoodsmen." Think about that for a moment. Yes, a significant portion of the Confederate Army was poor, uneducated, and illiterate. Some left-leaning historians have said, with some accuracy, that the poor whites of the South had more in common with the slaves than they did with the leading families who owned most of the land and the fabulous estates like the fictional Tara in *Gone with the Wind*.

What did that mean for the Confederate Army, though? Foot soldiers don't need to be smart or even literate, especially in the 1860s. What it meant to them was an army full of men who were used to hard work and hunting for their supper. Or, to put it more bluntly, the men of the South could shoot, and they could fight.

Of course, the Southerners made the same mistakes when it came to their view of the Northern soldiers. Not all of the Northern officers had paid their way into their positions, and many of the soldiers of the North also had to hunt to supplement their diets. As for the "city-boys" of New York, Chicago, Philadelphia, and Boston, it would be fair to say that they knew how to use their fists and didn't mind a fight.

Many with only a passing knowledge of the war sometimes make the mistake of thinking that the conflict was only the series of the large and more famous battles we read about in history books or see on television. However, if fighting did not take place every day, it came close. The battles of the Civil War are too long to expand on for our purposes here, so we will try to keep the battles before the Battle of Chancellorsville brief. Suffice it to say that within a short period of time, people on both sides realized this was likely going to be a long and costly war.

In 1861, the Civil War began, and it started with the southern siege of Fort Sumter in the harbor of Charleston, South Carolina. As most know, after a prolonged cannonade, the Union outpost surrendered, and secessionists throughout the South cheered wildly.

The first land battle of the Civil War was not actually the First Battle of Bull Run, as most believe, but an action at Philippi, in what was then western Virginia (West Virginia became a separate state during the war). Though relatively small in size and today considered to be a skirmish rather than a battle, the Union victory convinced many in the North that the war would be short.

The first large-scale land battle of the war was named after two geographical features. In the North, the battle was and is still known as the First Battle of Bull Run, named after the small river that runs through part of the battlefield. Southerners know the battle as the First Battle of

Manassas for the name of the town/road junction in the area. The battlefield was only 25 miles from Washington, DC, and it took place on July 21ˢᵗ, 1861. Famously, Washingtonian journalists, party-goers, and socialites gathered picnic baskets and went by carriage to the site of the battle, knowing full well that a battle was shaping up in the area (at this stage in the war, the troop movements were barely hidden). The observers expected an old-fashioned, well-organized Napoleonic battle (at least that's what they had chosen to believe) and a decisive Union victory.

Twenty thousand Southerners met thirty-five thousand Union troops at Bull Run, and after hours of fighting off many poorly led and costly Union attacks, the rebels counterattacked, outflanking the Union right and creating a panic in the Union lines. Terrified Union soldiers, some horribly wounded, ran or were carried away screaming through the terrified onlookers, who realized too late that war is not a spectator sport.

Despite their victory, the rebels were too few and too disorganized to push onto Washington, DC, but the battle showed that the Southerners were able to defeat the Union Army in battle and with fifteen thousand fewer men.

During the war, the rebels and their leaders developed a well-earned reputation for dashing and audacious attacks, but it was in the defense at Bull Run/Manassas that one of the most famous men of the Civil War earned his nom de guerre. Thomas Jonathan Jackson, a West Point graduate, Mexican-American War veteran, and an artillery instructor at the Virginia Military Institute, held back repeated Union attacks during the battle. Southern General Barnard Bee Jr. rallied his men by pointing out Jackson "standing like a stone wall."

The war also took place at sea, and on March 14ᵗʰ, 1862, the Union ironclad USS *Monitor* met the CSS *Virginia* at Hampton Roads, Virginia, in the world's first battle between armored ships. Most of the world knows this battle as *Monitor* v. *Merrimack*, but the latter had been renamed after iron plating had essentially changed the ship completely.

Between March and June 1862, "Stonewall" Jackson led a brilliant campaign in Virginia's Shenandoah Valley, a campaign that is still considered to be a masterpiece of mobile warfare. This campaign kept the Union off-balance and kept a vital supply area of theirs in chaos.

In the early summer of 1862, Union General George McClellan, outfitted with a powerful army, attempted to outflank the Confederates in

Virginia in order to capture the capital of Richmond. Believing himself to be outnumbered (he most definitely was not), McClellan moved slowly and cautiously after assuring President Abraham Lincoln he would capture the Southern capital in a rapid and overpowering dash up the peninsula between the James and York Rivers south of the city. During the battle, Confederate General Joseph E. Johnston was wounded, and Robert E. Lee took command of the Confederate Army of Northern Virginia.

This led to what is known as the Seven Days' Battles, which included the bloody Battle of Malvern Hill. The result was a Confederate victory and an embarrassing loss for the Union Army and its commander.

In August, the South won the Second Battle of Bull Run, also known as the Second Battle of Manassas, which opened the way to Lee's first invasion of the Northern territory. However, this push into the North ended with a bloody stalemate at Antietam (known as the Battle of Sharpsburg in the South), which Lincoln astutely and politically called a victory since the Union troops remained on the field.

During all of this, battles were raging in the west, along the Mississippi River and in Tennessee, such as those notable conflicts at Shiloh and Stone's River/Murfreesboro, whose casualties, like those at Antietam, shocked the nation. Also, in the west, a formerly washed-up officer named Ulysses S. Grant was given one last chance at command, and he began a brilliant campaign to take control of the Mississippi. He was joined there by another "washed-up" officer, William Tecumseh Sherman. The two would later work hand in hand to defeat the rebellion once and for all.

In December of 1862, the two sides concentrated large numbers of troops near Fredericksburg, Virginia. In a series of poorly planned, poorly executed, and poorly led attacks, the Union troops charged virtually unassailable Southern positions, leading to a slaughter of Northern men and the firing of yet another Union commander. The war went on, but the two sides remained engaged with or nearby each other in the Fredericksburg area for months, looking for a weakness or a mistake that would let them win a decisive victory or seize the enemy's capital. After all, Richmond and Washington, DC, lay just over one hundred miles apart.

Though a number of battles took place in the east during the winter and early spring of 1862/63, mostly on the coasts of the Carolinas and

Georgia, it was not until the late spring that the large decisive battles began again. And it was here that the Battle of Chancellorsville would take place, starting on the last day of April and ending during the first week of May 1863.

Chapter 4 – Leaders of Men

Robert E. Lee

Any chapter on the leaders in the Battle of Chancellorsville has to begin with Robert E. Lee. As was mentioned earlier, Chancellorsville is considered Lee's "masterpiece," and it is still considered one of the most influential battles in history, at least from the point of view of the military arts.

Robert E. Lee came from the American aristocracy, or at least as near to it as was possible in what was supposed to be an equal society. Lee's grandfather, Henry Lee II, had been an influential politician in the days before and during the American Revolutionary War. His father, known to history as "Light-Horse Harry" Lee, was an aide to George Washington during the Revolution and a skilled cavalry officer. Robert E. Lee himself was related to George Washington both by marriage and by blood—he married Mary Custis, the great-granddaughter of Martha Washington and George's step-great-granddaughter. He was also distantly related to the general himself, as they were third cousins twice removed. In Virginia, the Lee family was almost like royalty, and much was expected of their sons. However, like royalty, Lee's father was extremely bad with money, and Lee grew up in a comparatively deprived environment compared to his peers.

Lee in the Corps of Engineers, 1838
https://commons.wikimedia.org/wiki/File:Robert_E_Lee_1838.jpg

Lee was unable to afford a university education, so he sought an appointment to West Point. In 1829, he graduated second in his class, attained the highest rank of the cadets, and won the support of all around him—he had a quiet charm, dignified Southern manners, and was a natural leader of men.

He toiled away in the Corps of Engineers for years. At the time, the engineers were considered the elite of the army, tasked with helping to build the new nation and construct, among other things, its coastal forts. But that meant that advancement was slow since the competition was stiff. It was not until the Mexican-American War (1846-1848) that Lee was able to show his brilliance on the battlefield that he later became a legend for. Though performing exceedingly well throughout the campaign in Mexico, Lee is most famous in the Mexican-American War for the dangerous scouting trip he took through Mexican lines to find a weakness and allow the Americans to win the Battle of Veracruz in 1847.

Robert E. Lee and Ulysses S. Grant actually knew each other from their time they worked in concert in Mexico.

After the Mexican-American War, Lee held a variety of posts, including a position as the superintendent of West Point for three years from 1852 to 1855. Lee was on leave at his home in Arlington, Virginia, when John Brown's anti-slavery revolt began at Harper's Ferry in 1859; Lee was assigned to put it down, which he did swiftly. Much has been made of Lee's views of slavery, and extremists on both sides hold very simple views. One side says he was a cruel slave master, and there were certainly times when he could be, but on the other hand, he also freed some of his slaves and helped others move to Liberia, a fairly new nation in Africa that had been founded by ex-slaves.

Much of Robert E. Lee is an enigma, though. For example, he was quiet and the symbol of self-control, but those closest to him knew that he had a boiling temper. His views on slavery were somewhat at odds with each other as well. He believed that whites were superior to blacks; however, he also thought slavery was evil but that it was a necessary one, and he participated in it himself. He thought that "someday" it would die of its own accord, without political interference. Lee, like other Southerners, had a belief that slavery was decreed by God, and when God saw fit to remove it, He would. Lee did not believe that the Northerners could understand the predicament of the South and its "peculiar institution," as many called it.

Famously, when the Civil War broke out, Lee was asked to take the command of the Union Army, he but turned it down, and after much painful deliberation, he instead elected to fight for his home state, Virginia. He became Virginia's commanding officer, but it was a desk job, which mainly consisted of advising Confederate President Jefferson Davis. (Note: before the Civil War, most Americans referred to themselves from their state first and as Americans second, if at all. This sentiment held true in the North, too, but was more ingrained in the South.)

Initially, Lee was assigned a variety of busywork. He gathered supplies, helped to secure troops, and provided equipment where it was needed most. He worked at this for the first eleven months of the war. In the spring of 1862, he worked with Stonewall Jackson for the first time, helping him to plan his famous Shenandoah Valley Campaign. In May 1862, Confederate General Joseph E. Johnston was wounded fighting

Union Major General George McClellan on the James River peninsula, and so, Lee took command of the Army of Northern Virginia.

Lee took a group of heterogeneous men and whipped them into an army, and within a short time, after having fought a series of battles against McClellan that kept the Union general flummoxed and off-balance, he managed to form the Army of Northern Virginia into one of the most famous fighting forces in American history.

Stonewall Jackson

Thomas Jonathan "Stonewall" Jackson was born in 1824 in Clarksburg, Virginia, which is now West Virginia. Like Lee, he grew up poor, but he had no "name" or illustrious figures to follow in the steps of. His father and sister died early, followed later by his mother. Jackson was raised by relatives, moving from house to house as necessary.

Also, like Lee, Jackson sought an appointment to West Point, but he only got in when the student chosen before him decided to quit after one day. Jackson had a time of it at the academy. He was older than most of the others and was also from a much more modest background. Though he attended West Point decades after Napoleon Bonaparte went to the École Militaire in France, one could find similarities between the two, though not in stature. Jackson was poor and relatively uneducated. Napoleon, though from an upper-class family, was a "foreigner" from Corsica with little formal education at the time. Both were teased for it, as well as for their other differences. But in both cases, this bullying drove them on. Jackson graduated near the top of his class in 1846, the year the Mexican-American War began.

Jackson, like Lee and Grant, fought with distinction in Mexico, and he met Lee on a number of occasions, though Jackson was an artillery officer, and Lee was in the Corps of Engineers. When the war ended, Jackson was welcomed home as a hero and had risen to the rank of major from lieutenant. He served in New York and Florida, then retired from the military in 1851 when he was offered a professorship at the Virginia Military Institute (VMI).

Jackson as a young officer
Internet Archive Book Images, No restrictions, via Wikimedia Commons
*https://commons.wikimedia.org/wiki/File:First_lieutenant_Thomas_J._Jackson_sometime_after_*
West_Point_graduation_in_the_1840s,_from-
The_photographic_history_of_the_civil_war.._(1911)_(14739846876)_(cropped).jpg

In addition to teaching artillery tactics, Jackson also taught a variety of science classes, as well as philosophy. Unfortunately, Jackson's stay at the VMI, which lasted until the dawn of the Civil War, was much like his student career at West Point: He was a highly unpopular teacher. He was demanding, surprisingly unoriginal, and he was "peculiar," as the students and other teachers there likely put it. Today, we might just say "weird."

His quirks later endeared him to his men and to history, but this was before he was victorious on the battlefield. He sometimes taught with one arm up in the air, believing that one arm was longer than the other and that this might help even them out. He later did this on horseback during the war, and he likely took a bullet because of it. Jackson also believed that eating pepper weakened his left leg and avoided using the spice. A myth saying that Jackson sucked on lemons came after a postwar book was published on the man. This tale may have started because Jackson was an abstemious eater but a voracious eater of fruit.

Jackson married in 1853, but his wife Elinor died in childbirth the next year. He remarried three years later, but this marriage was also marked by tragedy. Though his wife lived into old age, their daughter died within one month of being born. Jackson and his second wife, Mary Anna Jackson, had another daughter in 1862, but she sadly never knew her father.

Jackson was there when John Brown was hanged, as he was representing the VMI. When the Civil War broke out, Jackson hoped Virginia would remain in the Union, but when that did not happen, he, like Lee, decided his loyalty lay with his home state and not the distant federal government and the North.

Jackson's exploits at Bull Run and in the Shenandoah Valley have already been recited, albeit briefly. Suffice it to say that by the end of the Shenandoah Campaign, Jackson had established a reputation as one of the most brilliant tactical officers of the war, one heralded in the South and respected, feared, and hated in the North.

Jackson before the Chancellorsville Campaign
https://commons.wikimedia.org/wiki/File:Stonewall_Jackson_by_Routzahn,_1862.png

Other Confederate Generals

Also present at Chancellorsville was a list of some of the most well-known generals of the war. There was the already famous cavalry commander James Ewell Brown Stuart, better known as Jeb, who had been running Union troops ragged since the start of the war, as well as

Jubal Early, who fought throughout the war and fled the country after the war ended. Early would later return and deliver speeches around the country, ennobling the cause of the South and helping give birth to the "noble underdog" sentiment that still lives on today. Besides these two distinguished men, there was also Lafayette McLaws, who led a stout defense at Fredericksburg and repeated charges at Gettysburg; A.P. Hill, who was one of Jackson's favorite officers and mentioned in his last words—it is notable to mention that Hill was killed just seven days before the end of the war; Richard Anderson, who, like many of the South's leading generals, had fought in Mexico in the 1840s; Raleigh Colston, who was born in France and whose adopted mother was of French nobility, and Robert E. Rodes, who was the first of Lee's coterie of general officers not to have been at West Point and who was chosen by Jackson to lead the decisive move at Chancellorsville. Lastly, General Ambrose Wright led a division of Georgians and distinguished himself enough to rise from colonel to brigadier general in a short time. After the war, he actually took part in US national politics for a short time.

Fightin' Joe Hooker

Facing Lee and Jackson at Chancellorsville was Joseph "Fightin' Joe" Hooker. A more unfortunate nickname would be tough to find. Today, Hooker is known primarily as the man Lee defeated in his "greatest battle," but prior to Chancellorsville, Hooker had distinguished himself well in some of the war's early major battles: Williamsburg, Antietam, and Fredericksburg.

The nickname was a mistake, a typo of sorts by a traveling journalist, but it stuck. Hooker had a pugnacious personality, and it seemed to fit. He was likely an alcoholic and may have shown more bluster than he actually had. His headquarters was famous for its drunken and raucous parties, and it's likely, but not assured, that the word "hooker," meaning "prostitute," came from these parties, as the girls there were of "easy virtue."

'Fightin' Joe
https://commons.wikimedia.org/wiki/File:Joseph_Hooker_-_Brady-Handy--restored.jpg

Hooker was a Massachusetts man who had fought in the Seminole Wars in Florida and held staff positions for future president Zachary Taylor and future general of the army Winfield Scott. In those positions, he likely came into contact with Lee, who served on Scott's staff in Mexico for a time. He also likely knew Grant and of Jackson. Hooker was not just a paper pusher—in Mexico, he was cited for gallantry in three battles.

In 1853, Hooker was involved in testifying against his former commander (and national hero) Scott in a trial concerning another officer. This likely damaged his chances for promotion at the time, and he increased his reputation for women and drink that he had started in Mexico. Eventually, he quit the army and moved to Sonoma County, California, trying his hand at farming and running unsuccessfully for the state legislature. Finding farming boring, he joined the state militia in 1859 and was on duty there when the Civil War began in 1861.

Hooker applied to rejoin the federal army but was rejected. On his own dime, he traveled to Washington to lobby those in power for a position. He was among those who went to view the First Battle of Bull Run, and he wrote a stinging detailed criticism of the leadership and conduct of the Union's failure. This article got him the commission he wanted, and Hooker was made a brigadier general and worked to reorganize the army under the newly appointed General George McClellan (who, despite having a reputation as a cautious commander today, is and was known as a great organizer).

During the Peninsula Campaign, Hooker proved himself and tried to push McClellan into a more aggressive policy, albeit unsuccessfully.

At Antietam, which is considered to be the Union's first major victory by many, Hooker engaged with Stonewall Jackson's unit for much of that bloody day. He led from the front and eventually had to be taken off the field under protest when he was wounded in the foot. After Antietam, Hooker was again critical of McClellan, who many were seeing as fainthearted and not willing to press the fight.

After the disastrous defeat at Fredericksburg, Hooker was named commander of the Union Army of the Potomac on January 26th, 1863, and set out to develop a plan to destroy the Confederate Army in Virginia and take Richmond. Perfecting his plans in May, he said, "I have the finest army on the planet. I have the finest army the sun ever shone on...If the enemy does not run, God help them. May God have mercy on General Lee, for I will have none."

Other Union Generals

In his planning to defeat Lee in the Chancellorsville area, Hooker was joined by several notable generals, including George Stoneman, who is noted to history as the leader of the last Union cavalry raid of the war in 1865, and George Meade, who would replace Hooker and go on to defeat Lee at Gettysburg. Dan Sickles also joined up; he made the term "(temporary) insanity defense" part of the American legal lexicon when he was acquitted for the murder of his wife's lover before the war. Incidentally, that lover was the son of Francis Scott Key, the author of the "Star-Spangled Banner," the national anthem of the United States. O.O. Howard, who became the namesake of Howard University; Henry Slocum, who was one of the youngest major generals of the war and who saw action at most of the more famous battles in the east; Darius Couch, who was later responsible for critically delaying Lee in his approach toward Gettysburg; and John Reynolds, who was a respected commander that was later killed on the first day of Gettysburg, were also among the prominent names that helped Hooker plan and fight in his campaign.

Chapter 5 – Prelude at Fredericksburg

Fightin' Joe Hooker's plan to defeat Robert E. Lee's Army of Northern Virginia was a good one. In actuality, it was sort of the mirror opposite of the one Lee was developing.

If you've read about the Civil War in books with pictures, or have seen pictures of the men of the period on the internet, you might notice an interesting phenomenon. Like today's "social media" where photographic trends and poses catch on fast and spread like wildfire, the Civil War era had its own fashionable trends. Perhaps the most recognizable was what we might call the "Napoleon pose."

The French general and emperor was famous for being depicted in paintings (photography did not exist at the time) standing erect in a dignified posture with one hand tucked inside the opposite side of his uniform's closure. Such a pose can be found in the painting by his favorite painter, Jacques-Louis David, below.

The Emperor Napoleon
https://commons.wikimedia.org/wiki/File:Jacques-Louis_David_-
The Emperor Napoleon in His Study at the Tuileries - Google Art Project.jpg

Napoleon revolutionized warfare, stressing the importance of audacity and mobility, and he frequently defeated armies many times his size. In the US, his military skill was revered, and his tactics and strategies were taught not only at West Point but at academies around the country. Military men wanted to be like him. Hence, portraits like the one below, this time of Union General George McClellan, whose nickname was "Little Napoleon."

George B McClellan
https://commons.wikimedia.org/wiki/File:George_B_McClellan_-_retouched.jpg

The point of this little example is to stress how much influence Napoleon Bonaparte had even some forty years after his death. And while we don't know for sure if Robert E. Lee and Stonewall Jackson, or even Joseph Hooker, were thinking of Napoleon as they planned for their spring campaign in 1863, his ghost was there without doubt, for as the generals sat down to their map tables, they planned maneuvers that easily could have been planned by the French master of war.

Let's begin with Joe Hooker. Hooker came to the command of the Army of the Potomac with the dismissal of General Ambrose Burnside, who had led the Union Army at the Battle of Fredericksburg in December 1862. Many historians consider Fredericksburg to be part of the Chancellorsville Campaign; though they took place months apart, they were fought in the same area for the same goals.

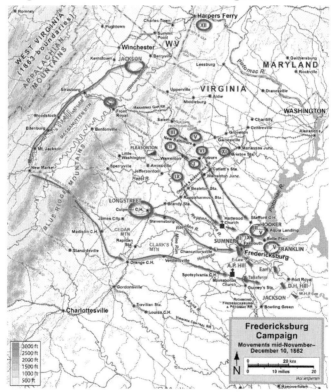

This shows the movements of both armies leading to the battles in the
Fredericksburg/Chancellorsville area of Virginia
Map by Hal Jespersen, www.posix.com/CW, CC BY 3.0
<https://creativecommons.org/licenses/by/3.0>, via Wikimedia Commons
https://commons.wikimedia.org/wiki/File:Fredericksburg_Campaign_initial_movements.png

The Battle of Fredericksburg marked a new low point in the Union war effort, which, with some few exceptions, had already experienced many low points. Burnside's armies faced Lee's across the important Rappahannock River in Virginia, only about sixty miles north from Richmond.

Virginia's rivers vary in size, from the small creek-like Bull Run to the wide Potomac. The Rappahannock was a medium-sized river. It was 184 miles long, and at Fredericksburg, it was deep enough and wide enough to need bridges to cross. The website of Fredericksburg today gives this warning about the river: *Although the river is very beautiful and seems calm and serene in most places, it can be very dangerous for those who enter it unprepared and without a life jacket.*

Just outside and west of the town itself, on the northern part of the Union lines, was a canal and a wide ditch that had to be crossed during any attack. In the center and south of the Union front was the Rappahannock. Before the two armies faced each other, the rebels destroyed the bridges leading from the town of Fredericksburg into the populated farmlands beyond, which was where they took up exceedingly strong positions that were helped by the topography—beyond the riverbank were slopes that the Union Army would have to scale before reaching the Southern lines. Though the battle took place along about a two-mile front, the most famous point along the Confederate lines was called Marye's Heights (pronounced "Marie's"), located at the northern end of the line.

On the cold, gray morning of December 13th, 1862, the Union began its assault on the Confederate lines outside Fredericksburg. Burnside's aides and fellow generals had lodged vociferous protests against the assault, as they were sure it was going to be virtual suicide. They were right, but Burnside, whether in the back or the forefront of his mind, decided that he was going to be the opposite of the fired George McClellan (whose cautious nature had gotten him dismissed) and attack the Southerners with "dash and elan," two of the favorite words of the time. His best course of action would have been caution—waiting out the weather and then moving his army in an attempt to get a better position. It was certainly unlikely, his aides argued, that the rebels were going to attack across the river themselves—they were outnumbered, and the Union occupied the stout buildings of the town (which they looted without mercy). In one of those buildings, Chatham Mansion, Lee had courted his wife decades earlier. In 1863, the house was Burnside's headquarters, and Lee could see it from his lines atop the heights opposite the town.

In warfare, especially in the 1860s, it was almost law that an attacker had to have at least a two to one advantage in men for a successful assault. Burnside didn't have that, though he came close. The Union forces numbered about 114,000 men, and the South had about 72,000 to 73,000. There was no way the Southerners were going to launch an attack on Burnside, and his best choice would have been to pick another place to fight.

But he didn't, and while Fredericksburg was not the bloodiest battle of the war, it might have been the most tragic of a war full of tragedy. In Ken Burn's award-winning documentary, *The Civil War*, a southern officer is quoted telling General James Longstreet (who would not be present at Chancellorsville) that when the North attacked his four-deep lines of riflemen at Marye's Heights, "General, a chicken could not live in that field when we open on it." He was right.

The Union men came in rows—thousands of them. When they got within cannon range, the Confederates opened up on them with cannonballs and canister shot (think giant shotguns at almost point-blank range). The wounds and screams were horrendous, but the Union men marched on. When they closed to within just yards of the Confederate riflemen, the rebels opened up with volley after volley from four ranks of men. The Northerners fell by the hundreds, but they still pressed on. In the back ranks of the rebels, as they reloaded and as their officers directed their fire, they actually cheered the bravery of the Union soldiers coming at them. They also raged against the stupidity of the Union officers that had ordered the assault. It wasn't a fight. As one of the Southern soldiers said afterward, "It was plain murder." The Union troops charged, fell back, and charged again *fourteen times.* Paraphrasing the preeminent Civil War historian Shelby Foote, "To this day, most people believe that the Southerners possessed the most dash and bravery, but I know of no greater example of bravery in the war than that of the Union troops fighting at Fredericksburg."

Though Marye's Heights is the most (in)famous part of the Battle of Fredericksburg, it was not the only part. To the south of Marye's Heights, another Union assault was supposed to take place in conjunction with the assault about a mile northward, but it was delayed due to the late arrival of the elements that made up the pontoon bridges the Union intended to use to cross the Rappahannock south of the town.

As you can see from the picture above, which was taken after the battle, the rebels could easily have blown the parts of this bridge to pieces as the Union brought them down to the river, but they didn't. They knew exactly how strong their positions were, and they were sure that no matter how many "bluejackets" (as the Union soldiers were sometimes called) Burnside threw over the bridge, they wouldn't make a dent in the Southern positions, so Lee, Jackson, and the other Southern commanders decided to let the Union "come on across." In actuality, they would pile atop each other in wave upon wave, crowding the area before the slopes where the Southerners were waiting. Eighty-two years later, men from both the North and the South, fighting together this time, would pile onto the beaches of Iwo Jima in much the same way, and they were slaughtered in staggering numbers when the Japanese opened up on the overcrowded beaches.

A contemporary painting of one of the Union charges at Fredericksburg
File:Battle of Fredericksburg 13. Dec 1862.png - Wikimedia Commons

One of the men making the attempt to dislodge the rebels above Fredericksburg was a professor at Bowdoin College in Maine. Joshua Lawrence Chamberlain, who would lead his men to glory at Gettysburg just a few months later, was part of the charge up the slopes. At the end of the day, he, like many other men, waited for nightfall to attempt to retreat. Before they did so, they lay among the dead and wounded, listening to men screaming, crying for their wives and mothers, and begging for their comrades to put them out of their misery. He used two dead bodies as a shield from the rifle fire that slowly petered out as night fell, using the lapels of one dead man's frock coat as a cover to try to sleep.

During the late afternoon and late evening, some rebel atop the heights would shout down to the Union men, "Jesus Christ! Shoot the poor bastard! We won't shoot!" They had enough of murder during the battle.

The Union sustained some 13,000 casualties compared to the South's 5,000. Many of those wounded later died or were removed from the war effort due to the nature of their wounds.

Oftentimes, people who are first learning about the American Revolution or the Civil War (or other contemporary wars in Europe) wonder: why did they march directly in groups right into enemy rifle and cannon fire? It's actually easy to answer. For centuries before the Civil War, the firearms of the time were notoriously inaccurate. For the best results, troops banded together, aiming in the direction of a group of men doing the same. Obviously, whoever was the most steadfast, loaded quicker, and developed new tactics (such as one rank firing while another loaded, and so on) got the most results. However, by the time of the Civil War, virtually all front-line troops were using rifles as opposed to muskets. Rifles are called that because the spiral in their inner barrel is called "rifling," which makes them much more accurate—and deadly. It's an unfortunate military axiom that nations always prepare for the *last* war because they don't anticipate a future one. And so, the men of the Civil War, even until the end, marched at each other row on row, which is one of the reasons this war was the deadliest in American history.

The next morning, General Burnside, likely feeling both guilt and anger over what had passed the day before, wanted to personally lead one more charge on Marye's Heights. His officers, though, talked him out of it. In an age before psychology, they probably knew enough about human nature to know that Burnside was trying to commit suicide—with glory. The only problem with that was that hundreds of more men would die.

Burnside sent a messenger under a white flag to General Lee, asking for a truce to remove the dead and wounded from the field, which Lee granted. Later that day, the Union Army moved out of Fredericksburg to the opposite side of the Rappahannock. Entering the town of Fredericksburg, Stonewall Jackson and his staff saw firsthand the looting and damage the Northern troops had done to the quaint Southern town. One of Jackson's aides asked him, "General, how we goin' to put an end to all this kind of thing?" and Jackson said, "Kill them. Kill them all."

On the night of December 14th, a rare show of the aurora borealis was seen over parts of Virginia, including Fredericksburg. The Confederates took it as a sign that God was pleased with their victory. The men of the Union probably thought the opposite.

Though Burnside was able to improve his reputation in the battles in Tennessee under Grant, he later was partially blamed for a colossal failure at the Battle of Petersburg and resigned just before the end of the war.

Chapter 6 – Two Plans, One Result

The armies of the North and the South remained in the Fredericksburg area after the battle. The risk to either side was grave. The Army of Northern Virginia held a strong position, as we have seen. There was no reason to give the enemy a chance to regain momentum and push toward Richmond. Should the Union forces retreat, they could possibly give Lee a chance to approach or assault Washington, DC–and any step back toward the Union capital might have grave political implications.

Though there were dissident voices in the South, they were much less numerous and far quieter than those in the North, where Abraham Lincoln had to deal with opposition to his leadership from Congress, his Cabinet, and from within the disparate ranks of his Republican Party. In other words, any retreat back toward Washington could jeopardize Lincoln's presidency.

Following the disaster at Fredericksburg, Burnside attempted another flanking move to get at Richmond in January, known to history as the "Mud March." This, too, was a failure, and desertions, which were already rife, increased. He also attempted to dismiss many of the staff officers of his army, which he did not have the authority to do. Already having to listen to grumblings from the sidelined McClellan (who, strangely enough, retained some popularity–enough to seek the presidency in 1864), Lincoln was not about to cede more control of the Army of the Potomac to Burnside. Rebuffed, Burnside resigned and was transferred west, as mentioned above.

Joe Hooker had made good arguments in his analysis of the First Battle of Bull Run and McClellan's abortive Peninsula Campaign. He showed confidence and an urge to fight. Some had doubts because of his reputation as a drinker, and Lincoln had gotten word of Hooker's off-the-cuff comment about the country "needing a dictator." He appointed Hooker anyway, saying to him, "I have heard, in such way as to believe it, of your recently saying that both the Army and the Government needed a Dictator. Of course it was not for this, but in spite of it, that I have given you the command. Only those generals who gain success can set up dictators. What I now ask of you is military success, and I will risk the dictatorship."

Hooker set about doing a number of things right away. Though today "Fightin' Joe" is sort of an object of ridicule for the disaster that was to follow, a number of the changes he installed were an improvement over the way things had been done with Burnside. Firstly, he fired a number of Burnside's officers and replaced them with men of his choosing.

Secondly, he reorganized the way the Army of the Potomac was structured. Burnside had organized the army into what he called "grand divisions." Readers familiar with World War II will know that a "corps" usually consists of somewhere between two and five divisions. In Burnside's system, the corps was subordinated to the "grand division" and proved, because the roots of the system were based on large units, to be unwieldy and slow to move in battle.

Third, Hooker instilled a new sense of discipline and pride in his men. Food and sanitary/medical conditions were improved, officers were given more rigorous training, and the quartermaster corps was reorganized and subject to greater oversight because of widespread corruption (which you might know if you've seen the movie *Glory*).

Hooker also made greater and better use of his cavalry to scout enemy positions, increased the use of observation balloons, and employed a greater number of scouts and spies than previous commanders. By the time of the Battle of Chancellorsville, which began in earnest in late April, Hooker could congratulate himself on a job well done because the army after Fredericksburg was a mess.

Hooker's Plan

Originally, Hooker had hoped that a bold drive of virtually all of his cavalry (some 10,000 men) around Lee's flanks toward Richmond and into Lee's supply lines would force Lee to retreat from the Fredericksburg/Chancellorsville area to protect the Confederate capital. When Lee retreated, Hooker would pursue him "with all vigor" as Lee moved toward Richmond, hopefully being able to bring his greater force to bear on a retreating and disorganized enemy. It was a good idea—on paper. And if the weather was good—which it wasn't. On April 13th, 1863, General Stoneman moved out, and it soon started to rain hard, turning the few roads, tracks, and fields into mud that made the use of cavalry impossible in any useful way. Within two days, he had barely covered a handful of miles and was forced to turn back. On hearing this, Abraham Lincoln, like a sports fan whose team had started the season with promise year after year and gone nowhere, told his aides, "I fear it is a failure already."

General Hooker was forced to draw up new plans after the failure of Stoneman's "raid." He and his staff came up with a plan that was in many ways bolder than anything the Union Army in the east had planned before. His intention was to hold Lee in place in the area of Fredericksburg with a sizable portion of his force, then move the rest of his army in a "double envelopment" of Lee, whose army was in the area between the small town of Chancellorsville and the Spotsylvania Court House (which had its own bloody battle in 1864).

Chancellorsville is about ten miles from Fredericksburg, and while today the countryside features the same rolling hills and pastoral countryside, in 1862/3, it was much more wooded, and only a few dirt tracks ran through it, making observation much more difficult than it would be today (all things being equal). But even today, Chancellorsville is a small town that is kind of in the middle of nowhere in a crowded state. The battlefield is the only reason most people have heard of it. In the 1860s, this was truly a rough territory, and it made maneuvering and deployment, at least for those unfamiliar with it, exceedingly difficult.

One section of Hooker's army would move northward from its base at Falmouth, just to the north of Fredericksburg, on the northern side of the Rappahannock River. This section would first swing north then west toward Rappahannock Station at Kelly's Ford and cross the river there. This branch of Hooker's forces would consist of the men under

Generals Meade, Howard, and Slocum, with General Sickles in reserve to the north of the main movement of the troops. Their job was to circle around Lee's western flank and strike him there, trapping his forces between Chancellorsville and Fredericksburg and destroying the Army of Northern Virginia for good.

At Falmouth and Fredericksburg, Generals Sedgwick (who was wounded at Antietam, took no action in Fredericksburg, and was later killed in action at the Battle of Spotsylvania in May 1864) and Reynolds would hold the mass of Confederate forces, feigning attacks but not "pressing them home" unless a real opportunity presented itself. In other words, they were to do just enough to worry the rebels and keep them in place, but they were not to expend their troops on another frontal assault, like what had happened in December. Hooker messaged Sedgwick, "It is not known, of course, what effect the advance will have upon the enemy, and the general commanding directs that you observe [Lee's] movements with the utmost vigilance, and should he expose a weak point, attack him in full-force and destroy him." When Hooker got word that his northern units were in position, the forces at Fredericksburg would do their bit.

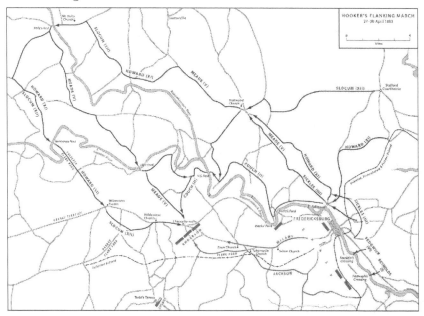

Illustration 8: Hooker's plan at Chancellorsville
https://commons.wikimedia.org/wiki/File:CH01_Hooker%27s_Flanking_March.jpg

It was a great plan, if it could be carried out in the manner in which it was designed. Though it is an overused phrase today, boxer Mike Tyson's quote about plans bears repeating here: "Everybody's got a plan until they get punched in the mouth." That quote could not be more appropriate for the situation at Chancellorsville in 1863.

As you can see, Southern General Thomas "Stonewall" Jackson was in overall command of the rebel troops in the Fredericksburg area. Jubal Early commanded the troops in and around Fredericksburg itself. Under him were Generals A.P Hill, Lafayette McLaws, and Raleigh Colston. Lee's headquarters was to the rear and to the west of this, with Generals Anderson and Wright protecting the western flank to the southeast of Chancellorsville.

As for Robert E. Lee, he listened while his aides and generals debated as to what General Hooker was up to. They knew something was afoot, for there was a great deal of movement reported and intelligence had come in about movement to the west, but there was nothing certain. On April 30th, Lee had his binoculars out and, along with his staff, was observing the Union positions. His men were debating on whether Hooker was going to come straight at them from the southeast or from the north. Lee lowered his glasses and said, "The main attack will come from above," meaning the north. He was exactly right.

For his part, Lee was concerned that he would have to deal with a force to his north and then worry consequently or concurrently about Hooker moving to his south between Lee's army and Richmond, depending on how Hooker's attack went. Lee determined that he would face the Union Army he believed was moving northward to flank him first, then file the armies of Jackson at Fredericksburg westward in a staggered manner, hopefully making the Union men in the town believe a sizable force still remained fixed there.

Jubal Early was to remain in place in Fredericksburg and the area around it, and he was given a brigade from McLaws in addition. Still, the rebels in Fredericksburg were drastically outnumbered by the Northern troops, but they had a strong position, and perhaps the Union men would not realize what was happening, especially since the blood-soaked heights would hide the Southern movement to the west.

Lee also believed that Hooker would not attack in just one place, but he did not have enough men to defend everywhere. An old military dictum goes something like this: "Defend everywhere, lose everywhere."

Lee would have about 45,000 men to move west to hopefully catch Hooker's force moving southeast from the west, which was still far fewer than his enemy, and 10,000 in the lines at Fredericksburg.

What Lee did went against military dictum, and much has been written about it since. What that means is that logic dictates that you shouldn't divide your force in the face of the enemy when he is stronger than you. However, if Hooker was doing what Lee believed he was, remaining in one place would only get him surrounded by a superior enemy, and retreating toward Richmond was both militarily and politically risky. In the mind of this writer, Lee did the only thing he could have done—but that is written with 20/20 hindsight.

All this time, Lee was receiving reports from his dashing cavalry commander, Jeb Stuart, who was saying that the Union forces were on the move to the northeast of Chancellorsville and were beginning to turn southeastward. Stuart had taken prisoners from three Union corps, and while these soldiers did not know the extent of Hooker's plans, just the fact that three corps were represented meant that a sizable army was approaching Lee from the west, just as he had anticipated. He told Stuart to keep scouting but to "anchor his forces at Chancellorsville."

On the night of May 30th, Lee ordered his generals to begin their movement out of Fredericksburg. General Richard Anderson was already digging trench lines about four miles to the east of Chancellorsville, and Lee ordered McLaws to move his men beginning at midnight to the area around Anderson's positions. Lee instructed Jubal Early, who was left with just one division along the entire front at Fredericksburg, to "keep up a bristling pretense of strength and aggressive intentions."

Jackson gave his orders to McLaws and Anderson at 11 a.m. By 11:20, the Battle of Chancellorsville had begun.

Hooker was not idle either. He had been issuing orders and coordinating as much as possible with his commanders in the field. Looking at the map above, you can see the "Tabernacle Church" below the red arrow marking Lee/Jackson's movement. At the tip of the arrow is where the forces of the North and the South first met. Hooker had given orders to Generals Slocum and Meade to march from Chancellorsville to find and defeat the rebels. He had also reaffirmed his orders to the men in Fredericksburg to make a demonstration to hold the Southerners in place. Hooker was not aware that most of the rebel troops had abandoned their Fredericksburg positions and were heading right at him.

General Meade, dubbed a "mean old goggle-eyed snapping turtle" by someone now unknown to history, and later the victor at Gettysburg, was to move with General Slocum in the direction of the Tabernacle Church with Generals Couch, Sickles, and Howard following behind. Meade was to lead his troops along the Orange Turnpike, to the north of the Plank Road, which was designated for Slocum's troops. Near the church, the two roads came together, and hopefully, the Union columns would meet there to strike the rebels in unison. It was a good plan. On paper, or in the mind, most plans seem good—that's why people begin them. But remembering Mike Tyson's quote, not all plans bear fruit.

Meade's and Slocum's troops were supposed to keep in contact with one another, which was seemingly easily done since the turnpike and the road were less than a mile apart at their farthest, about halfway between their starting point and the Tabernacle Church. However, the entire area from just east of Chancellorsville far to the west was called the "Wilderness."

And the Wilderness was just that, the North American version of a jungle. Trees were close together, and in between were masses of brush and bramble for miles on end. Somehow or another, these men, who had seen this area for much of the past year and a half at least, believed that messages could be speedily relayed through the Wilderness. They must have believed that the distance, which was less than a mile, could be covered quickly. Anyone who had tried to get through heavily forested and thorny terrain with no roads and no recognizable landmarks will know that a single mile can seem like ten, and instead of the twenty or so minutes it would take a man walking at three miles per hour, it might take an hour or more. Add the necessity for being vigilant and quiet, and more time is added to cover that distance. Meanwhile, the column you are looking for is moving, and the heavily wooded rolling hills have an additional feature as they sometimes mask sound or make it seem like it's coming from an entirely different direction. For an attacker, this can be a benefit, but when you are trying to find someone, it is not.

So, as one might surmise now, Meade's and Slocum's columns lost contact with one another. Making things more difficult, one of Meade's divisions was farther north on the River Road, its aim being to launch a left hook into the Southern right or rear flank, whichever presented itself.

As Meade's main force on the Orange Turnpike crested a hill and came into view of the eastern edge of the Wilderness, they came under fire from Confederate skirmishers. One of Meade's commanders, General George Sykes, marched down the turnpike and was the first to encounter the mass of Confederate troops under McLaws, who opened fire upon Sykes' men with all they had. Soon the rebels began moving toward Sykes' troops and began to swing left and right to envelope the Union men. Sykes sent word rearward that he was in trouble and began to retreat back down the turnpike in an organized fashion.

One of the rear columns, that of General Couch, was marching down the turnpike as planned, led by General Winfield Scott Hancock, another man who would go down in history at Gettysburg. Couch ordered Hancock to move up quickly to aid Sykes, but as Hancock got his men in ready order and Couch prepared to follow, word came from Hooker: "Withdraw both divisions to Chancellorsville." Both Hancock and Couch were confused. The battle had barely begun, and that by only part of the larger Union Army, and the Union men had the higher ground and more cover. Yet Hooker was ordering a withdrawal.

Couch sent word back to Hooker that the situation was advantageous and that the battle had not even truly begun. Couch could hear gunfire coming from his right, which meant that the men of Slocum's column were engaged with the enemy as well, but to him, they seemed to be holding their ground, which they were. To their left, Couch and Hancock could not hear anything, which meant that General Meade was likely not engaged yet, which was not a bad thing, for the ideal situation would be for Meade to strike the Confederate right or rear. Within thirty minutes, they all got the same order from Hooker: Retreat to Chancellorsville.

Couch and his aides debated disobeying the order, and his chief engineer rode back to Hooker's headquarters to explain to Fightin' Joe the benefits of staying in place. While he was gone, however, Couch's training kicked in, and he began to organize his men to follow orders, as he had learned at West Point, and to engage in a fighting retreat. Sykes fell back first, then Hancock. Two regiments were left to follow behind as a rearguard once the other formations had organized themselves and begun to move. As that was happening, it seems that Sykes' engineer, General Gouverneur K. Warren (who would be a hero later on at Gettysburg), had had an effect on Hooker, who sent back another order:

"Hold until 5 o'clock." By this point, it's likely that Couch and Hancock were getting the same feeling they had experienced before—an inept commander. Couch grabbed a messenger. "Tell General Hooker he is too late. The enemy are already on my right and rear. I am in full retreat." It was likely the process of trying to obey Hooker's orders that had moved the Union troops into a much less advantageous position. The fighting ability of the Union foot soldiers was up to the task, but once again, their high command was not.

To Couch's right (to the south), a similar situation was occurring. General Slocum had received similar orders and was being pursued by Confederate General Anderson. Additionally, in the north, General Meade had received the same orders that all of the other Union leaders had. He was even more mystified and disgusted. Meade had not even engaged the enemy yet, and he was in a position to cut south and perhaps appear at the enemy's rear. Meade was heard to remark the following about Hooker and the good positions that he was ordering his men to give up: "If he thinks he can't hold the top of a hill, how does he expect to hold the bottom of it?" Still, orders were orders. It was two o'clock in the afternoon. The battle was only three hours old, and the Union was already in retreat. Things were not going well, and they were going to get far, far worse.

Chapter 7 – Jackson's Last Charge

During the evening before, Lee had met Jackson to discuss his plans and give final orders. This was to be the last meeting of the two, and this meeting, today located and memorialized with a small stone marker in a fork in the road, has entered American, especially Southern, mythology. Paintings have been done, plays written, and movies made that included this scene. Here is one painting below, along with a picture of the marker.

Jackson himself was ordered to move out at daybreak but chose to do so at 3 a.m., before sunrise. When Jackson arrived to meet with McLaws and Anderson, whose men were digging in about four miles to the southeast of Chancellorsville, Jackson ordered them to stop and to follow him—he was going to attack at the first opportunity.

Lee's orders to Jackson were vague. That wasn't a mistake. Lee trusted Jackson enough to know that the man knew what he was doing. Jackson and his men had fought some forty battles in the last eight months, from the Shenandoah Valley to the heart of Virginia, most of them victoriously. To Jackson, he gave orders to proceed to where McLaws and Anderson were digging in. Digging in was not Stonewall Jackson's style, though. He knew there was a time and a place for it, such as at Fredericksburg, but this wasn't Fredericksburg. This was what was literally known as the "Wilderness" of Virginia—perfect for hiding movement and to outflank and surprise his enemies by using the terrain. Jackson's orders were "to proceed" to the Chancellorsville area. He had done that. But he wasn't ordered to stop there. In addition to McLaws' and Anderson's men, his own three divisions were coming up from Chancellorsville and would be there before mid-morning at the latest.

Jackson was sure the enemy was ahead, either at Chancellorsville proper (which at the time was less a "ville" than just one structure) or very close by. His men had seen Union soldiers in the woods that fled when they were spotted. Jackson was sure Hooker's main force was very, very close.

The Germans, considered to be the masters of military planning for centuries, have a term for a military leader who has a knack for moving his troops at just the right time and in just the right way. That term is "fingerspitzengefühl." The literal translation is "finger tips feeling," but that doesn't convey the true meaning. Definitions.net has a great definition: "It describes a great situational awareness, and the ability to respond most appropriately and tactfully." However it is defined, Jackson had it in spades. And Lee probably had more.

At that evening meeting, Lee had told Jackson of an audacious idea, which was Jackson's favorite kind. Earlier in this work, we mentioned the idea that military logic dictated that a weaker force should never divide its forces in the face of an enemy. When Lee moved part of his army out of Fredericksburg and its approximately 30,000 soldiers, leaving just 10,000 men, he did just that. No one questioned it—they knew Lee. They also

311

knew that the man would discuss his plans and listen to ideas, incorporating them if necessary, but once his orders were given, he expected them to be followed without hesitation.

So, Lee and Jackson decided that they would divide their forces yet again. Jackson would take his 26,000 men approximately fourteen miles to the west, then quickly turn east down the western branch of the Orange Turnpike directly at Hooker's right flank, which was commanded by General Howard. Lee and his corps commanders would remain in the southeast near the old smelting center of Catherine's Furnace. Lee would have 17,000 men with him. These 33,000 men would be trying to outmaneuver and surprise Hooker and his 73,000 troops.

Aside from the disadvantage in numbers, Lee and Jackson were faced with broken communications; any messages between the two would have to take a wide route, as the enemy would be between the two of them, known as "exterior lines" to military tacticians. Hooker possessed the "interior lines," where communication would be easier.

However, Jackson would have surprise on his side. He would also be attacking the end of the Union lines with a broad front of his men. In old naval warfare, this type of maneuver would be called "crossing the T." The illustration below shows this tactic.

As you can see, the ships in the top line would be able to bear the guns from six ships on the first enemy ship while the ships of the vertical formation would only be able to employ the guns on the first ship. Now, take a look at the map below, showing the situation at Chancellorsville on the late afternoon/evening of May 2nd, 1863. On the far left, you can see Jackson's divisions "crossing the T" of the right of the Union lines.

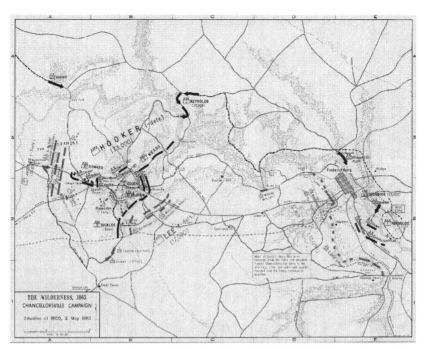

https://commons.wikimedia.org/wiki/File:02 CHANCELLORSVILLE, 1 May 1863.jpg

In the Union camp during the evening/night of May 1ˢᵗ and 2ⁿᵈ, there was discussion and much dejection about what had happened during the day. Why had Hooker ordered his men to retreat when they held such an advantage? Historian Shelby Foote, whose three-volume history of the Civil War (whose first volume was published in 1958 and has been revised over time) is still considered to be the definitive history of the conflict, believed Hooker's cautiousness had a number of reasons behind it. First, Lincoln, knowing Hooker, had warned him to "beware of rashness." Foote also put forward the idea that Hooker, a heavy drinker who had "sworn off" liquor for the battle, was feeling the effects of an alcoholic in withdrawal. He didn't face any severe pain, but without his emotional crutch, Hooker might have found himself second- and third-guessing himself. Other historians agree this might have been a factor. Third, Hooker might have wanted to succeed where others had failed, but his fear of failure may have outweighed his drive to succeed.

Aside from these somewhat uncertain but likely accurate assertions about Hooker's personality, he was also receiving information from his scouts, prisoners of war, and even spies he had within the Southern ranks. All of this information suggested that Lee was planning a strong attack with *all* of his forces on the center of Hooker's line, which was anchored on the Orange Turnpike on both sides of Chancellorsville and south to the area of Catherine's Furnace. If Lee did intend to do this, Hooker was more than ready for him: he had interior lines, his men had been digging entrenchments all night, and he had more men and guns. Hooker was hoping that Lee would repeat what Ambrose Burnside had done at Fredericksburg—a frontal assault on a very strong fortified position.

The problem was, Lee wasn't that stupid. Nothing in what he or Jackson had done up to that time suggested that he intended to attack Hooker's strongest point. Oddly enough, two months later, at Gettysburg, that's exactly what Lee did—and he regretted it to the day he died.

Meanwhile, while he was waiting on Jackson, Lee planned on keeping the Union men engaged. Throughout the day, the two sides engaged each other in a bloody fight, but Lee ordered his officers not to press the attack. He wanted Hooker to believe he would, which would keep the Union commanders' eyes fixed on him and not Jackson, whose forces peeled off for their fourteen-mile march at daybreak.

Jackson could not take a straight route to his destination. At one point, he would have to dogleg south in order to remain undercover. Jackson's attack would also benefit from three other things that he likely was not aware of in moving out. One, the men holding the Union right were made up mostly of recent immigrants from Germany, many of whom did not speak English well, if at all. This meant that their commanders' orders took much longer than they should have to be understood and obeyed. Two, their commanders, General Howard and Brigadier General Francis C. Barlow, were both highly unpopular martinets—high on discipline, low on skill. And thirdly, most of the regiments on the Union right had either never been in a winning battle or even seen action.

Hooker got reports that there was movement to his right, and he ordered a detachment to pursue. He thought, but was not positive, that Jackson's movement (Hooker did not know it was Jackson, however) was the beginning of a retreat back toward Richmond. In case it wasn't, he wanted to stay in contact with the enemy column, but Hooker was prevented in this by hard fighting at the end of Jackson's column by the 23rd Georgia Regiment. Jackson's main column was also screened on its northern flank by Jeb Stuart's cavalry, who moved between it and the Union, preventing the enemy from getting closer.

At 5:30 p.m., Jackson's men had reached their jumping-off place, screened by the woods and located along the Orange Turnpike and Ely Ford's Road to the north. Jackson's divisions were three-deep, with General Rodes leading, followed by Colston's and A.P. Hill's divisions.

The Union troops, at the conjunction of Ely Ford's Road and the Orange Turnpike, were commanded by General Charles Devens, who had his forces formed to anchor the far-right of the Union line. Despite all that was to follow, Devens personally acquitted himself well, being seriously wounded during the battle yet refusing to be taken from the field until the fighting was done. Here he is, pictured below, in the characteristic Napoleonic posture.

Devens during the war
https://en.wikipedia.org/wiki/File:GenChasDevens.jpg

Jackson's force covered just under two miles north to south abreast the two roads. Its final position before the attack was around one thousand yards from the Union forces, the first of which possessed only two cannons, which was a mistake in the extreme, for they were the end of Hooker's line. Should they be "rolled up," Jackson would hit each successive Northern unit in the flank, repeatedly "crossing the T." These men were also settling down to dinner, thinking another day had gone by (for them) without battle or injury.

At 5:15, Jackson sidled up to General Rodes on his horse Little Sorrel (who is actually stuffed and on display at the Virginia Military Institute today) and asked, "Are you ready, General Rodes?" Rodes replied, "Yes sir," and Jackson told him, "You can go forward then." All of Jackson's men had been ordered not to stop *for anything*. If they needed help, they were to send runners back but to keep advancing.

The Union men in the clearing near the conjunction of the two roads didn't hear a thing—at first. But they did see something. A lot of things, in fact, Dozens of deer running toward them, through their camp, in panic. Rabbits by the number, darting this way and that. Flocks of birds flying out of the trees overhead.

Suddenly, they were confronted with thousands upon thousands of rebels wearing their grey or (actually more common) butternut colored uniforms while letting loose the infamous "rebel yell," which by all accounts was a chilling series of high pitched yips and howls, all of which could (and often did) send chills up the spines of the Union men. Jackson and his aides remained in the rear as long as he could stand it, but Jackson soon joined his advancing, screaming men, ordering them to "Press on! Press on!" as he went.

Panic ensued. What few men that could turned and fired their weapons, then ran, if they weren't gunned down or bayoneted to death. The two cannons were fired, then abandoned—the Southerners turned them around and took them for themselves. As they advanced, the Southern ranks spread out, allowing Colston's and Hill's men to enter the fray, sending three Union divisions into a panic and driving them back toward the small settlement of Fairview. Hundreds of men were killed, many were grievously wounded, and many were taken prisoner. The Confederates suffered greatly as well, for some Union troops, especially among the veteran troops closer to the Union center, turned around and fought hard.

The battlefield was in complete darkness by 7:30. Though Jackson didn't want to, the darkness forced him to halt his attack. This also allowed the fleeing Union troops to reorganize and form lines in a U-shape around Chancellorsville. The men under Lee to the south had been fighting hard during the afternoon, pressing Hooker into a smaller and smaller area around the "town."

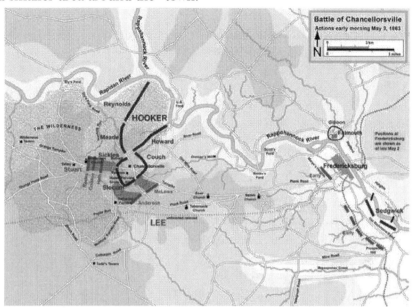

Illustration 14: The situation on the morning of May 3rd
*Map by Hal Jespersen, www.cwmaps.com, CC BY 3.0
<https://creativecommons.org/licenses/by/3.0>, via Wikimedia Commons
https://commons.wikimedia.org/wiki/File:Chancellorsville_May3a.png*

There would be more fighting the next day, and for a time, Chancellorsville would have the dubious distinction of being the costliest battle of the costliest war in US history. For the South, however, one of these casualties greatly tempered the joy they felt at their seeming victory. On the night of May 2nd, while reconnoitering his lines, Jackson and his men surprised a unit of North Carolinians, who had shortly before been engaged in a hard fight with men from Pennsylvania, including hand-to-hand combat. They fired on Jackson and his officers, who yelled, "Cease fire! Cease fire!" But the Carolinian commander believed it to be a Union ruse and ordered his whole unit to open fire, which they did. Among others, Jackson was hit, and badly. He took two bullets in his left arm and one in his right hand.

Entire volumes have been devoted to Jackson's last days. Suffice it to say that his left arm was amputated almost immediately upon reaching his own field hospital. He awoke not long after and gave his command to A.P. Hill, but Hill was also wounded. Command devolved to Jeb Stuart, who had never led infantry forces before; however, he performed very well the next day. On May 10th, despite appearing to improve for a time, Jackson died of pneumonia, which he may have had before the battle, but which his wounds had exacerbated. In his last hours, Jackson came in and out of lucidity, sometimes ordering men to do this or that. At other moments, he understood his doctors telling him that his time was short. "It is the Lord's Day," Jackson said. "My wish is fulfilled. I have always wanted to die on a Sunday." His very last words were, "Let us cross over the river, and rest under the shade of the trees." Upon hearing of Jackson's wounds, Lee said, "I would rather have lost my right arm."

Both sides had taken tremendous casualties, but there was more fighting to be done on May 3rd. Some of it took place at Fredericksburg, where Union General Sedgwick launched multiple attacks on Jubal Early's positions, realizing they were more thinly held than previously thought. Eventually, Early carried out an orderly retreat after another bloody battle at Fredericksburg, moving west to join Lee in his positions around three sides of the Union lines.

The fighting near Chancellorsville began at 5:30 a.m. with the Confederate cannons outnumbering the Union guns (for the only time in the war in Virginia) and pounding them mercilessly. The Union men acquitted themselves well, but since they were all but surrounded, and having their morale shattered by the events of the day before, they retreated at 9:30 to begin crossing the Rappahannock. During this fighting, Hooker was wounded when a cannonball struck his headquarters. A concussion knocked him out for over an hour. When he came to, he refused to be taken off the field, but for the rest of the day and into the Union retreat, Hooker was a beaten, timid man.

The rebel units, which had been pressing from west and east since Jackson's charge, now united in a solid front, but they, too, were weary of fighting. As Lee moved into the mass of troops in Chancellorsville, wild cheering went up, tempered only by the knowledge that Jackson had been seriously wounded.

For the next two days, fighting continued. By May 5th, the Union forces had been pushed back over the Rappahannock, and the rebels had pushed them away from Fredericksburg. In Washington, DC, Abraham Lincoln heard the news. "My God! My God! What will the people say?"

The Union losses at Chancellorsville were just over 17,000 killed, wounded, or missing. The Confederate totals were almost as bad: nearly

13,000 men killed, wounded, or missing. Though the South had won a great military and moral victory, the losses were tremendous, and the South had far fewer men. A few more "victories" like this, and the South might lose—or more hopefully from the South's point of view, the Union would lose heart. Robert E. Lee had a plan for making them do just that.

Conclusion

After the battle, Hooker was replaced by George Meade. A.P. Hill eventually recovered and took over Jackson's command.

Chancellorsville was Lee's crowning achievement of the war. He had defeated, in a shocking manner, a force over twice his size, and his reputation in both the South and the North grew. Some, in both parts of the country, started to feel as if he could not be beaten. Lee never succumbed to that idea, except perhaps briefly on the third day at Gettysburg, but that was two months away.

Chancellorsville had rocked the Union Army and dealt a blow to the Union cause. Politically, it weakened Lincoln and emboldened his enemies in Washington, many of whom wanted to come to terms with the South and end the war.

For Lee, the movement of the Army of the Potomac back toward Washington in relative disarray meant that the way was open for his planned invasion of the North, which he hoped would force the North to come to terms, but that is a story for another volume in this series.

Part 8: The Siege of Vicksburg

A Captivating Guide to the Final Battle of Ulysses S. Grant's Vicksburg Campaign during the American Civil War

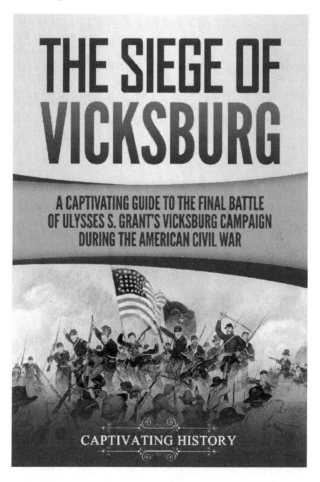

Introduction

The Siege of Vicksburg was debatably one of the most strategically critical events of the American Civil War. The standoff, which lasted from May 18th to July 4th, 1863, was ultimately a Union success, and its conclusion coincided with the Northern victory at Gettysburg, Pennsylvania, on July 3rd. This dual triumph by the federal government was considered the turning point of the Civil War, as the tide of victory began moving in favor of the North. After two years of intense fighting, the Confederacy was finally showing signs of weakening to the delight of President Abraham Lincoln, who received news of both successes on the same afternoon.

The Siege of Vicksburg was part of the more than three-month-long complicated Vicksburg campaign—a daring and unique strategy by Union General Ulysses S. Grant. The Union wanted control of the entire Mississippi River, and Vicksburg was considered the key to gaining the last piece of the waterway that served as a vital supply link to the Southerners. The Vicksburg campaign, which began at the end of March 1863, involved Northern troops penetrating deep into Louisianian enemy territory to circumnavigate the Confederate presence along the Mississippi and circle back east downstream from Vicksburg, crossing the waterways where they were not expected at Bruinsburg. Grant's risk ultimately paid off, but the impenetrable Vicksburg could not be breached. The only course open was for the Northerners to starve out, dig in, and shell the Confederate Army stationed within the fortress that was Vicksburg.

Forty-seven days later, Confederate General John Pemberton finally relented. His starving men had taken to eating rats, and diseases began to spread rapidly through the squalid conditions of the town. General Grant agreed to a conditional surrender, with the downtrodden Southern troops required to hand in their arms and return home as parolees. Within a week, the final stretch of the Mississippi that was still under Rebel control fell to the Union. Vicksburg remained under Union command for the remainder of the war, and the Southerners' main transport and communication routes through their territories straddling the Mississippi were officially blocked. The Vicksburg campaign was a coup for the Yankees, and it is historically considered the most decisive and influential series of events in the Civil War. The South would never recover.

Chapter 1 – Events Leading to the Vicksburg Campaign

The start of the American Civil War in the spring of 1861 would mark the entire term of President Abraham Lincoln (1809-1865, in off. 1861-1865) as one of domestic warfare. The federal government of the North, which supported the abolition of slavery, fought the Southern slave states, also known as the Confederate States of America (CSA), for four years until the spring of 1865. The Confederates (also referred to as the Rebels or the Southerners) drew the Yankees (also known as the Northerners or Federals) into their territory for most of the war. The Confederacy was formed by eleven states that seceded from the Union of the United States to form their own government. These states—South Carolina, Mississippi, Florida, Alabama, Georgia, Louisiana, Texas, Virginia, Arkansas, Tennessee, and North Carolina—occupied the southeastern extremities of the US. Other regions surrounding the CSA were contested or partly included in the Confederacy during the war, but in 1863, West Virginia split from Virginia to rejoin the Union.

The Vicksburg campaign of 1863 fell within what was known as the Western Theater of the Civil War. This was one of three official theaters, and it included operations in Alabama, Georgia, Florida, Mississippi, North Carolina, Kentucky, South Carolina, Tennessee, and Louisiana east of the Mississippi River. The Eastern Theater included activities east of the Appalachian Mountains, and those on the west of the Mississippi River fell within the Trans-Mississippi Theater—Missouri,

Oklahoma, Arkansas, Kansas, Texas, and Louisiana.

The Union experienced early successes in the war within the Western Theater, mostly due to the command of General Ulysses S. Grant's Army of the Tennessee. Ulysses Grant (1822–1885) had been born Hiram Ulysses Grant but was known to his friends as "Sam." Grant was from Ohio and graduated from West Point Military Academy in New York, along with most of the other commanders who served in the Civil War, whether under the banner of the North or South. However, Grant had a checkered career with the military until the Vicksburg campaign. Grant graduated in 1843 and went on to distinguish himself in the Mexican-American War (1846–1848) but resigned from the army in 1854. Apparently grappling with personal problems that led him to drink, Grant was unsuccessful at the various endeavors he undertook, such as farming, clerking, real estate, and politics. He leaped at the chance to join the Union for the Civil War in 1861, eventually receiving recognition with his twin victories at Forts Henry and Donelson in the Western Theater in February of 1862. His demands for unconditional surrender at Fort Donelson earned him the nickname of "Unconditional Surrender Grant" and led to his promotion to major general. (Grant went on to become the commanding general of the US Army from March 1864 to March 1869.)

Grant's initial failure at the Battle of Shiloh (April 6th-7th, 1862, southwestern Tennessee) forced President Lincoln to replace him with General Henry Halleck (1815–1872, a US army officer, lawyer, and scholar who served two terms with the military and went on to become the commanding general of the US Army). However, Lincoln refused to remove Grant from general command, stating that "I can't spare this man. He fights." Grant was reinstated as a general by July of 1862. He led the Army of the Tennessee and reestablished his reputation through dual victories in northern Mississippi (the Battles of Iuka and Corinth) in September and October of that year. After the end of the Civil War, President Andrew Johnson (1808–1875, in off. 1865–1869) made Grant the general of the US Army, and he also served briefly as the secretary of war before turning to politics as a member of the Republican Party. Grant went on to become the eighteenth president of the United States, serving two terms from 1869 to 1877. As president, he fought hard for justice. He created the Justice Department and worked to protect African Americans during the post-Civil War Reconstruction era.

The mighty Mississippi River that runs north-south, bisecting the US from beyond the Canadian border in the north to the Gulf of Mexico in the south, formed a natural division between the Southern states. Within the areas of fighting during the Civil War, the Mississippi River divided the states of Mississippi, Tennessee, and Kentucky on the eastern bank from Missouri and Arkansas on the western bank. Louisiana, at the far south on the Mexican Gulf, was divided by the river but fell mostly on the west. The Mississippi River provided critical access for naval warfare, the provision of men and supplies, and communications during the Civil War for both Yankees and Rebels alike. Union General William Tecumseh Sherman (1820-1891, American soldier, educator, author, and businessman who played a significant role in the war and who was promoted to major general in May of 1862) stated that the Mississippi was the spine of America. This proved true when the Federals took Vicksburg, thus breaking the backbone of the country.

The critically strategic town of Vicksburg, Mississippi, lay within Southern territory. It was located in Warren County, just south of the conjunction of the Mississippi River and Yazoo tributary, which drained from the northeast. Vicksburg was situated on high bluffs—the Walnut Hills—on the banks of the Mississippi River, overlooking Louisiana on the western bank. The town was located on a large bend of the Mississippi that circumnavigated the De Soto Peninsula, a part of Louisiana. (In 1876, flooding destroyed this meandering section of the Mississippi to form an oxbow lake—Centennial Lake—and De Soto became an island.)

Vicksburg held a commanding position not only geographically but also as a key Confederate river port during the Civil War, enabling manufactured goods, essential foods from plantations, and soldiers west of the Mississippi to reach the Western and Eastern Theater battlefields east of the mighty waterway. The Southern Railroad ran west-east through Vicksburg, enabling the transfer of these goods from the trans-Mississippi east.

Before the war, Vicksburg's key location in central-west Mississippi adjacent to the river made it a vital hub of trade for the steamboat traffic up and down the river. Large tributaries, such as the Red, Louisiana, and Yazoo Rivers that emptied from the southern states into the Mississippi, carried agricultural goods from far inland to waterfront trading towns. Cotton and other agricultural goods from the surrounding plantations were channeled through the bustling node of Vicksburg. This maritime trade utilized the main arterial route of the Mississippi, which exited into the open ocean of the Gulf of Mexico below New Orleans, Louisiana. The Southerners relied heavily on the ports around the gulf, as well as along the Atlantic seaboard, to transport their goods to the rest of America as well as abroad, particularly to Europe.

The Mississippi was the heart of the economic lifeblood of Southern trade. The North knew this, so one of the North's first strategies of attack at the start of the war in 1861 was to cut off this supply route. The plan had been abandoned in favor of piecemeal land battles, but after two years of fighting, President Lincoln realized that the war would be long and bloody. His attention was then drawn to more strategic approaches, such as controlling Vicksburg. Confederate President Jefferson Finis Davis (1808–1889, a US politician who had served two terms in the US military, served as the American secretary of war for four years, and served the US House of Representatives before joining the Confederacy for the entire Civil War as its) described the town as "the nailhead that holds the South's two halves together." and President Lincoln stated that "Vicksburg is the key! The war can never be brought to a close until that key is in our pocket."

With full knowledge of the importance of the Mississippi River, the Confederacy began fortifying the strategic towns along its banks, especially Vicksburg. The western extent of the town abutted the river, and its bluffs provided the perfect height for artillery batteries to point at the waterfront and riverway. The entire town, like its fellow settlements along much of the eastern bank of the Mississippi, was poised on a series of bluffs forming natural buttresses.

The Confederates further built up the land approaches to the town with earthworks and timber structures. These ramparts were built high, punctured with obstacles such as sharp timbers, and ended in deep ditches—a deathtrap for enemies who managed to get close enough to the fortified town. Batteries of cannons and heavy mortars protected all flanks of the town. The large hairpin bend in the river near Vicksburg forced boats to slow down as they moved past the town, making enemy vessels even more vulnerable to attack. It became increasingly apparent to both the North and South that the place most unlikely to be taken by force was Vicksburg because it was considered virtually impenetrable.

Starting in April of 1862, a series of river and land battles between the North and South saw a myriad of changes with the control points of the Mississippi, from its mouth near New Orleans to beyond Fort Pillow, Tennessee (north of Memphis and 463 kilometers, or 288 miles, upstream from Vicksburg). By the beginning of August 1862, the Union had beaten its way to victory and controlled the entire Mississippi along the battlelines except for a 229-kilometer (142-mile) stretch from Vicksburg downstream to Port Hudson, Louisiana, that became known as the Gibraltar of the South. Land battles in northeastern Mississippi and near Memphis, Tennessee, resulted in Union victories, and by early October of 1862, the time was right for the Federals to march on Vicksburg, as the town was vulnerable to a land attack.

The most likely approach to Vicksburg would have been from the north, northeast, or possibly the east. However, General Ulysses S. Grant was not a conventional man, and he was unlikely to do exactly as the enemy expected. Many senior commanders for both the Yankees and the Rebels had been chosen for leadership in the Civil War due to their particular engineering skills, and these skills would be excessively called upon in the campaign to come.

Chapter 2 – The Vicksburg Campaign

In planning the extraordinarily bold and risky Vicksburg campaign, General Ulysses S. Grant needed to consider the geography and terrain of Vicksburg's situation most seriously. Just north of Vicksburg and east of the Mississippi lay the delta region. This wet and marshy area was prone to flooding and was intersected by numerous streams, bayous, and tributaries to the Mississippi, such as the Yazoo River. Large parts of the delta were virtually impenetrable since the swampland was intersected by many creeks with steep banks and filled with disease-carrying mosquitoes, tangled undergrowth, and deadly beasts and reptiles, such as alligators and snakes.

On the west side of the Mississippi, in Louisiana, the ground was less marshy and flatter, but it would still require extensive corduroying—the laying of pontoons of log walkways across the wider rivers. The potential of heavy rains could turn the existing dirt roads of Mississippi into thick mud or create unexpected flash-flooding. The bluffs upon which Vicksburg was built dissipated northeastward (inland) but were part of a series of bluffs that extended from Columbus, Kentucky, in the north to Baton Rouge, Louisiana, in the south. (This vast stretch along the eastern bank of the Mississippi is more than eight hundred kilometers, or five hundred miles, long.) The bluffs proved to be an ideal natural defensive line for the Confederacy, as the Union had discovered.

General Grant was fortunate to have many good lieutenants under his command, including the controversial but effective Major General Sherman (known as "Cump" to his friends) who led the 15th Corps of the Army of the Tennessee during the Vicksburg campaign. Sherman was subject to severe mental conditions, including deep depression and hallucinations, but his erratic career tended to flourish under the broader command of General Grant, with whom he had an excellent relationship.

The Confederate man appointed to protect Vicksburg was Lieutenant General John Clifford Pemberton (1814-1881), a career army officer who chose to join the Confederacy at the start of the Civil War. Pemberton was placed at the helm of the newly formed Department of Mississippi and East Louisiana and arrived in Jackson on October 9th, 1862, to take charge of the Army of Mississippi. Jackson was about eighty kilometers, or fifty miles, directly east of Vicksburg and the state capital of Mississippi. General Pemberton had not enjoyed a successful career in the Confederate Army until that point, as he proved a better politician than tactician. However, Confederate President Davis had confidence that Pemberton could do better, particularly when placed in the center of the fighting.

Photograph of General Ulysses S. Grant as commander of the Army of the Tennessee for the Federal Army.
https://commons.wikimedia.org/wiki/File:Grant_crop_of_Cold_Harbor_photo.png

Photograph of John C. Pemberton, Lieutenant General of the Confederate Forces of the Army of Mississippi.

https://commons.wikimedia.org/wiki/File:John_C._Pemberton_(cropped).jpg

Between November of 1862 and March of 1863, the Union engaged in a series of amphibious and land-based attempts to either take Vicksburg or at least distract Pemberton and his approximately thirty-thousand-strong Army of Mississippi away from the prized town. Grant was known to be a master of diversionary tactics. Along with his supporting lieutenants, the Yankees arranged so many sideshow engagements during these five months that when they finally launched the Vicksburg campaign in late March of 1863, Pemberton refused to believe that reports of Grant's tricky maneuvers were possible or true.

In November of 1862, Confederate President Davis had given General Joseph E. Johnston (1807–1891, a career US Army officer who joined the Confederacy for the war and played a considerable part in the war) control of the Department of the West (the Western Theater). Johnston was not pleased about controlling such a large war arena, and he was also ill at ease with his two closest subordinate generals—Pemberton and Bragg.

Major General Braxton Bragg (1817–1876, a career US military officer who joined the Confederacy for the war) commanded the Confederate Army of Tennessee, which would be the last remaining full and functioning Rebel Army after the conclusion of the Siege of Vicksburg. However, both Pemberton and Bragg were required to report directly to Davis at the Confederate headquarters at Richmond, Virginia, and this indirect chain of command would prove problematic, ultimately becoming a major contributing factor to the Southern failure at Vicksburg. Johnston was also denied his request that Confederate forces be concentrated near Vicksburg—a short-sighted decision by the Confederacy that would cost them not only Vicksburg but also ultimately the Civil War. The various leaders of the Confederacy were despondent from the start of the Vicksburg campaign.

In contrast, the Union commanders and troops in the Western Theater were ready and eager for engagement. Some, such as Union General John Alexander McClernand (1812–1900, an American politician and lawyer and Union general in the Civil War), were too enthusiastic. McClernand explicitly wanted an independent command to capture Vicksburg quickly and blamed the entrenched professionalism of seasoned soldiers and their commanders as a major delay in the town's capture. On October 20th, 1862, McClernand received secret orders from the president and the War Office that he could raise a volunteer army to obliterate the "insignificant garrison" defending Vicksburg. But the commanding general of the Union Army, Henry Halleck, was quick in dispatching with McClernand's troops to other areas of fighting around Vicksburg to prevent the ignorant and hasty self-serving plans of the politically ambitious McClernand from being followed through.

McClernand's antics forced General Grant into action, who first began gathering Federal soldiers at the Grand Junction (the intersection of the Mississippi Central Railroad with the Memphis and Charleston Line) in Tennessee. He planned to perform a pincer-like attack with his most trusted commander, General Sherman, deep into Mississippi. Several problems plagued Grant at this point in the war. Besides the threat posed by McClernand, poor intelligence networks, interrupted supplies from the North, and continued resistance from the Confederates hampered the Union plans. However, Grant had been given permission by Halleck to "fight the enemy where you please," and by early December, the Blues (Northerners) had pushed the Grays (Southerners) south of Grenada, north-central Mississippi (225 kilometers, or 140 miles, northeast of

Vicksburg). Grant's and Sherman's land pushes had been aided by a Federal force moving east across the Mississippi River from Helena, Arkansas, toward Grenada. (Helena was about 114 kilometers, or 71 miles, south downriver from Memphis, Tennessee.)

General Grant kept Pemberton pinned below Grenada but sent General Sherman back north to Memphis to regroup and prepare for an amphibious attack against Vicksburg. (Memphis was 357 kilometers, or 222 miles, north of Vicksburg.) Grant was concerned about his tenuous supply line as he moved farther into enemy territory. The Confederates under Bragg were performing repeated raids on the Federal supply line, including destroying bridges, supply depots, and stations. Grant's plan at this point was to send Sherman down the Mississippi to land near the river mouth of the Yazoo, where it emptied into the Mississippi just north of Vicksburg. From that point, Sherman was instructed to cut the railroad supply line leading into Vicksburg from the north and begin siege operations.

Sherman moved south down the Mississippi with the promised protection of the Union navy and forty thousand men arranged into four infantry divisions of ten brigades, several batteries including fifty-four guns, and two cavalry (horse-mounted) brigades. But on December 18th, Confederate Major General Earl van Dorn (1820–1863, a career military man who joined the Confederacy for the war) led a cavalry raid with 3,500 horsemen on Grant's main supply depot at Holly Springs. The estimated damage of $1.5 million to Union supplies finally sent Grant retreating back to Memphis, which was eighty kilometers, or about fifty miles, to the northwest.

Sherman landed near Vicksburg in late December and approached the Walnut Hills from the north and northeast, attacking on December 27th. This skirmish was known as the Battle of Chickasaw Bayou. The Confederates had about half the number of men compared to the Union attackers. They were under General Martin Luther Smith (1819-1866, a soldier and civil engineer who joined the Confederacy for the war), but because of the robust fortifications and advantageous high ground, the Rebels managed to fend off the Union. Provisional Confederate divisions under Lieutenant General Stephen Dill Lee (1833-1908, an American soldier and politician who served the Confederacy for the war but no relation to Confederate General-in-Chief Robert E. Lee) and Major General Carter L. Stevenson Jr (1817-1888, a career military man who served the Confederacy for the war) took the major onslaught of the fight. By December 29ᵗʰ, Sherman had withdrawn his troops and placed them on transports to return to Memphis and rejoin General Grant's full Army of the Tennessee. Under Sherman, Colonel John De Courcy's and Major General Francis (Frank) Preston Blair Jr's units had suffered 1,315 casualties in a fruitless assault on Vicksburg, which would by no means be the Yankees' final attempt to storm the town's ramparts.

General Grant continued through the winter of 1862/63 and the spring of 1863 with a multitude of diversionary tactics to both confuse and distract the Confederates. Meanwhile, General John McClernand arrived to take command of Sherman's forces (being senior in rank to Sherman) and led the 13ᵗʰ and 15ᵗʰ Union Corps eighty kilometers (some fifty miles) up the Arkansas River, which is a major tributary to the Mississippi. The mouth of the Arkansas tributary was approximately 209 kilometers (130 miles) south of Memphis and 196 kilometers (122 miles) north of Vicksburg. The Battle of Fort Hindman (also known as the Battle of Arkansas Post) was fought from January 9ᵗʰ to the 11ᵗʰ, 1863, and it resulted in a Union victory and the capture of the fort. Although Union control of Fort Hindman would prevent Confederate naval forays from this point onto the Mississippi River, General Grant was not pleased with McClernand's independent and bold move against the Rebels, and he insisted that Union troops be concentrated to make a full onslaught against Vicksburg.

Federal ironclad gunboats pound Fort Hindman from January 9ᵗʰ to January 11ᵗʰ, 1863. This was a similar scene to that of Union General Porter's attack on Grand Gulf on April 29ᵗʰ, 1863.

https://commons.wikimedia.org/wiki/File:Battle_of_Fort_Hindman.png

After the Union's success on the Arkansas River, Grant undertook plans to divert the Mississippi River away from the shores of Vicksburg. He devised a way to do this by digging a canal along the base of the De Soto Peninsula where it abutted the Mississippi, just north of Vicksburg on the hairpin bend. This attempt at rerouting river traffic away from Vicksburg had been tried and failed by the Union in 1862 because of low water levels and the spread of diseases. Grant failed again in January of 1863 because of high water levels and flooding.

Grant's next ploy was to manipulate Lake Providence, 121 kilometers (75 miles) upriver from Vicksburg on the western Louisiana side of the Mississippi. The Union believed they could access a network of waterways from the lake that would emerge at the Red River, south of Vicksburg. The plan did not work, but the flooding caused by Union engineers would later produce a protective barrier to the right flank of Federal soldiers marching south through Louisiana. The Union continued through the first few months of 1863 with a series of amphibious (mostly digging canals) and land offensive tactics to snatch Vicksburg, but all of them failed. Valuable ships and troops were lost in these efforts.

The Federals also failed to take Fort Pemberton, upriver of the Yazoo River where the Tallahatchie and Yalobusha tributaries joined the Yazoo. During this operation, Union Rear Admiral David Dixon Porter's failed attempt to penetrate Steele's Bayou (just north of Vicksburg) and thus access the Yazoo was aborted when his ships became bogged down in the mud. (Porter, 1813-1891, was a US Navy career admiral from a distinguished naval family.) The Union fleet needed to be rescued by Sherman, who provided protection via land while Porter's boats untangled themselves and then abandoned the mission.

These failed efforts by General Grant at least kept his men fit and busy and simultaneously kept General Pemberton looking over his shoulder, constantly guessing at what Grant would try next. Finally, Grant decided on the most unlikely move of all: to send troops by foot south through Louisiana on the western bank of the Mississippi River. It was an outlandish and risky move, particularly since the Yankees would be marching through enemy territory. However, Grant was decided, and he began sending out decoys to detract from his real intentions. General Grant ordered skirmishes upriver from Vicksburg and raids on Confederate depots away from his main operation.

In the last two weeks of April 1863, Grant sent cavalry raids led by Colonel Benjamin Henry Grierson (1826-1911, a music teacher, businessman, and career army officer who did not like horses after he was kicked and nearly killed by a horse at the age of eight but somehow had a knack at leading cavalry charges) inland through Tennessee and Mississippi. Grant had instructed Grierson to "do all the mischief you can" to detract from the Louisiana march. Grierson, with his 1,700 riders, had an unlikely gift for cavalry raids and made a northeast to southwest dash through the enemy territory surrounding Vicksburg to distract and baffle the enemy. Grierson covered 965 kilometers (600 miles) during his conquests, which stretched from LaGrange (just south of Memphis) to Baton Rouge (just north of New Orleans). The main purpose of the raids, besides detracting from the Vicksburg campaign, was, of course, to destroy Confederate supply depots and infrastructure and prevent reinforcements from reaching Vicksburg.

To Pemberton, the Yankees seemed to be everywhere at once, and his unreliable intelligence network sent the Confederates scrambling to deal with Grierson. Pemberton was short of cavalry units and was virtually helpless to prevent Grierson's forays. The cavalier Federal colonel managed to capture over three thousand arms stockades, destroy ninety kilometers (fifty to sixty miles) of essential railway and tons of Confederate property, and capture one thousand Southern mules and donkeys that were crucial to the Rebel forces—all within sixteen days. Sherman referred to Grierson's shenanigans as "the most brilliant expedition of the war." Other skirmishes in northeastern Mississippi and northern Alabama, in which both the Northerners and Southerners were victorious, prevented the Rebels from sending further troops and reinforcements toward Pemberton near Vicksburg. The Union commanders were keeping the Confederates' attention well away from Grant's carefully devised plan.

On March 29th, Grant's Army of the Tennessee began the final phase of the Vicksburg campaign and began moving from western Mississippi across the Mississippi River to Louisiana above Vicksburg at Milliken's Bend—about twenty kilometers (twelve miles) upstream from Vicksburg. In Louisiana, they began building bridges and corduroy roads and even filled in swamps in preparation for a torturous 110-kilometer (70-mile) march south, which would take a month. This amphibious plan of attack took the troops deep into enemy territory and through wet and marshy lands replete with deadly reptiles and the potential for sudden flooding.

Grant would have his men march inland, away from the Rebel presence, along the western embankments of the Mississippi. The Federals then turned south, marching behind the enemy's backs through Louisiana to a point where they could once again recross the Mississippi at a place controlled by the Union. Once back in southern Mississippi, General Grant intended to make a pounce for Vicksburg from an unexpected direction—the south and the east. A requirement of the plan was to move empty Union gunboats downstream past the batteries at Vicksburg to be used to ferry the Federal troops from the western bank of Louisiana to the eastern bank of Mississippi.

This long, swampy march of the Vicksburg campaign and the movement of forty-two thousand men of the 13th and 17th Corps twice across the Mississippi River would be the largest amphibious military operation in history until the invasion of Normandy during World War II. Grant's tenacious maneuver sent the Yankees heading for the hamlet of Hard Times in Louisiana, located on a horseshoe lake of the river about five kilometers (three miles) west-northwest of Grand Gulf that was safely downriver of the Vicksburg guns. The troops marched on foot through the low ground of the Louisianan backwaters, taking a circuitous route inland away from any enemy presence along the riverbanks.

During the course of the Vicksburg campaign, one Northern newspaper commented that "the army was being ruined in mud-turtle expeditions, under the leadership of a drunkard [Grant], whose confidential adviser [Sherman] was a lunatic!" The ultimate success of a plan as outlandish as the campaign to take Vicksburg proved that perhaps the eccentricities of these leaders were an asset at the time. (In fact, Sherman had initially urged against Grant's unorthodox plans, but he eventually capitulated.)

Simultaneous to the Army of the Tennessee's hustle through enemy territory, the Union needed to open up a strategic node on the eastern bank of the Mississippi River to which the troops could be ferried. The fortified town of Grand Gulf—fifty-three kilometers, or thirty-three miles, south of Vicksburg—was chosen as the rendezvous point. Confederate Brigadier General John Stevens Bowen (1830–1863, a career US Army officer who joined the Confederacy) was in command of Grand Gulf, and he had been warning Pemberton of Union activity across the river in Louisiana. However, Pemberton had dismissed such notions as improbable rumors. Confederate General Pemberton was so confident that Grant had given up the fight for Vicksburg that he offered to send a contingent of his men from the Army of Mississippi located at Vicksburg to Major General Bragg's Army of Tennessee. It was only in mid-April that General Pemberton received hard intelligence that the Federals were indeed making a circuitous move through the trans-Mississippi, and by April 17th, there could be no doubt of the enemy's intentions.

During the dark, moonless night of April 16th, Rear Admiral Porter took the opportunity to move empty Union gunboats past Vicksburg south downriver to be used later as transports for the soldiers to recross the river. Porter successfully moved seven ironclad gunships, one armed ram, three army transport vessels, and a tugboat under the noses of the Rebels. Porter's ships ran the gauntlet past Vicksburg under heavy fire, and although many of the boats were somewhat damaged by Confederate artillery positioned on the bluffs, the Union vessels made it safely past. (Only 68 of the 525 rounds fired found a target.)

Porter sailed as close to the waterfront as possible, with the idea being that the long-range guns would fire over their heads. The Union gunboats extinguished their own lights and were additionally protected by coal barges lashed at the side that faced the Rebel batteries, as well as being packed with piles of straw, cotton, and grain to take the major impact of the shelling. Porter lost only one transport of his fleet during his daring midnight dash. The ladies who came out in Vicksburg to watch the passing of Porter reportedly created an ethereal scene, as their full white dresses were illuminated by the Confederate bonfires, cannon blasts, and smoke. (The citizens of Vicksburg had been celebrating with a grand ball on the same night due to the alleged withdrawal of the Yankees from their territory!)

On April 22nd, a second Union flotilla ran the gauntlet, again losing just one vessel but with no loss of life. This time, five of six vessels made it downstream, and, most importantly, so did 600,000 rations. (The sixth damaged vessel floated downstream with its crew, unharmed.) General Grant's audacious plan of attack now became paramount. It would be impossible to move Porter's naval contingent on the slow route back upstream and against the Mississippi current unharmed, as they would become fodder for the Vicksburg bluff batteries.

On April 29th, Admiral Porter's gunboats bombarded Grand Gulf for six hours but failed to take the stronghold, which, similar to Vicksburg, was built on high, easily defendable bluffs. The Yankee vessels were significantly damaged by heavy fire from eight heavy cannons under Bowen's command. The Union suffered seventy-five casualties, while the Confederates only had twenty-two. The smaller settlement of Bruinsburg, about fifteen kilometers (nine miles) south of Grand Gulf, was identified as a replacement landing point. Bruinsburg was nineteen kilometers (twelve miles) from Port Gibson, a small inland town that would provide an ideal staging point for the Union Army.

Sherman simultaneously created a ruckus at Snyder's Bluff north of Vicksburg to distract Pemberton. On April 29th and May 1st, Sherman engaged against the Confederates in what was essentially a Union feint, and he was easily repulsed. Snyder's Bluff was twenty kilometers (twelve miles) northeast of Vicksburg, alongside the Yazoo tributary and built upon an extension of the bluffs of Vicksburg. A Union captain named John Cheney who was stationed at Snyder's Bluff included the following passage in a letter home to his wife, describing the terrain in which the campaign was conducted:

"We are about 8 miles from V [Vicksburg], and can see it through our glasses...The Bluffs are very high, and the country very rough and heavy timbered...the weather is very hot indeed...The Yazoo is inhabited principally by Crockodiles [sic] which may be seen at any time."

On April 30th, Union gunboats began ferrying seventeen thousand troops across the Mississippi from Disharoon's plantation in Louisiana to Bruinsburg, Mississippi. The Federal troops had moved south from Hard Times to be able to cross the Mississippi River at Bruinsburg, which was too insignificant to put up resistance. By the late afternoon on that same day, the 13th Corps had been unloaded in Bruinsburg and begun the march east along the road to Port Gibson. Bayou Pierre was a river that lay north of Port Gibson, running northeast to southwest toward its mouth on the Mississippi at Bruinsburg. Bayou Pierre separated Port Gibson from the desired battleground to the north, as well as Vicksburg. General McClernand hurried his troops onward toward Port Gibson, worrying that the Confederates could destroy the bridges across Bayou Pierre since they must by now surely know of the Yankee plans.

Chapter 3 – The Race for Vicksburg

The Big Black River tributary of the Mississippi that emptied at Grand Gulf lay north of Bayou Pierre, stretching northeast past Vicksburg (south of the town). The Big Black and Bayou Pierre would serve as the main battlelines across which the Northerners made a push for Vicksburg, which took place from the beginning of May to mid-May 1863. When Federal troops began marching from Bruinsburg Landing on April 30th, their commander diverted them off the main road leading to Port Gibson and onto a subsidiary road running parallel to it that joined Rodney Landing (south of Bruinsburg on the Mississippi and Admiral Porter's alternative landing site before he was informed of Bruinsburg by an escaped slave) to Port Gibson. McClernand was sure that the Confederates must be aware of the Northerners' movements and plans, and he expected obstructions along the main route since the Rebels would have set up defenses to prevent the Northern march on Vicksburg.

The terrain around Port Gibson was treacherous, as it was full of steep ravines and high ridges, making it a poor and dangerous potential battleground. Besides the terrain, night was falling, and McClernand wanted to avoid trouble for the time being. Meanwhile, at Bruinsburg, a further twenty-five thousand Federal troops were being delivered at Bruinsburg after having made the Mississippi crossing. These soldiers of General McPherson's 17th Corps under Major General John Alexander

Logan (1826-1886, an American soldier and politician) provided a protective backstop to the 13th, which was moving ahead.

Confederate General Bowen, located at Grand Gulf, was by now well aware of the enemy's plans, and he called to Pemberton at Vicksburg for reinforcements. With the growing presence of abundant Yankee troops to his south, the most likely outcome for the Confederates would be to abandon Grand Gulf entirely in order to move outward and fight.

And as the Union columns marched up the Rodney-Port Gibson road, two Southern units were ready for them. Bowen had dispatched Brigadier General Martin E. Green's detachment to establish roadblocks west of Port Gibson. (Green, 1815-1863, was a politician, judge, and commander for the Confederacy, and he was killed by a Federal sharpshooter on June 27th during the Siege of Vicksburg.) Green's force was placed on the Rodney Road near Magnolia Church. A freshly arrived Alabama brigade dispatched from Vicksburg under Brigadier General Edward Tracy (1833-1863, a lawyer who joined the Confederacy for the war but was killed during the Battle of Port Gibson the next day by a Union sharpshooter) searched the road to Bruinsburg for the invaders. Backup brigades from Vicksburg—Brigadier General William Edwin Baldwin's Louisiana and Mississippi troops—hurried from Vicksburg to join the potential fight. Other Confederate units were dispatched from Vicksburg but would not arrive in time.

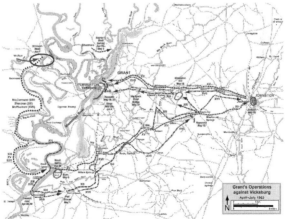

Union operations against the Confederacy in central Mississippi during the Vicksburg campaign from April to July 1863. (Blue for Northerners, red for Southerners.)
Map by Hal Jespersen, https://www.cwmaps.com/, CC BY 3.0
<https://creativecommons.org/licenses/by/3.0>, via Wikimedia Commons
https://commons.wikimedia.org/wiki/File:VicksburgCampaignAprilJuly63.png

As April 30th ticked into May 1st, a Federal column near Magnolia Church finally connected with General Green's men, and the Battle of Port Gibson began—one of the few engagements of the Civil War to occur partially at night. The Union men under Brevet Major General Eugene Asa Carr (1830-1910, a career military man who was awarded the Medal of Honor during the Civil War) engaged in artillery fire from the ravines west of Port Gibson, but the commander ultimately called off the fight, as it proved futile in the darkness.

The Battle of Port Gibson continued during the day from 8:30 a.m. to 5 p.m. on Friday, May 1st, as the vastly outnumbered Confederates attempted to prevent the Union from taking Port Gibson and Grand Gulf. The first movement at Port Gibson was Union Major General Peter Joseph Osterhaus's division moving north to meet Tracy's Alabamian regiment on the Federal's left flank. (Osterhaus, 1823-1917, was a German-American military man and diplomat.) At this point, Tracy's and Green's wings were widely separated, with Tracy's men fighting just south of Bayou Pierre and Green's men battling farther south near Magnolia Church. The Confederates started the day with a mere 2,500 men on the field.

When Tracy was killed, Colonel Isham Warren Garrott (1816-1863, who was killed on June 17th during the campaign by a Union sharpshooter just after his promotion to brigadier general) took command. Even though there was confusion over leadership, the Confederates managed to hold off the Union troops until late in the afternoon due to their advantageous tactical position on the tricky terrain. Around Magnolia Church, the Rebels under Green fought Brigadier Generals Carr and Alvin Peterson Hovey's (1821-1891, a politician, jurist, and military officer) divisions, ultimately forcing Green and his outnumbered men to retreat behind Center's Creek in alignment with the remaining Rebel Army. (Center's Creek ran north-south just west of Port Gibson, joining Bayou Pierre to the Rodney Road.)

As Green's troops joined to reinforce Garrott, Federal reinforcements under Logan's 17th were moved from Bruinsburg, along with General Grant, to face off against the Confederate grouping. These Union forces pushed the Rebels northeast. On a second front, east of Magnolia Church, McClernand and his divisions (including Carr and Hovey) had taken up the fight against Brigadier Generals Baldwin and Francis Marion Cockrell's divisions. (Baldwin, 1827-1864, was a bookstore owner and militia member who joined the Confederacy for the Civil War; Cockrell, 1834-1915, was a politician who served the Confederacy.) Cockrell's men included the Missouri Brigade, which had been released last and in haste from Grand Gulf where Bowen had held them in the event that further Federals would attempt a crossing. (General Bowen had not been sure until the last moment that most of the Army of the Tennessee was crossing just below his fortification of Grand Gulf.) Despite the Rebel additions to the Battle of Port Gibson, by the late afternoon, considerable Union surges forced the Rebels to retreat, particularly since daylight would soon begin fading. Overall, Bowen's men had been outnumbered three to one and had inflicted 875 casualties on the enemy but only suffered 787 themselves.

Although the Rebels fought valiantly, they eventually retreated north and east behind Bayou Pierre and then the Big Black River, leaving Grand Gulf open to the Federals. Despite losing the battle, Brigadier General Bowen had managed to delay the encroachment of the enemy for a day and had personally led two counterattacks at the Battle of Port Gibson. For this, he was promoted to major general later that month on May 25th, although this promotion was never ultimately approved by the Confederate Congress. Later, at the Battle of Champion Hill, Bowen led a counterattack that almost split Grant's army in two, but since reinforcements from Pemberton and Johnston failed to materialize, the Federals were eventually able to advance on Vicksburg.

After the Battle of Port Gibson, General Grant decided to head north toward the strategic Southern Railroad that linked Vicksburg to Jackson. He made feints toward the Big Black River en route to confuse the enemy, who was backed up between the Big Black and Vicksburg, remaining on the defensive. Grant marched with the combined corps of McClernand's 13th and General James Birdseye McPherson's 17th. McPherson (1828-1864) was a career US army officer, and he was killed the following year in the Battle of Atlanta; he was the second-highest-ranking Union officer killed in the Civil War. Sherman's 15th Corps was moving south from Snyder's Bluff overland, and when the Union army reunited, Grant would have a force forty-five thousand men strong, being supplied by wagons from a beachhead at Grand Gulf.

Confederate General Pemberton had called on two commanders: Major General William Wing Loring (1818-1886, a career military officer who served the US, the Confederacy, and then in Egypt), who took charge of the Confederates on the bluffs behind the Big Black River, and Brigadier General John Gregg (1828-1864, a Texan politician who served the Confederacy but was killed in 1864 during the Siege of Pittsburg). Gregg rode from Port Hudson with three thousand men toward Raymond. The town of Raymond formed the southern point of a triangle, with the town of Edwards nineteen kilometers (twelve miles) to the northwest and Jackson twenty-six kilometers (sixteen miles) to the northeast. (Edwards was twenty-seven kilometers, or seventeen miles, east of Vicksburg and about ten kilometers, or six miles, east of the Big Black River.)

The Battle of Raymond ensued on May 12th when Gregg's force stationed near the town were confronted with Federals they believed to be merely a contingent of the far wing of the Union Army marching north. Gregg believed that Grant was making a western feint toward the Southern Railroad near Edwards when, in fact, Gregg was facing the vanguard of McPherson's entire 17th Corps—the right wing of the full Union Army. Pemberton, assuming that Grant was marching on Jackson and that Gregg was in contact with Grant's rear troops, ordered Gregg to attack. This instruction was a mistake, and by the time Gregg realized he was facing the full might of the Army of the Tennessee, his tiny force of no more than four thousand men was heavily outnumbered. They engaged with the enemy along Fourteen Mile Creek.

After a few hours of fighting, from noon until 2:30 p.m., Gregg withdrew his troops toward Jackson. At Jackson, the main Confederate force had been gathering under General Johnston in anticipation of the Union's move toward Vicksburg. The unfortunate skirmish at Raymond prevented Gregg from joining Pemberton at Vicksburg and also convinced Union General Grant to march on Jackson and flush out the entire Confederate force. Grant had originally been heading northwest toward the Big Black River and on toward Vicksburg, but the thought of approaching Vicksburg with Johnston's army at his rear (to the east, in Jackson) resulted in a change of tactic. The Battle of Raymond had resulted in 515 Confederate and 446 Federal casualties.

The next day, on Wednesday, May 13th, McPherson's and Sherman's troops began moving toward Jackson. McPherson was to go via the settlement of Clinton, which was just west of Jackson. McClernand's 13th was required to remain near Raymond to protect the Union rear from Pemberton as they marched on the Mississippi capital of Jackson.

Confederate General Johnston arrived at Jackson on the same day, and realizing the town was not prepared to fend off the Yankees, he ordered an immediate evacuation. His words, "I am too late," proffered a defeatist attitude since Confederate reinforcements moving toward Jackson could have held off the enemy, allowing time for Pemberton to attack from the west and thus protect Vicksburg.

General Johnston was in Mississippi against his will, having been instructed to move his men by President Davis. Johnston's reticence at partaking in the Vicksburg campaign would signal a Confederate failure at this time in the western arena of the war, leading to the loss of Vicksburg and ultimately control of the Mississippi. The inability of Confederate Generals Pemberton and Johnston to work together and go on the offensive to each other's and to General Bowen's aid led to their inevitable failure.

The army and civilians of Jackson decamped to Canton, just northeast of Jackson. On May 14th, the Union began shelling the town, meeting with General Gregg's unit that had remained to hold the city until vital records and other paraphernalia were removed. A heavy thunderstorm in the morning prevented the Union from making a full assault, as roads turned to mud and artillery became problematic to move forward. Later that day, when the weather cleared, Sherman moved in from the south to find abandoned trenches. McPherson, who was approaching from the west, was able to capture the last remaining Confederates, those sacrificial lambs left to put up a fight during the Rebel withdrawal. The Battle of Jackson on May 14th was the first of two in the Vicksburg campaign, with the second ensuing after the end of the Siege of Vicksburg, which essentially closed off the campaign altogether. Unfortunately, this rather fruitless battle on a rainy day in May resulted in three hundred casualties for the Confederates and an estimated nine hundred for the Union.

However, General Grant had achieved his objective, as he had split the Southern Army and removed Johnston, for the time being, from the field. Grant turned his attention west to the enemy lying behind the Big Black River—his only obstacle in capturing Vicksburg. During the Battle of Jackson, Johnston had called for aid from Pemberton to attack the Yankees at Clinton, but Pemberton had hesitated. He did not want to leave Vicksburg vulnerable, and he was also aware that McClernand's troops would block any eastern advance along the Raymond-Edwards road. Pemberton ultimately made a half-hearted decision to move out from Vicksburg, leaving two divisions to defend the town, but he moved southeast, cutting off the Union supply line instead of making a full-frontal attack where he knew the enemy would be ready and waiting.

Departing Vicksburg on May 15th, Pemberton and his three divisions under Generals Loring, Bowen, and Stevenson made poor progress since Baker's Creek on the east of Edwards was flooded. General Pemberton was unaware that Jackson had been abandoned and that Sherman's troops were in the process of laying waste to the capital's government buildings, supply depots, and railroads. Having made little advancement that day, Loring's men camped just east of Baker's Creek at the vanguard of Pemberton's army. Bowen's and Stevenson's men formed a line northwest behind Loring.

Early on the morning of Saturday, May 16th, Pemberton finally received word from Johnston that Jackson had been lost to the Federals and that he must march his troops toward Clinton. As the Confederates began moving north, they clashed unexpectedly with McClernand's corps on the Raymond-Edwards road, as well as a middle road closer to the Jackson-Edwards road. Having not sent out advanced cavalry, Pemberton arranged his men in three defensive divisions along the Jackson Creek ridge for a stretch of approximately five kilometers (three miles). Jackson Creek ran parallel to Baker's Creek in a northeast-southwesterly direction just south of the Southern Railroad. Champion Hill was on the Jackson-Edwards road just to the west of Baker's Creek and north of the intersection with the middle road.

The battle that unfolded on May 16th is known as the Battle of Champion Hill or the Battle of Baker's Creek. The battle continued on two fronts, similar to the Battle of Port Gibson. Confederate General Stevenson and his commanders took on Union Generals Logan's, Hovey's, Carr's, and Osterhaus's units around Champion Hill—McPherson's corps on the Union's right wing. Confederate Generals Bowen and Loring fought a little farther south along the Jackson-Raymond road against Union Major General Andrew Jackson Smith (1815–1897, a career military man) and his units under a division of the 13th corps, with Major General Frank Blair's unit in support of Smith—McClernand's corps or the left wing.

The Blues and Grays fired at one another on a hot spring day in an exhausting series of charges and countercharges. By 1:00 p.m., Pemberton's far left flank was weakening, and as the Federals pushed back, the Rebel line was in danger of collapsing the entire army. Poor working relationships between the Confederate commanders meant that Generals Seth Maxwell Barton (1829–1900, a career military man who served the Confederacy for the war and went on to become a chemist) and Stephen D. Lee were not reinforced against McPherson's onslaught. Bowen finally rushed northeast, battering his way with Cockrell's Missourians onto the "Hill of Death" or Champion Hill, thus severely unsettling the Union and threatening their right wing. But the Blues had several reserve units to muster toward the fight, and Bowen's men found themselves isolated and unsupported upon the hill, with Bowen reportedly holding a magnolia flower in one hand and a sword in the other. Loring, however, had purposefully refused Pemberton's order to move forward to hold Champion Hill and the Rebels' left wing. Loring cited the presence of McClernand's forces as his reason for holding his ground, which was a seemingly futile excuse because McClernand never really seemed to engage in the battle that day at all, something that was particularly noted by General Grant.

Bowen was forced to retreat from Champion Hill, and this move signaled the final push by the Union, whose numbers simply overwhelmed the enemy, pushing them back toward Baker's Creek. Pemberton ordered an official retreat to be led by Bowen and Stevenson, with Loring holding the field to protect the withdrawing columns. The rearguard brigade assigned to hold off the enemy included a friend of Pemberton's, Brigadier General Lloyd Tilghman (1816–1863, an engineer and military man who had served the US Army before joining the Confederacy), who was killed by artillery fire. A clear path back to Vicksburg for the Confederates was blocked by the Federals, and the Rebels needed to divert slightly south toward the Raymond Road in order to get behind the safety of the Big Black River. Loring was so concerned that the Union divisions under Carr would block his exit route that he eventually led his troops south and then northeast to join with Johnston's forces, thus removing Loring's reinforcements from the final race to Vicksburg.

By late afternoon, Grant's men had taken Baker's Creek Bridge, and by midnight on the 16th, they controlled Edwards. In the early hours of Sunday, May 17th, Grant sent McPherson and Sherman north over the Southern Railroad to block the Confederate retreat to Vicksburg. McClernand was instructed to approach the enemy head-on at the intersection of the Big Black River and the railroad where they had camped for the night.

A temporarily constructed pontoon bridge over the Big Black River that was built for Union
General Sherman's men to cross on their way to Vicksburg, May 17th, 1863.
https://commons.wikimedia.org/wiki/File:Pontoon-bridge-big-black-river-1863.jpg

The exhausted and dejected Confederate troops in Bowen's corps
had disadvantageously camped on the eastern side of the Big Black as
they awaited Loring's division that was, by then, marching east toward
General Johnston. This delay by Pemberton would prove fatal. The
Union under Brigadier General Michael Kelly Lawler (1814-1882, an
Irish-born American who served two terms in the Civil War and was a
lawyer and farmer by trade), a unit of General Carr's divisions, struck
first at the enemy's left wing in the Battle of Big Black River (or the Battle
of Black River Bridge) on Sunday morning. The Confederates
proceeded with a panicky retreat across the river, and a Missourian
observed that many "either swam the river, were captured or killed in
trying to get over."

The Rebels managed to defend themselves by using artillery on the
bluffs along the western bank of the Big Black River. These defenses
provided sufficient time for most of Pemberton's men to escape, but the
fatalities in Bowen's division, particularly along the left flank, were high,
while the Union suffered few casualties that day. The battle was a rout
that sent the Confederates scurrying toward Vicksburg, burning bridges
as they retreated to delay the advancing Union.

One thousand eight hundred Confederate soldiers were captured near the Big Black as they hurried to cross two bridges near their encampments west toward Vicksburg. General Pemberton was once again acting contrary to Johnston's direct orders to escape to the northeast toward the remainder of the Confederate Army near Canton. Johnston was rightly concerned that Pemberton's army would be trapped at Vicksburg and ultimately be lost to the Union, which is precisely what happened. Pemberton reached Vicksburg in time to continue his dogged determination to defend the town at all costs by May 17th, but he was hotly pursued by the Federals. The utterly defeated ragtag Army of Mississippi still managed to establish bandstands on the town's hills, where they played the Southern tunes of "Dixie" and "Bonnie Blue Flag" and beat drums to encourage their men.

The Battle of Champion Hill had seen twenty-three thousand Confederate forces face thirty-two thousand Union men since Sherman's corps had arrived too late to join the fight. Confederate losses were 3,800, while Grant recorded 2,400 casualties. The entirety of Grant's Vicksburg campaign had resulted in a set of cascading events in his favor. After the blood-soaked day of Champion Hill, Vicksburg was almost entirely vulnerable to the Union approach. Had Grant lost the day, his supply lines into enemy territory would have been cut off and his army pressured from Pemberton to the west and Johnston to the east. It could have been inevitable that Grant would lose his Army of the Tennessee. But the victory of Baker's Creek (Champion Hill) and the removal of Loring's men from Grant's intended westward march had demoralized and weakened the Rebels standing between him and Vicksburg. Pemberton and Johnston's inability to work together would further muster Grant's cause. When Grant won Champion Hill, then overran the Big Black River, he won Vicksburg. When the Union won Vicksburg, they won the Mississippi. And once the Yankees had the Mississippi, it was simply a matter of time before they won the Civil War.

Chapter 4 – The Siege of Vicksburg

When Confederate General Pemberton and his commanders and men reached Vicksburg, he immediately began arranging his approximately thirty-thousand-strong force into four divisions to defend the town. General Martin Smith was positioned at the north end, or left flank, of the town. Major General Carter Stevenson was at the south, or right flank, of the defensive line, and Major General John Horace Forney's men held the east of Vicksburg, or the central flank. Bowen's division, just having fled the field, was kept in reserve, although they would ultimately serve the center. Smith's and Forney's men were the fresh reserve divisions that had been withheld at Vicksburg by Pemberton.

Grant marched his troops toward Vicksburg, disappointed he hadn't bagged the enemy before they settled into their considerable entrenchments. Having come upon the fortified town by Monday, May 18th, and after taking time to repair the bridges destroyed by the withdrawing Southerners, the Union soldiers arranged themselves to make a charge for the town in anticipation of bombarding the Rebels before they had time to arrange themselves. At this stage, the Blues had approximately thirty-five thousand men available for battle, but as the fight for Vicksburg raged on into early July, the Union numbers would swell to over seventy thousand men, as reinforcements were added to their original number, including the reserve 9th Corps under Major General John Parke and the 16th Corps, a detachment under Major

General Cadwallader C. Washburn. The Yazoo River was now available to the Federals to ship in fresh men as well as rations and supplies to keep Vicksburg surrounded.

General Pemberton had lost approximately half his men in the battles of the preceding two weeks, and considering the addition of Admiral Porter's naval units manning the Mississippi, the Confederates became hopelessly outnumbered and entirely surrounded by the Yankees. When the Federals first arrived on the scene, Pemberton had approximately half their number—18,500 able men—to defend Vicksburg since the remainder of his army needed to recover from the prelude to the siege. But the topography upon which Vicksburg was situated and the earthwork and fortification preparations along the ten-kilometer (six-and-a-half-mile) defensive line of the land approach had made it a fortress.

To the north, Fort Hill perched on a high bluff overlooking the great bend in the Mississippi. To the northeast, its neighbor, the highly elevated Stockade Redan, an arrow-shaped timber fortification of the embankment, boasted an impregnable approach along the Graveyard Road. Next, two redans, including the 3rd Louisiana, led on to the Great Redoubt, a four-sided square fortification that protected the road east from Jackson. Just south of the town, the 2nd Texas Lunette, a four-sided pointed fortification, covered the Baldwin's Ferry Road leading southeast into Mississippi, and just south of the lunette, the Railroad Redoubt protected the Southern Railroad exit. Square Fort (Fort Garrott) was situated at the southeastern extremity of the town's fortifications on the Hall's Ferry Road, and finally, South Fort abutted the Mississippi at the southern point of the perimeter.

At first, Sherman's 15th held the northern bluffs (Hayne's Bluff), or the right flank of the Union, adjacent McPherson's 17th Corps at the northeast surrounding the Jackson Road, covering the central-right flank. McClernand's 13th was positioned southeast of Vicksburg, manning the left Union flank around the Baldwin's Ferry Road and the Southern Railroad. The first Union attack on May 19th was from the north under General Sherman's corps, and it was led by Major General Frank Blair Jr, followed later by an impressive charge by Major General Hugh Boyle Ewing's brigade. (Ewing, 1826–1905, was a diplomat, attorney, author, and foster brother of General Sherman.) The Bluecoats charged down the northbound Graveyard Road toward the Rebels' formidable timber enforced Stockade Redan. They not only had to negotiate a treacherous ravine on the approach but also faced an impressive assortment of abatis—rows of sharp timbers pointed outward.

Along the north and northeast defense line, Smith's, Cockrell's, and Bowen's men pounded the Northerners with artillery and musket fire from their ramparts five meters (seventeen feet) above. When the enemy came as close as the deep ditches below the ramparts (the First Battalion of the 13th against the Confederate 36th Mississippi), they could do nothing but crouch in the 1.8-meter (6-foot) deep and 2.5-meter (8-foot) wide furrows. The Rebels above were forced to improvise by rolling and hurling fused six- and twelve-pound cannonballs down the slopes, as they were unable to discharge artillery at such close range. The Yankees made no real progress that day, and McPherson's and McClernand's men did not engage sufficiently to warrant any Yankee success. Federal losses (killed, wounded, and missing) for the day were a thousand men to the Confederates' two hundred casualties.

General Grant did not intend to engage in a long siege, and his relentless approach led him to attack the town a few days later. On May 22nd, Grant tried his luck again, sending his three main corps in a full assault against Vicksburg at about 10 a.m. after four hours of futile artillery bombardment from the land and river. The Federals approached across an intimidating five-kilometer (three-mile) front, equipped with ladders to scale the embankments, which would ultimately prove too short to do the job! At the north, Sherman was once again repulsed at Stockade Redan. McPherson's troops, which were approaching down the Jackson Road, recoiled under heavy Confederate fire after marching against the 3rd Louisiana Redan and the pivotal eastern Great Redoubt. McPherson suffered particularly heavy losses at the Great Redoubt. Only McClernand's units were successful in breaching the Southern barrier that day. The Yankees pushed through, overcoming the 2nd Texas Lunette on the Union's left flank. Further brigades under McClernand forced the Railroad Redoubt to be evacuated and put severe pressure on South Fort and Square Fort.

But McClernand needed assistance from Sherman and McPherson to persevere with his breakthroughs, and help was not forthcoming in time. Grant's open prejudice toward McClernand undermined the commanding general's belief that his subordinate had, in fact, made progress. Although a small contingent from McPherson's corps eventually helped, McClernand's troops were forced back by the Texans under General Stevenson, as well as Confederate General Green's division, in the late afternoon. The Rebels retook their forts and redoubts and flushed the Yankees from the field. McClernand's boasting to the press and his troops about his conquests led to his early and unfair dismissal on June 18th from the field of battle at Vicksburg, but it did not end his career.

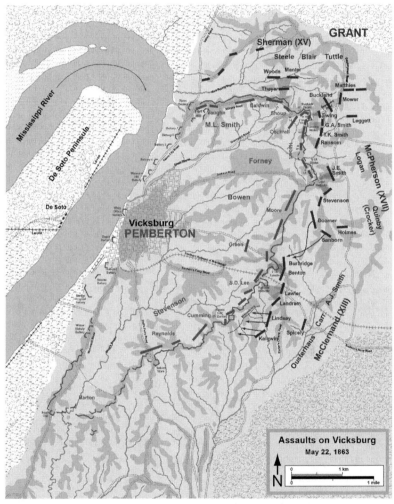

Arrangement of troops for the Union's second push against Vicksburg on May 22nd, 1863. This was a similar arrangement to the troop positions on May 19th. (Blue for Northerners, red for Southerners.)

Map by Hal Jespersen, https://www.posix.com/CW/, CC BY 3.0 <https://creativecommons.org/licenses/by/3.0>, via Wikimedia Commons https://commons.wikimedia.org/wiki/File:VicksburgMay22.png

General Grant's incomplete attack had cost him 3,200 men (killed, wounded, and missing), while the defenders of Vicksburg had lost less than 500. It was then that Grant decided to lay siege to the town rather than conduct further futile offensives. His field surgeons had convinced him that diseases amongst his men (similar to those afflicting the Confederates within the town), as well as the wounded in the field, needed attention. By May 25th, Grant agreed not to conduct further direct attacks on Vicksburg for the time being, but the stalwart general did not agree to a withdrawal. (On this day, a general ceasefire was called, during which the dead and wounded from both sides were retrieved, with the surviving soldiers intermingling as if nothing was amiss.)

Grant intended to set up a permanent camp to entrap the enemy in order to avoid as many causalities as possible. The Union general extended his siege line to twenty kilometers (twelve miles) around Vicksburg. Heavy siege mortar fire and shelling would continue from a distance, which was followed by random musket fire that eventually became a kind of game for the adversaries, as they fired across the battle lines at both fake and real targets. Finally, the lethal work of sharpshooters became the most strategic tactic, as the Blues and Grays positioned snipers to take out unfortunates whose heads rose too high above the parapets and ditches as they worked. The siege would last for six weeks, with devastating consequences for the Rebels.

The Federal move south through Mississippi during 1862 and the first half of 1863 had seen mass evacuations of civilians from those areas, as buggies laden with delicate, panicked ladies, their household possessions, and black slaves fled for safer areas as the Yankees drew toward them. Approximately half the citizens of Vicksburg had fled in the seventeen-day run-up to the Siege of Vicksburg, which had seen five overland engagements across their stretch of Mississippi and five Union victories.

The siege during the sweltering summer of 1863 made the remaining residents of Vicksburg and their slaves literally dig in to protect themselves from the almost continual bombardment of Minié balls (large bullets), Parrott shells, and further barrage. The Union continued firing on the town throughout the days, pausing only for meals. On land, the Northerners surrounded the town in a semicircle that covered the northern, eastern, and southern flanks of the town. From the west, Rear Admiral Porter's gunboats fired on Vicksburg from the Mississippi, and his naval convoy continued to supply the Union with food and supplies.

The residents of Vicksburg were forced to live in natural caves in the bluffs or in hurriedly constructed dugouts within the ground in shanty-style burrows. When the Civil War began in 1861, Vicksburg had a population of approximately 4,500 people—one of the largest towns in Mississippi—but at the time of the siege, this had diminished to approximately 2,000 civilians. The family plantation CC President Davis, Brierfield, was a short fifty-three kilometers (thirty-three miles) south of Vicksburg.

May 29th was a particularly brutal day of shelling, although it was just one of many that lived on in the memories of Vicksburg's citizens. The Union bombardments destroyed buildings and homes, killing civilians and soldiers in the process, including children asleep in their makeshift beds within the caves. Domestic homes temporarily being used as field hospitals were likewise hit, killing or further injuring the sick and wounded within. During the shelling, the citizens took to their cellars, shelters, and caves, but they emerged in the quiet periods to carry on life as usual.

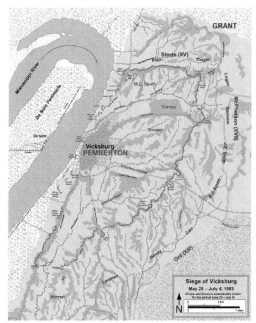

The final arrangement of troops during the Siege of Vicksburg from May 25th to July 4th, 1863.
(Blue for Northerners, red for Southerners.)
Map by Hal Jespersen, https://www.posix.com/CW/, CC BY 3.0
<https://creativecommons.org/licenses/by/3.0>, via Wikimedia Commons
https://commons.wikimedia.org/wiki/File:VicksburgSiege.png

Inside the ramparts, the Rebel forces had abundant ammunition, but food and water were running extremely low for everybody. The Union dammed off the creeks running into Vicksburg, and the Mississippi River could not easily be accessed because of the Union presence along the shores abutting the waterfront. Within the Southern entrapment, domestic dogs and cats began disappearing, and mule meat replaced the soldiers' rations when beef ran out. Rats became a delicacy in a dish called "squirrel stew" for starving soldiers who were eventually rationed to one handful of peas and rice and a single cup of water per day. (It should be noted these rats could have been the local muskrat, indigenous to the wetlands of North America, which would have been eaten by many before wartime.) By the end of June, the price of dry goods had skyrocketed within Vicksburg, and the soldiers were showing signs of scurvy. Dysentery, cholera, and malaria further wasted the emaciated Confederate soldiers.

The internal press of Vicksburg (the *Vicksburg Daily Citizen*) continued reporting on the siege, as well as the living conditions within the town. When paper ran out, they used wallpaper to both write and print on. On July 2nd, two days before the town surrendered, Vicksburg's press was still boasting about winning the standoff. Its editor, J. W. Swords, wrote in response to Grant's supposition that he would be dining in Vicksburg by July 4th. "Ulysses must get into the city before he dines in it. The way to cook a rabbit is first to catch it."

But a note in the *Vicksburg Daily Citizen* at the end of the siege reads as follows: July 4th, 1863: "Two days bring about great changes. The banner of the Union floats over Vicksburg. Gen. Grant has 'caught the rabbit;' he has dined in Vicksburg, and he did bring his dinner with him. The 'Citizen' lives to see it. For the last time it appears on 'Wall-paper.' No more will it eulogize the luxury of mule-meat and fricassed kitten—urge Southern warriors to such diet never more. This is the last wall-paper edition and is, excepting this note, from the types as we found them. It will be valuable hereafter as a curiosity."

This was the final insert of the *Vicksburg Daily Citizen*. The strange, ironic wording of the note is due to it having been engineered by the Union soldiers themselves. Upon entering Vicksburg on July 4th, they had found the printing tablet still laid out with the confident Confederate comments of July 2nd. The Northern soldiers took it upon themselves to rearrange the text, print fifty copies on the last remaining wallpaper, and sell them to fellow soldiers as keepsakes!

A photograph of the underground bombproof dugout dwellings in the yellow clay hills of the town during the Siege of Vicksburg, with the Shirley House (the "White House") in the background.
https://commons.wikimedia.org/wiki/File:ShirleysWhiteHouseVicksburg1863.jpg

During the siege, General Ulysses Grant kept a careful eye on General Johnston's movements near the Big Black River. Grant created a double line of entrenchments—one pointing toward Vicksburg and a second parallel but facing outward to guard against a Confederate encroachment from the land. He also reinforced his artillery by acquiring cannons from Union gunboats. However, Johnston was clearly reluctant to join the fight at Vicksburg and was more concerned with other Union activities around Mississippi. Northern reinforcements and troops continued to arrive at Vicksburg during the siege, and eventually, the Confederates within the town were outnumbered four to one.

The Union soldiers and sappers (quasi engineer soldiers employed to build bridges, dig trenches, and build abatis, etc.) busied themselves during the siege by continually extending and reinforcing their lines, tightening the noose around Vicksburg's neck and making it impossible for food and ordnance supplies to reach the town. They dug trenches toward the besieged town in zigzag patterns, hiding behind sap rollers to protect them as they worked. (Sap rollers were large cylinders of soft materials.) The zigzag trenches enabled the Federal soldiers to move ever closer to the ramparts of Vicksburg, with the erratic patterns making their movements more difficult to target by the Confederate sharpshooters above.

General Grant ordered mining operations below the ramparts, and on June 25th and July 1st, the Union exploded underground mines, with twenty hours of hand-to-hand combat continuing in the first instance in a four-meter (twelve-foot) deep crater. The 3rd Louisiana Redan on the Jackson Road leading east was severely damaged, and there were many Confederate casualties. The Northerners continued to burrow toward Vicksburg, and Pemberton's Confederates needed to countermine these efforts since they were infringed on many fronts by the digging activity. By the beginning of July, the Union had prepared a wide tunnel near the 3rd Louisiana Redan. It was large enough for a column of four men abreast to pass through, and rumors began sweeping through the Confederates that Grant would soon go on the offensive again. These efforts likely contributed to the surrender shortly thereafter.

During the siege, the Confederates continued forays to destabilize the Union, and one Rebel raid resulted in burning the ironclad *Cincinnati* warship that had already been considerably damaged on the Mississippi from Rebel artillery fire. (The ship was later salvaged and put back into Union service.) Confederate attempts to relieve Vicksburg from the western bank of the Mississippi in Louisiana continued throughout the siege. Confederate Major General John George Walker's Texas Division (known as "Walker's Greyhounds" for their speed and agility) had followed the Federals south in their pursuit of a river crossing that had ultimately been at Bruinsburg, but mismanagement by his subordinates saw the Yankees escape back into the Mississippi to continue with their campaign.

Walker led unsuccessful attacks west of the Mississippi on June 7th and July 4th, to no avail. The June assaults as Milliken's Bend and Young's Point saw savage fighting against untrained but highly motivated black troops from Mississippi and Louisiana. (Although the Union won this skirmish, they lost 652 men to the Confederates' 185.) Other encounters in Louisiana between the Blues and the Grays west of the Mississippi did not result in lasting success for the Southerners. In many instances, these encounters constituted enlisted black men protecting former slaves and newly acquired Union plantations or Union strongholds and supply depots. The final confrontation in early July at Helena, Arkansas, resulted in a disastrous defeat for the Rebels. As far as the Union was concerned, Vicksburg was safe from a river approach.

The siege that had begun in approximately mid-May of 1863 was proving too difficult for the Southerners to withstand. As July approached, General Pemberton needed to realistically abandon hope that help would come from the trans-Mississippi to the west or Johnston from the east. When he received a letter signed by "Many Soldiers" under his command that suggested surrender rather than their forced desertion, Pemberton had the good sense to begin planning a surrender. Both Generals Bowen and Martin Luther Smith advised against a breakout, citing an escape as impossible. Surrender was the only option available to the Southerners, and on July 3rd, two Confederate soldiers bearing a white flag finally rode out to the Union line. Negotiations for a surrender began.

Chapter 5 – Capturing the Mississippi River

At first, Union General Grant insisted upon unconditional surrender, as he had demanded at the Battle of Fort Donelson in February the year before. An unconditional surrender would require that all Rebel men, arms, and ordnances be turned over to the Yankees. Pemberton refused, threatening many more Union fatalities if Grant did not negotiate. With the assistance of generals on both sides, such as Bowen and Sherman, Grant and Pemberton finally agreed on terms. The Confederate soldiers were required to give up all battle arms, and they would be paroled rather than becoming prisoners of war. General Ulysses S. Grant correctly anticipated that sending the demoralized and emaciated Rebels home in shame would have more impact than capturing the men. Grant was convinced that the Union did not have the resources to care for tens of thousands of captives. The parolees were required to promise not to fight until such time as they were exchanged, a man for a man, for captured Federal prisoners being held by the Confederacy.

The official surrender was conducted near an oak tree on July 3rd in the afternoon, and although there are no photographs of the conversation, there are illustrations of the two generals meeting. In his memoirs, Grant described the fate of the poor tree, stating, "It was but a short time before the last vestige of its body root and limb had disappeared, the fragments taken as trophies." On July 4th–America's Independence Day–Grant and several divisions of his men marched into the surrendered town of Vicksburg, which they would permanently occupy for the remainder of the war. Despite having so recently been at each other's throats, Union soldiers reached out in extraordinary acts of humanity, providing their foes with food, water, and medical assistance.

As the Union flag of stars and stripes flew above Vicksburg, the dejected and angry Rebel soldiers were allowed to leave the town beginning on July 6th (it is not known how many days they needed to leave). After stacking their military weapons in immense piles (totaling seventy thousand rifles and muskets), furling their Confederate flags, and signing parole papers, they could make their way home. They were permitted to keep personal possessions, including sidearms and one horse per man. (Grant insisted that personal property was to specifically exclude slaves.) Many of the Rebel soldiers were inadvertently admitted back into the war by the following year against the agreement of the parole. Eventually, General Grant ceased all wartime exchanges and parole measures since the Confederates were not upholding their end of the bargain. The Confederate commanders captured after the siege were later exchanged for Union prisoners of similar rank, and Pemberton was returned to Richmond in mid-October of the same year.

Although records differ, the Siege of Vicksburg resulted in approximately three thousand Confederates killed, wounded, or missing, with the remainder of the Army of Mississippi (about twenty-seven thousand men) surrendering to the opposition. They were technically removed from the war unless they were later exchanged. Of these surrendered men, about two thousand were officers. During the siege, about eight hundred Northerners were killed, almost four thousand men were wounded, and two to three hundred were captured or went missing. Almost two hundred cannons were captured by the US in the siege alone, not counting those scooped up by Federal forces in the preliminary battles of the Vicksburg campaign. Sadly, an enormous number of horses (and one camel) were killed during the campaign, particularly those used to transport Confederate artillery. It was reported that the sheer volume of horse corpses around enemy batteries after the Battle of Champion Hill proved impossible for the Union to capture immediately.

During the Siege of Vicksburg, Confederate General Joseph E. Johnston had been gathering a force of thirty thousand men in Jackson. Johnston's intention was to relieve Pemberton and the town of Vicksburg from the siege, and he had been slowly encroaching on Vicksburg. However, Johnston tarried, complaining to Richmond (the Confederate headquarters in Virginia) that he did not have enough men. It was only by July 1ˢᵗ that the Jackson Confederates began inching their way west toward Vicksburg.

Communications between Pemberton and Johnston had always been poor. It was apparent that the generals rarely agreed and had continued to ignore each other's correspondence and requests throughout the campaign. It had also been extremely difficult for the Confederates to consult across the siege lines of Vicksburg and get messages in and out of the beleaguered town. At the time of the surrender, the Confederate troops from Jackson were positioned near the Big Black River. After Pemberton's capitulation, Johnston began marching his troops toward the Union's rear as they took command of Vicksburg.

On July 5ᵗʰ, Grant dispatched Sherman to confront Johnston, resulting in the Jackson Expedition, which was the final encounter of the Vicksburg campaign. Sherman's 9ᵗʰ, 15ᵗʰ, 13ᵗʰ, and part of the 16ᵗʰ Corps of the Army of the Tennessee chased Johnston's Confederate troops east over the Big Black River and farther beyond Champion Hill. This group of Southerners regrouped in Jackson. By July 10ᵗʰ, the Federal troops had surrounded Jackson and attacked two days later, albeit unsuccessfully. A standoff lasting from July 9ᵗʰ to July 17ᵗʰ ensued, as the Union surrounded the western extremities of the town in a semicircular arc reaching from north to south. This is known as the Siege of Jackson.

Johnston chose to evacuate the state capital for the second time in the Vicksburg campaign and removed his men by July 16ᵗʰ, abandoning the town to the Yankees. Jackson came under Federal command once again, which was yet another coup for the Northerners, who had spent 1862 and 1863 bagging strategic nodes in the Western Theater. The Siege of Jackson safeguarded Federal control over Vicksburg and officially ended the Vicksburg campaign. The completion of Sherman's Jackson Expedition was one of the highlights of his career, as it ensured that the Mississippi River remained in Union hands for the remainder of the war.

Simultaneous to the Siege of Vicksburg, the battle for Port Hudson in eastern Louisiana, 241 kilometers (about 150 miles) south downriver of Vicksburg, had continued from May 22ⁿᵈ to July 9ᵗʰ, 1863. Port Hudson lay just 32 kilometers (20 miles) north of Baton Rouge and 161 kilometers (100 miles) upriver from New Orleans—the closest major southern town before the Gulf of Mexico and the open ocean. Union General Nathaniel Prentice Banks (1816–1894, a politician who served in the Civil War) was tasked with overrunning Port Hudson before heading north to assist Grant with the Siege of Vicksburg. However, after several unsuccessful attacks on the fort, General Banks was forced to lay siege to Port Hudson for forty-eight days (one day longer than the Siege of Vicksburg). It was the longest siege in US military history at that time. (Banks's 19th Corps included black soldiers from Louisiana who were part of two desperate but failed assaults on Port Hudson on May 27th and June 11th.)

Five days after the surrender at the Siege of Vicksburg, Confederate General Franklin Kitchell Gardner (1823–1873, a career military man who served the Confederacy for the Civil War and has been heralded for his heroic stand during the siege) finally surrendered Port Hudson. Beginning on July 9th, 1863, the Union controlled the entire Mississippi, from its mouth at the gulf all the way north upstream into Northern territory, including all the major tributaries. It was a defining moment in the war. The Rebels would not regain this prized lost ground or the strategic nodes along the mighty Mississippi. The river that divided the western from the eastern Southern territories was now a major supply line for their adversaries.

Most of the Confederates who fought for Port Hudson were similarly paroled as those at Vicksburg. Approximately nine thousand Union soldiers were casualties of death, injury, disease, or severe sunstroke after the Siege of Port Hudson. Only approximately nine hundred men on Gardner's side were injured, dead, or incapacitated. General Banks kindly provided transport to the sick and diseased Confederate soldiers, returning home with extremely sick men who remained under the care of the Union. Almost six thousand Southern soldiers and civilians were paroled after this final Mississippi coup, with about four hundred men being imprisoned. By September of 1863, most of the parolees from Port Hudson had returned to duty, much to the fury of some Northern commanders. However, it was agreed on both sides that the terms of the parole had been unsubstantiated.

Chapter 6 – Outcome of the Vicksburg Campaign

Within these first few years of the Civil War, many Confederate successes in the Eastern Theater were attributed to poor appointments at the head of the Northern Army, the subsequent degeneration of communication between generals, and even insubordination. At the same time, in the Western Theater, in which the Siege of Vicksburg had transpired, incoherent communication and orders between the Southern leaders had been a significant contributing factor to the loss of Vicksburg and, as a result, the control of the Mississippi. General Pemberton showed consistent indecisiveness and hesitation as he attempted to please two masters: President Davis, who'd insisted that he hold Vicksburg at all costs, and General Johnston, who was attempting to make immediate tactical decisions in the heat of the campaign.

Pemberton's hesitation in following Johnston's orders during the Battle of Champion Hill could have potentially fed Johnston's reluctance to attack the Union's rear during the Siege of Vicksburg. It was apparent that Johnston made no real effort to relieve General Pemberton, his army, or the town of Vicksburg itself. After the fall of Vicksburg, fingers were pointed in all directions, and General John Pemberton demanded a court inquiry into General Johnston's delay in sending aid to Vicksburg, but a court-martial was never ordered.

The Union's success at the Siege of Vicksburg resulted in its domination of the Mississippi River, the crucially strategic arterial route through the Southern war theaters. The piece of river referred to as "Gibraltar" that had been under Confederate control systematically gave way to Union forces soon after the siege. The section that stretched from Vicksburg to Port Hudson was the main thoroughfare for food, men, and supplies from the western to the eastern states of the Southern territories. Blocking the easy flow of goods, particularly the products of agriculture grown in the trans-Mississippi, essentially cleaved the South in two. The conclusion of the Siege of Vicksburg was a dramatic and final turning point in the Civil War that saw the gradual demise of the Rebels. Coupled with the Union victory at Gettysburg the day before on July 3rd, 1863, in Northern territory (Pennsylvania), the war had turned in favor of the Federals, but it would take a further two years for the North to finally crush the indomitable South.

General John Pemberton was demoted in 1864, but he continued serving the war to its close in the Eastern Theater, albeit in unobtrusive roles. General Johnston assumed leadership of the Confederate Army of Tennessee in 1864 but was subsequently removed by President Davis during the Atlanta campaign (the summer of 1864, Western Theater). The truly outstanding Confederate individual from the Vicksburg campaign was General Bowen, who unfortunately died of dysentery shortly after the siege. He is considered as one of the greatest unsung Confederate heroes of the war, and he was accompanied everywhere by his wife, who refused to leave his side for the duration of the war.

For General Ulysses S. Grant, the Siege of Vicksburg paved the way for a glittering career and his immediate promotion to major general of the Regular Army (seasoned US soldiers). He was heralded as a national hero, and further wins in the Western Theater thereafter led to his appointment as the commanding general of the Union Army, an office he held from March 1864 until after the end of the Civil War in March of 1869. Confederate General-in-Chief Robert Edward Lee (1807-1870, a distinguished military soldier and engineer who commanded the Confederates for much of the Civil War) was required to make the final Southern surrender to Grant at Appomattox, Virginia, on April 9th, 1865, thus ending the Civil War. From 1869 to 1877, Ulysses S. Grant sat as the eighteenth president of the United States. Although several scandals tarnished his time in office, he was heralded as a symbol of national unity upon his death, and he has since been recognized for his considerable accomplishments, particularly with respect to civil, African American, and Native American rights and liberties.

General William T. Sherman's career was similarly made by the success of the Siege of Vicksburg, and he was appointed head of the Union Army in the Western Theater in 1864 once Grant was promoted. Sherman went on to enjoy military successes until the close of the war, and he succeeded Grant as the commander of the US Army, which he held for an astounding fourteen years until his retirement in 1883.

The Union's success at the Siege of Vicksburg is considered to be the most pivotal event in the Civil War. Capturing Vicksburg created a domino effect in which the last remaining piece of the Mississippi came under Union control. Once the Union held this mighty river that divided the country, they had fractured the South. Besides the militaristic and moral victory of Vicksburg, the Rebels could no longer use the north-south-running Mississippi nor the west-east-aligned Southern Railway to move men, supplies, and crucial communications to the battlefields east of the river. The North had broken the backbone of the South.

Unbeknownst to all who fought, the Civil War was at its midpoint. A further two years of fighting would finally see the crippled South capitulate. The Siege of Vicksburg had resulted in the disbanding of an entire Confederate Army—the Army of Mississippi. Now, only one army stood in the way of Union victory in the Western Theater: the Army of Tennessee.

Conclusion

The Siege of Vicksburg was arguably the most decisive battle of the American Civil War in that it swung the momentum of victory away from the South and toward the North. When the Union captured Vicksburg, they created insurmountable strategic and tactical difficulties for the Confederate forces. The Union success at Vicksburg and the resultant domination of the Mississippi meant that the cannons at Vicksburg remained silent for the remainder of the war—the town did not need to defend itself again, as it was permanently beaten. The Vicksburg campaign is described in US Army manuals as the most brilliant campaign ever waged on American soil and marks General Grant as the first amongst modern war tacticians.

Both presidents of the North and South had openly declared the strategic imperative of controlling Vicksburg. It was the crucial node on the eastern bank of the Mississippi that linked the Southern Railway that enabled the movement of troops, food, and supplies from Southern territories to the west of the Mississippi to the main battlefields east of the river. The high bluffs along the eastern bank of this mighty river meant that whoever controlled the towns on the high ground controlled the riverways, with the bluffs making for ideal artillery platforms aimed at the water.

In the winter of 1862, the race for Vicksburg began with the start of the Vicksburg campaign, which was initiated by General Ulysses S. Grant, who was both respected and chastised for his brilliance, bravery, and eccentricities. Grant was a master of diversionary tactics, and he ultimately chose the least likely strategy for gaining Vicksburg by sending tens of thousands of troops down the western side of the Mississippi, deep into enemy territory and knee-deep in mud, alligators, and deadly snakes. This sneak attack was considered so outlandish by the enemy that General Pemberton, who was in charge of protecting Vicksburg, did not believe it possible until it was too late.

The Confederates fought bravely for the first two weeks of May 1863 to prevent the Federals from reaching Vicksburg, but eventually, Pemberton and his men were forced behind the ramparts of the fortress-like town. For a further six weeks, the Rebels held firm, repelling the Union with all their might, and they never did manage to breach the fortifications. General Grant chose to starve and dig his enemy out, and they were finally willing to meet for negotiations to surrender on July 3rd. The Northern win at the Battle of Gettysburg on the same day may have contributed to General Pemberton's final decision to surrender.

Vicksburg saw the removal of an entire army from the Confederacy. One could see the visibly diminished morale of Southern troops as they piled their weapons on a heap with tears in their eyes before returning to their homes, no longer permitted to continue as Southern soldiers. In the words of President Abraham Lincoln, "[the Mississippi again rolled] unvexed to the sea," unaware that its loss was symbolic of the South's failure to rise again. The Rebel spine had been broken, and the Southern lands to the west of the river lay immobile, as they were unable to provide the support that the theater to the east would so desperately need in the years to come.

Part 9: The Gettysburg Campaign

A Captivating Guide to the Military Invasion of Pennsylvania That Culminated in the Battle of Gettysburg During the American Civil War

Introduction

Almost 160 years after the conclusion of the American Civil War, the conflict and its ramifications continue to preoccupy national interest. The bloodiest of all American wars, the four years of battle from 1861 to 1865 killed an estimated 650,000 to 850,000. Many of the simmering controversies that erupted into outright war had been present since the founding of the United States.

Abolitionists pointed to the amoral practice of African slavery, especially as it pertained to America's expansion into the western territories and matters of representation and taxation. Rather than deal with the hot-button issue, the delegates to the Constitutional Convention had settled on the Three-fifths Compromise in 1787, which allowed three out of five slaves to be counted as a person in determining a state's population. In side-stepping the problem, the founders all but guaranteed future conflicts over slavery that predictably erupted as the nation spread westward.

The economic roots of the war lay in an unbalanced burden of tariffs between the agricultural South and increasingly industrial North. This imbalance proved telling when the North successfully blockaded Southern ports, effectively denying the Confederacy the manufactured goods it could only obtain as imports.

Finally, during the Reconstruction years, adherents of the "Lost Cause" staunchly defended the war as a matter of constitutional interpretation. These apologists sought to mythologize and justify the Southern position, as evidenced by the persistence of the phrase "War of

Northern Aggression" in reference to the conflict. Even now, in the 21st century, opponents of a strong central government rail against federal overreach and speak of states' rights and secession.

In 1861, the motivations that led men to fight on either side ranged from a reckless desire for adventure to passionate advocacy for a given political position. Most did not understand, however, that advances in weaponry were quickly ending the days of gentlemanly warfare and chivalrous cavalry charges. For the first time in the 1860s, massed troops armed with weapons and ammunition produced by the Industrial Revolution faced one another in bloody, bludgeoning battles with staggering casualties numbering in the hundreds of thousands. The 1863 Gettysburg Campaign, culminating in the three-day battle of Gettysburg (July 1-3, 1863) surpassed them all.

No one can say for certain how the rank and file gathered in the fields of Pennsylvania felt about facing one another in battle so close to the eighty-seventh anniversary of the Declaration of Independence. Many of the accounts penned by veterans in the following years were colored by fading or convenient memories. Contemporaneous letters reflected fear, hunger, hope, and weariness.

In his epic 1974 fictional account of the Gettysburg campaign, *The Killer Angels: A Novel of the Civil War*, Michael Shaara attempted to capture the gravitas inherent in the pedigrees of some of the combatants. Crafting a scene that involved Confederate General Lewis Armistead and a British observer, Shaara had Armistead recite the Revolutionary War heritage of soldiers within his line of sight.

That conversation never happened, but the grandsons of distinguished patriots were there on those three hot days in July 1863—on both sides of the confrontation. Robert E. Lee himself was the son of "Light Horse" Harry Lee, who served as one of George Washington's officers.

Union Colonel Paul J. Revere, grandson of the eponymous patriot, suffered shrapnel to the throat on the second day at Gettysburg and died forty-eight hours later. Armistead, who died after being wounded in Pickett's Charge, was the nephew of Major George Armistead, who defended Ft. McHenry in the War of 1812 with such gallantry Francis Scott Key was moved to write "The Star-Spangled Banner."

President John Tyler's grandson, Private Robert Tyler Jones, fought for the Confederacy, as did the commander of the 53rd Virginia Infantry, Colonel William Aylett, the grandson of Patrick Henry. General

Alexander Webb, who commanded the Union Philadelphia Brigade, was the grandson of a minuteman who fought at Lexington in 1775.

Undoubtedly, countless others could trace their lineage to predecessors who were instrumental in founding the United States of America, if not by acts worthy of the history books, then certainly by the sweat of their brows.

Lee's Decision to Invade Pennsylvania

After racking up a string of victories in Virginia, Confederate General Robert E. Lee decided to take the fight to the North in the summer of 1863. He counted on growing anti-war sentiment on the northern home front to force the Union to negotiate a peace. Instead, Lee suffered a crippling defeat at Gettysburg that signaled the beginning of the end for the Southern cause.

The Confederacy would hold on until Lee's surrender at Appomattox Courthouse on April 9, 1865—approximately twenty-one months after the pivotal battle. Lee, however, never again went on the offensive after his ill-fated excursion into Pennsylvania. Going into the Gettysburg Campaign, the general believed the fight inside Union territory would determine the outcome of the war; he was right, but not in the way he anticipated.

Eight decades of simmering regional disputes preceded the Gettysburg campaign. The immediate precipitator of Lee's decision to move into Pennsylvania, however, lay in his victory over Maj. Gen. Joseph Hooker at Chancellorsville, a clash regarded as Lee's "perfect" battle. Waged in Virginia from April 30 to May 6, 1863, Chancellorsville set in motion the chain of events that led to Gettysburg. Buoyed by the victory, the Southern commander turned the 75,000 men of the Army of Northern Virginia northward into enemy territory.

Lee hoped to put enough pressure on Washington, D.C., to compel peace negotiations, but his strategy was also driven by the hunger of his men and their ragtag condition. Virginia's resources were spent. The North offered abundant crops and manufactured goods. The invasion meant the Confederates could eat off the land, confiscating food and badly needed supplies.

Hooker followed Lee as he moved north, but kept his distance, unwilling to see a repeat of Chancellorsville. Hooker's caution frustrated President Abraham Lincoln, who knew that support for the war in the

North was at an all-time low. In June, Lincoln replaced Hooker with Maj. Gen. George Gordon Meade, whose orders were to use the 90,000 men in the Army of the Potomac to prevent Lee from reaching Washington, D.C.

Three corps of Southern troops crossed the Potomac on June 15, 1863. By the 28th, they were on the banks of the Susquehanna River in Pennsylvania. Unfortunately, Lee's movements were hampered by a lack of on-the-ground intelligence from General Jeb Stuart's cavalry. Lee's decision to converge his forces on Gettysburg was thus made more on instinct than hard tactical data.

The area's major roads converged in Gettysburg, and Lee wanted control of those roads—a desire that committed 165,620 soldiers to participate in the largest battle ever to take place on American soil. Of those men, 93,921 were Union troops, and 71,699 were Confederate. All were Americans.

Chapter 1 – June 1863

After the Confederate victory at Chancellorsville in May 1863, the Army of Northern Virginia and the Army of the Potomac faced one another on either side of the Rappahannock River near Fredericksburg, Virginia. Though a Southern victory, Chancellorsville did not tip the scales of war definitively, resulting in a stalemate on the same ground the armies had held for five months. Ironically, the combatants were positioned almost equidistant from their capitals—Washington lay fifty-three miles to the north and Richmond fifty-seven miles south.

Any dissection of the Gettysburg campaign must begin with some attempt to understand General Robert E. Lee as both a commander and Southern figurehead.

Robert E. Lee

The son of Revolutionary War hero Henry "Light Horse Harry" Lee III, Robert Edward Lee spent the first thirty-two years of his career as an engineer with an excellent reputation. A graduate of the United States Military Academy at West Point, Lee served as the school's superintendent following his distinguished service in the Mexican-American War. His wife, Mary Anna Custis Lee, was George Washington's great-granddaughter.

Much has been made of Lee's anguish over the broken Union and his pained decision to resign his commission and join the Confederate Army after Virginia seceded in 1861. The fact that he did so, however, undeniably made him a traitor to the nation he had served so honorably.

Though a philosophical opponent of slavery (because he believed the institution harmed the white owners), Lee's conscience did not prevent him from listing several hundred human beings as his property. He admitted to the belief that enslaved African were his racial inferiors and that they did, in some ways, benefit from their forced servitude. In his eyes, slavery compelled blacks to develop a work ethic and introduced them to Christianity.

After serving as a military adviser to Confederate President Jefferson Davis in 1861, Lee assumed command of the Army of Northern Virginia in June 1862. He drove the Federal (Union) forces away from Richmond, the Confederate capital, and scored a victory at the Second Battle of Bull Run in August.

In September, Lee invaded Maryland only to retreat to Virginia after the Battle of Antietam, which showed no gains for either side. His subsequent victories in the summer of 1863 at Fredericksburg and Chancellorsville proved critical to his second invasion of the north, the Gettysburg Campaign.

Opinions of Lee's skill as a general range from the open worship of his soldiers and the hagiography of biographers to the critical evaluations of military historians. In retrospect, many of his decisions—including that to remain and fight for a third day at Gettysburg—appear to be sheer folly. Lee did not write a memoir to clarify his decisions, and his official dispatches were too impersonal to offer insights for posterity.

Most modern interpretations agree that although Lee provided a focal point of inspiration for his troops, he did not manage the Battle of Gettysburg well. Though there were moments throughout the war when Lee appeared to read the minds of his opponents—most of whom he knew personally—he was not a good communicator with his subordinates. That failure surfaced more than once at Gettysburg.

There are facts and suppositions about Lee during the Gettysburg campaign that are worthy of consideration. At age 56, he battled both heart trouble and rheumatism. Some scholars contend he suffered from dysentery. He was undoubtedly exhausted and arguably over-confident. At battle's end, however, Lee looked for no excuses to explain away his defeat. He assumed full responsibility for the debacle in Pennsylvania.

After the battle, Lee stayed on the defensive for the remainder of the war. He never mounted another head-on assault as he'd done with Pickett's Charge on July 3, 1863. In the end, Grant simply trapped Lee, forcing the general into a long series of retreats against superior forces, culminating in the Confederate surrender at Appomattox Courthouse on April 9, 1865. Lee refused all entreaties to continue the fight with guerilla forces, considering such a desperate move an ungentlemanly denial of defeat.

Many people continue to regard Lee as the Confederacy's finest general—perhaps one of the nation's greatest military minds—but that iconic status stems more from the personal respect Lee commanded than his tactical brilliance. By the standards of his day (his stance on slavery notwithstanding), Lee appears to have been an honorable man called to a dishonorable cause. He most certainly is a study in contrast.

After the war, Lee lost the right to vote, and his family home was confiscated to become Arlington National Cemetery. He was not, however, arrested or punished in any other way. Over time, Lee evolved into a symbol of national reconciliation, even visiting Ulysses S. Grant at the White House in 1869.

Yet Lee opposed giving the vote to formerly enslaved Africans. Though asked to condemn the Ku Klux Klan, he remained silent on that organization's violent tactics and on white supremacy in general. Critics argue that a public stance by Lee could have eased the worst excesses of the Reconstruction and post-Reconstruction eras, but that seems to accord almost super-human power to his influence.

As a civilian, Lee served as the president of Washington College from 1865 until his death in 1870 at age 63 following a stroke. The school is now Washington and Lee University, where Lee is buried.

Lee's Second Invasion

Lee's decision to invade the North for a second time represented what would become the most ambitious Southern offensive of the war. All other considerations aside, the campaign was, at its heart, a mass supply raid. War-ravaged Virginia was depleted of the needed resources to feed and equip an army, while the rich Northern farms were ripe for the taking.

By abandoning his defensive positions along the Rappahannock, Lee would upset the Union's planned summer campaigns by threatening the major cities of Philadelphia, Baltimore, and Washington, D.C. As mentioned, he hoped to capitalize on what he perceived to be growing anti-war sentiment in the North, an understanding gained primarily from reading Peace Democrat or "Copperhead" newspapers.

Those materials did not, however, give Lee an appreciation for President Abraham Lincoln's determination to win the war or for the effect of Major General Ulysses S. Grant's western campaigns on Northern morale. From May 1-17, Grant scored victories at Port Gibson, Raymond, Jackson, Champion Hill, and the Big Black River Bridge before cornering 30,000 Confederates under Lt. Gen. John C. Pemberton at Vicksburg. When a relief force commanded by General Joseph E. Johnson failed to rescue their Confederate compatriots, Grant settled in to wait out the siege.

Jefferson Davis called Lee to Richmond twice in May 1863 to discuss strategy. Given the location of the Federal troops, the two leaders had good reason to fear for the safety of the Southern capital. Additionally, the Confederate hold on the entire Tidewater region was called into serious question by a Union garrison of 20,000 troops in Suffolk that threatened Norfolk and Hampton roads.

With Vicksburg under siege and Virginia on tenuous ground, Davis had no single, comprehensive solution at his disposal. As his understanding of the situation evolved, he wanted Lee to take at least 20,000 men and go to Pemberton's relief at Vicksburg, but the general's thoughts were elsewhere.

In February, Lee had secretly asked Lt. Gen. Thomas J. "Stonewall" Jackson's chief engineer to craft a map of the valley of Virginia that would extend as far as Philadelphia. By April, Lee told Confederate Secretary of War James A. Seldon he was contemplating crossing into Maryland in May.

Despite all objections, Lee's position won out in the strategic talks. He insisted victory lay in concentrating his movements in the Northeast. The planned invasion reflected almost to the letter the general's execution of the Maryland Campaign in 1862.

Beyond his misreading of the Northern home front, Lee also placed an excessive degree of faith in the fighting spirit of his men after Chancellorsville. In his correspondence, Lee fantasized about his tested veterans creating a general panic in Pennsylvania, leading to the utter destruction of the Army of the Potomac. While ready for battle, Lee's men were hardly as "invincible" as their commander believed them to be.

Still, Davis approved the northern offensive, with Lee issuing his first orders ahead of the invasion on June 3. The Army of Northern Virginia moved away from Fredericksburg to concentrate around Culpepper. Though they marched with all stealth, Union General Joseph Hooker, in command of the Army of the Potomac, learned of their movements on June 5.

Joseph Hooker

Hooker, a native of Hadley, Massachusetts (born 1814), graduated twenty-ninth of fifty in the West Point Class of 1837. Known as a hard drinker with an eye for the ladies, Hooker served in the Seminole Wars and the Mexican-American War as a staff officer for Winfield Scott and future president Zachary Taylor.

He resigned his commission in 1853 after being involved in a controversy that put him at odds with General Scott. Hooker testified against Scott during a court-martial regarding insubordination—an act of disloyalty that Scott apparently did not forget or forgive.

As a civilian, Hooker was both bored and unsuccessful, failing as a farmer, land developer, and politician but standing out as a gambler and womanizer. By 1858, he wanted back in the army and wrote to the Secretary of War seeking a commission as a lieutenant colonel.

When nothing came of the request, he found a place with the California militia as a colonel. At the outbreak of the Civil War, Hooker again requested a commission but was rejected, likely because Scott was general-in-chief of the army.

Ultimately, Hooker appealed to Lincoln directly, gaining an appointment as a brigadier general of volunteers, organizing and training elements of the Army of the Potomac near Washington, D.C., under Maj. Gen. George B. McClellan.

During the 1862 Peninsula Campaign, Hooker earned a battlefield reputation for aggressive but exemplary action at Williamsburg and Seven Pines. Though his headquarters was always the scene of revelry, even in the heat of war, Hooker was known for putting the welfare of his men above all else, with special sensitivity for their morale.

After his promotion to major general in July 1862 and following the Second Battle of Bull Run, Hooker was given command of the troops that became the Army of the Potomac's I Corps. He led his men at South Mountain and Antietam, where they fought Confederate Lt. Gen.

Stonewall Jackson's forces to a standstill. Hooker, however, was forced to retire from the confrontation due to an injured foot. Afterward, he maintained the battle would have been a resounding Union victory had he remained on the field.

In September 1863, Hooker was promoted to brigadier general in the regular army. Throughout this period, he criticized the actions of his superiors, finding McClellan too slow and cautious and McClellan's replacement, Maj. Gen. Ambrose Burnside, a poor strategist. Some of Hooker's complaints trod the fine line of insubordination. Burnside even drafted a letter to Lincoln insisting Hooker was unfit for service in the current national crisis.

Fortunately for Hooker, however, Lincoln's patience with his generals had grown thin. The president fired Burnside and put Hooker at the head of the Army of the Potomac on January 26, 1863. The president counted on "Fighting Joe" Hooker's aggressive reputation to gain positive traction for the Union forces. The new commander started by improving the quality of his camp's food, sanitation, health care, and providing more generous furloughs for the men.

In other areas of innovation, Hooker established the army's first intelligence organization, the Bureau of Military Information, and approved a system of corps badges. The emblems were meant to create a sense of pride and ease unit identification during the chaos of battle. Officer training became more organized, and cavalry units were integrated into a designated corps.

Despite the effectiveness of these moves and the changes he made in command personnel, Hooker's personal conduct failed to meet the standard of his rank. One junior officer described the general's headquarters as little better than a brothel. Hooker surrounded himself with loyal cronies that added a layer of politics to his command, and he continued to drink.

Hooker planned an ambitious summer campaign that would result in the capture of Richmond. Instead, he suffered an embarrassing defeat at Chancellorsville, where proximity to a cannonball strike left him with a concussion. Refusing to relinquish command, Hooker made decisions that other officers found questionable in the aftermath of the fighting.

When Lee unexpectedly moved north, Hooker's mission was to protect Washington, D.C., at all costs before finding and defeating the Southerners. Yet again, Lincoln was losing confidence in his commander and would soon welcome the opportunity to replace him just as he'd ousted McClellan and Burnside.

Brandy Station

On June 5, when Hooker learned of Lee's movements, he dispatched Maj. Gen. Alfred Pleasonton with 4,000 infantry and artillery and 7,000 cavalrymen to pursue the Confederates. Pleasonton surprised Confederate Maj. Gen. Jeb Stuart at Brandy Station in the early morning hours of June 9.

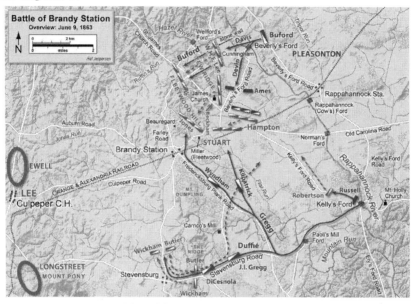

Map of the Battle of Brandy Station.
Map by Hal Jespersen, www.cwmaps.com, CC BY 3.0
<https://creativecommons.org/licenses/by/3.0>, via Wikimedia Commons;
https://commons.wikimedia.org/wiki/File:Brandy_Station_Overview.png

The fighting there evolved into one of the largest mounted confrontations of the war. Stuart commanded five cavalry brigades, approximately 9,500 men, under Brigadier Generals Wade Hampton, W.H.F. "Rooney" Lee, Beverly H. Robertson, William E. "Grumble" Jones, and Colonel Thomas T. Munford (in temporary command of Brig. Gen. Fitzhugh Lee's troops).

The flamboyant Stuart was almost captured but rallied to hold his ground. At the end of the day, the Union forces suffered 907 casualties to the Confederate's 523. In the fighting, Lee's son, Rooney, was seriously injured and captured later that month. While Stuart styled the confrontation as a victory, the Southern newspapers were less complimentary. Neither the close call in which his best cavalry general was surprised nor negative public opinion deterred Lee, however, in the execution of his ambitious plans for invasion.

James Ewell Brown "Jeb" Stuart

Jeb Stuart's name figures heavily among the officers whose conduct at Gettysburg received heavy post-war criticism. Stuart was a native Virginian born in 1833. Stuart's father was a War of 1812 veteran and a politician, serving in both houses of the Virginia General Assembly and the U.S. House of Representatives. His grandfather fought in the American Revolution.

Educated at home until age twelve, Stuart enrolled in Emory and Henry College at 15. He tried to enlist in the army for the first time in 1848 but was rejected due to his youth. In 1850, however, he received an appointment to West Point, where he prospered. When Robert E. Lee became the academy's superintendent in 1852, Stuart quickly became a friend of the family.

Stuart graduated 13th in a class of forty-six in 1854 and was dispatched to far West Texas, where he served at Fort Davis with the U.S. Regiment of Mounted Riflemen. He transferred to the cavalry in 1855 and was sent to Kansas. He saw action against various Native American tribes and during the outbreak of violence that preceded the Civil War, known as "Bleeding Kansas."

Stuart resigned his commission on May 3, 1861, and joined the Confederate Army as a lieutenant colonel with the Virginia Infantry. On July 4, Stuart assumed command of all cavalry companies in the Army of the Shenandoah under Thomas J. "Stonewall" Jackson. This consolidation led to the formation of the 1st Virginia Cavalry Regiment. By 1862, he held the rank of brigadier general and, a few months later, major general.

Known for his plumed hat and flowing cloak, Stuart performed admirably in all the major campaigns leading up to Gettysburg. There, however, his lack of contact with the main body of Lee's army for more than a week led to a rare rebuke from his commander and lingering post-war criticism. Like General James Longstreet, Stuart became a scapegoat for the Confederate defeat. Detractors insist that had Stuart kept Lee informed of Union troop movements, the battle would have resulted in a decisive victory.

Though not disciplined for his absence, Stuart was not promoted to lieutenant general when given a corps command in 1863. Unlike other Gettysburg general officers who lived to defend themselves, Stuart was struck down at the Battle of Yellow Tavern on May 11, 1864, dying the next day at only 31. A bullet had pierced Stuart's left side, and the projectile went through his stomach, missing the spine by only an inch. Taken to Richmond by ambulance, Stuart was coherent, ordering that his son receive his sword and spurs. The general received a visit from President Davis but died at 7:38 p.m. on May 12. His widow, Flora, wore black for the remainder of her life, passing in 1923. Known as one of the greatest cavalrymen in American history, Stuart received a sort of posthumous knighthood in the eyes of the very Southerners who had denounced his actions at Gettysburg.

Hooker's Resignation

In the wake of Brandy Station, Lee continued preparations to move north with his reconfigured army, changes put in place after the death of Stonewall Jackson on May 10. Adding a third corps to the Army of Northern Virginia, Lee would now rely on Lt. Gen. James Longstreet in command of the I Corps, Lt. Gen. Richard S. Ewell of the II Corps, and Lt. Gen. Ambrose Powell Hill of the III Corps. With the addition of Stuart's cavalry, Lee's combined strength was 75,000 men.

After concentrating at Culpepper, Lee planned to drive the Federals out of the Shenandoah Valley before moving north into the Cumberland Valley of Pennsylvania. By keeping the Blue Ridge Mountains to his right (east), Lee could shield his supply trains and those he intended to send south with confiscated goods.

On June 10, Lee directed Ewell to move into the Shenandoah Valley as the lead element of the invasion. The II Corps was home to most of Stonewall Jackson's troops, who had marched into the same region during the 1862 Valley Campaign.

After the Union defeat at Brandy Station, Hooker clearly understood that Lee was on the march north. In response, he wanted to move on Richmond, only to face a sharp rebuke from Lincoln, who reminded him that the objective was Lee's army, not the southern capital. Consequently, Hooker pursued of Lee on June 13 with 94,000 men comprised of seven infantries and one cavalry corps. Regardless of the numbers, however, Hooker believed that Lee (who had 75,000 men) outnumbered him.

The Union general's pessimism was fueled by the loss of thousands of veterans whose two-year enlistments had just ended. He was also nagged by the fact that some of his corps contained only two rather than three divisions. Hooker expressed his doubts by bombarding his higher-ups for reinforcements or permission to take control of units not currently under his command.

As Ewell moved north, he encountered Union Brig. Gen. Robert H. Milroy's garrison at Winchester on June 14. The Southerners assailed the position and scattered the Federals, capturing 4,000 prisoners, 300 wagons of supplies, and 23 cannons. Following a scouting mission by cavalry under the command of Brig. Gen. Albert G. Jenkins, Ewell's infantry marched into Pennsylvania on June 20.

Over the next week, Ewell's men made themselves at home in the south-central portions of the state. Raiding parties reached the vicinity of the state capital at Harrisburg. On June 21, Lee issued General Orders 72, in which the procedures for foraging were laid out. The officers in charge of supplies—quartermaster, commissary, ordnance, and medical— were directed to pay fair market prices for the goods they required. Soldiers were directed to exercise proper respect for private property.

Predictably, however, these directives were violated, leading Lee to issue a follow-up order scolding his men and reminding them of the conduct expected of them by the rules of civility and Christianity. Regardless, heavily laden wagons began to roll South, some carrying African Americans arrested regardless of their status as free or slave.

Many Pennsylvania residents snatched up all they could carry and ran from the Confederates. The chaotic response from the government and from troops whose protection the civilians should have rightly expected only worsened their distress. Neither the Lincoln administration's June 9 creation of the Department of the Susquehanna nor calls from Governor Andrew G. Curtain resulted in any substantive moves toward local defense.

When the 26th Pennsylvania Emergency Regiment attempted to confront Ewell's troops on June 26, they panicked after the first shots were fired. Those who weren't captured turned tail and ran. Moving toward Harrisburg, Ewell dealt with only sporadic and ineffective resistance.

Lee's troops, however, faced a different set of circumstances. Hooker, now aware of his adversary's presence, looked for a way to intercept the

Confederates through gaps in the Blue Ridge. On June 17 at Aldie, June 19 at Middleburg, and June 21 at Upperville, Jeb Stuart's cavalry clashed with mounted Federal units. Lee specifically ordered Stuart to engage in actions intended to harass and delay Hooker, especially if the Federal troops attempted to cross the Potomac.

If the Federal troops did get across the river, Stuart was to assume a position to the right of Lee's column as it continued north. In following his orders, Stuart was certainly an annoyance to the Federals and a worry to Washington. In picking his route, however, Stuart put Hooker between his own troops and Lee's for a week at the end of the month. This critical error deprived Lee of the high-quality intelligence necessary to plan his actions as circumstances increasingly put Gettysburg in the crosshairs of both armies.

Persistent in his belief that Lee outnumbered him, Hooker continued his calls for reinforcements, finally saying that if he did not receive additional troops, he would resign. Lincoln and Secretary of War Edwin M. Stanton called the general's bluff and accepted his resignation. Maj. Gen. George G. Meade was appointed to replace Hooker on June 28.

In his haste to leave the area, Hooker failed to give Meade a detailed assessment of the situation in Pennsylvania. Thus, Meade took command of the Army of the Potomac with scant knowledge of the forces he led and even less understanding of the enemy he faced. Making only essential changes regarding organization and administration, Meade immediately sent out multiple requests for information and tried to formulate a plan.

George Gordon Meade

Meade, born December 31, 1815, in Spain, grew up in Philadelphia, where he attended a private military school until his father's death in 1828. On July 1, 1831, Meade, who wanted to become a lawyer, entered West Point. He took little pleasure in his time there, though he graduated 19th in the Class of 1835.

After fulfilling his required year of army service, Meade resigned and sought employment with his brother-in-law in Florida as a railroad surveyor. He did similar work on the Texas-Louisiana border and the border between Maine and Canada. All these jobs had been in connection with the Army Corps of Topographical Engineers, which could no longer hire civilians after 1842.

Subsequently, Meade rejoined the army as a second lieutenant to continue his career. He saw battlefield service in the Mexican-American War and then assisted in putting down the Seminole tribe in Florida. In the early 1850s, Meade oversaw the construction of a lighthouse in the state before being assigned to survey Lake Huron and Lake Michigan.

At the outbreak of the Civil War, Meade was appointed a brigadier general of volunteers and given command of the 2nd Brigade of the Pennsylvania Reserves, assigned to construct defenses in Washington, D.C. When the Army of the Potomac was divided into four corps in March 1862, Meade served under Maj. Gen. Irvin McDowell in the I Corps.

After being wounded at Glendale in June 1862, he recuperated in Philadelphia, resuming command at the Second Battle of Bull Run. His men participated in the battles of South Mountain and Antietam. Meade assumed temporary command at the latter when Hooker, the corps commander, was wounded. In September 1862, after John Reynolds took command of the I Corp, Meade was placed in command of the Third Division.

The decision to place Reynolds over the I Corps left Meade, who had more combat experience, greatly frustrated. His feelings were somewhat improved with a promotion to major general in November ahead of the Battle of Fredericksburg, where Meade's men broke the Confederate lines even though his attack received no reinforcement. Meade led the V Corps at Chancellorsville, but his troops were held in reserve during the fighting, contributing to the Union defeat.

On the morning of June 28, Meade learned that he had been appointed to replace Hooker. He was not the president's first choice; John Reynolds turned down the job. In the end, however, Gettysburg proved to be a decisive victory for the North and led to Meade's promotion as a brigadier general in the regular army.

Meade retained command of the Army of the Potomac after Lt. Gen. Ulysses S. Grant was given command of all Union armies in March 1864. After the Battle of Spotsylvania Court House, Meade was promoted to major general. In the closing months of the war, Meade felt slighted on multiple occasions when less experienced generals received greater favor. Though present during the Appomattox Campaign, Meade was not on site for Lee's surrender. The Army of the Potomac disbanded on June 28, 1865.

Many of Meade's issues with his fellow generals lay in his political position. He opposed slavery only as the issue that caused the Union to be severed, not as a moral matter. To him, the war's only goal was preserving the United States, not freeing enslaved people.

Meade possessed a notoriously short temper and, though respected, was not an inspirational leader. Nicknamed "Old Snapping Turtle," Meade could be social and courteous when not under stress but abrasive and combative in the thick of war. He tended toward recklessness and paranoia.

After the war, as commander of the Department of the South, Meade oversaw the re-entry of Alabama, Florida, Georgia, North Carolina, and South Carolina into the Union. He died in Philadelphia in 1872.

Find and Fight the Enemy

On June 29, Meade ordered the Army of the Potomac to continue moving north, even though the general didn't know his opponent's location or goals for the next twenty-four hours. As a result, Meade opted to concentrate his troops on Pipe Creek in Maryland, south of the Pennsylvania border. Though this move was subsequently criticized as a reluctance to face Lee, Meade was fully prepared to take the offensive once he better understood the situation at hand.

Lee learned of Meade's appointment on June 29. He assumed Meade would initially be cautious in a new command but still ordered the Army of Northern Virginia to converge at Cashtown, seven miles northwest of Gettysburg. Lee instructed his corps commanders not to engage with Meade's forces until the entire Army of Northern Virginia was present. By the next day, the Southern III Corps had arrived in Cashtown. Longstreet was still west of the Blue Ridge, and Ewell was preparing to de-camp at Carlisle and march on July 1.

Chapter 2 – Tuesday, June 30, 1863

On Tuesday, June 30, 1863, Union Brigadier General John Buford, in command of the 1st Division of the Army of the Potomac, rode into Gettysburg. From a distance, Confederate soldiers under the command of General J. Johnston Pettigrew spotted Buford's troops.

Because of this chance encounter, Pettigrew and Buford came to separate but equally fateful conclusions. Pettigrew was convinced there was a significant Federal presence near Gettysburg but proved incapable of persuading his superiors of that fact. Buford recognized the importance of controlling the roadways that converged in Gettysburg and denying the Confederates access to the high ground south of town. Though uncertain of Lee's exact location, Buford knew the enemy he'd glimpsed west of town would be back in greater numbers.

Thanks to his decision to stay the night and hold his position with only two small brigades—approximately 2,800 men—and a battery of six guns, Buford chose the ground upon which the Battle of Gettysburg was fought.

John Buford, Jr.

Buford, a West Point graduate, was born to a slave-holding father in Woodford County, Kentucky, on March 4, 1826. He spent his boyhood in Rock Island, Illinois. After one year at Knox College, he was accepted into the West Point Class of 1848.

During his time at West Point, Buford's upperclassmen included future Southern generals Stonewall Jackson and George Pickett—the man destined to lead a fatal charge against the Union center on the third day of the Battle of Gettysburg.

Serving in Texas, Kansas, and Utah, Buford remained loyal to the Union and declined a commission in the Confederate Army. Like many Civil War commanders, however, his career and heritage provided striking twists in Buford's wartime experiences. His grandfather, Simeon Buford, served under Henry "Lighthorse" Lee during the American Revolution.

In 1854, Buford married Martha McDowell Duke, known as Pattie to her friends. They had two children, a son and a daughter. The bulk of Pattie's people sided with the South.

Buford distinguished himself at the Second Battle of Bull Run in August 1862, Antietam in September of the same year, and Stoneman's Raid in the spring of 1863. He was 37 in July 1863 and had only five months to live, succumbing to complications of typhoid in December 1863.

On the day of Buford's death, Lincoln promoted him to major general for his distinguished service at Gettysburg. Ironically, one of the people with the general when he died was his African-American servant, Edward.

Lincoln attended the funeral in Washington, D.C. Buford was buried at West Point next to another hero of Gettysburg, Lieutenant Alonzo Cushing, who died defending Cemetery Ridge, the very "high ground" that first attracted Buford's attention on June 30.

J. Johnston Pettigrew

A native of North Carolina, James Johnston Pettigrew was born on July 4, 1828. He studied law, taught at the United States Naval Observatory, and wrote a book about Spanish culture all before the age of 30.

When the Civil War broke out, he joined Wade Hampton's Legion as a private but soon accepted a colonel's commission with the 1st South Carolina Rifle Militia Regiment. By the summer of 1862, President Davis promoted Pettigrew to brigadier general.

At the Battle of Seven Pines in May and June 1962, Pettigrew nearly bled to death from a m wound to the throat and shoulder. He was also shot in the arm and suffered a bayonet wound to the leg. Though left for dead, he awakened a prisoner of war. Two months later, he was part of a prisoner exchange and returned to service.

At Gettysburg, Pettigrew commanded a brigade of 2,500 men in the Army of Northern Virginia as part of Major General Henry Heth's division in Lieutenant General A.P. Hill's Third Corps. On July 1, 1863, after Heth was wounded, Pettigrew assumed command of the division. During the retreat, Pettigrew's brigade served as the army's rear-guard unit. On the morning of July 14, they were among the last Confederate troops still in Union territory on the north side of the Potomac. While positioning his men on the front line, Pettigrew took a bullet to the abdomen fired by a cavalryman in the nearby Michigan Brigade. Refusing to be left behind and captured, Pettigrew was taken over the river. He died at Edgewood Manor plantation on July 17. The general was buried in North Carolina, where a day of mourning was observed in his honor.

Tuesday, June 30, 1863

Buford, at the head of two brigades of cavalry—approximately 3,000 men—rode into Gettysburg early on the morning of June 30. The locals greeted him joyously, relieved to see Union soldiers in the town's streets after having played brief host to Confederate General Jubal Early four days earlier. (Early's men marched out of Gettysburg on June 27.)

During his short occupation, Early had demanded the town fathers produce salt, flour, sugar, coffee, onions, bacon, and whiskey, along with a thousand pairs of shoes, 400 hats, and $5,000. The town council president, David Kendlehart, refused but told Early that Gettysburg's shops would be open for trade.

To the ragtag Southerners, Gettysburg looked like a prosperous town, but the lack of food was real and worsened thanks to their presence and the coming days of battle. With the destruction of the Rock Creek railroad bridge leading to Gettysburg, the populace would be cut off from its usual supply lines. As happy as they would be to see Lee's men retreat on July 4, they were happier still to see wagons arrive with badly needed provisions. One woman recalled grabbing an orange and eating every bite, including the seeds.

Still, the people of Gettysburg distributed food and drink to Buford's exhausted, hungry troopers. Local girls burst into patriotic songs to offer encouragement to the men. Young boys visited Buford's camp and offered to ride the horses to water. Anxious to keep his men in fighting form, Buford had the local newspaper print placards forbidding the sale or gifting of liquor to his men.

In addition to the demand for supplies, Early's presence had also struck terror among Gettysburg's African-American residents, who fled, rightfully fearing they would be rounded up and sent south. Most went east, with some sheltering near Culp's Hill. As recorded by Mary Elizabeth Montford, a woman known as Aunt Beckie declared she was going into the hills rather than be returned to slavery. A man called "Bow-Legged Jack" hid under a haystack for four days without food rather than face the Southerners.

It's unclear exactly how many material goods the Confederates confiscated in Gettysburg, although general ransacking certainly occurred. One thing they did not receive, however, was information from the populace. When questioned about the location of Union troops, the citizens professed to know nothing. Thus, their show of elation when Buford arrived was quite real.

A.P. Hill's Movements

As Buford arrived in Gettysburg, Confederate General A.P. Hill was forced to position his troops without the advantage of reports from advanced cavalry scouts. By then, General Jeb Stuart and his mounted troops had been out of touch with the main body of Lee's army for almost a week.

Instead, Hill sent Pettigrew toward Gettysburg on the Chambersburg Pike with about 2,700 infantrymen from North Carolina. Pettigrew had orders not to engage should he meet the enemy.

Dr. John William Crapster O'Neal

Along the way, the Confederates stopped and questioned Dr. John William Crapster O'Neal, who insisted there were no Union soldiers in Gettysburg. Rather than risk setting loose a spy, O'Neal was detained.

When Pettigrew spotted mounted Union cavalry on a ridgeline outside Gettysburg (John Buford's men), the doctor was forced to defend himself. O'Neal swore those Union soldiers had not been there when he left town to make a call on the Chambersburg Pike. He was telling the truth because he'd narrowly missed the arrival of Buford's men.

During the battle, O'Neal tended soldiers from both armies. He was largely responsible for recording Confederate gravesites in the aftermath, including names and regimental data when available. The doctor published this information in 1866, leading various southern groups to raise sufficient funds to repatriate large numbers of their war dead.

Pettigrew Backs Off

Regardless of when the Federals arrived in Gettysburg, Pettigrew saw them and obeyed his orders. He withdrew to Marsh Creek, where he met generals Hill and Henry Heth. The most recent intelligence indicated the Union Army was still in Maryland, leaving Hill to conclude Pettigrew had seen only scouts. Heth agreed but asked if he might take his division back to Gettysburg the next day. Hill gave his permission.

The decision to return to the town made Pettigrew uneasy, however. He was sure he'd seen Union cavalry in Gettysburg (and he had). Additionally, the Union infantry camp lay perilously close—only six miles away at Emmitsburg, Maryland, making rapid reinforcement in the face of an engagement a dangerous possibility.

Chapter 3 – Wednesday, July 1, 1863

At sunrise on July 1, a day that would prove to be hot and humid, Heth marched east from Cashtown on the Chambersburg Pike. There is a myth that he and his men wanted to confiscate shoes from a factory in Gettysburg, but no such enterprise existed in the town.

In arranging his marching column, Heth made the unconventional decision to lead with Major William J. Pegram's artillery battalion, followed by infantry under Brig. Gens. James J. Archer and Joseph R. Davis. In total, almost 14,000 Confederates set to march down Chambersburg Pike at 7 a.m.

Around 7:30 a.m., they encountered light resistance approximately three miles west of Gettysburg before engaging more aggressively with Union Colonel William Gamble's dismounted cavalry troopers. Credit for the first shot of the battle goes to Marcellus Jones, a lieutenant in the Eighth Illinois Cavalry.

The Federals, armed with breech-loading carbines, laid down rapid fire from behind fence posts and similar cover. The weapons allowed the Union soldiers to fire two to three times faster than men armed with muzzle-loaded rifles. Additionally, there was no need to stand to reload, which allowed the Federal troops to remain behind cover. Both factors created the false impression that a much larger force stood between the Confederates and Gettysburg.

Although Lee had ordered Hill not to engage the enemy until the entire Army of Northern Virginia was present, Heth had a fight on his hands. He outnumbered Buford's dismounted cavalry, but the Federals were deployed with the high ground at their backs—principally Oak Ridge, McPherson's Ridge, and Seminary Ridge.

Buford had chosen his positions well to execute a delaying action against superior forces. His men repeatedly stood their ground until the last possible second before imminent capture, then retreated and made a new stand—all in the name of buying time for Major General John F. Reynolds with the XI Corps to arrive, trailed by Major General Oliver O. Howard. Once on the field, Buford intended to assume even stronger defensive positions south of town on Cemetery Hill, Cemetery Ridge, and Culp's Hill.

Given the situation, Heth deployed his brigades rather than wait for the rest of the division. By about 10:20 a.m., the Southerners had reached Herr Ridge and pressed the Federals east to McPherson Ridge.

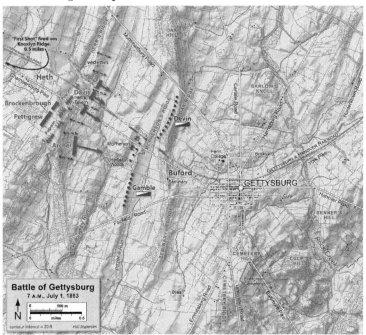

Map of the Battle of Gettysburg's actions on the first day.
This file is licensed under the Creative Commons Attribution 3.0 Unported license. Attribution:
Map by Hal Jespersen, www.posix.com/CW;
https://commons.wikimedia.org/wiki/File:Gettysburg_Day1_0700.png

John F. Reynolds

John Fulton Reynolds, a career army officer, would die later that day at only forty-two. A native of Pennsylvania born September 21, 1820, in Lancaster, he graduated in the West Point Class of 184; he and saw duty in Florida, South Carolina, and Texas. He was promoted to the rank of major in the Mexican-American War. During the conflict, he formed close friendships with Winfield Scott Hancock and Lewis A. Armistead.

From September 1860 to June 1861, Reynolds served as the Commandant of Cadets at West Point, where he taught tactics. At the outbreak of the Civil War, he declined a position as aide-de-camp to Lt. Gen. Winfield Scott, instead accepting an appointment as a lieutenant colonel in the 14th U.S. Infantry. Soon after, he was promoted to brigadier general and sent to Washington, D.C., but was diverted for service with the Army of the Potomac under Maj. Gen. George B. McClellan.

After participation in the Peninsula Campaign in 1862, Reynolds's brigade suffered a brutal Confederate attack at the Battle of Beaver Dam Creek on June 26-27. Reynolds was captured when he fell asleep after two days with no rest. He was sent to Libby Prison in Richmond only to be freed in a prisoner exchange on August 15.

On the second day of the Second Battle of Bull Run, Reynolds led a charge that stopped the Confederate advance and bought the Union Army time to execute an orderly retreat. Promoted to the rank of major general on November 29, 1862, after the Battle of Fredericksburg, he clashed with Hooker over the order to retreat at Chancellorsville.

President Lincoln met with Reynolds on June 2, 1863, to ask if he would assume command of the Army of the Potomac. Lincoln could not meet Reynold's request to act free of political restraint, however, and the post went to Meade on June 28.

At Gettysburg, Reynolds occupied the town on July 1, establishing defensive lines to the north and west. But, as he was supervising the placement of troops at Herbst Woods, a bullet struck, killing him instantly. The Union Army keenly felt the loss of the man widely considered the North's best general. Reynolds's actions on July 1 committed the outnumbered Army of the Potomac to the fight. He was buried in Lancaster, Pennsylvania, on July 4, 1863. Three statues at the Gettysburg National Military Park commemorate his participation in the battle.

Reynolds Arrives

The infantry exchanges during the morning of July 1 happened on the north and south sides of the Chambersburg Pike, with most of the fighting along McPherson Ridge. In this area, the Confederate brigade under General Joseph R. Davis fought the Federals under Brig. Gen. Lysander Cutler, with three Union regiments on the north side of the pike and two on the south.

Immediately to Cutler's left, the Federal Iron Brigade (1st Brigade, 1st Division, I Corps) under Brig. Gen. Solomon Meredith fought Confederate General James J. Archer's troops. Reynolds was responsible for positioning both Cutler and Meredith's brigades.

Most accounts place Reynolds on the battlefield by mid-morning. His arrival marked the end of the first of four phases of fighting on July 1 to the west of Gettysburg. From 7 a.m. until roughly 10:15, the fighting was relatively light and all under the command of officers with no greater seniority than division commander. The second phase began with the arrival of Reynolds and lasted until noon, with two brigade-level infantry actions to either side of the Chambersburg Pike on McPherson's Ridge.

Reynolds immediately met with Buford and then began deploying his infantry units. The timing of what happened next is up for considerable debate. After getting Cutler and Meredith in place and bringing up Captain James A. Hall's Maine battery, Reynolds was on horseback at the east end of Herbst Woods between 10:15 and 10:30 a.m.

The general was positioning the 2nd Wisconsin Infantry Regiment when he stood in the saddle to examine the terrain. Some witnesses said he was looking through a pair of field glasses. A musket ball struck Reynolds in the back of the neck, passing through his head and exiting the eye socket. (Other accounts say the shot struck him behind the ear.)

Reynolds fell forward, while his terrified horse galloped toward the open fields, only to be captured by the general's aides. A detail of men from the 76th New York carried the body, wrapped in an army blanket, to the nearby Lutheran Seminary. The source of the fatal shot remains in dispute, variously attributed to a sniper, random, and even friendly fire.

Reynolds was the highest-ranking officer of either army to die at Gettysburg. After the war, multiple Confederate veterans claimed to have killed Reynolds, but none of the accounts or alternative theories associated with his death have ever been conclusively verified.

With Reynold's death, command passed to Major General Abner Doubleday. The North had lost not only an inspirational leader but also a general with the acumen to effectively manage the unfolding battle. Although Reynolds's troop placements set the subsequent course of the day's battle, he was not there to oversee the outcome.

Doubleday in Command

As the fighting raged on after Reynold's death, Davis's Confederate brigade laid down fire on three of Cutler's Union regiments. Before the Federals could get in position, the Southern troops overlapped their line. The Federals fell back to Seminary Ridge. In what amounted to half an hour of fighting, Cutler's forces suffered a 45 percent casualty rate.

Meanwhile, Archer's Confederates faced heavy resistance from the Union Iron Brigade. When the Confederates reached the far side of Willoughby Run and began the climb into Herbst Woods, the longer Union line enveloped their position on the right.

During the fighting, Private Patrick Molony of the 2nd Wisconsin captured Archer when he discovered the general taking cover in a thicket. Archer was a slight man with a frail constitution but a tenacious disposition. He resisted, but Molony prevailed. Thus, Archer became the first of Lee's general officers to be taken prisoner. When escorted behind enemy lines, he encountered Doubleday, whom he knew from the regular army, and the two men exchanged greetings.

Imprisoned at Johnson's Island on the Lake Erie Coast, Archer suffered greatly from exposure to the poor weather. After a year, he was transferred to Fort Delaware, where he became one of the 600 officers shipped to Morris Island, South Carolina, to act as hostages to stop the constant Confederate shelling.

Exchanged in 1864, Archer rejoined the Confederate army, serving at the Siege of Petersburg before his health failed him completely. He died on October 26, 1864, at age 46.

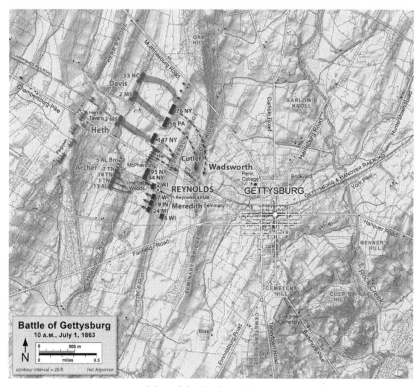

Map of the battle at 10 a.m.

Abner Doubleday

A career army officer, Abner Doubleday, fired the first shot of the Civil War in defense of Fort Sumter on April 12, 1861. His grandfathers served in the Revolutionary War, his mother's father riding as a messenger for George Washington at only fourteen.

Doubleday graduated 24th of fifty-six cadets in the West Point Class of 1842. He served in the Mexican-American War and the Seminole Wars and, as a captain, was second in command at Ft. Sumter under Major Robert Anderson. For the remainder of his life, Doubleday would refer to himself as the "hero" of Sumter.

An artilleryman by training, Doubleday commanded both the Artillery Department in the Shenandoah Valley in 1861 and Maj. Gen. Nathaniel Bank's artillery in the Army of the Potomac during the Peninsula Campaign. Known as a commander ready to seize the initiative for his actions at Brawner's Farm before the Second Battle of Bull Run, Doubleday fought gallantly at Antietam, where he was wounded by shrapnel from an exploding shell.

For his bravery at Antietam, Doubleday received the brevet rank of lieutenant colonel in the regular army and then major general of volunteers. His division remained mostly idle at the Battle of Fredericksburg and was held in reserve at Chancellorsville.

Doubleday's battlefield decisions at Gettysburg are considered his finest of the war. After John Reynold's death, Doubleday held off ten Confederate brigades for five hours. On July 2, however, Meade replaced Doubleday with Maj. Gen. John Newton based largely on the incorrect assertion by XI Corps commander Maj. Gen. Oliver O. Howard that Doubleday's corps had broken and caused the collapse of the Union line. In truth, Meade and Doubleday had long been at odds. Though he fought honorably for the remainder of the battle, Doubleday never forgot Meade's snub.

Sustaining a wound to the neck on July 2, Doubleday received a brevet promotion to the rank of colonel, but Meade refused to reinstate his corps command. Returning to Washington on July 7, Doubleday served out the war performing administrative duties in charge of court-martials with only one brief return to combat.

While in Washington, Doubleday testified against Meade to the Congressional Joint Committee on the Conduct of War. There, Doubleday harshly criticized Meade's actions at Gettysburg. A loyal Lincoln man, Doubleday rode with the president to Pennsylvania for the delivery of the Gettysburg Address on November 19, 1863.

After the war, as a colonel in the regular army, Doubleday served in San Francisco and Texas, where he commanded an African-American regiment stationed at Fort McKavett. Following retirement in 1873, Doubleday wrote two books about the Civil War, practiced law, and became an active member of the Theosophical Society. He died in January 1863 and is buried in Arlington National Cemetery.

In the end, Doubleday's greatest fame lies in the claim that he invented the game of baseball, but considerable evidence disputes this.

The Railroad Cut

With Davis's Southerners in disarray, Doubleday moved the 6th Wisconsin toward them around 11 a.m. Pausing at the fence running along the Chambersburg Pike, the Federals stalled Davis as he attacked Cutler's position. Joining the 84th and 95th New York, the three Union regiments charged the railroad cut where the Confederates had taken cover.

At the time, however, Davis was nowhere to be found. He had left his men in an untenable position in the cut, which was fifteen feet deep in places, preventing effective fire. Still, the Southerners fought tenaciously. As the Union continued to advance, hand-to-hand fighting broke out, with bayonets drawn. The bloodshed continued until Major John Blair, in command of the 2nd Mississippi, surrendered to Colonel Rufus Dawes of the 6th Wisconsin.

Confusion reigned on that section of the battlefield, where the Confederates could not engage in substantive fighting for the remainder of the day. Of the 1,707 Southern troops committed to that area, 500 were killed or wounded, with more than 200 taken prisoner.

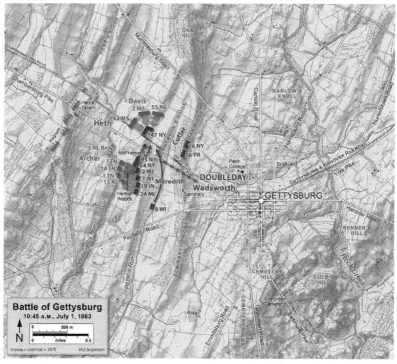

Map of the battle at 10:45 a.m.

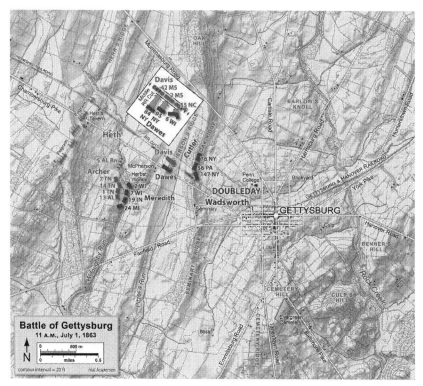

Fighting at the railroad.

This file is licensed under the Creative Commons Attribution 3.0 Unported license. Attribution: Map by Hal Jespersen, www.posix.com/CW; https://commons.wikimedia.org/wiki/File:Gettysburg_Dav1_1100.png

The Field at Midday

By 11:30 a.m., Confederate General Henry Heth, who had been ordered by Lee not to engage, had not only done so but appeared to be on the losing side of the ensuing battle. Southern reinforcements arrived by 12:30 p.m., however, under the command of General Pettigrew, Colonel John M. Brockenbrough, and Major General Dorsey Pender. Additionally, Ewell was marching on Gettysburg from the north, and Jubal Early's four brigades were moving toward the town along the Harrisburg Road.

Doubleday used the brief lull to reorganize the Union lines, strengthening both ends with newly arrived troops commanded by Brigadier General Thomas A. Rowley. It was not until 11:30 that Major General Oliver O. Howard learned of Reynold's death, which placed him in command of the Union troops. Calling for reinforcements from the III and XII Corps, Howard shored up his positions, placing two artillery batteries on Cemetery Hill, which was designated as a Federal rallying point should other positions fall.

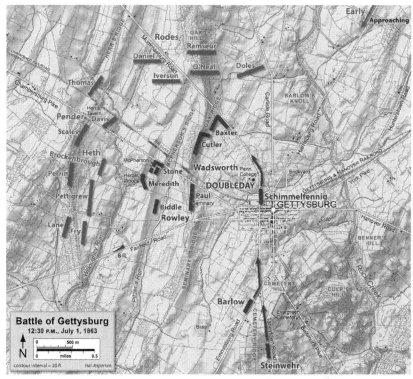

Position of forces at 12:30.

The third phase of the day's fighting opened at approximately 2 p.m. By that time, both sides benefited from the arrival of considerable reinforcements. The fighting that had begun west of town now extended to the north side, and General Lee had arrived to take tactical control of the Southern positions.

Ewell's Southerners were on the field and confronting Union troops positioned on Oak Hill. Seeing the Union placement as preparatory to an attack, Ewell set aside Lee's order regarding a general engagement—a somewhat moot point, as the battle had begun at 7 o'clock that morning.

The Confederates under Major General Robert E. Rodes attacked with three brigades (Doles, O'Neal, and Iverson), facing elements of the

Union I and XI Corps. Iverson and O'Neal's men fared poorly against six regiments under Union Brigadier General Henry Baxter.

Performing no reconnaissance, Iverson sent his men against Federal troops positioned behind a stone wall. The Federals waited until the Confederates were within a hundred yards to lay down withering fire that dropped the Confederates in almost perfect lines. The area of the battlefield, now known as Iverson's Pits, is regarded as one of the most haunted places at Gettysburg.

By 3 p.m., Baxter's exhausted Federals were replaced by Gabriel R. Paul's brigade, facing Confederate Brigadier Generals Junius Daniel and Dodson Ramseur. Paul held against Ramseur's initial attack but took a bullet through the temples that left him permanently blind. He did, however, survive to live another twenty years.

Daniel moved to the southwest to break the Federal I Corps line only to see the fighting devolve into a stalemate against the 149th Pennsylvania, known as the "Bucktail Brigade."

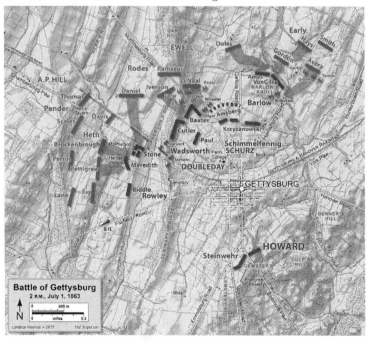

The attack at 2 p.m.

Lee Arrives on the Field

When Lee arrived around 2:30 p.m. and found a major battle in progress, he rescinded his previous order and gave Hill permission to attack. Heth was first in line with fresh brigades at his disposal under Pettigrew and Brockenbrough.

In some of the most intense fighting yet seen in the war, Pettigrew's North Carolina boys pushed the Federal Iron Brigade back to the Lutheran Theological Seminary. The Federal troops to the left on McPherson Ridge were decimated, and the Bucktails came under heavy attack.

Heth united with Major General Robert E. Rodes's division around 3 p.m., attacking with five brigades. During the fighting, a bullet struck Heth in the head, but he was saved by the newspapers he'd stuffed into his overly large hat to make it fit. The general lost consciousness for more than twenty-four hours and thus missed the remainder of the battle. Fragments of his division, under Pettigrew, fought through Pickett's Charge on July 3. Heth recovered sufficiently to command the army's retreat to Virginia.

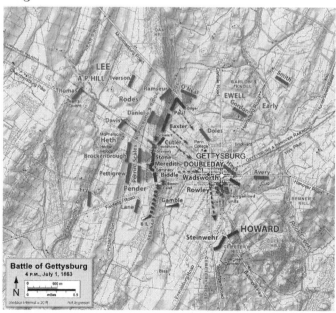

Rodes and Pender break through.

The fourth phase of the battle began at 4 p.m. when Jubal Early's Confederate division appeared on the battlefield, having moved northeast on the Harrisburg Road. Lee ordered a general assault. Early's men forced the right flank of the Union XI Corps to buckle, which caused a chain reaction down the Union line, then some two miles in length.

The Union troops retreated through the town, taking up positions on Culp's Hill and Cemetery Hill, where disarray reigned in the Federal ranks. Thousands of wandering soldiers searched for their units, gathering in small, exhausted groups around their tattered regimental flags. Around 5 o'clock, fortune shined on the Union Army with the arrival of Maj. Gen. Winfield Scott Hancock, who was deputized to act as Meade's personal representative.

Hancock possessed the authority to issue orders in Meade's name and to evaluate the battlefield. A man of decisive action, Hancock instantly ended the bickering between Doubleday and Howard over what to do next by simply assuming command. He ordered Howard to keep the XI Corps on Cemetery Hill, sent the I Corps to defend Culp's Hill, and dispatched word to Meade that the troops could retire or stand and fight as the ground was "not unfavorable." His decisive action proved advantageous. At roughly the same time Hancock reached the battlefield, Lee ordered Maj. Gen. Richard Ewell to push the tactical advantage the Confederates held and take both hills.

In one of the most controversial moments of the battle, however, Ewell backed down. His troops had fought hard all day, arriving already exhausted from hard marching. The general flinched when he saw both hilltops covered with Union artillery. Additionally, Lee's orders—in a stunning example of his often confusingly polite tone with subordinate commanders—gave Ewell an out. He was told to take the heights "if practicable" but to avoid a more general engagement.

That wording in the face of twelve hours of hard fighting in and around the town would, arguably, have left any commander scratching his head. Ewell's failure to act ended the day's fighting. The Confederates won the day but failed to deliver the death blow. Consequently, as the sun set on July 1, the Union had 27,000 men in place on the high ground and approximately eighty-five field pieces.

Richard S. Ewell

Like many of the combatants at Gettysburg, Confederate General Richard S. Ewell was the grandson of a Revolutionary War officer and a West Point graduate (Class of 1840). Ewell's friends called him "Old Baldy" thanks to his early hair loss.

Sewell served on the Santa Fe and Oregon Trails in his early army service. During the Mexican-American War, his bravery at Contreras and Churubusco resulted in a promotion to captain. At Churubusco, he served with Robert E. Lee. After the war, he explored portions of the Gadsden Purchase in the New Mexico Territory but was wounded fighting the Apache in 1859.

Returning to his home state of Virginia, where he was born in 1817, Ewell endured a long recovery but never fully regained his health. Although he held political views generally favorable to the Union, like Lee, he could not bear to fight against his birth state. Ewell resigned his commission on May 7, 1861, to join the Provisional Army of Virginia.

Wounded at Fairfax Court House on May 31, 1861, he was the first Confederate officer of field grade to be wounded during the war. Following a promotion to brigadier general, Ewell commanded a brigade at the First Battle of Bull Run.

Interestingly, within hours of the battle's end, Ewell told President Davis that the South must free its slaves and allow them to fight in the Confederate Army, expressing his willingness to lead African-American troops. Davis dismissed the idea, and the topic was never brought up again.

Ewell proved to be an inspirational leader despite an unassuming appearance and well-known eccentricities. Standing 5'8" with only a fringe of brown hair, the general had eyes that bulged on either side of a beak-like nose. He had an odd habit of letting his head droop to one side and spoke with a whistling lisp. During conversation, Ewell often came out with unintentional non sequiturs and had an impressive command of profanity. Nervous and given to hypochondria, the general slept in odd positions, sometimes wrapped around a stool, and ate a diet composed largely of wheat boiled in milk and sprinkled with sugar.

Oddities aside, however, he performed brilliantly on the field; he was promoted to major general and given a division in January 1862. He worked well with Stonewall Jackson, striking an odd contrast to the pious, stern commander. In his work with Jackson, it became clear that Ewell only functioned well when given precise instructions, something he would not receive from Lee at Gettysburg.

After seeing action in numerous battles, Ewell was wounded at Brawner's Farm on August 28, 1862, by a Minié ball to the left leg. After lying undiscovered on the battlefield for several hours, Ewell was taken to the field hospital, where doctors amputated the leg. He endured a painful recovery complicated by a fall on Christmas Day due to the poor fit of his wooden leg. When not in the saddle, he required crutches.

The general returned to fight with Lee at Chancellorsville. In May 1863, he was given command of the II Corps and promoted to lieutenant general. Though he performed well early in the Gettysburg Campaign, his failure to capture Cemetery Hill on July 1 tarnished his reputation, making him an attractive target for post-war Lee apologists who blamed Ewell for the defeat primarily to protect their hero.

His wound and nervous disposition continued to plague Ewell through the Battle of the Wilderness in 1864 and the Battle of Spotsylvania Court House. Lee removed him from field command, instead assigning the general to defend Richmond. Surrounded by Union troops after a fire that destroyed a third of the city, Ewell and his men were captured only days before Appomattox. The general was held in Boston Harbor at Fort Warren until July.

When released, Ewell retired to Tennessee. Though his leg stump had finally healed, Ewell suffered from numerous other complaints. Active in local education and the Episcopal Church, Ewell led an active life until he and his wife succumbed to pneumonia within days of each other in January 1872.

Winfield Scott Hancock

Hancock, born in 1824 in Montgomery Square, Pennsylvania, undoubtedly prevented a decisive rout of the Union forces on the first day of Gettysburg. His decision that day represented but one of many exemplary actions in a distinguished career as a military officer and future politician. An 1844 graduate of West Point, Hancock stood eighteenth in a class of twenty-five. His first posting in the 6th Infantry regiment was in the Red River Valley. He saw action in the Mexican-American War under his namesake, General Winfield Scott, in his largely unopposed campaign to take Mexico City. For actions at Contreras and Churubusco, Hancock received a brevet promotion to first lieutenant for meritorious and gallant service.

In 1850, he married Almira Russell. She and the couple's two children accompanied him to his 1855 posting at Fort Myers, Florida. Acting primarily as a quartermaster, Hancock saw no action in the Third Seminole War. Instead, he was sent to Fort Leavenworth, Kansas, and then Utah before being stationed in California, where he remained until the outbreak of the Civil War.

Choosing to remain loyal to the Union, Hancock returned east, receiving a September 1861 promotion to brigadier general and a brigade command under Brig. Gen. William F. Smith. After assuming command of the 1st Division II Corps when Maj. Gen. Israel B. Richardson fell at the Battle of Antietam, Hancock was promoted to major general of volunteers in November 1862.

He suffered an abdominal wound at the Battle of Fredericksburg and a second injury at Chancellorsville, where his division covered Hooker's withdrawal. Upon recovering, Hancock became the commander of the II Corps, participating in the Battle of Gettysburg, where he saw major action on July 2 and faced Pickett's Charge against Cemetery Ridge on July 3.

On the final day of the battle, Hancock, who insisted on remaining in the saddle to rally his troops, was wounded a third time—in the thigh—an injury that would plague him for the remainder of his life. He refused, however, to be removed from the field until the conclusion of the fighting. After recuperating, he commanded the II Corps under Lt. Gen. Ulysses S. Grant in the Overland Campaign despite his impaired mobility.

Hancock saw action at the Battles of the Wilderness, Spotsylvania Courthouse, and Cold Harbor. On August 12, 1864, he was promoted to brigadier general in the regular army. Following a humiliating defeat at Ream's Station during the Siege of Petersburg, Hancock gave up field command in November 1864.

He subsequently performed recruiting work, led the First Veteran Corps, and commanded the troops stationed in the Shenandoah Valley. In 1865, he received a brevet promotion to major general in the regular army. Following the Lincoln assassination on April 14, 1865, Hancock oversaw the execution of the conspirators on July 7.

Hancock's post-war accomplishments were impressive and many, including an 1880 presidential run as a Democrat. A charter director of the National Rifle Association, he was heavily involved with veterans' groups, wrote about his military career, and presided over the funeral of President Ulysses S. Grant in 1885. Hancock died in 1886 of an infection and complications of diabetes.

Of the many notable men who fought at Gettysburg on both sides, Hancock was arguably one of the most dedicated to military and civil service. Numerous statues memorialize the general, and his image graced the $2 series of silver certificates issued in 1886.

End of the Day

Had it not been for Hancock's take-charge attitude when he arrived on the disorganized battlefield on July 1, the Union Army would have found itself in far worse shape at the end of the day. As it was, the Union troops had been outnumbered and outflanked repeatedly.

By not pressing their advantage, the Confederates left their enemy in an unusually strong position for "losers." Around midnight, when Union General George Meade joined the Army of the Potomac, he took stock of the defensive position at his disposal and decided to stay and fight the next day.

Confederate General James Longstreet reached Lee's headquarters near the seminary at approximately 9 p.m. and learned of Lee's plan to do the same with considerable alarm. Before the invasion, Lee's stated intent had been to switch to tactical defensive operations on the ground of his choosing should he be forced into a major engagement. Now, he told Longstreet that if the Federal forces remained at Gettysburg the next day, the Confederates would attack.

The situation at the end of the first day's fighting continues to provide fodder for armchair generals. Without question, had the Confederates taken the high ground and positioned artillery there, the second day of the battle would have turned out far differently. These are the same ilk of theorists who insist that had Stonewall Jackson lived to fight at Gettysburg, victory would have been gained on day one.

The absence of Jeb Stuart's cavalry deprived Lee of valuable information and contributed to the accidental start of the battle on the morning of July 1. On the second day, with no cavalry to scout for him, Lee worked with an uncertain picture of the Union troop positions.

Through the night, the remaining participants on both sides joined the battle, including Johnson and Anderson's division for the South and two of Longstreet's divisions. The Union II and III Corps further strengthened the Union position on Cemetery Ridge, with the XII and V Corps to the east. That left only the Union VI Corps on the march to join the Army of the Potomac.

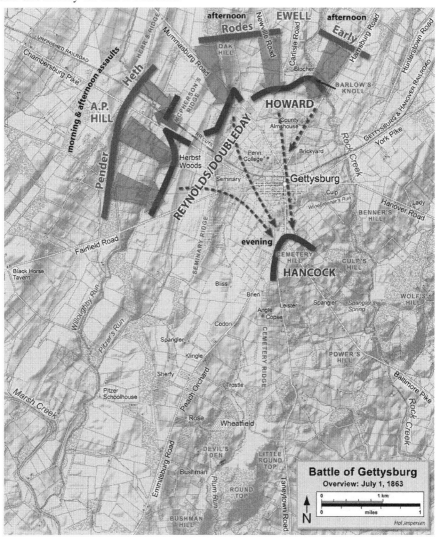

Overview of the first day of the battle.

Chapter 4 – Thursday, July 2, 1863

Around midnight on July 1, General Meade chose to headquarter in Lydia Leister's farmhouse, situated on the southwest slope of Cemetery Hill. After consulting with Buford, Hancock, and others, the general quickly reviewed his position during a dawn ride and formulated his defensive plan.

The XI Corps would remain on Cemetery Hill, with the XII Corps going to Culp's Hill. What remained of the I Corps would take up station between them. The II Corps under Hancock was moved to Cemetery Ridge, an elevation Meade intended to further reinforce as fresh troops arrived. Big Round Top and Little Round Top anchored the Union line. All told, Meade deployed six of his seven corps along a three-mile front that formed a giant fishhook.

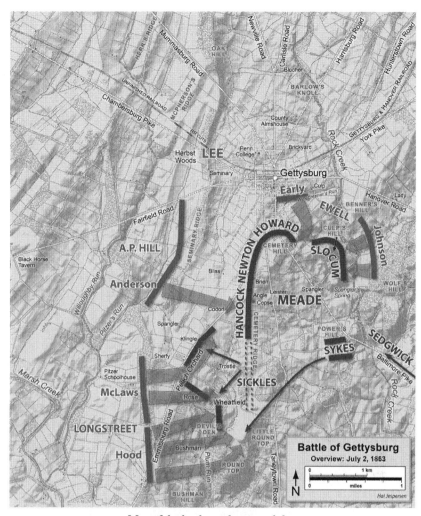

Map of the battle on the second day.
Map by Hal Jespersen, www.posix.com/CW, CC BY 3.0
<https://creativecommons.org/licenses/by/3.0>, via Wikimedia Commons;
https://commons.wikimedia.org/wiki/File:Gettysburg_Battle_Map_Day2.png

Lee's Army of Northern Virginia sat in a roughly parallel position on Seminary Ridge, forming an arc to the north of town. The Confederate II Corps (Ewell) and III Corps (Hill) were on the field, with the I Corps (Longstreet) arriving from Cashtown. The only one of Longstreet's divisions not to fight on July 2 were the men under the command of General George E. Pickett.

Ewell's failure to take either Culp's or Cemetery Hill at the end of the first day of the battle left Lee facing an enemy entrenched on high ground with interior lines ideal for moving reinforcements to strengthen weak spots. At first light, with the plan to attack still central in his thinking, Lee sent a staff engineer to examine the Union left flank.

The officer, Capt. Samuel R. Johnston, delivered a glaringly inaccurate report, claiming that the Union line ran south from Cemetery Ridge along the Emmitsburg Road and ended south of the Codori farm buildings, which were painted red. Johnston also said there were no Union troops on Little Round Top. Based on that flawed intelligence, Lee formulated his July 2 strategy.

Lee Issues His Orders

At approximately 9 a.m., the Confederate commander had solidified his vision for the day. Longstreet would attack on the Union left, Ewell would make a "demonstration" on the right, and Hill would move against the center. Both Longstreet and Ewell objected.

Longstreet argued for a move around the Union left to break Meade's lines of communication. After all, the general said, the original intent of the invasion had been to enter the enemy's territory and disrupt his operations through a series of harrying defensive battles. For his part, Ewell simply didn't want to move his men from positions they'd fought hard to capture the day before.

Lee ignored the concerns of both men. He felt that the troops could see Longstreet's proposal as a retreat in the face of victory, which would harm morale. As for Ewell, his instructions left him free to execute a real attack if the opportunity arose, which should satisfy the fighting spirit of his men. Lee insisted that Cemetery Hill must be captured to give the Confederates a commanding position over the town of Gettysburg, allowing them to disrupt the Federal supply lines and control the road to Washington, D.C.

When Longstreet realized that Lee would not change his mind, he tried to delay the start of the battle, protesting that John Bell Hood's division had not completely arrived on the field and Pickett was a half-day's march away. Lee insisted the attack proceed without Pickett but agreed that Longstreet could wait for Hood's last brigade. Lee also arranged for Maj. Gen. Richard H. Anderson's division from Hill's III Corps to cooperate with Longstreet.

After all the well-mannered bickering was resolved, Longstreet, with two divisions, was to straddle the Emmitsburg Road with Hood on the eastern side and Lafayette McLaws to the west, forming perpendicular lines. The goal was to collapse the Union defenders against themselves in an oblique or angled attack, leading to the capture of Cemetery Hill. Meanwhile, Anderson's division would stand ready to enter the fight at the center of the line.

Not realizing that Longstreet intended to put off the attack as long as possible, Lee rode to Ewell's headquarters and returned at 11 a.m. to find Longstreet right where he'd left him. Lee ordered his reluctant subordinate to attack at once. Dutifully, Longstreet began the march southeast, only to halt south of the Fairfield Road when advance units reported the presence of Union troops on Little Round Top.

This was the first indicator of Lee's faulty intelligence and the significance that misunderstanding would have for the day's events. Rather than the Federal left flank hanging in the air as Lee believed, the Federals held a line running the length of Cemetery Ridge anchored by Little Round Top.

Lee's plan was doomed before a single shot was fired. Longstreet's troops attacking up the road would face at least two Union corps on their right flank, with guns on the heights. Then, General Daniel E. Sickles and his Union III Corps altered the situation to the even greater detriment of the Southerners.

James Longstreet

Longstreet, born in Edgefield District, South Carolina, on January 8, 1821, was of Dutch descent. Described by his father as having a "rock-like" character, the boy picked up the lifelong nickname "Pete" after St. Peter, the rock upon which the Christian church was built.

Sent to live with relatives in Augusta, Georgia, Longstreet attended a neighboring military academy. Known for his rough manners and coarse language, Longstreet never cursed in the presence of women. He held no political convictions. His uncle, Augustus Longstreet, however, was a states' rights advocate who passed a love of whiskey and cards on to his nephew.

Entering West Point in 1838, Longstreet consistently ranked in the bottom third of his class. He absorbed significant tactical understanding, however—lessons evident in his emphasis on swift movement, protected interior lines, and strategic troop placements over showy encounters. He graduated 54th of 56 in the Class of 1842.

While serving in Missouri with the 4th Infantry, Longstreet befriended Ulysses S. Grant and may have been a member of the wedding party when Grant married Longstreet's fourth cousin, Julia Dent. From Missouri, Longstreet went to Louisiana, Florida, and Texas before serving in the Mexican-American War with the 8th Infantry.

At the Battle of Chapultepec, Longstreet was wounded in the thigh, falling with the regimental colors in his hand, which he passed to Lt. George Pickett. Unable to return home until December, Longstreet immediately married Louise Garland. With her, he fathered ten children.

In 1850, Longstreet became Chief Commissary for the Department of Texas, a position he resigned in 1851 to return to the 8th Infantry. He served on the frontier near Fredericksburg, Texas, and was posted in Albuquerque, New Mexico, when the first shot of the Civil War was fired. Longstreet resigned his commission and joined the Confederate States Army.

Immediately promoted to brigadier general and given command of three Virginia infantry regiments, Longstreet saw heavy action in the first two years of the war. He rose to the rank of major general in command of a division in the Army of Northern Virginia.

In January 1862, the general suffered immense personal tragedy when three of his children died of scarlet fever in rapid succession. Afterward, Longstreet became withdrawn, rarely drinking or playing cards with his officers, turning instead to religion for comfort.

By July 1863, he was a seasoned commander who enjoyed a close personal friendship with Lee. Regardless of their feeling for one another, however, the men disagreed at Gettysburg. Critics claim that Longstreet's delays on the second day led to the Confederate defeat.

Though not victorious in the pivotal battle, Longstreet survived the war and a treason conviction to become a prosperous businessman. In 1880, he was even appointed ambassador to the Ottoman Empire by President Rutherford B. Hayes. Longstreet retired to his Georgia farm in 1884, where he penned his memoirs over five years. Nothing that he wrote swayed his detractors.

The general died in January 1904, days shy of his eighty-third birthday. He left behind a second wife forty-two years his junior who adamantly defended his reputation until her own death in 1962.

Longstreet was one of only a handful of general officers from the Civil War to see the dawn of the 20th century.

While his actions at Gettysburg remain a matter of lengthy debate, one thing can be said with certainty: he did not expect to encounter Sickles' men in the Peach Orchard after a day of circuitous maneuvering to avoid observation by the enemy.

Sickles Makes a Unilateral Decision

Early on July 2, Meade had ordered General Daniel E. Sickles to position his men on Cemetery Ridge with the II Corps on his right and Little Round Top on the left. As the morning wore on, however, Sickles became fixated on a Peach Orchard in front of his placement, owned by the Sherfy family. At 11 a.m., Sickles rode to Meade's headquarters to request permission to move to the Peach Orchard, complaining that he'd been assigned a poor position. Meade, angry but calm, repeated his original orders. Having been forced to cede high ground at Chancellorsville, which was then used by artillery to bombard his forces, Sickles, however, could not shake the belief that he faced a crushing defeat at the hands of the enemy. Sickles ultimately decided—against orders—to occupy the orchard, ordering his two divisions to move 1,500 yards west of Cemetery Ridge into the orchard. In doing so, he put himself in a position to be attacked on multiple sides along lines too long for the men under his command to defend.

Though correct in his belief that there would be a significant Confederate assault in that area, Sickles, a politician with no military training, was mistaken that the Peach Orchard was a superior placement. He deployed his troops at a sharp angle—a salient—difficult to defend against a determined foe.

He exposed the Federal division along the Emmitsburg Road, under the command of Maj. Gen. Andrew A. Humphreys, to interlocking Confederate fire without sufficient artillery to respond. Maj. Gen. David B. Birney's division was spread out from the Peach Orchard to the Wheatfield and all the way to Devil's Den without enough men to cover the front. And, worse yet, Sickles left the Taneytown Road unguarded, imperiling one of Meade's essential lines of communication.

Longstreet Forced to Countermarch

After spying Federals on the summit of Little Round Top, Longstreet countermarched his columns. He adopted a serpentine route, using the intervening ridges to screen his troops from the Federal observers. Consequently, he didn't reach his position until four in the afternoon. Instead of the empty fields and orchards Longstreet expected, he found Sickles's Union III Corps in front of him on the Emmitsburg Road.

General Hood argued for a change in the Confederate battle plan, considering the unexpected developments. He wanted to swing around Little Round Top and attack the Federals from the rear. Longstreet refused. Although frustrated with Lee's refusal to reconceive his strategy in the light of what was now clearly bad intelligence, he ordered an immediate attack.

Hood was to lead the action, followed by McLaws and Anderson, moving from south to north. Still adamant that the plan was a mistake, Hood lodged a formal protest even as he prepared to engage the Federals. Before the assault, Longstreet opened the engagement with a thirty-minute artillery barrage comprised of thirty-six guns. The battery hit the Federal soldiers in the Peach Orchard hard and hammered their batteries on Houck's Ridge.

John Bell Hood

John Bell Hood, born in Kentucky in 1831, was an 1853 graduate of West Point known by the nickname "Sam." He nearly missed graduating altogether, running up 196 demerits in his final year at the academy.

Commissioned a brevet second lieutenant, he served as a cavalry officer in California and Texas, the latter under Lt. Col. Robert E. Lee. Throughout his military career, Hood was plagued by a series of wounds that began with a Comanche arrow through the hand while on patrol outside Fort Mason in 1857.

After Ft. Sumter, Hood resigned his commission and offered his services to Texas, where he joined the army as a captain. Soon promoted to major, Hood and his cavalry command headed east to see distinguished service in Virginia before becoming colonel of the 4th Texas Infantry on September 20, 1861.

In March 1862, Hood was promoted to brigadier general in charge of brigades comprised primarily of Texas regiments. Ever eager to personally lead his troops in battle, Hood was an aggressive commander who honed his command into an elite unit. At the Battle of Gaines' Mill on June 27, he led a charge that broke the Union line. The victory cost the Texans dearly, however. More than 400 of Hood's men—and most of his officers—were killed or wounded, a sight that reduced the general to tears.

In July, Hood's brigade was moved to Longstreet's corps and reduced from five to two brigades—the Texas brigade and Evander M. Law's Mississippians. At Second Bull Run, Hood's attack on the Federal left forced a retreat at the cost of more than a thousand casualties.

At Antietam, Hood relieved Stonewall Jackson's corps, turning back an assault by the Union I Corps that cost the division another thousand casualties. Though the price was bloody, the action resulted in Hood's elevation to major general in October 1862. His troops saw little action at either Fredericksburg or Chancellorsville, but fate awaited them at Gettysburg.

During the attack on Little Round Top on July 2, an artillery shell incapacitated Hood. His arm was not amputated, but Hood dealt with limited mobility for the rest of his life. He retained a decent grip with his left hand and motion at the elbow but could not raise his arm from the shoulder.

Recovering in Richmond, the tall, thin Hood with his blue eyes and blond beard made quite the impression on the ladies. He proposed to Sally Buchanan Preston, but she was noncommittal. Disappointed, Hood rejoined his men for the Battle of Chickamauga, September 18-20, 1863. On the 20th, he was injured again, a wound that forced the amputation of his right leg four inches below the hip.

The attending surgeon, convinced the general would die, loaded the severed leg onto the ambulance so it could be buried with Hood. Promoted to lieutenant general, Hood spent part of his second recuperation in Richmond, where he tried again to court Sally Preston. By February, he had a tentative "yes" from the girl, but as her family disapproved, he returned to the war in the spring of 1864 as a single man.

Although he had to be strapped in the saddle, Hood rode as far as twenty miles a day. An orderly stayed nearby, however, with the general's crutches ready. His artificial leg, along with at least two spares, had been given to Hood by the men of the Texas Brigade, who collected more than $3,000 in one day to aid their injured leader.

Hood saw serious action for the remainder of the war, fighting against Union General William T. Sherman's troops in the Atlanta Campaign and the March to the Sea. Assigned to the Trans-Mississippi Theater in March 1865, Hood surrendered in Natchez, Mississippi, receiving parole on Mary 31, 1865.

Following the war, Hood worked as a cotton broker in Louisiana. There, he finally married, but not to the elusive Sally. Hood and his wife, Anna Marie Hennan, had eleven children over ten years. Their family included three sets of twins. Philanthropic by nature, Hood worked to raise money for widows, orphans, and other wounded war veterans. He began but never finished his memoirs.

In 1879, an outbreak of yellow fever claimed the lives of Hood (age forty-eight), his wife, and their oldest daughter. The Texas Brigade Association supported the remaining ten children, who were adopted into seven families, for over twenty years.

The Attack Begins

As Hood protested the planned attack with Longstreet, Meade caught up with Sickles near Peach Orchard and delivered a blistering verbal reprimand emblematic of his famous temper. Sickles offered to return to Cemetery Ridge just as Longstreet's guns opened fire. Meade had no choice but to order Sickles to stay put and wait to be reinforced.

Hood's division deployed in two lines on the southern end of Seminary Ridge, with Brigadier General Jerome B. Robertson's Texas Brigade on the front left. Evander M. Law was positioned to the right front, George T. Anderson to the left rear, and Henry L. Benning to the right rear.

At 4:30 p.m., Hood ordered the Texas Brigade forward. Longstreet had instructed him to wheel left after crossing the Emmitsburg Road and then move north. Within minutes, however, while sitting astride his horse on Slyder Lane, an artillery shell exploded over Hood. The injury to the general's left arm was so severe he was removed from the field. His leaderless division continued moving east.

Several factors now came into play all at once. Regiments of the Union III Corps in the area known as Devil's Den threatened Hood's right flank. Law's brigade became distracted pursuing the 2nd U.S. Sharpshooters on Slyder Farm, pulling the Confederates to the right. The rough terrain fractured troop alignments, and Law, who had no idea he now commanded the division, failed to bring the situation under control. Consequently, the advance split, with the 1st Texas, 3rd

Arkansas, 44th and 48th Alabama moving toward Devil's Den. Law aimed the remaining five regiments toward Big and Little Round Top.

Devil's Den

The Devil's Den, an area littered with boulders, sits at the south end of Houck's Ridge. It anchored the III Corps line on the extreme left, where 2,200 men awaited the advancing Confederates. Union Brigadier General J.H. Hobard Ward commanded the position.

When the 3rd Arkansas and 1st Texas pushed through Rose Woods, they encountered Ward's men directly. The Federals had no time to erect defenses and stood facing their opponents for more than an hour of unusually vicious fighting. In only the first half hour, the 20th Indiana lost 50 percent of its men.

At the same time, two regiments of Law's brigade moved toward Big and Little Round Top through Plum Run Valley, where they menaced Ward's flank. They concentrated their attack against the 4th Maine and 124th New York, which protected the 4th New York Independent Battery firing on the Confederates from the heights.

Ward was forced to move the 99th Pennsylvania from his far right to shore up his left flank. Colonel Augustus Van Horne Ellis of the 124th New York and Major James Cromwell mounted their horses and led a charge down Houck's Ridge through the Triangular Field, repulsing the 1st Texas and moving the line back 200 yards.

The Texans rallied, however, unleashing a volley of fire that killed both Ellis and Cromwell and forced the New York troops back to their original positions. Of the 283 men who followed their officers down the slope, only a hundred returned. The Federals managed to hold the crest, however, due to the timely arrival of reinforcements from the 99th Pennsylvania.

In the second wave of the Southern attack, Benning and Anderson hit Ward's right flank, where a gap in the line had formed around the brigade commanded by Régis de Trobriand. Anderson's men converged on the southern edge of the area known as the Wheatfield, forcing the Union soldiers to fight from behind piles of their dead and wounded. The Southerners were forced to fall back, and Anderson suffered a leg wound that caused him to be removed from the field.

The 2nd and 17th Georgia moved around Ward's flank through Plum Run Valley, where they faced blistering fire from the guns atop

Little Round Top and the 99th Pennsylvania. In a scramble for reinforcements, the 40th New York and 6th New Jersey were pulled from the Wheatfield and sent to protect Ward's flank in Plum Run Valley.

There, they met the Confederates on a rocky piece of ground now known as the Slaughter Pen. As a testament to the bloody fighting of the second day, soldiers called Plum Run Valley the Valley of Death.

The Federal line along Houck's Ridge was collapsing, imperiling the 40th New York. This did not stop the Federals from attacking the Confederates seven times among the boulders strewn in the Slaughter Pen and Devil's Den. Ultimately, the 40th had no choice but to fall back, protected by the 6th New Jersey laying down covering fire.

In the end, Ward could not hold his position and retreated, allowing Hood's troops to take Devil's Den and the southern end of Houk's Ridge. The fighting then became concentrated on the northwest in Rose Woods and the Wheatfield, while, to the east, Law's five regiments moved against Little Round Top.

Little Round Top

Had Sickles not moved the III Corps into the Peach Orchard, he would have been in a position to defend Little Round Top at the south end of Cemetery Ridge. When Meade learned that Sickles had disobeyed his orders, he sent Brigadier General Gouverneur K. Warren, his chief engineer, to remedy the situation.

Standing on the summit of Little Round Top, Warren saw the sun glinting on Southern bayonets to the southwest. A Confederate assault was imminent. The general sent for help from any unit available. Major General George Sykes, in command of the Union V Corps, answered.

A messenger dispatched by Sykes to order Brigadier General James Barnes to move his 1st Division to Little Round Top first encountered the commander of the III Brigade, Colonel Strong Vincent. Understanding the gravity of the situation, Vincent took the initiative and ordered four regiments to the hill without waiting for instructions from Barnes.

Strong Vincent

Strong Vincent, born in Waterford, Pennsylvania, in 1837, was a Harvard-educated lawyer, graduating in 1859. He joined the Pennsylvania Militia at the start of the war as a first lieutenant but was promoted to lieutenant colonel of the 83rd Pennsylvania Infantry in September 1861. He assumed command of the regiment as a colonel in June 1862.

At Gettysburg, the 26-year-old commanded the 3rd Brigade, 1st Division, V Corps of the Army of the Potomac. Knowing his wife was pregnant with their first child, he wrote that, should he be killed, she must remember he died in service to "the most righteous cause that ever widowed a woman."

Although much has been written about Joshua Lawrence Chamberlain and the 20th Maine that day on Little Round Top, Vincent's valor is unquestioned. In the heat of the fighting, as the Union line was in danger of breaking, Vincent climbed atop a large boulder and admonished his men not to give an inch, emphasizing his words with a riding crop given to him by his wife. A bullet caught him in the thigh and groin. Carried from the field to a nearby farmhouse, Vincent died five days later. Meade promoted him to brigadier general on the evening of July 2, but the gravely injured man likely never knew of the honor. Sadly, his infant daughter was born two months later but lived only a year. She is buried next to Vincent in Erie, Pennsylvania.

Vincent Reinforces Little Round Top

Upon arrival, the four regiments Vincent ordered to Little Round Top took immediate fire from Confederate batteries. Starting on the western slope of the hill and moving counterclockwise, Vincent positioned the 44th New York, the 83rd Pennsylvania, and the 20th Maine. Vincent ordered Colonel Joshua Lawrence Chamberlain and the boys of the 20th Maine to hold the southern slope at the end of the line no matter what the Confederates threw at them. Chamberlain had 385 men at his disposal to make his stand.

Joshua Lawrence Chamberlain

Chamberlain's actions at Gettysburg immortalized his name in the history of the battle. He was born in 1828 in Brewer, Maine, and his ancestors fought in the French and Indian War, the American Revolution, and the War of 1812. Named Lawrence Joshua, Chamberlain, who planned to become a clergyman, changed the order of his name to emphasize the biblical "Joshua."

The eldest of five children, Joshua worked in the family's endeavors, principally farming and logging. His father, James, wanted to see his son pursue a military career. His mother, Sarah, favored a religious life for the boy. Both believed their child possessed the natural qualities of a leader.

Chamberlain set his sights on attending Bowdoin College, teaching himself Greek and honing his Latin during 1846 ahead of his entrance application. Ultimately, he mastered seven languages. Accepted in February 1847, Chamberlain overcame a stutter so completely he would go on to be regarded as an orator of considerable skill.

Active in church work throughout his college years, Chamberlain enrolled in Bangor Theological Seminary after graduating from Bowdoin in 1852. He married Fanny Adams in 1855, returning to Bowdoin that fall as an instructor and then professor. At the outbreak of the Civil War, he was granted a leave of absence, ostensibly to study in Europe. Instead, he enlisted as a lieutenant colonel and ultimately became colonel of the 20th Maine.

For his gallant defense of Little Round Top on July 2, 1863, Chamberlain received the Medal of Honor in 1893. After Gettysburg, he was awarded a brigade command before the Siege of Petersburg in 1864. At the Second Battle of Petersburg, a bullet pierced his right hip and groin, but Chamberlain drove his sword into the ground and held himself upright to rally his troops before finally collapsing from blood loss.

Though the wound was judged mortal, Chamberlain survived. He received a battlefield promotion to brigadier general, recuperated, and returned to his command in November. In 1865, during an engagement on Quaker Road, Chamberlain was shot again in the left arm and chest, nearly requiring the amputation of the limb. Again, he stayed on the field, encouraging his men to move forward. For these actions, he received a presidential promotion to major general.

In the morning hours of April 9, 1865, a Confederate staff officer approached Chamberlain with Lee's offer to surrender the Army of Northern Virginia. The next day, Chamberlain was selected to preside as the Confederate infantry paraded into Appomattox for the formal surrender that would take place on April 12. As the Southerners prepared to hand over their weapons and colors, Chamberlain ordered his men to attention and "carry arms" in respect for their defeated enemy.

In the twenty major battles in which he served, Chamberlain received four citations for bravery, suffered six wounds, and had six horses shot from under him. Returning to Maine after the war, he served four terms as the state's governor before returning to Bowdoin as the school's president from 1871 to 1883, resigning only when his health declined due to his wartime injuries. He subsequently practiced law and engaged in various business pursuits, including Florida real estate.

Chamberlain returned to Gettysburg many times after the battle, making his last trip to Pennsylvania in 1913 to plan the 50th anniversary commemoration of the engagement. Ill health kept him from attending the event two months later. He died in Portland, Maine, in 1914 at 85. His death was ruled a complication of the wound he suffered at Petersburg, making him, in the eyes of many, the last casualty of the American Civil War.

Confrontation on Little Round Top

General Evander M. Law, in command of the Alabama Brigade, sent the 4th, 15th, and 47th Alabama and the 4th and 5th Texas to take Little Round Top. The troops had marched more than twenty miles to reach the battlefield on a hot day. They were tired and out of water.

Striking the Federals on the crest, the attackers were repelled by them on the first volley. Regrouping, the 15th Alabama under Colonel William C. Oates shifted right to determine the location of the Federals' left flank—Chamberlain's position, which he held along with the 83rd Pennsylvania to his right.

Observing the Confederate move, Chamberlain elongated his position until the defenders on the hill stood in a single-file line. During a break in the assault, he ordered his troops at the far south end to swing back at an angle to the main line and stop the Southern flanking attempt.

Over an hour and a half, the 20th Maine held off two Confederate charges. In an audacious move, Chamberlain, with dwindling numbers and little to no ammunition, ordered a bayonet charge. His left flank advanced and wheeled to the right. When they came in line with the rest of the regiment, the rest of the troops charged—in effect, closing the door.

By pairing a frontal assault with a flanking maneuver, Chamberlain stopped and captured almost all the 15th Alabama. As the remaining Southerners retreated, Company B of the 20th Maine under Captain Walter G. Morrill and a handful of 2nd U.S. Sharpshooters kept up a volley of rifle fire. The effect was utter confusion in the Confederate ranks.

Elsewhere on the hill, however, the Alabama troops delivered punishing attacks on the Union left, while the 4th and 5th Texas assaulted the right. Vincent received a mortal wound during one of the charges, and command passed to Colonel James C. Rice.

The 140th New York arrived to assist in the defense of the hill, along with four guns of Battery D, 5th U.S. Artillery that were hauled up the rocky slopes by hand. However, the artillerymen, under the command of Lt. Charles E. Hazlett, faced constant sniper fire that hampered their movements. Additionally, they could not sufficiently lower the barrels of their pieces to gain a proper firing angle against the infantry attacks.

The arrival of the fresh New York troops saved the day. The Union held Little Round Top and would control the position for the remainder of the battle. Southern sharpshooters continued to pick off Union troops on the heights, however, killing General David Weed, who commanded a brigade of the Union V Corps. Hazlett, a friend of Weed's, moved to comfort the fallen man only to die by a sniper's bullet himself.

Skirmishes on Little Round Top continued into the evening. The stone breastworks on the hill constructed by the Federals to defend the position are still visible today. The hill was the starting point of the Union counterattack. At dusk, Brigadier General Samuel W. Crawford led the 3rd Division of the V Corps in an assault toward the Wheatfield.

The Wheatfield

In conceiving the day's plan of attack, Lee intended for Hood and Maj. Gen. Lafayette McLaws to launch a simultaneous attack. Longstreet, however, held McLaws back. By 5 p.m., with the enemy fully engaged in front of Hood's division, Longstreet saw that the troops were nearing their limit.

McLaws's men on Warfield Ridge were positioned in twin lines of two brigades each. Brig. Gen. William Barksdale faced the Peach Orchard on the front left with Brig. Gen. Joseph B. Kershaw on his right, and Brig. Gen. William T. Wofford was behind Barksdale with Brig. Gen. Paul Jones Semmes on his right.

Longstreet ordered the deployment of Kershaw's brigade, with Barksdale to follow in sequence. Some of the bloodiest fighting of the second day took place in the Wheatfield and the Peach Orchard.

John Rose owned the three major geographic features of the area designated as the "Wheatfield." These included the field itself (encompassing twenty acres), Rose Woods on the west side of the field, and a small rise called Stony Hill on the west. Houck's Ridge lay to the southeast and Devil's Den to the south.

For two hours in the Wheatfield, eleven brigades engaged in a series of attacks and counterattacks, earning the ground the name "Bloody Wheatfield."

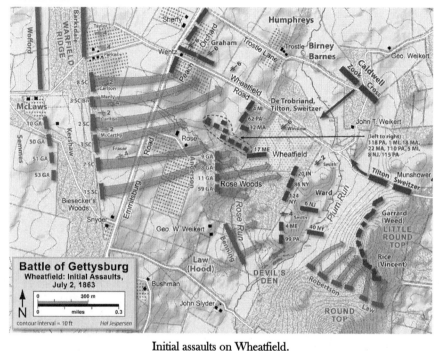

Initial assaults on Wheatfield.
*Map by Hal Jespersen, www.posix.com/CW, CC BY 3.0
<https://creativecommons.org/licenses/by/3.0>, via Wikimedia Commons;
https://commons.wikimedia.org/wiki/File:Gettysburg_Day2_Wheatfield1.png*

The first confrontation occurred when Anderson's brigade, as part of Hood's assault on Houck's Ridge, met the 18th Maine. The Federals, assisted by battery under Winslow, held and forced the Confederates to fall back.

By 5:30 p.m., as the Southern troops under Kershaw neared the Rose farmhouse, two brigades under colonels William S. Tilton and Jacob B. Sweitzer (part of Brig. Gen. James Barnes's 1st Division, V Corps) had reinforced Stony Hill.

The 17th Maine held again against the Confederates, but Barnes chose to withdraw 300 yards to the north, assuming a position near the Wheatfield Road. This forced the 17th Maine to pull back as well, allowing the Southerners to take Stony Hill and enter the Wheatfield en masse.

This area of the battlefield had been disorganized since Sickles made the poorly conceived decision to move to the Peach Orchard. Meade ordered General Winfield Scott Hancock to pull a division from the II Corps to reinforce the III. Hancock chose Brig. Gen. John C. Caldwell's 1st Division, then in a reserve location at the back of Cemetery Ridge.

Caldwell arrived around 6 p.m. with three brigades (Zook, Kelly, and Cross) and one in reserve (Brooke). Kelly's troops, known as the Irish Brigade, reclaimed Stony Hill while Cross pushed the Southerners out of the Wheatfield. In the fighting, both Zook and Cross were wounded and later died.

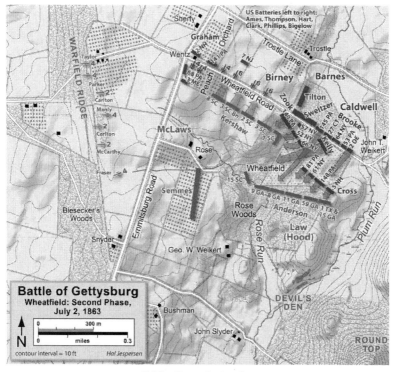

Caldwell counterattacks.
Map by Hal Jespersen, www.posix.com/CW, CC BY 3.0
<https://creativecommons.org/licenses/by/3.0>, via Wikimedia Commons;
https://commons.wikimedia.org/wiki/File:Gettysburg_Day2_Wheatfield2.png

When Cross's brigade ran low on ammunition, it was relieved by Brooke's men. The Union hold on the Peach Orchard fell apart, however, and the Confederates under Wofford once again took Stony Hill and pressed the Union flank in the Wheatfield. Brooke retreated into Rose Woods while Sweitzer's men slowed the Confederate attack in brutal hand-to-hand fighting.

With the Wheatfield once again in Union hands, reinforcements under Brig. Gen. Romeyn B. Ayres arrived (2nd Division, V Corps). As these Union men advanced, the Southerners came over Stony Hill and through Rose Woods in a swarm, flanking them and forcing an orderly retreat to Little Round Top.

This last Confederate attack of the day, around 7:30 p.m., continued through the Wheatfield, past Houck's Ridge, and into the Valley of Death. A counterattack was launched by Brig. Gen. Samuel W. Crawford from the north side of Little Round Top, led by a brigade of men under Colonel William McCandless that included a company of Gettysburg men. They drove the Southerners, now completely worn out from the day's fighting, back through the Wheatfield to Stony Hill before Crawford pulled back to the eastern boundary of the field. The area would, mercifully, remain quiet on the third day of the battle.

Six Confederate brigades fought thirteen Union brigades in the Bloody Wheatfield. A total of 20,244 men were involved, with a casualty rate of 30 percent. The wounded who tried to escape to Plum Run made the waters of the small stream run red. The vicious day of back-and-forth possession took such a heavy psychological toll on the troops that this small portion of the larger battle carried strong significance among Civil War veterans.

Peach Orchard

While Kershaw's right wing focused on assaulting the Wheatfield, the left hit Brig. Gen. Charles K. Graham's Pennsylvania troops, who were supported by thirty artillery pieces from the III Corps. The Confederates, mainly from South Carolina, endured heavy volleys until someone shouted a command to turn right into the Wheatfield. No such order had been issued. The mistake subjected the Southern left flank to brutal fire from the Union batteries. Hundreds fell to their deaths under the guns.

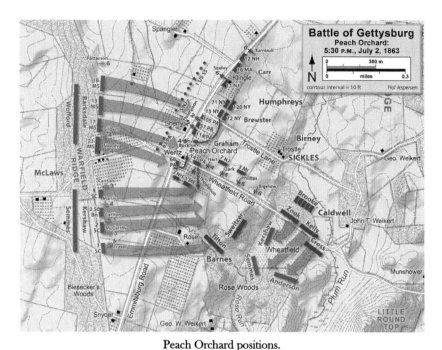

Peach Orchard positions.
Map by Hal Jespersen, www.posix.com/CW, CC BY 3.0
<https://creativecommons.org/licenses/by/3.0>, via Wikimedia Commons;
https://commons.wikimedia.org/wiki/File:Gettysburg_Day2_Peach_Orchard1.png

At the same time, the Confederate brigades on McLaws's left charged the Peach Orchard. General Barksdale, on horseback with sword drawn, led the attack. Roughly a thousand Union troops defended the position in a 500-yard line that ran north adjacent to the Emmitsburg Road and the lane of Abraham Trostle's farm.

With 1,600 Mississippi men behind him, Barksdale flanked the Union troops. Regiment by regiment, the line collapsed as the Federals fled toward Cemetery Ridge. Twice, Union General Graham's horses went down. Finally, the commander was hit by a bullet and shell fragment, leading to his capture by the 21st Mississippi.

Sickles, headquartered in the Trostle barn, was moving his men to the rear when a cannonball hit his right leg. Carried from the field on a stretcher, sitting upright and smoking a cigar, he attempted to rally his men. That evening, Sickles lost his leg, and command of the III Corps passed to General Birney.

The Union guns, endangered by infantry attacks in the Peach Orchard and Wheatfield Road, withdrew—some being dragged from the field while still firing. At the Trostle farmhouse, the 21st Mississippi captured three of the 9th Massachusetts Light Artillery's field pieces.

Late Evening Actions

Major General Richard H. Anderson's Confederate division (III Corps) attacked at 6 p.m. with five brigades. Humphrey could not maintain his position on the Emmitsburg Road, sealing the fate of the Union III Corps, though the general remained astride his mount and ensured a retreat in good order.

Meanwhile, on Cemetery Ridge, Meade and Hancock supervised a scramble of reinforcements. Meade sent almost all the men at his disposal to face Longstreet's attack, weakening the center of his line.

Hancock took Colonel George L. Willard's brigade (II Corps) to face Barksdale's Confederates on Seminary Ridge, driving the Mississippi men back to the Emmitsburg Road. Barksdale suffered multiple wounds in the fighting—a shot to the left knee, a cannonball to the left foot, and a bullet to the chest. When he finally fell from his horse, his troops had no choice but to leave him. He died the following morning in a Union field hospital.

Riding north in search of more reinforcements, Hancock detected a gap in the Union line, which the Confederates were set to exploit. He met the threat with the 1st Minnesota, ordering them to attack and seize the enemy flag. The Federal troops fixed bayonets and charged, forcing a Confederate retreat, but at the cost of an 82 percent casualty rate.

The Confederate brigade under Brig. Gen. Ambrose Wright advanced beyond Cemetery Ridge for a time, although many historians dispute the general's claim. Wright later told Lee that advancing to that point had been accomplished with relative ease but holding the position had been much harder. Some theories posit that Lee's conversation with Wright about the ease of his advance could have colored Lee's thinking ahead of Pickett's disastrous charge on the third day.

Around 4 p.m., Confederate General Ewell had begun an artillery barrage that inflicted light damage on the Union right flank but cost Ewell his most effective artillery officer, Maj. Joseph W. Latimer, who died of his wounds months later at only nineteen.

At 7 p.m., Ewell finally mounted an infantry assault, and around 8 p.m., two of Jubal Early's brigades reached East Cemetery Hill, only to be driven back by Federal reinforcements.

On Culp's Hill, men of the Federal XII Corps under Brig. Gen. George S. Greene inflicted heavy casualties on the Confederates under Maj. Gen. Edward "Allegheny" Johnson from behind entrenched breastworks. The costly attack gained only insignificant portions of the Union line.

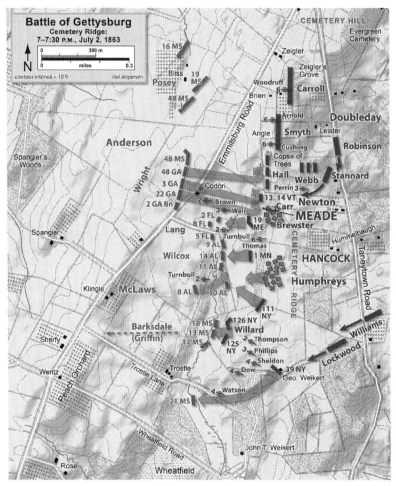

Anderson's assault on Cemetery Ridge.
Map by Hal Jespersen, www.posix.com/CW, CC BY 3.0
<https://creativecommons.org/licenses/by/3.0>, via Wikimedia Commons;
https://commons.wikimedia.org/wiki/File:Gettysburg_Day2_Cemetery_Ridge.png

Day Two Comes to an End

At 10:30 p.m., the second day of the Battle of Gettysburg finally ended, the sounds of the night punctuated by the pitiful cries of the wounded and dying men still lying on the field. Though Meade had taken a pummeling, that night he decided to hold his position and await fresh Confederate attacks the coming day. The Union general believed that should his opponent attack on the third day, the confrontation would be at the center of the line, as assaults on the right and left flanks had already failed.

In Lee's headquarters, distress reigned over the failure to rout the Federals. Still, the commander of the Army of Northern Virginia believed that by continuing to attack on the following day, victory was within his grasp. That confidence would prove to be ill-fated.

Chapter 5 – Friday, July 3, 1863, and Beyond

Around midnight on July 2, Meade met with his senior officers at his headquarters, still located in the Leister farmhouse. The general put three questions to the group, recorded by his chief of staff, Maj. Gen. Daniel A. Butterfield. Should the army stay or withdraw? The generals said stay. Should the army attack or wait for Lee to make his next move? After considerable discussion, most wanted to remain on the defensive. Finally, contingent on the previous decision, Meade asked how long they should wait. The consensus was twenty-four hours.

For his part, Lee worked alone that night, not consulting with his subordinates. The general decided to launch fresh attacks on the Union flanks, ordering assaults on both positions to begin in the early morning. Consequently, the Confederate cannon opened fire at 4:30 a.m. in a thunderous barrage.

As ordered, Ewell, reinforced overnight so that his forces were almost doubled, attacked. He did not know, however, that the Union XII Corps had been moved to face him along with a brigade from the VI Corps. The charging Confederates faced a solid wall of Federal fire that shattered their ranks. The Union right flank on Culp's Hill held.

As the firing died down, Lt. Col. Charles R. Mudge, commander of the 2nd Massachusetts, received a garbled order. The intent had been for his unit to probe the Confederate position at Spangler's Spring, but the colonel believed he received a directive to launch a full-scale attack. Even though he characterized the directive as tantamount to murder, Mudge ordered an advance into the open field. The Confederates, positioned behind stone walls, decimated the Federals, with Mudge himself suffering a mortal wound.

From his position on Seminary Ridge, Lee could hear the fighting on Culp's Hill. In short order, he learned that the Federals had taken the advantage there and Longstreet had made no move against the Union left. Lee assumed that if Meade had reinforced his right flank, he must have done the same on the left. Did that not indicate the weakest point in his enemy's line could be found in the center?

Lee considered moving against Cemetery Ridge, and Longstreet once again objected, saying that not even 15,000 men could overcome the Union center. Lee listened but did not change his mind, opting instead for an attack that has become infamous as "Pickett's Charge."

George Pickett

George Pickett, born in Richmond, Virginia, on January 16, 1825, was a career military officer before accepting a commission with the Confederate States Army. Though he had studied law at an early age, he accepted an appointment to West Point at age seventeen. Popular and mischievous, he was known for his pranks on fellow classmen, for which he earned countless demerits. He graduated last in the Class of 1846.

Pickett gained national recognition during the Mexican-American War when he carried the American flag over the wall at the Battle of Chapultepec in 1847. Pickett then fought his way to the roof and unfurled the colors. He received brevet promotions and commendations for gallant and meritorious conduct.

Pickett served on the Texas frontier and in the Washington Territory, where he married his second wife, Morning Mist, a member of the Haida tribe. She died in childbirth, but her infant son, James Tilton Pickett, lived. Known as "Jimmy," he died of tuberculosis in Portland, Oregon, in 1889 at age thirty-two.

After Fort Sumter, Pickett resigned his US Army commission. Seeing early service in the Department of Fredericksburg, Virginia, as a colonel in the Confederate States Army, Pickett was promoted to brigadier general on January 14, 1862. He cut a colorful figure astride his horse, Old Black. Known for his immaculate and well-tailored uniforms, the new general sported gold spurs on his polished boots and always carried a riding crop. Pickett wore a long, drooping mustache, and his hair hung in ringlets over his shoulders. He kept his beard meticulously trimmed and was fond of wearing cologne.

Though he appeared to be a dandy, Pickett saw impressive combat at Williamsburg and Seven Pines before being shot off his horse at Gaines' Mill while leading a charge. Though afoot, the general continued to lead his men despite a severe shoulder wound that kept him off the battlefield for three months. He suffered stiffness in the arm for a year after his recuperation.

Returning to the army in September 1862, Pickett was given command of a division consisting of two brigades under his old friend James Longstreet. In October, Pickett became a major general, and his division was upgraded with three additional brigades. Absent for the Confederate victory at the Battle of Chancellorsville, Pickett's name has come to be forever associated with defeat at Gettysburg.

Before his ill-fated charge, Pickett courted his third wife, teenage LaSalle "Sallie" Corbell, whom he married in November 1863. She was nineteen, the groom 38.

Following the debacle of Gettysburg, Picket commanded the Department of Southern Virginia and North Carolina, where he again faced defeat at the Battle of New Bern. Controversially, Pickett ordered the execution of twenty-two captured Union soldiers, all natives of North Carolina loyal to the United States. The youngest of the number was only fifteen.

For the remainder of the war, Pickett assisted with the defense of Richmond, fought in the Battle of Cold Harbor, and participated in the Battle of Five Forks. Some sources maintain that Pickett was relieved of his command in the closing days of the war, though if the orders were issued, they no longer exist. Regardless, Pickett was present at the Battle of Appomattox Courthouse and surrendered with Lee.

After the war, Pickett was haunted by the death of his men at Gettysburg, meeting only once with Lee in an exchange characterized as chilly. When reporters would question Pickett about his defeat on July 3, he often responded that the Yankees "had something to do with it."

When the war ended, Pickett fled to Canada rather than face prosecution for the Union soldier executions, returning only when he received General Grant's personal assurance of his immunity.

Pickett died of a liver abscess in Norfolk, Virginia, on July 30, 1875. Initially buried there, he was removed in October and taken to Richmond with more than 40,000 mourners lining the route of his casket. Some 5,000 participants marched in the subsequent procession. The memorial to Pickett dedicated in 1888 was not placed over his grave, the location of which remains disputed.

Sallie, who outlived her husband by fifty-five years, dedicated her life to creating a mythic portrait of Pickett. She wrote two books about him that were largely efforts in hagiography, but in the South, the general remains a tragic hero.

Preparing for Pickett's Charge

Selecting his only fresh troops for the assault, Lee committed Pickett's Virginia men to their fate—three brigades from the I Corps—totaling 5,500, including officers. To bolster their numbers, he added two brigades under the command of Maj. Gen. Isaac R. Trimble to Heth's division, now commanded by Pettigrew, for a total of 13,000 men.

Because the attack would take place over almost a mile of open ground, Lee ordered an artillery bombardment ahead of the infantry action. He focused the action on a group of trees near the middle of Cemetery Ridge. Finally, Lee put Longstreet in charge of the attack. To the general's surprise, the commander he referred to as "my old war horse" suggested Hill be put in charge instead, arguing that a third of the forces to be engaged came from the III Corps. After a withering look from Lee, however, Longstreet relented.

When the 1,300 Confederate guns opened fire, many of the shells overshot their target, striking the Union ambulances and supply chains behind Cemetery Ridge. Even Meade's headquarters came under fire and were evacuated after several staff members suffered wounds.

The shells that did strike the mark dismounted guns from their caissons, killing the gunners and draft horses. The Federals fired back, but the chief of artillery General Hunt argued with General Hancock, who wanted a steady barrage to bolster morale. Hunt wanted to conserve ammunition by firing only well-aimed shots. The II Corps gunners obeyed Hancock, exacting a definite toll on Lee's artillery. The shots that went long exploded in the ranks of the infantrymen waiting to begin the attack, killing or mutilating the troops.

Analysts of the battle point to the time distortion effect that often occurs in the heat of fighting. While locals listening to the bombardment at a distance describe minutes of sustained firing, participants estimated shelling that lasted from two to four hours. At one point, the artillery chief for the Confederate I Corps, Lt. Col. E. Porter Alexander, communicated with Longstreet, urging the general to start the attack before the ammunition was spent. But when the guns fell silent, Longstreet still hesitated. He did not believe the attack would succeed. When Pickett confronted him and asked for the order to begin the advance, Longstreet responded with a nod only. What happened next has both mythological and realistic elements in the retelling.

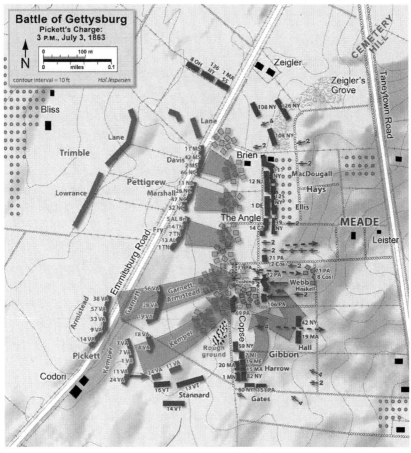

Map of Pickett's Charge.
Map by Hal Jespersen, www.posix.com/CW, CC BY 3.0
<https://creativecommons.org/licenses/by/3.0>, via Wikimedia Commons;
https://commons.wikimedia.org/wiki/File:Pickett%27s-Charge-detail.png

Illustrations of Pickett's charge tend to depict parade-ground straight lines emerging from the cover of the trees on Seminary Ridge. This battlefield art gives the impression of an advance over level ground. In truth, Pickett's men waited in the low depressions surrounding the Spangler farm buildings. This put them well behind the trees and to the right center of the Confederate line.

Brigadier generals Richard B. Garnett and James L. Kemper put their brigades in front of the farm structures, while Brig. Gen. Lewis A. Armistead's men were behind Garnett, sheltering behind a low ridge. The troops couldn't see the trees on Cemetery Ridge, and the Federals couldn't see them.

Pettigrew and Trimble were equally protected approximately 600 yards north of Pickett, also behind the trees. Thus, when the attack was ordered, two forces advanced—Pickett from the low ground and Pettigrew and Trimble from the trees on Seminary Ridge.

Pickett ordered a left oblique march to join his men with Pettigrew's line. Until the Confederates reached the halfway point, they suffered only light casualties, but when Pickett's men neared the Emmitsburg Road, Hancock's II Corps artillery and several Union batteries had a clear view of the advance.

The Union gunners switched from shell to canister. These short-range shells loaded with lead balls amounted to giant shotguns aimed at the Confederates. Adding to this deadly effect, the artillerymen fired double canister—two rounds loaded and fired with a single charge. As soon as the 8th Ohio Infantry found their range, they began a heavy musket barrage.

The fact that Pickett and Pettigrew's men found each other at the Emmitsburg Road was more of an accident than deliberate coordination. Their forward movement was broken by post and rail fencing. Once over, Garnett broke to the left, and Kemper swung to the right. In so doing, they passed two Union brigades that later claimed they'd driven the enemy from the area with intense fire.

Pettigrew and Trimble aimed for a section of the line held by Brig. Gen. Alexander Hays's division, positioned behind the rock walls that ran along Cemetery Ridge to the north and south. One wall, however, stood closer to the ridge, connected to the others by a perpendicular section, creating an area known as the Angle. If Pickett's men reached the northern ranks first, they would strike there.

After twenty minutes of crossing open ground, Garnett and Kemper's troops halted before the stone wall and traded shots with their Federal counterparts. When the Federals appeared to waiver before the Confederate onslaught, Lt. Alonzo H. Cushing, the commander of Battery A, 4th U.S. Artillery, moved his three intact guns forward in support. Wounded and weak, Cushing issued his orders through a subordinate.

When Pickett's boys broke the line in two places, the 1st New York Independent Battery responded with point-blank double canisters, sealing the breaches. Kemper fell wounded and Garnett was killed, leaving Armistead to lead the next Confederate penetration of the northern position. He went through the wall north of the cluster of trees, sending the Union troops reeling. Cushing, having expended his canister, lay dead on the field from a head wound.

Rallying, the Federals drove the Confederates back over the wall, but Armistead suffered a mortal wound and Hancock was severely injured. The Virginians needed reinforcements, but Hill's brigades marched toward the Union guns rather than the original target—the copse of trees. There, canister fire again halted the Confederate advance as Brig. Gen. George J. Stannard's brigade issued blistering fire against Pickett's right flank. After twenty minutes of hard fighting, many of the Virginians surrendered, while others fell back.

On Pickett's left, some of Pettigrew and Trimble's troops made it farther up the slope of Cemetery Ridge, but they could not get past the recessed stone wall where the Federals fired from four massed lines. The first volley caused such death and confusion in the Southern ranks that many of the soldiers threw down their arms and surrendered.

Though both North Carolina and Mississippi units claimed to have reached the farthest point during the doomed Confederate advance, the boasts rang hollow in the face of the slaughter. As the survivors straggled back to Seminary Ridge, General Lee met them astride his horse, Traveler, saying, "It's all my fault." At the same time, however, he expected Pickett to rally and try again. Stunned at the 60 percent casualty rate, Pickett told Lee he no longer had a division to field.

As the Confederate action raged, General Jeb Stuart, who arrived on July 2, skirmished with Union cavalry four miles east of town. Although Lee would have little to say about his errant general, Stuart maintained that his actions that day ensured complete security on Ewell's left and put him in place to disrupt the Union retreat—which never happened.

Dismounted troops in Union Brig. Gen. David M. Gregg's division fired on the Southerners near the Rummel farm. In the intense fighting, Confederate Brig. Gen. Wade Hampton's cavalrymen charged across the open fields near the Hanover Road, sabers drawn, with Brig. Gen. George Armstrong Custer's Michigan cavalry on an intercept course. The Union troops broke the charge, one of the greatest of the war.

At the same time, Union troops assaulted the Confederate right flank to the southwest. The actions harassed the enemy and forced some troop relocations but were largely unsuccessful. Union Brig. Gen. Elon J. Farnsworth fell during a futile cavalry charge repulsed by the Southerners to savage effect. Farnsworth was the last general officer to die in action at Gettysburg, and the charge ended the fighting on July 3.

Saturday, July 4, 1863

As July 4 dawned, the two armies remained on the battlefield, but only the occasional shot disrupted the eerie calm that had descended over the countryside. Meade congratulated his troops and directed the burial of Confederate dead lying within Union lines. By noon, the heat and intense humidity sparked thunderstorms. The rain brought on flash flooding by evening, with many severely wounded men drowning where they had fallen.

During the night, the Confederate II Corps had withdrawn from Culp's Hill to consolidate with Lee's remaining force on Seminary Ridge. When Union skirmishers ventured into Gettysburg on July 5, they found the town devoid of Confederate troops. The Southerners had begun the long march back to Virginia in defeat.

Lee ordered his infantry and artillery to make for the Potomac River crossings at Williamsport and Falling Waters. They took approximately 5,000 Union prisoners with them under the watch of Pickett's surviving troops. The Southern wounded were loaded in wagons and taken south along the Chambersburg Pike in a seventeen-mile-long caravan protected by a brigade of cavalry commanded by Brig. Gen. John D. Imboden.

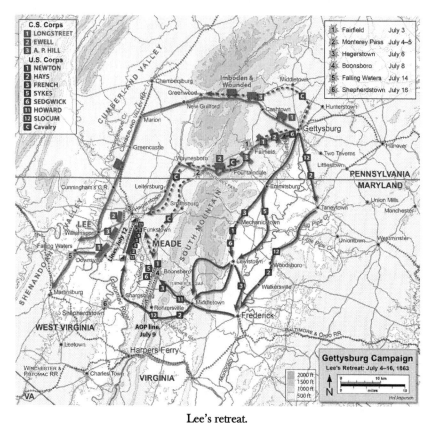

Lee's retreat.

Meade sent cavalry to disrupt Lee's retreat on July 4, striking the wagon trains, liberating Union soldiers, and taking the wounded captive. The next day, Meade sent the VI Corps under Maj. Gen. John Sedgwick along the Fairfield Road, but the general stopped when the Confederates turned and fought. Because the Southerners were moving through narrow breaks in the mountains, Sedgwick concluded the terrain favored his enemy. Meade agreed and gave up the idea of pursuing the Army of Northern Virginia, intending instead to thwart Lee's efforts to cross the Potomac.

Meade allowed Lee to move well ahead of the Union Army, but when the Confederates arrived at Williamsport on July 10, they discovered Union cavalry had destroyed the pontoon bridge at Falling Waters. Additionally, heavy rains had caused the river to flood. Lee had no choice but to dig in behind fortifications erected by his exhausted men while engineers rebuilt the bridge.

When Meade arrived at Williamsport on July 12, he found Lee's army waiting behind earthworks in a formidable line. Still, Meade wanted to attack, but his corps commanders counseled caution. Meade decided to wait, hoping for better weather. The next day, Lee's engineers finished the bridge. Under a driving rain, the Army of Northern Virginia reached the far shore of the Potomac. On the morning of the 14th, the Federals found themselves facing an empty position. Buford briefly skirmished at Falling Waters with Lee's rearguard, an engagement that resulted in the mortal wounding of Confederate General Pettigrew. Otherwise, Lee successfully retreated to the relative safety of Virginia.

Lincoln, buoyed by Grant's victory at Vicksburg, had hoped to see the war wrapped up with a decisive blow against the defeated Lee. When that didn't happen, the president vented his frustration, saying that no matter what he said or did, his army would not move. Lincoln did not grasp, however, that though victorious, the Army of the Potomac was almost as battered as that of Northern Virginia. The Union ranks had suffered heavy losses among the officer corps and the rank and file. The men were hungry, and many marched barefoot, their shoes worn out on the paved roads of Pennsylvania or lost to the sucking mud in Maryland.

Had reinforcements been dispatched from Washington, Meade might have been able to take more aggressive action, but no help was forthcoming. The Gettysburg campaign left both armies in tattered condition, with no end to the war in sight. Though beaten on the field at Gettysburg, the Confederates were not done and would indeed fight on for almost two more years.

Chapter 6 – Citizens, Doctors, Photographers, Posterity

Often absent in battlefield accounts of Gettysburg are considerations of how the town's citizens participated in or were affected by the events of those three days. They were not strangers to the threat of Confederate forces nearby. The town, then comprised of 2,400 residents, lies only ten miles north of the Mason-Dixon Line. Freed people in the area were often subject to kidnappings, and Southern troops conducted small-scale raiding actions into Pennsylvania. Though rumors had circulated of an invasion since the beginning of the war, those fears were realized in late June and early July 1863.

The epic battle transformed the lives and the landscape of Gettysburg, but the experiences of the residents ranged from tragic to heroic, with the occasional hint of macabre humor.

The morning of July 1 found Pennsylvania College student Robert McClean in class with professor of mathematics Dr. Michael Jacobs (who became one of the first authors to pen an account of the battle within months of its conclusion). To the professor's frustration, the sound of gunfire and artillery distracted his students so thoroughly that he gave in and dismissed the class. Anxious to see what was happening, McClean set out for Seminary Ridge only to have a cannon shot pass directly overhead. Later, McClean candidly admitted that the experience greatly improved his relationship with the Scriptures.

Sophia Culp Epley, a housewife and mother, had more immediate concerns than two battling armies. She found a gang of Confederates trying to make off with her cow. Yelling at the top of her lungs, she drove the interlopers away, oblivious to any personal danger. After all, Epley needed the milk for her children.

At the south end of Baltimore Street, John and Caroline Rupp lived with their six children near the base of Cemetery Hill. The home and adjacent tannery lay smack between the Union and Confederate lines. Correctly reading the danger, Rupp sent his family first to the neighbors and then to his father's home. Reluctant to leave his property, John Rupp hid in his basement for the rest of the battle while Confederate and Union snipers, oblivious to each other's presence, used the building as their base.

Catherine Garlach, on the other hand, directly faced the Confederate sniper who wanted to set up in her home. She lectured the man, chiding him for endangering innocents, until he hung his head in shame and left—without firing a shot.

Many residents kept journals during the fighting. Some, like Sallie Broadhead, confessed that the exercise was as much about relieving anxiety as creating a historical record. Though valuable for their insight into civilians caught in the thick of war, many such accounts are wholly inaccurate in their recollection of troop movements.

Still, the journals convey the writers' shocked disbelief that war had finally come to their doorstep, the fear and confusion of being caught between the armies, and the incredible relief when the whole thing was over. These sources and the stories published in the town's two weekly newspapers, *The Star and Sentinel* and *The Compiler*, collected eyewitness reports into the early 1900s that would have otherwise been lost.

Without them, we could not look through the eyes of Gates Fahnestock, a ten-year-old boy who peeked through the shutters of his home as Jubal Early's men rode through town firing their guns, officer's swords held high. To the child, the whole thing looked like "a Wild West show." At the same time, Sarah Barrett King could not help but note the ragged, filthy condition of the invaders, many of whom marched without shoes.

Perhaps Jennie McCreary put the town's stunned reaction best when she wrote to her sister, "We never expected a battle." But the battle arrived all the same, putting residents in the crosshairs. Some, like Jennie Wade, would simply be at the wrong place at the wrong time. In Jennie's case, she became the only local to die in the battle.

Jennie Wade

Wade, a Gettysburg native, worked with her mother as a seamstress. She had a sister and two younger brothers. The absent father resided in a mental institute. Born on May 21, 1843, Jennie was only twenty when she became an accidental casualty of war, felled by a stray bullet on July 3.

Ironically, on the first day of the battle, Jennie, her mother, and siblings were at the home of Georgia Anna Wade McClellan on Baltimore Street to help care for Georgia's newborn child. An estimated 150 bullets struck the building while they were there.

On Friday, July 3, 1863, still at her sister's house, Jennie was in the kitchen making bread. A Minié ball came through the door and struck Jennie in the back, passing through her left shoulder blade and striking her heart. She died instantly. The source of the shot has never been confirmed but is typically attributed to a Confederate sniper.

Mrs. Wade heard her daughter's body hit the floor. Two Union soldiers present in the house came downstairs when they heard screaming. The men buried Wade in the backyard; they used a coffin meant for General William Barksdale, mortally wounded after leading a charge on horseback through the Peach Orchard near Plum Run. He died on the morning of July 3.

Jennie's body was exhumed in January 1864 and buried in the graveyard of the German Reformed Church on Stratton Street. Since November 1865, she has rested in Gettysburg's Evergreen Cemetery. An American flag flies over her grave twenty-four hours a day; she's the only woman other than Betsy Ross to have been given this honor.

John Lawrence Burns

When Confederate General Jubal Early occupied Gettysburg briefly on June 26, 1863, his soldiers met the implacable will of Constable John Lawrence Burns, sixty-nine, a veteran of the War of 1812. He protested the Southern presence with such vehemence that the troops put him in a jail cell rather than deal with him. Released upon their departure, Burns, undeterred, gave chase and arrested a handful of stragglers.

On July 1, 1863, still determined to oppose the invasion, Burns walked toward the sound of the guns with a flintlock musket in hand.

Before he reached the thick of the fighting, he talked a wounded Federal soldier out of his Enfield rifle and cartridges. Armed and ready for action, Burns asked Maj. Thomas Chamberlin for permission to fight alongside the 150th Pennsylvania Infantry.

Chamberlin later described Burns as wearing dark pants and a matching waistcoat under a blue coat with brass buttons and sporting a well-worn top hat. Uncertain about what to do with the unlikely volunteer, Chamberlin sent Burns to Colonel Langhorne Wister, the regimental commander, who sent the old man into McPherson Woods.

There, Burns fought with the 7th Wisconsin before joining the 24th Michigan, or Iron Brigade, staying with them and functioning as a sharpshooter for the afternoon. Burns exhibited superior marksmanship, even knocking a charging Confederate officer from the saddle.

As the Union line broke, however, the Federals had no choice but to leave their new compatriot behind. Burns had been wounded in the arm and ankle, with minor injuries to his chest. Ever resourceful, Burns laid down his rifle, crawled some distance, and buried his ammunition.

When discovered by Confederate troops, he played the part of an innocent civilian who had ventured to the battlefield hoping to find a medic to treat his sick wife. The Southerners dressed his wounds, and later Burns made it to the cellar of a nearby house and ultimately home.

In the aftermath of the battle, Burns's story made him a national hero. After Lincoln delivered the Gettysburg Address on November 19, 1863, the president made time for a walk with the elderly combatant.

Burns lived ten years after the battle but suffered from dementia for the last two years of his life. Given to wandering, he reached New York City in December 1871, where he was found freezing and destitute on the streets. Burns was given medical attention and sent home, succumbing to pneumonia on February 4, 1872.

A statue commemorating Burns's participation in the battle sits atop a boulder on McPherson's Ridge. Dedicated forty years after his actions on July 1, 1903, the sculpture depicts Burns with a defiant air, rifle clutched in one hand, the other balled into a fist. The old man rests in Evergreen Cemetery, and, like Jennie Wade, his grave is marked by a perpetual American flag. His marker bears the simple epitaph "Patriot."

Elizabeth Salome "Sallie" Myers

Like many women in Gettysburg, schoolteacher Elizabeth Salome Myers nursed the sick and wounded—Federal and Confederate—despite her later admission that she couldn't bear the sight of blood. When the surgeon of the 143rd Pennsylvania Volunteers, Dr. James Fulton, put out a call for nurses, Myers answered, only to flee the hospital set up at St. Francis Catholic Church when her first patient declined her offer of help, saying he was dying.

Quick to recover from her shock, however, Myers went back to the bedside of the same patient, Sergeant Alexander Stewart, who wanted to hear the fourteenth chapter of the book of John. He explained that his family read the passage aloud before he and his brother left for the war. Soothing the dying man's last minutes strengthened her resolve. Myers continued working as a nurse throughout the summer. On the fortieth anniversary of the battle, she published *How a Gettysburg Schoolteacher Spent Her Vacation in 1863.*

Field Hospitals

As the battle raged, field medical stations were set up, sometimes less than 100 yards from the fighting. These stations had to be ready to move with little-to-no notice as the fighting drew closer. Marked by a red hospital flag, they served to apply rudimentary dressings before directing the wounded to hospitals where they could receive more care. In the extreme heat of the first three days of July and the torrential rains that followed, overtaxed doctors provided what care they could.

Doctors used lint to pack wounds and splints to stabilize broken bones. Tourniquets and pressure dressings were applied only as temporary measures for men in immediate need of surgery. Soldiers with bowel or chest wounds were given pain relief, usually opium. Partially severed fingers were amputated immediately.

As soon as these doctors could do so, they left the fighting and reported to field hospitals, where they worked all night by candlelight. The field hospitals used by the Army of the Potomac medical department included the following:

- I Corps, Lutheran Theological Seminary (July 1), White Church on the Baltimore Pike (July 2)
- II Corps – adjacent to Rock Creek east of the Bushman House (July 2)

- III Corps – Taneytown Road, White Run, and Rock Creek (July 2)
- V Corps – Taneytown Road west of Round Top (July 2), Two Taverns (July 3)
- VI Corps – Trostle House
- XI Corps – Spangler House
- XII Corps – Bushman House
- Cavalry Corps – Presbyterian Church and other buildings in Gettysburg

The wounded either straggled into these makeshift facilities of their own accord or were taken by ambulance. All bore the hideous wounds of modern warfare. Their bones shattered by exploding artillery and flesh rent by canister shot and bullets, many looked barely human.

Bloody, bruised, and in agony, they found themselves at the mercy of medical science that had not yet embraced the rudiments of germ theory. The knives and saws used by the doctors were, at most, dipped in buckets of bloody water between procedures.

Men who were gut shot or had suffered head wounds often had the greatest chance of surviving because the doctors considered them lost causes. Though in excruciating pain, the abdominal cases were at least spared the danger of infection inherent in the surgeries of the day. Gangrene killed as many soldiers as bullets. The survivors of head wounds, dazed and confused, were confined in pens to keep them from wandering off. A good percentage of those cases lived, though often suffering the symptoms of a traumatic brain injury for life.

With approximately 30,000 Union and Confederate patients needing medical attention, the field hospitals in and around Gettysburg operated into August 1863. On the first day of the battle, the casualty total had already reached 16,000. Many of these men were taken to a hospital set up in the McPherson barn. The adjacent farmhouse had been in the thick of the battle all day. Control of the property passed back and forth between the warring armies. Riddled with bullets, the building still provided shelter for the wounded and dying. There, Union and Confederate doctors worked side by side in blood-splattered aprons.

More of the wounded were taken to the barn, where surgeons labored to dress wounds and perform amputations. Thirst and hunger exacerbated the suffering of the soldiers. Some waited so long to get help they had to be pulled free of the congealed blood holding them fast to the floorboards.

Alerted to the suffering, Gettysburg residents prepared food and water, which they brought to the barn despite their natural fear of coming so close to the battlefront. William McClean, headed toward the McPherson Farm with biscuits, gruel, and fresh raspberries, passed burial parties interring soldiers where they had fallen while artillery fired in the distance.

(The work of burying the dead began immediately on the first day. With so many corpses lying on the field, the fear of contagion was real and serious. Burial parties hastily dug shallow graves. The dead, if identifiable, were recognized by penciled names on wooden boards as makeshift markers.)

Meanwhile, at Pennsylvania College on July 1, Confederate Chief Surgeon Samuel B. Morrison ordered that the buildings be used as field hospitals, including the home of college president Henry Baugher, whose wife (Clarissa) and daughter (Alice) worked as nurses. The Baughers' only son had died a year earlier at the Battle of Shiloh, which inspired the family to stay and help even as shells exploded around them.

One of the Confederates to be treated in Pennsylvania Hall was Colonel Waller Tazewell Patton of the 7th Virginia, whose great-nephew would be General George S. Patton of World War II fame. An artillery shell blew off Colonel Patton's lower jaw during Pickett's charge on July 3. The wound made breathing difficult, forcing the injured man to sit upright, leaning against a wall. When he became too weak to hold himself up, volunteer nurse Euphemia "Miss Effie" Goldsborough held him in place with the weight of her own body. Astonishingly and painfully, the colonel lived until July 21.

The level of dedication shown by Goldsborough was not the exception among these gallant medical professionals but rather the rule. When the battle was lost, Confederate Dr. Lewis E. Gott of the 49th Virginia Infantry and several of his colleagues refused to abandon their patients. The doctors stayed behind, working with the Union medical staff until they were sent to Fort McHenry in Baltimore as prisoners of war.

Pennsylvania Hall was used as a hospital until July 29, but the marks of its service lingered long after the last wounded man left the premises. For years, the floors remained stained with blood, as did many of the books used as headrests for the wounded. A number of those books now reside in the Musselman Library's Gettysburg College Special Collections.

In 1937, during excavations around the north portico of the building, workers unearthed bits of bone. It was common for surgeons to toss amputated limbs into piles—usually out a window or door—to be buried later.

Among the numerous sites in and around the battlefield considered to be haunted, Pennsylvania Hall has been the site of numerous encounters with the paranormal. Students report objects that move independently and sightings of a solitary soldier who circles the school's cupola late at night.

In the wake of the battle, Union leaders quickly realized that this network of makeshift hospitals, which had then expanded to some sixty sites, could not handle the incredible volume of recuperating men. While many were transported to Baltimore or Philadelphia, others were housed in what became, for a time, the largest field hospital in the Western Hemisphere.

Construction began on July 8 on eighty acres belonging to George Wolf a mile northeast of Gettysburg on the York Pike. The area was chosen for its proximity to the railroad, location on high ground, ample shade, and fresh spring water. Named for the medical director of the Army of the Potomac, Dr. Jonathan Letterman, the camp opened on July 22 and operated until January 1864. There, approximately 100 doctors treated more than 21,000 soldiers with only 1,200 deaths, a remarkable accomplishment for the time.

Patients were housed in more than 400 tents spaced at ten feet. Each could hold a dozen patients, with each doctor in charge of forty-seven men. Camp Letterman was, for all purposes, a small city, with separate quarters for officers and staff, an administrative building, a store run by the United States Christian Commission volunteers, and a delegation from the U.S. Sanitary Commission.

There were also funerary facilities for embalming and a nearby cemetery. Later, many of the Confederate dead were relocated to the South, while the Union soldiers were moved to the national cemetery. Today, the site is a shopping center off the Lincoln Highway.

Battlefield Photography

Many casual students of history believe that one of America's pioneering photographers, Mathew Brady, personally photographed the aftermath of the Gettysburg battlefield. In fact, Brady's eyesight had begun to deteriorate by the 1850s. He did, however, shoot thousands of portraits of young soldiers in his New York studio. Both an artist and a businessman, Brady posted ads in regional newspapers urging parents to secure photographs of their sons in case they were killed at war. To chronicle the fighting, Brady hired field assistants.

Brady was born to Irish immigrants in Warren County, New York, in either 1822 or 1824. Initially, he studied painting but switched to the emerging field of photography, which thoroughly captured his imagination.

Brady studied technique with Samuel Morse, who learned the daguerreotype method from Louis Jacques Daguerre in France in 1839. During the Civil War, however, the most popular method was albumen silver, which produced a paper photograph from a large glass negative.

Though his portraits of departing soldiers were popular and profitable, Brady yearned to capture the gritty reality of war itself. He first petitioned his friend General Winfield Scott for permission to work on the nation's battlefields, but the approval came from President Lincoln in 1861—with the caveat that Brady be self-financed.

At this early stage, Brady did travel to the front. He got so close to the fighting at the First Battle of Bull Run (July 21) he was very nearly captured. After that, and assessing the massive scope of the task at hand, Brady outfitted twenty-three assistants with mobile studios and dark rooms. For the remainder of the year, he directed their efforts at a distance from his New York studio.

In October 1862, Brady mounted an exhibition entitled "The Dead of Antietam," which brought the brutality of war home to the American public for the first time. In all previous wars, only eyewitnesses had seen the carnage of the battlefield. Now, average citizens were forced to confront the real cost of the conflict.

The images that most shocked the nation, however, were those taken by Timothy O'Sullivan, an Irishman who had begun working for Brady while still a teenager. O'Sullivan, along with Alexander Gardner and James Gibson, captured the horrors of Gettysburg for posterity.

O'Sullivan's most famous image, "A Harvest of Death," shows the rotting dead of Gettysburg lying where they had fallen, awaiting burial. That single photograph, however, was but a fraction of the pictures O'Sullivan shot in July 1863. In one vivid still after another, he captured the broken bodies of fallen soldiers, bloated in death, their limbs twisted at odd angles, lifeless hands reaching for help that never arrived.

Through his lens, Americans saw the ghastly wounds caused by artillery, counted the bodies of fallen soldiers lying limply over the boulders of Devil's Den, and beheld dead snipers resting beside their now silent rifles. O'Sullivan captured the grim jobs of burial parties and the brutal work of doctors in field hospitals. So acute was Sullivan's eye for the battlefield's salient landmarks that those photographs can be exactly matched with the same locations today in chilling "then and now" comparisons.

Action shots were not possible, as 19th-century cameras required the subjects to stand still, but something about the frozen quality of the surviving pictures make them even more poignant.

Though it fell from favor with the war-weary public after the fighting was over, Brady's body of work, paired with the efforts of his men in the field, constitutes one of the most visceral and compelling records of the American Civil War. Because of Brady, we have excellent portraits of generals from both armies, Abraham Lincoln, Jefferson Davis, and other significant political leaders. All are priceless national treasures.

Preserving the Battlefield

Four and a half months after the last shot was fired at Gettysburg, on the afternoon of November 19, 1863, President Abraham Lincoln delivered the sparse and well-crafted Gettysburg Address. He was not, however, the featured speaker at the Consecration of the Soldiers' National Cemetery at Gettysburg. That honor went to Reverend Edward Everett, a Unitarian minister from Massachusetts known for his work in education, diplomacy, and politics. The former secretary of state (for Millard Fillmore), congressman (in both the Senate and House), governor, and U.S. minister to the United Kingdom composed an oration of 13,607 words. He spoke for two hours, and no one remembers what he said.

Lincoln jotted down at least five drafts of his remarks—none on the back of an envelope, as legend would have us believe—and every version, including those reprinted in newspapers, is different. We don't even know exactly where the platform stood from which the president delivered his thoughts. Yet almost every American can quote all or some of Lincoln's Gettysburg Address.

The occasion was the reburial of Union soldiers taken from scattered graves across the countryside to the new Gettysburg National Cemetery. Less than half of that work, which began on October 17, had been completed.

Few knew that Lincoln was ill that day, complaining of nausea, dizziness, fever, and a headache. When he returned to Washington, D.C., on the 6:30 p.m. train, the president subsequently developed a rash characterized by blisters that led to a diagnosis of mild smallpox.

But regardless of his position on the day's program or his physical condition, Lincoln hit a note in his speech that resonated with Americans. When he said, "These dead shall not have died in vain," he touched a national chord that still sounds in Gettysburg today.

Residents of the Pennsylvania town, now surrounded by the Gettysburg National Military Park, readily admit they feel the presence of the men who died there in 1863. Every year, they celebrate the anniversary of Lincoln's speech on Remembrance Day, an occasion marked by a parade and the presence of thousands of Civil War re-enactors.

Others admit to seeing ghostly regiments in the dim light of dusk and dawn or phantom horsemen galloping across the silent fields. Tourist photos sometimes inexplicably show faces and figures not present when the shutter clicked. Though we might scoff at these ghost stories, Union troops on the battlefield in July 1863 swore they saw the ghost of George Washington leading them to victory.

Gettysburg is unquestionably a place where the dead play a role in everyday life. The national cemetery holds the graves of 3,512 combatants—979 unknown. There are also sections for the dead of the Spanish-American War (1898) and World War I (for American involvement, 1917-1918). The graves number more than 6,000. In the center of the site stands a sixty-foot granite monument, the work of sculptor Randolph Rogers and architect George Keller. Concentric half-circles of the Gettysburg dead grouped by state flank the memorial.

In the larger Gettysburg National Military Park, a site where the National Park Service is tasked with protecting and interpreting the battlefield, visitors can tour the areas where the fighting occurred, as well as those associated with supporting functions (field hospitals) and the aftermath. The adjacent museum and visitors center houses more than 43,000 artifacts. More are found each year.

Preservation of the site began as early as 1864 when the Gettysburg Battlefield Memorial Association was formed. Along with veterans' groups after the war, the Association acquired land and took up collections to create various memorials that now dot the landscape. In 1893, the federal government began purchasing these acquisitions. The future park was established by an act of Congress on February 11, 1895, under the direction of the secretary of war. Four other Civil War battlefields are maintained as parks, including Vicksburg, Shiloh, Chickamauga/Chattanooga, and Antietam.

The work of the park service at Gettysburg is ongoing, with efforts to restore the battlefield to its 1863 condition by thinning wooded areas absent in the 19th century and replanting key orchards and fields. Neither the men who died there nor the landscape on which they lost their lives is neglected, for, as Lincoln said, "The world will little note, nor long remember what we say here, but it can never forget what they did here."

Conclusion

Initially, the victory at Gettysburg on the heels of Vicksburg touched off a wave of euphoric celebration in the North. Only slowly did the public come to understand that the end of the war was not in sight. Lincoln expressed bitter disappointment in Meade's failure to definitively crush Lee.

The Army of the Potomac suffered immense loss during the Gettysburg campaign: 3,155 killed in action, 14,529 wounded. Two thousand of these died in the following weeks. Including the 5,365 missing, the number of casualties reached 23,049, or roughly a quarter of the Northern soldiers who participated in the battle.

Though criticized, Meade had fulfilled his orders. He protected Washington, D.C., and Baltimore and engaged Lee in battle. He also forced an invading army out of Union territory, capturing three large guns, the standards of forty-one units, small arms totaling 24,978 weapons, and taking 13,621 prisoners.

As a battlefield commander, Meade effectively used interior lines to support his troops in scattered positions in and around Gettysburg. He utilized the manpower at his disposal and sought the consensus of his subordinates before acting. In so doing, he cost the Army of Northern Virginia 20,451 casualties: 2,592 dead, 12,709 wounded, and 5,150 missing, equaling a third of Lee's troops.

Holding himself responsible for the defeat of his troops, Lee offered his resignation to Confederate President Jefferson Davis, but without success. Almost from the moment the Gettysburg Campaign ended, blame was apportioned, but less fell on Lee than his subordinates.

Newspapers in the south pointed to Jeb Stuart's long absence and criticized Ewell for failing to take Cemetery Hill. Editors alleged that General Richard Anderson hadn't committed sufficient troops to the action on July 2 and that Pettigrew hadn't effectively supported Pickett. Interestingly, Longstreet emerged largely unscathed in the court of public opinion. This is ironic since, in the post-war years, he was thoroughly condemned for his perceived failures at Gettysburg to the point of being made a scapegoat.

The campaign—and, most specifically, the July 1–July 3, 1863 battle— retains a mythic importance when examined in the context of the overall war. Gettysburg is now regarded as the turning point in the conflict, the beginning of the end for the Confederacy, though that end would be long and bloody in coming.

This examination has attempted to convey the major movement of troops from late June 1863 when Lee decided to cross into Pennsylvania until his retreat in early July. No work of this length can definitively dissect the Battle of Gettysburg, however, as the extensive bibliography that follows will show.

Gettysburg remains one of the most heavily studied confrontations of the American Civil War. There is a body of scholarship replete with unit histories and the evaluation of officers and their decisions up and down the chain of command on both sides. There are excellent biographies of all the major participants and many of the lesser-known but equally valiant combatants.

Armchair generals continue to ponder how different decisions at pivotal moments might have changed the outcome, pushing miniature soldiers around tabletop reconstructions or probing potential outcomes in realistic video simulations.

The Battle of Gettysburg has a way of getting into people's blood, compelling them to dig deeper, look back over the years, and truly understand what happened on the fields and craggy outcroppings of Pennsylvania. For many students, the battle becomes a lifelong obsession.

Lee, in his usual stoic manner, wrote to his wife on July 12, 1863, telling her that before she received his letter, she would learn that "...our success at Gettysburg was not so great as reported..." Astonishingly, in his correspondence with President Jefferson Davis, Lee's optimism appeared undaunted. He told Davis that reversals and defeats were to be expected in war and could be viewed as lessons in prudence and wisdom. Defeat, according to Lee, encouraged men to try harder, to learn from their mistakes, and to keep them from falling into even larger disasters. What mattered was the united nature of the Southern people who, through their forbearance of misfortune, would see all "come right in the end."

Though Lee could not see—or perhaps refused to see—the coming of the end for the Confederacy, the road to that end began at Gettysburg in a defeat from which the General and the Southern cause never recovered.

Part 10: The Battle of Chickamauga

A Captivating Guide to the Biggest Battle Ever Fought in Georgia and Its Impact on the American Civil War

Introduction

In September of 1863, the armies of the Union and Confederacy clashed along Chickamauga Creek in the northwest corner of Georgia. Rumor has it that "Chickamauga" means "river of death" in Cherokee or another Native American language. Historians have looked into this for nearly 160 years, and most of them believe this translation was likely added to the accounts of the battle for dramatic effect. After all, the Battle of Chickamauga was the second-most costly battle of the entire war in terms of casualties (men killed, wounded, and missing). Only Gettysburg, which had taken place just over two months earlier, was more costly.

The Battle of Chickamauga is a somewhat forgotten battle today. The reasons for this include the fact that over both the long- and the short-term, the battle did not decide much of anything, at least in terms of strategy or its effect on the war. The Confederate victory at Chickamauga did not turn the tide of the conflict, which so obviously had happened at Gettysburg in July, nor did it have an economic effect, such as the loss of Vicksburg, Mississippi, to the Union as the battle was beginning to take shape at Gettysburg.

Chickamauga did forestall the Union advance on Atlanta, and it did cause the Union to divert men and resources to defend the important river/rail hub at Chattanooga, Tennessee (fourteen miles to the north), but neither the battlefield nor its results had any real effect on the outcome of the war.

What the Battle of Chickamauga ultimately *did* do, however, was to further entrench and inflame both sides. Chickamauga was a costly Southern victory that only (perhaps) delayed the inevitable capture of Atlanta. It was also a humiliating Union defeat that caused the shuffling of command in that region, finally resulting in the appointment of William Tecumseh Sherman as the Union commander in the Southeast. The death toll at Chickamauga was just one more reason why the rest of the war was fought so bitterly.

Thank you for purchasing Captivating History's *Battle of Chickamauga*. We hope you enjoy reading about one of the largest battles of the American Civil War, one that has too often been overlooked.

Chapter 1 – Summer, 1863

Looking back, no one can really fault many of the Northern (Union or Federal) soldiers and civilians who began to believe the Civil War might soon be over. On July 4th, 1863, news reached most Union homes that two great victories had been won by the Federal forces at Vicksburg, Mississippi, and Gettysburg, Pennsylvania.

Union General Ulysses S. Grant had besieged the important Mississippi River port of Vicksburg for a brutal month and a half. His campaign to get to Vicksburg, which took him and his men through swamps and forests, had begun in December of the prior year. Many Northerners had almost forgotten about the campaign in the West until Grant and his second-in-command, William Tecumseh Sherman, had taken the port. With the capture of Vicksburg, Grant had seized the entire Mississippi River from the South. It was an important transport, supply, and communications highway. No one in either the North or the South could dismiss the fall of Vicksburg as inconsequential.

At Gettysburg, which lasted from July 1st to July 3rd, 1863, Confederate General Robert E. Lee had attempted to force the North to the negotiations table with a bold invasion of Pennsylvania (and perhaps even more cities if he had been successful). On Gettysburg's third day, Lee committed one of his few mistakes of the war by ordering the ill-fated "Pickett's Charge" against the distant and dug-in Union positions, costing him the battle and perhaps ultimately the war.

Still, despite these losses, the Confederacy still stood, albeit on shaky legs. Lee would retreat back to Virginia to defend his home state and

Richmond, the Confederate capital city. There, for almost two more years, Lee and his men would make the Union pay for every inch of Southern ground they took on their march to Virginia.

Further south and west, the Union armies had advanced south of Vicksburg and fought the savage Battle of Shiloh, which was just over one hundred miles east of Memphis, Tennessee. The Union Army of the Tennessee under Grant then began to move south toward New Orleans (another Union force would advance from that city northward). The Union Army of the Cumberland, which was formed in October 1862 and under the command of Major General William S. Rosecrans, marched southeastward toward Chattanooga and, more distantly, Atlanta, an all-important supply and transportation hub and one of the South's largest and most important cities.

Chapter 2 – Officers and Men

Major General William S. Rosecrans
https://commons.wikimedia.org/wiki/File:GenWmSRosecrans.jpg

Leading the Union effort to seize Chattanooga and move on Atlanta was
Union Major General William S. Rosecrans. Rosecrans, known to some
of his peers and men as "Old Rosy," had impressed his local

congressman so much that when Rosecrans was sixteen and applied to West Point, the politician bumped his own son off the West Point appointment list and gave his position to Rosecrans.

At West Point, Rosecrans was a top student, finishing fifth in his class of fifty-six in 1842, four years before the outbreak of the Mexican-American War. At West Point, he became well-acquainted with future Confederate foes James Longstreet, D. H. Hill, and Earl Van Dorn, all of whom he would meet on the battlefield at Chickamauga.

During the Mexican-American War, Rosecrans remained at West Point. He served on a variety of engineering posts around the country and resigned from the army in 1854. After this, he became a public engineer and successful inventor. However, one of his inventions, a safety lamp for mining/refining, exploded, leaving him with severe burns, some of which caused him to appear to always be grinning.

At the beginning of the Civil War, Rosecrans was in Ohio, and he was assigned by the governor to be the aide to General George McClellan, who would later gain fame and infamy on the battlefields of Virginia. Though McClellan got the credit, Rosecrans was the planner in the Union's two first victories of consequence in the summer of 1861. In 1862, Rosecrans was transferred to the Western Theater after criticizing the policies of Secretary of War Edwin Stanton, who became a lifelong political enemy.

At the victorious Battles of Iuka and Corinth, Mississippi, Rosecrans served under Ulysses S. Grant and played a major role in the Union victory at the bloody wintertime battle at Stones River, Tennessee, in 1862/63. Rosecrans was then given a corps command, which eventually became the Army of the Cumberland. He was tasked with driving the Confederates from Tennessee.

For six months, Rosecrans prepared his forces at Murfreesboro, south of Nashville, ignoring the urging of the lead Union commander in the West, Henry Halleck, and even President Abraham Lincoln. When he did move, he began a campaign that many Civil War historians rank as being up there with Grant's Vicksburg Campaign and the victory at Gettysburg. His campaign, the Tullahoma Campaign (named for a small town in central Tennessee), was more a series of carefully planned maneuvers. Rosecrans repeatedly outfoxed Confederate commander Braxton Bragg and forced him from Tennessee into Georgia, where the Battle of Chickamauga would take place.

Rosecrans's defeat at Chickamauga would forever stain the memory of his wartime career. The rest of his time in the war was spent as a military commander in Missouri, where he led troops in small actions against Confederate raiders. After the war, Rosecrans became a congressman from California, an ambassador to Mexico, and a successful businessman. He was even talked about as a potential vice-presidential candidate for Ulysses S. Grant. He died in 1898.

Braxton Bragg.
https://commons.wikimedia.org/wiki/File:Braxton_Bragg.jpg

Rosecrans's chief opponent on the battlefield at Chickamauga was Confederate Major General Braxton Bragg, one of the most unpopular generals in the secessionist army. Bragg's long friendship with

Confederate President Jefferson Davis allowed him to stay in command. Later on, he would become Davis's chief military adviser in Richmond.

Like Rosecrans, Bragg graduated from West Point, but he did so three years earlier, in 1837. Like Rosecrans and many other of the war's officers, Bragg met quite a few of his future opponents and comrades at the military academy. However, other than President Davis (whom he had served under with distinction in the Mexican-American War), most of his acquaintances, both in the North and the South, found Bragg to be an unpleasant and argumentative person.

In his post-war memoirs, Ulysses S. Grant tells a story about Bragg occupying two separate (and somewhat opposing) positions between the Mexican-American War and the Civil War. Bragg held the positions of both commander and quartermaster, and he argued with himself over supplies. In fact, he ended up rejecting his own requisition for supplies. His reputation for arguments, harsh discipline, and costly ineptitude would affect the upcoming clash at Chickamauga and cause noted Confederate cavalry commander Nathan Bedford Forrest to threaten Bragg's life should he attempt to give Forrest another order.

Although Bragg was victorious at Chickamauga, he was unable to retake Chattanooga. He was removed from his command to serve on Davis's staff in Richmond. He died in Galveston, Texas, in 1876, having held a number of positions in different businesses and attempting to defend his wartime career.

Rosecrans and Bragg were the overall commanders of their respective forces at Chickamauga, but, of course, their armies were organized into corps, divisions, and brigades. Many generals played a role at Chickamauga, but the most well-known today are Union General George Henry Thomas and Confederate General James Longstreet.

Thomas, a Virginian who had declared himself for the Union, would become known as the "Rock of Chickamauga" for the stout defense he led that allowed much of the Union Army to retreat peaceably to Chattanooga. Longstreet was already a famous general in the South. He was one of Robert E. Lee's righthand men in many of the famous battles in Virginia and at Gettysburg. Longstreet would be in command of the corps of Southerners that broke through the Union lines at Chickamauga and sent the bulk of Rosecrans's troops back to Chattanooga.

James Longstreet was one of the South's most respected generals. He was Robert E. Lee's righthand man at Gettysburg. (In fact, he notably warned Lee *not* to order Pickett's Charge, which may have cost the South the battle). He was a master in the use of artillery, having specialized in that branch at West Point and in the Mexican-American War. Longstreet sometimes suffered in comparison to Lee's former righthand, Thomas J. "Stonewall" Jackson, especially since Longstreet was a more cautious general. Still, despite his reputed caution (which, in reality, was simply being careful, unlike other generals in both armies who were cautious almost to the point of cowardice), Longstreet was one of the most able generals of the war.

George Henry Thomas.
https://commons.wikimedia.org/wiki/File:George_Henry_Thomas_-_Brady-Handy.jpg

James Longstreet.

All too often in Civil War histories, the lives and deeds of the soldiers of the Civil War are overlooked. While we cannot go into great detail about the lives and experiences of the soldiers at war, as this is meant to be purely an introduction on Chickamauga, we have included a number of sources in the bibliography. The American Battlefield Trust has a great site and allows you to control exactly how much information you want to absorb, from the general to the specific. Shelby Foote's *Civil War* trilogy is still one of the best sources on the Civil War, including information about the lives of the soldiers who fought. And Ken Burns's **PBS** series *The Civil War* is one of the best documentaries ever made, though it does contain some errors and at times appears dated, especially in the language used to describe slavery, enslaved peoples, and Confederate attitudes.

Chapter 3 – Before the Battle

Confederate General Bragg was determined to retake Chattanooga as soon as possible. Not only was the city immensely important to both sides as a rail/river and communications hub, but whoever was in possession of the city controlled a very important military position. By holding Chattanooga and the highlands around it, any occupying force had an immense advantage when it came to defense.

Aside from all the military reasons, Bragg was determined to retake the city, as it had been lost on September 9th in the most humiliating way. As was mentioned above, General Rosecrans had outmaneuvered the Southern armies outside and in Chattanooga. Bragg was forced to retreat before his forces were surrounded and besieged in the city. Though it was a necessary move to prevent disaster, Bragg's many critics (including himself) poured derision on him for being outmaneuvered and giving up the city and its environs without a major fight.

When Rosecrans occupied the city, he spent some time regrouping and resupplying before moving southeast in the direction in which Bragg had retreated. To Rosecrans, it made sense that Bragg would retreat toward the southeast to prevent an easy Union conquest of Atlanta, which was one of the most important cities in the Confederacy.

Rosecrans was not known for being especially vain, but at a time when generals, soldiers, politicians, and civilians alike often spoke about "glory," Rosecrans chafed a bit for not receiving much credit for his truly extraordinary Tullahoma Campaign. After all, Rosecrans pushed the bulk of the Confederate forces out of central and eastern Tennessee. His campaign occurred roughly at the same time as the intense and important Battle of Gettysburg and Grant's victory at Vicksburg. Thus, Rosecrans's campaign was overlooked, and the general and many of his men wanted the nation to know that they were making great strides in the fight against the Rebels. Taking Chattanooga was a real feather in Rosecrans's cap, and if he could take Atlanta? He might become the most acclaimed general in the Union. Rosecrans did receive much acclaim for taking Chattanooga, but he was now in a position (or so he thought) to either destroy Bragg's army or force it into an endless retreat to Atlanta.

On September 9th, Rosecrans telegraphed the overall Union commander in the West, Henry Halleck, saying, "Chattanooga is ours without a struggle, and East Tennessee is free." Unlike so many Union generals had before, Rosecrans intended to move after Bragg right away and not give him the chance to regroup. He immediately sent his army south of the city and into Georgia, convinced that Bragg's forces were in disarray.

Rosecrans hoped to catch Bragg's men in a large pincer movement or even envelop the Rebel forces before he could march away. He ordered the three corps of his army to take a variety of routes into the northwestern corner of the "Peach State." General Thomas Crittenden and his XXI Corps were to follow Bragg's line of retreat. Fifty miles to the south, General Alexander McCook and his XX Corps were ordered to march as rapidly as possible. They had to move around the Southern army and cut them off from the rest of Georgia (from both reinforcements and supplies). General George Henry Thomas was initially between the other two Union forces, and he was sent southward toward the Alabama-Georgia border with the intent of eventually looping north to meet the other Union forces and cut off Bragg from his possible retreat toward Atlanta.

The problem with this strategy was that it meant that the Union forces were separated by many miles. This could affect communications and, more seriously, allow a skilled Southern general to attack each force separately. And he would have more men to do it if he could attack each group on its own.

General Thomas, who had a reputation for both being quite reserved and rarely questioning orders, suggested to Rosecrans that the Union would be better served if Rosecrans moved his army out all at once instead of dividing his forces. They would surely have the numerical advantage, and they would not have to worry as much about being outmaneuvered and outgunned. Generally speaking, Rosecrans was a conservative general, but in this case, flush with victory, he brushed aside Thomas's suggestions, believing Bragg was fleeing all the way back to Atlanta, which was just under 125 miles away. He told one of the generals on his staff that he "didn't expect to get a fight out of Bragg this side of Atlanta." He ordered Thomas to proceed.

Braxton Bragg has been rated as one of the South's worst commanders since the end of the war, and in many ways, he was—especially when you consider the "competition," which included names like Robert E. Lee and Stonewall Jackson. But he wasn't a complete loss. He was an able organizer, and like most Southern generals, he was sometimes inclined to do the unexpected, though his reputation proclaims him as being a cautious man who all too often did not press his advantage. He would rely on his cautious side after Chickamauga, but before the battle, Bragg acted with uncharacteristic boldness.

Rosecrans believed that Bragg was in full retreat or, at the very least, would offer some resistance on the Union's drive to Atlanta. Indeed, it seemed to Rosecrans and a number of his subordinates that that was exactly what was happening. Southern prisoners told their captors that Bragg's force was panicking and on the retreat. The Union officers questioned Southern civilians, who let the Union forces believe they were tired of the conflict. They told them that the Southern officers who had slept in their homes admitted that the Confederates were panicking.

Like many commanders before and since, Rosecrans chose to believe what he *wanted* to believe. However, the truth was that the Confederate prisoners were lying. Some were actually taken prisoner in skirmishes or in the wildlands or pastures between Chattanooga and Chickamauga. They simply told the Union men what they wanted to hear. Other Southern soldiers claimed to be deserters. They weren't—they were volunteers who went into captivity with the express purpose of misleading Rosecrans and his men. Their mission was a success, and Rosecrans and many of his staff, along with many of his soldiers (who almost always want to believe what would be safest for them), fell for it. Though disheartened by the evacuation of Chattanooga, Bragg's men were not dispirited, at least not in any meaningful way, and they certainly were not disorganized and fleeing. Bragg and his corps, division, and brigade commanders worked to reorganize and resupply their men almost as soon as they left Chattanooga. Bragg's officers and men believed that their commander was going to try and do one or both of two things: move to retake Chattanooga or engage Rosecrans if he moved southeast. Shortly after the evacuation of Chattanooga, Rosecrans began to move his armies in the direction of Rome and Atlanta, Georgia, and Bragg meant to meet him sooner rather than later.

In addition to working on regrouping and resupplying his forces, Bragg asked Richmond for additional troops. In response, he was told that well-known and respected General James Longstreet would be detached from Lee's army in Virginia and sent to aid Bragg. It was Richmond's hope that Longstreet's departure would be missed by the Union, who were moving south slowly. Robert E. Lee was on the defensive in Virginia, and bad weather would be coming soon. It was also hoped that the addition of Longstreet's forces would give Bragg an advantage in numbers, which was something that the South rarely had during the war. With these numbers, Bragg could retake Chattanooga before Longstreet's men were missed in Virginia.

Rosecrans was hopeful, and for the most part, he was taken in by the misinformation fed to him by the "deserters" and locals. He also believed the reports of his scouts, who had told him that Bragg had fled Chattanooga in disarray. His successful Tullahoma Campaign had shown that he was the better field commander, and Rosecrans had begun to tell himself that his defeat of Bragg during the campaign would result in the Southerner's "panic."

Still, Rosecrans was not a fool. He had proven himself able up to that point and had served with distinction in a number of battles, including the important Corinth Campaign and in command (against Bragg) in the bloody Union victory at the Battle of Murfreesboro (also known as Stones River), which had allowed the Tullahoma Campaign to begin. On the other hand, Rosecrans was also frequently overcautious and had been within a hair's breadth of being dismissed for not moving sooner against Bragg before Stones River. Though he seemed to now believe that he had Bragg in full-scale retreat, which, in turn, made him uncharacteristically over-eager, he and his officers began to take note of the reports coming into his headquarters as his men moved east.

The area between Chattanooga and Chickamauga is marked by finger-like ridges that mostly run from the northeast to the southwest, running just over the Georgia border. In between these high ridges and hills are various coves that have few methods of easy exit and entry. The flat land just northwest of Chickamauga Creek and the town of Lafayette, the latter of which was a couple of miles to the south, consisted of sparsely populated farmland interrupted by sometimes dense woods.

As the Union troops made their way over these ridges, they began to see and hear signs of sizable Rebel forces. Contrary to the testimony of the "captured" Rebel soldiers and a number of the mountain people in the area, the Union officers began to get information from other sources, including from Washington (with which it was connected by telegraph in Chattanooga and beyond), that Bragg intended to cut them off from their supply base in Chattanooga and destroy them before reinforcements could arrive.

And this was exactly what Braxton Bragg intended to do. His plan was to force Rosecrans's army or at least a sizable portion of it into McLemore's Cove, which was pastureland surrounded on three sides by relatively dense woods. If Bragg could maneuver enough Union troops into the cove, which was a few miles to the southwest of the Chickamauga battlefield, they would likely have to surrender or be wiped out. If he could trap enough of them, Rosecrans might be forced to retreat back to Chattanooga.

Despite Union reports, Bragg's army had not gone into a panic after being evacuated from Chattanooga. Quite the opposite. Bragg, his officers, and his men were quite angry at having been outmaneuvered and were desperate for revenge. Though many of Bragg's generals did not personally like him (as mentioned previously, he was argumentative to an amazing degree and regarded himself as a better general than he was), they knew him to be an able organizer and quartermaster. Most of his personal enemies in the Southern forces disliked him for his abrasive personality and his seeming inability to finish off an enemy when he had him on the ropes.

However, as Rosecrans's men moved into Georgia, Bragg did a number of things to ensure the Rebels were ready for them. First, he reorganized his forces. He set up a new organizational system of corps and divisions. His army would consist of four corps, with two divisions each. Bragg's corps and divisions varied in size from one another. Generally speaking, they ranged from about ten thousand to twelve thousand men to over fifteen thousand.

Bragg's corps commanders included the cantankerous Leonidas Polk, who had been an Episcopal bishop before secession and was known to many as "Bishop Polk." Polk had attended West Point, graduating in 1827, but he resigned his commission shortly thereafter. He was also the cousin of former US President James K. Polk.

There was also General D. H. (Daniel Harvey) Hill, a very able general who had transferred west after a series of arguments and disagreements with Robert E. Lee in the east. After Gettysburg, Hill was sent to Bragg, with whom he proceeded to argue as well. But, of course, Bragg argued with everyone.

General William Henry Talbot Walker was called W. H. T. Walker for the same reason that D. H. Hill was called "D. H."; there were other generals named Walker and Hill in the Confederate Army. Walker was known (as were many Confederate generals) for being hyper-aggressive, but he was extremely competent and respected by his men. Walker often led from the front and had been wounded several times before Chickamauga.

The last commander was General Simon Bolivar Buckner. He lived to be almost one hundred, and his son and namesake fought in the Pacific in WWII, commanding forces on Okinawa. Unfortunately, he lost his life in the process, making him the highest-ranking US officer to lose his life in that conflict. The original General Buckner fought with distinction in the Mexican-American War and the Civil War. He fought exclusively in the West, fighting from one side of Tennessee to the other.

These commanders would soon be joined by James Longstreet, who came from Virginia. Longstreet's journey from the east, which would cover almost 1,900 miles, would take far longer than anticipated. This was due to both the mixed gauges (width) of Southern railways (meaning that his men and all their equipment had to change trains) and the scarcity of railroad engines. Still, a sizable portion of his force, along with himself, did arrive in Georgia in time for the battle. The first group of Longstreet's men was led by General John Bell Hood, one of the South's most lauded commanders. Hill had actually been a student of Union General Thomas at West Point, but he was not the best of students. Still, on the field, Hood was an able and popular commander, despite being possibly the most aggressive and sometimes reckless Confederate general of the war. Hood would eventually command most of the Confederate troops in Tennessee, leading a sizable force on Nashville. He was also severely wounded twice: once in his right arm, which became virtually useless thereafter and had to be carried in a sling, and to his right thigh, which happened at Chickamauga and resulted in the amputation of his leg. After recovering, Hood would fight until the Confederates surrendered in 1865.

One of the advantages these commanders enjoyed was knowing where most of Rosecrans's army was, especially the southwestern force of General Thomas, which was nearing the area of McLemore's Cove. Bragg had already moved a total of twenty-three thousand men in that direction.

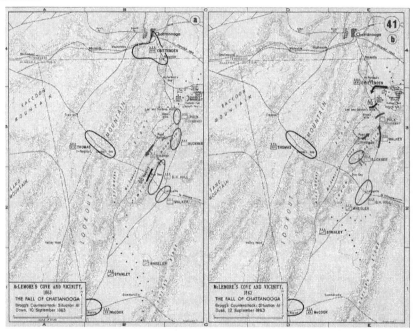

The forces of Thomas marching toward McLemore's Cove. The Southern armies cut off the eastern exits and filed in to block the north. Once Thomas entered, other CSA (Confederate States of America) forces would move south to cut off his western line of retreat. At least, that was the plan.

https://commons.wikimedia.org/wiki/File:CHICKAMAUGA_MAP_2.jpg

Throughout the run-up to the Battle of Chickamauga and the battle itself, you will see a pattern: poor communication, a rough landscape, and stubborn commanders resulted in missteps and mistakes.

Nothing about the Union move into Georgia was easy. The roads that did exist were almost all overgrown or rough dirt tracks. At times, their routes were blocked by trees cut down by the retreating Confederates. Throughout their movement east, the Rebels knew where the Union men were almost to the exact yard.

As Thomas's men moved east, Bragg gave instructions to one of Polk's division commanders, Major General Thomas C. Hindman, who had been called to join Polk's division after traveling from Arkansas. Hindman was to move into McLemore's Cove and strike Thomas's lead division. Also joining in the Confederate attack was one of D. H. Hill's divisions, which were led by noted General Patrick Cleburne, an Irish immigrant who had fought in the British Army before emigrating to the USA in 1846. Cleburne had risen from being a private in the Rebel army to division commander, and he was considered by many to be one of the South's best division commanders. Cleburne was to attack the southern part of McLemore's Cove, cutting off Negley's retreat as he was pushed in that direction by Hindman. Major General James S. Negley had led the Federal troops with skill in the Battle of Stones River (Murfreesboro) and had taken part in the Tullahoma Campaign. It was hoped that the destruction of Negley's division would cause Thomas to flood into McLemore's Cove, where Bragg could defeat him.

On September 9th, Bragg ordered Hindman to move into the cove and engage the enemy the next morning. He was to be joined by Cleburne, and together, they would destroy Negley's force. On the morning of the 10th, however, Hindman began to worry that Cleburne was being delayed for some reason or another. While his orders were to attack that morning, he began to dither, worrying that Cleburne's force would not arrive.

Hindman's gut feelings were right. D. H. Hill, Cleburne's commander, did not receive Bragg's orders for five hours. When he did receive them, Hill, who disliked Bragg intensely and who was almost as argumentative, sent out a message that was essentially a list of the reasons why Bragg's plan was a bad one. It took three hours for Cleburne's message to reach Bragg. By that time, the light was beginning to fade and, with it, Bragg's patience. By all accounts, he was pacing back and forth, occasionally cocking his ear in the direction where he intended the battle to take place. When he didn't hear any sounds, he would kick his heels into the ground and gouge out holes with his spurs.

Things didn't get any better for Bragg either. Tired of waiting for Hill's reply, he sent General Buckner and one of his divisions to aid Hindman in his attack. These two men met at 8 p.m., and after some discussion, they reached the conclusion that they would do nothing for the moment but attack some time the next day on September 11th.

Their Union counterpart in the area, General Negley, was also getting nervous. He had trailed telegraph lines along his route and signaled back to Rosecrans, saying, "There are indications of a superior force of the enemy being in position in Dug Gap [near McLemore's Cove]...My position is somewhat advanced and exposed." Negley decided that caution was the better option, and he led an organized withdrawal from the immediate area.

The next morning, Bragg decided to try again to trap a sizable Federal formation. Now it was Crittenden's XXI Corps' turn. Crittenden was moving straight from Chattanooga directly toward what would soon be the Chickamauga battlefield. Crittenden's lead division was led by General Thomas J. Wood, a West Point graduate from Kentucky who declared for the Union. This move would put him on the Chickamauga battlefield opposite his best friend, Confederate General Simon Bolivar Buckner. While Wood was moving forward, Crittenden would move the rest of his troops by rail to the small town of Ringgold, which lies a few miles southeast of Chickamauga Creek. This move put the Union troops close to Bragg's headquarters at Lafayette and a distance of fifteen miles from the rest of Crittenden's corps. If Wood came under sudden attack, no one would be able to help him and his men.

Bragg knew that there was a sizable Union force nearby and assembled the entire corps of "Bishop" Leonidas Polk to destroy it with the promise that if Polk "crushed that division...the others will be yours." Unfortunately, while Bragg knew a Union formation was in the area, he did not know *exactly* where. Polk was sent to a position that would have been ideal. Had he arrived an hour or two earlier, Wood's division would indeed have been "his," but by the time the mistake was realized, reports were already coming in saying that the rest of Crittenden's men were beginning to filter into Ringgold.

Polk was in a good position to attack a single division, but he was dangerously exposed to an attack by a greater or equally sized force. The Union corps were generally a bit larger than those of the Confederacy, of which the Confederates were well aware. The fact of the matter, however, was that Crittenden's corps was made up of three divisions, while Polk had four. Polk *did* have more men than the Union force, but he was convinced he was outnumbered. In a series of messages, Polk told Bragg he was moving back. Bragg promised him as many men as he wanted.

Early in the afternoon, Polk decided to pull back rather than risk what he believed might be a disaster.

Crittenden assembled his men at Ringgold and then moved them to a more defensible position north of the town near the Lee & Gordon's Mill, where he would unite with Wood. This forced Bragg to fall back to the town of Lafayette, yelling all the while over the lost opportunity. In the years after the war, many Southern officers wrote their memoirs. The generals, in particular, often defended their moves, especially controversial ones. Bragg did this, and so did D. H. Hill and Longstreet, among others. In Hill's account, Bragg had issued "impossible orders, and therefore those entrusted with their execution got in the way [habit] of disregarding them." He also said that Bragg had a nasty habit of blaming his subordinates for his mistakes and that, consequently, they were reluctant to show initiative. For his part, Bragg maintained that he issued clear orders that would have resulted in victory had they been followed in a timely manner.

Lee & Gordon's Mill shortly after the battle
https://commons.wikimedia.org/wiki/File:Lee_and_Gordon%27s_Mills,_Chickamauga_Battlefiel_d,_Tenn_-_NARA_-_528904.tif

Lee and Gordon's Mill today
https://commons.wikimedia.org/wiki/File:Lee_and_Gordon%27s_Mills.jpg

Interestingly enough, at the same time that Bragg was becoming increasingly irate about his missed opportunity, Rosecrans was doing the same. Possibly because his movements in the Tullahoma Campaign had been so successful and because he had bested Bragg a number of times, Rosecrans believed that the Southern general *must* be retreating in disarray. This idea was confirmed by the false reports he was receiving from the locals and Confederate "prisoners of war." It was a classic case of confirmation bias—going into a situation or facing a problem with a certainty that is constantly confirmed because one *wishes* it to be so.

Rosecrans had actually been told by Thomas that Negley had been right in moving away from McLemore's Cove, as reports were constantly coming in reporting of large Confederate forces in the area. Rosecrans sent a message to Thomas, telling the Virginian that he had read Thomas's message carefully but was convinced that Negley had moved out of the area before he could determine the size of the force that opposed him.

Still, through the days until September 13th, Rosecrans dismissed the reports coming in. General McCook reported that "Bragg's whole army" was at Lafayette, and Negley referred to a pass in the hills near him in the aforementioned report to Rosecrans. "There are indications of a superior force of the enemy being in position near Dug Gap. My position is somewhat advanced and exposed." Later, Negley saw large clouds of dust, indicating a large enemy force.

On September 13th, Rosecrans finally acknowledged that his unit commanders might be onto something and that his corps were deployed too far apart from each other. He realized they could be cut off and destroyed before the others could come to their aid. "Old Rosy" ordered his troops back and/or together. He then ordered his corps to form a north-south line anchored near Lee & Gordon's Mill. Wood's formation, in particular, was quite a distance away and had to retrace its painful steps across Lookout Mountain. He and his troops had to march back the way they had come, a total of fifty-seven miles of hard terrain.

Thankfully for Rosecrans, Bragg was still formulating a new plan and waiting for what he believed might be the key to the battle: the arrival of James Longstreet's corps from Virginia. The long and time-consuming journey of these men from Virginia gave Rosecrans time to reassemble his troops in such a way that they could support one another in defense and deliver a devastating blow to Bragg.

Bragg was chomping at the bit to get at Rosecrans, but he was still waiting for not only Longstreet but also units under the command of Simon Bolivar Buckner, who had been sent to the area northeast of Chattanooga after its fall. He was sent there in case the Union forces did something unexpected in that direction. Bragg was also waiting on two smaller divisions from noted Confederate commander Joseph E. Johnston, which numbered about nine thousand men divided into two divisions under John C. Breckinridge (former congressman and former US vice president under James Buchanan) and General William Walker. These men had to make a long journey from Mississippi but arrived by the 13th.

As for Longstreet's troops, they were making a long circuitous 900-mile journey on different sized railways that were not in the best condition. In total, sixteen different rail lines were used, and so the Southerners often had to disembark and get on a new train.

On September 15th, Union General Halleck telegraphed Rosecrans and reported to him that Longstreet's men were heading toward Georgia. Not only were the additional numbers a threat, but Longstreet's corps was also regarded as some of the best troops on either side during the war. Halleck told Rosecrans that in response to these reports, he was sending part of Ulysses S. Grant's Army of the Tennessee to him, as well as other troops that he could spare from other areas nearby.

One of the formations Rosecrans asked for was the Army of the Ohio, which was under the command of former overall Union commander Ambrose Burnside. He had been transferred after the dreadful US defeat at Fredericksburg, Maryland, in December 1862. Unfortunately, for Rosecrans, in this case, he, too, was the victim of his own overconfidence. Just a few days earlier, he had sent a message to Burnside, who was in northeastern Tennessee, that Bragg was in full retreat into Georgia and that Burnside could carry on with his plans to move into western Virginia. Rosecrans had asked Burnside for cavalry reinforcements to help scout the area ahead, which was done, but now with reports of Bragg seeming to be determined to make a stand, he asked Halleck to order Burnside south. But it was too late. Burnside was at Jonesboro, Tennessee, meaning he was too far away to arrive before the coming battle. He also moved slowly, which provoked President Lincoln (who followed the events on the field closely by telegraph) to exclaim, "Damn Jonesboro!" This preceded direct orders from the president to move to Rosecrans with "all haste." Burnside's men would not take part in the coming battle.

Longstreet's would.

Chapter 4 – Day One

Chickamauga was the second-most costliest battle in the entire Civil War, but as opposed to many other battles, such as Gettysburg, much of it and the events before it were accidental. As you have just read, the lead-up to the battle was marked by misinformation, misinterpretation, boldness, hesitancy, and just plain mistakes.

This was to continue until September 18th. Before we go further, remember that, generally speaking, in the Civil War, as in the Revolutionary War before it, the formations of soldiers on the battlefield were organized and lined up in ranks or rows—at least before panic set in, if it did. The first question that any student has upon learning about the Civil War for the first time is, "Why did they line up in rows like that?" The answer is quite simple. Though the weapons of the Civil War were more accurate than those of the Revolutionary War, they were largely inaccurate at any real distance over fifty or so yards. This was especially true at the beginning of the conflict. To increase accuracy and effect, troops massed together. This also allowed the individual ranks to fire, and they would then kneel to reload while the ranks behind them fired. By the time the war ended, however, technology and mass production had changed the way men fought on the field.

Since the troops typically marched in formation while on the battlefield, they had to respond to commands instantly. Today, soldiers are taught "about-face," "right-face," "left-face," and so on because it helps unit cohesion and teaches the soldiers how to respond to commands quickly and look sharp on the training ground. Militarily, it's useless today, but in 1863, the men needed to learn these commands and respond quickly while under fire. This was made more difficult, obviously, due to the sounds of battle. For centuries, men had used drums, flags, and horns to relay orders over the din of battle and over distances. It was the same in 1863, although sadly, many of the drummer boys were actually boys. Many of them suffered greatly or lost their lives in the war.

When the two opposing formations were facing each other, they referred to the ends of their positions or the position of their enemies by using the terms "right" and "left." For instance, at Chickamauga, the westward-facing Rebels' "right" was, generally speaking, northward, while their "left" was to the south. Obviously, this was the opposite for the Union. When writers or textbooks describe the battles of the era, they use phrases like "turn the enemy right" or "attack the enemy left." When the phrase "turn" is used, that usually refers to an attack on an enemy formation's flanks (the ends of the formation). It was hoped that they could force the enemy to "turn" part or all of their formation to meet the attack. In doing so, disorganization could set into undisciplined and/or badly trained troops. It could also leave a gap between the "turned" unit and its fellow unit next to it. This, in turn, could be exploited in a number of ways by the attacker.

Early on the morning of Tuesday, September 18th, Braxton Bragg was still fuming over his missed opportunities of the day before and sought to redeem them by attacking that morning. He planned to attack the forces of Union General Crittenden on the south end of the Union lines and "turn" his left flank, which would force the Union men to turn and face them on an east-west axis north of McLemore's Cove. Bragg's men would force them into the cove, where strong Confederate forces barred most exits, catching them in what Bragg called a "meat grinder." Bragg's orders to his army were clear: "The movement will be executed with the utmost promptness, vigor and persistence." In today's parlance, that would be "attack on schedule, press it, and don't lose contact with the enemy." But imagine it said with a bit of anger, as Bragg had smoke coming out of his ears due to the day before.

On the Confederate right was General Bushrod Johnson, who actually was born and raised in the North as a pacifist Quaker but rebelled and entered West Point. He had fought since the beginning of the war, beginning in the Tennessee Militia as a colonel and fighting through its end. Johnson and his troops, which were were on the far Confederate right, were to turn the Union left at Reed's Bridge over Chickamauga Creek. To his south (left), the Rebel forces under Walker and Buckner were to advance in the center and left, respectively.

Like it had the day before, fate had other ideas about Bragg's plans. Johnson initially marched in the wrong direction and had to retrace his steps, which wasted valuable time. To his south, Generals Walker and Buckner began their march to the creek, but they were miles from it. At one point, they were forced to share the same badly worn dirt road, again wasting time. General Buckner met the Union pickets (small forces sent out to prevent surprise attacks) and quickly defeated them. He waited for word of General Walker's actions, and after waiting through the afternoon, he set up camp for the night.

Both Walker and Johnson, who were to his north, were engaged with Union troops. As the Confederates approached Reed's Bridge, they met stiff resistance from Irish-born and raised cavalry Colonel H. G. Minty. He and his men fought Johnson's forces to a standstill on the narrow road. At Alexander Bridge to the south, Walker was met by the forces of another Union cavalry unit, one with a reputation for battle and surprise. It was commanded by Colonel John Wilder, and it was known as the "Lightning Brigade" for its swift movement and its ability to be seemingly at more than one place at a time. Though the Confederates eventually seized the bridge when Wilder's smaller unit retreated, it took them time to get over the bridge, for Wilder's men had removed the planking before they left. Meeting the Union cavalry in battle at Chickamauga and thereafter would not be something that many Southern units looked forward to. The Union horsemen were beginning to receive weapons that incorporated a new technology: repeating rifles. Depending on the make, these rifles could fire five or six bullets for every one fired by the Southerners.

By the afternoon, Bragg had only about nine thousand men across Chickamauga Creek. His forces, including those from Longstreet, which began to arrive in the late afternoon on the 18th, would eventually number sixty-five thousand for the coming battle. It was one of the few times in the war that the Confederates would have more men on the field than the "Yankees."

Longstreet's unit that arrived in the late afternoon was Hood's. Hood had been forced to take a different train than his men and had not seen his men since the Battle of Gettysburg in early July. There was a short, happy reunion, as Hood was immensely popular with his men. Then he led them into battle at Reed's Bridge, brushing aside the Union cavalry under Minty. The Southerners now began to send the rest of their army across the creek, and by dawn on the 19th, had about 75 percent of their forces over the water.

Chickamauga Creek and Reeds bridge.

On the Union side, Rosecrans was also busy. He had ordered Crittenden to spread his units more to the north (the Union "right") and ordered Thomas to take his XIV Corps northward. By sunrise, two of Thomas's divisions (commanded by Generals John Brannan and Absalom Baird) were in position, and two more (under James Negley and John Reynolds) were moving to the north.

However, despite their successful movements and a number of large skirmishes, both commanders had serious misapprehensions about the position of the enemy's forces. Rosecrans did not know that Bragg's men had crossed the creek, which was more like a small river. Bragg believed that the Union right was still three miles to the south. The movement of the Union troops during the day and evening meant that Bragg's planned flank attack for the 19th would not engage the Union right but move straight into the center of the Union lines.

The first truly heavy fighting in the Battle of Chickamauga took place by accident. At about 9 a.m. on September 19th, Colonel Dan McCook, the brother of Alexander McCook, the Union commander of the XX Corps, reported to General Thomas that a brigade-sized enemy force had crossed the creek in the area of Reed's Bridge. Thomas ordered General Brannan, the commander of the 3rd Division of the XIV Corps, to find, attack, and preferably capture this Rebel unit. That was easier said than done, of course, and in this case, that was doubly true. This Confederate force was the cavalry brigade of Brigadier General Nathan Bedford Forrest, who had already established himself as one of the best and most aggressive of the Confederate cavalry commanders.

Today, Forrest is a controversial figure, especially in Tennessee. His bust was removed in July 2021 from the Tennessee State House and moved to a museum. There was also a tremendously ugly statue of him erected on private land near a major highway approaching Nashville. This was removed in December 2021 (it is perhaps safe to say that even Forrest would have approved of this move). Forrest was a millionaire before the war at a time when being a millionaire was an almost unheard-of thing. He had made his fortune trading slaves, and when the war broke out, he enlisted as a private. But he soon wearied of the incompetence of his commanders. He then outfitted a unit completely on his own, and in a short time, he had established himself as an excellent military leader with an incredible feel for the battlefield. He was soon promoted all the way to the rank of general. After the Battle of Chickamauga, he would curse and threaten Braxton Bragg for his incompetence and go on to wage a brilliant campaign throughout Tennessee.

Thomas had sent a division after Forrest's brigade, and while Forrest was fighting a holding action against this larger force, he sent for reinforcements from General Walker's two-division corps, which was positioned to his south. Walker's men took McCook's men completely by surprise when they attacked the Federals' flank. The officer in charge of that attack had one of the most unique names of the war: States Rights Gist. No, that was not a nickname. His father was a staunch secessionist, going all the way back to the secession crisis of 1833 under President Jackson when South Carolina, Gist's home, threatened to leave the

Union.

Bragg received a message from the field and decided that the Federal move was an attempt to turn his right flank. It was not, but Bragg began to order more units to the north part of his line (the Confederate "right" and Union "left").

Commanding the lead brigade of the Union division was Colonel John Croxton, who, while being pushed back now by both Forrest and Gist, wryly sent back a message to Thomas reporting the presence of *two* Confederate brigades near Reed's Bridge. "Which brigade should I capture?" The Battle of Chickamauga had begun almost completely by accident, and now both commanders (Bragg and Rosecrans), as well as their field commanders, were forced to improvise on the fly.

General Brannan hurried his division to the aid of Colonel Croxton and was soon involved in heavy fighting with Gist's division and Forrest's brigade. Soon after arriving on the field, Brannan was forced to give ground against a fierce Rebel attack. General Thomas, who was not far from the fighting, then ordered the 1st Division of his corps under General Absalom Baird to aid Brannan and Croxton. Soon, the Union lines steadied, and Croxton pulled his men back to resupply ammunition.

The Union line would only hold for a short time, for Bragg had ordered yet another division to his right to reinforce those already involved in the fighting. This division was led by General St. John Liddell, a Louisianan who later advocated for the emancipation of the enslaved people of the South in order to secure British aid. After the war, Liddell was killed in a duel with another former Confederate officer. The addition of Liddell's brigade pushed the Union men all the way back to their jumping-off point, and it also resulted in the capture of a small number of Federal cannons. The capture of the guns came at a high cost. The Union artillery commander, who stood alone with his men after the infantry meant to protect him fled, fired sixty-four rounds of canister shot into the coming Rebels of the 8th Arkansas Brigade. For those of you unfamiliar with the term, "canister" was essentially a cannon-sized shotgun shell. The Rebels that made it to the Union guns would have seen their comrades ripped apart before their eyes. Other Confederate units would capture dozens of Federal guns and mountains of ammunition and other supplies once the Federal right began to crumble later in the day.

Much of the fighting at Chickamauga took place in heavily wooded areas that were interrupted by various sized farms and pastures. Both types of terrain led to heavy casualties, but the heavy woods hindered both commanding officers and their men from knowing what was going on, not only in the battle as a whole but also on the ground. On many occasions, especially as the light began to fade later in the day, soldiers from both sides would be surprised by additional enemy units seeming to appear "out of nowhere." This, as well as the number of men involved in the battle, would lead to the extremely high casualty rate at Chickamauga.

While the fighting was going on at the far end of the Union left, Thomas sent messages to Rosecrans, reporting what was happening and asking for reinforcements. Rosecrans sent the 2nd Division of McCook's XX Corps—men from Ohio, Indiana, Illinois, and Pennsylvania—to aid Brannan's and Baird's men. As the men from those units retreated in some disorder from the fighting, the men of the 2nd moved onto the edges of the road to let them pass. And then, undaunted, they marched into battle and began to push the Rebels back once more.

By this time, the battle was taking on a life of its own. Bragg sent more of his men to his right. This unit, led by respected commander Benjamin Cheatham, an upper-class Tennessean by birth who had relocated to California to take part in the Gold Rush for a time, entered the fray in the mid-morning. The fighting became exceedingly heavy and hard.

Forrest's cavalry was still involved in the fighting; they had been fighting on foot for about three hours when noon approached. One of Forrest's officers, Colonel Thomas Berry, later put his impressions of the battle to paper. "Neighing horses, wild and frightened, were running in every direction; whistling, seething, crackling bullets, the piercing, screaming fragments of shells, the whirring sound of shrapnel and the savage shower of canister, mingling with the fierce answering yells of defiance all united in one horrible sound." He left out the screaming, moaning, and crying of his own men but added that he had never seen, throughout his two years at war, a more terrible sight than this. "The ghastly, mangled dead and horribly wounded strewed the earth for over half a mile up and down the river banks." Chickamauga Creek had lived up to its name, he said. "It ran red with blood." Just to be clear, this last statement was not an exaggeration. The creek literally turned red with blood.

Union commander Rosecrans was out of touch with things at his headquarters, which was at the far right of the Union line, south of Lee & Gordon's Mill at Crawford Springs. More specifically, his headquarters was located in the home of a young widow named Eliza Glenn. This position was behind Thomas's right flank and closer to the battle, but Rosecrans still did not have a clear idea of what was going on. The confusion of battle and the heavy woods in the area muddied up the picture, but as in many battles before and after, the sound of heavy firing gave Rosecrans an indication of the direction and severity of the fighting. Even though telegraph lines connected Rosecrans with Thomas, the latter was too busy issuing orders of his own to give Rosecrans an exact and detailed update. Rosecrans was even more in the dark because his maps of the area were quite primitive and did not reveal many of the features of the area. So, while Rosecrans was attempting to get a clear picture of the battlefield, the battlefield kept inching closer to him, with both sides feeding more troops into the fighting on the Union left/Confederate right. Both sides had moved forward and back. At about the time Rosecrans was approaching the Widow Glenn's (he might have already been there by this time), Union troops under General Richard Johnson were attacking Cheatham's men and threatening to open a hole in the Confederate line that other Union troops could exploit. They could possibly turn the battle their way once and for all. One of Johnson's men, a Sergeant Young of the 79th Illinois, gave a frightful account of what he saw on the battlefield that day. "Men cheer, but in that awful roar the voice of a man cannot be heard 10 feet away. Men fall to the right and left. The line stumbles over corpses as it hurries on. There are flashes in the smoke cloud, terrible explosions in the air, and men are stepped on or leaped over as they throw up their arms and fall upon the grass and scream in the agony of mortal wounds."

Now it was Bragg's turn to reinforce, and he sent the division of Tennessean Alexander P. Stewart, who, at the end of the war, would be the last commander of the Confederate forces in the West. As his men moved forward into position on Cheatham's left, some of them saw one of their comrades from Cheatham's unit being carried on a stretcher with a mortal wound. His intestines were literally hanging from his body as he cheered his brothers-in-arms on. "Boys, when I left, we were driving 'em!" This was at about 2:30 in the afternoon. Stewart's division began a short but murderous fight with a Union division under Brigadier General Horatio Van Cleve and sent it back toward the Brotherton farmhouse on

Lafayette Road. In that short but brutal fight, one of Stewart's brigades, which numbered about 1,800 men, lost one-third of its men in just minutes—604 men were killed and wounded.

As Stewart was attacking, Thomas's call to his divisions under Negley and Reynolds was answered. These units were moving to the rear of Van Cleve's soldiers when it was attacked by the men in gray (and butternut) uniforms. Reynolds turned his men and came to Van Cleve's aid while Negley's men waited in the rear as a reserve. If they were not needed, they would continue their march toward Thomas.

The entry of Reynold's division was timely and accidental at the same time. It was also key; had the Confederates broken through, they would have cut the battlefield in two and moved forward to cut Dry Valley Road, which led to Chattanooga. This would have prevented any Union moves from or to that direction.

Van Cleve's men rallied alongside Reynold's before Dry Valley Road. They barely had time to catch their breath and take a quick drink before Stewart's men came roaring forward at them once again. The bloody fight continued for some time before the Union men began to fall back in a relatively orderly fashion to the north. This was the start of Thomas's stand in the area, and as troops arrived, he calmly arranged them in a horseshoe shape. During all of this, Bragg was feeding his men into the battle piece by piece. He still believed that the Yankees would try to attack and turn his left, so he kept units in place there until he needed them. This was something he was roundly criticized for during and after the war. While he was doing this, General Hood's Texans went against the Union right, which was south of Thomas on Lafayette Road. (The general had commanded the Texans personally throughout the war until taking command of Longstreet's corps until he arrived from Virginia, which he would do the next day.)

As a unit of tired, ragged, and wounded Tennesseans came toward the rear from the front lines, one cocky Texan exclaimed, "Rise up, Tennesseans, and see the men from Texas go in!" A bit later, after having been repulsed for the time being by a unit of Union cavalry, the Texans moved to the rear, where the Tennesseans were waiting. One man stood up and said, "Rise up, Tennesseans, and see the Texans COME OUT!"

Hood's troops went in again. This time, they met the Union division under Brigadier General Jefferson C. Davis. Yes, you read right. The

President of the Confederacy was Jefferson F. Davis, and he was safe in Richmond while the battle wore on. Davis's two brigades were in an unfortunate position. As the Union troops shifted from south to north, Davis's men were momentarily left with both flanks exposed. Hood's men, along with Johnson's men, inflicted heavy losses on the Union soldiers. Six hundred ninety-six were killed, wounded, or captured.

One of the men who was killed was brigade commander Hans Christian Heg, a Norwegian immigrant. A sizable percentage of the troops from both sides were immigrants. Most were Irish, but sizable contingents of Germans, Slovaks, English, Italians, and other European immigrants were fighting for their new country. Hood and Johnson began to approach Rosecrans's headquarters at the Widow Glenn's. The fighting got so close that the men in and around the building had to shout to make themselves heard. As you have read, the fighting at Chickamauga was one of attack and counterattack. So, when Hood's and Johnson's men surged forward, they were met by Union troops commanded by the unhorsed cavalry of Wilder's Lightning Brigade, who had begun the day's fighting on the north end of the Union line. Wilder's horsemen were joined by an artillery unit commanded by a man whose last name is still well-known today: chemist Eli Lilly, who began what is today the pharmaceutical giant that bears his name. Lilly set up his guns so that they faced the left flank of Johnson's men as they moved forward. Within minutes, scores of Confederate soldiers were dead or horribly wounded on the field. General Wilder blanched at the carnage and later wrote that he "had it in his heart to order the firing to cease, to end the awful sight."

By mid-afternoon, only two Union formations had not seen battle: General Gordon Granger's Reserve Corps, which was far to the north of the battlefield guarding the approach from that direction, and the division under General Philip Sheridan. Sheridan had already proved himself in battle, and he would go on to be Ulysses S. Grant's chief cavalry commander in Virginia shortly after Chickamauga. He did, however, have a bit of an inflated attitude about himself and his unit. This attitude spread to his staff officers, who cried out to other officers and men on the road to the field, "Make way for Sheridan! Make way for Sheridan!" as Sherman's division moved into position at the end of the Union line. They acted as if he was going to rescue the entire Union Army.

As his men moved into position, they were attacked by Hood's and Johnson's troops. Sheridan's defense was hindered by the savagery of the attack and the many Union troops fleeing the field, which slowed Sheridan's advance. Shortly after arriving on the field, Sheridan's unit was forced to retreat with haste. As they did, Union troops in the rear, who had watched Sheridan's grand entrance, exclaimed, "Make way for Sheridan! Make way for Sheridan!" There were comedians on both sides.

At the Federal headquarters, General Rosecrans was beginning to lose his cool. As the fighting raged nearby, a young Southern prisoner was brought to him. The prisoner told the general proudly that he was with Longstreet's corps. Rosecrans was notorious for receiving bad news poorly, and now that it seemed that even more Confederates were at Chickamauga than he had imagined, he lost his cool. He yelled and screamed in the face of the young prisoner, who quickly clammed up out of fear, believing he might be shot. Eventually, the Union commander calmed down, and as the boy was taken away, Rosecrans admitted that the youngster was probably right.

By this time, the sun was going down, and many men believed the fighting was done for the day. On the north flank of the Union forces, General Thomas began to reorganize his troops and set up a defense in the woods along the intersection of Alexander Bridge Road and Lafayette Road. Soon, this area, previously known as "Snodgrass Hill," would take on a new name based on the excellent defensive position of the troops there: Horseshoe Ridge.

As twilight fell, the men of Patrick Cleburne's division, which had been moving northward for some time from its position near Lee & Gordon's Mill, struck Thomas's position after crossing a freezing cold but only shoulder-deep ford of the Chickamauga Creek. The Southerners, mostly men from Alabama, Arkansas, Mississippi, and Texas, with a smattering of units from Tennessee, Louisiana, and Florida, unleashed a massive wall of fire at the Union lines. Cleburne had insisted on his men learning to fire rapidly, and the result was an almost continuous wall of fire. This also had the effect of making the Union men in blue believe there were many more Rebels than there actually were.

Soon, Cleburne's men and his artillery fire were pushing the Union troops rearward. One of the units in the Union front line, the 77th

Pennsylvania, virtually disappeared in the initial assault. As the Rebels moved forward in the dark, they began to yip and howl the infamous "Rebel yell." In the growing darkness, lit by the firing of the guns of both sides, the fighting became hand-to-hand. Cleburne's men pushed the Union line back a mile, capturing a number of guns in the process. Their advance stopped when it became too dark to see.

It was cold. Cleburne's men were freezing from the water and sweat. The fading of adrenaline also caused chills on both sides. Obviously, no fires could be lit. As dark as it was, picket troops on both sides, who were guarding against a possible surprise attack in the night, fired at each other often, waking those who could sleep and alarming those still awake. The soldiers on both sides also had to listen to the screams, cries, and moans of the wounded and dying all around them. No one could get up and help them. When they tried, rifle and even cannon fire burst out again.

General Thomas did not sleep either, at least not very much, nor did many of his men. During the night, the Union lines were reorganized into a coherent, connected wall of blue uniforms. By morning, a high percentage of the sixty thousand Union troops at Chickamauga were at Horseshoe Ridge. The remainder formed a line of corps and divisions aligned (roughly) east to west.

The approach toward Horseshoe Ridge today.
https://commons.wikimedia.org/wiki/File:Horseshoe_Ridge_Chickamauga.jpg

That night, Rosecrans called a war council at the Widow Glenn's house, which would burn to the ground the next day. Philip Sheridan recalled a depressing atmosphere. Rosecrans and the others knew that they had barely managed to hold back the Rebels that day and that the Southerners were preparing a massive assault for tomorrow. Not helping matters was the realization that the Confederates outnumbered them by a sizable margin. A Union attack was out of the question, but a strong defense would reduce the Rebels' advantage.

During the meeting, General Thomas occasionally nodded off, as he was exhausted after the long, bloody day. Thomas, who was known for being rather reserved anyway, was asked throughout the meeting for his recommendation. Each time, he would open his eyes for a moment, say, "I would strengthen the left," then go back to his light sleep.

The Confederates also had a meeting. General Hood, who was new to the Western Theater, noticed both a lack of formality and enthusiasm. The latter was especially true when General Bragg announced that he was reorganizing his command. The Southern right would be made up of Polk, Hill, and Walker. On the left would be Hood, Buckner, and the soon-to-arrive General Longstreet.

Longstreet had actually arrived at 2 o'clock in the afternoon, but when he got to the nearest depot, no one was there to greet him, brief him on the situation, or even tell him how to find General Bragg. Longstreet's horse hadn't arrived yet either, and until it did, the general paced back and forth at the depot, growing more frustrated by the moment. Finally, his horse and those of his staff arrived, and they decided to follow the sound of the distant battle, questioning soldiers along the way.

It took Longstreet until 11 p.m. to find Bragg, who was some twenty miles away. By the time Longstreet and his men found Bragg, they were already convinced of the rumors about the general's "unpleasantness" and had gradually worked themselves up against him as they traveled. When they arrived, Bragg had to be woken up, and he spent the next hour briefing Longstreet on the disposition of the troops and the plan for the coming day.

Bragg's plan for the next day was similar to that of the day before: he would order his right to swing south and push the Union right south into McLemore's Cove, where they would be forced to surrender or be annihilated. From the north of his position southward, each of the units on his right flank would swing south (to their left) as the Union was pushed into that direction.

In order to do that, many Southern formations would be repositioned northward during the night, with the attack beginning at first light. At least that was the plan. D. H. Hill's division of Polk's corps was supposed to move from the far Confederate left all the way north to the Rebel far right. This never happened because Hill never got Bragg's orders. He had not been at the meeting, and Polk did not relay the orders. The "Bishop" believed that Bragg would send word to Hill, which never happened.

Hill only learned about Bragg's plans the next morning—at about the time the attack was set to begin. His men were tired from the day before and had not yet eaten. When Hill got the orders to move, he sent word to Polk that he would attack in about an hour—*after* his men had their breakfast.

Polk did not send word to Bragg, who was pacing and swearing at his headquarters some miles away. Many Southerners criticized him for being away from the action, as they expected their generals to be near the front, like Lee and Jackson.

Bragg sent a man to Polk to find out what was happening. His courier returned to report that Polk was reading a newspaper in his tent and waiting on his breakfast. At that point, Bragg finally exploded, cursing in a most ungentlemanly manner about his generals and their incompetence. He then sent a very emphatic order to his officers to attack *immediately*.

Chapter 5 – Day Two

The battle resumed at 9:45, a good three hours after Bragg had intended. All along the line, the firing of rifles and cannons began to increase and move south until the entire line was aflame.

The Union left was attacked by three brigades under the overall command of General Breckinridge, the former US vice president. Two of those units moved around the end of the Union line and attacked the regiments of James Negley, whose lead brigade was forced back behind the Union left. This began the real horseshoe shape that would define the Union position on the far north of the battlefield.

One of Breckenridge's brigades had named itself the "Orphan Brigade." They were Kentuckians, whose state was completely under Union control. As long as the war went badly for the South, they could never return to their home state, hence their name. This unit was led by a man known personally to President Abraham Lincoln. Confederate Brigadier General Benjamin Hardin Helm was Mary Todd Lincoln's brother-in-law, and the president was quite fond of the West Point and Harvard graduate.

After the battle, Private John Green of the Orphan Brigade described the fighting that took place when his brigade engaged Thomas's lines. The Orphans were "giving and taking death blows which could only last but a few minutes without utter annihilation." Indeed, Mary Lincoln's brother-in-law was cut down, sadly and ironically, by the Union 15th Kentucky Brigade. Before the war, Kentucky, though a slave state, was divided almost in half between Union and Confederate sympathies, as was Tennessee. However, most pro-Union Tennesseans were in the rugged mountains of the far eastern quarter of the state. Interestingly, Delaware and Maryland, which were both Union states, were also slave states, which many do not know.

The final two brigades of Negley's division never made it to the far left of the Union line. They were farther south in the Union center, awaiting the arrival of General Thomas J. Wood. His division was still in reserve, despite receiving orders from Rosecrans to move into the front lines where Negley's two divisions were so that they could reunite with their comrades fighting on the left flank. When informed of this, General Rosecrans rode to Wood's position and let him have it quite publicly. "What is the meaning of this, sir? You have disobeyed my specific orders! By your damnable negligence you have endangered this entire army, and by God, I will not tolerate it! Move your division at once, as I have instructed, or the consequences will not be pleasant for yourself!" Rosecrans did not have time to couch his language, but he should not have delivered his rebuke in front of Wood's men. Still, it did result in Wood moving his troops into line and into the battle. Negley's men also joined their brother units on the left.

Another Confederate division, this one under Cleburne, assaulted the Union front south after Breckinridge's attack. As they advanced through the woods, they ran into log breastworks the Union men had cut down during the night. The fighting was intense and stopped Cleburne's attack. The Rebels then settled down behind whatever cover they could find and held on until General Polk sent Walker's and Cheatham's divisions to their aid. This time, all three units attacked the Union line, and all three were thrown back, suffering heavy losses.

At about this time, something crucial to the outcome of the battle occurred. General Thomas, who was under heavy pressure, was sending requests for reinforcements every few minutes. One of Rosecrans's men, Captain Kellogg, was traveling to survey Thomas's situation in the north, riding just behind the front line to do so. On the way, he noticed what he believed was a gap in the Union lines, which had been caused by a unit presumably sent to reinforce Thomas. When he arrived at General Thomas's headquarters, he reported the dangerous situation to the general, who telegraphed it back to Rosecrans's headquarters.

This supposed gap in the lines was between the units of General Reynolds (to the north) and General Wood's division, which was now in place near the center of the Union line. Rosecrans sent a message to Wood, ordering him to move his division to the north alongside Reynolds's men and close up the hole in the Federal lines. General Wood did not understand the order; there was no gap in the Union lines as far as he could see. But he had just received a stinging public rebuke and possible court-martial from Rosecrans not too long before, so he moved his unit as ordered. This created a division-sized gap in the Union lines.

At about 11:30 a.m., Rosecrans ordered the Union's Jefferson Davis into Wood's former position to the south. While this was happening, two of Philip Sheridan's brigades were sent north from the south of the "gap" to Thomas in the north. At this point in time, two Union divisions and half of another were in motion, moving sideways to the front, which created a gap a quarter-mile wide in the Union lines. There was no gap before—it was part of the "fog of war"—but there was one now.

Chickamauga was a strange battle in a number of ways. Many of the actions took place by accident or misunderstanding, and this situation was no different. Shortly after the Northern units began their shift northward, the Confederates under James Longstreet, who had finally made it to the front lines after his long journey, launched a massive attack at exactly where Wood's unit had pulled out. Three divisions (Hood and Johnson in front, with Brigadier General Joseph B. Kershaw in reserve) went charging into the gap in the Union lines. This was a total of twenty-three thousand men.

Though they took heavy losses from Union artillerymen, some of which actually threw pieces of grapeshot (chains, nails, etc.) by hand at the Rebels, the Southern men surged forward. They engaged in hand-to-hand fighting with the two batteries of Union artillery and moved on into a clearing near Dyer Farm to recoup and catch their breath.

At this point, General Hood rode up, using his one good arm to ride and ordering Johnson forward. Soon after, the Rebel yell went up, and the entire line of Southerners advanced over abandoned Union breastworks and into the fields beyond. Both Johnson's and Hood's divisions were moving forward when a surprise attack by a hidden Union brigade began. One Union rifleman struck a key target, that of General Hood, who took a .50 caliber Minié ball (a primitive bullet) in the upper thigh of his right leg, breaking his femur, which is one of the most painful places for a break. When he fell off his horse, the men from his old

Texas Brigade caught him. Orderlies brought him to the rear, where his leg was eventually amputated, and his division, along with Johnson's and Kershaw's men, surged forward.

To the left of Hood's position was Confederate Major General Thomas Hindman, who was also pushing forward. All of this combined to begin a rout of the Union forces on the front lines. Davis's men began to fall back, and they eventually panicked and fled to the rear. As they did so, they ran head-on into Sheridan's division, causing that unit to become disorganized and eventually panic themselves. One can only imagine the cries that went out toward Sheridan's men: "Run! Save yourselves! The entire Rebel army is coming this way!" With Davis's and now Sheridan's men in a state of irretrievable panic, other units around them began to flee to the rear, directly toward Rosecrans's headquarters.

The only unit in the area to stand fast was quickly enveloped on three sides. The situation was hopeless, so its commander, Brigadier General William H. Lytle, who had been a lawyer and author before the war and a hard fighter during it, ordered a desperate last gasp charge into the enemy lines to his unit's front. Lytle cried out, "All right men, we can die but once. This is the time and place. Let us charge!" As the Union line moved out, its general was shot in the spine, but he still rode forward until three more bullets blew him from his saddle. He died shortly after. With their popular commander dead, Lytle's men fled rearward as best they could, with the survivors joining the other Union formations surging backward.

One of the men in Rosecrans's headquarters was a man sent by President Lincoln to observe the Tennessee theater: Assistant Secretary of War Charles Dana. Dana kept notes on the battle and wrote extensively on his war experiences after the conflict. He had been awake for almost two days and had just about fallen asleep in the grass when he was awakened by the sound of Longstreet's attack starting. After he collected himself, he rose and saw a disturbing sight: General Rosecrans on his knees, crossing himself. Dana realized that if Rosecrans was doing that openly, the situation must be dire. And it was. Dana got on his horse and looked about. He then witnessed the collapse of the Union right flank firsthand.

Near Dana, Rosecrans assembled as many of his staff as he could and told them, "If you care to live any longer, get away from here." Then, according to Dana, "the entire headquarters around me disappeared.

The graybacks [Southern soldiers] came through in a rush, and soon the musket balls and cannon shot reached the place where Rosecrans had just recently stood. The whole right of the army had apparently been routed."

Naturally, the Confederates were ecstatic (at least its generals, especially Longstreet, who has been in command of the breakthrough). A nearby Rebel cannoneer heard Longstreet exclaim, "They have fought their last man, and *he* is running." General Bragg had called on his generals to push the Union right into McLemore's Cove and destroy it, but this was better—the entire Union right had disappeared. Now the key was to pivot his troops from his left around like a swinging door and move them north to destroy the Union general from Virginia: George Henry Thomas.

As for Rosecrans and the rest of the Union right, they fled toward Chattanooga through a narrow gap in the formidable Missionary Ridge behind the Union lines. There, a group of journalists took note of how "men, animals, vehicles became a mass of struggling, cursing, shouting, frightened life." The headlong rush through the gap eventually became a clogged 1863 version of a traffic jam. Luckily for these men, the Rebels attacked north toward Thomas and not them.

In the chaos, General Rosecrans, along with his chief aide, James A. Garfield, tried to salvage what he could of the situation and reach General Sheridan, perhaps in the hope of forming a Union line a bit to the rear. But as he did so, Rosecrans, Garfield, and the men around them came under intense cannon and rifle fire, preventing them from reaching Sheridan. Rosecrans and Garfield then tried to take a back road toward Thomas's position, but they were blocked by the men in gray. They rode northward another five miles through the Rossville Gap. They decided to take a road they knew would lead to Thomas, but at that moment, as they rested their horses and listened, they could hear no fighting. The men dismounted and put their heads to the ground, but they could only hear the occasional fire in the distance. They asked Union stragglers for information, but they had little to tell except that they believed the entire army was in retreat. Some soldiers from Negley's brigade told them that their unit had been shot to pieces.

At hearing this, Rosecrans began to lose himself. If Negley's unit had been destroyed, that meant that Thomas's flank had been breached and that the fighting had likely ended in a Confederate victory on that part of the battlefield too. Despite that, Rosecrans decided he would ride to Thomas's last known position and see if he could rally the men. Garfield was to ride back to Chattanooga to begin organizing the defense of the city. Garfield did the right thing and reminded Rosecrans that he was the army commander and that his place was organizing Chattanooga's defense. He should put himself at risk in an unknown situation. Garfield would go in his place. At 4 p.m., a few hours later, Rosecrans arrived in Chattanooga, his legs too tired to let him dismount his horse without help.

Garfield would arrive at Thomas's headquarters at 4 p.m. as well. The ride was dangerous. Garfield's two orderlies had been killed, and Garfield himself had been seriously wounded. "Garfield's Ride" would be the heroic action that would propel him into the presidency in 1880 (he would be assassinated a little over six months after his inauguration by a disgruntled man who had been denied a government position). Garfield was also the one who birthed the legend of General Thomas. Garfield had a message telegraphed to Chattanooga, saying Thomas "was standing like a rock." That information was picked up by every newspaper in the Union even before word of the defeat at Chickamauga was reported. From then on, General Thomas would be known as the "Rock of Chickamauga."

Through the late afternoon and early evening, repeated Confederate attacks had pushed Thomas's line back into the horseshoe shape that gave his position its name, at least for the Union soldiers on it: "Horseshoe Ridge" (formerly known as "Snodgrass Hill"). Despite repeated Confederate attacks on three sides, which pushed them into a narrower and narrower position, Thomas's men did hold fast. A monument honoring them stands at Horseshoe Ridge today.

Chickamauga Snodgrass Hill
Gary Todd from Xinzheng, China, CC0, via Wikimedia Commons
https://commons.wikimedia.org/wiki/File:Chickamauga_Snodgrass_Hill_(10494286314).jpg

With the news from Garfield, Thomas was sure there was no possibility of a Union counterattack to relieve him. So, he set about creating a plan to extricate his men from the ever-tightening Confederate ring. Starting at dusk, each unit was to move out in line starting from the southernmost unit, which was commanded by General Reynolds. Each unit was to move to the rear of the one to its left, which would cover it as it left. They headed for McFarland's Gap and Chattanooga.

At 5:30, just as Reynolds's division was about to move out, it was hit by a strong Confederate attack led by St. John Liddell. This attack came so suddenly and with such ferocity that it threatened to break through Reynolds's line and enter Thomas's defensive ring. If that happened, all the men with Thomas would be killed or captured. General Thomas himself took command of one of Reynolds's brigades, and just as they were about to break, he rallied them and told them to charge: "There they are! Clear them out!" The Union men did just that, pushing the Rebel unit to the rear and taking two hundred prisoners. They then rejoined Reynolds's lines and began to move to the rear.

In almost total darkness, three Union formations remained: the 21st and 22nd Ohio and the 22nd Michigan. They had been fighting almost all day and night, and they were asked to cover the retreat. Union General Brannan called to nearby General George Gordon Granger, "The enemy are forming for another assault; we have not another round of ammunition—what should we do?" Granger replied, "Fix bayonets and go for them." Down the remaining Union line, the dreaded command "Fix bayonets!" rang out. Soon, the Union charge was moving forward, and the men actually pushed the Confederates back a bit before they realized the Northerners were out of ammunition. Soon, the Rebel units surrounded the charging Union men. From those three valiant regiments, over three hundred men were killed and wounded, and over five hundred were taken prisoner.

Still, this sacrifice and the skill with which the retreat was carried out saved the Union's left wing under Thomas. The Union men disappeared so well that many Southern units were unaware they were gone and actually began firing on their own men, many of whom were in positions that had just been occupied by the North.

General Longstreet was irritated that Thomas had slipped away, but his men were elated—they had won a great victory. As he retreated, one Federal lieutenant, the future writer Ambrose Bierce, recollected that he heard the Rebel yell as he retreated. "It was the ugliest sound that any mortal ever heard—even a mortal exhausted and unnerved by two days of hard fighting, without sleep, without rest, without food and without hope." Along the line of the Federal retreat were many wounded who were too hurt and exhausted to go on. They simply laid down on the side of the road and waited to die.

Thomas collected as many men for a defense at Rossville as he could in case the Rebels were hard on their heels, but they were not. In yet another misstep, Braxton Bragg could not be convinced that he had won a great victory, even though his generals and staff told him so. They encouraged him to reorganize his forces and press the Union back to Chattanooga before they had time to organize a defense, but he was not convinced, and he would not be moved. His officers even brought up a Confederate private who had witnessed the Union retreat to tell Bragg that the Union was fleeing in disarray. Bragg still would not believe it. He asked the soldiers, "Do you even know what a retreat looks like?" The soldier, not caring who he was talking to after days of fighting, simply said, "I ought to, General; I've been fighting with you during your whole campaign."

During the war, in the years after, and in the history books since, Bragg has been chided for not following up on his victory. Some say that his losses were so severe in both men and horses that the Confederate Army in Tennessee was in no condition to continue the fight. Others say that the Union was in worse shape, having sustained heavy losses as well as a demoralizing defeat, and that, at the very least, Bragg should have moved toward Chattanooga. Bragg's generals were angry, and Longstreet was critical of him from that moment until the day he died. Cavalry commander Nathan Bedford Forrest soon separated his command from Bragg after threatening his commander's life. D. H. Hill was a personal enemy until the day he died, as were others.

Bragg decided to move onto Missionary Ridge, where he could observe the many routes into Chattanooga and send out scouts for more information. He believed that Rosecrans was too far for immediate relief and supply and that he would slowly grind the Union position into submission and retake the city. This never happened. Though Rosecrans was removed from command shortly thereafter, he and the Union forces in the city quickly reorganized and slowly built up their strength, not the other way around. Soon, they would move out of the Chattanooga area and push the enemy back into Georgia at the Battle of Missionary Ridge, which happened two months later at the end of November.

Conclusion

The Battle of Chickamauga, the second-most bloodiest battle of the American Civil War, is largely forgotten today. Since it came so soon after what many people realized at the time was a turning point at Gettysburg, the battle was seen by the Southerners as a wasted opportunity to recapture Chattanooga and perhaps recapture much of Tennessee. For the Union, the loss of life was tragic, and General Rosecrans's career was over. However, the Union defeat was only temporary. After Missionary Ridge, they drove the Confederates off the Chickamauga battlefield and pushed them back even farther.

Still, the idea that Tennessee was lost was a hard one for the South to bear. Tennessee was important not only for resources but also as a conduit between the Confederate West and East, as well as an important member of the secession. Additionally, fighting in Tennessee would prevent the Union from driving through Georgia to the Atlantic coast, cutting the Confederacy in half in the East.

In December 1864, the Confederacy appointed recovered General John Bell Hood to attack central Tennessee to hopefully force the Union drive under Sherman in Georgia to halt. Hood's reckless aggression at the Battles of Nashville and Franklin, with the latter being a particularly bloody affair, probably sped the Southern collapse rather than slowed it. Hood lost men in reckless attacks that could have been better deployed in defense.

Today, Gettysburg, Vicksburg, Chancellorsville, and a whole host of other battles are remembered more than Chickamauga, but the men who fought and died there should be remembered in the same way as the veterans from those other more famous battles.

Part 11: The Battle of Atlanta

A Captivating Guide to a Battle of the Atlanta Campaign That Changed the Course of the American Civil War

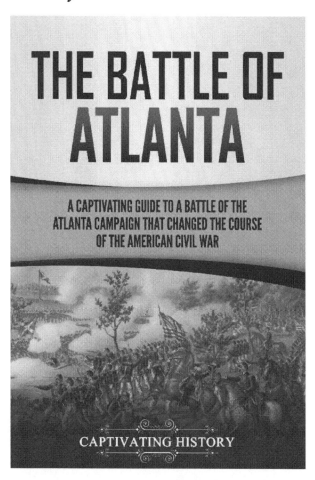

Introduction

"War is hell."

These three words encapsulate the raw brutality and unyielding suffering that accompanied the Battle of Atlanta. Ironically, Union General William Tecumseh Sherman said them. His brutal actions during the American Civil War reverberate through the annals of history because they showcase how true these words can be.

In 1864, a bloody reality descended upon the American South. What started as a fervent clash of principles transformed into an all-consuming war, with the Union Army representing the North and the Confederacy Army the South.

The flames of conflict engulfed the land, and Atlanta, Georgia, became a symbol of the Confederacy's resolve. Its capture or defense could sway the tide of the war. The Union general, known for his audacity and relentless "March to the Sea," firmly fixed his sights on the city. Although Atlanta's fate hung in the balance, Confederate General John Bell Hood fortified his defenses. He was determined to hold the city at all costs. All of this set the stage for a momentous battle as both armies converged on the war-torn area.

Our journey begins in the sweltering Georgia summer. Surrounded by the rolling hills and verdant landscapes of Atlanta, soldiers marched into history. These brave individuals hailed from all corners of the nation, donning blue and gray, united in their dedication to their respective causes. They were fathers, sons, brothers, and friends thrust into a crucible of fire and steel.

The soldiers had the type of grit that only war could summon. They braced themselves for the trials that lay ahead. Each of them endured the oppressive summer heat and thunderous cannon fire on the battlefield. They desired victory but also faced the ever-present specter of death and the longing for home.

However, the story of the Battle of Atlanta encompasses more than just the soldiers. The civilians found themselves swept in the maelstrom of war too. Men and women who called Atlanta home faced hardships that tested their resolve. The American Civil War was an encroaching danger that crept to their doorsteps and shattered their illusions of security. These civilians were forced to confront the brutal realities of conflict as the sound of artillery became a haunting lullaby.

Within Atlanta, families sought refuge and clung to fragments of normalcy amidst the chaos. Mothers consoled frightened children. Fathers braced themselves for the inevitable. Lovers clung to each other, their futures uncertain. Through their eyes, we witness the indomitable spirit that emerges when a city becomes a battleground. We share in their hopes and fears, losses and triumphs as they navigate the treacherous path between survival and despair.

The Battle of Atlanta stands as a testament to humans' capacity for both great heroism and profound tragedy. Get ready to journey into the heart of war, where echoes of the past resonate with haunting clarity. Better still, as you read this book, immerse yourself in the account by picturing yourself experiencing the events.

Imagine you're a soldier clad in the Union's blue or the Confederacy's gray. You're standing on the precipice of a battlefield. The air cracks with tension as the sun beats down mercilessly, mirroring the scorching turmoil that awaits. You can almost taste the acrid smoke that hangs heavy in the air, mingling with the stench of sweat and gunpowder. Can you hear the thunderous roar of cannons and the cries of your comrades-in-arms? Can you feel the weight of your weapon, your heart pounding in your chest, as you listen for the command to charge?

Maybe you're a woman who wants to fight as a soldier. No, you do not get a congratulatory pat on the back. Most people won't consider your becoming a soldier an honor. You don't even get the chance to enlist in the army even though you're fighting for your ideals and beliefs. Instead, you have to dress as a man, sneak out of the house, and pretend to be male.

Picture yourself as a wife watching your husband march off to battle. Anxiety grips your heart with each passing day. The silence of an empty home echoes with your worries and prayers, and you cling to memories, hoping they'll sustain you until his return. Or maybe you're a mother with the unbearable anguish of sending your young son off to war, a war he might never return from. Your heart clenches with each cannon's blast as you hope he is shielded from the horrors of battle.

Now, shift your perspective. You could be a husband bidding farewell to your beloved wife. Both of you know the uncertain fate that awaits. When your eyes meet, you see the love, fear, and longing in her. Can you sense the bittersweet ache of separation, the torment of not knowing if you'll ever hold each other again? You could be a father filled with pride and dread as you picture your son marching alongside seasoned soldiers. The weight of responsibility bears on your shoulders, and you can only hope he'll return to your embrace.

But war does not discriminate, nor does it spare the young. Imagine you're a young boy or girl peering through a cracked window as the battle rages on. Your mother tries to drag you off to the cellar, but you stay put. The world outside has transformed into a nightmarish symphony of chaos and destruction. The innocence of youth is shattered because you've witnessed the toll of war firsthand. The sight of wounded soldiers and the deafening cries of agony haunt your dreams, forever etching images of suffering onto your tender soul.

So, join me on this journey to step into the shoes of soldiers, husbands, wives, mothers, fathers, boys, and girls. Let us explore the Battle of Atlanta, not as distant spectators but as active participants in the tapestry of history.

Through the eyes of soldiers and civilians alike, we will unravel the threads of courage and desperation, tracing the contours of a battle that defined the American nation. Together, we'll discover the extraordinary stories of bravery and sacrifice, determination and resilience. We'll discover the enduring power of the human spirit in the face of unimaginable adversity. Welcome to the pages where history comes alive as we delve into a city where war became a literal hell.

Chapter 1 – Igniting the Fires of War

Let's travel back in time to the 19ᵗʰ century. Picture yourself standing at the crossroads of history where the fate of a nation teetered on a knife's edge. The year was 1864, and the American Civil War raged on with relentless fury.

But war doesn't begin in a day. It starts with differing opinions, opposing beliefs, unresolved conflicts, and skirmishes. The Civil War was no different. Although the nation's name was the *United* States of America, deep-seated tensions and conflicting ideologies divided it.

An Atlantan shop for auctioning and selling slaves (Negroes) in 1864.
https://commons.wikimedia.org/wiki/File:United_States_Colored_Troop_enlisted_African-American_soldier_reading_at_8_Whitehall_Street,_Atlanta_slave_auction_house,_Fall_1864-%27Auction_%26_Negro_Sales,%27_Whitehall_Street_LOC_cwpb.03351_(cropped).tif

It all began with a subject that would prove to be the powder keg of discord: slavery. The institution of slavery had become an increasingly divisive issue in America, pitting the North and South against each other like two rival siblings.

The North flourished with its factories and industrialized cities. Its burgeoning industrial economy and growing sense of moral outrage fueled a powerful anti-slavery sentiment. The South, on the other hand, depended on an agrarian economy. Slavery was an integral part of life in the Southern states. Farmers relied on enslaved labor to cultivate cotton and other cash crops, while others bought slaves to do menial jobs. The clash of these distinct economies created a deep rift that seemed insurmountable.

As sectional tensions rose, the question of states' rights versus federal authority loomed large. The Southern states staunchly defended states' rights to protect their individual liberties. They believed that each state had the autonomy to govern itself as it saw fit. Southern states wanted to be free from excessive interference from the federal government because they felt increasingly marginalized in national politics. Meanwhile, the North advocated for a more centralized authority to preserve the nation's unity.

Political factions emerged, with passionate individuals on both sides rallying behind their causes. Abraham Lincoln was elected president of the United States in 1860. This event served as a pivotal lightning rod that intensified the already simmering tensions. It set the stage for a conflict that would test the very fabric of the nation.

First, Lincoln was a Republican—a party that had little appeal to voters in the South. Almost all his votes came from the North. He won without even carrying a single Southern state. Second, he had an anti-slavery stance and a commitment to preserve the union of the states. So, he was a threat to the South's economic reliance on slavery.

To protect their interests, Southern states swiftly seceded from the Union. South Carolina took the lead, followed by six more states: Georgia, Mississippi, Alabama, Florida, Louisiana, and Texas. Four other Southern states joined them later. They united under a different flag and claimed their independence from the United States. The new nation was called the Confederate States of America.

The bombardment of Fort Sumter.

Finally, the die was cast for a conflict of epic proportions. The tension reached its breaking point at Fort Sumter on April 12th, 1861. This federal fort, situated in Charleston, South Carolina, became the site of the first shots fired in the Civil War. The Confederacy bombarded the military garrison at the fort, demanding its surrender, while President Lincoln sought to resupply and reinforce it. As negotiations broke down, cannons roared, and shells exploded. After thirty-four hours, the Union surrendered. No one was killed in the conflict, but this battle marked the beginning of the Civil War, the bloodiest conflict in American history.

Atlanta, Georgia, soon emerged as a critical hub of the South. It radiated both economic and military significance. This city was a symbol of the Confederacy's resilience, making it a prime target for the Union forces. What made Atlanta such a coveted prize, you may wonder? Well, let's rewind a little to the state of the bustling metropolis before the war.

Before the storm clouds of war rolled in, Atlanta was a city teeming with life and aspirations. Here, the old South mingled with progressive ambition, and the city beckoned dreamers and visionaries alike. It was the melding of old-world charm and burgeoning modernity. Victorian mansions whispered tales of Southern hospitality and charm, while factories and mills were the lifeblood of progress.

Think about the cobblestone paths of the late 1800s, the symphony of horse-drawn carriages and echoing footsteps dancing in harmony with the vibrant spirit of the city. Streets bustled with merchants, theaters echoed with laughter, and the neighborhoods hummed with the rhythm of daily life. Families, both Union and Confederate sympathizers, called this city their home, and dreams of a prosperous future resided in their hearts.

Atlanta boasted an intricate web of railroads that converged within its borders. It served as a linchpin holding the South together. It was a vital center for the Confederate Army's military operations and a critical transportation hub. Since the city was strategically located at the crossroads of several major rail lines, it connected the South to vital resources. Troops, supplies, and communication flowed through the city to support the Confederate forces on the front lines, enabling the Confederacy to wage war effectively.

But Atlanta was more than just a logistical stronghold. It was also a key supply center. It produced and warehoused vast quantities of provisions, ammunition, uniforms, and equipment, which sustained the Southern effort.

The city's communication network facilitated the dissemination of information. Its telegraph lines connected various command centers, enabling the faster transmission of orders and intelligence. Messages, orders, and other vital information from allies and spies quickly got to the Confederate Army. This web of communication allowed for swift coordination and response to Union movements. It gave the Confederacy an advantage in the ever-shifting tides of war.

The economic and industrial significance of Atlanta further solidified its importance. It had a diverse range of businesses and industries, including ironworks, foundries producing munitions, and mills churning out textiles. The city's industrial output fueled the Southern cause, providing the means to sustain the fight against the Union.

Beyond its military and economic importance, Atlanta held a symbolic weight that transcended its physical attributes. It represented the heart and soul of the Confederacy. It was a resilient bastion of Southern values, culture, determination, and defiance. Capturing the city would be a blow to the South's morale, as its defense had become a point of pride.

The city fueled the Southern war machine, making it a prime target of the Union. Its capture or defense had great importance to both sides.

Preparing to face the impending storm of Union aggression, Confederate forces bolstered Atlanta's defenses by constructing fortifications. Meanwhile, Union General William Tecumseh Sherman was unwaveringly resolved to cripple the South. Atlanta was the key to unlocking the North's ultimate victory. It was a formidable obstacle in his path.

Now that the stage had been set and the players assembled, it was only a matter of time before the Battle of Atlanta occurred. To understand the battle better, we need to look at the events that led to it and its key players.

Chapter 2 – The Key Players

The Battle of Atlanta had three prominent commanders: General William Tecumseh Sherman, General Joseph Eggleston Johnston, and General John Bell Hood. Each man had unique attributes, background, personality, and outlook on the Civil War, which shaped his plans and strategies. Let us delve into their minds as they prepared for the cataclysmic confrontation that awaited them.

General William Tecumseh Sherman.
No known restrictions; https://www.loc.gov/resource/cwpb.03379/

Born in 1820 in Ohio, General William T. Sherman's early life was marked by tragedy and hardship. His father died when he was just nine, leaving his family in financial distress. Luckily, his father's friend and neighbor, Thomas Ewing, informally adopted him. Sherman later secured a congressional appointment to the United States Military Academy at West Point. There, he cultivated his military knowledge and honed his leadership skills.

General Sherman was physically imposing. He had a sturdy and tall frame. A graying beard and receding hairline framed his face. His weathered features depicted a man hardened by the trials of war. His piercing, steely gaze held an intensity that revealed a man constantly calculating and searching for the best course of action.

Sherman had a unique blend of boldness and pragmatism. He was fiercely determined and focused. He possessed a relentless drive to achieve victory. Beneath his stern exterior lay a man of keen intellect, sharp wit, and a gift for strategy. He wasn't afraid to take risks, seize opportunities, or adapt swiftly to changing circumstances.

During the Civil War, Sherman distinguished himself at the Battle of Bull Run in 1861. He later served under General Ulysses S. Grant at Shiloh, where he was promoted to major general.

Once he understood the importance of Atlanta, the general began the Atlanta Campaign. His plan was audacious yet calculated. He wanted to outflank and outmaneuver the Confederate forces defending the city. By cutting off supply lines and weakening defenses, he planned to force the Southern army into a vulnerable position and seize control of Atlanta, ultimately securing the prize he sought.

Sherman employed the strategy of total war to achieve his aim. This concept involved uncompromising aggression toward the enemy's armies and civilian populations. He believed in striking at the heart of the Confederate war effort by targeting military installations and civilian infrastructure and resources. He planned to destroy the economic resources of the Southern population, break their will, and cripple their capacity to continue the fight. It was a brutal but what he believed necessary approach to achieving a swift Union victory.

General Joseph Eggleston Johnston.

Initially opposing Sherman in the Atlanta Campaign was General Joseph E. Johnston. He was born in 1807 to a prominent military family in Virginia. Johnston also attended the Military Academy at West Point. He demonstrated his aptitude for military studies and then served in the Mexican-American War, where he earned accolades for bravery and leadership.

General Johnston was a respected military commander with a dignified appearance that commanded attention and exuded an air of confidence. He had a neatly trimmed beard and a lean and athletic frame that belied his years. Johnston was a master of defensive warfare. He was well known for his meticulous planning and keen sense of military tactics. He employed caution, intellect, and acumen in battle. He was calm and composed under pressure. The general possessed a quiet resolve that earned him the respect and admiration of his troops.

Johnston's approach to the war contrasted starkly with Sherman's aggressive mindset. He understood that the South had limited manpower and resources. So, he advocated attrition rather than attack.

The Confederate general aimed to protect Atlanta with carefully constructed defensive lines. He believed in preserving his forces by avoiding direct confrontations unless conditions were favorable. Johnston sought to wear down the Union Army through guerilla tactics and defensive maneuvers.

His ultimate goal was to force Sherman into a costly and protracted siege. This would weaken the Union's resolve, encouraging them to make mistakes. The Southern army would then exploit the enemy's weaknesses and win.

However, Johnston's cautious approach occasionally brought him into conflict with Confederate President Jefferson Davis and other leaders who sought more aggressive action. Johnston's tendency to retreat and avoid decisive battles led to strained relationships. It also resulted in occasional reassignments during the war. That was what happened during the Atlanta Campaign, just before the Battle of Atlanta. Johnston was reassigned because his battle tactics were too defensive.

Despite these challenges, the general remained highly respected among his fellow officers. His reputation as a skilled strategist, commitment to his soldiers' well-being, and compassionate leadership endeared him to his troops, who affectionately called him "Uncle Joe."

General John Bell Hood.
https://commons.wikimedia.org/wiki/File:Lt._Gen._John_B._Hood.jpg

General John Bell Hood took over command of the Confederate Army of Tennessee from General Johnston. Hood was born in 1831 in Kentucky to a physician. He graduated from the United States Military Academy at twenty-two and joined the Confederate Army during the Civil War.

Possessing a sturdy build, prominent chin, and strong jawline, Hood had a rugged appearance that contributed to his commanding presence. He was a courageous risk-taker known for his audacity and bravery on the battlefield. He exhibited a strong sense of duty and loyalty to the Confederate cause.

Hood willingly partook in the dangers his troops faced by leading them from the front lines. He ended up sustaining injuries before the Battle of Atlanta. His left arm got wounded at Gettysburg, rendering the arm unusable. The next month, his leg was severely wounded in the Battle of Chickamauga, which led to amputating it four inches below the hip. Hood then had to rely on a manservant to help with daily tasks and crutches for movement.

Yet, even in the face of overwhelming odds, the general fought actively to defend the South. And it paid off. He was one of the most rapidly promoted officers in the Confederate Army.

Hood's leadership style was marked by his offensive-minded approach. He sought decisive victories on the battlefield by favoring direct assaults over cautious defensive strategies. He believed that taking the fight to the Union forces would enable his army to give them a decisive blow, which could weaken Northern resolve and pave the way for Confederate success. While he demonstrated tactical skill, his aggressive strategies often came at a high cost. However, his style was in line with what the Confederate president and leaders favored.

As a proud and determined commander, Hood resolved to hold onto Atlanta at all costs. He intended to rely on the city's fortifications. Then, he would engage in an offensive battle by drawing out the Union Army, attacking them, and inflicting heavy casualties. The general hoped to exploit the rugged terrain. If his army could wear down the Northern forces, he would outlast Sherman's advance and maintain control of Atlanta.

It was a risky gambit, but Hood was solely focused on the defense of Atlanta. He was willing to stake everything in his quest for victory, even if it meant sacrificing his own troops.

These three generals were instrumental in the Atlanta Campaign, especially William Sherman and John Hood, who fought against each other. Other key players were the Union and Confederate soldiers.

A variety of things pushed the Union soldiers to take up arms. Many of them went to war out of duty and patriotism. They believed it was their responsibility to defend the Union. These men saw the Confederate cause as a threat to the very idea of the Union. They also saw the battle as an opportunity to end slavery and create a more just society. Lincoln's Emancipation Proclamation allowed African Americans to enlist in the Union Army.

But it wasn't just big ideas that motivated these soldiers. Many fought to protect their homes. They didn't want Confederate forces to invade their communities, and they were willing to risk everything to keep their families safe.

Others enlisted for the promise of a regular paycheck. They hoped to escape the hardships of civilian life by earning money in the army. As soldiers, they would secure a stable income and provide for their families.

On the Confederate side, the motivations were slightly different but no less powerful. The soldiers saw the Union invasion as a threat to their property and the traditions they held dear, and they wanted to protect their families, land, and communities. To them, the battle was a pivotal moment in their struggle against Northern aggression.

Southern loyalty and patriotism were powerful driving forces for Confederate soldiers. Their allegiance to the South influenced their actions on the battlefield. A good example of such a soldier is Samuel Rush Watkins. He served in Company H in the Tennessee infantry regiment during the Atlanta Campaign. Watkins had a deep attachment to his homeland and a sense of duty to defend it against the North or the Yankees.

For some Confederate soldiers, the defense of slavery was a key motivation. They believed in preserving the institution of slavery because it was integral to their economic prowess.

Others stood by honor and duty. They were guided by principles of chivalry, courage, and loyalty and saw themselves as guardians of Southern heritage. They fought with unwavering determination. Surrender or retreat wasn't an option for them.

As soldiers from both sides fought during the Atlanta Campaign, they were driven by duty, patriotism, family, and deeply held convictions. Their motivations were constantly tested on the battlefield.

Besides the soldiers and famous battle heroes of Atlanta, there were unsung heroes who must be mentioned.

Within the city, people and institutions emerged as towers of support. As far back as 1862, hotels and municipal buildings became makeshift hospitals. Even the Atlanta Medical College suspended its classes to tend to wounded soldiers. A sprawling hospital complex was built on the fairgrounds by the Georgia Railroad. It provided aid to the countless casualties of war and helped relieve the already overcrowded hospitals.

Businesses like the Atlanta Rolling Mill were also key players. The mill was one of two in the South that could produce railroad rails, and it shifted its focus during the Civil War. Once re-rolling old rails, it now churned out iron sheets for Confederate ships, iron rails for the railroads, and cannons for the battlefields. It was a symbol of Southern industry and resilience. The mill was bought out and renamed the Confederate Rolling Mill in 1863.

Unfortunately, Georgia was wrought with problems. The Civil War's relentless march led to food shortages, particularly for yeoman or non-slaveholding farmers' families. Riots and looting erupted, as people, driven by the hunger gnawing in their stomachs and the desire to provide for their families, saw no other option for survival. Some women in Atlanta faced the agonizing decision to stay and endure the horrors of war or flee to safety. They took their children and journeyed away from the turmoil.

But in that same Atlanta, other women emerged as pillars of strength. The elite white women used their influence to encourage enlistment into the army. They appealed to the men's sense of masculinity and honor to inspire them to fight for the Confederacy.

While their husbands and sons ventured off to the battlefields, Atlanta's women took charge of their homes. Women of all classes took on roles that had been previously denied to them and became the backbone of the family. They became the managers of family farms, homes, plantations, and businesses. Working-class women found jobs in factories and arsenals. However, these opportunities were often limited to white women.

Other women helped their struggling neighbors by creating fundraising groups to support them. They formed aid societies to craft essentials for soldiers, which included socks, shirts, gloves, bandages, and blankets.

However, their contributions extended far beyond the realm of helping soldiers or families. Brave women operated as spies and scouts who gathered intelligence. Despite the constant threat of discovery, they moved past enemy lines and then conveyed crucial information about troop movements, supplies, and strategies. In doing so, they exhibited a kind of courage that challenged the norms of their time.

Some took their commitment even further. They disguised themselves as men and enlisted in the Union or Confederate army and donned the uniforms of soldiers. These women embraced the call of duty with a fervor that defied societal norms. They marched into battle, shouldered rifles, and shared the same dangers as their male counterparts.

Some females worked as nurses and volunteers in hospitals. A sixteen-year-old girl named Augusta "Gussie" King Clayton volunteered in a military hospital. In these hospitals, countless lives hung in the balance. Gussie provided a ray of hope by caring for wounded soldiers, nursing the sick, reading to the wounded, offering words of comfort, and writing letters to their loved ones. She fell victim to typhoid, a fatal disease during the Civil War. When Sherman's army arrived at the outskirts of Atlanta, Gussie was fighting for her life.

African Americans were not left out. Born into a world that had enslaved them for generations, all they knew was the bitter taste of oppression. But on January 1st, 1863, President Abraham Lincoln issued the Emancipation Proclamation that freed all slaves living in the Confederate States.

This decree was a beacon of hope for African Americans in the South. To them, the war was no longer just a fight between the North and South but a catalyst for liberation. It was a war for their very humanity, a battle to break the chains of bondage that had bound them for so long. Now, they could fight for the right to be treated as equals. Many African American men eagerly joined the Union Army, forming regiments known as the United States Colored Troops (USCT).

Unfortunately, General Sherman did not let USCT soldiers fight in his ranks. His decision did not deter some African Americans. They decided to become teamsters, general laborers, and cooks for the Union Army. At least four hundred African American cooks actively worked on the war front during the Battle of Atlanta as stretcher-bearers.

All these men and women played an active role in the Battle of Atlanta. While some of them were at the battlefront, others helped with the smooth running of operations and the well-being of soldiers during the war. Some others were on the home front, contributing in whatever way they could.

Chapter 3 – Prelude to the Battle

The sweltering summer of 1864 set the backdrop for the Battle of Atlanta. But before the clash of arms commenced, a series of events shaped the course of the conflict.

In May 1864, the Atlanta Campaign was born. General Sherman gathered his forces—the Union Army of the Cumberland, Army of the Tennessee, and Army of the Ohio—and began the relentless advance toward Atlanta. He was on a mission to seize control of the city.

The air was thick with anticipation as the Union soldiers pressed forward, their hearts filled with a thirst for victory. Their boots stirred up clouds of dust that clung to their uniform and coated their weary bodies. Sweat trickled down their faces, merging with the dirt and leaving salty trails on their skin. The scent of dirt and sweat mingled together, creating a distinctive aroma that permeated the air, a testament to the physical toll the soldiers endured.

The men trudged through heat and torrential downpours, their bodies weary, their spirits tested. They endured the sting of insect bites and the discomfort of damp uniforms. With each step, they felt the harsh terrain beneath their worn-out boots. The uneven ground, littered with rocks and tree roots, challenged their balance.

Yet, they pressed on, their minds aflame with the desire to see this campaign through. The determination to seize Atlanta and bring an end to the Confederacy's grip on the region fueled their spirits. From May to July, they fought battles along the way, such as the Battle of Resaca and the Battle of Kennesaw Mountain. In each battle, Union forces clashed with Confederate defenders.

General Sherman employed flanking strategies to outmaneuver General Johnston's defensive positions. He used swift strikes to keep the Southern forces off balance. His army launched a series of frontal assaults but faced fierce resistance. The Northern forces continued their flanking maneuvers, forcing the Confederates to retreat repeatedly. However, Sherman's path wasn't without its trials. As the campaign wore on, he faced setbacks and challenges that tested his mettle.

The Confederate Army of Tennessee, under the command of General Joseph Johnston, faced the daunting task of repelling the Union advance. Johnston recognized the numerical advantage, tenacity, and resourcefulness of his adversary. So, he refused to engage in a direct confrontation.

In an attempt to delay the Union Army's progress, he combined defensive tactics with strategic retreats. The formidable terrain and natural landscape barriers of Georgia served as valuable assets in the South's defense. Johnston used defensive warfare to buy time while waiting for the opportune moment to strike a decisive blow.

These were battles of wit as the two generals sought to outmaneuver each other, each vying for the upper hand. The campaign stretched on, the tension building with each passing day.

Confederate fortifications at Atlanta.
No known restrictions; <u>*https://www.loc.gov/item/2012646711/*</u>

Meanwhile, the Southern army had been building fortifications around Atlanta for more than a year. They intensified their efforts earlier in the summer when they heard that Sherman's forces had left Chattanooga and were marching toward Atlanta.

The Southern forces embarked on a feverish effort to transform the city into a fortress. The Confederate soldiers made slaves toil tirelessly as they raced against time to fortify their position for the inevitable battle. The civilians could hear the sound of hammers and shovels echo through the streets as men dug trenches and erected earthworks. The enslaved laborers' hands grew calloused and blistered, their muscles aching.

By July 1864, the landscape around Atlanta had transformed into a network of trenches and fortifications. Two concentric rings of fortifications arose from the Georgia soil. The inner ring was the defensive bulwarks. Stern-faced soldiers armed with glinting musket barrels stood inside the ring. They were always alert, their eyes fixed on the horizon where the Union forces approached.

The outer ring was a giant maze, a labyrinth of earthen palisades and winding trenches that snaked their way around Atlanta's outskirts. This was a cunning device intended to slow the relentless advance of the Union troops. It would serve as a barrier between the Confederates and the Union onslaught.

The Southern army stored ammunition, food, and other essential provisions in several places in the city. Artillery became the heartbeat of their defense. They handpicked cannon placements to provide maximum coverage and firepower. The soldiers positioned their cannons on high ground, allowing them to rain devastating fire on the Northern troops as they advanced. These strategically placed artillery pieces formed a formidable barrier.

However, Confederate President Jefferson Davis was dissatisfied with General Johnston's performance. Despite Johnston's cautious approach, Sherman's forces gained ground and pressed southward toward Atlanta.

Davis and other high-ranking officials favored aggressive strategies and believed Johnston wasn't doing enough to defend Atlanta. Prior to his command in Atlanta, the general had lost key battles, including the Peninsula Campaign and the defense of Richmond. His past record in battle eroded confidence in his leadership abilities. Besides, the Confederates had lost important strongholds, such as Chattanooga and

Vicksburg. The Confederate government faced mounting pressure to defend Atlanta, a vital transportation and industrial center for the Confederacy.

Wagon train leaving Atlanta in 1864.
https://en.m.wikipedia.org/wiki/File:LastTrainAtlantaDepot1864crop1.jpg

As the Union forces closed in on the city, Johnston ordered the evacuation of the military hospitals and ammunition machinery in Atlanta. Residents were distressed about the approaching Northern troops, and some fled. The urgency to defend Atlanta intensified.

There was a growing belief that Confederate forces needed a change in command to bolster Atlanta's defenses and mount a more aggressive resistance. The government felt that a more offensive-minded commander would prevent the loss of the city by confronting the Northern forces head-on. A week later, President Davis relieved Johnston of his command. Davis replaced him with General John Bell Hood, a lieutenant general and corps commander in the Army of Tennessee.

Hood, known for his more assertive approach, was seen as a better fit for defending Atlanta. He assumed his new position on July 17th, 1864, and was made a full general with temporary rank the next day.

By this time, the Union Army was five miles away from the outskirts of Atlanta. Once Hood took over the reins of the Confederate Army of Tennessee, he sought to shift the strategy of his forces from defense to offense. He hoped to take the fight directly to Sherman and inflict a crippling blow that would drive the Union Army from the gates of Atlanta.

While Sherman's forces were advancing toward the city from other directions, the Army of the Cumberland, commanded by General George H. Thomas, was crossing Peach Tree Creek. This was one of the three armies that had combined to form the Union forces under Sherman. General Hood saw this event as an opportunity to devastate the enemy's forces. His aim was to isolate and destroy the Cumberland troops before the other two armies could render assistance. On the night of July 19th, Hood met with his generals and planned an attack on Thomas's army.

The stage was set for a decisive confrontation. The Union's disposition on that fateful night seemed to beckon the Confederates to attack. The plan, in theory, was sound. Thomas's troops were spread thin and were vulnerable in their unfortified positions while crossing Peach Tree Creek. They were also miles away from other Union troops.

But as the first rays of dawn bathed the battlefield on July 20th, General Hood's grand design began to unravel. The Battle of Peach Tree Creek unfolded with a series of missteps that sent his plan spiraling into disarray. Thomas's forces had made staggering progress under cover of night, forcing the Confederate right flank to reposition itself, which wasted precious time. Within that period, the Union Army boldly established its defensive positions.

The sun hung high in the sky, casting a golden glow upon the battlefield. But time wasn't on Hood's side. It wasn't until 3:30 p.m. that the South's right flank launched an attack. The crack of musket fire filled the air as Union soldiers unleashed a storm of lead upon the advancing Confederates. The Southerners, unfettered, pressed on, launching relentless charges.

For a short while, the Confederate attackers threatened to envelop the Union lines. In a brief glimmer of hope, the Southerners temporarily overran a portion of the Northern lines. But their triumph was short-lived. The Union Army regrouped and pushed back with a vengeance. They swiftly adjusted their defenses, holding the line with unwavering resolve. Their counterattack forced the Confederate troops to retreat.

As the sun set, the Confederates recognized the futility of further engagement and withdrew. The Battle of Peach Tree Creek had come to a bitter end. Hood's plan had crumbled beneath the weight of fierce Union resistance. The once-promising attack had faltered, leaving behind the memory of failure.

The battlefield lay cloaked in an eerie stillness, broken only by the soft moans of the wounded and the rumble of retreating Confederate soldiers. The dust and smoke, once stirred by the relentless clashes, now hung in the air like a somber shroud. The sun set on a landscape marred by the carnage of battle, casting long shadows over the fallen. Hood's aspiration of victory had been dashed. The brave souls who fought under his command were left to grapple with the bitter taste of defeat.

The casualty count told a grim tale. Around 2,500 Confederate lives were lost, while the Union forces mourned approximately 1,750 comrades. The Battle of Peach Tree Creek drew blood on both sides. It was a clash where dreams of victory collided with the harsh realities of war. It foreshadowed the intensity of the conflict yet to come.

The sights and sounds of the battlefield, the cries of bravery, and the stench of gunpowder were etched into the memories of the soldiers involved. For Hood, it was a bitter setback and a blow that tested his resolve.

On the other hand, the Battle of Peach Tree Creek further strengthened Sherman's position. Although the Union forces achieved a tactical victory, it wasn't without cost.

As the Union forces drew close to Atlanta, a sense of anticipation filled the air. The city loomed on the horizon, a beacon of Confederate pride and defiance. The Northern soldiers could almost taste victory, a bittersweet taste on their tongue, knowing that it would come at a great cost.

The once-thriving Atlanta, known as the gate city of the South, now lay under the shadow of impending doom. The lives of civilians far from the front lines weren't less harrowing. From the porch of her home, nine-year-old Carrie Berry could hear the war. Quiet days had become increasingly rare. Instead, they were replaced with the distant rumble of cannons and the sharp crack of muskets. Carrie dreaded the shells the most. They broke through structures, causing many deaths.

There was only one sanctuary when the shells descended—the cellar. The walls were a bit thicker, the air a tad more breathable. It offered a fragile shield against the onslaught. Carrie and her family huddled together in there when the shells descended, but that didn't stop them from experiencing the destruction the shells brought. One busted under their dining room. Another passed through the smokehouse and fell through the top of their house. Luckily, they were in Carrie's aunt's home when the shells damaged their house.

This was the grim reality for Atlantan civilians. Streets that once bustled with commerce were now filled with danger and hushed whispers. The state of Atlanta mirrored the state of its people. It was a city teetering between hope and despair. The tension was palpable. In this raging war, the fate of Atlanta hung precariously in the balance.

Chapter 4 – The Midnight March

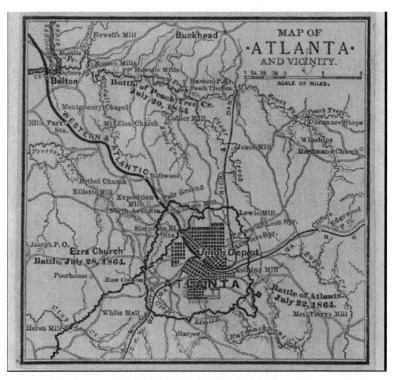

Map of Atlanta during the Civil War.

After the Union victory at the Battle of Peach Tree Creek, General Sherman shifted his focus to the Army of Tennessee commanded by Major General James B. McPherson. He needed a vantage point for his soldiers, somewhere he and his commander could easily observe Atlanta and fight with a higher chance of victory. The most logical place to set up camp was Bald Hill, which overlooked the Georgia Railroad junction connecting Atlanta to Decatur.

General Hood, anticipating the move, sent his troops to Bald Hill. About two thousand cavalrymen from his army got there first and occupied the hill. The Union troops descended on them like a tempest, attacking at mid-morning on July 21st. The Confederates fought fiercely, but they were forced to withdraw to a nearby wooded tract, leaving Bald Hill to the Federals.

Hood did not give up, though. He was resolute and determined to win Bald Hill back, so he drew up plans for a daring maneuver. He arranged for some soldiers to guard Atlanta from the inner ring fortification, then ordered the rest of his troops to embark on a long night march, aiming to come in behind the Northern forces. This would disrupt the Union position and turn the tide of the battle.

However, in the fog of war, the Southern general had overlooked a crucial detail. His plan hinged on his commander withdrawing his men from battle, a task easier said than done. Hours passed, and the night grew darker before the Confederate forces assembled and began their fifteen-mile march. The Confederate skirmishers held their positions to mask the withdrawal of the seventeen thousand to eighteen thousand soldiers.

There must have been a seemingly endless column of weary men, their boots shuffling on the dusty road. Remember, they had fought the Battle of Peach Tree Creek on July 20th and fought off the attacking Union forces the next day. Yet, that same night, they were trekking to attack the Northern army's left flank. Maybe the moon was out that night, and the twinkling stars were the Confederate soldiers' guiding light. Or it could have been a night of thick darkness. The path ahead would have been illuminated by the occasional flicker of a lantern casting eerie shadows on the marching brigade of soldiers.

The night was filled with hushed footfalls and jingling equipment. The rifles' carry-on straps pressed into the soldiers' shoulders. The ever-present humidity clung to their skin. The soldiers' gray uniforms were stained with sweat and dust from the road. With each step in the dense, shadowy woods, the chill of the night crept into their uniforms.

These soldiers couldn't stop their trek to even make a campfire for the night because they had an audacious goal in their minds. They would attack the weakened rear of the Union Army's left flank in the morning and then destroy Sherman's supply train. But by the time morning light crept over the battlefield, Hood's troops had barely reached the halfway point of their journey.

Sherman had his own gambit unfolding. He had moved his headquarters to Augustus Hurt House, Decatur, which was strategically located on a nearby hill just two miles east of Atlanta. He surveyed the city's fortifications from the high ground. It was a commander's view of the battlefield, which could be likened to a chessboard.

Sherman believed that conquering Atlanta would hasten the end of the Civil War, and he had to do everything possible to take the city from the Confederates and annihilate its power. So, he sent the Army of the Tennessee to destroy the Georgia Railroad that came into Atlanta from the east.

As dawn's first light illuminated the sky, Sherman received good news: Hood's forces had vacated the outer ring of the city's defenses. Not wanting to waste such an awesome opportunity, the general ordered his troops to pursue them. He was about to send an infantry corps away from his left flank when McPherson cautioned him that it would make the army vulnerable. Sherman listened to McPherson's counsel and rescinded his orders, a decision that would prove to be the salvation of the Union forces.

McPherson arranged his thirty-five thousand troops in a sprawling L-shaped formation. The vertical section faced north-south, while the horizontal section extended east-west. Bald Hill, later to be named Leggett's Hill, was fortified with cannons and a sentinel overlooking the battlefield.

Unfortunately for Hood, fate had other designs for him and his audacious attack strategy. His army was hampered by the harsh terrain. He also didn't know the full extent of McPherson's formidable line. When the general's infantry took their positions, they were six agonizing hours behind schedule, and McPherson was ready for him.

The Battle of Atlanta was about to begin. The night march had brought the Confederate forces to a moment that would define their lives and the course of history. Although the troops met a different situation from what they expected, they stood ready to face whatever the day would bring.

Chapter 5 – A Bloody Battle of Crimson

July 22nd, 1864, dawned with a palpable sense of anticipation. General Hood had strategized for the Battle of Atlanta by planning to catch the weakened rear of the Union troops unawares. But as the day unfolded, it became clear that his attack faced insurmountable challenges.

The rugged terrain, which had been an advantage during General Johnston's command, slowed the Southern army's advance to a crawl. So, the attack Hood planned as a dawn assault was delayed until the afternoon.

Sweat-soaked uniforms clung to the skin of the Southern soldiers. The Confederates were weary from their nightlong journey by the time they arrived, but they found themselves facing well-entrenched Northern troops. The Confederates were directly in front of fortified Union soldiers. McPherson had also extended his line eastward. The front lines were etched along Flat Shoals Road and Moreland Avenue, stretching from the vibrant East Atlanta Village to where the Inman Park MARTA station stands today.

The over seventy-five thousand soldiers wearing the Northern blue and Confederate gray stood before each other, and both sides began to battle. Commanders shouted orders, and each army moved as a unit. While the heat from the sun pressed down upon them, the soldiers focused on winning the battle.

General Hood watched the battle from the home of Atlanta Mayor James Calhoun. The house, which was at the highest point of where Historic Oakland Cemetery stands today, provided a commanding view of the clash. Sherman watched the battle from his vantage point, which was opposite Hood's location. His mind calculated every move as the soldiers fought.

For a brief moment, Hood's troops breached the Union lines. The Confederate soldiers exploited the newly gained position by attacking the Yankees with a visceral intensity. McPherson noticed that there was a chink in that position and galloped toward it to inspect the ongoing battle. Hood's infantry noticed him and shot him. He died a short while later.

Despite McPherson's death, the Union soldiers' spirits were not broken. They held their positions atop Bald Hill. They drove the Confederates back, and the South's newly gained position quickly slipped through the Southern troops' grasp.

As the sun beat down mercilessly, the cacophony of war prevailed. The deafening roar of cannon and musket fire drowned out natural sounds in the environment. The acrid stench of spent gunpowder mingled with the heavy, sweat-soaked air. Union and Confederate forces clashed with primal fury. Wave after wave of Hood's troops surged up the hill, their battle cries loud and unrelenting. The Northern soldiers met the onslaught with unwavering resolve. Despite the ferocity and relentless push of the South's infantry, they held the line.

By late afternoon, the sun cast long shadows on the battlefield. The Confederates exploited another weak spot in the Union lines. They attacked a vulnerable spot at an exposed railroad to the north. Aware of their precarious position, Sherman's forces retreated eastward.

However, a Union commander led a valiant counterattack, preventing reinforcements from reaching Hood's soldiers. The Confederate forces were repulsed again and again, their ranks thinning with every futile charge.

As the day wore on, the nice green fields turned a gruesome shade of crimson with the blood of the fallen. The bodies of Southern and Northern soldiers lay in macabre piles, their forms twisted and mingled by the merciless hail of bullets. It was a tableau of death and destruction. It was a chilling sight, even for those who had seen the horrors of war before. The battle, which lasted around nine hours, exacted a heavy toll on both sides. The Confederate troops were forced to retreat when they could no longer bear any more losses.

When the dust and smoke finally settled, the full extent of the battle's devastation became painfully clear. The South suffered approximately 5,500 causalities (either dead, wounded, captured, or missing). The Union forces also paid a steep price for victory, with about 3,700 casualties. The cost of this battle was dire. Two major generals, James Birdseye McPherson of the Union Army and William Henry Talbot Walker of the Confederate Army, never left the battlefield alive. Their loss was keenly felt by both armies.

But the toll extended beyond the battlefield. On that same fateful day, Augusta "Gussie" King Clayton, who had been volunteering in Atlanta's military hospitals, died from typhoid. Her passing was a heart-wrenching loss deeply felt by her family and the city. With shells still raining upon Atlanta, Gussie's family couldn't hold a proper funeral for her. Instead, they laid her to rest in the family garden. It was a somber and makeshift farewell to a young life cut short too soon.

To Sherman, the battle had not reached a decisive conclusion. Although Atlanta wasn't an easy prize, it was a much-needed one. The Civil War, which had lasted for more than three years by this point, had steadily eroded President Abraham Lincoln's popularity. There was a looming election, and the electorate was losing hope in Lincoln. The president had to secure Atlanta, a symbol of Southern defiance, to tip the scales in his favor. And it was Sherman's job to deliver it to him.

While the Confederates had done a great job of fortifying Atlanta, the fortification was too close to the city center. It left the city vulnerable to the maximum range of the Union cannons. After the battle, Sherman gazed at the earthworks and trenches. He realized that raining cannon fire on Atlanta was necessary for a Union victory. So, he laid siege and bombarded the city with artillery.

The Battle of Atlanta was the second time in a mere three days that General Hood's efforts to dislodge the Union grip on Atlanta had failed. His relentless drive to reclaim Bald Hill (or Leggett's Hill) had met resolute opposition as the Yankees clung tenaciously to their prize. The Confederates' already-outnumbered army paid dearly for the battle.

The victory of the Northern soldiers on July 22nd, 1864, marked a turning point in the war. It didn't lead to the Confederates giving up the city, but it set the stage for Atlanta's eventual fall.

Chapter 6 – The Clash Continues

After a long battle, what do soldiers do? They rest. If they have won, they jubilate and celebrate. If they are losing or expect another battle after winning, they rest and re-strategize to anticipate the enemy's next move.

And that was what the Union and Confederate armies did. The Northern Army of the Tennessee remained at Bald Hill and placed some soldiers at the perimeter to guard it. The Southerners retreated back to the Atlanta fortifications outside the city. In each army, soldiers regrouped to ensure that they were accounted for and that their chain of command remained intact. Units that suffered heavy casualties were reorganized.

Meanwhile, medics and medical personnel treated wounded soldiers, prioritizing the critically injured. They transported soldiers who required extensive medical care to hospitals or medical facilities and treated the rest on the battlefield.

The soldiers gathered information from intelligence personnel and captured enemy soldiers, then sent reports to their respective generals. Some recovered, while others identified the dead or wounded. Some focused on checking their ammunition and supply needs. Food, water, and other supplies were distributed to replenish the fighting men's resources while they inspected and conducted maintenance on their weapons and equipment.

Since McPherson had passed away, General Sherman put the Union Army of the Tennessee under the command of Major General Oliver O. Howard. Sherman decided to prevent supplies from entering Atlanta. He sent the Army of the Ohio to the east edge of the city and the Army of the Cumberland to the north. Then, he maneuvered the Army of the Tennessee into position on the city's western flank. The mission was clear: cut the Atlanta and West Point Railroad, a transport route that brought in supplies from East Point, Georgia, into Atlanta. This strategy would strangle the life out of the city and force the Confederates to evacuate. Howard's troops set out on the morning of July 27th.

But General Hood had held a vise-like grip on Atlanta. Resolute in his defense, his indomitable spirit refused to yield. He aimed to relieve the mounting pressure on the city and disrupt Sherman's siege. It wasn't surprising that the Confederate cavalry detected the Northern troops' advance with precision. At 4.15 a.m., a few hours after Howard's departure, a warning reached Hood's headquarters. The message said, "Indications are that the enemy will attack our left."

Howard's troops, undeterred by the predawn hour, kept marching until they extended the Union line to the railroad. By nightfall, the Confederate cavalry's predictions had manifested into reality. Howard's men shifted Sherman's right flank nearly two miles to the south, positioning themselves due west of Atlanta. By July 28th, the soldiers had dug into the earth to place artillery as fortifications.

Determined to thwart the Union plan, Hood dispatched two formidable corps to intercept the Federal threat. They were to march westward along Lick Skillet Road, seize the crossroads near Ezra Church, and entrench facing north. Ezra Church was a modest yet strategically placed Methodist church located about five miles southwest of downtown Atlanta.

Hood wanted his men to launch a surprise attack on the enemy. Catching them unprepared could spell victory for the South and alter the course of the Atlanta Campaign. Nevertheless, maintaining the element of surprise in the fluid dynamics of a Civil War campaign was exceedingly challenging.

Some Union soldiers at the Battle of Ezra Church.
https://commons.wikimedia.org/wiki/File:BattleOfEzraChurchHarpersWeekly.jpg

Howard, who had been Hood's classmate at West Point, had anticipated the attack. He had placed one of his corps in the Confederate Army's path. They piled rails and logs to fashion makeshift breastworks and earthworks before the Southern army arrived. The Union infantry now held Ezra Church and Lick Skillet junction, rendering General Hood's plan obsolete.

The Confederate corps commander, Lieutenant General Stephen D. Lee, impulsively decided to attack head-on. He believed they could seize the crossroads before the Yankees could become entrenched. The clash that followed was a chaotic symphony of musket fire, the woods echoing with the cries of men locked in desperate combat.

The Union infantry, ensconced behind their makeshift defenses, unleashed a torrent of bullets. Simultaneously, Union artillery units unleashed a devastating crossfire upon the advancing Southern troops. The Confederate division, which was attempting a frontal assault, bore the brunt of the storm. It was a devastating charge met with withering fire. So, the Confederates were compelled to fall back, leaving the field strewn with their fallen comrades. Undaunted by the casualties, they called upon reinforcements.

In the midst of the tumult, the Northern army clung tenaciously to Ezra Church. Desperate to enforce their defenses, the men even dismantled the pews within the church to bolster the barricades.

Another division joined the Southerners, and their attacks began to unravel. Their assaults became uncoordinated and disjointed as each unit arrived piecemeal on the battlefield. The result was more carnage, with musket volleys felling Confederates by the hundreds.

Hours later, the day drew to a close, but the conflict raged on. The Battle of Ezra Church spiraled into a maelstrom of violence. The fighting was brutal, often dissolving into close-quarters combat. Southern soldiers confronted overwhelming odds as they tried to breach the Union lines. They launched multiple assaults, but each was met with fierce resistance from the Northerners. Despite their valor and determination, the Confederate attackers struggled to make headway against the Union defenders.

As day turned into night, the intensity of the battle gradually waned. Skirmishes continued until cover of darkness allowed the Confederates to slip away, leaving the place to the Union forces.

When the dust finally settled, the fields and woods surrounding Ezra Church were strewn with the lifeless and wounded. Both Union and Confederate forces retrieved their fallen and cared for the injured. Field hospitals bustled with activity as medical personnel worked tirelessly to save lives and offer solace to the suffering.

The Battle of Ezra Church concluded with a Union victory. The South suffered grievous losses, with estimates exceeding between 2,800 and 3,000 casualties. In contrast, the Northern forces recorded fewer than 650 men lost. Howard's defenses, though resolute, had not cut the rail tracks. While a tactical defeat for the Confederates, the battle prevented the Union troops from reaching the coveted rail line. Lee and his corps marched on and guarded the railroad.

The battle was over, yet war raged on. The struggle for Atlanta, with its symbolic and strategic significance, remained far from decided. The South had once again defended its ground, but the city's ultimate fate still hung precariously in the balance.

Chapter 7 – The Desperate Dash to Cut Supply Lines

All through this time, Carrie Berry still lived in Atlanta. But all she could think about was the shelling and the muskets shooting. Whenever the shelling became too much, she and her family hid in their small cellar. Carrie's ten-year birthday was on August 3rd, but she couldn't celebrate with a cake because times were too hard. She only had one birthday wish—let there be peace in the land on her next birthday so she could have a nice dinner.

Meanwhile, General Sherman was still trying to cut off supplies from Atlanta and the Confederates. While his artillery bombarded Atlanta, he decided to keep trying to cut off the Macon and Western Railroad, which was between Atlanta and East Point. By July 31st, Howard was almost at the railroad. The general sent the Army of the Ohio to take up a position at Howard's right. The Army of the Ohio marched out on August 2nd. They settled into their new position two miles away from the rail tracks, approximately a mile south of Ezra Church and just beyond Utoy Creek.

General Hood, however, knew the Northern army's goal. He received regular intelligence from his cavalry, which diligently tracked the Union troops' movements. Hood ordered another division to reinforce Lee's troops, stretching the line of soldiers from the main Confederate perimeter to the South Fork of Utoy Creek. The Southern forces then built rifle pits and artillery bastions that reached a mile or more below

East Point.

On August 4th, Sherman decided that the time had come to seize the railroad. He ordered his soldiers not to stop until they had control of it. The first fight between the Union and Confederate soldiers led to 83 Northern soldiers killed and 140 captured Southern soldiers. Unperturbed by the modest advance, the Army of the Ohio, supported by one corps from the Army of the Cumberland, started crossing Utoy Creek.

The next day, the Union soldiers had to halt for the army to regroup. This pause, while necessary, allowed the Confederate forces to reinforce their defenses. The Southern troops went the extra mile by felling trees and using them to build an abatis.

When the Northern troops charged to fight, the Southern army responded with a tempest of musket and cannon fire. The charge was repulsed, and the Confederates got the upper hand. Seventy-six Union soldiers were killed, 199 were wounded, and 31 were captured, compared to 15 to 20 casualties on the Confederate side. That was over three hundred casualties for the Union forces and a maximum of twenty for the Confederates.

Undaunted, Sherman kept adjusting his strategy so his men could cut off the railroad. Despite the Union men's unwavering courage, the Northern assault faltered. The Confederate soldiers, though outnumbered, stood resolute. Their defenses proved impregnable. The Union soldiers couldn't breach them unassisted. Even when reinforcements came, their valorous effort led to almost two hundred casualties.

By the time the Battle of Utoy Creek was over, the Union losses ranged from between close to one thousand and as many as two thousand soldiers killed, wounded, captured, or missing. The South, on the other hand, lost about 250.

The Battle of Utoy Creek, in terms of casualties, might not have been a major engagement. But its importance lay in its strategic implication. The South had successfully thwarted the North's attempt to sever a critical supply line into Atlanta. The victory convinced General Sherman that infantry assaults against obstacles and trenches were futile. These frontal assaults on Confederate soldiers were not the path to victory. As the dust of the battle settled, Sherman's armies settled into their encirclement of Atlanta, besieging the city with more determination.

The Confederates kept guarding the railroad. They had won the battle and hoped to continue winning. Their victory bolstered them, and soon, the Southern army decided to launch a counterattack.

Desperate to break the siege, General Hood sent a Confederate cavalry commander, Major General Joseph Wheeler, on a daring raid. He decided to go to northern Georgia to cut Sherman's supply lines and destroy railroad tracks, which would halt the Union Army's relentless advance to Atlanta. On August 14th, Confederate forces closed in on a Union garrison at Dalton, Georgia, commanded by Colonel Bernard Leybold. They demanded the surrender of the garrison, but the Union commander refused to yield.

Outnumbered and facing insurmountable odds, the Union garrison retreated to fortifications atop a hill outside the town's boundaries. The two cavalries sporadically fought through the night, their gunfire punctuating the darkness like angry fireflies.

As dawn broke on the horizon, the Confederate raiders renewed their onslaught, but Leybold's men held firm. When all seemed lost for the Northern garrison, reinforcements from Chattanooga arrived. A four-hour skirmish ensued. By the end of the clash, Wheeler's cavalry reluctantly withdrew from the battlefield. The extent of the Confederates' damage to the railroad track is debatable. However, repairs began almost immediately. Within two days, trains rode along those rails. This skirmish came to be known as the Second Battle of Dalton.

There is also no record of the number of casualties in the battle. Although it was inconclusive by traditional measures, the Second Battle of Dalton could be counted as a Union victory. The Confederates had chosen to withdraw and had been unable to completely cut off the Union Army's supplies.

With Wheeler's cavalry absent, General Sherman set out to cripple General Hood's supply lines. He sent Union Brigadier General Judson Kilpatrick on that mission. On August 18th, 1864, Kilpatrick's cavalry arrived at the Atlanta and West Point Railroad. Tools clutched in determined hands, they destroyed parts of the railroad tracks with fervor. The metallic screech of twisted steel echoed in the air. They burned the Confederate supplies at the Jonesborough depot the next day. The precious Southern army supplies that had been piled high sent plumes of smoke billowing into the sky.

The Union forces continued their destruction at Lovejoy's Station on August 20th but were interrupted by Confederate forces, who fought with them into the night. Eventually, Kilpatrick was forced to flee to avoid being encircled by the enemy troops.

The Union and Confederate casualties were almost equal—almost 240 men on each side. But the battle was a Confederate victory since the Union soldiers withdrew. The Southern forces had thwarted the Northern troops. They prevented further destruction to the railroad and ensured it was in good working condition two days later.

General Sherman needed a decisive victory, and time was no longer on his side. The presidential election was in November. If he didn't capture Atlanta, President Abraham Lincoln could possibly not be reelected. On August 25th, Sherman ordered six divisions to march south of the city. Their destination was the Macon and Western Railroad, nestled near Jonesborough, Georgia.

General Hood thought it was business as usual. Unaware of the large number of the Northern troops, he discharged two corps to disrupt their advance. On August 31st, the Confederate forces launched a ferocious assault on two Union corps. However, the Federal soldiers were not easily swayed. They stood their ground and forced the Southern troops to retreat.

With a sinking heart, Hood realized the enormity of the Union presence gathering south of Atlanta. Since his army was vastly outnumbered, he had to make an agonizing decision: focus on the battle at Jonesborough or strongly defend Atlanta. Fearing a Union assault, Hood ordered one of the Confederate corps to return to defend the city.

Meanwhile, Sherman's forces relentlessly fought at Jonesborough. The Union soldiers eventually won. Hood's corps had about 2,000 casualties, and the Union had 1,149.

Now that the Union had won the railroad, the soldiers set to the task that would doom the Confederates. They ripped and tore at the iron sinews of the Macon and Western Railroad. They made good work of it, destroying one rail after the other until they were drenched in sweat. Each rail wrenched was a victory for which they had fought long and hard. Each torn piece of the rail track was a sure sign of complete victory.

While the soldiers rendered the railroad unusable, they heard a distant whistle. Soon, a train from Atlanta hurtled toward them. Upon sighting the destroyed rail lines, the train came to an abrupt halt. To flee from the impending danger, it reversed its course and went back to Atlanta, taking with it the news that the Confederate supply line had been cut. The enormity of the Union triumph dawned on the soldiers when they saw the looks on the faces of those on the train. Meanwhile, a sense of defeat clawed into the Confederate forces when they realized that their supply line had been severed.

Hood faced a reality of doom. Sixty thousand Federal troops now massed on the southern part of Atlanta. His communication and supply lines were also severed, a problem that would prove devastating for the Confederates. Atlanta, once a mighty stronghold and symbol of Southern pride, now teetered on the precipice of surrender. There was only one choice left for General Hood and his Confederate Army—abandon the city they had fought so fiercely to defend.

Chapter 8 – The Fall of Atlanta

Whitehall Street, a business district in Atlanta in the 1860s before Union soldiers burned down.
No known restrictions; https://www.loc.gov/item/2018666987/

Atlanta's citizens experienced the grim battles from within the city. Young Carrie Berry had to endure the trauma of war at such a young age. Sherman's army had constantly been bombarding Atlanta since July.

When the Union and Confederate forces battled or were involved in skirmishes, the shells landing on the city increased, and Carrie had to hide out in their small cellar. And when the shelling wasn't as intense, they cleaned up the house, cooked, knitted, visited the scarce number of friends and relatives left in Atlanta, or went to church if possible.

While the Confederate raiders retreated on August 15th, the morning started like any other for Carrie. She was already used to the shells falling in her city and hoped that she would get some reprieve that day.

She'd just finished eating breakfast and left the dining room when a monstrous shell filled with steel balls landed with a sinister thud by the garden gate. It made a large hole in the ground, then burst with a roar as it scattered dirt all over the yard. Some fragments from the shell flew from the garden and fell into the dining room. Carrie went pale. With trembling limbs and a racing heart, she fled to the cellar, where she stayed until it was time for dinner. Unfortunately, the shells did not relent. The next day, a shell flew into her mother's room and fell on the bed. Luckily, they were in the cellar when the shell fragments burst; otherwise, they might not have lived to see another day.

The shells kept landing in the city and increasing in intensity. On August 20th, a shell passed through her uncle's house and burned it down. That prompted her family to move downtown for a while. They lived in the cellar of Jacob's store at Five Points, a district where five streets intersected.

By the time Sherman had focused on destroying the railroad, he moved most of his soldiers to face the Confederates. The Union forces abandoned their breastworks to march on where they would win the war against Atlanta. The shelling on the city reduced drastically, and Carrie's family moved back home on August 27th. Carrie even looked for her schoolteacher so she could resume school.

On September 1st, Carrie's cousin Emma told her family that the Confederates would leave Atlanta that evening and that the Union Army would occupy it the next day. That night, the Southern army set fire to its ammunition to prevent Northern soldiers from acquiring them and using the weapons against the South. The Confederate mill was burned and razed to the ground. Then, the soldiers broke into stores, trying to get all they could before leaving.

After the Confederates abandoned Atlanta and left, the Union troops marched into defenseless Atlanta on September 2nd, 1864. Two days later, Sherman declared the end of the Atlanta Campaign. His proclamation, which was Special Field Order No. 64, signaled that Atlanta was theirs. The city, once a symbol of defiance, now stood under a new banner.

But in mid-November, Sherman gave a devastating order. It was toward the end of fall when leaves turned orange, yellow, and brown, and the trees shed their leaves. Just like leaves that change color are dying, the general's order changed Atlanta for the worse.

Before he began his "March to the Sea," Sherman sent his soldiers to set fire to the city's munitions factories, railway yards, and clothing mills. The flames did not stop at burning military resources; they consumed everything in their path. The fire turned into a relentless inferno that left Atlanta in ruins.

Conclusion

The Battle of Atlanta was a defining moment in the American Civil War and in American history. It was filled with bravery, sacrifice, and untold human resilience. There were smoke-filled skies and blood-soaked fields. There were men and women, soldiers and civilians who fought for their beliefs, their homes, and their very existence.

Think about President Abraham Lincoln, who got reelected after Atlanta was defeated. Think about General Sherman and General Hood, as well as the Union and Confederate soldiers. Now, imagine Gussie's short life because she volunteered at the military hospitals and contracted typhoid. Her sister, Sarah Clayton, wrote a memoir years later about the dangers they encountered during the war, and Gussie's remains were interred at Oakland Cemetery.

How about Carrie Berry, whose trials didn't end with the Union Army taking over Atlanta? First, two Union soldiers took their hog and made a meal out of it in early November. Her relations, neighbors, and friends left the city. Then, on November 12th, the soldiers began to burn stores and houses. By November 16th, the whole town was on fire, and the Yankees left in the afternoon. Carrie and her family endured the smoke and inferno. Luckily, their house did not burn, and they went on to rebuild their lives in Atlanta.

The Battle of Atlanta had far-reaching effects. It was a pivotal event in the Civil War. For President Lincoln, the victory breathed life into his reelection campaign. But what is more important is how Atlanta handled the rampage and destruction.

The Civil War eventually ended on April 9th, 1865. The citizens of Atlanta, once ravaged by the flames of war, began to rebuild. In 1868, Atlanta became the capital of Georgia as a symbol of rebirth and renewal. In 1877, it became the permanent capital by popular vote. Today, there are no pre-Civil War buildings in the city. The scars of war will always mark Atlanta's history, but its spirit has remained unbroken as it has risen from the ashes of war.

Here's another book by Captivating History that you might like

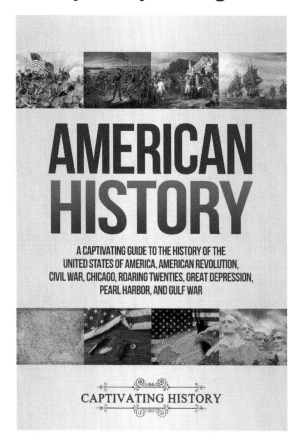

Free Bonus from Captivating History (Available for a Limited time)

Hi History Lovers!

Now you have a chance to join our exclusive history list so you can get your first history ebook for free as well as discounts and a potential to get more history books for free! Simply visit the link below to join.

Captivatinghistory.com/ebook

Also, make sure to follow us on Facebook, Twitter and Youtube by searching for Captivating History.

References

American Battlefield Trust:

Fort Sumter Animated Battle Map, Video, https://www.youtube.com/watch?v=Hfn5BZZBpoU, accessed October, November 2021,

Fort Sumter, Charleston Harbor, SC, April 12 – 14, 1861, https://www.battlefields.org/learn/civil-war/battles/fort-sumter, accessed October, November 2021.

American History TV:

Fort Sumter History – National Park Service Historian Rick Hatcher, Video, https://www.youtube.com/watch?v=zoj_fNAn9OE, accessed via C-Span, October,

November, 2021.

Bordewich, Fergus M., 2011. *Fort Sumter: The Civil War Begins*, accessed via The

Smithsonian Magazine, https://www.smithsonianmag.com/history/fort-sumter-the-civil-war-begins-1018791/, October, November 2021.

History.com:

Fort Sumter, https://www.history.com/topics/american-civil-war/fort-sumter, accessed

October, November 2021.

Mr. Droste History:

Battle of Fort Sumter Explained (Civil War History), Video, https://www.youtube.com/watch?v=PRWrZ236cxI, accessed October, November 2021.

National Park Service:

Battle of Fort Sumter, https://www.nps.gov/articles/battle-of-fort-sumter-april-1861.htm, accessed October, November 2021,

October, November 2021.

Wikipedia:

American Civil War, https://en.wikipedia.org/wiki/American_Civil_War, accessed .

October, November 2021,

Battle of Fort Sumter, https://en.wikipedia.org/wiki/Battle_of_Fort_Sumter, accessed October, November 2021,

Fort Pickens, https://en.wikipedia.org/wiki/Fort_Pickens, accessed October, November, 2021,

Fort Sumter, https://en.wikipedia.org/wiki/Fort_Sumter, accessed October, November 2021,

List of American Civil War generals (Confederate),
https://en.wikipedia.org/wiki/List_of_American_Civil_War_generals_(Confederate), accessed October, November 2021,

List of American Civil War generals (Union),
https://en.wikipedia.org/wiki/List_of_American_Civil_War_generals_(Union), accessed October, November, 2021.

Battlefields,org:

Second Manassas, Second Bull Run, Brawner's Farm,
https://www.battlefields.org/learn/civil-war/battles/second-manassas, accessed June, July 2021.

Britannica.com:

Second Battle of Bull Run, https://www.britannica.com/event/Second-Battle-of-Bull-Run-1862, accessed June, July 2021.

Historynet.com:

Second Battle of Bull Run, https://www.historynet.com/second-battle-of-bull-run, accessed June, July 2021.

National Park Service:

Battle of Second Manassas (Second Bull Run), February 2011,

https://www.nps.gov/mana/learn/historyculture/second-manassas.htm, accessed June, July 2021,

Civil War Series, The Second Battle of Manassas, Section 1-7, https://www.nps.gov/parkhistory/online_books/civil_war_series/18/sec7.htm, accessed June, July 2021.

Townsend, Jan, 2011, Ed. Burgess, James. *The Civil War in Prince William County.*, Prince William County Historical Commission, accessed via Prince William County Government, https://www.pwcva.gov/assets/documents/planning/HistComm_Book_The_Civil_War_in_PWC.pdf, June 2021.

TravelBrains.com:

Travelbrains Second Manassas Expedition Guide, accessed via AmericanCivilWar.com, https://americancivilwar.com/manassas2_travelbrains.html, June, July 2021.

Weapons and Warfare: History and Hardware of Warfare:

Lee Divides and Conquers at the Second Battle of Bull Run, https://weaponsandwarfare.com/2017/10/22/lee-divides-and-conquers-at-the-second-battle-of-bull-run/, accessed June, July 2021.

Wikipedia.com:

A.P. Hill's Light Division, https://en.wikipedia.org/wiki/A._P._Hill%27s_Light_Division, accessed June, July 2021,

American Civil War, https://en.wikipedia.org/wiki/American_Civil_War, accessed June, July 2021,

Battle of Cedar Mountain, https://en.wikipedia.org/wiki/Battle_of_Cedar_Mountain, accessed June, July 2021,

Emancipation Proclamation, https://en.wikipedia.org/wiki/Emancipation_Proclamation, accessed June, July 2021,

Fitz John Porter, https://en.wikipedia.org/wiki/Fitz_John_Porter, accessed June, July 2021,

Iron Brigade, https://en.wikipedia.org/wiki/Iron_Brigade, accessed June, July 2021,

John Gibbon, https://en.wikipedia.org/wiki/John_Gibbon, accessed June, July 2021,

John Pope, https://en.wikipedia.org/wiki/John_Pope_(military_officer)#Civil_War, accessed June, July 2021,

Northern Virginia Campaign,

https://en.wikipedia.org/wiki/Northern_Virginia_campaign, accessed June, July 2021,

Peninsula Campaign, https://en.wikipedia.org/wiki/Peninsula_campaign, accessed June, July 2021,

Rufus King, https://en.wikipedia.org/wiki/Rufus_King_(general)#Civil_War, accessed June, July 2021,

Second Battle of Bull Run,
https://en.wikipedia.org/wiki/Second_Battle_of_Bull_Run, accessed June, July 2021.

American Battlefield Trust:

Washington, D.C. during the Civil War,
https://www.battlefields.org/learn/articles/washington-dc-during-civil-war, accessed June 2021.

Battlefields.org:

An End to Innocence, The First Battle of Manassas,
https://www.battlefields.org/learn/articles/end-innocence, accessed June 2021,

The Battle of Bull Run, First Manassas,
https://www.battlefields.org/learn/articles/bull-run, accessed June 2021,

Fairfax County and Prince William County, VA, July 21 1861,
https://www.battlefields.org/learn/civil-war/battles/bull-run, accessed June 2021.

Britannica.com:

First Battle of Bull Run, https://www.britannica.com/event/First-Battle-of-Bull-Run-1861, accessed June 2021,

Gould, Kevin, 2015. *Balloon Corps*, https://www.britannica.com/topic/Balloon-Corps, accessed June 2021.

Furgurson, Ernest B., 2011. *The Civil War, The Battle of Bull Run: The End of Illusions*, accessed via the Smithsonian Magazine,
https://www.smithsonianmag.com/history/the-battle-of-bull-run-the-end-of-illusions-17525927/, June 2021.

History.com:

First Battle of Bull Run, https://www.history.com/topics/american-civil-war/first-battle-of-bull-run#section_1, accessed June 2021,

:*The First Battle of Bull Run*, https://www.history.com/this-day-in-history/the-first-battle-of-bull-run, accessed June 2021.

National Park Service:

Civil War Series, *The First Battle of Manassas*, Sections 1-7,

https://www.nps.gov/parkhistory/online_books/civil_war_series/17/sec1.htm, accessed
June 2021.

Ruane, Michael E., 2011. *Battle of Bull Run provided a surprising start to the bloody Civil War*, The Washington Post, https://www.washingtonpost.com/local/battle-of-bull-run-provided-a-surprising-start-to-the-bloody-civil-war/2011/06/30/gIQAa7OOGI_story.html, accessed June 2021.

The Ohio State University, *Manassas I (First Bull Run)*, https://ehistory.osu.edu/battles/manassas-i-first-bull-run, accessed June 2021.

Townsend, Jan, 2011, Ed. Burgess, James. *The Civil War in Prince William County.*, Prince William County Historical Commission, accessed via Prince William County Government, https://www.pwcva.gov/assets/documents/planning/HistComm_Book_The_Civil_War_in_PWC.pdf, June 2021.

Wikipedia: *American Civil War*, https://en.wikipedia.org/wiki/American_Civil_War, accessed June 2021,

Confederate States of America, https://en.wikipedia.org/wiki/Confederate_States_of_America, accessed June 2021,

First Battle of Bull Run, https://en.wikipedia.org/wiki/First_Battle_of_Bull_Run, accessed June 2021,

List of Weapons of the American Civil War, https://en.wikipedia.org/wiki/List_of_weapons_in_the_American_Civil_War, accessed
June 2021,

Union Army Balloon Corps, https://en.wikipedia.org/wiki/Union_Army_Balloon_Corps, accessed June 2021.

American Battlefield Trust:

Pea Ridge, Elkhorn Tavern, Benton County, Arkansas, Mar 6-8, 1862, https://www.battlefields.org/learn/civil-war/battles/pea-ridge, accessed September, October, 2021.

Beckenbaugh, Terry, 2020. *Battle of Pea Ridge*, Contemporary Operations Studies Team, Combat Studies Institute, Fort Leavenworth, Kansas, accessed via the Encyclopedia of Arkansas, https://encyclopediaofarkansas.net/entries/battle-of-pea-ridge-508/, September, October, 2021.

Beckenbaugh, Terry, 2020. *Pea Ridge Campaign*, U.S. Army Command and General Staff College, accessed via the Encyclopedia of Arkansas, https://encyclopediaofarkansas.net/entries/pea-ridge-campaign-507/, September, October, 2021.

National Park Service:

Civil War Series, The Campaign for Pea Ridge, Section 1-8, https://www.nps.gov/parkhistory/online_books/civil_war_series/19/sec1.htm, accessed September, October 2021,

Southern Battle Flags, https://www.nps.gov/peri/learn/historyculture/southern-battle-flags.htm, accessed September, October 2021.

Owens, Richard H., 2000. *Battle of Pea Ridge*, accessed via History.net, https://www.historynet.com/battle-of-pea-ridge.htm, September, October 2021.

Shea, Prof. William, 1993. University of Arkansas at Monticello. The Arkansas Historical Quarterly, Volume 52, No. 2 (Summer, 1993) pp. 129-155, Published by the Arkansas Historical Association, *The Confederate Defeat at Cache River*, accessed via JSTOR, https://www.jstor.org/stable/40019246?read-now=1&seq=1#page_scan_tab_contents, September, October 2021.

Shea, Prof. William, 2012. University of Arkansas at Monticello. American History TV, *The Civil War, Civil War Battle of Pea Ridge*, Saline County Library, Benton, https://www.c-span.org/video/?304869-1/civil-war-battle-pea-ridge, accessed September, October 2021.

The Historical Gamer, YouTube video, *Scourge of War: Battle of Pea Ridge – Elkhorn Tavern (March 7th 1862)*, https://www.youtube.com/watch?v=WMZN8fCiGyI, accessed July, August 2021.

Wikipedia: *Albert Pike*, https://en.wikipedia.org/wiki/Albert_Pike, accessed September, October 2021,

Army of the Southwest, https://en.wikipedia.org/wiki/Army_of_the_Southwest, accessed September, October 2021,

Army of the West (1862), https://en.wikipedia.org/wiki/Army_of_the_West_(1862), accessed September, October 2021,

Battle of Cotton Plant, https://en.wikipedia.org/wiki/Battle_of_Cotton_Plant, accessed September, October 2021,

Benjamin McCulloch, https://en.wikipedia.org/wiki/Benjamin_McCulloch, accessed September, October 2021,

Franz Sigel, https://en.wikipedia.org/wiki/Franz_Sigel, accessed September, October 2021,

Henry Halleck, https://en.wikipedia.org/wiki/Henry_Halleck#Civil_War, accessed September, October 2021,

Missouri State Guard, https://en.wikipedia.org/wiki/Missouri_State_Guard, accessed September, October 2021,

Samuel Ryan Curtis, https://en.wikipedia.org/wiki/Samuel_Ryan_Curtis, accessed September, October 2021,

The Battle of Pea Ridge, https://en.wikipedia.org/wiki/Battle_of_Pea_Ridge, accessed September, October 2021,

Trans-Mississippi Theater of the American Civil War, https://en.wikipedia.org/wiki/Trans-Mississippi_Theater_of_the_American_Civil_War, accessed September, October 2021.

"Account of the Battle of Shiloh." HistoryNet. Last modified June 12, 2006. https://www.historynet.com/account-of-battle-of-shiloh.htm.

Allen, Stacy D. "Shiloh." *Blue & Gray Magazine*, 2018.

"The Battle of Shiloh in Quotes." The Historians Manifesto. Last modified September 6, 2012. https://thehistoriansmanifesto.wordpress.com/2012/09/06/the-battle-of-shiloh-in-quotes/.

Catton, Bruce, and James M. McPherson. *American Heritage History of the Civil War*. New Word City, 2014.

Daniel, Larry J. *Shiloh: The Battle That Changed the Civil War*. New York: Simon & Schuster, 2008.

"Digital History." UH - Digital History. Accessed May 25, 2021. https://www.digitalhistory.uh.edu/disp_textbook.cfm?smtID=3&psid=403.

Foote, Shelby. *The Civil War: A Narrative. Fort Sumter to Perryville*. New York: Vintage, 1986.

McPherson, James M., *Battle Cry of Freedom: The Civil War Era*. New York: Oxford University Press, 1988.

Nevin, David. *The Road to Shiloh: Early Battles in the West*. Morristown, NJ: Time-Life, 1983.

"Our Wish for a Hard Battle A Chicago Artilleryman's Account of the Battle of Shiloh." Illinois Periodicals Online at Northern Illinois University - (Main Page). Accessed May 25, 2021. https://www.lib.niu.edu/1998/ihwt9827.html.

Southern veterans giving the Rebel yell: https://www.youtube.com/watch?v=s6jSqt39vFM&ab_channel=SmithsonianMagazine.

"Shiloh: Primary Sources." Spartacus Educational. Accessed May 25, 2021. https://spartacus-educational.com/USACWshiloh.htm.

(Despite its political leanings, this website has some extraordinary primary documents and accounts available.)

"A Soldier's Story: Battle of Shiloh." Belle on the Battlefield. Last modified January 27, 2019. https://belleonthebattlefield.wordpress.com/2019/01/30/a-soldiers-story-battle-of-shiloh/.

Academic Accelerator. (n.d.). *Second battle of Dalton.* https://academic-accelerator.com/encyclopedia/second-battle-of-dalton

America's Library. (n.d.). *Atlanta's role in the civil war.* https://www.americaslibrary.gov/es/ga/es_ga_atlanta_1.html

American Battlefield Trust. (n.d.). *Battle of Ezra Church.* https://www.battlefields.org/learn/articles/battle-ezra-church

American Battlefield Trust. (n.d.). *Battle of Peach Tree Creek.* https://www.battlefields.org/learn/articles/battle-peach-tree-creek

American Battlefield Trust (n.d.). *Battle of Utoy Creek.* https://www.battlefields.org/learn/articles/battle-utoy-creek

American Battlefield Trust. (n.d.). *Fulton County, GA / Jul 20, 1864.* https://www.battlefields.org/learn/civil-war/battles/peach-tree-creek

Atlanta in the American Civil War. (2023, February 28). In *Wikipedia.* https://en.wikipedia.org/w/index.php?title=Atlanta_in_the_American_Civil_War&oldid=1142067860

Battle of Atlanta. (2023, May 24). In *Wikipedia.* https://en.wikipedia.org/w/index.php?title=Battle_of_Atlanta&oldid=1156674045

Berry, C. M. (1897). *Carrie Berry's diary.* Atlanta History Center. https://dlg.galileo.usg.edu/turningpoint/ahc/cw/pdfs/ahc0029f-001.pdf

Cutrer, T. W. (2018, March 29). *Hood, John Bell (1831-1879).* Texas State Historical Association. https://www.tshaonline.org/handbook/entries/hood-john-bell

Davis, S. (2018, September 17). *Atlanta campaign.* New Georgia Encyclopedia. https://www.georgiaencyclopedia.org/articles/history-archaeology/atlanta-campaign/

ExploreATL. (n.d.). *Battle of Atlanta: Civil War tipping point.* https://sites.google.com/exploreatl.com/battle-of-atlanta/

Gordy, J. (2019, February 20). *5 things to know about the Battle of Atlanta cyclorama.* Atlanta History Center. https://www.atlantahistorycenter.com/blog/5-things-to-know-about-the-battle-of-atlanta-cyclorama/

Greenwalt, P. (2014, August 31). *Jonesborough, Georgia: The battle that doomed Atlanta.* Emerging Civil War. https://emergingcivilwar.com/2014/08/31/jonesborough-georgia-the-battle-that-doomed-atlanta/

Haber, E. (2018, August 29). *Spotlight on the women of Atlanta during the Civil War.* Historic Oakland Foundation. https://oaklandcemetery.com/spotlight-on-the-women-of-atlanta-during-the-civil-war/

Harper's New Monthly Magazine. (1865, October). *Atlanta in ruins* [Illustration]. New Georgia Encyclopedia. https://www.georgiaencyclopedia.org/articles/history-archaeology/atlanta-campaign/

Hickman, K. (2017, March 6). *American Civil War: Battle of Ezra Church.* ThoughtCo. https://www.thoughtco.com/battle-of-ezra-church-2360231

Hudson, M. (2022, July 15). *Battle of Atlanta.* Encyclopedia Britannica. https://www.britannica.com/event/Battle-of-Atlanta

Library of Congress. (n.d.). *William T. Sherman.* https://www.loc.gov/exhibits/civil-war-in-america/biographies/william-t-sherman.html

Library of Congress. (1864). *Destruction of the depots, public buildings, and manufactories at Atlanta, Georgia, November 15. 1864. The fourteenth and twentieth corps moving out of Atlanta, November 15, 1864.* https://www.loc.gov/item/00652832/

McPherson, J. M. (Ed.). (1994). *The atlas of the Civil War.* Macmillan.

Monovisions Black & White Photography Magazine. (n.d.). *Vintage: Everyday life of Atlanta, Georgia (19th century).* https://monovisions.com/vintage-everyday-life-of-atlanta-georgia-19th-century/

N-Georgia. (n.d.). *The Civil War battle at Lovejoy Station.* https://www.n-georgia.com/lovejoy-station-civil-war-battle.html

N-Georgia. (n.d.). *The second Civil War battle in Dalton.* https://www.n-georgia.com/dalton-civil-war-battle2.html

National Geographic. (n.d.). *Apr 12, 1861 CE: Battle of Fort Sumter.* https://education.nationalgeographic.org/resource/battle-fort-sumter/

New York Historical Society Museum & Library. (n.d.). *Surviving the siege of Atlanta.* https://wams.nyhistory.org/a-nation-divided/civil-war/surviving-siege-of-atlanta/

Ohio Civil War Central. (n.d.). *Battle of Ezra Church.* https://www.ohiocivilwarcentral.com/battle-of-ezra-church/

Ohio Civil War Central. (n.d.). *Battle of Lovejoy's Station.*
https://www.ohiocivilwarcentral.com/battle-of-lovejoys-station/

Ohio Civil War Central. (n.d.). *Battle of Utoy Creek.*
https://www.ohiocivilwarcentral.com/battle-of-utoy-creek/

Onion, A., Sullivan, M., Mullen, M., ... Zapata, C. (2020, July 21). *Battle of Atlanta continues.* https://www.history.com/this-day-in-history/battle-of-atlanta-continues

Onion, A., Sullivan, M., Mullen, M., ... Zapata, C. (2020, August 31). *Atlanta falls to Union forces.* History. https://www.history.com/this-day-in-history/atlanta-falls-to-union-forces

Pollock, D. A. (2014, May 30). *The Battle of Atlanta: History and remembrance.* Southern Spaces. https://southernspaces.org/2014/battle-atlanta-history-and-remembrance/

Robertson, J. (2019, July 18). *John Bell Hood.* Radio IQ.
https://www.wvtf.org/civil-war-series/2019-07-08/john-bell-hood

Searles, H. (2022, May 5). *Second battle of Dalton.* American History Central.
https://www.americanhistorycentral.com/entries/second-battle-of-dalton/

Searles, H. (2022, May 6). *Battle of Jonesborough.* American History Central.
https://www.americanhistorycentral.com/entries/jonesborough-battle-of/

Searles. H. (2023, April 29). *The Battle of Lovejoy's Station, 1864.* American History Central. https://www.americanhistorycentral.com/entries/battle-of-lovejoys-station/

Searles, H. (2023, August 10). *Battle of Utoy Creek facts.* American History Central. https://www.americanhistorycentral.com/entries/battle-of-utoy-creek-facts/

The Army Historical Foundation. (n.d.). *General William Tecumseh Sherman.*
https://armyhistory.org/general-william-tecumseh-sherman/

The Editors of Encyclopedia Britannica. (2021, October 13). *Battle of Atlanta summary.* Encyclopedia Britannica.
https://www.britannica.com/summary/Battle-of-Atlanta

The Editors of Encyclopedia Britannica. (2023, March 17). *Joseph E. Johnston.* Encyclopedia Britannica. https://www.britannica.com/biography/Joseph-E-Johnston

The Ohio State University. (n.d.). *John Bell Hood.*
https://ehistory.osu.edu/biographies/john-bell-hood

The Ohio State University. (n.d.). *Ezra church (Battle of the poor house).*
https://ehistory.osu.edu/battles/ezra-church-battle-poor-house

United States Senate. (n.d.). *Civil War begins.*
https://www.senate.gov/artandhistory/history/minute/Civil_War_Begins.htm

Bailey, Ronald H. *The Bloodiest Day: The Battle of Antietam*. Time Life Education, 1984.

Foote, Shelby. *The Civil War: A Narrative: Volume 2: Fredericksburg to Meridian*. New York: Vintage, 2011.

McPherson, James M. *Battle Cry of Freedom: The Civil War Era*. New York: Oxford University Press, 2003.

"Chickamauga." American Battlefield Trust. https://www.battlefields.org/learn/civil-war/battles/chickamauga

"Civil War Weapons." Civil War Academy. Last modified July 21, 2020. https://www.civilwaracademy.com/civil-war-weapons

The Civil War. Directed by Ken Burns. PBS, September 1990.

Foote, Shelby. *The Civil War: A Narrative. Fredericksburg to Meridian*. New York: Vintage, 1986.

"Life of the Civil War Soldier in the Army." American Battlefield Trust. Last modified March 26, 2021. https://www.battlefields.org/learn/articles/life-civil-war-soldier-army

McPherson, James M. *Battle Cry of Freedom: The Civil War Era*. New York: Oxford University Press, 2003.

Foote, Shelby. The Civil War, a Narrative: Fredericksburg to Meridian. New York: Vintage, 1986.

Holmes, Richard, Hew Strachan, Chris Bellamy, Hugh Bicheno, and Professor of the History of War and Fellow Director Oxford Program on the Changing Character of War Hew Strachan. *The Oxford Companion to Military History*. New York: Oxford University Press, USA, 2001.

McPherson, James M. *Battle Cry of Freedom: The Civil War Era*. New York: Oxford University Press, 2003.

American Battlefield Trust:

Vicksburg, https://www.battlefields.org/learn/civil-war/battles/vicksburg, accessed July, August 2021,

: *Vicksburg: Animated Battle Map*, YouTube video, https://www.youtube.com/watch?v=1eSgimZ8GKQ, accessed July, August 2021.

Britannica.com:

Vicksburg Campaign, https://www.britannica.com/event/Vicksburg-Campaign, accessed July, August 2021.

DePue, Dr. Mark, 2015. Abraham Lincoln Presidential Library and Museum. YouTube Video, *The Civil War Battle Series: Vicksburg*, https://www.youtube.com/watch?v=hyTVOPTTa6k, accessed July, August 2021.

History.com:

Grant: Massive Siege of Vicksburg Leads to Union Victory, YouTube video, https://www.youtube.com/watch?v=qnq-df4MQzI, accessed July, August 2021.

Mann, Meredith, June 30, 2016. *The Writing on the Wall: Documenting Civil War History*, New York Public Library, Manuscripts and Archives Division, Stephen A. Schwarzman Building, https://www.nypl.org/blog/2016/06/30/vicksburg-daily-citizen, July, August 2021.

National Park Service:

Civil War Series 24, Section 1-9, https://www.nps.gov/parkhistory/online_books/civil_war_series/24/sec1.htm, July, August 2021,

Here Brothers Fought, The Siege of Vicksburg, The Official NPS Theater Film, https://www.nps.gov/vick/index.htm, July, August 2021.

Ohio History Central:

Siege of Vicksburg, https://ohiohistorycentral.org/w/Siege_of_Vicksburg, accessed July, August 2021.

U.S. Army Heritage & Education Center:

Siege of Vicksburg, https://ahec.armywarcollege.edu/exhibits/CivilWarImagery/cheney_vicksburg.cfm, accessed July, August 2021.

Wikipedia.com:

Battle of Champion Hill, https://en.wikipedia.org/wiki/Battle_of_Champion_Hill, accessed July, August 2021

Confederate States of America, https://en.wikipedia.org/wiki/Confederate_States_of_America, accessed July, August 2021,

John S. Bowen, https://en.wikipedia.org/wiki/John_S._Bowen#American_Civil_War, accessed July, August 2021,

John C. Pemberton, https://en.wikipedia.org/wiki/John_C._Pemberton#Vicksburg, accessed July, August 2021,

Siege of Port Hudson, https://en.wikipedia.org/wiki/Siege_of_Port_Hudson, accessed July, August 2021,

Siege of Vicksburg, https://en.wikipedia.org/wiki/Siege_of_Vicksburg, accessed July, August 2021,

Ulysses S. Grant, https://en.wikipedia.org/wiki/Ulysses_S._Grant, accessed July, August 2021,

Vicksburg Campaign, https://en.wikipedia.org/wiki/Vicksburg_campaign, accessed July, August 2021,

Vicksburg, Mississippi, https://en.wikipedia.org/wiki/Vicksburg,_Mississippi, accessed July, August 2021,

Western Theater of the American Civil War,
https://en.wikipedia.org/wiki/Western_Theater_of_the_American_Civil_War, accessed July, August 2021,

William Tecumseh Sherman,
https://en.wikipedia.org/wiki/William_Tecumseh_Sherman#Vicksburg, accessed July, August 2021.

Adkin, Mark. *The Gettysburg Companion: The Complete Guide to America's Most Famous Battle.* Harrisburg, Pennsylvania: Stackpole Books, 2008.

Albright, Harry. *Gettysburg: Crisis of Command.* Hippocrene Books, 1991.

Archer, John M. *Culp's Hill at Gettysburg: The Mountain Trembled.* Gettysburg, Pennsylvania: Thomas Publications, 2002.

Backus, Paige Gibbons. "Camp Letterman at Gettysburg," 6 December 2021, Battlefields.org.

Barthel, Thomas. *Abner Doubleday – A Civil War Biography.* Jefferson, North Carolina: McFarland & Company, 2010.

Bates, Samuel P. *The Battle of Gettysburg.* Philadelphia, Pennsylvania: T. H. Darrs & Co., 1875.

Beattie, Dan. *Brandy Station 1863: First Step Towards Gettysburg.* United Kingdom: Osprey Publishing, 2009.

Bennett, Gerald R. *Days of "Uncertainty and Dread": The Ordeal Endured by the Citizens of Gettysburg.* Littlestown, Pennsylvania: 1994.

Blair, Jayne E. *The Essential Civil War: A Handbook to the Battles, Armies, Navies and Commanders.* Jefferson, North Carolina: McFarland & Company, Inc., 2006.

Bledsoe, Andrew S. *Citizen-Officers: The Union and Confederate Volunteer Junior Officer Corps in the American Civil War.* Baton Rouge, Louisiana: Louisiana State University Press, 2015.

Bloom, Robert L. *We Never Expected a Battle: The Ordeal Endured by the Citizens at Gettysburg.* Littlestown, Pennsylvania: 1988.

Bonekemper, III, Edward H. *McClellan and Failure: A Study of Civil War Fear, Incompetence and Worse.* Jefferson, North Carolina: McFarland & Company, Inc., 2010.

Bowden, Scott and Bill Ward. *Last Chance for Victory: Robert E. Lee and the Gettysburg Campaign.* New York: Savas Beatie, 2001.

Brown, Kent Masterson. *Retreat from Gettysburg: Lee, Logistics, and the Pennsylvania Campaign.* Chapel Hill: University of North Carolina Press, 2005.

Busey, Travis W. and John W. Busey. *Union Casualties at Gettysburg: A Comprehensive Record.* Jefferson, North Carolina: McFarland & Co., 2011.

Carpenter, John A. *Sword and Olive Branch: Oliver Otis Howard.* Fordham University Press, 1999.

Casdorph, Paul D. *Lee and Jackson.* New York: Paragon House, 1992.

_____. *Confederate General R. S. Ewell: Robert E. Lee's Hesitant Commander.* University Press of Kentucky, 2004.

Catton, Bruce. *Gettysburg: The Final Fury.* New York: Random House, 1974.

Chamberlain, Joshua Lawrence. *Bayonet! Forward: My Civil War Reminiscences.* Stan Clark Military Books, 2003.

Coco, Gregory A. *A Vast Sea of Misery: A History and Guide to the Union and Confederate Field Hospitals at Gettysburg, July 1-November 20, 1863.* Gettysburg, PA: Thomas Publications, 1988.

_____. *A Strange and Blighted Land - Gettysburg: The Aftermath of a Battle.* Gettysburg, Pennsylvania: Thomas Publications, 1995.

_____. *Gettysburg's Confederate Dead.* Gettysburg, Pennsylvania: Thomas Publications, 2003.

Coddington, Edwin B. *The Gettysburg Campaign: A Study in Command.* New York: Scribner's, 1968.

Cooling, Benjamin Franklin. *Jubal Early: Robert E. Lee's "Bad Old Man."* Rowman & Littlefield, 2014.

Crain, Caleb. "How Soon It May Be Too Late." *The New York Times,* 4 August 2013.

Creighton, Margaret S. *The Colors of Courage: Gettysburg's Forgotten History.* New York: Basic Books, 2005.

Dorwart, Dr. Bonnie Brice. "Civil War Hospitals," *Essential Civil War Curriculum.* Essentialcivilwarcurriculum.com.

Dreese, Michael A. *The Hospital on Seminary Ridge and the Battle of Gettysburg.* Jefferson, North Carolina: McFarland & Company, Inc., 2002.

Eicher, David J. *The Longest Night: A Military History of the Civil War.* New York: Simon & Schuster, 2001.

Freeman, Douglas S., *R. E. Lee, A Biography,* four volumes. New York: Charles Scribner's Sons, 1934.

Gallagher, Gary W., ed. *The First Day at Gettysburg: Essays on Confederate and Union Leadership*. Kent, Ohio: Kent State University Press, 1992.

Gindlesperger, James. *Bullets and Bandages: The Aid Stations and Field Hospitals at Gettysburg*. Blair, 2020.

Gordon, Lesley J. *General George E. Pickett in Life and Legend*. Chapel Hill, North Carolina: University of North Carolina Press, 1998.

Gottfried, Bradley M. *The Maps of Gettysburg*. New York: Savas Beatie, 2010.

Gragg, Rod. *The Illustrated Gettysburg Reader: An Eyewitness History of the Civil War's Greatest Battle*. New York: Regnary House, 2013.

Guelzo, Allen C. *Robert E. Lee: A Life*. New York: Penguin Random House, 2022.

Hagan, Neil and Stephen Hyslop. *Atlas of the Civil War: A Comprehensive Guide to the Tactics and Terrain of Battle*. National Geographic, 2009.

Hebert, Walter H. *Fighting Joe Hooker*. Old Soldier Books, 1987.

Hessler, James A. *Sickles at Gettysburg: The Controversial Civil War General Who Committed Murder, Abandoned Little Round Top, and Declared Himself the Hero of Gettysburg*. Savas Beatie, LLC, 2010.

_____ and Britt C. Isenberg. *Gettysburg's Peach Orchard: Longstreet, Sickles, and the Bloody Fight for the "Commanding Ground" Along the Emmitsburg Road*. Savas Beatie, 2019.

Hood, Stephen M. *John Bell Hood: The Rise, Fall, and Resurrection of a Confederate General*. Savas Beatie, LLC, 2013.

Horan, James D. *Timothy O'Sullivan, America's Forgotten Photographer*. Garden City, New York: Doubleday & Company, 1966.

Hunt, Jeffrey W. *Meade and Lee After Gettysburg: The Forgotten Final Stage of the Gettysburg Campaign, from Falling Waters to Culpeper Court House, July 14–31, 1863*. Savas Beatie, 2017.

Jordan, David M. *Winfield Scott Hancock: A Soldier's Life*. Bloomington: Indiana University Press, 1988.

Jorgenson, Jay. *Gettysburg's Bloody Wheatfield*. Shippensburg, Pennsylvania: White Mane Books, 2002.

Kernek, Clyde B. *Field Surgeon at Gettysburg*. Indianapolis: Guild Press of Indiana, 1998.

LaFantasie, Glenn. W. *Twilight at Little Round Top: July 2, 1863 – The Tide Turns at Gettysburg*. Hoboken, New Jersey: John Wiley & Sons, Inc., 2005.

Longacre, Edward G. *General John Buford: A Military Biography*. Conshohocken, Pennsylvania: Combined Books, 1995

Luvaas, Jay, and Harold W. Nelson. *The U.S. Army War College Guide to the Battle of Gettysburg.* 1986.

Mackowski, Chris, Kristopher D. White, and Daniel T. Davis. *Don't Give an Inch: The Second Day at Gettysburg, July 2, 1863 - From Little Round Top to Cemetery Ridge.* El Dorado Hills, California: Savas Beatie, 2016.

Mosby, John S. *Stuart's Cavalry in the Gettysburg Campaign.* New York: Moffat, Yard & Co., 1908.

Nelson, A. H. *The Battles of Chancellorsville and Gettysburg.* Minneapolis, Minnesota: no publisher listed, 1899.

Nesbitt, Mark. *Saber & Scapegoat: J.E.B. Stuart and the Gettysburg Controversy.* Mechanicsburg, Pennsylvania: Stackpole Books, 1994.

Nevins, James H. and William B. Styple. *What Death More Glorious: A Biography of General Strong Vincent.* Kearny, New Jersey: Belle Grove Publishing Co., 1997.

Newton, Steven H. *McPherson's Ridge: The First Battle for the High Ground, July 1, 1863.* Cambridge, Massachusetts: DaCapo Press, 2002.

Nichols, Edward J. *Toward Gettysburg: A Biography of General John F. Reynolds.* University Park Pennsylvania: Pennsylvania State University Press, 1958.

O'Neill, Jr. Robert F. *The Cavalry Battles of Aldie, Middleburg and Upperville, Small but Important Riots, June 10-27, 1863.* Lynchburg, Virginia: H.E. Howard Co., 1993.

Peterson, John S and Michael Phipps. *"The Devil's to Pay": General John Buford, USA.* Gettysburg: Farnsworth Military Impressions, 1995.

Pfanz, Harry W. *Gettysburg: The Second Day.* Chapel Hill: University of North Carolina Press, 1987.

_____. *Gettysburg: Culp's Hill and Cemetery Hill.* Chapel Hill: University of North Carolina Press, 1993.

_____. *Gettysburg: The First Day.* Chapel Hill: University of North Carolina Press, 2001.

Priest, John Michael. *"Stand to It and Give Them Hell": Gettysburg as the Soldiers Experienced It from Cemetery Ridge to Little Round Top, July 2, 1863.* El Dorado Hills, California: Savas Beatie, 2014.

Pritzker, Barry *Mathew Brady.* East Bridgewater: JG Press, 1992.

Reardon, Carol. *Pickett's Charge in History and Memory.* Chapel Hill: University of North Carolina Press, 1997.

Redd, Rea Andrew *Altars to Amputations: From Gettysburg Churches to Battlefield Hospitals: A History and Walking Tour.* Savas Beatie, 2020.

Robertson, James I. *General A.P. Hill: The Story of a Confederate Warrior.* New York: Random House, 1987.

Sauers, Richard. A. *Gettysburg Campaign, June 3 - August 1, 1863: A Comprehensive, Selectively Annotated Bibliography.* Greenwood Publishing Group, 1982.

_____. *A Caspian Sea of Ink: The Meade-Sickles Controversy.* Baltimore, Maryland: Butternut and Blue, 1989.

_____. *Meade: Victor of Gettysburg.* Potomac Books, 2004.

Sears, Stephen W. *Gettysburg.* New York: Houghton Mifflin Company, 2003.

Smithsonian Institution. *The Civil War: A Visual History.* New York: DK Publishing, 2011.

Spruill, Mark. *Decisions at Gettysburg: The Nineteen Critical Decisions That Defined the Campaign.* Knoxville, Tennessee: University of Tennessee Press, 2011.

Symonds, Craig L. and William J. Clipson. *Gettysburg: A Battlefield Atlas.* Charleston, SC: The Nautical & Aviation Publishing Company of America, 1992.

Tagg, Larry R. *The Generals at Gettysburg: The Leaders of America's Greatest Battle.* Mason City, Iowa: Savas Publishing Co., 1998.

Trudeau, Noah Andre. *Gettysburg: A Testing of Courage.* New York: Harper Collins Publishers, 2002.

Trulock, Alice Rains. *In the Hands of Providence: Joshua L. Chamberlain and the American Civil War.* The University of North Carolina Press, 1992.

Tucker, Leslie R. *Major General Isaac Ridgeway Trimble: Biography of A Baltimore Confederate.* McFarland, 2005.

Tucker, Philip Thomas. *Storming Little Round Top: The 15th Alabama and Their Fight for the High Ground, July 2, 1863.* Conshohocken, Pennsylvania: Combined Books, 2001.

_____. *Barksdale's Charge: The True High Tide of the Confederacy at Gettysburg, July 2, 1863.* Casemate Publishers, 2013.

Walker, Paula and Robert Girardi. *The Soldiers' General: Major General Gouverneur K. Warren and the Civil War.* Savas Beatie, 2015.

Weigley, Russell F. *A Great Civil War: A Military and Political History, 1861-1865.* Bloomington and Indianapolis: Indiana University Press, 2000.

Wert, Jeffry D. *Cavalryman of the Lost Cause: A Biography of J.E.B. Stuart.* New York: Simon & Schuster, 2008.

_____. *General James Longstreet: The Confederacy's Most Controversial Soldier.* New York: Simon & Schuster, 1993.

Wilson, Clyde Norman. *The Most Promising Young Man of the South: James Johnston Pettigrew and His Men at Gettysburg.* McWhiney Foundation Press, 1998.

Wilson, Robert. *Mathew Brady: Portraits of a Nation.* London: Bloomsbury, 2013.

Wittenberg, Eric J and J. David Petruzzi. *Plenty of Blame to Go Around: Jeb Stuart's Controversial Ride to Gettysburg,* 2nd ed. New York: Savas Beatie LLC, 2006.

_____. *Gettysburg's Forgotten Cavalry Actions.* New York: Savas Beatie LLC, 2011.

Wynstra, Robert J. *The Rashness of the Hour: Politics, Gettysburg, and the Downfall of Confederate Brigadier General Alfred Iverson.* New York: Savas Beatie, 2011.

Made in the USA
Columbia, SC
23 June 2024

37404566R10320